# SAT PREP

## For the Thoughtful Christian

**James P. Stobaugh**

For Such A Time As This Ministries

Hollsopple, Pennsylvania

**SAT PREP FOR THE THOUGHTFUL CHRISTIAN**

For Such A Time As This Ministries
510 Swank Rd., Hollsopple, PA 15935
Phone: 814-479-7710
E-mail: JPSTOBAUGH@AOL.COM
Web site:
http://forsuchatimeasthis.com
http://forsuchatimeasthis.com/blog
http://twitter.com/jamespstobaugh
http://facebook.com/jpstobaugh

*Acknowledgments:* I wish to thank Karen, my wife, and S. David Garber, copy editor, for their editorial assistance. I also honor my troubleshooting MIT friends who checked and corrected the math lessons. In addition, I thank the students who let their essays and responses be included here.

Book design by James P. Stobaugh
Cover design and printing by Masthof Press LLC
219 Mill Road, Morgantown, PA 19543
www.masthof.com
Printed in the United States of America

Printed on acid-free paper, SFI and FSC Certified

International Standard Book Number: 978-1-60126-466-4

10 9 8 7 6 5 4 3 2 1    25 24 23 22 21 20 19 18 17 16

*To my students*
*who have journeyed and learned with me*
*for over 25 years*


You are the most strategic generation in human history!
With the inspiration of the Holy Spirit, it is my firm conviction that
you can and will transform the future of world culture and history,
through knowing and loving the Word of God and
by knowing and understanding human culture.
Come, let us learn together!
Let us draw the world to our Lord Jesus Christ!

# About the Author

James P. Stobaugh met his future wife at Harvard University. Jim and Karen Stobaugh were married and have four home-educated adult children. Jim's education includes a BA cum laude, Vanderbilt; MA, Rutgers; MDiv, Princeton Seminary; Charles E. Merrill Fellow, Harvard University; DMin, Gordon-Conwell Seminary.

For nearly half a century, Jim has been a counselor for SAT preparation and college admission. His students are recruited by the most competitive universities in the world.

Meanwhile, Jim is the pastor of an evangelical church at Boswell, Pennsylvania. In the Laurel Highlands, Jim and Karen reside on their farm, the Shepherd's Glen. They enjoy playing with their three fuzzy cats and two black Labrador retrievers.

You can see more of Jim's ministry and literary works at www.forsuchatimeasthis.com.

James P. Stobaugh's works include the following:

Preparing Thoughtful Christians to Be World-Changers for Christ Literature Series (6 vols., grades 6–12)

*Skills for Language Arts*
*Skills for Rhetoric*
*Skills for Literary Analysis*
*American Literature*
*British Literature*
*World Literature*

Preparing Thoughtful Christians to be World-Changers for Christ History Literature (6 vol., grades 6–12)

*Studies in World History*, vol. 1
*Studies in World History*, vol. 2
*Studies in World History*, vol. 3
*American History: Observations and Assessments*
*British History: Observations and Assessments*
*World History: Observations and Assessments*

Other books:

*ACT and College Preparation for the Christian Student*
*Companion for 50 Classics*
*Handbook for Literary Analysis*
*African-American History*
*Growing Up White*
*SAT Prep for the Thoughtful Christian*

All of the above resources can be obtained by visiting www.forsuchatimeasthis.com.

# Contents

# Preface

God has great plans for your lives, young people! "'For I know the plans I have for you,' declares the LORD, 'plans to prosper you and not to harm you, plans to give you hope and a future'" (Jeremiah 29:11). If God is calling you to attend college, this book is for you!

College graduates assume most of the leadership roles of this country. They make most of the decisions, write most of the literature, and adjudicate most of the court cases. In short, college graduates make most high culture! Christian college graduates can be world-changers for Christ!

The term "high culture" was introduced into English largely by Matthew Arnold in *Culture and Anarchy* (1869). Around the same time, German scholars wrote of *Kultur*, meaning that there is a mystical spirit permeating society, something that is more profound than Western civilization itself. Indeed!

High culture creates the best that has been said and thought in the world. It is a force for moral and political good. It promotes and creates the way of life that a civilization enjoys—the art that it views, the movies it enjoys, the books it reads. I am not talking about fads and froth but about the things that determine how we think, govern, and worship. The term is contrasted with popular culture, as well as with traditional cultures. I want you to create a wholesome, godly high culture, something more profound and ubiquitous than anything in Western culture.

To reach this goal, you need to be the best you can be for our God. Join the high-culture creation epicenters of education, government, entertainment, health, law, and religion; go to those spheres, and make a difference.

The *SAT Prep for the Thoughtful Christian* will prepare you for college and therefore to be world-changers for Christ, to create a new high culture. This book, practically speaking, prepares you for the new SAT, debuting in March 2016. Here are some nuances of the new Scholastic Aptitude Test:

1. *No penalty for wrong answers.* You and your fellow students will no longer be penalized for wrong answers while taking the new SAT.
2. *Revamped essay.* Instead of composing a personal essay for the writing section, you will read a passage and then analyze how the author persuades the readers. Although content passages will change, the essay question itself will be the same on all tests.
3. *Evidence-focused reading.* Just like the essay section, the reading section will also be more focused on content evidence. You will be asked a question about the text and then need to give evidence best supporting your answer. If you get the first question wrong, it could be difficult to answer the second and third questions correctly.
4. *Context-based vocabulary.* The new SAT will ask you to define a word based on how it is used in context. Sample questions show familiar words that can have various meanings. More than ever, learning Greek and Latin roots trumps vocabulary memorization every time.
5. *More graphs and charts.* The new test will have an increased emphasis on questions that make students gather information from graphs and charts.
6. *More emphasis on grammar, syntax, and dictions.* You will also be asked to revise sentences in order to make them consistent with standard English practices.
7. *Primary-source texts.* The new SAT reading section will include excerpts from U.S. founding documents like the Declaration of Independence and the Bill of Rights. You will not be expected to be familiar with the documents beforehand, but that would not hurt!
8. *Stress reduction.* Scripture memorization will calm your fears and help you focus!

You will face an SAT quite different from earlier ones. So this book must be different from other prep books. From an increase in content-based questions to a revamped essay section, this *SAT Prep* will make sure you are ready.

This book includes a devotion and five lessons per chapter. The devotion includes a memory verse and a journal question. Memorizing Scripture and analyzing Scripture in a journal will build your Christian life and will increase your SAT score. In each chapter the five lessons comprehensively review all SAT skills:

Lesson 1: Evidence-Based Reading and Writing
Lesson 2: Critical Reading and Writing
Lesson 3: SAT Essay
Lesson 4: Reading: Document-Based Analysis
Lesson 5: Math: Algebra, Arithmetic Problem Solving and Data Analysis, and Passport to Advanced Math

Day after day and lesson after lesson, you will mature in your Christian faith as you practice test items while preparing for the new SAT. When you and other thoughtful Christian students finish this book, you will be prepared for such a time as this! I am excited! "Now, God be thanked Who has matched us with His hour, and caught our youth, and wakened us from sleeping" (Rupert Brooke, who died in World War I, in 1915).

—James P. Stobaugh

# Chapter 1   Love's Choices
# John 10

> *Memory Verses:* I am the good shepherd. The good shepherd lays down his life for the sheep. The hired hand is not the shepherd and does not own the sheep. So when he sees the wolf coming, he abandons the sheep and runs away. Then the wolf attacks the flock and scatters it. The man runs away because he is a hired hand and cares nothing for the sheep. —John 10:11–13

A sixteen-year-old boy who lives in Westbury, Long Island, was picked up by the police several years ago for defacing a synagogue. It seems that the boy went on a Halloween tear with some friends. They sprayed obscenities on the front door of the synagogue while a service was going on.

The young man, a Roman Catholic, was caught. He was fined $150 and ordered to give one hundred hours of service to his hometown church. His parents publically deplored what their son had done. Their pain drew letters of understanding support from people near and far.

But most touching of all was a letter that had to do with court costs and expenses of legal counsel. The family incurred a deficit of $1,000 to defend their son. They were finding it hard to come up with the money. One day a letter arrived. It contained a check for $1,000. It was from a Jewish lawyer in Manhattan. We consciously, deliberately, choose to love or to hate; love is not something that we unconsciously wander into.

A train pulls into Auschwitz concentration camp. Even before the steam has ceased from hissing from the brakes of the engine, the hapless, forlorn Jews are being unloaded. An SS captain stands erect, with two ominous police dogs at his side. A motion with his right hand to the right means life in the work camp nearby, called Birkenau. A motion with left hand means instant death in the gas chambers. The Jews knew what was up—no one could ignore the ominous smoke billowing from the stacks of the crematorium, and the awful stench of flesh burning was unavoidable. Yet no one could move. Everyone hoped to be motioned to the right: the desperate effort of escape should at least be postponed until each saw to which side they would be sent. The line moved ever so slowly toward the captain. Right, right, and then a whole string of people were sent left. A couple was perceivably nervous as the line moved closer to the captain. The couple had been newly married only a month before. What a honeymoon! The persons ahead of them were sent to the right. They felt hope! And then the horror of hopelessness hit them. The woman was sent to the right and the man to the left.

Suddenly a man, a prisoner, approached the captain. He interjected, "Excuse me, Herr Captain, but may I take the place of the young man you are sending to the left? I am a broken, unhealthy, man. He is strong. Wouldn't it be better if he lived and I died?" The young man was spared. The prisoner (a priest) was gassed.

A Good Shepherd willingly gives his life for the sheep if a danger arises. In theological jargon, we call this atonement. Atonement happens when the age-old pattern of transgression and revenge is broken. When the offended one absorbs an indignity and resists the urge to retaliate, forgiveness and reconciliation—the two purest forms of love—have a chance. The death of Jesus on the cross has been the subject of theological speculation for centuries. All of my theology courses at seminary explored theories of atonement, and it comes down to this: Christ met our evil with his good. When he was reviled, he did not revile again. We gather at the foot of the cross, expecting to hear him say, "This is my body, broken." Instead we hear a word of grace, "This is my body, *broken for you.*"

In the Christian sense, love is not primarily an emotion but an act of the will. When Jesus tells us to love our neighbors, he is not telling us to love them in the sense of responding to them with a cozy emotional feeling. You can as well produce a cozy emotional feeling on demand as you can a yawn or a sneeze. On the contrary, he is telling us to love our neighbors, our family, and our enemies, in the sense of being willing to work for their well-being even if it means sacrificing our own well-being. Thus in Jesus' terms we can love our neighbors without necessarily liking them. In fact, liking them may stand in the way of loving them by making us overprotective sentimentalists instead of reasonably honest friends. When Jesus talked to the Pharisees, he didn't say, "There, there, everything's going to be all right." He said, "You brood of vipers! How can you speak good when you are evil!" (cf. Matt. 12:34) And he said that because He loved them.

This does not mean that liking may not be a part of loving, only that it doesn't need to be. Sometimes liking follows on the heels of loving. It is hard to work for somebody's well-being very long without coming in the end to rather like that person too.

John 10:17–18 tells us that Jesus saw his whole life as an act of obedience to God. God had given him a task to do, and he was prepared to carry out that task to the end, even if doing so meant death. Jesus was in a unique relationship to God. We can only describe that relationship by saying that he was the Son of God. But that relationship did not give him the right to do what he liked; it depended on the fact that, cost what it may, he always did what God liked. For Jesus, to be the Son of God was at one and the same time the greatest of privileges and the greatest of responsibilities. Sonship for him, and sonship for us, can never be based on anything except obedience. And we are commanded to love one another as we love ourselves. But we must choose, as Jesus did, to obey our heavenly Father.

Our Scripture also tells us that Jesus always saw the cross and the glory together. He never doubted that he must die; and he equally never doubted that he would rise again. The reason for this confidence was Jesus' confidence in God. He never believed that God would abandon him. Jesus believed that obedience to God was bound to bring suffering; but he also believed that obedience to God was bound to bring glory. And further, he believed that suffering was for only a moment and that the glory was for all eternity. All life is based on the fact that anything worth getting is hard to get. There is a price to be paid for anything. Scholarship can only be bought at the price of study; skill in any craft or technique can only be obtained at the price of practice; eminence in any sport can only be achieved at the price of training and discipline. The world is full of people who have missed their destiny because they would not pay the price. No one can take the easy way and enter into any kind of glory or greatness; no one can take the hard way and fail to find glory and greatness.

Love in our families is nurtured as we make quality decisions each day—a hundred times a day. Do I work late or spend time with my family? Do I move and leave people and family I love, or do I stay and face a demotion? Do I refuse to take a job that forces me to be away from my family? If I do so, I can kiss my career good-bye. These are hard choices, and there are no easy answers. These are love's choices.

I am reminded of my own father, who died in 1982. Dad was not a very important man according to the standards of the world. First, he was a custodian at a large oil refinery; then, after returning to school, he became a teacher. He never made money. Not many people knew him. But he was the most important man in my life, and he highly influenced me and therefore you. He made quality decisions in his life. He put his family first. When he was dying in St. Vincent's Hospital, what do you think mattered most to him? The fact that he may or may not have fame and money? Or the fact that a son loved him so much that he would have given his own life to let his dad live?

Finally, we cannot possibly mistake that Christ's death was entirely voluntary. That is a fact that Jesus stresses again and again. In the garden, he bade his would-be defender to put down his sword. If he had wished to do so, he could have called the hosts of heaven to his defense. Before Pilate, Jesus made it quite clear that Pilate was not condemning him, but that he was accepting death. Jesus was not the victim of circumstances. He was not like some animal, dragged to the sacrifice, unwilling to go, struggling against the hands of the priest, not knowing what was happening. Jesus voluntarily laid down his life for you and me because he chose to do so. Barclay, in his commentary on John, tells a story about a World War I French soldier who was seriously wounded. His arm was so badly smashed that it had to be amputated. He was a healthy young man, and the surgeon was grieved that the boy must go through life maimed. So he waited beside the bedside of the man to tell him the bad news when he recovered consciousness. When the lad's eyes opened, the surgeon said to him, "I am sorry to tell you that you have lost your arm." The young soldier replied, "I did not lose it; I gave it for France." Jesus was not helplessly caught up in a mesh of circumstances from which he could not break free. Apart from anything else, apart from any divine power and aid that he might have called in, it is abundantly clear that to the end he could have turned back and saved his life. He did not lose his life; he gave it for you and me. He was not killed; he chose to die a hideous death for you and me. As our Good Shepherd, Jesus Christ, the Jewish lawyer in Brooklyn, the young priest in Auschwitz, we are called to give our lives day in and day out for the lovely and unlovely, for those hard to love, for those whom we love and those whom we are tempted to hate. We are called to make quality decisions for our families: love demands that we make hard choices. The way of the cross offers no other alternatives.

"His death was not a defeat canceled by a resurrection triumph," wrote Archbishop William Temple, "It is itself a triumph."

## Journal Question

Do you love someone by choice—someone who is not related, someone you do not have to love? Why?

# Lesson 1
## Evidence-Based Reading and Writing

### Literary Choice
Gabriel García Márquez was the most famous writers of Magical Realism. Marquez resisted predetermined, predictable plot structures and used Magic Realism to tease out the most profound realism his plots could sustain.

### A Very Old Man with Enormous Wings

1   On the third day of rain they had killed so many crabs inside the house that Pelayo had to cross his drenched
2   courtyard and throw them into the sea, because the newborn child had a temperature all night and they thought it
3   was due to the stench. The world had been sad since Tuesday. Sea and sky were a single ash-gray thing, and the
4   sands of the beach, which on March nights glimmered like powdered light, had become a stew of mud and rotten
5   shellfish. The light was so weak at noon that when Pelayo was coming back to the house after throwing away the
6   crabs, it was hard for him to see what it was that was moving and groaning in the rear of the courtyard. He had to go
7   very close to see that it was an old man, a very old man, lying face down in the mud, who, in spite of his tremendous
8   efforts, couldn't get up, impeded by his enormous wings.
9        Frightened by that nightmare, Pelayo ran to get Elisenda, his wife, who was putting compresses on the sick
10   child, and he took her to the rear of the courtyard. They both looked at the fallen body with a mute stupor. He was
11   dressed like a ragpicker. There were only a few faded hairs left on his bald skull and very few teeth in his mouth,
12   and his pitiful condition of a drenched great-grandfather took away any sense of grandeur he might have had. His
13   huge buzzard wings, dirty and half-plucked, were forever entangled in the mud. They looked at him so long and so
14   closely that Pelayo and Elisenda very soon overcame their surprise and in the end found him familiar. Then they
15   dared speak to him, and he answered in an incomprehensible dialect with a strong sailor's voice. That was how they
16   skipped over the inconvenience of the wings and quite intelligently concluded that he was a lonely castaway from
17   some foreign ship wrecked by the storm. And yet, they called in a neighbor woman who knew everything about life
18   and death to see him, and all she needed was one look to show them their mistake.
19        "He's an angel," she told them. "He must have been coming for the child, but the poor fellow is so old that
20   the rain knocked him down."
21        On the following day everyone knew that a flesh-and-blood angel was held captive in Pelayo's house.
22   Against the judgment of the wise neighbor woman, for whom angels in those times were the fugitive survivors of a
23   celestial conspiracy, they did not have the heart to club him to death. Pelayo watched over him all afternoon from
24   the kitchen, armed with his bailiff's club, and before going to bed he dragged him out of the mud and locked him up
25   with the hens in the wire chicken coop. In the middle of the night, when the rain stopped, Pelayo and Elisenda were
26   still killing crabs. A short time afterward the child woke up without a fever and with a desire to eat. Then they felt
27   magnanimous and decided to put the angel on a raft with fresh water and provisions for three days and leave him to
28   his fate on the high seas. But when they went out into the courtyard with the first light of dawn, they found the
29   whole neighborhood in front of the chicken coop having fun with the angel, without the slightest reverence, tossing
30   him things to eat through the openings in the wire as if he weren't a supernatural creature but a circus animal.
31        Father Gonzaga arrived before seven o'clock, alarmed at the strange news. By that time onlookers less
32   frivolous than those at dawn had already arrived, and they were making all kinds of conjectures concerning the
33   captive's future. The simplest among them thought that he should be named mayor of the world. Others of sterner
34   mind felt that he should be promoted to the rank of five-star general in order to win all wars. Some visionaries hoped
35   that he could be put to stud in order to implant the earth with a race of winged wise men who could take charge of
36   the universe. But Father Gonzaga, before becoming a priest, had been a robust woodcutter. Standing by the wire, he
37   reviewed his catechism in an instant and asked them to open the door so that he could take a close look at that pitiful
38   man, who looked more like a huge decrepit hen among the fascinated chickens. He was lying in the corner, drying
39   his open wings in the sunlight among the fruit peels and breakfast leftovers that the early risers had thrown him.
40   Alien to the impertinences of the world, he only lifted his antiquarian eyes and murmured something in his dialect
41   when Father Gonzaga went into the chicken coop and said good-morning to him in Latin. The parish priest had his
42   first suspicion of an imposter when he saw that he did not understand the language of God or know how to greet his
43   ministers. Then he noticed that, seen close up, he was much too human: he had an unbearable smell of the outdoors,
44   the back side of his wings was strewn with parasites, and his main feathers had been mistreated by terrestrial winds,
45   and nothing about him measured up to the proud dignity of angels. Then he came out of the chicken coop and in a
46   brief sermon warned the curious against the risks of being ingenuous. He reminded them that the devil had the bad
47   habit of making use of carnival tricks in order to confuse the unwary. He argued that if wings were not the essential

48  element in determining the difference between a hawk and an airplane, they were even less so in the recognition of
49  angels. Nevertheless, he promised to write a letter to his bishop so that the latter would write his primate
50  [archbishop] so that the latter would write to the Supreme Pontiff in order to get the final verdict from the highest
51  courts.

52      His prudence fell on sterile hearts. The news of the captive angel spread with such rapidity that after a few
53  hours the courtyard had the bustle of a marketplace, and they had to call in troops with fixed bayonets to disperse the
54  mob that was about to knock the house down. Elisenda, her spine all twisted from sweeping up so much marketplace
55  trash, then got the idea of fencing in the yard and charging five cents admission to see the angel.

56      The curious came from far away. A traveling carnival arrived with a flying acrobat who buzzed over the
57  crowd several times, but no one paid any attention to him because his wings were not those of an angel but, rather,
58  those of a sidereal bat. The most unfortunate invalids on earth came in search of health: a poor woman who since
59  childhood has been counting her heartbeats and had run out of numbers; a Portuguese man who couldn't sleep
60  because the noise of the stars disturbed him; a sleepwalker who got up at night to undo the things he had done while
61  awake; and many others with less serious ailments. In the midst of that shipwreck disorder that made the earth
62  tremble, Pelayo and Elisenda were happy with fatigue, for in less than a week they had crammed their rooms with
63  money, and the line of pilgrims waiting their turn to enter still reached beyond the horizon.

64      The angel was the only one who took no part in his own act. He spent his time trying to get comfortable in
65  his borrowed nest, befuddled by the hellish heat of the oil lamps and sacramental candles that had been placed along
66  the wire. At first they tried to make him eat some mothballs, which, according to the wisdom of the wise neighbor
67  woman, were the food prescribed for angels. But he turned them down, just as he turned down the papal lunches that
68  the penitents brought him, and they never found out whether it was because he was an angel or because he was an
69  old man that in the end he ate nothing but eggplant mush. His only supernatural virtue seemed to be patience.
70  Especially during the first days, when the hens pecked at him, searching for the stellar parasites that proliferated in
71  his wings, and the cripples pulled out feathers to touch their defective parts with, and even the most merciful threw
72  stones at him, trying to get him to rise so they could see him standing. The only time they succeeded in arousing him
73  was when they burned his side with an iron for branding steers, for he had been motionless for so many hours that
74  they thought he was dead. He awoke with a start, ranting in his hermetic language and with tears in his eyes, and he
75  flapped his wings a couple of times, which brought on a whirlwind of chicken dung and lunar dust and a gale of
76  panic that did not seem to be of this world. Although many thought that his reaction had not been one of rage but of
77  pain, from then on they were careful not to annoy him, because the majority understood that his passivity was not
78  that of a hero taking his ease but that of a cataclysm in repose.

79      Father Gonzaga held back the crowd's frivolity with formulas of maidservant inspiration while awaiting the
80  arrival of a final judgment on the nature of the captive. But the mail from Rome showed no sense of urgency. They
81  spent their time finding out if the prisoner had a navel, if his dialect had any connection with Aramaic, how many
82  times he could fit on the head of a pin, or whether he wasn't just a Norwegian with wings. Those meager letters
83  might have come and gone until the end of time if a providential event had not put an end to the priest's tribulations.

84      It so happened that during those days, among so many other carnival attractions, there arrived in the town
85  the traveling show of the woman who had been changed into a spider for having disobeyed her parents. The
86  admission to see her was not only less than the admission to see the angel, but people were also permitted to ask her
87  all manner of questions about her absurd state and to examine her up and down so that no one would ever doubt the
88  truth of her horror. She was a frightful tarantula the size of a ram and with the head of a sad maiden. What was most
89  heartrending, however, was not her outlandish shape but the sincere affliction with which she recounted the details
90  of her misfortune. While still practically a child, she had sneaked out of her parents' house to go to a dance, and
91  while she was coming back through the woods after having danced all night without permission, a fearful
92  thunderclap rent the sky in two, and through the crack came the lightning bolt of brimstone that changed her into a
93  spider. Her only nourishment came from the meatballs that charitable souls chose to toss into her mouth. A spectacle
94  like that, full of so much human truth and with such a fearful lesson, was bound to defeat, without even trying, that
95  of a haughty angel who scarcely deigned to look at mortals. Besides, the few miracles attributed to the angel showed
96  a certain mental disorder, like the blind man who didn't recover his sight but grew three new teeth, or the paralytic
97  who didn't get to walk but almost won the lottery, and the leper whose sores sprouted sunflowers. Those consolation
98  miracles, which were more like mocking fun, had already ruined the angel's reputation when the woman who had
99  been changed into a spider finally crushed him completely. That was how Father Gonzaga was cured forever of his
100  insomnia and Pelayo's courtyard went back to being as empty as during the time it had rained for three days and
101  crabs walked through the bedrooms.

102      The owners of the house had no reason to lament. With the money they saved, they built a two-story
103  mansion with balconies and gardens and high netting so that crabs wouldn't get in during the winter, and with iron
104  bars on the windows so that angels wouldn't get in. Pelayo also set up a rabbit warren close to town and gave up his

job as a bailiff for good, and Elisenda bought some satin pumps with high heels and many dresses of iridescent silk, the kind worn on Sunday by the most desirable women in those times. The chicken coop was the only thing that didn't receive any attention. If they washed it down with creolin and burned tears of myrrh inside it every so often, it was not in homage to the angel but to drive away the dunghill stench that still hung everywhere like a ghost and was turning the new house into an old one. At first, when the child learned to walk, they were careful that he not get too close to the chicken coop. But then they began to lose their fears and got used to the smell, and before they child got his second teeth, he'd gone inside the chicken coop to play, where the wires were falling apart. The angel was no less standoffish with him than with the other mortals, but he tolerated the most ingenious infamies with the patience of a dog who had no illusions. They both came down with the chicken pox at the same time. The doctor who took care of the child couldn't resist the temptation to listen to the angel's heart, and he found so much whistling in the heart and so many sounds in his kidneys that it seemed impossible for him to be alive. What surprised him most, however, was the logic of his wings. They seemed so natural on that completely human organism that he couldn't understand why other men didn't have them too.

When the child began school, it had been some time since the sun and rain had caused the collapse of the chicken coop. The angel went dragging himself about here and there like a stray dying man. They would drive him out of the bedroom with a broom and a moment later find him in the kitchen. He seemed to be in so many places at the same time that they grew to think that he'd been duplicated, that he was reproducing himself all through the house, and the exasperated and unhinged Elisenda shouted that it was awful living in that hell full of angels. He could scarcely eat, and his antiquarian eyes had also become so foggy that he went about, bumping into posts. All he had left were the bare cannulas of his last feathers. Pelayo threw a blanket over him and extended him the charity of letting him sleep in the shed, and only then did they notice that he had a temperature at night, and was delirious with the tongue twisters of an old Norwegian. That was one of the few times they became alarmed, for they thought he was going to die, and not even the wise neighbor woman had been able to tell them what to do with dead angels.

And yet he not only survived his worst winter, but also seemed improved with the first sunny days. He remained motionless for several days in the farthest corner of the courtyard, where no one would see him, and at the beginning of December some large, stiff feathers began to grow on his wings, the feathers of a scarecrow, which looked more like another misfortune of decrepitude. But he must have known the reason for those changes, for he was quite careful that no one should notice them, that no one should hear the sea chanteys that he sometimes sang under the stars. One morning Elisenda was cutting some bunches of onions for lunch when a wind that seemed to come from the high seas blew into the kitchen. Then she went to the window and caught the angel in his first attempts at flight. They were so clumsy that his fingernails opened a furrow in the vegetable patch, and he was on the point of knocking the shed down with the ungainly flapping that slipped on the light and couldn't get a grip on the air. But he did manage to gain altitude. Elisenda let out a sigh of relief, for herself and for him, when she watched him pass over the last houses, holding himself up in some way with the risky flapping of a senile vulture. She kept watching him even when she was through cutting the onions, and she kept on watching until it was no longer possible for her to see him, because then he was no longer an annoyance in her life but an imaginary dot on the horizon of the sea.

(trans. Gregory Rapasso,
https://www.ndsu.edu/pubweb/~cinichol/CreativeWriting/323/MarquezManwithWings.htm)

## Student Response 1

### Magic Realism

1    In his description of magical realism, M. H. Abrams (*A Glossary of Literary Terms*) says, "These writers
2    interweave, in an ever-shifting pattern, a sharply etched realism in representing ordinary events and descriptive
3    details together with fantastic and dreamlike elements, as well as with materials derived from myth and fairy tales."
4    Another description by Matthew Strecher defines Magic Realism as "what happens when a highly detailed, realistic
5    setting is invaded by something 'too strange to believe'" (Princeton.edu). This literary style, magical realism, is very
6    evident in Gabriel García Márquez's "A Very Old Man with Enormous Wings."
7        Here is the first and most important question to ask about this short story: "Is there an event that cannot be
8    explained by universal laws or logic?" (*Margin Magazine*). Obviously, Marquez's short story opens with an
9    unexplainable event: what appears to be a human man with angel wings. This is the most apparent example of
10   magical elements being accepted as a natural part of an otherwise mundane and realistic world.
11       Another example of magic realism is the "miracle-quality" the angel-man appears to possess. These so-
12   called miracles attributed to the angel "showed a certain mental disorder." In other words, the miracles never went
13   quite right. There was always something that went askew. For example, there was "the blind man who didn't recover
14   his sight but grew three new teeth, or the paralytic who didn't get to walk but almost won the lottery, and the leper
15   whose sores sprouted sunflowers." These "consolation miracles" turned out to be more like "mocking fun" of the
16   angel more than anything.
17       Lastly, the final example of magical realism is the spider-girl. This was a girl who was turned into a large
18   spider after disobeying her parents. "She was a frightful tarantula the size of a ram and with the head of a sad
19   maiden." The angel and the spider-girl were attractions in an otherwise mundane world. These examples are clear
20   proof of magical realism. (Callie)

## Student Response 2

### Magic Realism

1    Gabriel García Márquez wrote "A Very Old Man with Enormous Wings" in 1968. It is a story about a family who
2    finds an old man lying in the mud outside their house. The man has wings, and the people take him to be an angel.
3    They keep the angel with them, first locked in a chicken coop and then around the house until one day he flies away.
4    Márquez wrote this story using Magic Realism, a style of writing that contains supernatural elements while
5    depicting things plainly as they appear without focusing extensively on emotions. Three examples of Magic Realism
6    in the story are the angel, the spider woman, and the miracles dealing with the people's ailments.
7        The angel's appearance in the story is a fantastic element, but he is depicted as a simple man with wings.
8    Instead of describing the angel with qualities that people would normally associate with angels, Márquez chose to
9    plainly state the simple facts.

10       [Pelayo and Elisenda] looked at the fallen body with a mute stupor. He was dressed like a ragpicker. There
11       were only a few faded hairs left on his bald skull and very few teeth in his mouth, and his pitiful condition
12       of a drenched great-grandfather took away any sense of grandeur he might have had. His huge buzzard
13       wings, dirty and half-plucked, were forever entangled in the mud.

14   Because he is using Magic Realism, Márquez didn't even bother to address the question of who he was, where he
15   came from, or how he got there. He only wrote of what the people saw.
16       In the case of the spider woman, Márquez did write about who the woman used to be. When she was very
17   young, she sneaked out of her house to go to a dance, against her parents' permission. On the way back home, she
18   was struck with a "lightning bolt of brimstone" that changed her into a huge spider. Once again, there is no
19   explanation of why or how she was transformed, only the events that occurred and her appearance.
20       Another example of Magic Realism in "A Very Old Man with Enormous Wings" is the miracle ailments of
21   the people who went to see the angel. They thought that by touching him or by rubbing his feathers on them, they
22   would be cured. Instead, unusual miracles occurred.
23       Besides, the few miracles attributed to the angel showed a certain mental disorder, like the blind man who
24   didn't recover his sight but grew three new teeth, or the paralytic who didn't get to walk but almost won the lottery,
25   and the leper whose sores sprouted sunflowers. Those consolation miracles, which were more like mocking fun, had
26   already ruined the angel's reputation when the woman who had been changed into a spider finally crushed him
27   completely.

28       As is characteristic of this story, these strange happenings are described as commonplace. Instead of the
29 angel possessing fantastic abilities, these events are merely a sidenote.
30       By his use of Magic Realism, Márquez trivialized supernatural occurrences and made them ordinary and
31 realistic. By describing the angel, spider woman, and miracles that affected people in the way that he did, Márquez
32 turned an unbelievable story into one that, aside from outlandish events, almost seems normal. (Kory)

## Close Reading

1. "A Very Old Man" is a
   A. Drama
   B. Poetry
   C. Short Story
   D. Novelette

2. The narrative technique?
   A. Omniscient
   B. Limited Omniscient
   C. First Person
   D. Third-Person Objective

3. The tone of most of "A Very Old Man" is?
   A. Serious Whimsy
   B. Sanguine
   C. Choleric
   D. Phlegmatic

4. Márquez creates the tone by
   A. Humorous scenes
   B. Character reactions to the angel
   C. Tense interpersonal rivalries
   D. Antagonistic characters

5. This world view of the novel?
   A. Romanticism
   B. Theism
   C. Naturalism
   D. Realism

6. A central motif of the narrative?
   A. Unrequited Love
   B. Forgiveness
   C. Revenge
   D. Magic Realism

7. A narrative with a similar motif?
   A. *Oedipus Rex*
   B. *Julius Caesar*
   C. *Plutarch's Lives*
   D. *The Odyssey*

8. Father Gonzaga suspects the creature is not a real angel because
   A. He is injured.
   B. He is weeping.
   C. He has parasites and generally is smelly
   D. He cannot perform any miracles

9. What is the purpose of the character Elizondo?
   A. The author uses Elizondo to comment on the state of things
   B. Elizondo makes religious observations
   C. Elizondo is a confident of the angel
   D. Elizondo is an antagonist of the angel

10. Elizondo is best described as a
    A. Cynic
    B. Romantic
    C. Saint
    D. Realist

11. "Glimmered like" in Line 4 is an example of
    A. Simile
    B. Paradox
    C. Hyperbole
    D. Personification

12. What is "it was awful living in that hell full of angels"?
    A. Paradox
    B. Hyperbole
    C. Contradiction
    D. Syllogism

13. Lines 21–30 imply that the angel
    A. Is Satan
    B. Is a fraud.
    C. Has healing powers
    D. Is crazy

## Command of Evidence (Student Response 1)

1. The first time the Student Response presents its thesis?
   A. Lines 1–2
   B. Lines 5–6
   C. Lines 15–16
   D. Lines 19–20

2. A general strategy that the essay employs
   A. State an argument and defend it with text
   B. Define the term and offer multiple examples
   C. Offer multiple examples
   D. Discuss what it is not

3. A major flaw of this essay?
   A. Gross generalizations
   B. Inadequate textual evidence
   C. Conclusion introduces new themes (the thesis) of the short story
   D. Incredulous foils

## Command of Evidence (Student Response 2)

1. The first time the Student Response presents its thesis?
   A. Lines 5–6
   B. Lines 8–9
   C. Lines 12–13
   D. Lines 19–20

2. A general strategy that the essay employs:
   A. Asks several rhetorical questions that it answers
   B. Defines Magic Realism and then offers examples
   C. Uses episodic adventures
   D. Promotes a thesis and then defends it

3. A major flaw of this essay?
   A. Gross generalizations
   B. Inadequate textual evidence
   C. The conclusion introduces tangential arguments
   D. The essay is partisan (lacks objectivity)

## Words in Context (Narrative)

1. What is the meaning of *magnanimous* in Line 27?
   A. Angry
   B. Benevolent
   C. Malevolent
   D. Generous

2. What is the meaning of *decrepitude* in Line 131?
   A. Vigor
   B. Simplicity
   C. Unhappiness
   D. Feebleness

# Lesson 2

## Critical Reading and Writing

### Command of Evidence

Read the following passages and answer the accompanying questions:

### Passage 1

1　Benjamin Franklin, affectionately deemed "The First American," was born in Boston, Massachusetts, to a Puritan
2　family of seventeen siblings and overcame meager beginnings to become one of the most influential and important
3　figures in American history, combining his Puritan roots with new Enlightenment ideas promoting individual
4　freedoms. He made significant scientific discoveries, such as how to harness electricity, and invented a great many
5　useful things like the lightning rod and bifocals, all while prolifically writing eloquent works such as his
6　autobiography and regular publications like *Poor Richard's Almanac*. Franklin's writing style is a composite of the
7　Puritan Plain style of his roots, with journalistic construction that modeled both clarity and brevity from his early
8　career; he used dynamic though not lofty or unattainable diction, sophisticated prose with unexpectedly practical and
9　self-effacing conclusions contributing to his humorous and serious tone, so that with Franklin's insight and counsel,
10　the nation's posterity might grow to a higher level of intellectual, practical, and spiritual maturity.

11　　　Franklin wrote in "lucid and serviceable prose . . . [and shows] the happy results . . . in his solid expository
12　pieces and above all in his incomparable letters treasured by all of his correspondents" (Aaron, xii). In his numerous
13　letters, Franklin used familiar language that was lofty but accessible and endearing. In the beginning of his
14　autobiography, Franklin addressed his son, William, "I have ever had pleasure in obtaining any little anecdotes of
15　my ancestors. . . . Imagining it may be equally agreeable to you to know the circumstances of my life, . . . I sit down
16　to write them for you. . . . Having emerged from the poverty and obscurity in which I was and bred, to a state of
17　affluence and some degree of reputation in the world, . . . my posterity may like to know, as they may find some of
18　them suitable to their own situations" (Stobaugh, 58). Franklin's prose is both high-minded and personal, showing a
19　deep sympathy and passion for the welfare of not only his son, but also all future generations.

20　　　Franklin created the beloved annually published pamphlet *Poor Richard's Almanac*, filled with a
21　smorgasbord of poems, aphorisms, practical advice, puzzles, and new scientific discoveries. The almanac was
22　crafted with engaging illustrations, folksy humor, dry unexpected wit, and colorful epigrams to explore human
23　frailty and offer practical advice to pursue the best kind of living and success. To this end, Franklin wrote such
24　brilliant truisms as these: "Three can keep a secret, if two are dead" and "If you would not be forgotten, as soon as
25　you are dead and rotten, either write things worth reading, or do things worth writing." These publications enriched
26　the culture and formed idiosyncrasies of American society.

27　　　**A motivator of incredible intelligence, Franklin crafted his *Autobiography* with careful word and**
28　**diction choice, using colloquial language; creating a work that appeals to the masses with brevity, clarity, and**
29　**didactic genius; and giving the gift of knowledge to his reader, rather than just propagating his own**
30　**achievements.** Franklin describes a relatable journey toward self-improvement: "As I knew, or thought I knew,
31　what was right and wrong, I did not see why I might not *always* do the one and avoid the other. But I soon found I
32　had undertaken a Task of more Difficulty than I had imagined: While my Care was employ'd in guarding against
33　one Fault, I was often surpriz'd by another" (Franklin, 80). Here the author uses plain language within complex
34　sentence structure and a didactic and earnest tone to connect with his readers and describe the human tendency of
35　minimizing and avoiding the relentless adversity of life. Franklin then outlines "Thirteen Virtues" that he found
36　effective in combating one's nature, including temperance, industry, sincerity, humility, and ironically: chastity.
37　Though Franklin was a known philanderer, he included chastity in his list of ideals, failing on a personal level, he
38　was the "ambivalent ally of flawed mankind" (Aaron xi).

39　　　Benjamin Franklin, America's first celebrity, philosophe, and true Renaissance man, proved that through
40　industry and perseverance, one can rise from obscurity to prominence, wealth, and knowledge. Most important to
41　Franklin was his intent to empower posterity through the how-to effects of lists and illustrations to inspire youth to
42　achieve the rags-to-riches American Dream. Immensely public spirited and foresighted, Franklin, "America's
43　Philosophe," "signed all four critical documents which marked the birth of the American nation" (Allison et al. 5);
44　with his inimitable writing style of epigrammatic, journalistic, logical, and colloquial panache, he helped birth the
45　American identity of pragmatic idealism, altruism, and the spirit of freedom to pursue one's best self. (Zach)

**Works Cited**

Allison, Andrew M., M. Richard Maxfield, and W. Cleon Skousen. *The Real Benjamin Franklin*. Washington, DC: National Center for Constitutional Studies, 1982. Print.

Franklin, Benjamin, Daniel Aaron. *The Autobiography, with an Introduction by Daniel Aaron*. New York: Random House, 1990. Print.

Stobaugh, Dr. James P. *American Literature*. Green Forest, AR: Master Books, 2012. Print.

1. What would be the best title of this essay?
   A. Poor Richard's Almanac
   B. The Story of Electricity
   C. Rags to Riches
   D. Ben Franklin: Witty Statesman

2. What is the purpose of the first paragraph?
   A. The author wishes to increase readers' understanding of the 18th century.
   B. The author gives a general overview of Ben Franklin's life and his contribution to history.
   C. The author begins a chronological history of Franklin.
   D. The author asks a rhetorical question.

3. What organizational plan does the author employ?
   A. He offers a thesis at first and then argues the opposite.
   B. He defines the perimeters of his argument and then gives textual examples.
   C. He states his thesis and then offers arguments from the writings of Franklin and secondary sources.
   D. He asks a series of rhetorical questions.

4. How does the author "move" the reader through the essay?
   I. He gives a series of anecdotes.
   II. He gives a few quotes.
   III. He offers secondary source analyses.
   IV. He compares Franklin to Thomas Jefferson.

   A. I and II
   B. III and IV
   C. I and IV
   D. I, II, III, and IV

5. The author finishes his essay with
   A. A summary of Franklin's contribution to American History
   B. A new conclusion
   C. A Christian warning
   D. With a quote from *Poor Richard's Almanac*

6. This essay can best be described as
   A. Essay
   B. Biography
   C. Polemic
   D. Apology

7. The author
   A. Criticizes Franklin for his immoral behavior
   B. Clearly admires Ben Franklin
   C. Laments that Franklin never makes a public confession of faith
   D. Criticizes the *Autobiography* for its untrue claims

# Passage 2

1  Voltaire wrote about the French and Indian War, "A torch lighted in the forests of America set all Europe in
2  conflagration" (K/C 98). As the French began to spread out into North America, the English were angered by their
3  invasion. French-English skirmishes began to happen more and more frequently during King William's War and

4  Queen Anne's War. The Ohio Valley, needed by the French in order to maintain their empire in North America and
5  needed by the English in order to allow their colonists to spread westward, was also the source of many clashes
6  between France and England. This rivalry was the main cause of the French and Indian War, as two empires fought
7  for predominance in the New World. Ultimately, England won the French and Indian War because of two main
8  reasons: the French wasted much of their strength in Germany at the beginning of the war, and the English general
9  William Pitt was a brilliant strategist.
10      First, the English victory was due in part to the unwise French action in Germany. Kennedy and Cohen
11  write, "Luckily for the British colonists, the French wasted so much strength in this European bloodbath that they
12  were unable to throw an adequate force into the New World. 'America was conquered in Germany,' declared
13  Britain's great statesman William Pitt" (K/C 105). The distraction of the French in Europe ultimately became their
14  downfall, as William Pitt, the English general, took advantage of their preoccupation and concentrated on
15  conquering French forts in the New World colonies.
16      In fact, mostly because of Pitt's impressive strategic skills, the British won the French and Indian War. The
17  general before Pitt, Edward Braddock, was condescending toward the colonists and too traditional in his methods.
18  Braddock, an elderly general who insisted on marching his troops in lines after the customary methods (causing
19  many casualties), was eventually killed in one of the first battles of the war. The new general Pitt was a "splendid
20  orator endowed with a majestic voice, [who] believed passionately in his cause, in his country, and in himself" (K/C
21  106). This "Organizer of Victory" began to pull troops away from attacking the French West Indies, since the
22  distraction was slowly weakening the British cause. He concentrated on Canada, attacking Louisbourg first (present-
23  day Cape Breton Island). The (second) siege of Louisbourg (1758) was a success, bolstering British morale and
24  significant in the conquering of New France. Québec was next, and under the direction of a young officer named
25  James Wolf, it surrendered to the British (1759). It was only a matter of years before France surrendered its colonies
26  completely. **In 1763, the French and Indian War ended, with the British as victors.**
27      England won the French and Indian War because of their brilliant leader and their unwise opponents.
28  Kennedy and Cohen state, "By the peace settlement at Paris, French power was thrown completely off the continent
29  of North America, leaving behind a fertile French population that is to this day a strong minority in Canada" (107).
30  Even though French traces were left in North America, the British would ultimately be known as the true controllers
31  of the New World (Madison).

1.  What would be the best title of this essay?
    A.  A German Victory                 C.  Why England won the French and Indian War
    B.  The Victories of Pitt               D.  The French and Indian War

2.  How does the author begin the essay?
    A.  Summary of Argument             C.  Rhetorical Questions
    B.  Introduction to the Argument        D.  A quote from a 19th Century French philosopher

3.  Why?
    A.  It credibly emphasized the importance of     C.  It draws the reader into the argument.
        this war.                              D.  It develops the main purpose.
    B.  It is interesting.

4.  What is a possible criticism of such a beginning?
    A.  American literature is the best resource to discover human nature
    B.  Never mention an author's name
    C.  Weak quote
    D.  Weak analogy

5.  What organizational plan does the author employ?
    A.  Argument, Evidence, Counterargument     C.  Thesis, Supporting Historical Data
    B.  Thesis, Supporting Textual Evidence,      D.  Anecdotes, Commentary, Conclusion
        Conclusion

6.  The evidentiary strength of this essay?
    A.  Primary Sources                   C.  Extensive Textual Evidence
    B.  Credible Secondary Sources         D.  Conflict and Resolution

7.  The author's primary strategy of creating transitions?
    I.   Using guide words like "First"
    II.  To pause for affect
    III. Double indent
    IV.  To mention a word or thought from the preceding paragraph

    A.  I and II          C.  II and III
    B.  III and IV        D.  I and IV

8.  At the same time, a problem in this use of transitions?
    A.  Too many examples
    B.  There cannot be a "first" without a "second."
    C.  It is boring.
    D.  The transitions are not clear.

## Grammar and Usage

Choose the best grammar/usage form in bold sentence(s).

1.  Passage 1, Lines 27–29
    A.  NONE
    B.  Brilliant and appealing Franklin crafted his *Autobiography* carefully, with different diction choices that included colloquial expression and formal English. As a result, he created an appealing work to all, a work with brevity, clarity, and didactic genius, giving the gift of knowledge to his reader, rather than just propagating his own achievements.
    C.  A motivator of incredible intelligence, Franklin crafted his *Autobiography* with inspired diction choices using colloquial language, creating a work that appeals to the masses with brevity, clarity, and didactic genius, giving the gift of knowledge to his reader, rather than just propagating his achievements.
    D.  A motivator of incredible intelligence, Franklin crafted his *Autobiography* using colloquial language, creating a work that appeals to the masses with brevity, clarity, and didactic genius, giving the gift of knowledge to his reader, rather than just propagating his achievements.

2.  Passage 2, Lines 25–26
    A.  NONE
    B.  England won the French and Indian War because of its brilliant leaders and their unwise opponents.
    C.  England won the French and Indian War because of brilliant leaders and their unwise opponents.
    D.  England won the French and Indian War because of its brilliant leader and its unwise opponents.

# Lesson 3
## SAT Essay

### Student Response 1

*Prompt:* Does one have to fail to be successful?

1     Is failure necessary to have success? Many successful people believe so. The answer can be found in two
2 very different places: the life of a famous inventor and my own personal experiences.
3     Thomas Edison, the inventor of the lightbulb, tried for years to harness electricity to produce light. **Many**
4 **of those who worked with him wanted to give up as failure after failure rocked their confidence in Edison.**
5 However, he responded with surprising foresight in the face of such disappointment. "I have not failed. I've just
6 found 10,000 ways that won't work," he stated, and began another experiment. Finally, Edison reached his dream—
7 the invention of the lightbulb. He had learned from his failures and achieved success.
8     Like Edison, I have had success only because of the presence of failures. When I was younger, I struggled
9 with my weight. Every time I tried to exercise self-control, I failed. However, these failures taught me what I needed
10 to do differently. Every time I failed to meet my exercise goal or stay consistent to my diet, I planned how I would
11 overcome that habit next time. Soon I began to have success surmounting my mountains. Finally I reached my
12 fitness goal. Again, it is only through failures that success met me.
13     Failure is vital to having success. Each time a person fails, one can either give up or learn from the
14 mistakes. It is through disappointment—and the correct response to that failure—that true success is found. In the
15 words of George Cukor, "You can't have any successes unless you can accept failure" (Madison).

### Student Response 2

*Prompt:* Are good decisions worth the cost?

1     In life, we face decisions. In fact, everything that we do is a result of a decision. However, some decisions
2 have weighty, momentous implications on us and on others. Good choices in these situations are sometimes costly.
3     For instance, an acquaintance of mine tried to cull a tree. The tree fell in a direction other than my
4 acquaintance intended, and he felt that he had to stop it. On an impulse, he reached his arm out in front of the falling
5 tree. The tree exerted an inexorable force that bore down on his arm and drove it into a spike on a nearby fence. This
6 decision was costly, but he needed to stop the tree. Although he ultimately failed, it was something that he had to
7 attempt.
8     **Aristotle, in his treatise aptly called *Rhetoric*, said that since public oratory depends on predicting**
9 **future events, the events of the past must be analyzed.** Decision makers for countries need to look at historical
10 examples. Philosopher George Santayana said something with the following import: "Those who don't know history
11 are destined to repeat it." If leaders refuse to appeal to history, they will not only make bad decisions, but they will
12 be costly as well.
13     The Founding Fathers of America knew that the British government was unreasonably tyrannical. They
14 threw off that burdensome yoke of government with firm resolve by enouncing in the Declaration of Independence
15 that their colonies were free and independent states. We know, looking back on what the Founders did, that they
16 made a good decision. They formed a great country called America. However, the great result came at a terrible
17 cost: a war. Yet they persevered and won.
18     Personal experience, philosophy, and history tell us that good decisions are costly. Although they may be
19 costly to us, good decisions will ultimately be worth it. The freedom we enjoy today is a result of a costly decision.
20 (Matthew)

1. In Student Response 1
   A. Failure comes gently and unavoidably.
   B. Failure should be avoided at all cost.
   C. Failure is a distraction, not a necessity.
   D. Failure is generally necessary for lasting success to occur.

2. In Response 2 the author organizes the essay
   A. By stating a rhetorical question and then developing the thesis
   B. By offering a series of anecdotes
   C. By stating a thesis and offering several examples
   D. By a series of bullet points

3. Student Response Essay 1 can be improved by
   I. Giving more specific examples.
   II. Strengthening transitions
   III. Remove personal examples

   IV. Make essay longer
   V. Clearly state the thesis and tie to the topic

   A. I, II, IV, and V
   B. III and IV
   C. II and III

   D. V
   E. All

4. Problems in Student Response Essay 2 include
   I. Examples are not tied closely to the thesis.
   II. Transitions are weak.
   III. There are too many personal examples.
   IV. The essay is too short.
   V. The thesis is not clearly stated nor tied to the topic.

   A. I and II
   B. III and IV
   C. II and III

   D. I, II, IV, and V
   E. NONE

5. The main point of the Student Response 1?
   A. Lines 1–2
   B. Lines 8–9

   C. Lines 13–15
   D. Line 15

6. The main point of the Student Response 2?
   A. Lines 2–4
   B. Lines 8–9

   C. Lines 18–19
   D. Line 20

7. A significant stylistic problem in Student Essay 2?
   A. First person and third person are used interchangeably.
   B. Second-person pronouns are used.
   C. Transitions are weak.
   D. There are agreement problems.

8. Criticism of Student Response 2:
   I. The essay's position is unclear or limited. The critical thinking in the essay is weak and not supported by sufficient or relevant examples and details.
   II. The central idea is poorly defined.
   III. The essay is poorly organized and in general the essay lacks coherence.
   IV. The language is ordinary and uninspiring.
   V. The sentence structure lacks variety and complexity.
   VI. There are serious grammar mistakes.

   A. I, II, and III
   B. I, II, III, IV, and V

   C. IV, V, and VI
   D. NONE

9. What score would the student responses receive?
Student Response 1 receives a __. Student Response 2 receives a __.

## Grammar and Usage

Choose the best grammar/usage form in bold sentence(s).

1. Student Response 1, Lines 3–4
   A. NONE
   B. Many of those who worked with him wanted to give up as failure after failure rocked their confidence in him.
   C. Edison's failures caused many to lose confidence in him.
   D. Many of those who worked with him wanted to give up after failure rocked their confidence in Edison.

2. Student Response 2, Lines 8–9
   A. NONE
   B. Aristotle, in his treatise aptly called *Rhetoric*, argued that since public oratory depends on predicting future events, the events of the past must be analyzed.
   C. Since public oratory depends on predicting future events, Aristotle, in his treatise aptly called *Rhetoric*, said the events of the past must be analyzed.
   D. Aristotle's *Rhetoric* argued that the events of the past must be analyzed in order to make public oratory effective.

---

The essay gives you an opportunity to show how effectively you can read and comprehend a passage and write an essay analyzing the passage. In your essay, you should demonstrate that you have read the passage carefully, present a clear and logical analysis, and use language precisely.

Your essay must be written on the lines provided in your answer booklet; except for the planning page of the answer booklet, you will receive no other paper on which to write. You will have enough space if you write on every line, avoid wide margins, and keep your handwriting to a reasonable size. Remember that people who are not familiar with your handwriting will read what you write. Try to write or print so that what you are writing is legible to those readers.

You have 50 minutes to read the passage and write an essay in response to the prompt provided inside this booklet.

A. Do not write your essay in this booklet. Only what you write on the lined pages of your answer booklet will be evaluated.

B. An off-topic essay will not be evaluated. —College Board <https://collegereadiness.collegeboard.org/sample-questions/essay>

---

# Lesson 4
## Reading: Document-Based Analysis

### John Quincy Adams Defends the Amistad Captives before the U.S. Supreme Court (1841)

1  I appear here on the behalf of thirty-six individuals, the life and liberty of every one of whom depend on the decision
2  of this Court. . . . Three or four of them are female children, incapable, in the judgment of our laws, of the crime of
3  murder or piracy, or, perhaps, of any other crime. Yet, from the day when the vessel was taken possession of by one
4  of our naval officers, they have all been held as close prisoners, now for the period of eighteen long months. . . .
5  The Constitution of the United States recognizes the slaves, held within some of the States of the Union,
6  only in their capacity of persons—persons held to labor or service in a State under the laws thereof—persons
7  constituting elements of representation in the popular branch of the National Legislature—persons, the migration or
8  importation of whom should not be prohibited by Congress prior to the year 1808. The Constitution no where
9  recognizes them as property. The words *slave* and *slavery* are studiously excluded from the Constitution.
10  Circumlocutions are the fig-leaves under which the parts of the body politic are decently concealed. Slaves,
11  therefore, in the Constitution of the United States are persons, enjoying rights and held to the performance of
12  duties. . . .
13  The persons aforesaid, described as slaves, are Negroes and persons of color, who have been transported
14  from Africa in violation of the laws of the United States. . . . The Court should enable the United States to send the
15  Negroes home to Africa . . . in pursuance of the law of Congress passed March 3, 1829, entitled "An act in addition
16  to the acts prohibiting the slave-trade." . . .
17  The President . . . signed [an] order for the delivery of MEN to the control of an officer of the navy to be
18  carried beyond sea. . . . The District Judge, contrary to all [the] anticipations of the Executive, decided that the
19  thirty-six Negroes . . . brought before the Court . . . were FREEMEN; that they had been kidnapped in Africa; that
20  they did not own . . . Spanish names; . . . that they were not correctly described in the passport, but were new
21  Negroes . . . fully entitled to their liberty.
22  Well was it for the country—well was it for the President of the United States himself that he paused before
23  stepping over this Rubicon! The indignation of the freemen of Connecticut might not tamely endure the sight of
24  thirty-six free persons, though Africans, fettered and manacled in their land of freedom, to be transported beyond the
25  seas, to perpetual hereditary servitude or to death, by the servile submission of an American President to the insolent
26  dictation of a foreign minister. . . .
27  [President Van Buren informed his subordinates that] if the decree of the Judge should be in our favor, and
28  you can steal a march upon the Negroes by foreclosing their right of appeal, ship them off without mercy and
29  without delay: and if the decree should be in their favor, fail not to enter an instantaneous appeal to the Supreme
30  Court, where the chances may be more hostile to self-emancipated slaves.
31  Was ever such a scene of Lilliputian trickery enacted by the rulers of a great, magnanimous, and Christian
32  nation? Contrast it with that act of self-emancipation, by which the savage, heathen barbarians Cinqué and Grabeau
33  liberated themselves and their fellow suffering countrymen from Spanish slave traders, and which the Secretary of
34  State . . . denominates lawless violence. . . . Cinqué and Grabeau are uncooth and barbarous names. Call them
35  Harmodius and Aristogiton, and go back for moral principle three thousand years to the fierce and glorious
36  democracy of Athens. They too resorted to lawless violence, and slew the tyrant to redeem the freedom of their
37  country. . . .
38  I said, when I began this plea, that my final reliance for success in this case was on this Court as a court of
39  JUSTICE; and in the confidence this fact inspired, that, in the administration of justice, in a case of no less
40  importance than the liberty and the life of a large number of persons, this Court would not decide but on a due
41  consideration of all the rights, both natural and social, of everyone of these individuals. . . . I have avoided,
42  purposely avoided, . . . a recurrence to those first principles of liberty which might well have been invoked in the
43  argument of this cause. I have shown that [the Amistad's crew members] . . . were acting at the time in a way that is
44  forbidden by the laws of Great Britain, of Spain, and of the United States, and . . . that these Negroes were free and
45  had a right to assert their liberty. . . . .
46  On the 7th of February, 1804, now more than thirty-seven years past, my name was entered, and yet stands
47  recorded, on both the rolls, as one of the Attorneys and Counsellors of this Court. . . . I stand before the same Court,
48  but not before the same judges—nor aided by the same associates—nor resisted by the same opponents. As I cast
49  my eyes along those seats of honor and public trust, now occupied by you, they seek in vain for one of those

50 honored and honorable persons whose indulgence listened then to my voice. Marshall—Cushing—Chase—
51 Washington—Johnson—Livingston—Todd—Where are they? . . . Gone! Gone! All gone! . . . In taking, then, my
52 final leave of this Bar, and of this Honorable Court, I can only ejaculate a fervent petition to Heaven, that every
53 member of it may go to his final account with as little of earthly frailty to answer for as those illustrious dead. . . .
54 (http://www.digitalhistory.uh.edu/disp_textbook.cfm?smtID=3&psid=294)

1. The purpose of this message?
   A. To argue that the Amistad slaves should be acquitted of all charges
   B. To ask for a lighter jail sentence
   C. To argue that America owed these freed slaves reparations
   D. To argue that these slaves should be manumitted

2. Why would this act be necessary in 1841?
   A. The slave trade was legal.       C. Slave importation was legal
   B. Slavery was legal.               D. Slavery was abolished

3. Why do you suppose John Quincy Adams was chosen as the defense attorney?
   I. He was old and wise.
   II. He was a famous abolitionist.
   III. He was the only living statesmen who knew intimately the Founding Fathers.
   IV. He had friends on the Supreme Court.

   A. I and IV        C. II and IV
   B. II and III      D. All

4. What is true about his arguments?
   I. Africans had "vindicated their own right of liberty" by "executing the justice of Heaven" upon a "pirate murderer, their tyrant and oppressor."
   II. Slavery was inevitable, but slave trade must end.
   III. This court case started the American Civil War.

   A. I        C. III        E. II and III
   B. II       D. I and II

5. Which group would benefit for this case?
   A. Slaves              C. Slaves who escaped
   B. Northern Laborers   D. Abolitionists

6. Where does Adams argue that slaves are persons, not property?
   A. Lines 1–5       C. Lines 40–45
   B. Lines 5–11      D. Lines 46–51

7. Opponents to Adams might offer the following relevant arguments:
   I. Slavery is legal in the United States.
   II. Slave trade is illegal, but that does not justify murder (Amistad and his peer murdered the ship's crew).
   III. Slavery is unprofitable.

   A. I        C. III
   B. II       D. All

# Lesson 5

## Math: Algebra, Arithmetic Problem Solving and Data Analysis, and Passport to Advanced Math

**Data Analysis**

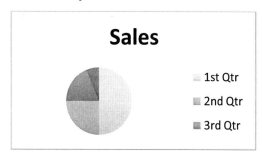

| | Sales |
|---|---|
| 1st Qtr | 16 |
| 2nd Qtr | 8 |
| 3rd Qtr | 6 |
| 4th Qtr | 2 |

What is true about this chart?

  I.  1st quarter sales were equal to all the other quarters combined
 II.  2nd quarter sales are equal to 3rd and 4th quarter sales combined
III.  Sales declined 50% in the 2nd quarter

A. I

B. II and III

C. I and IV

D. All

## Algebra

1. Take the sum of $x^3 + 3x - 2$, $2x^3 + x^2 - x + 5$, and $4x^3 + 2x^2 - 7x + 4$ from the sum of $2x^3 + 9x$ and $5x^3 + 3x^2$.
   A. $12x - 6$
   B. $14x - 7$
   C. $10x - 5$
   D. $19x - 3$

2. Multiply $b^4 - 2b^2$ by $b^4 + 2b^2 - 1$.
   A. $b^6 - 2b^4 + 1$
   B. $b^8 - 2b^2 + 1$
   C. $b^6 - 2b + 1$
   D. $b^8 - 5b^4 + 2b^2$

3. Simplify $11x + 4y^2 - (2xy - 3y^2) + (2x^2 - 3xy) - (3x^2 - 5xy)$.
   A. $11x + 7y^2 - x^2$
   B. $10x + 7y$
   C. $8x^2 + 4y^2$
   D. $12x^2 + 8y^2$

4. Divide $300 among A, B, and C, so that A shall have twice as much as B, and B $20 more than C.
   A. $160; $80; $60
   B. $140; $60; $40
   C. $180; $90; $70
   D. $150; $70; $50

5. Find two numbers differing by 8 such that four times the less may exceed twice the greater by 10.
   A. 14; 22
   B. 12; 20
   C. 13; 21
   D. 10; 19

6. What must be added to $3a^3 - 4a^2 - 4$ to produce $5a^3 + 6$?
   A. $3a^3 + 6a^2 + 12$
   B. $4a^3 + 8a^2 + 16$
   C. $3a^3 + 9a^2 + 18$
   D. $2a^3 + 4a^2 + 10$

# Chapter 2  A Time for Covenant Renewal

# Joshua 4

*Memory Verses:* So Joshua called together the twelve men he had appointed from the Israelites, one from each tribe, and said to them, "Go over before the ark of the Lord your God into the middle of the Jordan. Each of you is to take up a stone on his shoulder, according to the number of the tribes of the Israelites, to serve as a sign among you. In the future, when your children ask you, 'What do these stones mean?' Tell them that the flow of the Jordan was cut off before the ark of the covenant of the Lord. When it crossed the Jordan, the waters of the Jordan were cut off. These stones are to be a memorial to the people of Israel forever." —Joshua 4:4–7

After being in bondage for over four hundred years and wandering in the wilderness for almost fifty, a new generation of Israelites was preparing to cross the Jordan River into the Promised Land, a land—a way of life—promised to them for over three generations by their God, Yahweh, Elohim, Adonai, their beloved Lord.

Less than a month earlier, their leader Moses had died. Moses, the covenant maker, the mediator, the founder of Israel, the intercessor—Moses was dead. Almost single-handedly, he had taken a group of ragtag, stiff-necked people, loosely knit together by religion and ethnic ties, welded them into a nation, and led them across some of the most difficult terrain of the known world. Moses' passion had won their confidence and solidified them. His complete dedication to God had inspired them to deeds they never would have deemed possible. Around nocturnal campfires, inspiring stories were shared, stories of crossing the mighty Red Sea and the destruction of Pharaoh's army. Heroic tales—stories of Moses' military prowess and astute leadership. Gentle laughter was heard as the uneasy Israelites fondly remembered their beloved leader.

But these were only haunting memories passed down from their deceased relative. What had God done for them recently? Now, directly in front of them was an anemic version of the Red Sea, the muddy, unpretentious Jordan River, but nevertheless a formidable obstacle. Looming on the horizon were the hills of unfriendly Canaan and before that the well-defended citadel of Jericho—all reminders of the difficult road lying ahead.

There was an uneasiness in the camp of Israel, an uneasiness not unlike the uneasiness a bride feels after her wedding. For all of her life she has planned for this special day—and it has been all that she had hoped it to be and more. But that special day is over, over forever. After she has packed up her wedding dress, she sighs as she considers the coming days—days full of fattening waistlines or crabby husbands. Hardly the stuff of which dreams are made! Is this the best she will know all her life? Is this the pinnacle of life's experiences? Likewise the Israelites must have thought, "Are the good old days gone forever? Will God show us the miracles as he so faithfully did for our fathers and grandmothers?"

The most teasingly uncomfortable thought of all, though, was the fact that Moses, predictable dependable Moses, was dead. Moses had died and was buried in the land of Moab (Deut. 34:5–6), but they were told to cross the Jordan River and possess this most unappetizing Canaanite land. Again, around many twilight campfires, no doubt whiskered Hebrews whispered, "Who will lead us now?"

Dawn, the last dawn that they were to spend on the east bank of the Jordan River, brought no new confidence into the Israeli camp. As the fog slowly lifted from the silently flowing Jordan River, no one seemed to be in a hurry to stir. For the first time in over fifty years, they were a people without a leader. Where is the bridge? It would be easy enough for the people to wade across, but what about the wagons, the tents, the tabernacle? As breakfast was being prepared, no one dared ask, yet everyone wondered, "How is this aging and rather lackluster son of Nun going to pull it off?"

Joshua, son of Nun, was also nervous. Although Joshua was around sixty, he had never led this nation: Moses had always taken care of that. And until recently, Joshua had supposed that one of Moses' heirs would take over at Moses' death. That was just fine with Joshua. Although Joshua loved to cast his spear into the enemies of God, he detested the duties of political leadership. Leave all that to the priests and tribal elders, full of wise words. Joshua, the warrior, preferred the exhilaration of warfare to the nuts and bolts of administration. Nevertheless, here he was: in a dramatic calling, God had declared that he was to lead this hopeless excuse of an army and a notoriously unpredictable, recalcitrant nation. A nation indeed! They did not even have a homeland.

That promised homeland protruded ominously out of the dissipating morning mist. What lay ahead? Joshua must have sighed as he thought about the prospects.

Yet even deeper than these unspoken fears was Joshua's love for God. He paused for a moment and remembered that his God really loved him. If Joshua mistrusted his armies, he certainly trusted God. "I will be your God, and you will be my people" were words spoken to and memorized by Joshua and every Hebrew child since Abraham's times. He knew that the Israelites had a special relationship with God, a bond that transcended time and circumstances. God had made a covenant with them, so they were not operating merely from their own resources.

Through all of Israel's history runs the awareness that it has a covenant with and relates to its God. Covenants were quite common in the ancient Middle East, but only the Jewish people had a covenant with their God, the Creator of all. Simply put, a covenant is an agreement, a contract between two parties. "If you do this," it begins, "I will do this." The contract is abrogated only when one or both parties do not uphold their side of the bargain. They were a chosen, special people because God had chosen to tie his purposes with their personal history.

Paul, the earliest New Testament writer, develops the covenant theme even more. In Romans, Paul unravels this idea and calls it *adoption*. By understanding adoption, we should be able to garnish fruitful insights into the biblical concept of covenant.

Karen and I understand adoption. Almost thirty-five years ago, Karen and I received a phone call from the Goodwill Home and Missions Christian Adoption Service. Within a month we were to receive our second daughter. To say that we were excited is a great understatement. It was as if we had to complete nine months of preparation in only three weeks!

Jessica Ruth, our precocious fireball, finally came a few days after Thanksgiving. As we were quickly swallowed by her deep blue eyes and flirtatious dimples, we covenanted our lives to her as long as we and she should live. Keep in mind that we, not she, initiated this contract, this covenant. Jessica had no say in the matter.

God took the initiative with Israel. In his grace he turned to a group of nomadic tribes and made them Israel. The covenant rested on his free favor (Berkhof, *Theology*). Abram, a man with no past or future, was drawn by God into the vortex of history; his name was changed, and he was given a new future. Jane Doe, a female infant with no name, no past or future, was suddenly, inextricably, and permanently drawn into our lives and given a new name: Jessica Ruth. A little fuzzy haired black girl who looks nothing like us became our child. She became our inheritance. Not only did she take our name, but our parents also became her grandparents, and her children will be our grandchildren. And so it was with Israel. God chose this unlikely band of nomads to be his people; He gave them a name, a history, and a future. His inheritance became their inheritance. They bore his name.

In Romans 8:15 we read that the believer is adopted; at conversion we are given a covenant, a contract. Adoption has four consequences: (1) the adopted person loses all rights in the old family and gains all the rights of a legitimate child in the new family. We no longer belong to the world, nor must we answer to its demands. We belong to God; we carry his name.

It followed that (2) the adopted persons become heir to their new father's estate. Even if other sons or daughters are born afterward, it does not affect their rights. All the adoptees are inalienably coheirs with Christ (Rom. 8:17). The old life of those adopted is wiped out. We are all equally coheirs in God's family.

Also, (3) all debts are canceled. The adoptees are regarded as new persons, entering into a new life disconnected from past mistakes. Our old sins, although serious, should not affect our lives today. For we are forgiven and brought into covenant relationship by the vicarious sacrifice of our Lord Jesus Christ.

Finally, (4) in the eyes of the law, each adoptee is absolutely the child of the new father. That meant that if the adopted son or daughter has committed a crime or incurred an obligation, the adoptive family is responsible. And so we stand before our heavenly Father when we sin. Fortunately, our Father God sees us through the blood of his Son.

I emphasize that this covenant is irrevocable, permanent. Once consummated, nothing can change it: nothing! Permanence is a difficult concept for us to grasp. So much of our world is impermanent. Our world is full of discarded Cheerio boxes and dysfunctional automobiles. We live five years in Chicago and eight in Pittsburgh and then move to New York. We buy a toaster, it wears out, and we buy another: nothing is permanent in our lives. When we begin something new, we jettison the memories of the old as quickly as possible.

But adoption is permanent. Jessica is not a puppy that we can discard if she wets in the corner or if she cries at night. No, for better or for worse, as long as history is recorded, Jessica will be known as our little girl.

It was this same adopted, covenant relationship with God, this love affair with the Almighty, that warmed Joshua's heart as he broke camp to cross the Jordan. His confidence was not in flesh and blood, in chariots, in spears, but in God and his permanent promise to support the children of Israel as long as they followed his law.

But here is the fly in the ointment. So far I have only indicated how God acts in this covenant. And it is true that God initiates his covenant, but the covenant cannot function without humankind's faithful response to God's commands. The covenant with Israel, fulfilled in the Christian covenant, is unilateral in origin but bilateral in purpose. God demands trust and obedience from his covenant partner. The Jewish nation must act—step into the cold foreboding stream, possess the land—in response to God's command. The covenant is inoperative until the Israelites move, break camp, begin to cross the Jordan into the Promised Land. Promises are merely promises unless they are possessed, grasped by God's covenant partner, meaning Israel then and all of us believers today.

Into the Jordan step the priests this early morning. Bearing the ark of the covenant, a symbolic reminder of God's irrevocable covenant with his people, they are assured that God will part the waters. Why? Because God has promised to do so. Suddenly the waters stop. As the priests stand in intercession, the Jewish nation, led by Joshua, effortlessly cross the Jordan River.

Believers, we all are stepping into the Jordan River. We know the waters will part because our God, our covenant God, has promised that they will. We will not trust in programs, slogans, impressive degrees, or money: we trust only in God. Look! We are standing in the river! Will you join us? Will you join us as we possess the land? The land is ours, promised to us, but we must possess it.

Later, in quieter moments, the Hebrews made camp on the western side of the Jordan River. Joshua had entered the Jordan as an inexperienced, unknown leader, but he walked out the other side as a respected man of God. He was what the Hebrews call a "servant of God," a most honorific term reserved for the greatest Jewish leaders; Abraham and Moses were servants of God. "That day the Lord exalted Joshua in the sight of all Israel; and they stood in awe of him all the days of his life, just as they had stood in awe of Moses" (Josh. 4:14) The Israelites had a new leader, a leader every bit as capable as Moses. There was new confidence in the camp of Israel.

Joshua's first orders to the Israelites were to remember what God had done:

> In the future when your descendants ask their parents, "What do these stones mean?" tell them, "Israel crossed the Jordan on dry ground." For the LORD your God dried up the Jordan before you until you had crossed over. The LORD your God did to the Jordan what he had done to the Red Sea when he dried it up before us until we had crossed over. He did this so that all the peoples of the earth might know that the hand of the Lord is powerful and so that you might always fear the LORD your God. (Josh. 4:21–24)

As the Israelites did at Gilgal with their twelve stones, let us do with our lives (Josh. 4:20). Let us make this a special day; let us build a memorial to God in the next few weeks, a memorial of which our children will speak someday. As our Lord dried up the waters of the Red Sea and the Jordan River, as he healed the sick in Galilee, so also he has promised to do for us. Let us impact our town and country so that all may know that the hand of the Lord is mighty; that we may fear the Lord our God forever.

This crossing is a sacred moment, one we should remember for the rest of our lives. How blessed we are to be part of this sacred moment! Let us pause and savor God's presence in our midst. As the Israelites paused on the west bank of the Jordan, they listened to the muffled sounds of the morning. Looming in front of them was a foreboding, unconquered land, but a Promised Land, a land flowing with milk and honey. Let us be silent before God, before the magnitude of our task, but let us not falter; let us not forget our covenant partner. We bring nothing that can help us to overcome our formidable obstacles, no messianic cure for all programs, nothing but our Lord Jesus Christ. Insofar as we allow Christ to control our lives and ministry, that is the degree to which we shall be successful.

On that first night, on the edge of the Promised Land, the children of Israel gathered around the priests to sing psalms and to hear heroic stories of God's faithfulness. In those days there were no books, and the people relied on the priests to recall accurately the exploits of God. No doubt these Hebrews had heard the same stories countless times. But each time they were told, new excitement vibrated through the group: in a real sense, in the Hebrew mind, every time the story was retold, part of it came alive again. This is the way we experience Scripture. As we gather and retell some marvelous stories of our wonderful, faithful, powerful God—journey stories, so to speak—we possess the land. This God we serve is the same God whom our faithful forebears served. God has made great promises, and we must keep our obligations to God. We will not become complacent. The land is not yet ours; we are only camped on the edge. But the land is ours to possess, and with God's guidance and power we will do so. We may need to walk seven dusty days around Jericho, but we will possess the land. There will be no giving in to evil as long as we are alive. We will not compromise. We will grow, no matter how painful, until that day when our Lord shall return. Yes, there are giants in the land; yes, the "Canaanites" are powerful. But remember, Jericho is ahead of us and the Red Sea is behind us. Let us join to break camp and possess the Promised Land!

## Journal Question

What evidence do you have that you are adopted into the Christian family?

# Lesson 1
## Evidence-Based Reading and Writing

### Literary Choice

Edgar Lee Masters is best remembered for his great collection *Spoon River Anthology*, a sequence of over two hundred free-verse epitaphs spoken from the cemetery of the town of Spoon River.

**Lucinda Matlock**

1     I went to the dances at Chandlerville,
2     And played snap-out at Winchester.
3     One time we changed partners,
4     Driving home in the moonlight of middle June,
5     And then I found Davis.
6     We were married and lived together for seventy years,
7     Enjoying, working, raising the twelve children,
8     Eight of whom we lost
9     Ere I had reached the age of sixty.
10    I spun, I wove, I kept the house, I nursed the sick,
11    I made the garden, and for holiday
12    Rambled over the fields where sang the larks,
13    And by Spoon River gathering many a shell,
14    And many a flower and medicinal weed—
15    Shouting to the wooded hills, singing to the green valleys.
16    At ninety-six I had lived enough, that is all,
17    And passed to a sweet repose.
18    What is this I hear of sorrow and weariness,
19    Anger, discontent, and drooping hopes?
20    Degenerate sons and daughters,
21    Life is too strong for you—
22    It takes life to love Life.

### Student Response

**Lucinda Matlock Analysis**

1    "Life is too strong for you—it takes life to love Life." These words, penned by poet Edgar Lee Masters, are from his
2    poem "Lucinda Matlock." It starts out simply, telling of the young Lucinda's romance with her husband, Davis.
3    Moving on to her cramped but not unhappy middle life, filled with worldly cares of raising children, providing for
4    her family, and escaping to the woods for a few joyful, carefree moments. When she reaches the age of ninety-six,
5    she passes to a "sweet repose." Masters ends the poem with the line " It takes life to love Life." Why does Lucinda
6    so passionately assert this fact? Branching from the worldview Realism reflected in Master's poem, Matlock comes
7    to realize that a person must experience all of the ups and downs of life to truly appreciate living.
8         In the first part of the poem, Matlock is just beginning to live life: she is young and inexperienced:
9
10          I went to the dances at Chandlerville
11          And played snap-out at Winchester.
12          One time we changed partners
13          Driving home in the moonlight of middle June,
14          And then I found Davis.
15
16    After she finds Davis, her life is changed as she begins the responsible life of a homemaker and mother:
17
18          We were married and lived together for seventy years,
19          Enjoying, working, raising the twelve children,
20          Eight of whom we lost
21          Ere I had reached the age of sixty.

| 22 | I spun, I wove, I kept the house, I nursed the sick, |
|---|---|
| 23 | I made the garden, and for holiday |
| 24 | Rambled over the fields where sang the larks, |
| 25 | And by Spoon River gathering many a shell |
| 26 | And many a flower and medicinal weed— |
| 27 | Shouting to the wooded hills, singing to the green valleys. |
| 28 | |
| 29 | Here Matlock goes through the humdrum, normal duties of life, loving, working, and losing, joy and sorrow. She |
| 30 | lives her life interspersed by short periods of rest found in the natural setting around her: the woods, streams, and |
| 31 | valleys. |
| 32 | Finally, Matlock "passes to a sweet repose" after a life filled with toil, joy, and pain. |
| 33 | |
| 34 | At ninety-six I had lived enough, that is all, |
| 35 | And passed to a sweet repose. |
| 36 | What is this I hear of sorrow and weariness, |
| 37 | Anger, discontent, and drooping hopes? |
| 38 | Degenerate sons and daughters, |
| 39 | Life is too strong for you— |
| 40 | It takes life to love Life. |
| 41 | |
| 42 | Lucinda surprisingly questions the discontent of those around her, telling them that truly, you must experience the |
| 43 | ups and downs of life in order to love it. |
| 44 | Edgar Lee Master in his poem "Lucinda Matlock" wishes to tell the reader that in order to truly love life, |
| 45 | you must live through all of it. His protagonist goes through love, joy, sorrow, work, and play in a calm fashion, |
| 46 | experiencing what is sent her way. Indeed, Lucinda truly gives the message that "Life is too strong for you— / It |
| 47 | takes life to love Life." |

## Close Reading

1. This literary piece is
   A. Drama
   B. Poetry
   C. Short Story
   D. Novelette

2. Specifically, this literary piece is a/an
   A. Epitaph
   B. Aphorism
   C. Soliloquy
   D. Diatribe

3. The narrative technique?
   A. Omniscient
   B. Limited Omniscient
   C. First Person
   D. Third Person Objective

4. The tone of most of the literary piece?
   A. Serious Reflective
   B. Sanguine
   C. Anger
   D. Phlegmatic

5. The author creates the tone by:
   A. Humorous scenes
   B. Dialogue and aphorisms
   C. Tense interpersonal rivalries
   D. Stream of consciousness

6. This worldview of the literary piece?
   A. Romanticism
   B. Theism
   C. Naturalism
   D. Realism

7. The literary type is best described as
   A. Realism
   B. Romanticism
   C. Existentialism
   D. Deism

8. A central motif of the literary piece?
   A. Unrequited Love
   B. Disappointment
   C. Revenge
   D. Celebration of Life

9. Literature with a similar motif?
   A. *The Book of Ruth*
   B. *The Book of Ecclesiastes*
   C. *Go Down, Moses*
   D. *The Odyssey*

## Command of Evidence (Student Response)

1. The first time the Student Response presents its thesis is where?
   A. Lines 1–2
   B. Lines 6–7
   C. Lines 26–27
   D. Lines 28–30

2. A general strategy that the Student Response employs:
   A. State an argument and defend it with text
   B. Define the term and offer multiple examples
   C. Offer multiple examples
   D. Discuss what it is not

3. A major flaw of the Student Response?
   A. Gross generalizations
   B. Inadequate textual evidence
   C. The conclusion introduces new heretofore unmentioned themes (the thesis) of the short story
   D. Superficial Analysis

4. A major syntax/grammar problem?
   A. Second-person pronouns
   B. Run-on sentences
   C. Weak evidence
   D. Misspelled words

# Lesson 2
## Critical Reading and Writing

### Command of Evidence

Read the following passages and answer the accompanying questions:

### Passage 1

1   Nathaniel Hawthorne utilizes the characters of Arthur Dimmesdale, Roger Chillingworth, and Hester Prynne in *The*
2   *Scarlet Letter* to represent moral qualities and characteristics. Reverend Arthur Dimmesdale is cowardly, never
3   publicly repenting of his adultery, although he is deeply aware of his sin. Roger Chillingworth stands out in the
4   novel as the amoral villain. Only seeking revenge, he cares most about himself rather than his wife. Hester Prynne
5   stands as not only the protagonist but also the heroine. Remaining strong throughout the literary work, she repents of
6   her sin and accepts the punishment, which eventually brings her restoration. These three distinct main characters
7   bring to the reader a wide array of moral characteristics and concepts.
8            Throughout *The Scarlet Letter*, Reverend Arthur Dimmesdale struggles with his sin of committing adultery
9   with Hester Prynne. However, unlike Hester, Dimmesdale does not publicly repent of his sin until the very end of
10  the novel. For most of the work, he remains timid and cowardly. In chapter 11, "The Interior of a Heart,"
11  Dimmesdale achieves great respect and popularity in the village because of his fervent preaching. His great
12  messages are due to his personal struggles with sin. "While thus suffering under bodily disease, and gnawed and
13  tortured by some black trouble of the soul, . . . the Reverend Mr. Dimmesdale had achieved a brilliant popularity in
14  his sacred office. He won it, indeed, in great part by his sorrows." However, while he was delivering these powerful
15  messages, he tormented himself, wanting to confess to his congregation. "He longed to speak out, from his own
16  pulpit, at the full height of his voice, and tell the people what he was: . . . 'I, your pastor, whom you so reverence
17  and trust, am utterly a pollution and a lie!'" Yet he does not admit to his sins; instead, he literally beats himself in
18  private. "His inward trouble drove him to practices, more in accordance with the old, corrupted faith of Rome, than
19  with the better light of the church in which he had been born and bred. In Mr. Dimmesdale's secret closet, under
20  lock and key, there was a bloody scourge. Oftentimes this Protestant and Puritan divine had plied it on his own
21  shoulders. . . . He kept vigils, likewise, night after night, sometimes in utter darkness. . . . He thus typified the
22  constant introspection wherewith he tortured, but could not purify, himself." Dimmesdale's desperation and guilt
23  haunt him for the most of the literary work. It is not until one of the last chapters that he confesses to the town. Even
24  then, he recognizes his lateness in doing so. "'People of New England!' cried he. . . . 'At last! At last! I stand upon
25  the spot where, seven years since, I should have stood; here, with this woman.'" Arthur Dimmesdale is a man with a
26  great conviction, yet he is too spineless to admit what he has done.
27           Roger Chillingworth, a European scholar, is the husband of Hester Prynne. **When he arrives in America,**
28  **he discovers her on the town scaffold with an illegitimate child, accused of adultery.** Chillingworth is the villain
29  of the novel, representing pure evil. He is only concerned with himself, and his primary goal is to seek revenge.
30  Hester is in prison when he meets with her in chapter 4, "The Interview." He shares with her that he will seek and
31  find the man who committed adultery with her. "His fame, his position, his life, will be in my hands. Beware!"
32  Hearing his plans, Hester accuses him of possibly being the Black Man. "Art thou like the Black Man that haunts the
33  forests round about us?" The Black Man was considered to be the devil in Christian folklore, associated with
34  witchcraft in America. He places himself as the judge and punisher of Hester's sin, yet he never wishes to help or
35  forgive her. After Dimmesdale dies, in the conclusion, Hawthorne shares with the reader that Chillingworth soon
36  died as well, simply because the object of his revenge was gone and he had no more purpose to his life. "Nothing
37  was more remarkable than the change which took place, almost immediately after Mr. Dimmesdale's death, in the
38  appearance and demeanour of the old man known as Roger Chillingworth. All his strength and energy . . . seemed at
39  once to desert him. . . . This unhappy man had made the very principle of his life to consist in the pursuit and
40  systematic exercise of revenge; and when . . . that evil principle was left with no further material to support it, when,
41  in short, there was no more devil's work on earth for him to do, it only remained for the unhumanized mortal to
42  betake himself whither his Master would find him tasks enough, and pay him his wages duly." The author clearly
43  viewed Chillingworth as the Devil's helper, the picture of evil.
44           Hester Prynne is not only the protagonist of *The Scarlet Letter*; she is the heroine as well. She does not hide
45  her sin like Dimmesdale; instead, she accepts the punishment. Hester understands that her public repentance and
46  punishment will eventually bring restoration. Throughout the literary work, she remains strong, courageous, and
47  faithful. Because of her strength, in chapter 13, "Another View of Hester," many of the townspeople have

48 reinterpreted the meaning of her scarlet letter. "She was self-ordained a Sister of Mercy. . . . The letter was the
49 symbol of her calling. Such helpfulness was found in her—so much power to do, and power to sympathize—that
50 many people refused to interpret the scarlet A by its original signification. They said that it meant Able; so strong
51 was Hester Prynne, with a woman's strength." When Dimmesdale publicly announces his sin from seven years
52 earlier, Hester is by his side, there to support him. She remained faithful to him for those seven years, always loving
53 him. "'Hester Prynne,' cried he, with a piercing earnestness, 'in the name of Him, so terrible and so merciful, who
54 gives me grace, at this last moment, to do what—for my own heavy sin and miserable agony—I withheld myself
55 from doing seven years ago, come hither now, and twine thy strength about me!'"
56       Arthur Dimmesdale, Roger Chillingworth, and Hester Prynne interact with one another throughout *The*
57 *Scarlet Letter*, yet their characters represent distinctly different moral characteristics. Dimmesdale is cowardly,
58 waiting till the very end of the novel to publicly confess. Chillingworth is driven by evil and a passion for revenge.
59 Hester, the true heroine of the novel, is strong and faithful throughout Hawthorne's literary work. (Claire)

1.  What would be the best title of this essay?
    A.  The Adulterer and the Doctor
    B.  The Rose in the Thorns
    C.  Four Characters in *The Scarlet Letter*
    D.  Ben Franklin: Witty Statesman

2.  What is the purpose of the first paragraph?
    A.  The author wishes to increase readers' understanding of Puritan New England
    B.  The author gave a history of the Hawthorne corpus
    C.  The author offers a summary of the characters in *The Scarlet Letter*
    D.  The author asks a rhetorical question

3.  What organizational plan does the author employ?
    A.  He offers a thesis at first and then argues the opposite
    B.  He defines the perimeters of his argument and then gives textual examples
    C.  He states his thesis and then offers supporting anecdotes
    D.  He asks a series of rhetorical questions

4.  How does the author "move" the reader through the essay?
    I.    She gives a few quotes.
    II.   She gives a series of anecdotes.
    III.  She compares this novel to several other Hawthorne works.
    IV.   She systematically discusses each character.

    A.  I and II
    B.  III and IV
    C.  I and IV
    D.  IV

5.  The author finishes his essay with
    A.  A summary of the novel
    B.  A new conclusion: Hester Prynne is the most winsome character
    C.  A Christian warning
    D.  With a quote from *The Scarlet Letter*

6.  The author:
    A.  Criticizes Dimmesdale for his immoral behavior
    B.  Clearly admires Hester Prynne
    C.  Laments that Chillingworth never makes a public confession of faith
    D.  Criticizes Hawthorne for his faith

## Passage 2

1 Stemming from Romanticism, the philosophical movement of Transcendentalism is uniquely American, gaining
2 popularity in the mid-1800s. This movement, spread by such writers as Ralph Waldo Emerson and Henry David
3 Thoreau, had a significant impact on American thought. It crafted the notion that people should be able to follow

4    their own feelings, going with what they personally believed was right. An omniscient God was absent from this
5    philosophy, replaced instead with nature. Transcendentalism encouraged subjectivity and intuition.

6           Preceding the growth of Transcendentalism, America was still entrenched in a theistic worldview. Yet
7    Transcendentalism was completely at odds with the Judeo-Christian worldview. Instead of encouraging the worship
8    of an omniscient God, transcendentalists encouraged the reverence of omniscient nature. Because of this, Henry
9    David Thoreau and Ralph Waldo Emerson, along with other supporters of this philosophy "engaged in the social
10   experiments of Brook Farm, Fruitlands, and Walden," according to the *Stanford Encyclopedia of Philosophy*. In
11   these "experiments," Thoreau and Emerson lived alone with nature. Their years spent in such secluded places as
12   Walden also highlighted the element of individualism in Transcendentalism. Not only was God not a part of this
13   romantic-like vision; other humans and institutions were also considered not absolutely necessary in one's life. Such
14   societal structures as the church and community were not needed for a person's spiritual walk and life. The
15   transcendentalists also viewed the church and other components of the community as extremely based in tradition,
16   which they viewed as bondage. R. Lundin, writing for the *Elwell Evangelical Dictionary*, explains, "According to
17   Thoreau, it is not man's sin but his boredom and weariness that are 'as old as Adam.' The American Adam needs to
18   exchange his bondage to tradition for a freedom to experiment: 'old deeds for old people, and new deeds for new.'"
19   This call for "a freedom to experiment" was essentially a rejection of the past.

20         Transcendentalism affected American thought, particularly by encouraging subjectivity. Because of the
21   fierce individualism taught by the supporters of this movement, people were also taught that whatever they believed
22   was right. R. Lundin writes, "[Transcendentalists] were committed to intuition as a way of knowing." They believed
23   that a person should go with whatever they believed to be right in their own eyes. Instead of God or fate determining
24   a person's life, it was the person's own feelings and perceptions that would guide their steps. In Duke University's
25   outline of central concepts for Transcendentalism, individualism is again highlighted: "An individual is the spiritual
26   center of the universe. Within the self or the individual are found the clues or the secrets to nature, history, and the
27   cosmos. . . . All knowledge begins with self-knowledge."

28         Moving away from the theistic worldview, Transcendentalism embraced an omniscient nature. **Followers**
29   **of this philosophical movement threw off traditions and the past, instead encouraging individualism.**
30   Transcendentalists encouraged Americans to follow their own feelings and intuitions, proceeding with what they
31   personally believed to be right. (Claire)

1. What would be the best title of Passage 2?
   A. Romanticism
   B. Emerson and Thoreau
   C. Why the Light Shines Brightly
   D. The Origin of Transcendentalism

2. How does the author begin her essay?
   A. Summary of Argument
   B. Introduction to the Argument
   C. A Definition of Transcendentalism
   D. A Story

3. Why?
   A. She likes Thoreau.
   B. She wanted to differentiate Transcendentalism from Romanticism.
   C. She placed Transcendentalism in the context of American history.
   D. She wants to clarify American Romanticism versus German Romanticism.

4. What organizational plan does the author employ?
   A. Argument, Evidence, Counter-Argument
   B. Thesis, Supporting Textual Evidence, Conclusion
   C. Thesis, Supporting Historical Data, Textual Evidence
   D. Anecdotes, Commentary, Conclusion

5. The evidentiary strength of this essay?
   A. Primary Sources
   B. Credible Secondary Sources
   C. Extensive Textual Evidence
   D. Conflict and Resolution

6. The author's primary strategy of creating transitions?
   I. To pause for affect
   II. Using guide words like "Transcendentalism."
   III. Double indent
   IV. To mention a word or thought from the preceding paragraph

   A. I and II
   B. III and IV
   C. II and III
   D. I and IV

## Grammar and Usage

Choose the best grammar/usage form in bold sentence(s).

1. Passage 1, Lines 27–28
   A. NONE
   B. When he arrives in America, he discovers Hester on the town scaffold with an illegitimate child, accused of adultery.
   C. When he arrives in America, his adulterous wife is standing on the town scaffold with her illegitimate son.
   D. When he arrives in America, he finds her on the town scaffold with an illegitimate child, accused of adultery.

2. Passage 2, Lines 28–29
   A. NONE
   B. Encouraging individualism, followers of this philosophical movement rejected past traditions.
   C. Followers of this philosophical movement threw past traditions, instead encouraging individualism.
   D. Followers of this philosophical movement threw rejected the past, instead encouraging individualism.

# Lesson 3
## SAT Essay

### Student Response 1

*Prompt:* What are the benefits of a people-centered philosophy?

1  Humanistic ideology affected the human psyche in multiple ways, including people's ability to be content
2  with themselves, their more independent persona in relation to the church, and a newfound motivation to simply do
3  more with themselves as opposed to their originally bleak and desolate condition during the Dark Ages. Humanism
4  was a revolutionary concept that characterized the Renaissance. Its core belief was that humanity should be able to
5  celebrate for all the things they have accomplished. We are not as bad as the church would like us to think. In fact,
6  humanity is rather neat. As a result, there was a drastic rise in the egos of the individual citizens of the Renaissance.
7  During the Dark Ages, the concept of self-worth was in deep malpractice if not nonexistent. People were
8  scared, superstitious, and obsessed with pleasing Jesus with their suffering. The Renaissance brought a complete and
9  utter alteration to this bleak train of thought. People were suddenly capable of appreciating what they had and even
10  rising up in the world and obtaining more. People were happy. Granted, not all were happy, but there was still a
11  marked change in overall consumer satisfaction. Entrepreneurs and merchants saw a rise in the acceptability of free
12  enterprise. They created and invented with high hopes and starstruck eyes. They were content and not bogged down
13  by the bleak self-sacrificial nature of the church or the fear of catching some rat disease.
14  More than art and industry came out of the Renaissance. The church had had a firm grasp on the people of
15  Europe for a long time. However, the Renaissance saw a group of people rise up with their own ideologies brought
16  about by Humanism. Thinkers like Hume, Rousseau, Nietzsche, and Voltaire began publishing their works. Each
17  one hinted at the need for humanity to realize that the church held them back from their potential. Nietzsche went so
18  far as to say "god is dead." Concepts such as this were previously viewed as taboo and even illegal, as far as the
19  church's power goes. However, the Renaissance saw a rise in the acceptability of Deism, Atheism, and
20  Existentialism. All this happened because the idea of humanism paved the way for self-reliance in the people as well
21  as a newfound courage to stand up for their personal beliefs and opposed to using religion as a crutch.
22  Finally, humanism was a self-motivator. It inspired people to simply do more. Artists, musicians, scientists,
23  mathematicians, and even writers saw opportunities and milestones that were previously unattainable. People
24  actually wanted things that others created. Art and music filled the halls of not only the wealthy, but the working
25  class as well. Humanism gave people a chance to find their inner creator. To be an artist was now a highly respected
26  and attainable occupation, not just something restricted to monks and clergymen. Everyone was now able to do what
27  they wanted and actually make a good profit of it. Humanism was the escape, the emancipator, the way out. It freed
28  people from the muck of the Dark Ages and allowed people to do more with their lives than just lie around and pray
29  for a quick death. (Alonzo)

### Student Response 2

*Prompt:* Should the government fund art and literature that is offensive?

1  Although the National Endowment for the Arts is a controversial program, a thorough examination of the
2  evidence suggests that the government should stop awarding artistic grants and thereby promote fiscal responsibility,
3  private giving, and individual rights.
4  As the current American debt continues to soar, the American government should do all it can to cut
5  spending and remove the debt burden from future generations. Unfortunately the government continues to support
6  controversial programs like the National Endowment for the Arts (NEA). The NEA spent over 102 million dollars in
7  2004. Despite the fact that artists need funds, now is not the time to give out millions of taxpayer money. By cutting
8  this program, the government would make an important step toward fiscal responsibility.
9  Additionally, the abolishment of the NEA would promote private giving. This might seem odd, yet since
10  the NEA is paid for by higher taxes, individuals have less disposable income and hence do not donate as much as
11  they otherwise might. Although the NEA does incent private gifts through matching funds, it takes away from

12 money that could have otherwise been directly given by the citizens. Therefore, if the concern is truly for the artists,
13 then the NEA should be abolished to allow more private giving.
14     Besides promoting fiscal responsibility and additional private giving, the removal of the NEA would also
15 promote individual rights. Under the current NEA system, the government appoints "panels" to decide how to
16 allocate funds. The government's decisions on how to distribute the money have been highly criticized. One
17 promising solution to this controversy would be to eliminate the NEA and let the people choose for themselves how
18 best to spend their own money. In this author's opinion, the constitution establishes no federal power to take
19 taxpayer money and spend it on good art as defined by the government. Therefore, the NEA should be abolished to
20 promote individual rights.
21     In conclusion, the current NEA system is adding to the national debt, hindering private donations, and
22 stepping on the rights of the American people. A simple solution to these terrible problems would be to eradicate the
23 NEA and therefore empower America. (Jacqueline)

1. In Student Response 1,
   A. The Renaissance was desirable.
   B. The Church was a negative organization.
   C. The world moved away from God in the Renaissance.
   D. The plague killed thousands of people.

2. In Response 2 the author organizes the essay
   A. By stating a rhetorical questions and then developing the thesis.
   B. By offering a series of anecdotes.
   C. By stating a thesis and offering several examples.
   D. By a series of bullet points.

3. Student Response 1 can be improved by

   I. Strengthening transitions.
   II. Giving more specific examples.
   III. Including a personal example.
   IV. Making the essay longer.
   V. Clearly stating the thesis and tying it to the topic.

   | | |
   |---|---|
   | A. I, II, IV, and V | C. II and III |
   | B. III and IV | D. IV and V |

4. Problems in Student Response 2 include

   I. Transitions are weak.
   II. There are too many personal examples.
   III. The essay is too short.
   IV. The thesis is not clearly stated nor tied to the topic.

   | | |
   |---|---|
   | A. I and II | D. I, II, and IV |
   | B. III and IV | E. NONE |
   | C. II and III | |

5. The main point of the Student Response 1?
   | | |
   |---|---|
   | A. Lines 3–5 | C. Lines 13–15 |
   | B. Lines 8–9 | D. Line 27–29 |

6. The main point of the Student Response 2?
   | | |
   |---|---|
   | A. Lines 1–3 | C. Lines 18–20 |
   | B. Lines 8–9 | D. Line 20–22 |

7. Criticism of Student Response 1:
   I. The essay's position is unclear or limited. The critical thinking in the essay is weak and not supported by sufficient or relevant examples and details.
   II. The central idea is poorly defined.
   III. The essay is poorly organized, and in general the essay lacks coherence.
   IV. The language is ordinary and uninspiring.
   V. The sentence structure lacks variety and complexity.
   VI. There are serious grammar mistakes.

   A. I, II, and III
   B. I, II, III, IV, and V
   C. VI
   D. IV, V, and VI

8. What score would the student responses receive?
   Student Response 1 receives __.          Student Response 2 receives __.

---

Students' essays are evaluated (Score 1–4) in terms of reading, analysis, and writing:

**Reading:** Successful essays demonstrate thorough comprehension of the passage, including the interplay of central ideas and important details, and use textual evidence effectively.

**Analysis?** Successful essays demonstrate skill in evaluating the author's use of evidence, reasoning, style, and other stylistic or persuasive techniques and support and develop claims with well-chosen evidence from the passage.

**Writing:** Successful essays are focused, organized, and precise, with an appropriate style and tone that varies sentence structure and follows the conventions of standard written English. —COLLEGE BOARD (https://collegereadiness.collegeboard.org/sat-suite-assessments/practice/essay)

# Lesson 4
## Reading: Document-Based Analysis

**First Inaugural Address**
**Thomas Jefferson (1801)**

1    Called upon to undertake the duties of the first executive office of our country, I avail myself of the presence of that
2    portion of my fellow-citizens which is here assembled to express my grateful thanks for the favor with which they
3    have been pleased to look toward me, to declare a sincere consciousness that the task is above my talents, and that I
4    approach it with those anxious and awful presentiments which the greatness of the charge and the weakness of my
5    powers so justly inspire. A rising nation, spread over a wide and fruitful land, traversing all the seas with the rich
6    productions of their industry, engaged in commerce with nations who feel power and forget right, advancing rapidly
7    to destinies beyond the reach of mortal eye—when I contemplate these transcendent objects, and see the honor, the
8    happiness, and the hopes of this beloved country committed to the issue and the auspices of this day, I shrink from
9    the contemplation, and humble myself before the magnitude of the undertaking. Utterly, indeed, should I despair did
10    not the presence of many whom I here see remind me that in the other high authorities provided by our Constitution
11    I shall find resources of wisdom, of virtue, and of zeal on which to rely under all difficulties. To you, then,
12    gentlemen, who are charged with the sovereign functions of legislation, and to those associated with you, I look with
13    encouragement for that guidance and support which may enable us to steer with safety the vessel in which we are all
14    embarked amidst the conflicting elements of a troubled world.
15        During the contest of opinion through which we have passed, the animation of discussions and of exertions
16    has sometimes worn an aspect which might impose on strangers unused to think freely and to speak and to write
17    what they think; but this being now decided by the voice of the nation, announced according to the rules of the
18    Constitution, all will, of course, arrange themselves under the will of the law, and unite in common efforts for the
19    common good. All, too, will bear in mind this sacred principle, that though the will of the majority is in all cases to
20    prevail, that will, to be rightful, must be reasonable; that the minority possess their equal rights, which equal law
21    must protect, and to violate would be oppression. Let us, then, fellow-citizens, unite with one heart and one mind.
22    Let us restore to social intercourse that harmony and affection without which liberty and even life itself are but
23    dreary things. And let us reflect that, having banished from our land that religious intolerance under which mankind
24    so long bled and suffered, we have yet gained little if we countenance a political intolerance as despotic, as wicked,
25    and capable of as bitter and bloody persecutions. During the throes and convulsions of the ancient world, during the
26    agonizing spasms of infuriated man, seeking through blood and slaughter his long-lost liberty, it was not wonderful
27    that the agitation of the billows should reach even this distant and peaceful shore; that this should be more felt and
28    feared by some and less by others, and should divide opinions as to measures of safety. But every difference of
29    opinion is not a difference of principle. We have called by different names brethren of the same principle. We are all
30    Republicans, we are all Federalists. If there be any among us who would wish to dissolve this Union or to change its
31    republican form, let them stand undisturbed as monuments of the safety with which error of opinion may be
32    tolerated where reason is left free to combat it. I know, indeed, that some honest men fear that a republican
33    government cannot be strong, that this Government is not strong enough; but would the honest patriot, in the full
34    tide of successful experiment, abandon a government which has so far kept us free and firm on the theoretic and
35    visionary fear that this Government, the world's best hope, may by possibility want energy to preserve itself? I trust
36    not. I believe this, on the contrary, the strongest Government on earth. I believe it the only one where every man, at
37    the call of the law, would fly to the standard of the law, and would meet invasions of the public order as his own
38    personal concern. Sometimes it is said that man cannot be trusted with the government of himself. Can he, then, be
39    trusted with the government of others? Or have we found angels in the forms of kings to govern him? Let history
40    answer this question.
41        Let us, then, with courage and confidence pursue our own Federal and Republican principles, our
42    attachment to union and representative government. Kindly separated by nature and a wide ocean from the
43    exterminating havoc of one quarter of the globe; too high-minded to endure the degradations of the others;
44    possessing a chosen country, with room enough for our descendants to the thousandth and thousandth generation;
45    entertaining a due sense of our equal right to the use of our own faculties, to the acquisitions of our own industry, to
46    honor and confidence from our fellow-citizens, resulting not from birth, but from our actions and their sense of
47    them; enlightened by a benign religion, professed, indeed, and practiced in various forms, yet all of them inculcating

honesty, truth, temperance, gratitude, and the love of man; acknowledging and adoring an overruling Providence, which by all its dispensations proves that it delights in the happiness of man here and his greater happiness hereafter—with all these blessings, what more is necessary to make us a happy and a prosperous people? Still one thing more, fellow-citizens—a wise and frugal Government, which shall restrain men from injuring one another, shall leave them otherwise free to regulate their own pursuits of industry and improvement, and shall not take from the mouth of labor the bread it has earned. This is the sum of good government, and this is necessary to close the circle of our felicities.

About to enter, fellow-citizens, on the exercise of duties which comprehend everything dear and valuable to you, it is proper you should understand what I deem the essential principles of our Government, and consequently those which ought to shape its Administration. I will compress them within the narrowest compass they will bear, stating the general principle, but not all its limitations. Equal and exact justice to all men, of whatever state or persuasion, religious or political; peace, commerce, and honest friendship with all nations, entangling alliances with NONE; the support of the State governments in all their rights, as the most competent administrations for our domestic concerns and the surest bulwarks against antirepublican tendencies; the preservation of the General Government in its whole constitutional vigor, as the sheet anchor of our peace at home and safety abroad; a jealous care of the right of election by the people—a mild and safe corrective of abuses which are lopped by the sword of revolution where peaceable remedies are unprovided; absolute acquiescence in the decisions of the majority, the vital principle of republics, from which is no appeal but to force, the vital principle and immediate parent of despotism; a well-disciplined militia, our best reliance in peace and for the first moments of war till regulars may relieve them; the supremacy of the civil over the military authority; economy in the public expense, that labor may be lightly burthened; the honest payment of our debts and sacred preservation of the public faith; encouragement of agriculture, and of commerce as its handmaid; the diffusion of information and arraignment of all abuses at the bar of the public reason; freedom of religion; freedom of the press, and freedom of person under the protection of the habeas corpus, and trial by juries impartially selected. These principles form the bright constellation which has gone before us and guided our steps through an age of revolution and reformation. The wisdom of our sages and blood of our heroes have been devoted to their attainment. They should be the creed of our political faith, the text of civic instruction, the touchstone by which to try the services of those we trust; and should we wander from them in moments of error or of alarm, let us hasten to retrace our steps and to regain the road which alone leads to peace, liberty, and safety.

I repair, then, fellow-citizens, to the post you have assigned me. With experience enough in subordinate offices to have seen the difficulties of this the greatest of all, I have learnt to expect that it will rarely fall to the lot of imperfect man to retire from this station with the reputation and the favor which bring him into it. Without pretensions to that high confidence you reposed in our first and greatest revolutionary character, whose preeminent services had entitled him to the first place in his country's love and destined for him the fairest page in the volume of faithful history, I ask so much confidence only as may give firmness and effect to the legal administration of your affairs. I shall often go wrong through defect of judgment. When right, I shall often be thought wrong by those whose positions will not command a view of the whole ground. I ask your indulgence for my own errors, which will never be intentional, and your support against the errors of others, who may condemn what they would not if seen in all its parts. The approbation implied by your suffrage is a great consolation to me for the past, and my future solicitude will be to retain the good opinion of those who have bestowed it in advance, to conciliate that of others by doing them all the good in my power, and to be instrumental to the happiness and freedom of all.

Relying, then, on the patronage of your good will, I advance with obedience to the work, ready to retire from it whenever you become sensible how much better choice it is in your power to make. And may that Infinite Power which rules the destinies of the universe lead our councils to what is best, and give them a favorable issue for your peace and prosperity.

1. What is the purpose of this message?
   I. Jefferson warns the British to desist from border demands.
   II. Jefferson sought to reach out to his political opponents and heal the breach between Federalists and Republicans.
   III. Jefferson strongly states his belief in freedom of religion.
   IV. Jefferson promises to extend equal rights to women.

   A. I and II                    C. II and IV
   B. III and IV                  D. I and IV

2. Why would this conciliatory speech be necessary in 1801?
   I. Jefferson won by the slimiest of majorities
   II. England was about to invade the United States
   III. Jefferson wanted to obtain the Louisiana Purchase from France
   IV. The 1800 election was the first time a nation had switched governments between two radically dissenting parties, peacefully without a revolution

      A.  I and II          C.  III and I
      B.  III and IV       D.  I and IV

## Words in Context

1. What is the meaning of *commerce* in Line 6?
   A. Discussions          C. Business
   B. Treaties             D. Remorse

2. What is the meaning of *countenance* in Line 24?
   A. Visage              C. Retrospection
   B. Demeanor          D. Reflection

3. What is the meaning of *benign* in Line 47?
   A. Malevolent         C. Benevolent
   B. Malfeasance        D. Neutrality

4. What is the meaning of *inculcating* in Line 47?
   A. Damaging          C. Remarking
   B. Sustaining          D. Instilling

5. What is the meaning of *frugal* in Line 51?
   A. Prudent            C. Outstanding
   B. Staid               D. Ostentatious

6. What is the meaning of *acquiescence* in Line 64?
   A. Remonstration      C. Demonstration
   B. Compliance         D. Subjugation

7. What is the meaning of *approbation* in Line 86?
   A. Reticence           C. Retention
   B. Approval            D. Abstinent

# Lesson 5

## Math: Algebra, Arithmetic Problem Solving and Data Analysis, and Passport to Advanced Math

### Passport to Advanced Math

1. When throwing two dice, what is the probability that one of the two at least turns up a 6?

   A. 12/36
   B. 11/36

   C. 10/36
   D. 9/36

A            B            C

_____

2. If AC is a straight line and B is the midpoint of that straight line, what is true?

   I.   AC = AB + BC
   II.  AC − AB > BC
   III. AC > AB
   IV.  AC = 2BC

   A. I and II
   B. I, III, and IV

   C. I, II, and III
   D. All

### Arithmetic Problem Solving

1. If *a* and *b* are positive integers, what is the difference between *a* and *b*.

   I.   $a - b$
   II.  $b - a$
   III. $2a - 2b$
   IV.  $a(b)$

   A. I and II
   B. II and III

   C. I and III
   D. NONE

2. By how much is *b* greater than 10?

   A. b + 10
   B. b − 10

   C. 10 − b
   D. 2b − 10

3. Express the sum of a and b diminished by c.

   A. a + b − c
   B. b + a + c

   C. b − a − c
   D. a + b + c

4. Write five numbers in order of magnitude so that x shall be the middle number.

   A. x − 2, x − 1, x, x + 1, x + 3
   B. x − 2, x − 2, x, x + 1, x +

   C. x − 2, x − 1, x, x + 1, x + 2
   D. x − 2, x − 1, x, x + 2, x + 3

5. A man has an income of *a* dollars. His expenses are *b* dollars. How much has he left?

   A. b − a                           C. a − (-b)
   B. a − b                           D. a(b)

6. How much less than *c* is 8?

   A. 8− c                            C. − c + −8
   B. c − (−8)                        D. c − 8

7. A man has four daughters, each of whom is 3 years older than the next younger. If *x* represents the age of the oldest, what will represent the age of the others?

   A. x − 3, x − 6, x − 9             C. x − 6, x − 12, x − 18
   B. x − 3, x − 9, x − 12            D. x − 3, x − 9, x − 12

8. At a certain election 1,065 ballots were cast for two candidates, and the winning candidate had a majority of 207. How many votes did each receive?

   A. 441; 636 votes                  C. 429; 636 votes
   B. 429; 678 votes                  D. 432; 638 votes

# Chapter 3   Shiny Iron Chariots
# Joshua 17

> *Memory Verse:* "Though the Canaanites have chariots fitted with iron and though they are strong, you can drive them out." —Joshua 17:18

Our enemies are formidable; they have shiny iron chariots. We therefore are afraid of the future. We want as little change as possible, as if postponing change delays the inevitable future. In spite of the fact that no tribes except Judah had received such rich and large areas of land, they felt growing pains and needed more land. That is good; no matter how blessed we may be, we should always want more of God, more of his word to be a reality in our lives. We eternally need to be holy dissatisfied. Perhaps that is partly what being "led by the Spirit" is all about.

"If you are so numerous [and they were]," Joshua, their leader, responded, "and if the hill country of Ephraim is too small for you, go up into the forest and clear land for yourselves there in the land of the Perizzites and Rephaites" (Joshua 17:15). The Ephraimites and Manassehites were insulted! Imagine! The same people who merely had to walk around Jericho seven times, who had conquered an entire country against overwhelming odds, these same people are called to clear land! Without the benefit of chainsaws and heavy equipment, clearing land is a demeaning, onerous task at best. The chosen people of God are being called to the nitty-gritty of everyday life.

During these hard times, when we struggle, we seem to grow the most. Lawrence Kohlberg, a child psychologist, and a man under whom I studied while a seminarian at Harvard, argues that human beings grow emotionally and spiritually when we face conflict. Only when we are forced to reevaluate our circumstances are we free to grow. As we look back on our own Christian lives, the hard times, the broken times, were often the best times. At these moments, as we walked through "the valley of the shadow of death," as we faced conflict, as we had to feel the grit of life in our beds, in our hearts, these were the times in which we grew the most. When we thought that marriage would end, when our son or daughter failed, when we faced that death of our husband/wife, at that moment we grew like never before. When we found ourselves naked in our vulnerability and sinfulness and helplessness, then we saw that God is our source of strength—and we grew. As we clear the forests of our lives, we experience the real, solid, and permanent growth for which we long.

So Joshua suggests that they clear the wood country. They must carve out their own future. And so must you. That is the law of life. What comes easily goes easily. The things we struggle for are what we value and appreciate. The rewards of life come not to those who have their hands out, but to those who are willing to sacrifice in order to gain their objective. There is much talk about giving people freedom, and people asking to be made free. The simple fact is that freedom cannot be given; it is something for which every race and nation has to struggle. It is not something that can be given, but it is something that must be attained.

Before and as the Israelites clear the hill country, they first must displace the Canaanites. And while we are still in the Bronze Age, our tools and weapons are made of bronze, yet they have iron chariots! They have B-2 bombers, and we only have machine guns.

The Israelites were a Bronze Age people. They did not know how to make or shape iron, much less iron chariots. They were a simple people whose specialty was herding sheep and worshiping God, not fighting. In Joshua, chariots are mentioned for the first time in chapter 11. Chariots were the Sherman tanks of that age. The light war chariot had been introduced to western Asia by the Aryans, about one hundred years before Joshua. Normally the chariot carried a team of three: a driver, a shield bearer, and a bowman. No army could defeat another army with chariots unless it also had chariots—or a resourceful God. Imagine, Joshua says in a rather nonchalant way, "Oh, by the way, you are numerous and very powerful. . . . Though the Canaanites have iron chariots and though they are strong, you can drive them out." One can imagine the Israelite elders looking at one another in disbelief. Although it is not recorded in Scripture, one can imagine the elders responding, "Sure, Joshua. Do you want to lead us?"

This Scripture reminds us of a fact that we often forget: The issues facing you will not be settled by shiny iron chariots or horses or social programs or how much we give God or what we do not give him. Ultimately victory depends upon the faithfulness of our God and our ability to hear and to respond to his voice.

## Journal Question
Describe an obstacle(s) that you need God's help to overcome.

# Lesson 1
## Evidence-Based Reading and Writing

### Literary Choice

*A Modest Proposal*, by English author Jonathan Swift, is a satirical, anonymously written essay criticizing British eighteenth-century policy toward Ireland. Swift suggests that the impoverished Irish might ease their economic troubles by selling their children as food for rich English gentlemen and ladies. Here is an excerpt:

1     It is a melancholy object to those, who walk through this great town, or travel in the country, when they see
2 the streets, the roads and cabin-doors crowded with beggars of the female sex, followed by three, four, or six
3 children, all in rags, and importuning every passenger for an alms. These mothers, instead of being able to work for
4 their honest livelihood, are forced to employ all their time in strolling to beg sustenance for their helpless infants
5 who, as they grow up, either turn thieves for want of work, or leave their dear native country, to fight for the
6 Pretender in Spain, or sell themselves to the Barbados.
7     I think it is agreed by all parties, that this prodigious number of children in the arms, or on the backs, or at
8 the heels of their mothers, and frequently of their fathers, is in the present deplorable state of the kingdom, a very
9 great additional grievance; and therefore whoever could find out a fair, cheap. and easy method of making these
10 children sound and useful members of the commonwealth, would deserve so well of the public, as to have his statue
11 set up for a preserver of the nation.
12     But my intention is very far from being confined to provide only for the children of professed beggars: it is
13 of a much greater extent, and shall take in the whole number of infants at a certain age, who are born of parents in
14 effect as little able to support them, as those who demand our charity in the streets.
15     As to my own part, having turned my thoughts for many years upon this important subject, and maturely
16 weighed the several schemes of our projectors, I have always found them grossly mistaken in their computation. It is
17 true, a child just dropped from its dam may be supported by her milk for a solar year, with little other nourishment:
18 at most not above the value of two shillings, which the mother may certainly get, or the value in scraps, by her
19 lawful occupation of begging; and it is exactly at one year old that I propose to provide for them in such a manner,
20 as, instead of being a charge upon their parents, or the parish, or wanting food and raiment for the rest of their lives,
21 they shall, on the contrary, contribute to the feeding, and partly to the clothing, of many thousands.
22     There is likewise another great advantage in my scheme, that it will prevent those voluntary abortions, and
23 that horrid practice of women murdering their bastard children, alas! too frequent among us, sacrificing the poor
24 innocent babes, I doubt, more to avoid the expense than the shame, which would move tears and pity in the most
25 savage and inhuman breast.
26     The number of souls in this kingdom being usually reckoned one million and a half, of these I calculate
27 there may be about two hundred thousand couple whose wives are breeders; from which number I subtract thirty
28 thousand couple, who are able to maintain their own children, although I apprehend there cannot be so many, under
29 the present distresses of the kingdom; but this being granted, there will remain an hundred and seventy thousand
30 breeders. I again subtract fifty thousand, for those women who miscarry, or whose children die by accident or
31 disease within the year. There only remain an hundred and twenty thousand children of poor parents annually born.
32 The question therefore is, How this number shall be reared, and provided for? which, as I have already said, under
33 the present situation of affairs, is utterly impossible by all the methods hitherto proposed. For we can neither employ
34 them in handicraft or agriculture; we neither build houses (I mean in the country) nor cultivate land: they can very
35 seldom pick up a livelihood by stealing till they arrive at six years old; except where they are of cowardly parts,
36 although I confess they learn the rudiments much earlier; during which time they can however be properly looked
37 upon only as probationers: As I have been informed by a principal gentleman in the county of Cavan, who protested
38 to me, that he never knew above one or two instances under the age of six, even in a part of the kingdom so
39 renowned for the quickest proficiency in that art.
40     I am assured by our merchants, that a boy or a girl before twelve years old, is no saleable commodity, and
41 even when they come to this age, they will not yield above three pounds, or three pounds and half a crown at most,
42 on the exchange; which cannot turn to account either to the parents or kingdom, the charge of nutriments and rags
43 having been at least four times that value.
44     I shall now therefore humbly propose my own thoughts, which I hope will not be liable to the least
45 objection. I have been assured by a very knowing American of my acquaintance in London, that a young healthy

46  child well nursed, is, at a year old, a most delicious nourishing and wholesome food, whether stewed, roasted,
47  baked, or boiled; and I make no doubt that it will equally serve in a fricassee or a ragoust.
48      I do therefore humbly offer it to public consideration, that of the hundred and twenty thousand children,
49  already computed, twenty thousand may be reserved for breed, whereof only one-fourth part to be males; which is
50  more than we allow to sheep, black cattle, or swine, and my reason is, that these children are seldom the fruits of
51  marriage, a circumstance not much regarded by our savages, therefore one male will be sufficient to serve four
52  females. That the remaining hundred thousand may, at a year old, be offered in sale to the persons of quality and
53  fortune, through the kingdom, always advising the mother to let them suck plentifully in the last month, so as to
54  render them plump and fat for a good table. A child will make two dishes at an entertainment for friends, and when
55  the family dines alone, the fore or hind quarter will make a reasonable dish, and seasoned with a little pepper or salt,
56  will be very good boiled on the fourth day, especially in winter.

## Analysis

1.  Which of the following statements best describes Swift's thesis?
    A.  The Irish are harmless but mostly lazy people.
    B.  England should send the Irish to America.
    C.  England can solve the Irish famine crisis by curtailing imports of Irish food stuffs.
    D.  This satirical hyperbole mocks heartless attitudes toward the poor, as well as England's Irish political policy in general.

2.  The author uses: the following evidence to support the above argument:
    A. Lines 54–56                      C. Lines 36–39
    B. Lines 12–14                      D. NONE

3.  What is the meaning of *sustenance* in Line 4?
    A. Comfort                          C. Nourishment
    B. Angst                            D. Warmth

4.  What is the meaning of *rudiments* in Line 36?
    A. Wardrobe                         C. Extravagance
    B. Fundamentals                     D. Paltriness

## Source Analysis

In this passage, which of the following statements best describes the author's attitude/tone toward the British government's Irish policy?

   I. The English government is being cruel and selfish in its policies.
  II. The Irish are naturally lazy.
 III. While the English government is not without its faults, there is really no comprehensive solution to the Irish problem.

        A. I only                       C. III only
        B. II only                      D. II and III

# Lesson 2
## Critical Reading and Writing

### Command of Evidence

Read the following passage and answer accompanying questions:

1   When on board *H.M. S. Beagle* as naturalist, I was much struck with certain facts in the distribution of the organic
2   beings inhabiting South America, and in the geographical relations of the present to the past inhabitants of that
3   continent. These facts, as will be seen in the latter chapters of this volume, seemed to throw some light on the origin
4   of species—that mystery of mysteries, as it has been called by one of our greatest philosophers. On my return home,
5   in 1837, it occurred to me that something might perhaps be made out on this question by patiently accumulating and
6   reflecting on all sorts of facts which could possibly have any bearing on it. After five years' work, I allowed myself
7   to speculate on the subject, and drew up some short notes; these I enlarged in 1844 into a sketch of the conclusions
8   which then seemed to me probable. From that period to the present day I have steadily pursued the same object. I
9   hope that I may be excused for entering on these personal details, as I give them to show that I have not been hasty
10  in coming to a decision.
11      In considering the origin of species, it is quite conceivable that a naturalist, reflecting on the mutual
12  affinities of organic beings, on their embryological relations, their geographical distribution, geological succession,
13  and other such facts, might come to the conclusion that species had not been independently created, but had
14  descended, like varieties, from other species. Nevertheless, such a conclusion, even if well founded, would be
15  unsatisfactory, until it could be shown how the innumerable species inhabiting this world have been modified so as
16  to acquire that perfection of structure and co-adaptation which justly excites our admiration.
17      Naturalists continually refer to external conditions, such as climate, food, etc., as the only possible cause of
18  variation. In one limited sense, as we shall hereafter see, this may be true; but it is preposterous to attribute to mere
19  external conditions the structure, for instance, of the woodpecker, with its feet, tail, beak, and tongue, so admirably
20  adapted to catch insects under the bark of trees. In the case of the mistletoe, which draws its nourishment from
21  certain trees, which has seeds that must be transported by certain birds, and which has flowers with separate sexes
22  absolutely requiring the agency of certain insects to bring pollen from one flower to the other, it is equally
23  preposterous to account for the structure of the parasite, with its relations to several distinct organic beings, by the
24  effects of external conditions, or of habit, or of the volition of the plant itself.
25      It is, therefore, of the highest importance to gain a clear insight into the means of modification and co-
26  adaptation. At the beginning of my observations it seemed to me probable that a careful study of domesticated
27  animals and of cultivated plants would offer the best chance of making out this obscure problem. Nor have I been
28  disappointed; in this and in all other perplexing cases I have invariably found that our knowledge, imperfect though
29  it be, of variation under domestication, afforded the best and safest clue. I may venture to express my conviction of
30  the high value of such studies, although they have been very commonly neglected by naturalists.
31      Although much remains obscure, and will long remain obscure, I can entertain no doubt, after the most
32  deliberate study and dispassionate judgment of which I am capable, that the view which most naturalists until
33  recently entertained, and which I formerly entertained—namely, that each species has been independently created—
34  is erroneous. I am fully convinced that species are not immutable, but that those belonging to what are called the
35  same genera are lineal descendants of some other and generally extinct species, in the same manner as the
36  acknowledged varieties of any one species are the descendants of that species. Furthermore, I am also convinced that
37  Natural Selection has been the most important, but not the exclusive, means of modification.

(Charles Darwin, *Origin of the Species*, in *The World's Greatest Books*,
edited by Arthur Mee and J. A. Hammerton, vol. 15, *Science*, 43)

1. A natural conclusion drawn from this statement—"In considering the origin of species, it is quite conceivable that a naturalist, reflecting on the mutual affinities of organic beings, on their embryological relations, their geographical distribution, geological succession, and other such facts, might come to the conclusion that species had not been independently created, but had descended, like varieties, from other species" might be that
   A. God created living things to satisfy his will.
   B. A divine purpose and will is controlling everything.
   C. Animal and plant species evolve independent from a higher power, but not from other species.
   D. Animal and plant species evolved independent from a higher power, and independently from each other.

2. Creation literalists offer the following counterargument(s):
   A. Independent of naturalistic processes, God created the world and all that live in it.
   B. To posit that species evolved by happenstance and were selected (or not) by natural processes—such a proposal implies there is no divine design.
   C. While some species are similar, their similarities in no way proves a link of causation.
   D. ALL.

3. Evidence to counter Darwin's theory could include
   A. The extinction of dinosaurs.
   B. The existence of an appendix in homo sapiens.
   C. The fact that all animal species participate in some sort of play.
   D. The fact that mules are sterile.

## Words in Context

What is the meaning of *immutable* in Line 34?
   A. Adaptable
   B. Imperfect
   C. Unchangeable
   D. Indomitable

## Analyzing a Source

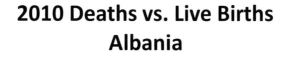

# 2010 Deaths vs. Live Births
# Albania

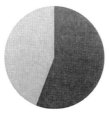

■ Male Live Births/1000

▨ Female Live Briths/1000

Based upon the above graph, the following conclusions are true:
I. More male babies are born alive than female babies.
II. Female infants die from pneumonia more than male babies.
III. There are more male adults in Albania than female adults.
IV. There are 15.11 average infant deaths in Albania.

   A. I
   B. II and IV
   C. I and III
   D. I and IV

# Lesson 3
## SAT Essay

*Prompt:* Perhaps the most famous scientist of the twentieth century, Albert Einstein (1879–1955), is responsible for the theory of relativity. He won the Nobel Prize in Physics in 1921. In 1936, he wrote the following letter to a sixth-grade student, Phyllis Wright, in response to her question as to whether or not scientists pray, and if so, what they pray for. How rhetorically effective do you find Einstein's response?

1  The Riverside Church
2  January 19, 1936
3
4  My dear Dr. Einstein,
5      We have brought up the question Do scientists pray? in our Sunday school class. It began by asking
6  whether we could believe in both science and religion. We are writing to scientists and other important men, to try
7  and have our own question answered.
8      We will feel greatly honored if you will answer our question: Do scientists pray, and what do they pray for?
9      We are in the sixth grade, Miss Ellis's class.
10  Respectfully yours,
11  Phyllis

---------------------

1  January 24, 1936
2  Dear Phyllis,
3      I will attempt to reply to your question as simply as I can. Here is my answer:
4      Scientists believe that every occurrence, including the affairs of human beings, is due to the laws of Nature.
5  Therefore a scientist cannot be inclined to believe that the course of events can be influenced by prayer, that is, by a
6  supernaturally manifested wish.
7      However, we must concede that our actual knowledge of these forces is imperfect, so that in the end the
8  belief in the existence of a final, ultimate spirit rests on a kind of faith. Such belief remains widespread even with the
9  current achievements in science.
10      But also, everyone who is seriously involved in the pursuit of science becomes convinced that some spirit
11  is manifest in the laws of the universe, one that is vastly superior to that of man. In this way the pursuit of science
12  leads to a religious feeling of a special sort, which is surely quite different from the religiosity of someone more
13  naive.
14  With cordial greetings,
15  Your A. Einstein

(http://www.lettersofnote.com/2012/05/dear-einstein-do-scientists-pray.html)

### Student Response

1  Albert Einstein, gifted in science, and well known for his accomplishments, exhibits a large portion of his appeal to
2  logos solely through his reputation. His letter to Phyllis Wright is a good demonstration of how to write in a
3  rhetorically effective way, as it has elements of logos, ethos, and pathos, as well as concern for audience.
4      Through his experience as a scientist, Einstein appeals to ethos, answering a question about scientists, as a
5  scientist himself.
6      **Because he is writing a letter, Albert Einstein uses first person, which boosts pathos, allowing the**
7  **reader to feel a closer connection with the writer.** Einstein does not attempt to convince his audience through the
8  use of much emotion-evoking language, and in his letter he displays a view that is encompassing of both the
9  sciences and religion, avoiding, whether unintentionally or intentionally, nearing the polemical. Although the letter
10  is not purely based on the emotional, Einstein makes use of strong connotations, such as: humble, superior, vastly,
11  etc. Appealing to logos by using his scientific knowledge along with the reader's knowledge of his reputation, he
12  begins to explain his worldview.

13      Scientific research is based on the idea that everything that takes place is determined by laws of Nature, and
14      therefore this holds for the actions of people. For this reason, a research scientist will hardly be inclined to
15      believe that events could be influenced by a prayer, i.e., by a wish addressed to a supernatural being.
16
17      **There is an added credibility, or logos, in the fact the Albert Einstein maintains his focus upon the question**
18      **asked, attempting merely to answer, in his words, "as simply as I can."**
19      Einstein goes on to speak of the wonders of Nature (which he capitalizes, suggesting a possible romantic or
20 naturalistic view), and the fact that through science, he has come to the conclusion that there is a spirit or being
21 superior to man, saying,
22
23      In this way, the pursuit of science leads to a religious feeling of a special sort, which is indeed quite
24      different from the religiosity of someone more naive.
25
26 Instead of insulting or outright denying the religious, Einstein avoids the polemical by stressing the origins of his
27 opinions upon religion. This appeals to logos, because he does not use emotional or controversial statements to
28 prove his point; instead he is confident in what he believes.
29      The last sentence of Einstein's letter is remarkable though appearing basic, as it appeals to logos and pathos
30 at the same time. Einstein says, "I hope this answers your question," returning to the personal through the use of the
31 words "I" and "hope," which appeal to pathos, or emotion. The sentence is also a reaffirmation of the man's wish to
32 answer the question, rather than straying from the subject.
33      The letter that Albert Einstein wrote in response to student Phyllis Wright is evidence showing that Einstein
34 was not only proficient in science, but he was a skilled writer as well. In the letter, Einstein shows great concern for
35 his audience, his ability to stay focused, and his ability to use logos, ethos, and pathos to his advantage, to convince
36 the reader, and maneuver through a contentious subject without angering the audience. (Jasmine)

## Score: __.

Score the above essay based on the Student Response evaluation rubric (College Board®):

| Score | Reading | Analysis | Writing |
|---|---|---|---|
| 1 | **Inadequate:** The response demonstrates little or no comprehension of the source text. The response fails to show an understanding of the text's central idea(s) and may include only details without reference to central idea(s). The response may contain numerous errors of fact and/or interpretation with regard to the text. The response makes little or no use of textual evidence (quotations, paraphrases, or both), demonstrating little or no understanding of the source text. | **Inadequate:** The response offers little or no analysis or ineffective analysis of the source text and demonstrates little or no understanding of the analytic task. The response identifies without explanation some aspects of the author's use of evidence, reasoning, and/or stylistic and persuasive elements, and/or feature(s) of the student's choosing. Or numerous aspects of the response's analysis are unwarranted based on the text. The response contains little or no support for claim(s) or point(s) made, or support is largely irrelevant. The response may not focus on features of the text that are relevant to addressing the | **Inadequate:** The response demonstrates little or no cohesion and inadequate skill in the use and control of language. The response may lack a clear central claim or controlling idea. The response lacks a recognizable introduction and conclusion. The response does not have a discernible progression of ideas. The response lacks variety in sentence structures; sentence structures may be repetitive. The response demonstrates general and vague word choice; word choice may be poor or inaccurate. The response may lack a formal style and objective tone. |

| | | | |
|---|---|---|---|
| | | task. Or the response offers no discernible analysis (e.g., is largely or exclusively summary). | The response shows a weak control of the conventions of standard written English and may contain numerous errors that undermine the quality of writing. |
| 2 | **Partial:** The response demonstrates some comprehension of the source text. The response shows an understanding of the text's central idea(s) but not of important details. The response may contain errors of fact and/or interpretation with regard to the text. The response makes limited and/or haphazard use of textual evidence (quotations, paraphrases, or both), demonstrating some understanding of the source text. | **Partial:** The response offers limited analysis of the source text and demonstrates only partial understanding of the analytical task. The response identifies and attempts to describe the author's use of evidence, reasoning, and/or stylistic and persuasive elements, and/or feature(s) of the student's own choosing, but merely asserts rather than explains their importance, or one or more aspects of the response's analysis are unwarranted based on the text. The response contains little or no support for claim(s) or point(s) made. The response may lack a clear focus on those features of the text that are most relevant to addressing the task. | **Partial:** The response demonstrates little or no cohesion and limited skill in the use and control of language. The response may lack a clear central claim or controlling idea or may deviate from the claim or idea over the course of the response. The response may include an ineffective introduction and/or conclusion. The response may demonstrate some progression of ideas within paragraphs but not throughout the response. The response has limited variety in sentence structures; sentence structures may be repetitive. The response demonstrates general or vague word choice; word choice may be repetitive. The response may deviate noticeably from a formal style and objective tone. The response shows a limited control of the conventions of standard written English and contains errors that detract from the quality of writing and may impede understanding. |
| 3 | **Proficient:** The response demonstrates effective comprehension of the source text. The response shows an understanding of the text's central idea(s) and important details. The response is free of substantive errors of fact and interpretation with regard to the text. The response makes appropriate use of textual evidence (quotations, paraphrases, or both), demonstrating an understanding of the source text. | **Proficient:** The response offers an effective analysis of the source text and demonstrates an understanding of the analytical task. The response competently evaluates the author's use of evidence, reasoning, and/or stylistic and persuasive elements, and/or feature(s) of the student's own choosing. The response contains relevant | **Proficient:** The response is mostly cohesive and demonstrates effective use and control of language. The response includes a central claim or implicit controlling idea. The response includes an effective introduction and conclusion. The response demonstrates a clear progression of ideas both within paragraphs and throughout the essay. |

| | | | |
|---|---|---|---|
| | | and sufficient support for claim(s) or point(s) made. The response focuses primarily on those features of the text that are most relevant to addressing the task. | The response has variety in sentence structures. The response demonstrates some precise word choice. The response maintains a formal style and objective tone. The response shows a good control of the conventions of standard written English and is free of significant errors that detract from the quality of writing. |
| 4 | **Advanced:** The response demonstrates thorough comprehension of the source text. The response shows an understanding of the text's central idea(s) and of most important details and how they interrelate, demonstrating a comprehensive understanding of the text. The response is free of errors of fact or interpretation with regard to the text. The response makes skillful use of textual evidence (quotations, paraphrases, or both), demonstrating a complete understanding of the source text. | **Advanced:** The response offers an insightful analysis of the source text and demonstrates a sophisticated understanding of the analytical task. The response offers a thorough, well-considered evaluation of the author's use of evidence, reasoning, and/or stylistic and persuasive elements, and/or feature(s) of the student's own choosing. The response contains relevant, sufficient, and strategically chosen support for claim(s) or point(s) made. The response focuses consistently on those features of the text that are most relevant to addressing the task. | **Advanced:** The response is cohesive and demonstrates a highly effective use and command of language. The response includes a precise central claim. The response includes a skillful introduction and conclusion. The response demonstrates a deliberate and highly effective progression of ideas both within paragraphs and throughout the essay. The response has a wide variety in sentence structures. The response demonstrates a consistent use of precise word choice. The response maintains a formal style and objective tone. The response shows a strong command of the conventions of standard written English and is free or virtually free of errors. |

## Grammar and Usage

Choose the best grammar/usage form in bold sentence(s).

1. Einstein, Lines 7–8
   A. NONE
   B. Using first person, Albert Einstein connects with the reader and thereby increases pathos.
   C. Because he is writing a letter, Albert Einstein uses first person, which increases pathos, enabling the reader to feel a closer connection with the writer.
   D. Albert Einstein uses first person, which boosts pathos, allowing the reader to feel a closer connection with the writer.

2. Student Response, Lines 17–18
   A. NONE
   B. There is an added credibility, or logos, in the fact the Albert Einstein maintains his focus upon the question, attempting merely to answer, in his words, "as simply as I could."
   C. There is an added credibility, or logos, in the fact the Albert Einstein maintains his focus upon the question asked.
   D. There is an added credibility, or logos, because Albert Einstein remains focused upon the question asked, attempting merely to answer, in his words, "as simply as I could."

# Lesson 4
## Reading: Document-Based Analysis

**Letter to the Hebrew Congregation at Newport**
**George Washington (August 21, 1790)**

Gentlemen:

1  While I received with much satisfaction your address replete with expressions of esteem, I rejoice in the opportunity
2  of assuring you that I shall always retain grateful remembrance of the cordial welcome I experienced on my visit to
3  Newport from all classes of citizens.
4       The reflection on the days of difficulty and danger which are past is rendered the more sweet from a
5  consciousness that they are succeeded by days of uncommon prosperity and security.
6       If we have wisdom to make the best use of the advantages with which we are now favored, we cannot fail,
7  under the just administration of a good government, to become a great and happy people.
8       The citizens of the United States of America have a right to applaud themselves for having given to
9  mankind examples of an enlarged and liberal policy—a policy worthy of imitation. All possess alike liberty of
10  conscience and immunities of citizenship.
11      It is now no more that toleration is spoken of as if it were the indulgence of one class of people that another
12  enjoyed the exercise of their inherent natural rights, for, happily, the Government of the United States, which gives
13  to bigotry no sanction, to persecution no assistance, requires only that they who live under its protection should
14  demean themselves as good citizens in giving it on all occasions their effectual support.
15      It would be inconsistent with the frankness of my character not to avow that I am pleased with your
16  favorable opinion of my administration and fervent wishes for my felicity.
17      May the children of the stock of Abraham who dwell in this land continue to merit and enjoy the good will
18  of the other inhabitants—while every one shall sit in safety under his own vine and fig tree and there shall be NONE
19  to make him afraid.
20      May the father of all mercies scatter light, and not darkness, upon our paths, and make us all in our several
21  vocations useful here, and in His own due time and way everlastingly happy.

1. Which of the following conclusions can be surmised by reading this letter?
   I.   George Washington is an anti-Semite.
   II.  George Washington considers all American citizens equal.
   III. George Washington is considering converting to Judaism.
   IV.  George Washington thinks slaves should have the same rights as all Americans

   A. NONE                                    C. II
   B. I, III, & IV                            D. II and III

2. Which choice provides the best evidence for the answer to the previous question?
   A. Lines 8–10                              C. Lines 2–5
   B. Lines 1–2                               D. Lines 17–19

## Words in Context

1. What is the meaning of *replete* in Line 1?
   A. Incomplete                              C. Secure
   B. Unknown                                 D. Abounding

2. What is the meaning of *felicity* in Line 16?
   A. Mischievousness                         C. Unhappiness
   B. Contentment                             D. Loyalty

# Lesson 5

## Math: Algebra, Arithmetic Problem Solving and Data Analysis, and Passport to Advanced Math

### Arithmetic Problem Solving

A sail boat has 7,000 square feet of surface that needs to be painted. If 1 gallon of paint will cover 300 square feet, what is the least whole number of gallons that must be purchased in order to have enough paint to apply one coat to the surface? (Assume that only whole gallons of paint can be purchased.)

|   |   |   |   |
|---|---|---|---|
| A. | 22 | C. | 26 |
| B. | 24 | D. | 40 |

### Algebra

Which of the following is equal to 2?

A. [8 / (8 - 6)] x 2          C. 8 / [(8 - 6) x 2]

B. [(8 / 8) - 6] x 2          D. (8 / 2) - (6 x 2)

### Data Analysis

A dealer who sells multiple brands of automobiles created the following chart of his yearly sales:

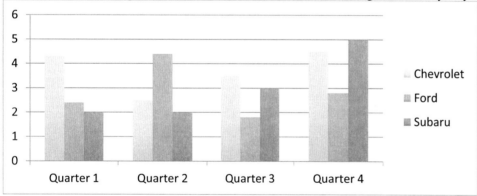

1. Which of the following conclusions are correct?
   I.   Chevrolet is the best-selling brand in Quarter 1.
   II.  Customers bought more Fords than Subarus in Quarter 2.
   III. Compared to Quarter 1, Subaru sales more than doubled in Quarter 4.
   IV.  The economy was experiencing a recession.
   V.   Fords were cheaper in cost than Subarus.

   A. I, II, and III          C. III, IV, and V
   B. IV and V               D. All

2. What are possible reasons that Subaru dominated 4th Quarter sales?
   I.   There was a major Ford recall in the 3rd Quarter.
   II.  Quarter 4 snowfall exceeded previous records (Subarus have all-wheel drive).
   III. Chevrolet had a huge promotion sale in the 4th Quarter.

   A. I                       C. III
   B. II                      D. II and III

# Chapter 4   Generic Christianity
# Mark 12

---

*Memory Verse:* "You do not know the Scriptures or the power of God." —Mark 12:24

---

During the last decades of the twentieth century, a fortuitous development occurred in the drug and supermarket businesses: generic pricing. Removing all frills, expunging expensively adorned packing, and thereby lowering advertising costs, drugstores and grocery stores were able to offer a profitable alternative to name brand products. The results have been astounding: food prices and drug prices have essentially frozen in the last ten years.

But, if generic strategies are a good idea in the consumer marketplace, they fare poorly in the religious marketplace. Too many of us have tried, with perfectly pure intentions, to distill Christianity to its noncontroversial if unexciting basics. As we sought to find common ground with our world, we have reached for the basics, for the least common denominator. We have sacrificed theological efficacy for mass appeal. As we navigate through treacherous waters, we grope for some commonality to still the storm that our Lord, his cross, our faith seem eventually to engender.

What does this propensity, this overwhelming urge toward a digestible, decent, noncontroversial Christianity mean to us? What it means is that some of us have transformed the most revolutionary message of all time into a ho-hum litany of respectable, manageable, politically correct religion. Categorizing and crystallizing our religious lives into neat little packages of do's and don'ts, we boldly wave our Bibles and hum the choruses of our religious gurus as we march through the kingdom. No risk, no challenge: we have everything neatly tied together in our meaningless phrases such as "I believe in the Word!" or "I'm covered in the blood!" Or we substitute our loyal attendance at Sunday morning service for genuine spirituality. Have we become twentieth-century Sadducees?

Representing most of the prestigious priestly class, the Sadducees were perhaps the most powerful religious and political group in Christ's world. They were the epitome of decorum, religious decency, and proper spirituality. The Sadducees, though, were called old believers: they clung tenaciously to tradition, to older beliefs, older ways of doing things.

They were biblical literalists. In other words, they rejected all interpretations of the Word except their own. While praising Torah (the sacred first five books of the Old Testament), they rejected the Pharisees' oral tradition, as eventually recorded in the Talmud (scholarly commentary on Torah). They had not accepted a new idea in over three hundred years; inspiration died with Moses and the prophets. But unlike Moses, they took no risks: they never trembled before a burning bush. Their Judaism was decent, respectable, and . . . . sterile. In their fervency to consume the Word, they had forgotten how to love. Their God was not the God of the living. Their religion was a cold, distasteful, anemic version of Judaism, indigestible for all but haughty, pretentious souls.

They were quintessentially religious people who were virtually devoid of spirituality. They would have gladly given their tithes and offerings for an organ-repair fund but would have considered giving for a Brazil mission to be a bad investment. These same Sadducees are now asking Jesus a probing question—a question whose answer they already know. They ask Jesus this particular question to force him to show his knowledge or lack of knowledge of Scripture. With great relish they have created a picayune scenario to embarrass him.

Then the Sadducees, who say there is no resurrection, came to him with a question. "Teacher," they said, "Moses wrote for us that if a man's brother dies and leaves a wife but no children, the man must marry the widow and raise up offspring for his brother. Now there were seven brothers. The first one married and died without leaving any children. The second one married the widow, but he also died, leaving no child. It was the same with the third. In fact, none of the seven left any children. Last of all, the woman died too. At the resurrection whose wife will she be, since the seven were married to her?" (Mark 12:18–23)

I want you to feel the sting of Christ's reply. The Greek is much stronger than I can render in English, but it goes something like this, "You are positively, without a doubt, absolutely wrong. You are wrong, self-deceived because you know neither the Scripture or the power of God." His response stuns these old men. They were never wrong! Until now!

Perhaps we are bothered by his response, too, on two levels. First, we do not like absolute statements such as we find here. Our relativistic generation feels violated by such dogmatic statements. Second, what does Christ mean by suggesting, no, insisting that the Sadducees do not know Scripture? Has our Lord been in the sun too long? The Sadducees know Scripture more than anyone in the world. They had even memorized most of the Old Testament—certainly all of Torah (the first five books of the Old Testament).

This peculiar forceful reply is an unusual flare for our Lord, who characteristically is always seeking to bring peace and reconciliation. But at this juncture, he is faced with such a dangerous heresy, such a formidable threat to all for which he stood, that he had to release a powerful, unambiguous response.

The Sadducees, in their selective reading of Scripture and their arbitrary limits for God, brought Jesus to this violent moment. They worshiped a book, a good book, a sacred book, but still only a book. They must worship their Lord! The bottom line, the result of their idolatry, Christ tells them, is that they have no power.

Our Bible is the clearest, most unambiguous testimony to God's presence. But I do not serve a book: I serve a risen Lord. The Sadducees had begun to serve a book, a generic religion, a decent, respectable, scholarly, antiseptic religion. And in the process, they were deceived, they were powerless. Power must flow from a relationship, not from knowledge of a book. Power divorced from Christ and his cross becomes human manipulation, veiled powerlessness. Powerlessness is the natural offspring of generic Christianity.

The Sadducees know Scripture, but they really do not know the Bible. The Word they know has become a fossilized story of nice men and women who saw God do powerful things in their lives— but of course, God does not do that sort of thing anymore. In one of the most supremely ironical moments in Scripture, Christ reminds us that knowledge of God's Word is not good enough: we must also know the author. The Sadducees loved to parade their ample knowledge of the Scriptures before their willing audiences. But in the final analysis, they were deceived: they really did not know the Word because they did not know their God. Perhaps now we understand how biting was the criticism the Sadducees had to swallow when Christ finishes, "My God is not the God of the dead, but of the living!" Again he repeats his venomous point? "You are quite wrong!" (cf. Mark 12:24).

The generic Christianity of the Sadducees is Christianity that takes and takes and takes. It shakes everything down to a few voguish expressions of theological jargon. It becomes fat and sassy, stagnant and mean, hardheaded and pseudospiritual. Ultimately, Sadducees destroy themselves, but not before they confuse and sidetrack a few good folks.

Every time we put limits on God with our hidden agendas, we play the Sadducee. Every time we camouflage our rebellion and spiritual decadence with phrases like "I listen only to Jesus," we play the Sadducee. Every time we hide behind our worn, well-read, memorized, and blessed Bibles instead of carrying our crosses and getting down to the hard business of loving one another, well, we play the Sadducee. When we allow our pseudospiritual knowledge about the Bible, when we play our proof-texting games called "Let's impress everyone else by how many passages we can show to prove our point," when we do not allow God to use that knowledge of his Word to change our lives and other lives—then we play the Sadducee. We are stagnated with our catchy theological slogans and late-afternoon Bible teachers who massage our shattered egos. When we revel in religious games and avoid any real spiritual challenges, we are enjoying generic Christianity. Day in and day out, the Holy Spirit continually seeks to move us out of our false, puffed-up spirituality and force us to be real. The Spirit forces us to stop talking about how Moses acted or Hannah prayed or Elijah preached. Now the Spirit is asking us, "How will you act? What does Scripture mean to you? Will you stop playing your games?"

So here we sit, stunned. God's needle has deflated our balloons. No more games. Let's be about our Lord's business. He is teaching us to give, to receive. God is showing us that we will find him among the poor; but we must discard our Sadducee games or we will be unworthy to serve the poor. God does not want an acting guild to represent him, no matter how spiritual they may claim to be. No, God wants you and me. You and me! Not our facades, not our representatives, not our cantankerous selves, but broken, crucified, alive Christians—perhaps tired Christians, who have purposed to tuck their Bibles under their arms, look up into the sky, lift open their arms, and whisper with as much emotion and power as they can muster, "Give me all, O Lord, give me all. Show me how to be real; then, O God Almighty, show me how to be like Jesus." And when we do that, when we can stop playing our Sadducee games, when we reject generic Christianity, then, and only then, we will turn our world upside down.

## Journal Question

In what ways do we hinder the move of God by our "religious" behavior?

# Lesson 1
## Evidence-Based Reading and Writing

### Literary Choice

"The Yellow Wallpaper," by Charlotte Perkins Gilman, is a haunting short story, published in 1892. The story is told from a first-person perspective as the narrator, suffering from mental illness, writes in her journal. The themes within the story are representative of Victorian Era gender roles and cultural practices.

### The Yellow Wallpaper
### Charlotte Gilman (1892)

1  It is very seldom that mere ordinary people like John and myself secure ancestral halls for the summer.
2  A colonial mansion, a hereditary estate, I would say a haunted house, and reach the height of romantic
3  felicity—but that would be asking too much of fate!
4  Still I will proudly declare that there is something queer about it.
5  Else, why should it be let so cheaply? And why have stood so long untenanted?
6  John laughs at me, of course, but one expects that in marriage.
7  John is practical in the extreme. He has no patience with faith, an intense horror of superstition, and he
8  scoffs openly at any talk of things not to be felt and seen and put down in figures.
9  John is a physician, and *perhaps*—(I would not say it to a living soul, of course, but this is dead paper and a
10  great relief to my mind)—*perhaps* that is one reason I do not get well faster.
11  You see he does not believe I am sick!
12  And what can one do?
13  If a physician of high standing, and one's own husband, assures friends and relatives that there is really
14  nothing the matter with one but temporary nervous depression—a slight hysterical tendency—what is one to do?
15  My brother is also a physician, and also of high standing, and he says the same thing.
16  So I take phosphates or phosphites—whichever it is, and tonics, and journeys, and air, and exercise, and am
17  absolutely forbidden to "work" until I am well again.
18  Personally, I disagree with their ideas.
19  Personally, I believe that congenial work, with excitement and change, would do me good.
20  But what is one to do?
21  I did write for a while in spite of them; but it *does* exhaust me a good deal—having to be so sly about it, or
22  else meet with heavy opposition.
23  I sometimes fancy that in my condition if I had less opposition and more society and stimulus—but John
24  says the very worst thing I can do is to think about my condition, and I confess it always makes me feel bad.
25  So I will let it alone and talk about the house.
26  The most beautiful place! It is quite alone, standing well back from the road, quite three miles from the
27  village. It makes me think of English places that you read about, for there are hedges and walls and gates that lock,
28  and lots of separate little houses for the gardeners and people.
29  There is a *delicious* garden! I never saw such a garden—large and shady, full of box-bordered paths, and
30  lined with long grape-covered arbors with seats under them.
31  There were greenhouses, too, but they are all broken now.
32  There was some legal trouble, I believe, something about the heirs and coheirs; anyhow, the place has been
33  empty for years.
34  That spoils my ghostliness, I am afraid, but I don't care—there is something strange about the house—I can
35  feel it.
36  I even said so to John one moonlight evening, but he said what I felt was a *draught*, and shut the window.
37  I get unreasonably angry with John sometimes. I'm sure I never used to be so sensitive. I think it is due to
38  this nervous condition.
39  But John says if I feel so, I shall neglect proper self-control; so I take pains to control myself—before him,
40  at least, and that makes me very tired.
41  I don't like our room a bit. I wanted one downstairs that opened on the piazza and had roses all over the
42  window, and such pretty old-fashioned chintz hangings! but John would not hear of it.

43 He said there was only one window and not room for two beds, and no near room for him if he took
44 another.
45 He is very careful and loving, and hardly lets me stir without special direction.
46 I have a schedule prescription for each hour in the day; he takes all care from me, and so I feel basely
47 ungrateful not to value it more.
48 He said we came here solely on my account, that I was to have perfect rest and all the air I could get. "Your
49 exercise depends on your strength, my dear," said he, "and your food somewhat on your appetite; but air you can
50 absorb all the time." So we took the nursery at the top of the house.
51 It is a big, airy room, the whole floor nearly, with windows that look all ways, and air and sunshine galore.
52 It was nursery first and then playroom and gymnasium, I should judge; for the windows are barred for little children,
53 and there are rings and things in the walls.
54 The paint and paper look as if a boys' school had used it. It is stripped off—the paper—in great patches all
55 around the head of my bed, about as far as I can reach, and in a great place on the other side of the room low down. I
56 never saw a worse paper in my life.
57 One of those sprawling flamboyant patterns committing every artistic sin.
58 It is dull enough to confuse the eye in following, pronounced enough to constantly irritate and provoke
59 study, and when you follow the lame uncertain curves for a little distance they suddenly commit suicide—plunge off
60 at outrageous angles, destroy themselves in unheard of contradictions.
61 The color is repellent, almost revolting; a smouldering unclean yellow, strangely faded by the slow-turning
62 sunlight.
63 It is a dull yet lurid orange in some places, a sickly sulphur tint in others.
64 No wonder the children hated it! I should hate it myself if I had to live in this room long.
65

## Close Reading

The narrator is obviously distressed, if not insane. How does the author convey this fact?
    I.  The narrator's garrulousness
    II.  The narrator's self-absorption
    III.  The narrator's obsession with the color yellow

    A. I                               C. III
    B. II                              D. All of the Above

## Words in Context

    1. What is the meaning of *congenial* in Line 19?
    A. Satisfied                        C. Friendly
    B. Stubborn                      D. Hungry

    2. What is the meaning of *flamboyant* in Line 57?
    A. Ostentatious                  C. Rapacious
    B. Reserved                      D. Parsimonious

## Source Analysis

From this text the reader can make the following assumptions about gender roles in Victorian England:

    I.  Husbands are the head of most families.
    II.  Women are loquacious, men are not.
    III.  It is common for women to be physicians (like the narrator's mom).

    A.  I                                 D.  I and II
    B.  II                              E.  NONE of Above
    C.  III

# Lesson 2
## Critical Reading and Writing

### Command of Evidence

Read the following passage and answer accompanying questions:

1    It was this nationalizing tendency of the West that transformed the democracy of Jefferson into the national
2    republicanism of Monroe and the democracy of Andrew Jackson. The West of the War of 1812, the West of Clay,
3    and Benton and Harrison, and Andrew Jackson, shut off by the Middle States and the mountains from the coast
4    sections, had a solidarity of its own with national tendencies. On the tide of the Father of Waters, North and South
5    met and mingled into a nation. Interstate migration went steadily on—a process of cross-fertilization of ideas and
6    institutions. The fierce struggle of the sections over slavery on the western frontier does not diminish the truth of this
7    statement; it proves the truth of it. Slavery was a sectional trait that would not down, but in the West it could not
8    remain sectional. It was the greatest of frontiersmen who declared: "I believe this Government cannot endure
9    permanently half slave and half free. It will become all of one thing or all of the other." Nothing works for
10    nationalism like intercourse within the nation. Mobility of population is death to localism, and the western frontier
11    worked irresistibly in unsettling population. The effect reached back from the frontier and affected profoundly the
12    Atlantic coast and even the Old World.
13        But the most important effect of the frontier has been in the promotion of democracy here and in Europe.
14    As has been indicated, the frontier is productive of individualism. Complex society is precipitated by the wilderness
15    into a kind of primitive organization based on the family. The tendency is anti-social. It produces antipathy to
16    control, and particularly to any direct control. The tax-gatherer is viewed as a representative of oppression. Prof.
17    Osgood, in an able article, has pointed out that the frontier conditions prevalent in the colonies are important factors
18    in the explanation of the American Revolution, where individual liberty was sometimes confused with absence of all
19    effective government. The same conditions aid in explaining the difficulty of instituting a strong government in the
20    period of the confederacy. The frontier individualism has from the beginning promoted democracy.
21        The frontier States that came into the Union in the first quarter of a century of its existence came in with
22    democratic suffrage provisions, and had reactive effects of the highest importance upon the older States whose
23    peoples were being attracted there. An extension of the franchise became essential. It was western New York that
24    forced an extension of suffrage in the constitutional convention of that State in 1821; and it was western Virginia
25    that compelled the tide-water region to put a more liberal suffrage provision in the constitution framed in 1830, and
26    to give to the frontier region a more nearly proportionate representation with the tide-water aristocracy. The rise of
27    democracy as an effective force in the nation came in with western preponderance under Jackson and William Henry
28    Harrison, and it meant the triumph of the frontier—with all of its good and with all of its evil elements.
    (Frederick Jackson Turner, *The Frontier in American History* [New York: Henry Holt & Co., 1920], 1–2).

1. The thesis of this passage?
    A. Lines 21–22            C. Lines 13–14
    B. Lines 1–2             D. Lines 24–25

2. Which of the following arguments are supported by the passage?
    I.  Native American opposition to European settlements stimulated the frontier spirit.
    II.  The frontier encouraged an entrepreneurial bent among early settlers.
    III.  The frontier is a ubiquitous presence in early American history.

        A. I                C. III
        B. II              D. All

3.  The best explanation for the statement "The frontier States that came into the Union in the first quarter of a century of its existence came in with democratic suffrage provisions, and had reactive effects of the highest importance upon the older States whose peoples were being attracted there"?
    A.  Immigrants from existing states found new freedom in the emerging frontier and after the fact encouraged emerging democratic tendencies from their home states.
    B.  The frontier shamed the extant states into wanting more democracy.
    C.  When the older states saw women gaining voting rights on the frontier, the older states resisted democratic movements.
    D.  NONE.

4.  The election of which of the following presidents would support Turner's thesis?
    A.  John Quincy Adams              C.  Andrew Jackson
    B.  Franklin Roosevelt             D.  James Buchanan

5.  The Turner thesis might be an explanation for which of the following historical events?
    I.    The 19th-century Populist Movement
    II.   The 1960s Feminist Movement
    III.  The Alaskan Settlement Period of 1890 and following

          A. I                        D. I and II
          B. II                       E. I and III
          C. III

## Words in Context

1. What is the meaning of *solidarity* in Line 4?
    A. Disparity                      C. Unity
    B. Comfort                        D. Disunity

2. What is the meaning of *prevalent* in Line 17?
    A. Ubiquitous                     C. Dispersed
    B. Marginal                       D. Submerged

3. What is the meaning of *preponderance* in Line 27?
    A. Multitude                      C. Tangential
    B. Dominance                      D. Magnanimity

# Lesson 3
## SAT Essay

*Prompt:* Are sports figures paid too much? As you read the passage below, consider how the author uses

    A.  Evidence, such as facts or examples, to support claims.
    B.  Reasoning to develop ideas and to connect claims and evidence.
    C.  Stylistic or persuasive elements, such as word choice or appeals to emotion, to add power to the ideas expressed.

1    **Professional sports are a big business. They contribute to the welfare of our economy.** They provide jobs for
2    thousands and entertainment for millions. Although professional sports help to further economic stability for many,
3    many denigrate the exorbitant salaries that professional ballplayers make. They find it horrible that a ballplayer
4    should be making millions while others are starving on the streets. These nay-sayers, however, fail to realize that
5    professional ball creates many jobs for those who would be otherwise unemployed or relying on government
6    assistance. They also do not seem to understand the workings of a capitalist society. Professional ball is capitalism at
7    its best, and some hate it for this very reason.
8          Professional sports help boost the economy by creating jobs. **Many only acknowledge the jobs created**
9    **for the players and coaches; however, they fail to see the "hotdog man," the security guards, the grass cutters,**
10    **the line markers, the custodians, the light engineers, the ushers and others.** The number of jobs created is not
11    only confined to the stadium. Hotels also become jammed-packed, and restaurants thrive during ball seasons.
12    Consequently, hotels and restaurant managers are forced to hire more employees to keep up with the high demand.
13    The creation of jobs can be further highlighted by the absence of a professional sport, basketball. Currently,
14    professional basketball players of the NBA are on strike. Not only is this obviously hurting the players' income, but
15    it is also hurting everyone involved in the NBA revenue stream. The banner man is not able to sell his posters and
16    banners at games. The hotdog man is unable to sell his hotdogs. The custodians cannot clean up after the game.
17    Hotels and restaurants are forced to lay off employees because customers are dwindling, and the list goes on.
18    Clearly, professional ball helps everyone involved.
19          Not only does professional ball have a widespread beneficial impact on its surroundings, but it is also a
20    perfect example of capitalistic system. Or maybe, because professional ball is a capitalist system, it has a widespread
21    beneficial impact on its surroundings. No one "loses" in the professional ball system. Everyone is paid according to
22    how much money they are able to bring to the professional ball system. Team owners are paid the most because they
23    do the most work and consequently produce the most money. They organize the games, ensure television time,
24    organize television ads, produce professional ball merchandise, manage income and taxes, and hire players. They
25    make the most because they rake in the most money for the team and do all the nitty-gritty work. Ballplayers are the
26    next tier down from the team owners. If it were not for the players, the games would not even exist. Ballplayers are
27    the reason for the professional ball system, and consequently, they also produce exorbitant amounts of money for the
28    system. The amount of money paid becomes successively less as the money produced also decreases. For example,
29    the hotdog man is paid much less because he produces much less income for the system. Many may think it very
30    unfair that although the hotdog man works the same amount of time as the players, his income is a fraction of theirs.
31    However, the fact is, this is how a capitalist system works. The more value an individual contributes to a system, the
32    more capital the individual receives.
33          This fact of capitalism may sound cruel to many, but they fail to realize that money in a capitalist society
34    does not have a limit. Capitalism is not a zero-sum game. Just because a professional ballplayer becomes
35    progressively richer does not mean that another individual has to become progressively poorer. There is not a fixed
36    ratio of rich to poor in a capitalist society. In fact, because ballplayers produce exorbitant amounts of money, and are
37    consequently paid exorbitant salaries, many other individuals are able to share in this production. Unlike
38    professional ball games where one has to lose for the other to win, all can win in a capitalist society. (Sarah)

    1. What is the thesis of this essay?
        A. Capitalism is the best political system.
        B. Sports figures are paid too much.
        C. Professional sports are quintessentially the best of capitalism.
        D. Fans should boycott professional sports.

2. Evidence to support this claim would include
    I. Professional sports help boost the economy by creating jobs.
    II. Currently, professional basketball players of the NBA are on strike.
    III. Many may think it very unfair that although the hotdog man works the same amount of time as the players, his income is a fraction of theirs.

    A. I                          C. III
    B. II                         D. All

3. What is the counterargument:
    A. Lines 28-31                C. Lines 8–10
    B. Lines 19–20               D. NONE

4. Stylistic or persuasive elements, such as word choice or appeals to emotion, add power to the ideas expressed. How?
    I. Using words like "buzz" and "capitalism" connote positive concepts.
    II. Using examples that include the best-paid ballplayer and the lowly hotdog vendor increase the passage's ethos (credibility).
    III. The absence of women sports figures causes the reader to find the passage more credible.

    A. I                          D. I and III
    B. II                         E. I and II
    C. III

5. The passage would receive a score of __ .

## Grammar and Usage

Choose the best grammar/usage form in bold sentence(s).

1. Line 1
    A. NONE
    B. Professional sports are a big business, but they contribute to the welfare of our economy.
    C. Professional sports are a big business but they contribute to the welfare of our economy.
    D. Professional sports are a big business, and they contribute to the welfare of our economy.

2. Lines 8–10
    A. NONE
    B. Many only acknowledge the jobs created for the players and coaches; they fail to see the "hotdog man," the security guards, the grass cutters, the line markers, the custodians, the light engineers, the ushers and others.
    C. Many only acknowledge the jobs created for the players and coaches and they fail to see the "hotdog man," the security guards, the grass cutters, the line markers, the custodians, the light engineers, the ushers and others.
    D. Many only acknowledge the jobs created for the players and coaches even as they fail to see the "hotdog man," the security guards, the grass cutters, the line markers, the custodians, the light engineers, the ushers and others.

# Lesson 4
## Reading: Document-Based Analysis

### "Property"
### James Madison (March 29, 1792)

1  This term in its particular application means "that dominion which one man claims and exercises over the external
2  things of the world, in exclusion of every other individual." In its larger and juster meaning, it embraces every thing
3  to which a man may attach a value and have a right; and which leaves to everyone else the like advantage. In the
4  former sense, a man's land, or merchandize, or money is called his property. In the latter sense, a man has property
5  in his opinions and the free communication of them. He has a property of peculiar value in his religious opinions,
6  and in the profession and practice dictated by them. He has a property very dear to him in the safety and liberty of
7  his person. He has an equal property in the free use of his faculties and free choice of the objects on which to
8  employ them. In a word, as a man is said to have a right to his property, he may be equally said to have a property in
9  his rights. Where an excess of power prevails, property of no sort is duly respected. No man is safe in his opinions,
10 his person, his faculties, or his possessions. Where there is an excess of liberty, the effect is the same, tho' from an
11 opposite cause. Government is instituted to protect property of every sort; as well that which lies in various rights of
12 individuals, as that which the term particularly expresses. This being the end of government, that alone is a just
13 government, which impartially secures to every man, whatever is his. According to this standard of merit, the praise
14 of affording a just security to property, should be sparingly bestowed on a government which, however scrupulously
15 guarding the possessions of individuals, does not protect them in the enjoyment and communication of their
16 opinions, in which they have an equal, and in the estimation of some, a more valuable property. More sparingly
17 should this praise be allowed to a government, where a man's religious rights are violated by penalties, or fettered
18 by tests, or taxed by a hierarchy? Conscience is the most sacred of all property; other property depending in part on
19 positive law, the exercise of that, being a natural and unalienable right. To guard a man's house as his castle, to pay
20 public and enforce private debts with the most exact faith, can give no title to invade a man's conscience which is
21 more sacred than his castle, or to withhold from it that debt of protection, for which the public faith is pledged, by
22 the very nature and original conditions of the social pact. That is not a just government, nor is property secure under
23 it, where the property which a man has in his personal safety and personal liberty, is violated by arbitrary seizures of
24 one class of citizens for the service of the rest. A magistrate issuing his warrants to a press gang, would be in his
25 proper functions in Turkey, under appellations proverbial of the most complete despotism. That is not a just
26 government, nor is property secure under it, where arbitrary restrictions, exemptions, and monopolies deny to part of
27 its citizens that free use of their faculties, and free choice of their occupations, which not only constitute their
28 property in the general sense of the word; but are the means of acquiring property strictly called. What must be the
29 spirit of legislation where a manufacturer of linen cloth is forbidden to bury his own child in a linen shroud, in order
30 to favor his neighbor who manufactures woolen cloth; where the manufacturer and wearer of woolen cloth are again
31 forbidden the economical use of buttons of that material, in favor of the manufacturer of buttons of other materials!
32 A just security to property is not afforded by that government, under which unequal taxes oppress one species of
33 property and reward another species: where arbitrary taxes invade the domestic sanctuaries of the rich, and excessive
34 taxes grind the faces of the poor; where the keenness and competitions of want are deemed an insufficient spur to
35 labor, and taxes are again applied, by an unfeeling policy, as another spur; in violation of that sacred property, which
36 Heaven, in decreeing man to earn his bread by the sweat of his brow, kindly reserved to him, in the small repose that
37 could be spared from the supply of his necessities. If there be a government then which prides itself in maintaining
38 the inviolability of property; which provides that *none* shall be taken directly even for public use without
39 indemnification to the owner, and yet directly violates the property which individuals have in their opinions, their
40 religion, their persons, and their faculties; nay more, which indirectly violates their property, in their actual
41 possessions, in the labor that acquires their daily subsistence, and in the hallowed remnant of time which ought to
42 relieve their fatigues and soothe their cares, the influence will have been anticipated, that such a government is not a
43 pattern for the United States. If the United States mean to obtain or deserve the full praise due to wise and just
44 governments, they will equally respect the rights of property, and the property in rights: they will rival the
45 government that most sacredly guards the former; and by repelling its example in violating the latter, will make
46 themselves a pattern to that and all other governments.

(*James Madison: Writings*, ed. Jack N. Rakove [New York: Library of America, 1999], 515–17).

1. Which of the following conclusions can be surmised by reading this document?
   I. Property is very valuable.
   II. Slavery is a just and valuable institution.
   III. Conscience is the most sacred of all property.

   A. NONE          C. I and III          E. II and III
   B. All           D. II

2. What does "According to this standard of merit, the praise of affording a just security to property, should be sparingly bestowed on a government which, however scrupulously guarding the possessions of individuals, does not protect them in the enjoyment and communication of their opinions, in which they have an equal, and in the estimation of some, a more valuable property" mean?
   A. Government is owned like property, but government does not own the religion and opinions of its people.
   B. Public property is always more important than private property.
   C. Citizens must be careful to fight for their property.
   D. Ownership of property does not give citizens the right to violate the rights of others.

3. What does "A just security to property is not afforded by that government, under which unequal taxes oppress one species of property and reward another species: where arbitrary taxes invade the domestic sanctuaries of the rich, and excessive taxes grind the faces of the poor" mean?
   A. All taxes are evil.
   B. Taxes are a necessary evil.
   C. Private property is onerous.
   D. Secure property is only justified by a fair and just government that lays an equal burden on all its citizens.

4. In what document would this essay be supported?
   A. A pamphlet on liberty          C. A defense of Communism
   B. A sermon on law                D. All

5. Which of the following statements would James Madison not support?
   A. Property, understood in its broad scope, is the foundation of all liberty, and "as a man is said to have a right to his property, he may equally be said to have a property in his rights."
   B. Conscience is not the property of the state.
   C. Ultimately the needs of the state come before any individual.
   D. Property embraces everything to which a man may attach a value and have a right; and which he leaves to everyone else the like advantage.

## Words in Context

1. What is the meaning of *scrupulously* in Line 14?
   A. Superficially          C. Carelessly
   B. Carefully              D. Painstakingly

2. What is the meaning of *hierarchy* in Line 18?
   A. Control                C. Protocol
   B. Order                  D. Magnanimity

3. What is the meaning of *despotism* in Line 25?

   A. Absolutism             C. Banking
   B. Democracy              D. Forgiveness

4. What is the meaning of *arbitrary* in Line 33?
   A. Capricious             C. Random
   B. Indiscriminate         D. Orderly

# Lesson 5
## Math: Algebra, Arithmetic Problem Solving and Data Analysis, and Passport to Advanced Math
**Passport to Advanced Math**

1. Points X, Y, and Z are collinear, and XZ = YZ. If the coordinates of X are (7, 2) and the coordinates of Y are (3, 6), what are the coordinates of Z?

   A. (2, 2)              C. (4, 4)                      E. (5, 4)
   B. (-4, 4)             D. (4, -4)

2. In the figure below, if AB is a line segment and OA = OB, what are the coordinates of point B?

   A. (-5,3)             C. (-3,-5)                    E. (-5,-3)
   B. (3, 5)             D. (-3,5)

A (5, 3)

O

B

3. In the same figure, if AB is a line segment and AO = BO what is the length of AB?

   A. 4                  C. 2                          E. 68
   B. 8                  D. 16

4. In the figure shown, W is the midpoint of line segment PZ, and S and T are midpoints of PW and WZ, respectively. If the length of ST is c, what is the length of PZ?

P     S     W     T     Z

   A. 2C                                  D. C/2
   B. C                                   E. 3A
   C. 3C/2

# Chapter 5   The Legacy of Leprosy
# 2 Kings 5

> *Memory Verse:* Elisha sent a messenger to say to him, "Go, wash yourself seven times in the Jordan, and your flesh will be restored and you will be cleansed." —2 Kings 5:10

The story of the healing of Naaman is well known to every Sunday school graduate. Gehazi's story is not as well known, even though it directly follows the account of Naaman and is actually a part of the Naaman narrative. One reason why the Gehazi part is not as well publicized is that it has such a sad ending. It's the story of a man who left leprosy as his legacy to his family.

The very leprosy that was miraculously lifted from Naaman settled upon Gehazi and his descendants (2 Kings 5:27).Gehazi was the servant, or assistant, of Elisha, the prophet of God. It seems that he started out well. As we read 2 Kings 4 we could even say that Gehazi appears to be a model servant. Every time he's mentioned, he's doing what every good servant would be expected to do for his master. In fact, in many ways Gehazi was a partner with Elisha in the ministry. But when we come to the end of 2 Kings 5 we read of Gehazi's legacy of leprosy. What happened?

Gehazi committed some very serious sins. When Elisha refused to take any payment or gift from Naaman, Gehazi could not resist the temptation to try to relieve Naaman of some of his all-too-available wealth! In 5:20 we see that Gehazi said to himself, "As the LORD lives, I will run after Naaman and take something from him." Can you believe it? Doing something wrong in the name of the Lord! It seems that Gehazi didn't even have much of a guilty conscience as he planned his course of action. As far as Gehazi was concerned, Naaman had come prepared to pay big money for a cure from his leprosy. Now Naaman was returning to the pagan land of Syria with all that ready silver and gold! Why not lighten the load a little for Naaman, as he traveled back to Damascus, and keep some of that treasure in the Holy Land? So what if he had to make up just a little story to exaggerate the needs of the ministry in order to twist Naaman's arm? Didn't the ends justify the means. The ends, in this case, were for Gehazi to get a little of this world's goods! But wasn't this money, at least indirectly, going to be used for the Lord's work, since it was providing for one of the Lord's servants? Maybe, Gehazi reasoned, "I should put something away for retirement since the prophet doesn't have a pension plan!" The fact that a little cover-up lie also had to be told to Elisha wasn't all that bad, was it? We too might question why God would give leprosy to a man and all his descendants for such an action. Admittedly it was wrong and foolish behavior, but why did God consider this sin so serious that he imposed a legacy of leprosy on Gehazi?

Gehazi's sins were serious because the testimony of the Lord was directly and negatively affected. Gehazi defiled the Lord's work. Gehazi dishonored the Lord's servant. And Gehazi distorted the Lord's gospel. Gehazi's actions were not confined to his own private world, but affected others as well. They would not only discredit the testimony of the Lord in Israel, but would also disgrace the testimony of the Lord internationally! Gehazi's sins were very serious indeed.

Gehazi defiled the Lord's work because he lied about the ministry. He told Naaman that two young prophets had dropped in on Elisha unexpectedly (5:22). They were poor servants of the Lord from the backwoods country and were in need of a little cash and some new clothes, especially there in the big city of Samaria. Nothing could have been further from the truth! It was a made-up story, yet it sounded believable precisely because it had to do with the Lord's work.

Gehazi's legacy of leprosy should be a warning to everyone involved in Christian ministry. We must remember: in Christian ministry the ends do not justify the means. The way we do things is as important as what we do.

In 1 Timothy 6:9–10 we read that people "who want to get rich fall into temptation and a trap and into many foolish and harmful desires that plunge them into ruin and destruction. For the love of money is the root of all kinds of evil. Some people, eager for money, have wandered from the faith and pierced themselves with many griefs." The love of money, even for a ministry, defiles the Lord's work and leads to a legacy of leprosy. The "many griefs" in this text are all part of that legacy of leprosy. The godly heritage of many Christian families has been lost because of a love of money and any other goal that is not centered on our Lord. It has not only defiled the work of the Lord, but the fallout of the love of money has also had devastating effects on the families of those involved.

Gehazi also dishonored the Lord's servant. He lied about Elisha. In concocting his story about the prophets in need, Gehazi actually put words into the mouth of Elisha. He told Naaman that Elisha told him about the two young prophets who had come from Ephraim, and that Elisha had told him to go to Naaman with this need. Putting words into the mouth of Elisha certainly gave the story more credibility, but this story slandered the prophet of the Lord—a serious sin.

Not only did Gehazi, lie about Elisha, he also lied directly to Elisha. When Elisha asked Gehazi where he had been, Gehazi responded without hesitation, "Your servant went nowhere" (5:25). God was giving Gehazi one last chance to repent and tell Elisha what a terrible thing he had done. If Gehazi had confessed his sin to Elisha right then, the situation could have been rectified, and we would have had a wonderful story of repentance and restoration! But Gehazi compounded his sin with cover-up. When we have fallen short of God's standards in some area, and we are gently confronted by a fellow believer asking us, "Where have you been?," how do we react? How many times do pride and the desire to "always be right" cause us to compound our sins by rationalizing our actions or attempting to cover them up? The Bible is warning us here that while God is always seeking to restore us, if we refuse to humble ourselves to his restoring process, we have chosen his judgment!

Dishonoring the Lord's servants is a sin that's very easy to commit. In most churches or ministries, the Lord's servants do a lot of the "up-front" work and are therefore subject to a lot of criticism. Criticism of the Lord's servants is dangerous business: let's be especially careful that our comments do not put into their mouths words that were never actually spoken!

Lying to or about anyone is a sin. Lying about a servant of the Lord is a particularly serious sin, however, because it's not only the Lord's servant who is dishonored: it's also the Lord Himself who is dishonored! God may need to remove those who continue to misrepresent and criticize the Lord's servants from their church or area of service. And many times it is quite obvious when God steps into the situation and disciplines with the "leprosy of Gehazi." God does not allow the sin of dishonoring his servants to be masked indefinitely. The "mark of Gehazi" not only renders the believer unclean to serve the Lord; it is also a reminder to fellow believers that dishonoring the Lord's servants involves serious consequences! The legacy of leprosy becomes God's warning to every potential Gehazi.

Gehazi's sin was also serious because it distorted the Lord's gospel. The gospel is God's good news. God's good news is that salvation and all of his gifts are free! In Isaiah 55:1 we read, "Come, all you who are thirsty, come to the waters; and you who have no money, come, buy and eat! Come, buy wine and milk without money and without cost." By lying and taking money, Gehazi distorted the good news that God's gift of healing is free. Moreover, Gehazi caused the spiritual picture in this story to be distorted. The free gift of cleansing from the fatal disease of leprosy pictures the truth that salvation, God's cleansing from the fatal disease of sin, is a free gift! "For the gift of God is eternal life through Jesus Christ our Lord" (Romans 6:23). Gehazi's greed distorted the great truth that "it is by grace you have been saved, through faith—and this is not from yourselves, it is the gift of God" (Ephesians 2:5–6).

We can be sure that when word rippled out in Damascus about Naaman's cure, the good news was distorted. The servants who were with Naaman would have told the story about the miraculous cure, but when they were asked "How much did it cost him?," they would have had to report that a price was paid. They may have emphasized that the life-saving cure cost Naaman only 300 pounds of silver—what a deal! But they were not able to say, "It was free!" The good news of God's free gift was distorted, and the truth that all Naaman had to do was humble himself in obedience to the Lord God of Israel was lost in the distortion. How sad!

And what bad news for Gehazi! Gehazi's legacy of leprosy should make us more aware of the seriousness of sins that negatively affect the testimony of our Lord Jesus Christ. Defiling the Lord's work, dishonoring the Lord's servants and distorting the Lord's gospel—these are very serious sins indeed. They not only bring God's necessary discipline on the individuals who commit these sins. They also result in negative fallout in the family for generations to come. Don't leave behind a legacy of leprosy.          (adapted from a teaching by Dr. David Reid, *Devotions for Growing Christians* [Neptune, NJ: Loizeaux Brothers, 1986]).


## Journal Question

We live in an age when many people consider "sin" to be a psychological maladjustment or a misinterpretation of an event. How does one take sin seriously without gravitating into a sort of religious legalism?

# Lesson 1
## Evidence-Based Reading and Writing

### Literary Choice

*Father Goriot*, by Honoré de Balzac, is a peculiar novel written by one of the leading authors of the nineteenth century. Owing to his powerful observation of detail and intrepid observations of society, Balzac is one of the founders of realism in literature. His characters are replete with complexity and moral ambiguity.

1     Mme. Vauquer (née de Conflans) is an elderly person, who for the past forty years has kept a lodging-
2 house in the Rue Nueve-Sainte-Geneviève, in the district that lies between the Latin Quarter and the Faubourg Saint-
3 Marcel. Her house (known in the neighborhood as the Maison Vauquer) receives men and women, old and young,
4 and no word has ever been breathed against her respectable establishment; but, at the same time, it must be said that
5 as a matter of fact no young woman has been under her roof for thirty years, and that if a young man stays there for
6 any length of time it is a sure sign that his allowance must be of the slenderest. In 1819, however, the time when this
7 drama opens, there was an almost penniless young girl among Mme. Vauquer's boarders.
8     That word *drama* has been somewhat discredited of late; it has been overworked and twisted to strange
9 uses in these days of dolorous literature; but it must do service again here, not because this story is dramatic in the
10 restricted sense of the word, but because some tears may perhaps be shed *intra et extra muros* [inside and outside
11 walls] before it is over.
12     Will any one without the walls of Paris understand it? It is open to doubt. The only audience who could
13 appreciate the results of close observation, the careful reproduction of minute detail and local color, are dwellers
14 between the heights of Montrouge and Montmartre, in a vale of crumbling stucco watered by streams of black mud,
15 a vale of sorrows which are real and joys too often hollow; but this audience is so accustomed to terrible sensations,
16 that only some unimaginable and well-nigh impossible woe could produce any lasting impression there. Now and
17 again there are tragedies so awful and so grand by reason of the complication of virtues and vices that bring them
18 about, that egotism and selfishness are forced to pause and are moved to pity; but the impression that they receive is
19 like a luscious fruit, soon consumed. Civilization, like the car of *Juggernaut*, is scarcely stayed perceptibly in its
20 progress by a heart less easy to break than the others that lie in its course; this also is broken, and Civilization
21 continues on her course triumphant. And you, too, will do the like; you who with this book in your white hand will
22 sink back among the cushions of your armchair, and say to yourself, "Perhaps this may amuse me." You will read
23 the story of Father Goriot's secret woes, and, dining thereafter with an unspoiled appetite, will lay the blame of your
24 insensibility upon the writer, and accuse him of exaggeration, of writing romances. Ah! once for all, this drama is
25 neither a fiction nor a romance! *All is true,*—so true, that every one can discern the elements of the tragedy in his
26 own house, perhaps in his own heart.
27     The lodging-house is Mme. Vauquer's own property. It is still standing in the lower end of the Rue Nueve-
28 Sainte-Geneviève, just where the road slopes so sharply down to the Rue de l'Arbalete, that wheeled traffic seldom
29 passes that way, because it is so stony and steep. This position is sufficient to account for the silence prevalent in the
30 streets shut in between the dome of the Pantheon and the dome of the Val-de-Grace, two conspicuous public
31 buildings which give a yellowish tone to the landscape and darken the whole district that lies beneath the shadow of
32 their leaden-hued cupolas.
33     In that district the pavements are clean and dry, there is neither mud nor water in the gutters, grass grows in
34 the chinks of the walls. The most heedless passer-by feels the depressing influences of a place where the sound of
35 wheels creates a sensation; there is a grim look about the houses, a suggestion of a jail about those high garden
36 walls. A Parisian straying into a suburb apparently composed of lodging-houses and public institutions would see
37 poverty and dullness, old age lying down to die, and joyous youth condemned to drudgery. It is the ugliest quarter of
38 Paris, and, it may be added, the least known. But, before all things, the Rue Nueve-Sainte-Geneviève is like a bronze
39 frame for a picture for which the mind cannot be too well prepared by the contemplation of sad hues and sober
40 images. Even so, step by step the daylight decreases, and the cicerone's droning voice grows hollower as the traveler
41 descends into the Catacombs. The comparison holds good! Who shall say which is more ghastly, the sight of the
42 bleached skulls or of dried-up human hearts?

# Close Reading

1. Which of the following statements are true?
   I.   The novel begins with an accumulation of minute detail that accentuates the decay and dilapidation of the boardinghouse.
   II.  The characters are realistically examined, but in a facile way.
   III. The author develops physical traits and reactions to environment which give insights into their moral behavior.

   A. I
   B. II
   C. III

   D. II and III
   E. All of the Above

2. What is the purpose of this statement? "Will anyone without the walls of Paris understand it? It is open to doubt. The only audience who could appreciate the results of close observation, the careful reproduction of minute detail and local color, are dwellers between the heights of Montrouge and Montmartre, in a vale of crumbling stucco watered by streams of black mud, a vale of sorrows which are real and joys too often hollow."
   A. The author wishes to convey the deteriorated physical and mental condition of his characters.
   B. This scene of is a foreshadowing of the catastrophic events that will surely follow.
   C. This setting really has no relevance to the novel.
   D. The author is merely warning the reader of an upcoming earthquake.

3. Which of the following beginnings is similar to the beginning of this novel?
   A. True!—nervous—very, very dreadfully nervous I had been and am; but why will you say that I am mad? The disease had sharpened my senses—not destroyed—not dulled them. Above all was the sense of hearing acute. I heard all things in the heaven and in the earth. I heard many things in hell. How, then, am I mad? Hearken! and observe how healthily—how calmly I can tell you the whole story. (Edgar Allan Poe, "The Tell-Tale Heart")
   B. During the whole of a dull, dark, and soundless day in the autumn of the year, when the clouds hung oppressively low in the heavens, I had been passing alone, on horseback, through a singularly dreary tract of country; and at length found myself, as the shades of the evening drew on, within view of the melancholy House of Usher. I know not how it was—but, with the first glimpse of the building, a sense of insufferable gloom pervaded my spirit. I say insufferable; for the feeling was unrelieved by any of that half-pleasurable, because poetic, sentiment, with which the mind usually receives even the sternest natural images of the desolate or terrible. I looked upon the scene before me—upon the mere house, and the simple landscape features of the domain—upon the bleak walls—upon the vacant eye-like windows—upon a few rank sedges—and upon a few white trunks of decayed trees—with an utter depression of soul which I can compare to no earthly sensation more properly than to the after-dream of the reveller upon opium—the bitter lapse into everyday life—the hideous dropping off of the veil. (Edgar Allan Poe, "The Fall of the House of Usher")
   C. The "Red Death" had long devastated the country. No pestilence had ever been so fatal, or so hideous. Blood was its Avatar and its seal—the redness and the horror of blood. There were sharp pains, and sudden dizziness, and then profuse bleeding at the pores, with dissolution. The scarlet stains upon the body and especially upon the face of the victim, were the pest ban which shut him out from the aid and from the sympathy of his fellow-men. And the whole seizure, progress, and termination of the disease were the incidents of half an hour. (Edgar Allan Poe, "The Masque of the Red Death")
   D. The thousand injuries of Fortunato I had borne as I best could; but when he ventured upon insult, I vowed revenge. You, who so well know the nature of my soul, will not suppose, however, that I gave utterance to a threat. At length I would be avenged; this was a point definitively settled—but the very definitiveness with which it was resolved, precluded the idea of risk. I must not only punish, but punish with impunity. A wrong is unredressed when retribution overtakes its redresser. It is equally unredressed when the avenger fails to make himself felt as such to him who has done the wrong. (Edgar Allan Poe, "The Cast of Amontillado")
   *(The Works of Edgar Allan Poe*, vol. 2, http://www.gutenberg.org/files/2148/2148-h/2148-h.htm#link2H_4_0010)

## Words in Context

1. What is the meaning of *juggernaut* in Line 19?
   A. Powerful Force
   B. Compelling Thought
   C. Persuasive Argument
   D. Soothing Feeling

2. What is the meaning of *conspicuous* in Line 30?
   A. Subtle
   B. Remarkable
   C. Prominent
   D. Belated

## Source Analysis

From this text the reader can make the following assumptions about the author:

   I. He uses the setting to develop characters.
  II. His plots are often minimally important.
 III. He usually writes Gothic novels.

    A. I
    B. II
    C. III

    D. I and II
    E. NONE of Above

# Lesson 2
## Critical Reading and Writing

### Command of Evidence

Read the following passage and answer accompanying questions:

1   Smallpox is unquestionably a highly infectious or communicable disease, and in the language of a past day, there is
2   a virus or poison which can pass from the sick to the unaffected; when this transference occurs on a large scale, we
3   speak of an epidemic of smallpox. . . . There seems very little doubt that the home of smallpox was somewhere on
4   the continent of Africa, although it is true that there are traditions pointing to its existence in Hindustan at least 1000
5   B.C. One Hindu account alludes to an ointment for removing the cicatrices of eruption. Africa has certainly for long
6   been a prolific source of it: every time a fresh batch of slaves was brought over to the United States of America,
7   there was a fresh outbreak of smallpox. It seems that the first outbreak in Europe in the Christian era was in the latter
8   half of the sixth century, when it traveled from Arabia, visiting Egypt on the way. The earliest definite statements
9   about it come from Arabia and are contained in an Arabic manuscript now in the University of Leyden, which refers
10   to the years A.D. 570 and 571. There is a good deal of evidence that the Arabs introduced smallpox into Egypt at the
11   sacking of Alexandria in A.D. 640. Pilgrims and merchants distributed it throughout Syria and Palestine and along
12   the north of Africa; then, crossing the Mediterranean, they took it over to Italy. The Moors introduced it into Spain
13   whence, via Portugal, Navarre, Languedoc, and Guienne it was carried into western and northern Europe. The
14   earliest physician to describe smallpox is Ahrun, a Christian Egyptian, who wrote in Greek. He lived in Alexandria
15   from A.D. 610 to 641. The first independent treatise on the disease was by the famous Arabian physician Rhazes,
16   who wrote in Syriac in A.D. 920, but his book has been translated into both Greek and Latin. The first allusion to
17   smallpox in English is in an Anglo-Saxon manuscript of the early part of the tenth century; the passage is
18   interesting—"Against pockes: very much shall one let blood and drink a bowl full of melted butter; if they [pustules]
19   strike out, one should dig each with a thorn and then drop one-year alder drink in, then they will not be seen"—this
20   was evidently to prevent the pitting dreaded even at so early a date. Smallpox was first described in Germany in
21   1493, and appeared in Sweden first in 1578. . . . To many of [the originator of a smallpox vaccination] Jenner's
22   contemporaries the view that vaccinia had at one time been a disease of human beings seemed unlikely; but we are
23   now in a far better position to admit its probability than were those of Jenner's time. We have since then learned that
24   man shares many diseases with the lower animals, tuberculosis, plague, rabies, diphtheria, and pleuro-pneumonia, to
25   mention only a few. We have also learned that certain lower animals, insects for instance, are intermediary hosts in
26   the life-cycle of many minute parasites which cause serious diseases in the human being, amongst which malaria,
27   yellow fever, and the sleeping sickness are the most familiar.
28       It appears to have been understood before Jenner's time that persons who had acquired cowpox by handling
29   cattle, but especially by milking cows, were immune from smallpox. In the reign of Charles II, it is well known that
30   the court beauties envied the dairy-maids because having had cowpox, they could not take smallpox, which all
31   women so dreaded. Dr. Corlett tells us that the Duchess of Cleveland, one of the King's mistresses, on being told
32   that she might lose her place in the royal favor if she were disfigured by smallpox, replied that she had nothing to
33   fear as she had had cowpox. In 1769 a German, Bose, wrote on the subject of cowpox protecting from smallpox. In
34   the year 1774 a cattle dealer, Benjamin Jesty, at Yetminster, in Dorset, inoculated his wife and three children with
35   cowpox. *None* of them ever took smallpox during the rest of their lives although frequently exposed to its infection.
36   Jesty died in 1816, and it is recorded on his tombstone that he was the first person who inoculated cowpox to protect
37   from smallpox. Cowpox, or vaccinia, though infectious for cows, is not transmissible among human beings, in other
38   words, as a disease of man it is not infectious. Edward Jenner, the Englishman of Berkeley in Gloucestershire, was
39   the first person to think scientifically on the fact that cowpox protected from smallpox. John Hunter had said to him,
40   "Jenner, don't think, try." Luckily, however, he did both. Thinking alone avails little, experimentation alone avails
41   not much, but the one along with the other has removed mountains. Just as Newton thought scientifically about that
42   falling apple and reduced our conceptions of the universe to order, just as Watt thought scientifically about that
43   kettle-lid lifted by the steam and so introduced the modern era of mechanical power brought under man's control, so
44   Jenner thought about and experimented with cowpox until he had satisfied himself that he had discovered something
45   which would rid the human race forever of the incubus of an intolerable pestilence.
46       It was in 1780 that Jenner set himself to study cowpox in a way that had never before been attempted, for
47   he was convinced that in the having had an attack of the disease lay the secret of the conquest of that world-scourge.
48   He confided in his friend Edward Gardner about "a most important matter . . . which I firmly believe will prove of

49  essential benefit to the human race. . . . Should anything untoward turn up in my experiments, I should be made,
50  particularly by my medical brethren, the subject of ridicule." Luckily he was quite prepared for both ridicule and
51  opposition; for has not everything new been ridiculed and opposed? Galileo was opposed, Bruno was opposed,
52  Copernicus was opposed, Harvey was opposed, George Stevenson was opposed, Pasteur was ridiculed and opposed,
53  and so were Darwin, Simpson, and even Lister. The physiological inertia even of the educated has too often blocked
54  the path of advancement: but Jenner is in illustrious company, a prince amongst the hierarchy of the misunderstood.
55  . . . In 1788 Jenner had a careful drawing made of the hand of a milkmaid suffering from cowpox to demonstrate to
56  Sir Everard Home how exceedingly similar were vaccinia and variola. Home agreed it was "interesting and
57  curious," and the subject began to attract some attention in medical circles.
58        In November, 1789, Dr. Jenner inoculated his eldest child Edward, aged 18 months, with some swinepox
59  virus, and as nothing untoward happened, he inoculated him again with swinepox on April 7, 1791. The child had a
60  slight illness, very like vaccinia, from which he rapidly recovered. The moment for the crucial experiment was not
61  yet; it came in due time, but Jenner had to wait five years for it, and five years are a long time to a man who is
62  yearning to perform his crucial experiment. Happily for suffering humanity, in the early summer of 1796 the
63  opportunity came; the hour and the man were there together. . . . Early in 1797, through another outbreak of cowpox,
64  Jenner was able to inoculate three persons with variola, only to find as before that they were immune from smallpox.
65  He now felt himself justified in preparing a paper for the Royal Society, the highest scientific tribunal in England.
66  The council, however, returned him his paper with the remark that in their opinion the amount of evidence was not
67  strong enough to warrant its publication in the *Transactions*. Jenner was wise enough not to be discouraged, and so
68  in June, 1798, he published the paper himself under the title, "Inquiry into the causes and effects of the Variolae-
69  Vacciniae, a disease discovered in some of the western counties of England, particularly Gloucestershire, and known
70  by the name of cowpox." This historic pamphlet, which ranks with the great classics of medicine, was dedicated to
71  Dr. O. H. Parry, of Bath. Later on the Royal Society was sagacious enough to elect the very man whose paper it had
72  previously refused. . . . Dr. Jenner's views were now becoming known, and the critics and the doubters had
73  appeared: St. Thomas has always had a large following. The most formidable of the early objectors was Dr.
74  Igenhouz, who had come to London to study inoculation for variola, and had already inoculated, among other
75  notable persons, the Archduchess Theresa Elizabeth of Vienna. The careless vaccinations of Doctors Pearson and
76  Woodville at the London Smallpox Hospital brought much apparent discredit on Jenner's work. In all his early work
77  Jenner used lymph obtained directly from papules on the cow or calf, but Woodville in 1799 showed that excellent
78  results could be got from arm-to-arm vaccination. As this latter method is a very convenient one, the technique was
79  widely adopted. We have to remember that we are speaking of a period about sixty years before Lister gave to
80  suffering humanity that other great gift, antisepsis: and so many arms "went wrong," not because of being
81  vaccinated, but because the scratches were afterwards infected by the microorganisms of dirt. Jenner knew well the
82  difference between the reaction of clean vaccination and that of an infected arm, but a great many medical men of
83  his time did not, and so he was constantly plagued with reports of vaccinations "going wrong" when it was *septic*
84  infection of uncleansed skin that had occurred. The explanation of these things by letter consumed a very great deal
85  of his valuable time. By the end of 1799 a large number of persons had, however, been successfully vaccinated. As
86  one Pearson proved troublesome by starting an institution for public vaccination on principles which Jenner knew to
87  be wrong, and as Jenner found himself virtually supplanted and misrepresented, he came up to London in 1800 to
88  vindicate his position. The King, the Queen, and the Prince of Wales, to whom he was presented, materially helped
89  on the cause by countenancing the practice of vaccination. Lord Berkeley, his Lord of the Manor, was in this as in
90  all things a kind and wise patron. In the United States of America vaccination made rapid progress, having been
91  introduced there under the good auspices of Dr. Waterhouse, professor of medicine at Cambridge, Mass. The
92  discovery was announced with true American informality as "Something curious in the medical line," on March 12,
93  1799. . . . Many people at the present time allow themselves to be persuaded into being anti-vaccinators because
94  neither they nor their deluders have ever known what an epidemic of smallpox is, have never seen with their own
95  eyes the awful spectacle of a person suffering from smallpox in any of its forms—discrete, confluent, or
96  hemorrhagic. Thanks to this very Jenner, the world has now for 100 years been almost free from epidemic, virulent
97  smallpox and most perfectly so in the vaccinated countries, so that millions, the majority, of Englishmen, have never
98  seen a case of smallpox at all. Not knowing the awful danger they have escaped, through Great Britain having had
99  compulsory vaccination since 1853, they have become lax in their belief in the necessity for the continuance of that
100 precaution. "They jest at scars that never felt a wound." Towns such as Gloucester in England, in which a large
101 number of children have been allowed to grow up unvaccinated, have always been visited sooner or later by a
102 serious outbreak of smallpox. It must be so; the laws of natural phenomena cannot be changed to suit the taste of
103 those persons who are mentally incapable of understanding them. They cannot be evaded; ignorance of the law is no
104 more an excuse in the realm of natural than of man-made law.

105     We now come to that undesirable product of present-day, grandmotherly legislation, the *conscientious*
106 objector. As I am not a politician, I shall not say anything for or against the policy of inserting in a bill which makes
107 vaccination compulsory a clause giving to the conscientious objector the power or right to refuse to have his child
108 vaccinated, but as a medical man who knows a little of the history of medicine, I can only describe it as gratuitous
109 folly. I am one of those who believe that the laity should have no say in the matter of whether any given procedure is
110 or is not advantageous for the public health. The efficacy of universal inoculation of vaccinia as a prophylactic
111 against variola is a question of scientific medicine to be decided on technical grounds and ought not to be a matter
112 open to debate by the public at all. It is perfectly monstrous to suppose that the ordinary person, quite untrained to
113 weigh evidence for or against the advisability of the carrying out of a particular form of national immunization
114 against a horrid disease, is qualified to form any opinion. He might as well be consulted on the advisability of
115 making the channel tunnel or on the safest type of aeroplane or on any other subject involving the technical training
116 of the engineer. To permit the so-called "man in the street" to say whether he shall or shall not permit the carrying
117 out of some important piece of civic hygiene is to introduce a principle subversive of all system and obstructive of
118 all progress in the science of public health. It is absurd that in a case like this the pronouncements of the judges are
119 to be submitted to the criticisms of the jury. England has already had one or two pretty severe lessons through
120 allowing such places as Gloucester and Leicester to exercise their right of private judgment on the question of
121 vaccination. In Gloucester, where there was at one time a vigorous anti-vaccination movement, a serious epidemic
122 overtook the city a few years ago (1896). What science pronounces to be beneficial, the layman must submit to.
123 What we want in these days is less superstition and more faith—in science. I am informed that there are more than
124 2,000 unvaccinated children in the schools of this city at the present moment, and all because a piece of legislation
125 allows any unintelligent, prejudiced, or credulous parent to decide on the momentous question of the vaccination of
126 his children. . . . The "conscience clause" should be immediately removed from the act in which it was inserted on
127 the grounds that it is weak and reactionary in principle, not in the interests of the development of the legislative
128 aspect of the science of public health, and that it permits in certain unintelligent communities quite a considerable
129 number of unvaccinated children to grow up as a permanent menace to their town and district.
130     When the history of medicine becomes more widely known, when the principles of protective inoculation
131 are more generally understood, when respect for science is the rule rather than the exception, when great
132 achievements in the saving rather than the destroying of life are objects of national veneration, then we may hope to
133 see the day when it will be unhesitatingly admitted that the discovery by Dr. Edward Jenner, the Englishman, was
134 one of the most momentous in the history of the human race, and that his life was one of the noblest, most unselfish
135 and, in its far-reaching effects, most important that has ever been lived on this planet.

(D. Fraser Harris, MD, DSc, "Edward Jenner and Vaccination," *Scientific Monthly* 1 (1915): 66–85,
http://www.gutenberg.org/cache/epub/987/pg987.htm)

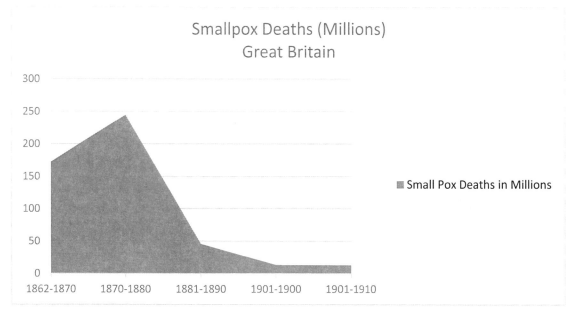

1. The thesis of this passage?
   A. Lines 1–4                             C. Lines 105–8
   B. Lines 24–25                         D. Lines 129-134

2.  Which of the following arguments are supported by the passage?
    I.   Good hygiene is helpful but will not completely eradicate smallpox.
    II.  Jenner's vaccination is important, but the disease was more or less disappearing anyway.
    III. Smallpox vaccination should be compulsory.

    A. I                      D. I and III
    B. II                     E. All
    C. III

3.  Why did Dr. Igenhouz oppose Dr. Jenner's inoculation?
    A. It violated Scripture.                C. At least two physicians incorrectly administered
    B. Many inoculated patients died.            the smallpox inoculation.
                                             D. All of the Above

4.  What counterargument does the author offer?
    A. The Bible is opposed to inoculation.
    B. Conscientious objections to inoculation.
    C. Administration of the inoculation by government agencies.
    D. Administration of the inoculation by female nurses.

5. Jenner could have influenced the following scientists:
    I.   Louis Pasteur
    II.  Isaac Watts
    III. Benjamin Franklin

    A. I                      D. I and II
    B. II                     E. I and III
    C. III                    F. All

6. What can be surmised by examining the chart illustrating the eradication of smallpox in Great Britain.
    I.   Compulsory smallpox vaccinations began around 1880.
    II.  Smallpox rates dropped after 1880.
    III. Opposition to smallpox vaccinations dropped after 1880.

    A. I                      D. I and II
    B. II                     E. I and III
    C. III                    F. All

7. The smallpox occurrence rate stayed about the same from 1900 to 1910. What is one plausible explanation?
    I.   The smallpox inoculation had lost its effectiveness.
    II.  The British government stopped inoculating its citizens.
    III. Smallpox had been almost completely eradicated.

    A. I                      D. I and II
    B. II                     E. I and III
    C. III                    F. All

8. While the text does not address this issue, what are possible reasons why smallpox deaths increased from 1870 to 1880?
    I.   Universal inoculation was not practiced until 1881.
    II.  The birth rate of Great Britain sharply dropped.
    III. There was a severe outbreak of flu.

    A. I                      D. I and II
    B. II                     E. I and III
    C. III                    F. All

## Words in Context

1. What is the meaning of *inertia* in Line 53?
   A. Dissolution
   B. Inaction
   C. Momentum
   D. Confusion

2. What is the meaning of *septic* in Line 83?
   A. Malignant
   B. Benign
   C. Putrefying
   D. Harmless

3. What is the meaning of *conscientious* in Line 105?
   A. Imaginative
   B. Obdurate
   C. Apathetic
   D. Conscience-driven

4. What is the meaning of *credulous* in Line 125?
   A. Believable
   B. Unbelievable
   C. Smart
   D. Clever

# Lesson 3
## SAT Essay

Examine the following picture and answer the questions:

World War II Poster
(http://www.archives.gov/atlanta/exhibits/item243-exh.html)

1. A purpose of this photograph/poster could be:
  I.   To sell war bonds
  II.  To recruit more female workers to factories
  III.  To encourage Americans to enlist in the military

        A. I                        D. I and II
        B. II                      E. I and III
        C. III

2. Which group(s) might find this photograph objectionable?
   A. American soldiers                  C. Daughters of the American Revolution
   B. American women                 D. NONE

3. Which of the following strategies does the photographer employ to influence his audience?

  I. The young lady worker looks sufficiently feminine to offer no threat to possible returning male soldiers but sufficiently "male" to assure everyone that she is competent and thorough in her work.

  II. Presumably the female worker can do some things—oil machinery—but must rely on male coworkers to do more technical and sometimes more physically demanding work.

  III. The object receiving oil appears to be a submarine, or some sort of war machinery that will advance the war effort and at the same time is a way for this mother or daughter to offer support for her loved one.

  IV. The female worker, in her natural, competent composure, is making a statement that she is there to stay: no returning war veteran will take her place!

  V. The female worker's gentle smile implies that she is thinking of the day when her husband, father, or brother will return to stand again at her side.

  A. I and II
  B. I, II, and III
  C. IV and V

  D. I, II, III, and V
  E. All

## Student Essay 1

*Prompt:* Assess the effect of modern media on society.

1    As television began to gain popularity in the late 1940s, the public and private sectors were awed at this
2 new medium of communication. **Little did they know that the TV would transform entertainment, news,**
3 **sports, and politics and eventually the entire globe.** Obviously television has changed the world; however, the
4 more obscure implications of this new technology must now be considered, especially in regards to elections and
5 politics. Because of the image-emphasizing nature of television and the passive nature of humankind, TV has had a
6 negative impact on presidential elections.
7    To understand the effects of television upon humans, they must first be understood. Because of sinful
8 tendencies, humankind is often lazy instead of hardworking and passive instead of active. When it comes to decision
9 making and elections, people in general prefer to be told whom to chose rather than take time and effort to search for
10 the best candidate themselves. Political news networks understand this temptation in humans and often seek to
11 impose their opinions and biases upon the passive and often uneducated population. Some would argue that
12 television is great because it allows nearly all citizens of every economic level to listen and chose for themselves
13 whom to elect. However, this viewpoint fails to understand that although the passive viewers may think they are
14 choosing for themselves, it is often the bias of the commentator who ultimately influences and determines their vote.
15    Not only do news networks influence who lives at 1600 Pennsylvania Avenue, but also once the president
16 moves in, the television media continues to influence and persuade the wayward public. For example, Walter
17 Cronkite convinced Americans that the Vietnam War could not be won and that President Johnson foreign policy
18 was flawed. "We always knew . . . that Cronkite had more authority with the American people than anyone else,
19 [including the president]." Although the so-called purpose of news networks is to accurately report unbiased facts,
20 TV often deceptively leads the public by overemphasizing unimportant points, taking short phrases out of context,
21 oversimplifying concepts, and leading their attention away from the bigger issues. If the public continues to be
22 swayed by twelve-second clips and talking heads, the U.S. Presidency will become a pitiful puppet manipulated by
23 the mighty hands of the television media.
24    The third major problem with television's coverage of American politics is the increasing emphasis of
25 image over issues. For instance, the first televised debates were criticized because "'victory' in the debates was
26 largely a triumph of image over content." Because television is visual, successful candidates were those who
27 focused on their image and crafted persuasive words that seemed appealing in short video clips. Entertainment and
28 politics began to merge as the networks focused on the superficial rather than on the significant issues that would
29 determine the course of America. This further encouraged the public to watch the presidential debates the same way
30 they would watch a comedy or suspense film—for pleasure. **Television only encouraged people to seek a**
31 **superficial understanding of the issues, instead of critically analyzing and researching to fully understand the**
32 **important, complicated issues.**
33    Granted, television in itself is an efficient means of raising awareness and communicating important facts
34 in a timely manner. However, when newscasters twist information to support their bias or when people passively
35 accept whatever the media says, then television becomes a negative influence upon American politics .(Jacqueline)

1. Generally speaking, the author claims what?
   A. TV has had a laudable effect on society.
   B. TV in moderation has had a laudable effect on society.
   C. TV has potentially positive effects, but the media has irresponsibly used it to advance its agendas.
   D. She fondly remembers Saturday morning TV.

2. The following are examples of evidence, such as facts or examples, to support claims.
   I. Lines 1–2                    III. Lines 16–18
   II. Lines 7–8                   IV. Lines 25–26

      A. I                    C. I, II, and III              E. II, III, IV
      B. II                   D. II and III

3. Which of the above choices are reasoning to develop ideas and connect claims and evidence?
   A. I                    D. II and III
   B. II                   E. IV
   C. I, II, and III       F. NONE

4. Which of the above choices provide stylistic or persuasive elements, such as word choice or appeals to emotion, to add power to the ideas expressed:
   A. I                    D. II and III
   B. II                   E. IV
   C. I, II, and III       F. NONE

5. The author is probably
   A. A born-again Christian          C. Someone who loves television
   B. A young writer                  D. NONE

6. What score would this essay receive? __

## Grammar and Usage

Choose the best grammar/usage form in bold sentence(s).

1.  Lines 2–3
    A.  NONE
    B.  Little did they know that the TV would transform global entertainment, news, sports, and politics.
    C.  Little did they know that the TV would transform entertainment, news, sports, and politics—the entire globe,
    D.  Little did they know that the TV would transform entertainment, news, sports, and politics around the entire globe.

2.  Lines 30–32
    A.  NONE
    B.  Television only encourages people to seek a superficial understanding of the issues, instead of critically analyzing and researching to fully understand the important, complicated issues.
    C.  Instead of critically analyzing and researching to fully understand the important complicated issues, television encourages people to be satisfied with only a superficial understanding of the issues.
    D.  Television only encourages people to seek a superficial understanding of the issues, but not critically analyze and research the important, complicated issues.

# Lesson 4

## Reading: Document-Based Analysis

### National Foundation on the Arts and the Humanities Act of 1965 (Public Law 89–209)

(As amended through P.L. 113–76, enacted January 17, 2014)

1 The Congress finds and declares the following: (1) The arts and the humanities belong to all the people of the United
2 States. (2) The encouragement and support of national progress and scholarship in the humanities and the arts, while
3 primarily a matter for private and local initiative, are also appropriate matters of concern to the Federal Government.
4 (3) An advanced civilization must not limit its efforts to science and technology alone, but must give full value and
5 support to the other great branches of scholarly and cultural activity in order to achieve a better understanding of the
6 past, a better analysis of the present, and a better view of the future. (4) Democracy demands wisdom and vision in
7 its citizens. It must therefore foster and support a form of education, and access to the arts and the humanities,
8 designed to make people of all backgrounds and wherever located masters of their technology and not its unthinking
9 servants. (5) It is necessary and appropriate for the Federal Government to complement, assist, and add to programs
10 for the advancement of the humanities and the arts by local, State, regional, and private agencies and their
11 organizations. In doing so, the Government must be sensitive to the nature of public sponsorship. Public funding of
12 the arts and humanities is subject to the conditions that traditionally govern the use of public money. Such funding
13 should contribute to public support and confidence in the use of taxpayer funds. (6) The arts and the humanities
14 reflect the high place accorded by the American people to the nation's rich cultural heritage and to the fostering of
15 mutual respect for the diverse beliefs and values of all persons and groups. (7) The practice of art and the study of
16 the humanities require constant dedication and devotion. While no government can call a great artist or scholar into
17 existence, it is necessary and appropriate for the Federal Government to help create and sustain not only a climate
18 encouraging freedom of thought, imagination, and inquiry but also the material conditions facilitating the release of
19 this creative talent. (8) The world leadership which has come to the United States cannot rest solely upon superior
20 power, wealth, and technology, but must be solidly founded upon worldwide respect and admiration for the Nation's
21 high qualities as a leader in the realm of ideas and of the spirit. (9) Americans should receive in school, background
22 and preparation in the arts and humanities to enable them to recognize and appreciate the aesthetic dimensions of
23 our lives, the diversity of excellence that comprises our cultural heritage, and artistic and scholarly expression.
24 (10) It is vital to a democracy to honor and preserve its multicultural artistic heritage as well as support new ideas,
25 and therefore it is essential to provide financial assistance to its artists and the organizations that support their work.
26 (11) To fulfill its educational mission, achieve an orderly continuation of free society, and provide models of
27 excellence to the American people, the Federal Government must transmit the achievement and values of
28 civilization from the past via the present to the future, and make widely available the greatest achievements of art.
29 (12) In order to implement these findings and purposes, it is desirable to establish a National Foundation on the Arts
30 and the Humanities. (20 U.S.C. 951, enacted Nov. 5, 1990, P.L. 101–512, sec. 101, 104 Stat. 1961)

### A Criticism of the NEA (National Endowment for the Arts)

1 A fine line exists between government benevolence, government intervention, and government control. Although it
2 seems benevolent for our government to support the arts through the NEA-funding program, such benevolence has
3 led to government intrusion and control, to the chagrin of many tax-paying citizens. Art critics and enthusiasts alike
4 have found the saying "With shekels come shackles" to be very true in the art realm. Because of government
5 funding, the arts have received shekels or funding, but shackles have quickly followed. The NEA has caused tension
6 between the people's wants and the government restrictions with regard to what should be accepted and displayed in
7 the art world. Because of this government-citizen discrepancy, and the overpowering control government has begun
8 to wield over the arts, government funding for the arts should not use reluctant taxpayer money to fund and control
9 something that runs against the desires of the people.
10 Because the government funds art projects and displays through the NEA program, many government
11 officials have decided to become art critics. For example, New York Mayor Rudolph Giuliani threatened "to bring
12 the Brooklyn Museum to its knees if it went ahead with an art exhibition that he finds sick." Giuliani, however, was

13  not the first who tried to control the arts. A few years earlier, Sen. Jesse Helms "objected vociferously to . . . an
14  exhibition." The NEA also refused to fund an exhibition in New York titled "Witnesses," an exhibition on AIDS,
15  despite grief from citizens and artists alike. These government officials were able to disparage and control these art
16  exhibitions and become "art critics" because they felt like they owned, and they partly did own, the art exhibitions
17  that they were funding. However, although through NEA funding, government officials feel like they can control a
18  large part of the art business, it must be remembered where the funding money comes from in the first place. The
19  government is using taxpayer money to fund a program that usually shuts down exhibitions against the will of the
20  people. Also, if the government can control self-expression through art, will they stop at that? What about self-
21  expression in speech, religion, and politics? Clearly, if government can intrude on art self-expression, the gateway is
22  open for other government intrusion and intervention.
23      Many citizens are willing to cede their free will to the government with regard to art because they believe
24  that private philanthropy depends positively on public subsidies. In other words, they believe that government,
25  through the NEA, is generating more than ten times as much in non-NEA donations. But is this realistic? Do
26  Americans really increase art contributions because the government is involved? How does government funding of
27  the arts really look to the American people? According to Arthur Brooks in "Do Public Subsidies Leverage Private
28  Philanthropy to the Arts," The American people may see government funding of the arts as an attempt to bail out a
29  failing or failed project. The American people may also diminish their enthusiasm and support for the arts "if the
30  government takes responsibility for its funding." So government funding of the arts does not only cause government
31  intrusion; it may also hurt private philanthropy.
32      Undoubtedly, Government funding of the arts has overstepped the fine line from benevolence to
33  intervention and control. Because the government is funding art, they can also control art expression. Government
34  funding may also cause Americans to see arts as a failing and losing project. Americans should be wary of this
35  funding and refuse to "give up liberty [of self-expression] for [art] security" (Benjamin Franklin). (Jacqueline)

1. Congress offered the following reasons for passage of the NEA:
   I.   Democracy demands wisdom and vision in its citizens. It must therefore foster and support a form of
        education, and access to the arts and the humanities, designed to make people of all backgrounds and
        wherever located masters of their technology and not its unthinking servants.
   II.  Government supports the arts and humanities as a last resort—when private support is insufficient.
   III. In school, Americans should receive background and preparation in the arts and humanities to enable
        them to recognize and appreciate the aesthetic dimensions of our lives, the diversity of excellence that
        comprises our cultural heritage, and artistic and scholarly expression.

   A. NONE                          C. I and III
   B. All                           D. II

2. Postmodernism is a late-twentieth-century movement in the arts and literature that was a departure from
   modernism. Postmodernism includes skeptical interpretations of culture, literature, art, philosophy, history,
   economics, architecture, fiction, and literary criticism. It was, as it were, an antimodernist (or antiscience)
   movement. Which of the following statements in the Humanities Acts seems to support the fact that the NEA
   is postmodern legislation.
   A. Lines 13–15                   C. Lines 25-30
   B. Lines 19–21                   D. ALL

3. What is the thesis of "A Criticism of the NEA?"
   A. Lines 11–12                   C. Lines 23–24
   B. Lines 1–4                     D. Lines 32–35

4. How does the author develop the argument?
   I.   The NEA funded by Congress is necessary.
   II.  The NEA is a problem because it is influenced too much by politics.
   III. Government funding of the NEA discourages private benevolence.

   A. NONE                          D. II
   B. All                           E. II and III
   C. I and III

5. What is an example of this statement? "Because the government funds art projects and displays through the NEA program, many government officials have, decided to become art critics".
   A. The Mayor of New York City visits an art exhibit.
   B. Congress refuses to fund expensive art deco paintings on a Sante Fe bridge.
   C. A famous playwright refuses to accept an award from Congress because of the War in Afghanistan.
   D. Congress refuses to fund a art exhibit because it includes the Ten Commandments.

# Lesson 5
## Math: Algebra, Arithmetic Problem Solving and Data Analysis, and Passport to Advanced Math

### Arithmetic Problem Solving

1. 12:30 a.m. is how many minutes past 9:45 a.m.?
   A. 105      C. 155      E. 175
   B. 125      D. 165

2. The number a - 6 is how much less than a + 6?
   A. 6      C. - 12      E. 2
   B. 12      D. - 6

3. To enter preschool, children must be no more than 4 years old on the start date of August 1. What is the oldest, in months, that a child can be on April 1 and still start school on the following August 1?
   A. 42      C. 44      E. 46
   B. 43      D. 45

4. How many three-digit numbers have the hundreds digit equal to 4 and the units digit equal to 5?
   A. 10      C. 20      E. 200
   B. 19      D. 190

5. There are fewer than 40 students enrolled in a certain class. If, at a certain time, 1/7 of the students are members of the band and another 1/5 are members of sports teams, what is the total class enrollment?
   A. 10      C. 25      E. 35
   B. 14      D. 28

6. How many different positive integral divisors does 24 have including 1 and 24?
   A. 8      C. 6      E. 2
   B. 7      D. 4

7. A number is divisible by 3 if the sum of its digits is divisible by 3. Which of the following numbers is divisible by 15?
   A. 21,115      C. 32,715      E. 72,365
   B. 24,048      D. 33,333

## Data Analysis

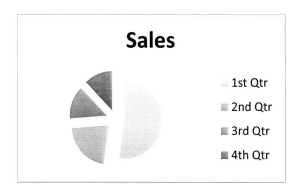

| 1st Qtr | 80 |
| 2nd Qtr | 33 |
| 3rd Qtr | 21 |
| 4th Qtr | 19 |

What is true about this chart?

   I.   1st Quarter sales were double any two other quarters.
  II.   1st Quarter sales were more than all the other quarters combined.
III.   2nd Quarter sales were larger than 3rd and 4th Quarter sales combined.

     A. NONE           C. I and II           E. II and III
     B. All              D. II

# Chapter 6   The Miracle at Cana
# John 2

> *Memory Verses:* The master of the banquet tasted the water that had been turned into wine. He did not realize where it had come from, though the servants who had drawn the water knew. Then he called the bridegroom aside and said, "Everyone brings out the choice wine first and then the cheaper wine after the guests have had too much to drink; but you have saved the best till now."
> —John 2:9–12

How does the kingdom of God grab you? Jesus does not speak of the kingdom of God as a reorganization of a society. No, he says that we will be excited about the kingdom of God the way my sister-in-law was excited when a stranger returned her lost wedding ring from a Burger King parking lot in Annapolis, Maryland. And, no, the Good Samaritan did not expect a reward. John 2:1–12 shows that the kingdom of God is like a wedding.

This is an incredible story! The story of the wedding at Cana! I heard a story about a kid who, when asked what he learned in Sunday school, replied, "We learned that Pharaoh wouldn't let the Hebrew children go free, so Moses called in some F-16 fighters, cruise missiles, and stealth bombers and blew up Cairo."

"Come on," his mom replied, "Tell me what she really said."

"If I did, Mom," the smiling child replied, "you would not believe me!"

Believe it or not, this is a marvelous, sensational story of the transforming power of Jesus Christ!

I remember my wedding day. We were so young, so full of energy—and skinny. I really enjoyed getting married.

In John 2, we have a picture of Jesus at a wedding in Cana. With his mother and his disciples, we see him sharing one of the happiest events in Judaism.

Then, as today, a wedding was a notable occasion. It was Jewish law that the wedding of a virgin should take place on a Wednesday. But the wedding celebration lasted far more than one day. It could last for a week! The wedding ceremony itself occurred late in the evening, usually after a feast. After the ceremony the young couple—the girl might be only 13 or 14 years old, and her husband somewhat older—were conducted to their new home. By then it was dark, and they were carried through the village streets by the light of flaming torches, with a canopy over their heads. The wedding couple traveled the most circuitous route possible so that as many people as possible could see the happy couple.

But a newlywed couple did not go away for a honeymoon. Hardly! They stayed at home and hosted a weeklong party, during which they wore crowns and stayed dressed in their wedding clothes. Thus they were king and queen for a week! In a land where life was so unforgiving and harsh, this was a joyous week indeed!

Our story opens today with Jesus returning from the wilderness. He was at a very important juncture in his ministry. He must choose his disciples and begin his ministry. But he found time for frivolity! He graced the occasion with his appearance.

But Jesus did more than grace the wedding. He saved it. A real crisis developed when the wedding party ran out of wine. For a Jewish feast, wine was essential. For the provisions to fail was a severe humiliation for the bridal party and their families. Jesus truly saved the day! And today Jesus does not merely visit us: he either becomes Lord of our lives or he is nothing.

Mary came to Jesus to alert him of the need.

"O Woman," he replied, "my hour has not yet come."

But nonetheless, he turned water into wine. This is one miracle at Cana.

You may have trouble believing in this miracle. I have no trouble! It sounds like the Jesus I know. He would not turn stones into bread for himself, but he did turn water into wine for others. He would not save himself, but he died for others.

Yet, he saved my soul! He gave me a reason for living. My faith does not exactly rest on this story, but hey, it confirms what I know about my Lord: He cares about the little things in life.

At Hampton Court Palace, not far from London, England, is the famous Black Hamburg vine planted in 1796. For nearly 200 years it has been producing annually about 650 bunches of grapes. Where does it get its nutrients? Its roots are bedded deeply into a culvert from which flows the most disgusting raw sewage in all of England. From the garbage of England flows the very best wine in the world!

And so, we produce all this garbage in our lives. And it somehow turns out to be good wine—but only because God knows how to do it! He is the vine; we are merely the branches. He uses us with all our faults to do his will. Now, that is a miracle!

No, I have no problem believing in miracles. I have seen him produce wine from water in my life. He has taken hopeless situations and made them hopeful, taken my sinful life and saved it. Yes, I can believe in miracles.

"He touched nothing that he did not adorn," the English writer Oliver Goldsmith wrote. What sin touches, what the devil touches, he defiles. But God in Jesus Christ touches us, and he gives life. An Elizabethan poet says it well: "The modest water saw its God and blushed." Charles Wesley writes: "When wine they want, the Almighty Lord / Water instead of wine demands. / He both created by his Word, / Nothing his sovereign power withstands. / And every year in every vine, / He changes water into wine."

Yes, most of us need a miracle. Every day. A miracle to go to work, to stay alive, to live with that person. A miracle!

From seminary, I remember that old George Williams needed a miracle. It was the winter of 1976. Remember? Thirty below. A foot of snow. I was sitting in a drafty building in Harvard Yard listening to Dr. Williams, the most famous medieval Church historian in America. He was lecturing on the Venerable Bede, one of the first British church historians. Williams was notorious for his criticism of miracles: in fact, he did not believe in God at all.

But in 1976, Williams was dying of cancer. He knew it too. And he was tired and cold. As he lectured on Venerable Bede, he reached a point in his lecture where he paused and looked out the window at Widener Library. We all sat and waited. He was lecturing on an alleged miracle that had happened to Bede.

"You know," he finally said, still looking out the frosted window, "I used to laugh at people who believed in miracles. But now, it is not funny. I need a miracle. And now, laugh at me too, but now I believe in them, too."

It is the shortage of wine that causes Christ to perform a miracle: the recognition that there was a need. Are you willing to admit to Christ that you need a miracle?

Jesus told Mary that his "hour" had not yet come, referring to his self-disclosure. He knew that once his mission was out of the bag, it was only three short years, and then the cross. . . . Jesus turned water into wine, but the greatest miracle was yet to come. When he died on the cross.

Several years ago there was a fire in Chicago. Every person in one family died except a five-year-old boy. During the fire, a stranger ran into the fire and saved the little boy. The little boy suffered smoke inhalation, and the stranger's hands were badly burned. The boy and the man went to separate hospitals and never saw each other at that time. In fact, no one knew who the stranger was.

Finally the child recovered, and the courts tried to decide who could adopt him. Several relatives were contacted and *none* of them were interested. Finally he was about to be turned over to the State. But during the hearing to determine the future of the little boy, a man entered the courtroom. He proceeded to ask the judge politely if he could adopt the child.

"Who are you?" the judge asked. "And what right do you have to adopt this child?"

The man said nothing but he took his hands out of his pockets and showed the judge what was left of his severely burned hands. It was the man who had rushed in and saved the child's life.

Young people, Jesus Christ can turn water into wine. Christ can take us out of our burning houses; he can empower us in hostile, secular universities and save us. But he wants us to give him our hearts. He has adopted us. And Christ alone deserves to own us. For the sake of needing a miracle, because of the cross. Trust Christ. Give him everything.

## Journal Question

Describe a miracle that you need in your life.

# Lesson 1
## Evidence-Based Reading and Writing

### Literary Choice

*Growing Up White*, by James P. Stobaugh, gifted me with soft memories that expatriate southerners have: rendezvous with suntanned southern boys at soda fountains, and family gatherings in pecan groves. I am also reminded of some memories I would like to forget: stringy barbecued squirrel, for one, and racist comments for another. Yet I share with Jake the joy of the journey. And there are days when I close my eyes and yearn again for one more Delta dawn that Stobaugh so eloquently describes in this tour de force. (Lisa Mormon)

### *Growing Up White* (chap. 1)

1      The spring sunrise silhouetted scraggly sugar maples guarding my ten-acre Pennsylvania Laurel Highlands
2  farm.
3      A soft May spring breeze teased juvenile leaf buds struggling to make up for lost time at the end of a winter
4  that began before Veterans Day and extended beyond Memorial Day. The beginning of the Laurel Highlands winter
5  saluted living warriors, and the end honored the dead ones. Until late May, frosty cold impeded solstial warmth.
6  May in the Laurel Highlands was just a slightly warmer version of March, and 80 degrees warmed the Highlands
7  only once or twice a year. It was as if summer never arrived. Or, if it arrived, it stayed so briefly that no one noticed.
8      Or so it seemed to this expatriate southerner.
9      Sunrises came and went effortlessly and with no fanfare. They came and went too quickly for my liking. I
10  no longer contemplated their going and their coming. My world was rich with other things, but not allegory.
11  Corporeal existence in the real-time world dulled my perspicuity in ways that I had not anticipated.
12      It was my birthday, and I was 59.
13      My grey farmhouse was on the edge of a rolling hill whose bottom abutted my musty basement and whose
14  top stroked God's azure grandeur. My bedroom was somewhere between musty and azure.
15      In my bed was my lover, my wife for 34 years. Her slumbered magnificence, undiluted by pasty make-up
16  and morning sobriety, nonetheless brightened dim morning light. Even in vulnerable repose this woman was supple
17  and sinuous! I was tempted to ravish the fair maiden but denied myself in tribute to faithful sleep.
18      I tiptoed down the creaky stairs to the kitchen.
19      The kitchen was the command post of my ailing, ancient Mennonite-built farm. The farm and the kitchen
20  were the very essence of practicality. No granite counter top or shiny modern faucet adorned this kitchen. There
21  were no enticements to worldliness or pride; no, this kitchen drew aspiring cooks to plain cooking and faithful diners
22  to godly living.
23      One fortunate gift from my former Anabaptist owner was frequent and mammoth kitchen windows. Built
24  when coal heat was cheap and abundant, the kitchen was sincere about blessing its visitors with plentiful sunlight.
25  Light cascaded into the inviting kitchen where the former and present tenants spent most days contemplating the
26  Holy Scriptures and the beauty of God's creation.
27      I walked in sock feet toward the stainless steel sink.
28      I filled the teakettle and put it on the stove. I first moved the start knob to the right, wrong way—as I have
29  done since we got the darn thing—and then back to the left, the right way. It exploded into a cascade of burning blue
30  propane gas, searing the hairs on my right hand.
31      "Good morning, world!"
32      Surrounded by leviathan whales, ship crews will throw out a tub in order to divert the attention of their
33  behemoth sentinels. The whales amuse themselves by tossing the tub into the air, as children do with a soccer ball.
34  While their attention is diverted, the formerly endangered ships sail away. Hence, "Throwing a tub to the whales!"
35      On my 59th birthday, I, Jake Stevens, was surrounded by a myriad of whales, and I was throwing my tub to
36  the Goliaths. Outside the kitchen window an irascible female cardinal was tapping on my window. Two years before
37  a cardinal couple was building a nest outside our side kitchen window in a privet hedge. Too low, in my estimation,
38  to escape our ferocious barn cats. These birds would become redbird take-out if I did not intervene.
39      I did. I tore down the nest before the stupid cardinals could birth cat food.
40      Unfortunately, the proprietors, especially the female, did not appreciate my thoughtful act. In fact, every
41  morning, for two years, she waited until I came down the stairs and tapped in angry clatter at my entrance.
42      Tap! Tap! Tap!

43    "I thought cardinals only lived about 18 months," I growled.

44    I was an incongruity. A study in contradictions. A southerner, who married a northerner. An alumnus of
45    several elite universities, who lived below the poverty line. Overweight due to my morbid lifestyle, I nonetheless
46    was effusively healthy. My family physician, which looked and lived a lot like me, was obviously disappointed: he
47    himself suffered under sundry maladies and wondered why I didn't. Yet last week, with some satisfaction, he
48    warned me that my vitamin $D_3$ levels were low. Glad to throw a tub to my doctor's whale.

49    I was a part-time Presbyterian minister, who wrote nonfiction books that only nerdy precocious prodigies
50    read. It was one of the smallest niche markets in the history of humankind, which my paltry pocketbook and choleric
51    publisher could attest.

52    By this time, though, the kettle was whistling. And the lovely maiden, Anna, came down the stairs.

53    Anna descended with a certainty in Providence that gave her gait a strong assurance: there was no creak on
54    the stairs when she descended. Anna approached the new day with more than a modicum of caution though. She was
55    unwilling to commit to unbridled optimism until she identified and measured the obstacles before her and the
56    resources that she could marshal to meet them. Anna was disinclined to embrace luck, or chance, for my careful
57    wife did not believe in such things. Her God controlled her future, and he would show her the path to follow this
58    new day. She trusted her God, but her husband, Jake Stevens, was an entirely different matter. God only knew what
59    he would do, especially on his birthday.

60    "Happy birthday, Jacob," she smiled as she entered the kitchen.

61    "Good morning, Sweetie," I responded.

62    I placed one Earl Gray, three PG Tips tea bags in the teapot and wrapped it in a tea cozy. As Anna, whose
63    parents were from Raasy, Skye, Scotland, were fond of saying, "The tea is stewing."

64    And so it was.

65    Anna joined me at the stove.

66    She measured out half a cup of steel-cut oatmeal and put it into a pot.

67    I kissed her. "Morning."

68    The effervescent mist of the stewing tea mingled with Anna's silver hair reflecting the morning sun.

69    Anna's hair started turning grey when she was 38 and had progressed into a processional of hoary splendor.

70    "Let's sit down," I invited.

71    Our solid oak oval kitchen table was cluttered with strewings. Anna was an inveterate note taker. She went
72    through realms of sticky notes every year. They decorated napkin holders and saltshakers and even her Bible. Sticky
73    notes organized, alerted, and scolded us with epistemological pretension that offered very little metaphysical
74    comfort but helped us organize our kaleidoscopically complicated lives.

75    Out our window gluttonous gold finches consumed overpriced striped sunflower seeds. For thirty-four
76    years we had held hands, prayed together, lived together. For twenty of those years we had greeted the morning
77    sheen at this kitchen table.

78    We quietly enjoyed the commencement of this new day.

79    Timid whitetail deer moved from thicket to spring. Stripped chippies dodged spiteful blue jays and scurried
80    along stone fences. Conscientious crows hopped among pokeberry bushes tossing hard blackberries into ravenous
81    beaks. To plume their nests, swooping orange-crowned chipping sparrows snatched whispy hair from our dozing
82    barn cats.

83    I recklessly held my teacup with two fingers and blew my steaming tea until it cooled; Anna held her cup in
84    two hands. She was unwilling to invest effort into something that God and circumstances would bring about
85    naturally.

86    The brown, orange-beaked ADHD female cardinal moved to the bird feeder, which we also provided gratis
87    to my avian friends. The visitor was not welcome, but how does one racially profile cardinals?

88    "Jacob, what are you doing? Are you daydreaming?"

89    While everyone else called me "Jake," Anna used my formal name, "Jacob." "Jake" reminded her of
90    tobacco-chewing NASCAR fans. "Jacob" was an investment of faith. She wanted to be married to an erudite, arcane
91    "Jacob," not a parochial hick named "Jake," which in truth was what I was. Anna did not believe what she saw, nor
92    was she moved by what she felt. She was only moved by what she believed. Faith annihilated mutability, destroyed
93    vastness, and brought history at once into possession.

94    "No, of course not. I am hypnotized by your radiant beauty."

95    And what I could see was beautiful. She was wearing her favorite L. L. Bean green-checkered flannel
96    nightgown that revealed nothing and was more resistant to wandering hands than a flak jacket.

97    "What are you thinking, Jacob?"

98    Anna returned to the kitchen counter to fill two blueberry-decorated bowls with oatmeal, Greek yogurt, and
99  home-made granola. The delicious mixture was Anna's creation and appreciated by this hungry boy on most days,
100 but not on my birthday. I had higher expectations.
101    "It is hard to be 59," I whined.
102    "Come on, Jacob. Eat your breakfast. Do you want some more tea?"
103    "I love oatmeal, Anna, but it is my birthday. Why can't I have eggs, grits, country ham, biscuits, and red-
104 eye gravy?"
105    "When did I ever cook you eggs, grits, country ham, biscuits, and red-eye gravy?"
106    "Never."
107    "Do you look like you need eggs, grits, country ham, biscuits, and red-eye gravy?"
108    "No?" she continued. "Looks to me like you need oatmeal, yogurt, and granola."
109    At the same time, Anna announced my absolution with a smile.
110    Anna's smile was epic. It began on the edge of her red cheek and ended in my heart. Nothing pleasured me
111 more than an Anna smile. Meanwhile, my plaid-flannel-shirt-covered belly had conveniently captured about two
112 grams of porridge that had escaped from my roguish spoon. I deftly scooped the absconder before it despoiled
113 Anna's imported Persian carpet.
114    Anna was observing all with amused annoyance.
115    "Indeed."
116    Yes, Anna could do two things at once. Even three or four. She dazzled everyone at the Harvard Graduate
117 School of Education while I was slumming at the Harvard Divinity School.
118    "It is hard to be 59," I repeated. "Is it harder being 61?"
119    I loved teasing my slightly older Anna about marrying a "younger man."
120    "Cougar," I smiled.
121    "You have acted like an 80-year-old since I first met you," Anna came back. "You were the only Harvard
122 man I know who could not wait to attend the 'oldies but goodies' Boston Pop concert."
123    "It was memorable—especially 'Moon River.' Remember?"
124    "How can I forget?"
125    "God, that woman is beautiful," I thought.
126    Scottish Raasy Anna had a ruddy complexion and piercing brown eyes, with a feisty disposition to match
127 both. Her tight curly silver hair, somewhat tamed by childbirth, accentuated her earnestness and sincerity. Anna had
128 a sense of humor, but it was uncorrupted by frivolous exaggeration. There was no connotation in her denotation.
129    Idealism was realism to this woman. I doubt that she had ever told a lie. Surely our galaxy would *catapult*
130 out of the universe if she did! The problem was that the woman was nearly perfect and expected an approximation
131 thereof from her spouse. Still, Anna, like a vintage red wine, grew mellower with each new vicissitude of life.
132    Anna accompanied me through my 59th year, a time when I found myself in Alighieri Dante's darksome
133 wood. The darkness of Dante's forest was intimidating: growing old is no fun, but it can be tolerable if one has a
134 friend growing old with oneself. I was glad to have had the companionship for these 34 years.
135    Anna was my Beatrice, Dante's ideal woman, and like Beatrice, Anna no doubt would guide me to
136 Paradiso.
137    "Sweetie, you are my Beatrice!"
138    "Who?" She exclaimed.
139    "What exactly do you want for your birthday?" She asked without waiting for an answer.
140    "You know." I smiled.
141    Anna scooped the remainder of her granola into her mouth.
142    An angry blue jay drove away all his cousins. The wasteful interloper scattered more striped sunflower to
143 the ground than he ate.
144    Anna was obviously restless. She still worked for a living.
145    "Honey, this is interesting, but I have work to do. Can we talk later?"
146    "Absolutely."
147    "Happy birthday again!" Anna said as she kissed me with centennial enthusiasm.
148    As Anna wandered upstairs, I wandered back in time.
                    (James P. Stobaugh, *Growing Up White* [New York: Harvard Square Editions, 2014], 1–10)

## Close Reading

1. The author is developing the theme of mutability by using these details.
   I.   Lines 1–7
   II.  Lines 9–22
   III. Lines 32–39

        A. I                  C. III               E. All of the Above
        B. II                 D. II and III

2. Based on the author's description of Anna, the following conclusions seems likely:
   I.   Anna is an ostentatious person.
   II.  Anna is a religious person.
   III. Anna is a choleric person.

        A. I                   D. I and III
        B. II                 E. All of the above
        C. III

3. What is the best way to describe Jake's feelings toward Anna?
   A. Love approaching awe            C. Fear
   B. Cautious affection                D. Indifference

4. "Idealism was realism to this woman. I doubt that she had ever told a lie. Surely our galaxy would *catapult* out of the universe if she did" means
   A. Anna was an obdurate person.       C. Anna was a moral person who would not
   B. Anna was a dreamer.                     exaggerate anything—even the truth.
                                              D. NONE

## Words in Context

1. What is the meaning of *leviathan* in Line 32?
   A. Monster                 C. Plant
   B. Mouse                  D. Dilettante

2. What is the meaning of *effusively* in Line 46?
   A. Remarkably            C. Fulsomely
   B. Guardedly             D. Purposely

3. What is the meaning of *precocious* in Line 49?
   A. Challenged            C. Exuberant
   B. Retarded               D. Advanced

4. What is the meaning of *effervescent* in Line 68?
   A. Pallid                  C. Shaky
   B. Vibrant                D. Bubbly

5. What is the meaning of *gluttonous* in Line 75?
   A. Spartan               C. Insatiable
   B. Expeditious           D. Malevolent

## Source Analysis

From this text the reader can make the following assumptions about the author:
   I.   He uses the setting to develop the theme.
   II.  He uses dialogue to develop characters.
   III. Plot is a secondary consideration.

        A. I                  C. III               E. NONE of Above
        B. II                 D. I and II

# Lesson 2

## Critical Reading and Writing

### Command of Evidence

Read the following passage and answer the accompanying questions:

1    *The Significance of Land Tenure.* —The way in which land may be acquired, held, divided among heirs,
2    and bought and sold exercises a deep influence on the life and culture of a people. The feudal and aristocratic
3    societies of Europe were founded on a system of landlordism which was characterized by two distinct features. In
4    the first place, the land was nearly all held in great estates, each owned by a single proprietor. In the second place,
5    every estate was kept intact under the law of primogeniture, which at the death of a lord transferred all his landed
6    property to his eldest son. This prevented the subdivision of estates and the growth of a large body of small farmers
7    or freeholders owning their own land. It made a form of tenantry or servitude inevitable for the mass of those who
8    labored on the land. It also enabled the landlords to maintain themselves in power as a governing class and kept the
9    tenants and laborers subject to their economic and political control. If land tenure was so significant in Europe, it
10   was equally important in the development of America, where practically all the first immigrants were forced by
11   circumstances to derive their livelihood from the soil.
12   *Experiments in Common Tillage.* —In the New World, with its broad extent of land awaiting the white
13   man's plow, it was impossible to introduce in its entirety and over the whole area the system of lords and tenants
14   that existed across the sea. So it happened that almost every kind of experiment in land tenure, from communism to
15   feudalism, was tried. In the early days of the Jamestown colony, the land, though owned by the London Company,
16   was tilled in common by the settlers. No man had a separate plot of his own. The motto of the community was:
17   "Labor and share alike." All were supposed to work in the fields and receive an equal share of the produce. At
18   Plymouth, the Pilgrims attempted a similar experiment, laying out the fields in common and distributing the joint
19   produce of their labor with rough equality among the workers.
20   In both colonies the communistic experiments were failures. Angry at the lazy men in Jamestown who
21   idled their time away and yet expected regular meals, Captain John Smith issued a manifesto: "Everyone that
22   gathereth not every day as much as I do, the next day shall be set beyond the river and forever banished from the fort
23   and live there or starve." Even this terrible threat did not bring a change in production. Not until each man was given
24   a plot of his own to till, not until each gathered the fruits of his own labor, did the colony prosper. In Plymouth,
25   where the communal experiment lasted for five years, the results were similar to those in Virginia, and the system
26   was given up for one of separate fields in which every person could "set corn for his own particular." Some other
27   New England towns, refusing to profit by the experience of their Plymouth neighbor, also made excursions into
28   common ownership and labor, only to abandon the idea and go in for individual ownership of the land. "By degrees
29   it was seen that even the Lord's people could not carry the complicated communist legislation into perfect and
30   wholesome practice."
31   *Feudal Elements in the Colonies—Quit Rents, Manors, and Plantations.* —At the other end of the scale
32   were the feudal elements of land tenure found in the proprietary colonies, in the seaboard regions of the South, and
33   to some extent in New York. The proprietor was in fact a powerful feudal lord, owning land granted to him by royal
34   charter. He could retain any part of it for his personal use or dispose of it all in large or small lots. While he
35   generally kept for himself an estate of baronial proportions, it was impossible for him to manage directly any
36   considerable part of the land in his dominion. Consequently he either sold it in parcels for lump sums or granted it to
37   individuals on condition that they make to him an annual payment in money, known as "quit rent." In Maryland, the
38   proprietor sometimes collected as high as £9000 (equal to about $500,000 to-day) in a single year from this source.
39   In Pennsylvania, the quit rents brought a handsome annual tribute into the exchequer of the Penn family. In the royal
40   provinces, the king of England claimed all revenues collected in this form from the land, a sum amounting to
41   £19,000 at the time of the Revolution. The quit rent,—"really a feudal payment from freeholders,"—was thus a
42   material source of income for the crown as well as for the proprietors. Wherever it was laid, however, it proved to be
43   a burden, a source of constant irritation; and it became a formidable item in the long list of grievances which led to
44   the American Revolution.
45   Something still more like the feudal system of the Old World appeared in the numerous manors or the huge
46   landed estates granted by the crown, the companies, or the proprietors. In the colony of Maryland alone there were
47   sixty manors of three thousand acres each, owned by wealthy men and tilled by tenants holding small plots under

48 certain restrictions of tenure. In New York also there were many manors of wide extent, most of which originated in
49 the days of the Dutch West India Company, when extensive concessions were made to patroons to induce them to
50 bring over settlers. The Van Rensselaer, the Van Cortlandt, and the Livingston manors were so large and populous
51 that each was entitled to send a representative to the provincial legislature. The tenants on the New York manors
52 were in somewhat the same position as serfs on old European estates. They were bound to pay the owner a rent in
53 money and kind; they ground their grain at his mill; and they were subject to his judicial power because he held
54 court and meted out justice, in some instances extending to capital punishment.

55 The manors of New York or Maryland were, however, of slight consequence as compared with the vast
56 plantations of the Southern seaboard—huge estates, far wider in expanse than many a European barony and tilled by
57 slaves more servile than any feudal tenants. It must not be forgotten that this system of land tenure became the
58 dominant feature of a large section and gave a decided bent to the economic and political life of America.

59 *The Small Freehold.* —In the upland regions of the South, however, and throughout most of the North, the
60 drift was against all forms of servitude and tenantry and in the direction of the freehold; that is, the small farm
61 owned outright and tilled by the possessor and his family. This was favored by natural circumstances and the spirit
62 of the immigrants. For one thing, the abundance of land and the scarcity of labor made it impossible for the
63 companies, the proprietors, or the crown to develop over the whole continent a network of vast estates. In many
64 sections, particularly in New England, the climate, the stony soil, the hills, and the narrow valleys conspired to keep
65 the farms within a moderate compass. For another thing, the English, Scotch-Irish, and German peasants, even if
66 they had been tenants in the Old World, did not propose to accept permanent dependency of any kind in the New. If
67 they could not get freeholds, they would not settle at all; thus they forced proprietors and companies to bid for their
68 enterprise by selling land in small lots. So it happened that the freehold of modest proportions became the cherished
69 unit of American farmers. The people who tilled the farms were drawn from every quarter of western Europe; but
70 the freehold system gave a uniform cast to their economic and social life in America.

71 *Social Effects of Land Tenure.* —Land tenure and the process of western settlement thus developed two
72 distinct types of people engaged in the same pursuit—agriculture. They had a common tie in that they both
73 cultivated the soil and possessed the local interest and independence which arise from that occupation. Their
74 methods and their culture, however, differed widely.

75 The Southern planter, on his broad acres tilled by slaves, resembled the English landlord on his estates
76 more than he did the colonial farmer who labored with his own hands in the fields and forests. He sold his rice and
77 tobacco in large amounts directly to English factors, who took his entire crop in exchange for goods and cash. His
78 fine clothes, silverware, china, and cutlery he bought in English markets. Loving the ripe old culture of the mother
79 country, he often sent his sons to Oxford or Cambridge for their education. In short, he depended very largely for his
80 prosperity and his enjoyment of life upon close relations with the Old World. He did not even need market towns in
81 which to buy native goods, for they were made on his own plantation by his own artisans who were usually gifted
82 slaves.

83 The economic condition of the small farmer was totally different. His crops were not big enough to warrant
84 direct connection with English factors or the personal maintenance of a corps of artisans. He needed local markets,
85 and they sprang up to meet the need. Smiths, hatters, weavers, wagon-makers, and potters at neighboring towns
86 supplied him with the rough products of their native skill. The finer goods, bought by the rich planter in England, the
87 small farmer ordinarily could not buy. His wants were restricted to staples like tea and sugar, and between him and
88 the European market stood the merchant. His community was therefore more self-sufficient than the seaboard line of
89 great plantations. It was more isolated, more provincial, more independent, more American. The planter faced the
90 Old East. The farmer faced the New West.

91 *The Westward Movement.* —Yeoman and planter nevertheless were alike in one respect. Their land hunger
92 was never appeased. Each had the eye of an expert for new and fertile soil; and so, north and south, as soon as a
93 foothold was secured on the Atlantic coast, the current of migration set in westward, creeping through forests, across
94 rivers, and over mountains. Many of the later immigrants, in their search for cheap lands, were compelled to go to
95 the border; but in a large part the path breakers to the West were native Americans of the second and third
96 generations. Explorers, fired by curiosity and the lure of the mysterious unknown, and hunters, fur traders, and
97 squatters, following their own sweet wills, blazed the trail, opening paths and sending back stories of the new
98 regions they traversed. Then came the regular settlers with lawful titles to the lands they had purchased, sometimes
99 singly and sometimes in companies.

100 In Massachusetts, the westward movement is recorded in the founding of Springfield in 1636 and Great
101 Barrington in 1725. By the opening of the eighteenth century the pioneers of Connecticut had pushed north and west
102 until their outpost towns adjoined the Hudson Valley settlements. In New York, the inland movement was directed
103 by the Hudson River to Albany, and from that old Dutch center it radiated in every direction, particularly westward
104 through the Mohawk Valley. New Jersey was early filled to its borders, the beginnings of the present city of New

105  Brunswick being made in 1681 and those of Trenton in 1685. In Pennsylvania, as in New York, the waterways
106  determined the main lines of advance. Pioneers, pushing up through the valley of the Schuylkill, spread over the
107  fertile lands of Berks and Lancaster counties, laying out Reading in 1748. Another current of migration was directed
108  by the Susquehanna, and, in 1726, the first farmhouse was built on the bank where Harrisburg was later founded.
109  Along the southern tier of counties a thin line of settlements stretched westward to Pittsburgh, reaching the upper
110  waters of the Ohio while the colony was still under the Penn family.
111      In the South the westward march was equally swift. The seaboard was quickly occupied by large planters
112  and their slaves engaged in the cultivation of tobacco and rice. The Piedmont Plateau, lying back from the coast all
113  the way from Maryland to Georgia, was fed by two streams of migration, one westward from the sea and the other
114  southward from the other colonies—Germans from Pennsylvania and Scotch-Irish furnishing the main supply. "By
115  1770, tide-water Virginia was full to overflowing and the 'back country' of the Blue Ridge and the Shenandoah was
116  fully occupied. Even the mountain valleys . . . were claimed by sturdy pioneers. Before the Declaration of
117  Independence, the oncoming tide of home-seekers had reached the crest of the Alleghenies."

(Charles and Mary Beard, *History of the United States* [New York: MacMillan Co., 1921], chap. 2,
http://www.gutenberg.org/files/16960/16960-h/16960-h.htm#Page_28)

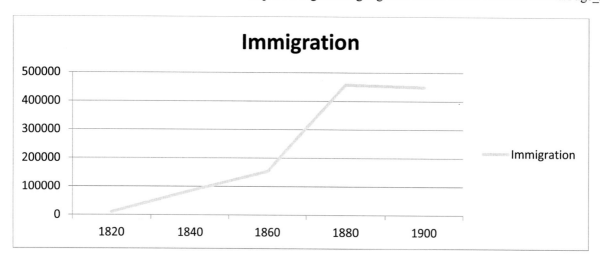

1. The historians probably think the following impulses of history are most important:
   A. Political history
   B. Religious history
   C. Social history
   D. Economic history

2. Which of the following arguments are supported by the passage?
   I.    The way in which land may be acquired, held, divided among heirs, and bought and sold exercises a deep
         influence on the life and culture of the United States.
   II.   Land tenure and the process of western settlement thus developed two distinct types of people engaged in
         the same pursuit—agriculture.
   III.  The waterways determined the main lines of immigration.
   IV.   Native American accommodation greatly impacted western expansion.

   A. I
   B. II and IV
   C. II and III
   D. I, II, and III
   E. All

3. Which of the following are supported by the passage?
   I.    Slavery was profitable.
   II.   Immigration was a powerful force in American history.
   III.  Farming created products and increased markets.

   A. I
   B. II
   C. III
   D. I and III
   E. All

## Data Analysis

1. The above chart implies:
   I.   The years 1860–1880 showed the most precipitous increase in immigration.
   II.  The Irish potato famine drove immigration in 1880–1900.
   III. Asian immigration increased after 1900.

   A. I                     D. II and III
   B. II                    E. All
   C. III

2. Which statements are true?
   I.   The American Civil War did not diminish immigration.
   II.  The completion of the Transcontinental Railroad may have contributed to immigration.
   III. The Great Flu Epidemic slowed immigration after 1900.

   A. I                     D. I and II
   B. II                    E. All
   C. III

3. These two historians make a point to argue that the early American colonies were not communistic: "Some other New England towns, refusing to profit by the experience of their Plymouth neighbor, also made excursions into common ownership and labor, only to abandon the idea and go in for individual ownership of the land. 'By degrees it was seen that even the Lord's people could not carry the complicated communist legislation into perfect and wholesome practice.'" What is the most likely reason this is emphasized?
   A.  The authors are Communists.
   B.  The authors are Anarchists.
   C.  During the 1920s, when this history text was written, Communism was thriving in the Soviet Union and was perceived as a threat.
   D.  This history was written during the McCarthy Era and Communism really was a threat to the American experiment.

4. What sort of evidence would refute this argument? "Their land hunger was never appeased. Each had the eye of an expert for new and fertile soil; and so, north and south, as soon as a foothold was secured on the Atlantic coast, the current of migration set in westward, creeping through forests, across rivers, and over mountains."
   A.  An historian discovers that Georgia expansion began in Savannah and spread toward the Appalachians.
   B.  An historian discovers that in spite of a navigable river and fertile land to the west, Native American opposition stopped expansion into the interior.
   C.  While available land was abundantly available in eastern Kentucky, no one settled there. While the outside of Charleston, VA (now West Virginia) was mostly ignored, pioneers streamed into the bluegrass country surrounding Lexington.
   D.  Eastern Maine continued to grow in population and industry while the more fertile and western Maine remained sparsely populated.

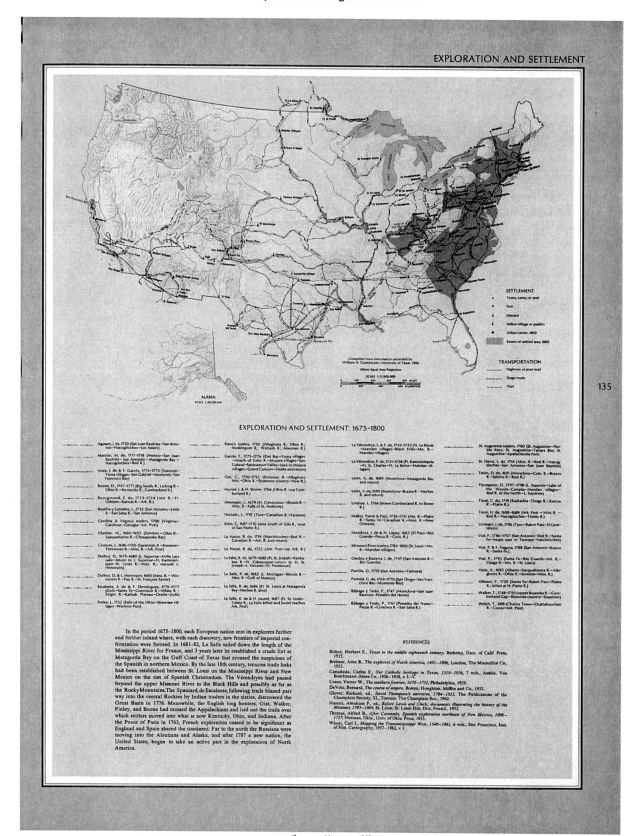

EXPLORATION AND SETTLEMENT: 1675–1800

135

In the period 1675–1800, each European nation sent its explorers further and further inland where, with each discovery, new frontiers of imperial confrontation were formed. In 1681–82, La Salle sailed down the length of the Mississippi River for France, and 3 years later he established a crude fort at Matagorda Bay on the Gulf Coast of Texas that aroused the suspicions of the Spanish in northern Mexico. By the late 18th century, tenuous trade links had been established between St. Louis on the Mississippi River and New Mexico on the rim of Spanish Christendom. The Vérendryes had passed beyond the upper Missouri River to the Black Hills and possibly as far as the Rocky Mountains. The Spaniard, de Escalante, following trails blazed part way into the central Rockies by Indian traders in the sixties, discovered the Great Basin in 1776. Meanwhile, the English long hunters, Gist, Walker, Finley, and Boone had crossed the Appalachians and laid out the trails over which settlers moved into what is now Kentucky, Ohio, and Indiana. After the Peace of Paris in 1763, French exploration ceased to be significant as England and Spain shared the continent. Far to the north the Russians were moving into the Aleutians and Alaska, and after 1787 a new nation, the United States, began to take an active part in the exploration of North America.

REFERENCES

Bolton, Herbert E., *Texas in the middle eighteenth century*, Berkeley, Univ. of Calif. Press, 1915.
Brebner, John B., *The explorers of North America, 1492–1806*, London, The Macmillan Co., 1933.
Castañeda, Carlos E., *Our Catholic heritage in Texas, 1519–1936*, 7 vols., Austin, Von Boeckmann-Jones Co., 1936–1958, v. I–V.
Crane, Verner W., *The southern frontier, 1670–1732*, Philadelphia, 1929.
DeVoto, Bernard, *The course of empire*, Boston, Houghton, Mifflin and Co., 1952.
Glover, Richard, ed., *David Thompson's narrative, 1784–1812*, The Publications of the Champlain Society, XL, Toronto, The Champlain Soc., 1962.
Nasatir, Abraham P., ed., *Before Lewis and Clark; documents illustrating the history of the Missouri, 1785–1804*, St. Louis, St. Louis Hist. Doc. Found., 1952.
Thomas, Alfred B., *After Coronado; Spanish exploration northeast of New Mexico, 1696–1727*, Norman, Okla., Univ. of Okla. Press, 1935.
Wheat, Carl I., *Mapping the Transmississippi West, 1540–1861*, 6 vols., San Francisco, Inst. of Hist. Cartography, 1957–1963, v. I.

5. On the above map, what would be a logical reason why areas of Western Virginia remained unsettled.
    I.   Intransigent, hostile Native Americans were present.
   II.   The land was not particularly fertile.
  III.   The land was too mountainous

        A. I                    D. I and II
        B. II                  E. All
        C. III

6. Speculate upon why Florida was not settled until well after 1800.
    I.   Malaria
   II.   The hostile Spanish claimed to own it until the middle of the 1800s.
  III.   Santa Anna of Mexico claimed ownership.
  IV.   The Seminole Native Americans would not allow anyone to settle in this territory.

        A. I and II            C. I and IV
        B. II and III         D. II and IV

# Lesson 3

## SAT Essay

*Prompt:* As you read the passage below, consider how the author uses

    A. Evidence, such as facts or examples, to support claims.

    B. Reasoning to develop ideas and to connect claims and evidence.

    C. Stylistic or persuasive elements, such as word choice or appeals to emotion, to add power to the ideas expressed.

In Lines 1–4, Emerson makes the following assertion about education in his time: "I believe that our own experience instructs us that the secret of Education lies in respecting the pupil. It is not for you to choose what he shall know, what he shall do. It is chosen and foreordained, and he only holds the key to his own secret. By your tampering and thwarting and too much governing, he may be hindered from his end and kept out of his own." What does he mean? Do you think that public education today still resembles Emerson's description? Explain.

| | |
|---|---|
| 1 |     I believe that our own experience instructs us that the secret of Education lies in respecting the pupil. It is |
| 2 | not for you to choose what he shall know, what he shall do. It is chosen and foreordained, and he only holds the key |
| 3 | to his own secret. By your tampering and thwarting and too much governing, he may be hindered from his end and |
| 4 | kept out of his own. Respect the child. Wait and see the new product of Nature. Nature loves analogies, but not |
| 5 | repetitions. Respect the child. Be not too much his parent. Trespass not on his solitude. |
| 6 |     But I hear the outcry which replies to this suggestion—Would you verily throw up the reins of public and |
| 7 | private discipline; would you leave the young child to the mad career of his own passions and whimsies, and call |
| 8 | this anarchy a respect for the child's nature? I answer—Respect the child, respect him to the end, but also respect |
| 9 | yourself. Be the companion of his thought, the friend of his friendship, the lover of his virtue—but no kinsman of his |
| 10 | sin. Let him find you so true to yourself that you are the irreconcilable hater of his vice and the imperturbable |
| 11 | slighter of his trifling. |
| 12 |     The two points in a boy's training are, to keep his *naturel* and train off all but that—to keep his *naturel*, but |
| 13 | stop off his uproar, fooling, and horseplay—keep his nature and arm it with knowledge in the very direction to |
| 14 | which it points. Here are the two capital facts, Genius and Drill. This first is the inspiration in the well-born healthy |
| 15 | child, the new perception he has of nature. Somewhat he sees in forms or hears in music or apprehends in |
| 16 | mathematics, or believes practicable in mechanics or possible in political society, which no one else sees or hears or |
| 17 | believes. This is the perpetual romance of new life, the invasion of God into the old dead world, when he sends into |
| 18 | quiet houses a young soul with a thought which is not met, looking for something which is not there, but which |
| 19 | ought to be there: the thought is dim but it is sure, and he casts about restless for means and masters to verify it; he |
| 20 | makes wild attempts to explain himself and invoke the aid and consent of the by-standers. Baffled for want of |
| 21 | language and methods to convey his meaning, not yet clear to himself, he conceives that though not in this house or |
| 22 | town, yet in some other house or town is the wise master who can put him in possession of the rules and instruments |
| 23 | to execute his will. Happy this child with a bias, with a thought which entrances him, leads him, now into deserts |
| 24 | now into cities, the fool of an idea. Let him follow it in good and in evil report, in good or bad company; it will |
| 25 | justify itself; it will lead him at last into the illustrious society of the lovers of truth. |
| 26 |     In London, in a private company, I became acquainted with a gentleman, Sir Charles Fellowes, who, being |
| 27 | at Xanthos, in the Aegean Sea, had seen a Turk point with his staff to some carved work on the corner of a stone |
| 28 | almost buried in the soil. Fellowes scraped away the dirt, was struck with the beauty of the sculptured ornaments, |
| 29 | and, looking about him, observed: more blocks and fragments like this. He returned to the spot, procured laborers, |
| 30 | and uncovered many blocks. He went back to England, bought a Greek grammar, and learned the language; he read |
| 31 | history and studied ancient art to explain his stones; he interested Gibson the sculptor; he invoked the assistance of |
| 32 | the English Government; he called in the succor of Sir Humphry Davy to analyze the pigments; of experts in coins, |
| 33 | of scholars and connoisseurs; and at last: in his third visit brought home to England such statues and marble reliefs |
| 34 | and such careful plans that he was able to reconstruct, in the British Museum where it now stands, the perfect model |
| 35 | of the Ionic trophy-monument, fifty years older than the Parthenon of Athens, and which had been destroyed by |

36 earthquakes, then by iconoclast Christians, then by savage Turks. But mark that in the task he had achieved an
37 excellent education, and become associated with distinguished scholars whom he had interested in his pursuit; in
38 short, had formed a college for himself; the enthusiast had found the master, the masters, whom he sought. Always
39 genius seeks genius, desires nothing so much as to be a pupil and to find those who can lend it aid to perfect itself.

40      Nor are the two elements, enthusiasm and drill, incompatible. Accuracy is essential to beauty. The very
41 definition of the intellect is Aristotle's: "that by which we know terms or boundaries." Give a boy accurate
42 perceptions. Teach him the difference between the similar and the same. Make him call things by their right names.
43 Pardon in him no blunder. Then he will give you solid satisfaction as long as he lives. It is better to teach the child
44 arithmetic and Latin grammar than rhetoric or moral philosophy, because they require exactitude of performance; it
45 is made certain that the lesson is mastered, and that power of performance is worth more than the knowledge. He
46 can learn anything which is important to him now that the power to learn is secured: as mechanics say, when one has
47 learned the use of tools, it is easy to work at a new craft.

48      Letter by letter, syllable by syllable, the child learns to read, and in good time can convey to all the
49 domestic circle the sense of Shakespeare. By many steps each just as short, the stammering boy and the hesitating
50 collegian, in the school debates, in college clubs, in mock court, comes at last to full, secure, triumphant unfolding
51 of his thought in the popular assembly, with a fullness of power that makes all the steps forgotten.

52      But this function of opening and feeding the human mind is not to be fulfilled by any mechanical or
53 military method; is not to be trusted to any skill less large than Nature itself. You must not neglect the form, but you
54 must secure the essentials. It is curious how perverse and intermeddling we are, and what vast pains and cost we
55 incur to do wrong. Whilst we all know in our own experience and apply natural methods in our own business—in
56 education our common sense fails us, and we are continually trying costly machinery against nature, in patent
57 schools and academies and in great colleges and universities.

58      The natural method forever confutes our experiments, and we must still come back to it. The whole theory
59 of the school is on the nurse's or mother's knee. The child is as hot to learn as the mother is to impart. There is
60 mutual delight. The joy of our childhood in hearing beautiful stories from some skillful aunt who loves to tell them,
61 must be repeated in youth. The boy wishes to learn to skate; to coast, to catch a fish in the brook, to hit a mark with a
62 snowball or a stone; and a boy a little older is just as well pleased to teach him these sciences. Not less delightful is
63 the mutual pleasure of teaching and learning the secret of algebra, or of chemistry, or of good reading and good
64 recitation of poetry or of prose, or of chosen facts in history or in biography.

65      Nature provided for the communication of thought by planting with it in the receiving mind a fury to impart
66 it. 'Tis so in every art, in every science. One burns to tell the new fact, the other burns to hear it. See how far a
67 young doctor will ride or walk to witness a new surgical operation. I have seen a carriage-maker's shop emptied of
68 all its workmen into the street, to scrutinize a new pattern from New York. So in literature, the young man who has
69 taste for poetry, for fine images, for noble thoughts, is insatiable for this nourishment, and forgets all the world for
70 the more learned friend—who finds equal joy in dealing out his treasures.

(Ralph Waldo Emerson, "Education," in *Complete Writings*,
http://transcendentalism-legacy.tamu.edu/authors/emerson/essays/education.html)

## Student Response

1 The well-known author Ralph Waldo Emerson influenced American writers and thinkers. In a short essay titled
2 "Education," Emerson expressed his view of an ideal education. Emerson's conclusion was called "the natural way"
3 of education.

4      Toward the end of this essay, Emerson said, "Our modes of Education aim to expedite, to save labor; to do
5 for masses what cannot be done for masses, what must be done reverently, one by one: say rather, the whole world
6 is needed for the tuition of each pupil." Emerson noted how education was a system of efficiency; a "cookie-cutter"
7 structure of learning; a method of mass-produce knowledge. According to Emerson, this image of education was not
8 working and not efficient, even though the claimed end aim of education was efficiency. Quite oppositely, Emerson
9 described education as a tender place of growth; an ignition for the love of learning; a one-on-one mentoring time.

10      The last sentence of his quote is probably the most meaningful. Upon first glance it appears that Emerson
11 proposed that the whole world pay the fees for a child's schooling. Most think of tuition as "a sum of money
12 charged for teaching or instruction by a school, college, or university" (*Oxford American Dictionary*). Emerson had
13 a different meaning in mind. Rather, he meant tuition as "[the] teaching or instruction, esp. of individual pupils or
14 small groups." (*Oxford American Dictionary*). Emerson was far from advocating that the world pay for a child's
15 tuition. Rather, this phrase went back to Emerson's conclusion of the natural way of education. He meant that the
16 world was the place of true education, of true learning. In other words, the world was an instructor to each individual

17 student. The natural desire to learn, aroused in the hearts of young pupils, should be a guiding force in the learning
18 process.

19      Emerson went on to explain his "natural way" of education. He said, "The natural method forever confutes
20 our experiments, and we must still come back to it. The whole theory of the school is on the nurse's or mother's
21 knee. The child is as hot to learn as the mother is to impart. There is a mutual delight. . . .The boy wishes to learn."
22 Education, therefore, should be synonymous with an enthusiastic desire to learn. The natural yearning of a child (to
23 know) is fulfilled by parents as they reveal their knowledge of the world. As soon as the child reaches the age of
24 formal schooling, they enter a "departmental, routinary, [and] military" system, snuffing out the joy and enthusiasm
25 of learning and discovery.

26      As Emerson described, education should be the process of mentorship: "One burns to tell the new fact, the
27 other burns to hear it." Emerson reminded the reader that great minds like Plato and Socrates were educated under
28 this model. "Happy the natural college thus self-instituted around every natural teacher; the young men of Athens
29 around Socrates; of Alexander around Plotinus." Basically, Emerson argued that the moment this model of
30 mentorship was organized for the masses, difficulties arose. Instead of one-on-one instruction—a teacher pouring
31 solely into one student—"instruction seems to require skillful tutors, of accurate and systematic mind, rather than
32 ardent and inventive masters." Wisdom should be imparted, not drilled like the education system of today.

33      What about drills? What about the systematic learning of mathematics, science, or grammar? Emerson's
34 response to the hierarchy of learning that schools have put in place was clear: "Nor are the two elements, enthusiasm
35 and drill, incompatible. Accuracy is essential to beauty. . . . It is better to teach the child arithmetic and Latin
36 grammar than rhetoric or moral philosophy, because they require exactitude of performance. . . . When one has
37 learned the use of drills, it is easy to work at a new craft." The only purpose of these training drills and exercises is
38 to set boundaries and terms for which true learning can thrive. A child who masters the drills will master the art of
39 learning.

40      Emerson did not entirely discount the education system he saw. Rather, he recognized that there was an
41 imbalance between the military drilling system of education and the natural instinct of mentors who imparted
42 wisdom to the young. Education should be a desire to learn where mentors guide a child through the sea of
43 knowledge awaiting them in the world. Forcing children to learn in such a dogmatic system would eradicate any
44 love of learning they began with. Instead, the child needs respect, patience, and investment by a wiser mentor. In
45 summary Emerson said, "Leave this military hurry and adopt the pace of Nature. Her secret is patience."

46      A sixth-grader is seated in science class among thirty other students. She raises her hand: she has
47 something to say. The teacher anxiously glances at the clock. There are only two minutes until school will be
48 dismissed for the day. The curious child starts to share something exciting that she has discovered. Only two
49 minutes into the story, the bell rings and the class ends. Parents are waiting outside to pick up their children, and the
50 teacher cannot detain the students past school hours. The child does not finish her story. Everyone rushes out.

51      Ralph Waldo Emerson would refer to this hypothetical situation as unnatural; however, such situations
52 happen every day in school. Emerson urges us to "leave this military hurry and adopt the pace of Nature." However,
53 this action is impossible in a situation that has "to do for masses what cannot be done for masses." Trying to educate
54 the "masses" requires teachers to adopt a "mechanical or military method." Because of this, the geniuses are held
55 back, and the "dull sailors" are helplessly pulled along. The child is not "respected," and neither are their needs and
56 talents. Education is confined by school hours, and all children are forcefully molded into identical soldiers,
57 marching to the beat of the clock. Emerson's solution to this devastating problem is to "cherish mother-wit." Of
58 course, only a mother herself can fully cherish the "mother-wit" and consequently fully respect the child. This is
59 why homeschooling is so successful and avoids the inevitable militant situation present in schools. Mothers love
60 their children's individual strengths and weaknesses. They have the time to cherish their child's individuality. They
61 are able to respect their curiosity. They have freedom with their children. They do not have to put a time limit on
62 education. They do not need or try "to do for masses what cannot be done for masses."

63      My personal experience helps to make these observations a reality. As a homeschooled student, I and my
64 individual strengths have been "respected." I have not been "trespassed on my solitude." I have been encouraged to
65 share my experiences. My wise sayings were greeted. My understanding of a "good book" was applauded. My
66 education was not restrained to eight in the morning to three in the afternoon—it was a continual experience. In
67 essence, I have had a "natural" education. I remember constantly working out a math problem or a science question
68 with my mom/teacher and finding myself thirty minutes later in a deep conversation about ethics, politics, literature,
69 or even life in general. I remember going to pick blueberries on a school day and the whole while discussing great
70 books with my grandma. I remember building a catapult with my granddad and learning about force, levers, and
71 even the history of the catapult itself. I remember going on a walk with my dad and learning the names of at least
72 twenty different types of trees. Although I am referring to my education as a past experience, my "natural
73 education" is still occurring. Only last summer I had the opportunity to travel to Italy. During this trip, I learned

74 about Italy's rich history through osmosis. I was fully immersed in its culture. I learned more in this summer than I
75 ever would have learned in a classroom. This trip was so educational because it was natural. I did not have to
76 memorize dry facts out of a textbook. The same can be said for my entire educational experience.
77      Children involved in the masses rarely have this opportunity. They are not able to naturally learn because a
78 natural education involves time and individuality. Teachers are "unable to wait for him, as Nature and Providence
79 do." Education becomes "departmental, routinary, [and] military." Homeschooling is the antithesis of school.
80 Homeschooling is so successful in ensuring a rich and natural educational environment because children do not have
81 to be unnaturally placed with their own age group, but can become closely associated with various age groups and
82 learn from the more experienced. School is based on the masses; homeschooling is based on the individual. School
83 functions on a time limit; homeschooling is a continual process. School is artificial; homeschooling is natural.
84 (Callie)

1. What is the thesis of Emerson's "Education"?
    I.   Lines 1–2
    II.  Lines 12–14
    III. Lines 52–55
    IV. Lines 65–66

      A. I                                   D. II and III
      B. II                                  E. IV
      C. I, II, and III                 F. NONE

2. Which of the above choices connects claims and evidence.
    A. I                   C. I, II, and III            E. IV
    B. II                 D. II and III              F. All of the Above

3. Which of the above choices involves a personal example:
    A. I                   C. I, II, and III            E. IV
    B. II                 D. II and III              F. NONE

4. The purpose of the above personal story is
    A. To refute Emerson's position.
    B. To offer an alternative, but persuasive example.
    C. To support Emerson's position.
    D. To advocate standardized testing.

5. In Emerson's essay on education, the following are stylistic or persuasive elements, such as word choice or appeals to emotion, that add power to the ideas expressed:
    A. Line 1                      C. Line 65
    B. Lines 6–7                D. NONE

6. What is the purpose of the story of Sir Charles Fellowes?
    A. To illustrate that education is based upon interest, ingenuity, and industriousness.
    B. To refute the claim that education is superfluous.
    C. To advocate an Oxford University education.
    D. To denigrate homeschooling.

7. The Student Response
    A. Mostly agrees with Emerson.              C. Is neutral toward Emerson's arguments.
    B. Vociferously disagrees with Emerson.      D. NONE

8. A rhetorical device used in the Student Response Line 32 is
    A. Simile.                     C. Paradox.
    B. Antithesis.              D. Rhetorical Question.

9. The author is probably
   A. A born-again Christian.
   B. A homeschooler.
   C. Someone who watches a lot of television.
   D. NONE

11. What is true about the Student Response?
    A. The author likes Emerson's poetry more than his essays.
    B. The author begins with a critique of Emerson's essay but ends with a defense of homeschooling.
    C. The author begins with acriticism of Emerson but ends with a diatribe against public education.
    D. The author argues that private Christian education is superior to all other pedagoby.

12. What score would this essay receive? __ Why? _____

# Lesson 4
## Reading: Document-Based Analysis

### George Washington's Farewell Address (1796)

1   The period for a new election of a citizen to administer the executive government of the United States being not far
2   distant, and the time actually arrived when your thoughts must be employed in designating the person who is to be
3   clothed with that important trust, it appears to me proper, especially as it may conduce to a more distinct expression
4   of the public voice, that I should now apprise you of the resolution I have formed, to decline being considered
5   among the number of those out of whom a choice is to be made.
6       I beg you, at the same time, to do me the justice to be assured that this resolution has not been taken
7   without a strict regard to all the considerations appertaining to the relation which binds a dutiful citizen to his
8   country; and that in withdrawing the tender of service, which silence in my situation might imply, I am influenced
9   by no diminution of zeal for your future interest, no deficiency of grateful respect for your past kindness, but am
10  supported by a full conviction that the step is compatible with both.
11      The acceptance of, and continuance hitherto in, the office to which your suffrages have twice called me
12  have been a uniform sacrifice of inclination to the opinion of duty and to a deference for what appeared to be your
13  desire. I constantly hoped that it would have been much earlier in my power, consistently with motives which I was
14  not at liberty to disregard, to return to that retirement from which I had been reluctantly drawn. The strength of my
15  inclination to do this, previous to the last election, had even led to the preparation of an address to declare it to you;
16  but mature reflection on the then perplexed and critical posture of our affairs with foreign nations, and the
17  unanimous advice of persons entitled to my confidence, impelled me to abandon the idea.
18      I rejoice that the state of your concerns, external as well as internal, no longer renders the pursuit of
19  inclination incompatible with the sentiment of duty or propriety, and am persuaded, whatever partiality may be
20  retained for my services, that, in the present circumstances of our country, you will not disapprove my determination
21  to retire.
22      The impressions with which I first undertook the arduous trust were explained on the proper occasion. In
23  the discharge of this trust, I will only say that I have, with good intentions, contributed towards the organization and
24  administration of the government the best exertions of which a very fallible judgment was capable. Not unconscious
25  in the outset of the inferiority of my qualifications, experience in my own eyes, perhaps still more in the eyes of
26  others, has strengthened the motives to diffidence of myself; and every day the increasing weight of years
27  admonishes me more and more that the shade of retirement is as necessary to me as it will be welcome. Satisfied
28  that if any circumstances have given peculiar value to my services, they were temporary, I have the consolation to
29  believe that, while choice and prudence invite me to quit the political scene, patriotism does not forbid it.
30      In looking forward to the moment which is intended to terminate the career of my public life, my feelings
31  do not permit me to suspend the deep acknowledgment of that debt of gratitude which I owe to my beloved country
32  for the many honors it has conferred upon me; still more for the steadfast confidence with which it has supported
33  me; and for the opportunities I have thence enjoyed of manifesting my inviolable attachment, by services faithful
34  and persevering, though in usefulness unequal to my zeal. If benefits have resulted to our country from these
35  services, let it always be remembered to your praise, and as an instructive example in our annals, that under
36  circumstances in which the passions, agitated in every direction, were liable to mislead, amidst appearances
37  sometimes dubious, vicissitudes of fortune often discouraging, in situations in which not unfrequently want of
38  success has countenanced the spirit of criticism, the constancy of your support was the essential prop of the efforts,
39  and a guarantee of the plans by which they were effected. Profoundly penetrated with this idea, I shall carry it with
40  me to my grave, as a strong incitement to unceasing vows that heaven may continue to you the choicest tokens of its
41  beneficence; that your union and brotherly affection may be perpetual; that the free Constitution, which is the work
42  of your hands, may be sacredly maintained; that its administration in every department may be stamped with
43  wisdom and virtue; that, in fine, the happiness of the people of these States, under the auspices of liberty, may be
44  made complete by so careful a preservation and so prudent a use of this blessing as will acquire to them the glory of
45  recommending it to the applause, the affection, and adoption of every nation which is yet a stranger to it.
46      Here, perhaps, I ought to stop. But a solicitude for your welfare, which cannot end but with my life, and the
47  apprehension of danger, natural to that solicitude, urge me, on an occasion like the present, to offer to your solemn
48  contemplation, and to recommend to your frequent review, some sentiments which are the result of much reflection,

49  of no inconsiderable observation, and which appear to me all-important to the permanency of your felicity as a
50  people. These will be offered to you with the more freedom, as you can only see in them the disinterested warnings
51  of a parting friend, who can possibly have no personal motive to bias his counsel. Nor can I forget, as an
52  encouragement to it, your indulgent reception of my sentiments on a former and not dissimilar occasion.

53  Interwoven as is the love of liberty with every ligament of your hearts, no recommendation of mine is
54  necessary to fortify or confirm the attachment.

55  The unity of government which constitutes you one people is also now dear to you. It is justly so, for it is a
56  main pillar in the edifice of your real independence, the support of your tranquility at home, your peace abroad; of
57  your safety; of your prosperity; of that very liberty which you so highly prize. But as it is easy to foresee that, from
58  different causes and from different quarters, much pains will be taken, many artifices employed to weaken in your
59  minds the conviction of this truth; as this is the point in your political fortress against which the batteries of internal
60  and external enemies will be most constantly and actively (though often covertly and insidiously) directed, it is of
61  infinite moment that you should properly estimate the immense value of your national union to your collective and
62  individual happiness; that you should cherish a cordial, habitual, and immovable attachment to it; accustoming
63  yourselves to think and speak of it as of the palladium of your political safety and prosperity; watching for its
64  preservation with jealous anxiety; discountenancing whatever may suggest even a suspicion that it can in any event
65  be abandoned; and indignantly frowning upon the first dawning of every attempt to alienate any portion of our
66  country from the rest, or to enfeeble the sacred ties which now link together the various parts.

67  For this you have every inducement of sympathy and interest. Citizens, by birth or choice, of a common
68  country, that country has a right to concentrate your affections. The name of American, which belongs to you in
69  your national capacity, must always exalt the just pride of patriotism more than any appellation derived from local
70  discriminations. With slight shades of difference, you have the same religion, manners, habits, and political
71  principles. You have in a common cause fought and triumphed together; the independence and liberty you possess
72  are the work of joint counsels, and joint efforts of common dangers, sufferings, and successes.

73  But these considerations, however powerfully they address themselves to your sensibility, are greatly
74  outweighed by those which apply more immediately to your interest. Here every portion of our country finds the
75  most commanding motives for carefully guarding and preserving the union of the whole.

76  The North, in an unrestrained intercourse with the South, protected by the equal laws of a common
77  government, finds in the productions of the latter great additional resources of maritime and commercial enterprise
78  and precious materials of manufacturing industry. The South, in the same intercourse, benefiting by the agency of
79  the North, sees its agriculture grow and its commerce expand. Turning partly into its own channels the seamen of the
80  North, it finds its particular navigation invigorated; and, while it contributes, in different ways, to nourish and
81  increase the general mass of the national navigation, it looks forward to the protection of a maritime strength, to
82  which itself is unequally adapted. The East, in a like intercourse with the West, already finds, and in the progressive
83  improvement of interior communications by land and water, will more and more find a valuable vent for the
84  commodities which it brings from abroad, or manufactures at home. The West derives from the East supplies
85  requisite to its growth and comfort, and, what is perhaps of still greater consequence, it must of necessity owe the
86  secure enjoyment of indispensable outlets for its own productions to the weight, influence, and the future maritime
87  strength of the Atlantic side of the Union, directed by an indissoluble community of interest as one nation. Any other
88  tenure by which the West can hold this essential advantage, whether derived from its own separate strength, or from
89  an apostate and unnatural connection with any foreign power, must be intrinsically precarious.

90  While, then, every part of our country thus feels an immediate and particular interest in union, all the parts
91  combined cannot fail to find in the united mass of means and efforts greater strength, greater resource,
92  proportionally greater security from external danger, a less frequent interruption of their peace by foreign nations;
93  and, what is of inestimable value, they must derive from union an exemption from those broils and wars between
94  themselves, which so frequently afflict neighboring countries not tied together by the same governments, which their
95  own rival ships alone would be sufficient to produce, but which opposite foreign alliances, attachments, and
96  intrigues would stimulate and embitter. Hence, likewise, they will avoid the necessity of those overgrown military
97  establishments which, under any form of government, are inauspicious to liberty, and which are to be regarded as
98  particularly hostile to republican liberty. In this sense it is that your union ought to be considered as a main prop of
99  your liberty, and that the love of the one ought to endear to you the preservation of the other.

100  These considerations speak a persuasive language to every reflecting and virtuous mind, and exhibit the
101  continuance of the Union as a primary object of patriotic desire. Is there a doubt whether a common government can
102  embrace so large a sphere? Let experience solve it. To listen to mere speculation in such a case were criminal. We
103  are authorized to hope that a proper organization of the whole with the auxiliary agency of governments for the
104  respective subdivisions, will afford a happy issue to the experiment. It is well worth a fair and full experiment. With
105  such powerful and obvious motives to union, affecting all parts of our country, while experience shall not have

106 demonstrated its impracticability, there will always be reason to distrust the patriotism of those who in any quarter
107 may endeavor to weaken its bands.

108     In contemplating the causes which may disturb our Union, it occurs as matter of serious concern that any
109 ground should have been furnished for characterizing parties by geographical discriminations, Northern and
110 Southern, Atlantic and Western; whence designing men may endeavor to excite a belief that there is a real difference
111 of local interests and views. One of the expedients of party to acquire influence within particular districts is to
112 misrepresent the opinions and aims of other districts. You cannot shield yourselves too much against the jealousies
113 and heartburnings which spring from these misrepresentations; they tend to render alien to each other those who
114 ought to be bound together by fraternal affection. The inhabitants of our Western country have lately had a useful
115 lesson on this head; they have seen, in the negotiation by the Executive, and in the unanimous ratification by the
116 Senate, of the treaty with Spain, and in the universal satisfaction at that event, throughout the United States, a
117 decisive proof how unfounded were the suspicions propagated among them of a policy in the General Government
118 and in the Atlantic States unfriendly to their interests in regard to the Mississippi; they have been witnesses to the
119 formation of two treaties, that with Great Britain, and that with Spain, which secure to them everything they could
120 desire, in respect to our foreign relations, towards confirming their prosperity. Will it not be their wisdom to rely for
121 the preservation of these advantages on the Union by which they were procured ? Will they not henceforth be deaf
122 to those advisers, if such there are, who would sever them from their brethren and connect them with aliens?

123     To the efficacy and permanency of your Union, a government for the whole is indispensable. No alliance,
124 however strict, between the parts can be an adequate substitute; they must inevitably experience the infractions and
125 interruptions which all alliances in all times have experienced. Sensible of this momentous truth, you have improved
126 upon your first essay, by the adoption of a constitution of government better calculated than your former for an
127 intimate union, and for the efficacious management of your common concerns. This government, the offspring of
128 our own choice, uninfluenced and unawed, adopted upon full investigation and mature deliberation, completely free
129 in its principles, in the distribution of its powers, uniting security with energy, and containing within itself a
130 provision for its own amendment, has a just claim to your confidence and your support. Respect for its authority,
131 compliance with its laws, acquiescence in its measures, are duties enjoined by the fundamental maxims of true
132 liberty. The basis of our political systems is the right of the people to make and to alter their constitutions of
133 government. But the Constitution which at any time exists, till changed by an explicit and authentic act of the whole
134 people, is sacredly obligatory upon all. The very idea of the power and the right of the people to establish
135 government presupposes the duty of every individual to obey the established government.

136     All obstructions to the execution of the laws, all combinations and associations, under whatever plausible
137 character, with the real design to direct, control, counteract, or awe the regular deliberation and action of the
138 constituted authorities, are destructive of this fundamental principle, and of fatal tendency. They serve to organize
139 faction, to give it an artificial and extraordinary force; to put in the place of the delegated will of the nation the will
140 of a party, often a small but artful and enterprising minority of the community; and, according to the alternate
141 triumphs of different parties, to make the public administration the mirror of the ill-concerted and incongruous
142 projects of faction, rather than the organ of consistent and wholesome plans digested by common counsels and
143 modified by mutual interests.

144     However combinations or associations of the above description may now and then answer popular ends,
145 they are likely, in the course of time and things, to become potent engines, by which cunning, ambitious, and
146 unprincipled men will be enabled to subvert the power of the people and to usurp for themselves the reins of
147 government, destroying afterwards the very engines which have lifted them to unjust dominion.

148     Towards the preservation of your government, and the permanency of your present happy state, it is
149 requisite, not only that you steadily discountenance irregular oppositions to its acknowledged authority, but also that
150 you resist with care the spirit of innovation upon its principles, however specious the pretexts. One method of
151 assault may be to effect, in the forms of the Constitution, alterations which will impair the energy of the system, and
152 thus to undermine what cannot be directly overthrown. In all the changes to which you may be invited, remember
153 that time and habit are at least as necessary to fix the true character of governments as of other human institutions;
154 that experience is the surest standard by which to test the real tendency of the existing constitution of a country; that
155 facility in changes, upon the credit of mere hypothesis and opinion, exposes to perpetual change, from the endless
156 variety of hypotheses and opinion; and remember, especially, that for the efficient management of your common
157 interests, in a country so extensive as ours, a government of as much vigor as is consistent with the perfect security
158 of liberty is indispensable. Liberty itself will find in such a government, with powers properly distributed and
159 adjusted, its surest guardian. It is, indeed, little else than a name, where the government is too feeble to withstand the
160 enterprises of faction, to confine each member of the society within the limits prescribed by the laws, and to
161 maintain all in the secure and tranquil enjoyment of the rights of person and property.

162      I have already intimated to you the danger of parties in the State, with particular reference to the founding
163 of them on geographical discriminations. Let me now take a more comprehensive view, and warn you in the most
164 solemn manner against the baneful effects of the spirit of party generally.

165      This spirit, unfortunately, is inseparable from our nature, having its root in the strongest passions of the
166 human mind. It exists under different shapes in all governments, more or less stifled, controlled, or repressed; but, in
167 those of the popular form, it is seen in its greatest rankness, and is truly their worst enemy.

168      The alternate domination of one faction over another, sharpened by the spirit of revenge, natural to party
169 dissension, which in different ages and countries has perpetrated the most horrid enormities, is itself a frightful
170 despotism. But this leads at length to a more formal and permanent despotism. The disorders and miseries which
171 result gradually incline the minds of men to seek security and repose in the absolute power of an individual; and
172 sooner or later the chief of some prevailing faction, more able or more fortunate than his competitors, turns this
173 disposition to the purposes of his own elevation, on the ruins of public liberty.

174      Without looking forward to an extremity of this kind (which nevertheless ought not to be entirely out of
175 sight), the common and continual mischiefs of the spirit of party are sufficient to make it the interest and duty of a
176 wise people to discourage and restrain it.

177      It serves always to distract the public councils and enfeeble the public administration. It agitates the
178 community with ill-founded jealousies and false alarms, kindles the animosity of one part against another, foments
179 occasionally riot and insurrection. It opens the door to foreign influence and corruption, which finds a facilitated
180 access to the government itself through the channels of party passions. Thus the policy and the will of one country
181 are subjected to the policy and will of another.

182      There is an opinion that parties in free countries are useful checks upon the administration of the
183 government and serve to keep alive the spirit of liberty. This within certain limits is probably true; and in
184 governments of a monarchical cast, patriotism may look with indulgence, if not with favor, upon the spirit of party.
185 But in those of the popular character, in governments purely elective, it is a spirit not to be encouraged. From their
186 natural tendency, it is certain there will always be enough of that spirit for every salutary purpose. And there being
187 constant danger of excess, the effort ought to be by force of public opinion, to mitigate and assuage it. A fire not to
188 be quenched, it demands a uniform vigilance to prevent its bursting into a flame, lest, instead of warming, it should
189 consume.

190      It is important, likewise, that the habits of thinking in a free country should inspire caution in those
191 entrusted with its administration, to confine themselves within their respective constitutional spheres, avoiding in the
192 exercise of the powers of one department to encroach upon another. The spirit of encroachment tends to consolidate
193 the powers of all the departments in one, and thus to create, whatever the form of government, a real despotism. A
194 just estimate of that love of power, and proneness to abuse it, which predominates in the human heart, is sufficient to
195 satisfy us of the truth of this position. The necessity of reciprocal checks in the exercise of political power, by
196 dividing and distributing it into different depositaries, and constituting each the guardian of the public weal against
197 invasions by the others, has been evinced by experiments ancient and modern, some of them in our country and
198 under our own eyes. To preserve them must be as necessary as to institute them. If, in the opinion of the people, the
199 distribution or modification of the constitutional powers be in any particular wrong, let it be corrected by an
200 amendment in the way which the Constitution designates. But let there be no change by usurpation; for though this,
201 in one instance, may be the instrument of good, it is the customary weapon by which free governments are
202 destroyed. The precedent must always greatly overbalance in permanent evil any partial or transient benefit which
203 the use can at any time yield.

204      Of all the dispositions and habits which lead to political prosperity, religion and morality are indispensable
205 supports. In vain would that man claim the tribute of patriotism, who should labor to subvert these great pillars of
206 human happiness, these firmest props of the duties of men and citizens. The mere politician, equally with the pious
207 man, ought to respect and to cherish them. A volume could not trace all their connections with private and public
208 felicity. Let it simply be asked: Where is the security for property, for reputation, for life, if the sense of religious
209 obligation *desert* the oaths which are the instruments of investigation in courts of justice ? And let us with caution
210 indulge the supposition that morality can be maintained without religion. Whatever may be conceded to the
211 influence of refined education on minds of peculiar structure, reason and experience both forbid us to expect that
212 national morality can prevail in exclusion of religious principle.

213      It is substantially true that virtue or morality is a necessary spring of popular government. The rule, indeed,
214 extends with more or less force to every species of free government. Who that is a sincere friend to it can look with
215 indifference upon attempts to shake the foundation of the fabric?

216      Promote then, as an object of primary importance, institutions for the general diffusion of knowledge. In
217 proportion as the structure of a government gives force to public opinion, it is essential that public opinion should be
218 enlightened.

219    As a very important source of strength and security, cherish public credit. One method of preserving it is to
220    use it as sparingly as possible, avoiding occasions of expense by cultivating peace, but remembering also that timely
221    disbursements to prepare for danger frequently prevent much greater disbursements to repel it, avoiding likewise the
222    accumulation of debt, not only by shunning occasions of expense, but by vigorous exertion in time of peace to
223    discharge the debts which unavoidable wars may have occasioned, not ungenerously throwing upon posterity the
224    burden which we ourselves ought to bear. The execution of these maxims belongs to your representatives, but it is
225    necessary that public opinion should cooperate. To facilitate to them the performance of their duty, it is essential that
226    you should practically bear in mind that towards the payment of debts there must be revenue; that to have revenue
227    there must be taxes; that no taxes can be devised which are not more or less inconvenient and unpleasant; that the
228    intrinsic embarrassment, inseparable from the selection of the proper objects (which is always a choice of
229    difficulties), ought to be a decisive motive for a candid construction of the conduct of the government in making it,
230    and for a spirit of acquiescence in the measures for obtaining revenue, which the public exigencies may at any time
231    dictate.

232    Observe good faith and justice towards all nations; cultivate peace and harmony with all. Religion and
233    morality enjoin this conduct; and can it be that good policy does not equally enjoin it? It will be worthy of a free,
234    enlightened, and at no distant period, a great nation, to give to mankind the magnanimous and too novel example of
235    a people always guided by an exalted justice and benevolence. Who can doubt that, in the course of time and things,
236    the fruits of such a plan would richly repay any temporary advantages which might be lost by a steady adherence to
237    it? Can it be that Providence has not connected the permanent felicity of a nation with its virtue ? The experiment, at
238    least, is recommended by every sentiment which ennobles human nature. Alas! is it rendered impossible by its
239    vices?

240    In the execution of such a plan, nothing is more essential than that permanent, inveterate antipathies against
241    particular nations, and passionate attachments for others, should be excluded; and that, in place of them, just and
242    amicable feelings towards all should be cultivated. The nation which indulges towards another a habitual hatred or a
243    habitual fondness is in some degree a slave. It is a slave to its animosity or to its affection, either of which is
244    sufficient to lead it astray from its duty and its interest. Antipathy in one nation against another disposes each more
245    readily to offer insult and injury, to lay hold of slight causes of umbrage, and to be haughty and intractable, when
246    accidental or trifling occasions of dispute occur. Hence, frequent collisions, obstinate, envenomed, and bloody
247    contests. The nation, prompted by ill-will and resentment, sometimes impels to war the government, contrary to the
248    best calculations of policy. The government sometimes participates in the national propensity, and adopts through
249    passion what reason would reject; at other times it makes the animosity of the nation subservient to projects of
250    hostility instigated by pride, ambition, and other sinister and pernicious motives. The peace often, sometimes
251    perhaps the liberty, of nations has been the victim.

252    So likewise, a passionate attachment of one nation for another produces a variety of evils. Sympathy for the
253    favorite nation, facilitating the illusion of an imaginary common interest in cases where no real common interest
254    exists, and infusing into one the enmities of the other, betrays the former into a participation in the quarrels and wars
255    of the latter without adequate inducement or justification. It leads also to concessions to the favorite nation of
256    privileges denied to others, which is apt doubly to injure the nation making the concessions; by unnecessarily
257    parting with what ought to have been retained, and by exciting jealousy, ill-will, and a disposition to retaliate, in the
258    parties from whom equal privileges are withheld. And it gives to ambitious, corrupted, or deluded citizens (who
259    devote themselves to the favorite nation), facility to betray or sacrifice the interests of their own country, without
260    odium, sometimes even with popularity; gilding, with the appearances of a virtuous sense of obligation, a
261    commendable deference for public opinion, or a laudable zeal for public good, the base or foolish compliances of
262    ambition, corruption, or infatuation.

263    As avenues to foreign influence in innumerable ways, such attachments are particularly alarming to the
264    truly enlightened and independent patriot. How many opportunities do they afford to tamper with domestic factions,
265    to practice the arts of seduction, to mislead public opinion, to influence or awe the public councils? Such an
266    attachment of a small or weak [nation] towards a great and powerful nation dooms the former to be the satellite of
267    the latter.

268    Against the insidious wiles of foreign influence (I conjure you to believe me, fellow-citizens) the jealousy
269    of a free people ought to be constantly awake, since history and experience prove that foreign influence is one of the
270    most baneful foes of republican government. But that jealousy to be useful must be impartial; else it becomes the
271    instrument of the very influence to be avoided, instead of a defense against it. Excessive partiality for one foreign
272    nation and excessive dislike of another cause those whom they actuate to see danger only on one side, and serve to
273    veil and even second the arts of influence on the other. Real patriots who may resist the intrigues of the favorite are
274    liable to become suspected and odious, while its tools and dupes usurp the applause and confidence of the people, to
275    surrender their interests.

276      The great rule of conduct for us in regard to foreign nations is in extending our commercial relations, to
277 have with them as little political connection as possible. So far as we have already formed engagements, let them be
278 fulfilled with perfect good faith. Here let us stop. Europe has a set of primary interests, which to us have none or a
279 very remote relation. Hence she must be engaged in frequent controversies, the causes of which are essentially
280 foreign to our concerns. Hence, therefore, it must be unwise in us to implicate ourselves by artificial ties in the
281 ordinary vicissitudes of her politics, or the ordinary combinations and collisions of her friendships or enmities.

282      Our detached and distant situation invites and enables us to pursue a different course. If we remain one
283 people under an efficient government, the period is not far off when we may defy material injury from external
284 annoyance; when we may take such an attitude as will cause the neutrality we may at any time resolve upon to be
285 scrupulously respected; when belligerent nations, under the impossibility of making acquisitions upon us, will not
286 lightly hazard the giving us provocation; when we may choose peace or war, as our interest, guided by justice, shall
287 counsel.

288      Why forego the advantages of so peculiar a situation? Why quit our own to stand upon foreign ground?
289 Why, by interweaving our destiny with that of any part of Europe, entangle our peace and prosperity in the toils of
290 European ambition, rival ship, interest, humor, or caprice?

291      It is our true policy to steer clear of permanent alliances with any portion of the foreign world; so far, I
292 mean, as we are now at liberty to do it; for let me not be understood as capable of patronizing infidelity to existing
293 engagements. I hold the maxim no less applicable to public than to private affairs, that honesty is always the best
294 policy. I repeat it, therefore, let those engagements be observed in their genuine sense. But, in my opinion, it is
295 unnecessary and would be unwise to extend them.

296      Taking care always to keep ourselves by suitable establishments on a respectable defensive posture, we
297 may safely trust to temporary alliances for extraordinary emergencies.

298      Harmony, liberal intercourse with all nations, are recommended by policy, humanity, and interest. But even
299 our commercial policy should hold an equal and impartial hand; neither seeking nor granting exclusive favors or
300 preferences; consulting the natural course of things; diffusing and diversifying by gentle means the streams of
301 commerce, but forcing nothing; establishing (with powers so disposed, in order to give trade a stable course, to
302 define the rights of our merchants, and to enable the government to support them) conventional rules of intercourse,
303 the best that present circumstances and mutual opinion will permit, but temporary, and liable to be from time to time
304 abandoned or varied, as experience and circumstances shall dictate; constantly keeping in view that it is folly in one
305 nation to look for disinterested favors from another; that it must pay with a portion of its independence for whatever
306 it may accept under that character; that, by such acceptance, it may place itself in the condition of having given
307 equivalents for nominal favors, and yet of being reproached with ingratitude for not giving more. There can be no
308 greater error than to expect or calculate upon real favors from nation to nation. It is an illusion which experience
309 must cure, which a just pride ought to discard.

310      In offering to you, my countrymen, these counsels of an old and affectionate friend, I dare not hope they
311 will make the strong and lasting impression I could wish; that they will control the usual current of the passions, or
312 prevent our nation from running the course which has hitherto marked the destiny of nations. But, if I may even
313 flatter myself that they may be productive of some partial benefit, some occasional good, that they may now and
314 then recur to moderate the fury of party spirit, to warn against the mischiefs of foreign intrigue, to guard against the
315 impostures of pretended patriotism—this hope will be a full recompense for the solicitude for your welfare, by
316 which they have been dictated.

317      How far in the discharge of my official duties I have been guided by the principles which have been
318 delineated, the public records and other evidences of my conduct must witness to you and to the world. To myself,
319 the assurance of my own conscience is, that I have at least believed myself to be guided by them.

320      In relation to the still subsisting war in Europe, my proclamation of the 22nd of April 1793 is the index of
321 my plan. Sanctioned by your approving voice and by that of your representatives in both houses of Congress, the
322 spirit of that measure has continually governed me, uninfluenced by any attempts to deter or divert me from it.

323      After deliberate examination, with the aid of the best lights I could obtain, I was well satisfied that our
324 country, under all the circumstances of the case, had a right to take, and was bound in duty and interest to take, a
325 neutral position. Having taken it, I determined, as far as should depend upon me, to maintain it, with moderation,
326 perseverance, and firmness.

327      The considerations which respect the right to hold this conduct, it is not necessary on this occasion to
328 detail. I will only observe that, according to my understanding of the matter, that right, so far from being denied by
329 any of the belligerent powers, has been virtually admitted by all.

330      The duty of holding a neutral conduct may be inferred, without anything more, from the obligation which
331 justice and humanity impose on every nation, in cases in which it is free to act, to maintain inviolate the relations of
332 peace and amity towards other nations.

333     The inducements of interest for observing that conduct will best be referred to your own reflections and
334 experience. With me a predominant motive has been to endeavor to gain time to our country to settle and mature its
335 yet recent institutions, and to progress without interruption to that degree of strength and consistency which is
336 necessary to give it, humanly speaking, the command of its own fortunes.
337     Though, in reviewing the incidents of my administration, I am unconscious of intentional error, I am
338 nevertheless too sensible of my defects not to think it probable that I may have committed many errors. Whatever
339 they may be, I fervently beseech the Almighty to avert or mitigate the evils to which they may tend. I shall also
340 carry with me the hope that my country will never cease to view them with indulgence and that, after forty-five
341 years of my life dedicated to its service with an upright zeal, the faults of incompetent abilities will be consigned to
342 oblivion, as myself must soon be to the mansions of rest.
343     Relying on its kindness in this as in other things, and actuated by that fervent love towards it, which is so
344 natural to a man who views in it the native soil of himself and his progenitors for several generations, I anticipate
345 with pleasing expectation that retreat in which I promise myself to realize, without alloy, the sweet enjoyment of
346 partaking, in the midst of my fellow-citizens, the benign influence of good laws under a free government, the ever-
347 favorite object of my heart, and the happy reward, as I trust, of our mutual cares, labors, and dangers.

    Geo. Washington           United States           19th September 1796

(http://www.gpo.gov/fdsys/pkg/GPO-CDOC-106sdoc21/pdf/GPO-CDOC-106sdoc21.pdf)

1. George Washington warns against

    A. Women's Rights                  C. Political parties

    B. States' rights                     D. Phony treaties

2. Washington fails to mention a looming problem between the South and the North:

    A. Slavery                         C. Federal funding of education

    B. Civil rights                      D. Interstate transportation

3. Washington's comments, "In contemplating the causes which may disturb our Union, it occurs as matter of serious concern that any ground should have been furnished for characterizing parties by geographical discriminations, Northern and Southern, Atlantic and Western; whence designing men may endeavor to excite a belief that there is a real difference of local interests and views" express a concern about

    A. Women's rights                  C. Sectional strife

    B. The tyranny of England          D. Foreign invasion

4. This quote "There can be no greater error than to expect or calculate upon real favors from nation to nation. It is an illusion which experience must cure, which a just pride ought to discard" warns against

    A. Domestic building projects        C. Veteran affairs

    B. Foreign alliances                D. State governments

5. This speech would refute the notion that

    A. Washington was an atheist.        C. Washington was a Federalist.

    B. Washington was a Mason.          D. Washington planned to free his slaves.

6. In the future, what political argument might benefit from this speech?

    I.   An isolationist foreign policy position.

    II.   A pro-slavery status quo position.

  III.   An antislavery position.

  IV.   A strong military position.

    V.   A pro-political party stand.

        A. I                           D. III and IV

        B. II                        E. V

        C. I and II

# Lesson 5

## Math: Algebra, Arithmetic Problem Solving and Data Analysis, and Passport to Advanced Math

### Arithmetic Problem Solving

1.  Margaret and Jane have the same amount of money. If Margaret should give Jane 40 cents, she would have one-third as much as Jane. What amount of money has each?
    A.  $.80
    B.  $.60
    C.  $.40
    D.  $.30

2.  Jim, Harry, and Adam picked berries and sold them; Jim and Harry received $4.22, Jim and Adam $3.05, Harry and Adam $3.67. How much did each receive for his berries?
    A.  J., $1.80; H., $2.44; A., $1.25
    B.  J., $ 1.80; H., $2.42; A., $1.26
    C.  J., $1.80; H., $2.42; A., $1.25
    D.  J., $1.80; H., $2.42; A., $1.28

3.  David can build a stone wall in 10 days, and Susan in 12 days. How long would it take them to do it working together?
    A.  10 days
    B.  9 days
    C.  11 days
    D.  5.5 days

4.  Six years ago James was five times as old as Suzanne. If he is twice as old as Suzanne now, what are their ages?
    A.  J. 36, S. 18
    B.  J. 24, S. 12
    C.  J., 18, S. 9
    D.  J., 16; S., 8

5.  How long will it take a man to walk X miles if he walks 15 miles in $B$ hours?

    A.  BX x 2 hours
    B.  —
    C.  X=2B hours
    D.  –      hours

6.  A father gave his son four times as many dollars as he then had, and his mother gave him $25, when he found that he had nine times as many dollars as at first. How many dollars had he at first?
    A.  $5.25
    B.  $6.00
    C.  $6.25
    D.  $6.50

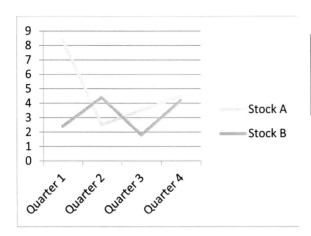

| | Stock A | Stock B |
|---|---|---|
| Quarter 1 | 8.4 | 2.4 |
| Quarter 2 | 2.5 | 4.4 |
| Quarter 3 | 3.5 | 1.8 |
| Quarter 4 | 4.5 | 4.2 |

1. What is true about this chart (above)?
   I.   Stock A in Quarter 1 is double Stock B in Quarter 4
   II.  Sometime in Quarter 2, Stock A and B are equal
   III. Stock B dropped in price proportionately more than Stock A

    A. I                                  C. III
    B. I and II                         D. NONE

2. In what quarter was the best time to sell Stock A? Stock B?

  A. A, 2nd Quarter; B, 2nd Quarter            C. A, 3rd Quarter; B, 1st Quarter
  B. A, 1st Quarter; B, 2nd Quarter            D. A, 1st Quarter; B, 1st Quarter

# Chapter 7   The Fatal Campsite
# Genesis 13

> *Memory Verse:* So Lot chose for himself the whole plain of the Jordan and set out toward the east. The two men parted company: Abram lived in the land of Canaan, while Lot lived among the cities of the plain and pitched his tents near Sodom. —Genesis 13:11–12

Christians fail for a number of reasons, but one thing is common to all cases: failure does not happen instantaneously. Failure is a process.

The story of Lot in Genesis 13 is a sad case of a believer who failed. Lot is mentioned in 2 Peter 2:7–8 three times as a "righteous" person. But righteous Lot failed to use his life for God. He traveled the road to failure. How can a mature Christian believer so easily ruin his life as Lot did?

The first step toward failure came because Lot looked at things from the wrong perspective. He made a selfish decision as he "chose for himself" (Genesis 13:11). His choice was based only on what looked like the best deal: Lot saw that all the valley of the Jordan "was well watered" (13:10). Lot's decision did not take into account the fact that the wicked cities of the valley were also alive and kicking and enticing unwary believers into destruction. Lot served God when it was convenient and comfortable—but he was not yet making decisions that took him into situations that were challenging and difficult. And never was Lot able to delay his own pleasures for the sake of obedience. The road to failure begins with bad choices that grow out of our best intentions but not out of obedience to God's command.

We also may begin our road to failure by taking the easy way, the road that fits our agendas and our pleasure. And we have all sorts of rationalizations! One of the best examples I have is the wrong choice I find many young people making. The late Elizabeth Eliott, a great Christian teacher and widow of Jim Eliott, warns young people that sexual intimacy does not show us one thing about the character of a person. Many young people erroneously make the wrong assumption that such intimacy will be a good preparation for marriage. Therefore they choose to live together before marriage. The road of failure is paved with good intentions and wrong assumptions.

Although both Abraham and Lot were believers, Abraham chose the right road. He chose God's best for him, not following selfish desires. In Hebrews 11:10 we read that Abraham "was looking forward to the city with foundations, whose architect and builder is God." Abraham was not interested in earthly man-made cities like Sodom and Gomorrah, no matter how appealing they might be. Give Abraham the wilderness if it means God is with him!

Abraham was not concerned about what land he had or did not have. He was more concerned about building on the solid foundations he had in God. What kind of city are we moving our tents next to? The city of God? Or the city of our selfish choices?

Lot's second step on the road to failure occurs in Genesis 13:12. Lot "pitched his tents near Sodom." He did not move into Sodom—not yet. But he was flirting with evil. And at first glance sin always appears more appealing than the ways of God.

"Chill out, Stobaugh," you may be thinking. "After all, he only lived near the city, not in it."

But Lot was moving in the wrong direction. His decision mechanisms were set to produce self-centered decisions, not decisions based on what God wants. It is never a matter of living in open sin in the beginning. Satan is too smart for that: he grabs us in bits and pieces! Or tries anyway!

Young saints, I am afraid some of us have pitched our tents too close to Sodom, on fatal campgrounds. We are flirting with sin. We live double lives—a righteous life to assuage our consciences, and a fun life to make the righteous life more bearable. Taking a high-paying job, for instance, that involves us in unethical practices is pitching our tents next to Sodom. Cheating on taxes? "Everyone does it," we mutter to ourselves. As in Lot's case, it may be only a short while before we move right into the evil city (14:12).

By contrast, Abraham moved to unappetizing Hebron, in the high country, and "there he built an altar to the LORD" (13:18). And at the same time, while God gave him the less fertile high country, he also gave him the whole world!

The promises of God, which Abraham possessed, belong to those who are motivated by obedience. Not to those who are motivated by good intentions—or sincerity. Lot was sincerely wrong!

As our story continues, in Genesis 19 we see that Lot is fully ensnared in the affairs of Sodom. Lot probably married a Sodomite; no doubt he was making a good living. And compromise, with all its earthly rewards, had become a way of life. Lot got rid of his tent and bought a four-bedroom duplex in the best section of Sodom. He conveniently winked at the sin around him—what else could he do? He at least did not participate in the sin. But as so often happens, others suffer as a result of our bad choices (e.g., his wife).

How slowly but deadly sin can be. We really never do any one big thing wrong. But all the little things add up and ultimately destroy us. Our good intentions and self-centered decisions do not rob us of heaven (for we are saved by grace), but they create for us a hell on earth.

We as a society have lost our way. According to the theologian Leslie Newbigin, Euro-American culture has in large part lost its interaction with the transcendent word to which it owes its origin and vitality, and wanders about seeking human absolutes to take its place. Slowly, then, Lot and his family replace God's absolutes with substitute human absolutes. Instead of keeping God's commandments, Lot began to live for self, to practice minimal human decency, in the mode of "Live and let live," or a not-golden rule, "Don't do to others what you don't want them to do to you."

In the beautiful book about Welsh coal miners called *How Green Was My Valley*, we see a wonderful pastor destroyed by folks full of good intentions but short on discernment and obedience. Although this pastor was above reproach concerning a young lady in church, gossipers and rumormongers slowly, but effectively, ruined his ministry and career. Slowly, one sin at a time, folks moved closer and closer to Sodom. And this pastor and his church both suffered.

The final scene we have of Lot is indeed tragic. By the mercy of God his life was spared. But he lost everything—job, home, possessions, and his wife. It is true that Lot was able to take his two daughters out of Sodom, but he was not able to take Sodom out of his daughters (Genesis 19:30–38). From incestuous relationships came the dreaded Moabites and Ammonites, nations that were to plague the people of God for years to come. Lot's failure, which began with a bad choice, had disastrous effects upon himself and all his loved ones. The story of Lot is a clear and solemn warning for every growing Christian: Don't travel the road to failure! From the very beginning, make choices informed by the Holy.

## Journal Question

As you prepare for college how can you prepare to avoid Lot-like decisions?

# Lesson 1
## Evidence-Based Reading and Writing

### Literary Choice

Alexis de Tocqueville was a French political thinker and historian, a sociologist of sorts, best known for his work *Democracy in America* (2 vols., 1835–40). This groundbreaking work set the standard for demographic and sociological studies for a generation.

### Parties in the United States

1  A great distinction must be made between parties. Some countries are so large that the different populations which
2  inhabit them have contradictory interests, although they are the subjects of the same Government, and they may
3  thence be in a perpetual state of opposition. In this case the different fractions of the people may more properly be
4  considered as distinct nations than as mere parties; and if a civil war breaks out, the struggle is carried on by rival
5  peoples rather than by factions in the State.
6      But when the citizens entertain different opinions upon subjects which affect the whole country alike, such,
7  for instance, as the principles upon which the government is to be conducted, then distinctions arise which may
8  correctly be styled parties. Parties are a necessary evil in free governments; but they have not at all times the same
9  character and the same propensities.
10      At certain periods a nation may be oppressed by such insupportable evils as to conceive the design of
11  effecting a total change in its political constitution; at other times the mischief lies still deeper, and the existence of
12  society itself is endangered. Such are the times of great revolutions and of great parties. But between these epochs of
13  misery and of confusion there are periods during which human society seems to rest, and mankind to make a pause.
14  This pause is, indeed, only apparent, for time does not stop its course for nations any more than for men; they are all
15  advancing towards a goal with which they are unacquainted; and we only imagine them to be stationary when their
16  progress escapes our observation, as men who are going at a foot-pace seem to be standing still to those who run.
17      But however this may be, there are certain epochs at which the changes that take place in the social and
18  political constitution of nations are so slow and so insensible that men imagine their present condition to be a final
19  state; and the human mind, believing itself to be firmly based upon certain foundations, does not extend its
20  researches beyond the horizon which it descries. These are the times of small parties and of intrigue.
21      The political parties which I style great are those which cling to principles more than to their consequences;
22  to general, and not to especial cases; to ideas, and not to men. These parties are usually distinguished by a nobler
23  character, by more generous passions, more genuine convictions, and a more bold and open conduct than the others.
24  In them private interest, which always plays the chief part in political passions, is more studiously veiled under the
25  pretext of the public good; and it may even be sometimes concealed from the eyes of the very persons whom it
26  excites and impels.
27      Minor parties are, on the other hand, generally deficient in political faith. As they are not sustained or
28  dignified by a lofty purpose, they ostensibly display the egotism of their character in their actions. They glow with a
29  factitious zeal; their language is vehement, but their conduct is timid and irresolute. The means they employ are as
30  wretched as the end at which they aim. Hence it arises that when a calm state of things succeeds a violent revolution,
31  the leaders of society seem suddenly to disappear, and the powers of the human mind to lie concealed. Society is
32  convulsed by great parties, by minor ones it is agitated; it is torn by the former, by the latter it is degraded; and if
33  these sometimes save it by a salutary perturbation, those invariably disturb it to no good end.
34      America has already lost the great parties, which once divided the nation; and if her happiness is
35  considerably increased, her morality has suffered by their extinction. When the War of Independence was
36  terminated, and the foundations of the new Government were to be laid down, the nation was divided between two
37  opinions—two opinions which are as old as the world, and which are perpetually to be met with under all the forms
38  and all the names which have ever obtained in free communities—the one tending to limit, the other to extend
39  indefinitely, the power of the people. The conflict of these two opinions never assumed that degree of violence in
40  America which it has frequently displayed elsewhere. Both parties of the Americans were, in fact, agreed upon the
41  most essential points; and neither of them had to destroy a traditionary constitution, or to overthrow the structure of
42  society, in order to ensure its own triumph. In neither of them, consequently, were a great number of private interests
43  affected by success or by defeat; but moral principles of a high order, such as the love of equality and of
44  independence, were concerned in the struggle, and they sufficed to kindle violent passions.

45     The party which desired to limit the power of the people endeavored to apply its doctrines more especially
46 to the Constitution of the Union, whence it derived its name of Federal. The other party, which affected to be more
47 exclusively attached to the cause of liberty, took that of Republican. America is a land of democracy, and the
48 Federalists were always in a minority; but they reckoned on their side almost all the great men who had been called
49 forth by the War of Independence, and their moral influence was very considerable. Their cause was, moreover,
50 favored by circumstances. The ruin of the Confederation had impressed the people with a dread of anarchy, and the
51 Federalists did not fail to profit by this transient disposition of the multitude. For ten or twelve years they were at the
52 head of affairs, and they were able to apply some, though not all, of their principles; for the hostile current was
53 becoming from day to day too violent to be checked or stemmed. In 1801 the Republicans got possession of the
54 Government; Thomas Jefferson was named President; and he increased the influence of their party by the weight of
55 his celebrity, the greatness of his talents, and the immense extent of his popularity.

(Alexis de Tocqueville, *Democracy in America*, chap. 10,
http://www.gutenberg.org/files/815/815-h/815-h.htm#link2HCH0026)

## Close Reading

1.   Generally speaking, the author
    A. Approves of political parties
    B. Disapproves of political parties
    C. Believes that slavery is necessary
    D. Prefers the French Monarchy to the American Republic

2. The author prefers "great" parties to "minor" parties. Why?
   I.  Minor, or parochial parties, cause dissension and put in danger the spirit of liberty.
  II.  Major parties are driven by ideology and the larger good of the country.
 III.  Minor parties encourage petty bickering and disagreements and have no larger vision of the good.

        A. I                            D. NONE
        B. II                           E. All
        C. III

3.   Which of the following statements is true?
    A.  Tocqueville loved America and saw its diversity as a strength. At the same time, it did not hold a
       candle to the Napoleonic regime that he enjoyed in France.
    B.  Tocqueville marveled at the apparent contradiction that existed in American society. On one hand,
       Americans were committed to a higher, ubiquitous vision. On the other hand, every small township
       managed its own affairs and happily organized committees and meetings on every subject. Tocqueville
       recognized the country's deep strain of individualism.
    C.  Tocqueville recognized that tension of American pluralism—everyone liked it but no one knew how to
       live with it. Ultimately, Tocqueville predicted, this would lead to a great war.
    D.  In spite of the great progressive ideology that permeated all aspects of American life, there were still
       glaring injustices, especially in relation to slavery and to women's rights.

4.   "America has already lost the great parties, which once divided the nation; and if her happiness is
considerably increased, her morality has suffered by their extinction" means that
    A.  America no longer had any parties: the Republican Party had removed all opposition.
    B.  The resurgent Whig Party was growing but did not really have a legitimate voice in American politics.
    C.  In the 1830s, it appeared to Tocqueville that the Jacksonian Democratic Republican Party had more or
       less supplanted the healthy dialogue that was occurring between the Federalists and anti-Federalists in
       the Constitution-debate era.
    D.  Slavery had so dominated American politics that there was no studied debate over any other issue.

5.   A group that might take issue with the above statement would be
    A.  The Whig Party.                 C.  The Know Nothing Party.
    B.  The Democratic Republican Party.     D.  The Progressive Party.

6. "The political parties which I style great are those which cling to principles more than to their consequences; to general, and not to especial cases; to ideas, and not to men. " An example(s) of a political party that would not be described in this statement would be
   I. The Whig Party, which preferred a small government and a strict interpretation of the Constitution.
   II. The Democratic Republican Party, which preferred a big government and a loose interpretation of the Constitution.
   III. The Know Nothing Party, which vociferously opposed immigration and foreigners in general.
   IV. The Free Soil Party, which advocated free labor versus slavery.

   A. I                    C. III                    E. II and III
   B. II                   D. I and II

7. An example(s) of groups described in Lines 1–3 include
   I. The Serbs, Hungarians, and Austrians in the Austrian-Hungarian Empire
   II. The Native Americans and Europeans in the United States
   III. The Huguenots and Roman Catholics in France
   IV. The Turks and the Armenians in the Ottoman Empire

   A. I and II               D. I and IV
   B. II and III             E NONE
   C. III and IV

8. Tocqueville makes the following point about morality and party politics:
   A. Political parties may disagree but they all share the same moral base.
   B. American was more moral before it had political parties.
   C. Political parites have a tendency to scrifice its morals to win elections.
   D. The Founding Fatherts were more moral than Jacksonian Democrats

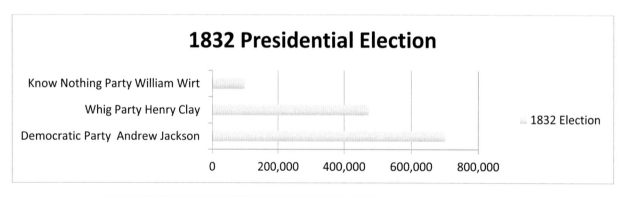

## 1832 Presidential Election

| Party and Candidate | Votes |
| --- | --- |
| Democratic Party Andrew Jackson | 702,735 |
| Whig Party Henry Clay | 474,107 |
| Know Nothing William Wirt | 99,817 |

1. Based upon the above chart, the following are true:
   I. Andrew Jackson received more votes than all the other candidates combined.
   II. If William Wirt had withdrawn from the election, Henry Clay would have won.
   III. Over 2 million American voted in the 1832 election

   A. I                    D. I and II
   B. II                   E. All
   C. III

2. If the author could vote, which candidate would he avoid?

  A. Jackson                      C. Wirth
  B. Clay                         D. All

## Source Analysis

From this text the reader can make the following assumptions about the author.

  I.   Tocqueville was a monarchist.
  II.  Tocqueville was a republican (one who prefers republican government).
  III. Tocqueville was an Anglophile.

  A. I                            D. II and III
  B. I and II                     E. NONE of above
  C. III

# Lesson 2

## Critical Reading and Writing

### Command of Evidence

Read the following passage and answer accompanying questions:

### Passage 1

#### Themes in *The Adventures of Huckleberry Finn*

1   "We said there warn't no home like a raft, after all. Other places do seem so cramped and smothery, but a raft don't.
2   You feel mighty free and easy and comfortable on a raft." Huckleberry Finn and a fugitive slave named Jim both
3   seek freedom from society and the problems which it brings. For Jim, society means slavery. For Huck, society
4   means the constraints of civilization and cultural norms. Thus, the two unlikely companions set out on a raft down
5   the Mississippi River. And yet, as they run from the society they have known, they float further south and further
6   into the heart of that very same culture which they fear. Through his attempt to flee from the troubling problems of
7   civilization, Huckleberry Finn discovers that there is no physical escape from the world in which he lives, but that he
8   can create his own worldview and outlook on life.

9      Near the outset of Twain's novel, Huckleberry Finn searches for freedom and appears to find it on a raft
10  floating down the Mississippi River. "It's lovely to live on a raft. We had the sky, up there, all speckled with stars,
11  and we used to lay on our backs and look up at them, and discuss about whether they was made, or only just
12  happened." Huck often revels in his glorious freedom, floating down a river on a raft, with no one ordering him
13  around and nothing to care about except staying alive. Yet, even when reflecting on this glorious situation, Huck
14  sometimes reveals that all is not entirely well.

15      "When it was dark I set by my camp fire smoking, and feeling pretty satisfied; but by-and-by it got sort of
16  lonesome, and so I went and set on the bank and listen to the currents washing along, and counted the stars and drift-
17  logs and rafts that come down, and then went to bed."

18      He speaks of satisfaction alongside a loneliness which he can't shake off. Perhaps this freedom is not
19  entirely free after all.

20      Time proves that Huck and Jim's journey down the Mississippi is headed ultimately toward re-civilization
21  and re-enslavement. The original plan which Huck and Jim formulate when they begin traveling together is that they
22  will head downstream to Cairo, where they will land and purchase tickets for a steamboat headed up the Ohio River
23  and into free territory. Huck and Jim will then both be free. However, they pass Cairo one night in an intense fog.
24  By the time they realize their mistake, attempting to walk back up North is out of the question. Shortly after this
25  catastrophe, two con-men referred to as the king and the duke board Huck and Jim's raft and force their company
26  upon the two refugees. As they land at every town along the river and hoodwink the people who live there, Huck
27  and Jim's freedom lies constantly at stake. Ultimately, the king and the duke betray Jim to a group of slave hunters
28  for a price. "All kings is mostly rapscallions, as fur as I can make out." Huck's care for Jim prevents him from
29  abandoning the runaway slave, and thus his brave attempt to flee from the constraints of society appears to be
30  unsuccessful.

31      Despite Huck's technical failure to escape civilization, he does succeed in emotionally and intellectually
32  rejecting society. In one of the most famous scenes of Twain's novel, Huck has written a letter to Jim's captors
33  notifying them of Jim's real master and warning them of his escape plan. Huck feels that this act will cleanse his
34  guilty conscience which remembers his old Sunday school lessons. These lessons taught him that disobeying the law
35  (i.e., freeing a slave) would send a person to Hell.

36      "[But then I remembered] the time I saved him by telling the men we had small-pox aboard, and he was so
37  grateful, and said I was the best friend old Jim ever had in the world, and the only one he's got now; and then I
38  happened to look around and see that paper. It was a close place. I took it up, and held it in my hand. I was a-
39  trembling, because I'd got to decide, forever, betwixt two things, and I knowed it. I studied a minute, sort of holding
40  my breath, and then says to myself: 'All right, then, I'll go to hell'—and tore it up."

41      In his own words, "What's the use you learning to do right, when it's troublesome to do right and ain't no
42  trouble to do wrong, and the wages is just the same?" Even as Huck faces his failed attempt at freedom, he
43  successfully breaks the intellectual boundaries that his culture has attempted to impose upon him. In this sense,
44  Huck does successfully flee from society.

45      In *The Adventures of Huckleberry Finn*, the title character discovers the impossibility of escaping from the
46 problems created by civilization. He simultaneously finds that through facing his troubles instead of running away
47 from them, he can overcome them mentally and construct his own view of morality. "It don't make no difference
48 whether you do right or wrong, a person's conscience ain't got no sense, and just goes for him anyway." (All quotes
49 from Mark Twain, *The Adventures of Huckleberry Finn* (New York: Barnes and Noble Classics, 2003) (John)

## Passage 2

### Huck's Journey

1     In his tour de force, *Huckleberry Finn*, Mark Twain chronicles the journey of Huck Finn from somewhat of a
2 Romantic to a confirmed Realist. As the novel progresses, Huck Finn changes from a romantically idealistic to a
3 decidedly pragmatic young man. Huck's idealism early on can be seen in his altruistic plans to turn in criminals he
4 meets along the Mississippi:

5         "Quick, Jim, it ain't no time for fooling around and moaning; there's a gang of murderers in yonder, and if
6         we don't hunt up their boat and set her drifting down the river so these fellows can't get away from the
7         wreck there's one of 'em going to be in a bad fix. But if we find their boat we can put ALL of 'em in a bad
8         fix—for the sheriff'll get 'em. Quick—hurry! I'll hunt the labboard side, you hunt the stabboard. You start
9         at the raft, and—"

10 Rather than choosing the safe and expedient course of action, using the raft to get off the boat, Huck decides to take
11 the Romantic, idealistic course of action, put them "in a bad fix," and in about a sentence, to "put ALL of 'em in a
12 bad fix." Of course, finding the criminals' skiff involved searching for the boat, wasting valuable time, and
13 increasing the risk of discovery.
14     In contrast, by the end of the book, Huck wants to do everything as quickly and safely as possible. When
15 Jim is captured as a runaway slave, he constantly takes the simplest, most pragmatic course of action. On the other
16 hand, Tom Sawyer never fails to make things as complicated and Romantic as possible.

17         Then we started for the house, and I went in the back door—you only have to pull a buckskin latch-string,
18         they don't fasten the doors—but that warn't romantical enough for Tom Sawyer; no way would do him but
19         he must climb up the lightning-rod. But after he got up half way about three times, and missed fire and fell
20         every time, and the last time most busted his brains out, he thought he'd got to give it up; but after he was
21         rested he allowed he would give her one more turn for luck, and this time he made the trip.

22 By this incident, which is rather late in his interactions with Tom Sawyer, Huck begins to be a touch cynical about
23 Tom's romantic idealism, stating that going in through the door "warn't romantical enough for Tom Sawyer," and
24 then poking fun at the outcome of Tom's exploits, saying that he "fell every time, and the last time most busted his
25 brains out." By this point in the novel, Huck is a confirmed pragmatist.
26     Throughout the course of Tom Sawyer, Huck Finn changes from an idealistic Romantic to a pragmatic
27 Realist. Early on in his journey, Huck prefers the idealistic course of action, choosing to foil criminals instead of
28 prioritizing his and Jim's safety. However, by the end of his travels, he is thoroughly pragmatic, always suggesting
29 the quickest and safest course of action to save Jim, while poking fun at the failures of the romantic Tom Sawyer.
30 (Alouette)

    1. Both passages agree on the following statement(s):
      I.   The interior life of Huck Finn changes as the novel progresses.
     II.   Huck Finn's decision to help the slave Jim escape was a correct, moral decision.
   III.   Huck Finn was the opposite in personality from Tom Sawyer.

        A. I                                   D. I and II
        B. II                                 E. II and III
        C. III

    2. Which passage would agree with this statement: Huck Finn does not embrace any particular moral code but
      more or less embraced a sort of existentialism where he is the center of the universe.
        A. Passage 1                       C. Both
        B. Passage 2                       D. Neither

3. Based on Passage 2, Huck would be

A. Pragmatist.  C. Cynic.

B. Realist.  D. Absurdist.

4. Based on Passage 1, why is it ironical that Huck and Jim are floating down the Mississippi River to freedom?

A. Their pursuers are waiting in Arkansas to apprehend the pair.

B. The farther they float south or down the Mississippi River, the farther they are from freedom in Canada.

C. Jim is terminally ill and will not survive the journey.

D. Huck cannot escape his nefarious father.

5. What does this Passage 1 statement mean? "Even as Huck faces his failed attempt at freedom, he successfully breaks the intellectual boundaries that his culture has attempted to impose upon him. In this sense, Huck does successfully flee from society."

A. Even as Huck faces his failed attempt at freedom, he nonetheless escapes the moral and cognitive boundaries placed on him by his society.

B. Huck will never be able to escape the fear he has of being on his own.

C. Huck cannot forgive himself for killing his father.

D. Huck is deeply discouraged by the Arkansas feud.

6. From the scoffing superiority of sixth-form year and success Amory looked back with cynical wonder on his status of the year before. He was changed as completely as Amory Blaine could ever be changed. Amory plus Beatrice plus two years in Minneapolis—these had been his ingredients when he entered St. Regis'. But the Minneapolis years were not a thick enough overlay to conceal the "Amory plus Beatrice" from the ferreting eyes of a boarding-school, so St. Regis' had very painfully drilled Beatrice out of him, and begun to lay down new and more conventional planking on the fundamental Amory. But both St. Regis' and Amory were unconscious of the fact that this fundamental Amory had not in himself changed. Those qualities for which he had suffered, his moodiness, his tendency to pose, his laziness, and his love of playing the fool, were now taken as a matter of course, recognized eccentricities in a star quarter-back, a clever actor, and the editor of the St. Regis' *Tattler*: it puzzled him to see impressionable small boys imitating the very vanities that had not long ago been contemptible weaknesses. (F. Scott Fitzgerald, *This Side of Paradise*, book 1, http://www.gutenberg.org/files/805/805-h/805-h.htm)

The character described in the above passage is most like Huck as described in

A. Passage 1  C. NONE

B. Passage 2  D. BOTH

## Words in Context

1. What is the meaning of *refugees* in Passage 1, Line 26?

A. Morning  C. Expatriates

B. Natives  D. Enemies

2. What is the meaning of *tour de force* in Passage 2, Line 1?

A. Fatal Event  C. Disconcerting Solution

B. Impressive Achievement  D. Soothing Moment

3. What is the meaning of *pragmatic* in Passage 2, Line 3?

A. Mendacious  C. Obdurate

B. Impractical  D. Practical

4. What is the meaning of *expedient* Passage 2, Line 10?

A. Perfunctory  C. Supercilious

B. Superfluous  D. Advantageous

5.  What is the meaning of *idealistic* Passage 2, Line 26?
    A.  Principled
    B.  Pejorative
    C.  Remorseful
    D.  Effusive

6.  What is the meaning of *romantic* Passage 2, Line 27?
    A.  A cultural movement that emphasized rationalism.
    B.  A cultural movement that extolled the virtues of nature.
    C.  A literary movement that emphasized the ordinary versus extraordinary.
    D.  A cultural movement that had an unnatural fascination with death.

7.  What is the meaning of *foil* Passage 2, Line 27?
    A.  Resist
    B.  Prevent
    C.  Eradicate
    D.  Emphasize

# Lesson 3

## SAT Essay

*Prompt:* As you read the passage below, consider how the author uses

A. Evidence, such as facts or examples, to support claims.
B. Reasoning to develop ideas and to connect claims and evidence.
C. Stylistic or persuasive elements, such as word choice or appeals to emotion, to add power to the ideas expressed.

Read the following passage by Albert Camus, from his novel *The Stranger* (New York: Vintage, 1989), and discuss his worldview.

## Passage 1

1　The chaplain gazed at me with a sort of sadness. I now had my back to the wall and light was flowing over my
2　forehead. He muttered some words I didn't catch; then abruptly asked if he might kiss me.
3　　　　I said, "No."
4　　　　Then he turned, came up to the wall, and slowly drew his hand along it. "Do you really love these earthly
5　things so very much?" he asked in a low voice.
6　　　　I made no reply.
7　　　　For quite a while he kept his eyes averted.
8　　　　His presence was getting more and more irksome, and I was on the point of telling him to go, and leave me
9　in peace, when all of a sudden he swung round on me, and burst out passionately: "No! No! I refuse to believe it.
10　I'm sure you've often wished there was an afterlife."
11　　　　Of course I had, I told him. Everybody has that wish at times. But that had no more importance than
12　wishing to be rich, or to swim very fast, or to have a better-shaped mouth. It was in the same order of things. I was
13　going on in the same vein, when he cut in with a question. How did I picture the life after the grave? I fairly bawled
14　out at him: "A life in which I can remember this life on earth. That's all I want of it." And in the same breath I told
15　him I'd had enough of his company.
16　　　　But, apparently, he had more to say on the subject of God. I went close up to him and made a last attempt
17　to explain that I'd very little time left, and I wasn't going to waste it on God. Then he tried to change the subject by
18　asking me why I hadn't once addressed him as "Father," seeing that he was a priest. That irritated me still more, and
19　I told him he wasn't my father; quite the contrary, he was on the others' side. "No, no, my son," he said, laying his
20　hand on my shoulder. "I'm on your side, though you don't realize it—because your heart is hardened. But I shall
21　pray for you."
22　　　　Then, I don't know how it was, but something seemed to break inside me, and I started yelling at the top of
23　my voice. I hurled insults at him, I told him not to waste his rotten prayers on me; it was better to burn than to
24　disappear. I'd taken him by the neckband of his cassock, and, in a sort of ecstasy of joy and rage, I poured out on
25　him all the thoughts that had been simmering in my brain. He seemed so cocksure, you see. And yet *none* of his
26　certainties was worth one strand of a woman's hair. Living as he did, like a corpse, he couldn't even be sure of being
27　alive. It might look as if my hands were empty. Actually, I was sure of myself, sure about everything, far surer than
28　he; sure of my present life and of the death that was coming. That, no doubt, was all I had; but at least that certainty
29　was something I could get my teeth into—just as it had got its teeth into me. I'd been right, I was still right, I was
30　always right. I'd passed my life in a certain way, and I might have passed it in a different way, if I'd felt like it. I'd
31　acted thus, and I hadn't acted otherwise; I hadn't done *x*, whereas I had done *y* or *z*. And what did that mean? That,
32　all the time, I'd been waiting for this present moment, for that dawn, tomorrow's or another day's, which was to
33　justify me. Nothing, nothing had the least importance and I knew quite well why. He, too, knew why. From the dark
34　horizon of my future a sort of slow, persistent breeze had been blowing toward me, all my life long, from the years
35　that were to come. And on its way that breeze had leveled out all the ideas that people tried to foist on me in the
36　equally unreal years I then was living through. What difference could they make to me, the deaths of others, or a
37　mother's love, or his God; or the way a man decides to live, the fate he thinks he chooses, since one and the same
38　fate was bound to "choose" not only me but thousands of millions of privileged people who, like him, called

39 themselves my brothers. Surely, surely he must see that? Every man alive was privileged; there was only one class
40 of men, the privileged class. All alike would be condemned to die one day; his turn, too, would come like the
41 others'. And what difference could it make if, after being charged with murder, he were executed because he didn't
42 weep at his mother's funeral, since it all came to the same thing in the end? The same thing for Salamano's wife and
43 for Salamano's dog. That little robot woman was as "guilty" as the girl from Paris who had married Masson, or as
44 Marie, who wanted me to marry her. What did it matter if Raymond was as much my pal as Celeste, who was a far
45 worthier man? What did it matter if at this very moment Marie was kissing a new boy friend? As a condemned man
46 himself, couldn't he grasp what I meant by that dark wind blowing from my future? . . .
47     I had been shouting so much that I'd lost my breath, and just then the jailers rushed in and started trying to
48 release the chaplain from my grip. One of them made as if to strike me. The chaplain quietened them down, then
49 gazed at me for a moment without speaking. I could see tears in his eyes. Then he turned and left the cell. Once he'd
50 gone, I felt calm again. But all this excitement had exhausted me and I dropped heavily on to my sleeping plank. I
51 must have had a longish sleep, for, when I woke, the stars were shining down on my face. Sounds of the countryside
52 came faintly in, and the cool night air, veined with smells of earth and salt, fanned my cheeks. The marvelous peace
53 of the sleepbound summer night flooded through me like a tide. Then, just on the edge of daybreak, I heard a
54 steamer's siren. People were starting on a voyage to a world which had ceased to concern me forever.
55     Almost for the first time in many months I thought of my mother. And now, it seemed to me, I understood
56 why at her life's end she had taken on a "fiancé"; why she'd played at making a fresh start. There, too, in that Home
57 where lives were flickering out, the dusk came as a mournful solace. With death so near, Mother must have felt like
58 someone on the brink of freedom, ready to start life all over again. No one, no one in the world had any right to
59 weep for her. And I, too, felt ready to start life all over again. It was as if that great rush of anger had washed me
60 clean, emptied me of hope, and, gazing up at the dark sky spangled with its signs and stars, for the first time, the
61 first, I laid my heart open to the benign indifference of the universe. To feel it so like myself, indeed, so brotherly,
62 made me realize that I'd been happy, and that I was happy still. For all to be accomplished, for me to feel less
63 lonely, all that remained to hope was that on the day of my execution there should be a huge crowd of spectators and
64 that they should greet me with howls of execration.

    (http://archive.org/stream/ost-english-camusalbert-thestranger/CamusAlbert-TheStranger_djvu.txt)

## Passage 2: Student Response

### The Existential Worldview of Camus

1 "You will never be happy if you continue to search for what happiness consists of. You will never live if you are
2 looking for What is the meaning of life." —Albert Camus
3     *The Stranger*, written by Albert Camus, is a book about Meursault's feelings about his mother's death and
4 his crime. Meursault's feelings about life exhibit Albert Camus's existential worldview.
5     Existentialism, a philosophical movement, attempts to validate human knowledge as a basis for reality.
6 Existentialists believe that humans make decisions based on need and function rather than knowledge. These
7 decisions can be good or evil; it just depends if it suits one's needs. Existentialists have quite a selfish view. Every
8 action that they do is for their own behalf. They believe that human nature is made through life choices and that
9 worldly desire is futile. Existentialists view the world as hostile and indifferent. Camus's protagonist Meursault
10 displays these qualities.
11     Meursault believes that he was right, is right, and will always be right. This clearly shows the selfish beliefs
12 of Camus. "I had been right, I was still right, I was always right." Also, Meursault says he took one path in life, but
13 he could have just as well taken any other path. He believes that human nature is made through life choices. He
14 could have had another way of life if he had made different choices. "I had lived my life as one way and I could just
15 as well have lived it another. I had done this and I hadn't done that."
16     Meursault shows that Camus does not care for worldly desires. He does not even care for the world around
17 him. "What did other people's deaths or a mother's love matter to me; what did his God of the lives people choose
18 or the fate they think elect matter to me when we're all elected by the same fate, me and billions of privileged people
19 like him who also called themselves my brothers?"
20     Camus also writes about the indifference of the world. He even relates the indifference to himself. Camus
21 portrays his view through Meursault that human life is unexplainable and apathetic. "I opened myself to the gentle
22 indifference of the world. Finding it so much like myself—so like a brother, really—I felt that I had been happy and
23 that I was happy again."
24     *The Stranger*, written by Albert Camus, is a book about Meursault's feelings after his mother's death and
25 his crime. Meursault's feelings about life exhibit Albert Camus's existential worldview. (Hannah)

1. What is the main plot action in Passage 1?
   A. A condemned man is praying with a priest before he is executed.
   B. A sick, dying man is taking last rites.
   C. A condemned man is arguing with a chaplain/priest who has come to comfort the condemned man
   D. A condemned man misses his mother.

2. How do you characterize the narrator in Passage I?
   A. Omniscient                          C. Third-person objective
   B. Limited omniscient                   D. First person

3. Which of the following chaplain/pastor/priest scenes is similar to Passage 1:
   A. If in vain the good Chaplain sought to impress the young barbarian with ideas of death akin to those conveyed in the skull, dial, and cross-bones on old tombstones; equally futile to all appearance were his efforts to bring home to him the thought of salvation and a Saviour. Billy listened, but less out of awe or reverence perhaps than from a certain natural politeness; doubtless at bottom regarding all that in much the same way that most mariners of his class take any discourse abstract or out of the common tone of the work-a-day world. And this sailor-way of taking clerical discourse is not wholly unlike the way in which the pioneer of Christianity full of transcendent miracles was received long ago on tropic isles by any superior savage so called—a Tahitian say of Captain Cook's time or shortly after that time. Out of natural courtesy he received, but did not appropriate. It was like a gift placed in the palm of an outreached hand upon which the fingers do not close.

   (Herman Melville, *Billy Budd*, chap. 25, University of Virginia E-Texts, https://www.library.virginia.edu/organization/etext/)

   B. And thus, while standing on the scaffold, in this vain show of expiation, Mr. Dimmesdale was overcome with a great horror of mind, as if the universe were gazing at a scarlet token on his naked breast, right over his heart. On that spot, in very truth, there was, and there had long been, the gnawing and poisonous tooth of bodily pain. Without any effort of his will, or power to restrain himself, he shrieked aloud; an outcry that went pealing through the night, and was beaten back from one house to another, and reverberated from the hills in the background; as if a company of devils, detecting so much misery and terror in it, had made a plaything of the sound, and were bandying it to and fro. "It is done!" muttered the minister, covering his face with his hands. "The whole town will awake, and hurry forth, and find me here!"

   (Nathaniel Hawthorne, *The Scarlet Letter*, chap. 12, http://www.bartleby.com/83/12.html)

   C. I had not been seated very long ere a man of a certain venerable robustness entered; immediately as the storm-pelted door flew back upon admitting him, a quick regardful eyeing of him by all the congregation, sufficiently attested that this fine old man was the chaplain. Yes, it was the famous Father Mapple, so called by the whalemen, among whom he was a very great favourite. He had been a sailor and a harpooneer in his youth, but for many years past had dedicated his life to the ministry. At the time I now write of, Father Mapple was in the hardy winter of a healthy old age; that sort of old age which seems merging into a second flowering youth, for among all the fissures of his wrinkles, there shone certain mild gleams of a newly developing bloom—the spring verdure peeping forth even beneath February's snow. No one having previously heard his history, could for the first time behold Father Mapple without the utmost interest, because there were certain engrafted clerical peculiarities about him, imputable to that adventurous maritime life he had led. When he entered I observed that he carried no umbrella, and certainly had not come in his carriage, for his tarpaulin hat ran down with melting sleet, and his great pilot cloth jacket seemed almost to drag him to the floor with the weight of the water it had absorbed. However, hat and coat and overshoes were one by one removed, and hung up in a little space in an adjacent corner; when, arrayed in a decent suit, he quietly approached the pulpit.

   (Herman Melville, *Moby Dick*, chap. 8, www.gutenberg.org)

   D. The congregation being fully assembled, now, the bell rang once more, to warn laggards and stragglers, and then a solemn hush fell upon the church which was only broken by the tittering and whispering of the choir in the gallery. The choir always tittered and whispered all through service. There was once a church choir that was not ill-bred, but I have forgotten where it was, now. It was a great many years ago, and I can scarcely remember anything about it, but I think it was in some foreign country. The minister gave out the hymn, and read it through with a relish, in a peculiar style which was much admired in that part of the country. His voice began on a medium key and climbed steadily up till it reached a certain point, where it bore with strong emphasis upon the topmost word and then plunged down as if from a spring-board.

   (Mark Twain, *Tom Sawyer*, chap. 5, www.gutenberg.org).

4. The chaplain in Passage 1 is a
   A. Protagonist
   B. Antagonist
   C. Foil
   D. Narrator

5. What rhetorical device is used in Passage 1?
   A. Simile
   B. Antithesis
   C. Paradox
   D. Stream of consciousness

6. The author of Passage 2 is
   A. Opposed to existentialism
   B. A fan of Camus
   C. Likes Camus but likes Franz Kafka more
   D. Is neutral toward existentialism

7. At what point in Passage 2 does the student switch from an analysis of Camus's novel to a criticism of existentialism?
   A. Lines 1–3
   B. Lines 5-10
   C. Lines 28-37
   D. Lines 79–82

8. A better ending to this passage might be
   A. The protagonist experienced an uneventful execution, which to the self-centered, egotistical, existential Meursault made sense.
   B. Nothing mattered to Meursault; nothing mattered to anyone.
   C. Meursault wept in terror and remorse; but it was too late.
   D. Nothing mattered to Meursault—not as he entered oblivion.

9. Which of the following passages is written by Camus?

   A. Highbury, the large and populous village, almost amounting to a town, to which Hartfield, in spite of its separate lawn, and shrubberies, and name, did really belong, afforded her no equals. The Woodhouses were first in consequence there. All looked up to them. She had many acquaintance in the place, for her father was universally civil, but not one among them who could be accepted in lieu of Miss Taylor for even half a day. It was a melancholy change; and Emma could not but sigh over it, and wish for impossible things, till her father awoke, and made it necessary to be cheerful. His spirits required support. He was a nervous man, easily depressed; fond of every body that he was used to, and hating to part with them; hating change of every kind.

   B. Think what it must be for a dying man, trapped behind hundreds of walls all sizzling with heat, while the whole population, sitting in cafes or hanging on the telephone, is discussing shipments, bills of lading, discounts! It will then be obvious what discomfort attends death, even modern death, when it waylays you under such conditions in a dry place.

   C. I am by birth a Genevese, and my family is one of the most distinguished of that republic. My ancestors had been for many years counsellors and syndics, and my father had filled several public situations with honour and reputation. He was respected by all who knew him for his integrity and indefatigable attention to public business. He passed his younger days perpetually occupied by the affairs of his country; a variety of circumstances had prevented his marrying early, nor was it until the decline of life that he became a husband and the father of a family.

   D. But he, Siddhartha, was not a source of joy for himself, he found no delight in himself. Walking the rosy paths of the fig tree garden, sitting in the bluish shade of the grove of contemplation, washing his limbs daily in the bath of repentance, sacrificing in the dim shade of the mango forest, his gestures of perfect decency, everyone's love and joy, he still lacked all joy in his heart. Dreams and restless thoughts came into his mind, flowing from the water of the river, sparkling from the stars of the night, melting from the beams of the sun, dreams came to him and a restlessness of the soul, fuming from the sacrifices, breathing forth from the verses of the Rig-Veda, being infused into him, drop by drop, from the teachings of the old Brahmans.

10. What score would Passage 2 receive? __

# Lesson 4
## Reading: Document-Based Analysis

**The Monroe Doctrine**
**James Monroe (1823)**

### Seventh Annual Message to Congress

1  A precise knowledge of our relations with foreign powers as respects our negotiations and transactions with each is
2  thought to be particularly necessary. Equally necessary is it that we should form a just estimate of our resources,
3  revenue, and progress in every kind of improvement connected with the national prosperity and public defense. It is
4  by rendering justice to other nations that we may expect it from them. It is by our ability to resent injuries and
5  redress wrongs that we may avoid them. . . .
6  At the proposal of the Russian Imperial Government, made through the minister of the Emperor residing
7  here, a full power and instructions have been transmitted to the minister of the United States at St. Petersburg to
8  arrange by amicable negotiation the respective rights and interests of the two nations on the North West coast of this
9  continent. A similar proposal had been made by His Imperial Majesty to the Government of Great Britain, which has
10  likewise been acceded to. The Government of the United States has been desirous by this friendly proceeding of
11  manifesting the great value which they have invariably attached to the friendship of the Emperor and their solicitude
12  to cultivate the best understanding with his Government. In the discussions to which this interest has given rise and
13  in the arrangements by which they may terminate the occasion has been judged proper for asserting, as a principle in
14  which the rights and interests of the United States are involved, that the American continents, by the free and
15  independent condition which they have assumed and maintain, are henceforth not to be considered as subjects for
16  future colonization by any European powers. . . .
17  A strong hope has been long entertained, founded on the heroic struggle of the Greeks, that they would
18  succeed in their contest and resume their equal station among the nations of the earth. It is believed that the whole
19  civilized world take a deep interest in their welfare. Although no power has declared in their favor, yet *none*
20  according to our information, has taken part against them. Their cause and their name have protected them from
21  dangers which might ere this have overwhelmed any other people. The ordinary calculations of interest and of
22  acquisition with a view to aggrandizement, which mingles so much in the transactions of nations, seem to have had
23  no effect in regard to them. From the facts which have come to our knowledge there is good cause to believe that
24  their enemy has lost forever all dominion over them; that Greece will become again an independent nation. That she
25  may obtain that rank is the object of our most ardent wishes.
26  It was stated at the commencement of the last session that a great effort was then making in Spain and
27  Portugal to improve the condition of the people of those countries, and that it appeared to be conducted with
28  extraordinary moderation. It need scarcely be remarked that the result has been so far very different from what was
29  then anticipated. Of events in that quarter of the globe, with which we have so much intercourse and from which we
30  derive our origin, we have always been anxious and interested spectators.
31  The citizens of the United States cherish sentiments the most friendly in favor of the liberty and happiness
32  of their fellow men on that side of the Atlantic. In the wars of the European powers in matters relating to themselves
33  we have never taken any part, nor does it comport with our policy so to do.
34  It is only when our rights are invaded or seriously menaced that we resent injuries or make preparation for
35  our defense. With the movements in this hemisphere we are of necessity more immediately connected, and by
36  causes which must be obvious to all enlightened and impartial observers.
37  The political system of the allied powers is essentially different in this respect from that of America. This
38  difference proceeds from that which exists in their respective Governments; and to the defense of our own, which
39  has been achieved by the loss of so much blood and treasure, and matured by the wisdom of their most enlightened
40  citizens, and under which we have enjoyed unexampled felicity, this whole nation is devoted.
41  We owe it, therefore, to candor and to the amicable relations existing between the United States and those
42  powers to declare that we should consider any attempt on their part to extend their system to any portion of this
43  hemisphere as dangerous to our peace and safety. With the existing colonies or dependencies of any European
44  power we have not interfered and shall not interfere, but with the Governments who have declared their
45  independence and maintained it, and whose independence we have, on great consideration and on just principles,
46  acknowledged, we could not view any interposition for the purpose of oppressing them, or controlling in any other

47  manner their destiny, by any European power in any other light than as the manifestation of an unfriendly
48  disposition toward the United States.
49      In the war between those new Governments and Spain we declared our neutrality at the time of their
50  recognition, and to this we have adhered, and shall continue to adhere, provided *none* shall occur which, in the
51  judgment of the competent authorities of this Government, shall make a corresponding change on the part of the
52  United States indispensable to their security.
53      The late events in Spain and Portugal shew that Europe is still unsettled. Of this important fact no stronger
54  proof can be adduced than that the allied powers should have thought it proper, on any principle satisfactory to
55  themselves, to have interposed by force in the internal concerns of Spain. To what extent such interposition may be
56  carried, on the same principle, is a question in which all independent powers whose governments differ from theirs
57  are interested, even those most remote, and surely *none* more so than the United States.
58      Our policy in regard to Europe, which was adopted at an early stage of the wars which have so long
59  agitated that quarter of the globe, nevertheless remains the same, which is, not to interfere in the internal concerns of
60  any of its powers; to consider the government de facto as the legitimate government for us; to cultivate friendly
61  relations with it, and to preserve those relations by a frank, firm, and manly policy, meeting in all instances the just
62  claims of a very power, submitting to injuries from *none*.
63      But in regard to those continents circumstances are eminently and conspicuously different. It is impossible
64  that the allied powers should extend their political system to any portion of either continent without endangering our
65  peace and happiness; nor can anyone believe that our southern brethren, if left to themselves, would adopt it of their
66  own accord. It is equally impossible, therefore, that we should behold such interposition in any form with
67  indifference. If we look to the comparative strength and resources of Spain and those new Governments, and their
68  distance from each other, it must be obvious that she can never subdue them. It is still the true policy of the United
69  States to leave the parties to themselves, in the hope that other powers will pursue the same course. . . .

(http://www.presidency.ucsb.edu/ws/index.php?pid=29465&st=&st1=)

1.  What is the thesis of this passage?
    A.  Lines 1–5
    B.  Lines 31–32
    C.  Lines 38–40
    D.  Lines 41–43

2.  What nations most concern Monroe?
    A.  Canada
    B.  Asian
    C.  European
    D.  South American

3.  What reason does Monroe offer to support his argument?
    A.  Lines 31–32
    B.  Lines 37–40
    C.  Lines 50–54
    D.  Lines 59–63

4.  Which of the following arguments would be a violation of the Monroe Doctrine?
    I.   The Cuban Missile Crisis
    II.  Santa Anna attacking the Alamo
    III. The Spanish ownership of Cuba
    IV.  The French invasion of Mexico in 1862

        A.  I and II
        B.  II and III
        C.  III and IV
        D.  I and IV

## Words in Context

1.  What is the meaning of *amicable* in Line 41?
    A.  Hungry
    B.  Friendly
    C.  Obstinate
    D.  Vague

2.  What is the meaning of *eminently* in Line 63?
    A.  Signally
    B.  Famously
    C.  Marginally
    D.  Unhappily

# Lesson 5

## Math: Algebra, Arithmetic Problem Solving and Data Analysis, and Passport to Advanced Math

### Algebra

1. The greater of two numbers is twice the less, and the sum of the numbers is 129. What are the numbers?
   A. 23, 46     B. 43, 86     C. 33, 66     D. 42, 84

2. A man walked 24 miles in a day. If he walked twice as far in the forenoon as in the afternoon, how far did he walk in the afternoon?
   A. 8 miles     B. 6 miles     C. 4 miles     D. 12 miles

3. If a coin collector receives 2 cents for his first Lincoln-head cent, 4 cents for his second one, 8 cents for the third one, and so on for 12 sales, what will his gross amount be?
   A. $71.80     B. $61.70     C. $80.89     D. $81.90

4. If the population of a small town is 10, 000, and increases 10% a year for four years, what will be its population at the end of the four years?
   A. 10, 400     B. 14,000     C. 14, 641     D. D. 16,000

5. What is the best way to solve this problem? A cistern has two pipes. By one of them it can be filled 6 hours sooner than by the other, and by both together in 4 hours. Find the time it will take each pipe alone to fill it.

   A. Let $x$ = the number of hours it takes the smaller pipe. Then $x - 6$ = the number of hours it takes the larger pipe. Therefore    + ── the part both can fill in one hour.

   B. Let $x$ = the number of hours it takes the smaller pipe. Then $x - 6$ = the number of hours it takes the larger pipe. Therefore    + ── the part both can fill in one hour.

   C. Let $x$ = the number of hours it takes the larger pipe. Then $x - 6$ = the number of hours it takes the larger pipe. Therefore    +         = the part both can fill in one hour.

   D. Let $x$ = the number of hours it takes the smaller pipe. Then $x - 6$ = the number of hours it takes the larger pipe. Therefore    + ── the part both can fill in one hour.

6. What is the answer?
   A. It takes one pipe 6 hrs. and the other 3 hrs.
   B. It takes one pipe 8 hrs. and the other 4 hrs.
   C. It takes one pipe 16 hrs. and the other 8 hrs.
   D. It takes one pipe 12 hrs. and the other 6 hrs.

### Data Analysis

|  | Unemployed | Employed | Total |
|---|---|---|---|
| Americans | 20 | 69 | 89 |
| Germans | 39 | 42 | 81 |
| Swedes | 59 | 111 | 170 |

What is the closest percentage of the unemployed (among all nationalities)?
   A. 35%          B. 28%          C. 33%          D. 53%

# Chapter 8   An Unclenched Moment
# 2 Chronicles 20

> *Memory Verse:* "You will not have to fight this battle. Take up your positions;
> stand firm and see the deliverance the LORD will give you." ——2 Chronicles 20:17

As the sun teasingly nestled beneath the western horizon, King Jehoshaphat's short reign was also sinking. "God," he cried, "What am I to do?" God was going to tell Jehoshaphat to do some things he would rather not do. Time-honored solutions to problems of the past were not going to solve future problems. And I am sure that he wondered if there was anyone else up there!

Young Jehoshaphat, a good king himself but the successor of evil Asa, shivered as he considered this new challenge: earlier that day he had heard that the dreaded Moabites, Ammonites, and their allies were invading Judah. Any one of these dreaded Arabian tribes was a formidable enemy—and all of them were attacking tiny Judah!

The Moabites and Ammonites were too much for poor Jehoshaphat. He had the good sense at least to know it. So he did what we all should do when we face obstacles: he turned to time-honored ways to solve his problems.

Like all previous generations, Jehoshaphat naturally looked to old solutions to solve problems. No doubt he asked the army, "Can you defeat these armies?" After all, Deborah and Gideon had led the scrappy Hebrew forces to victory once before, so why not now? What they needed, Jehoshaphat clearly understood, was an old-time miracle. Perhaps the army could provide this miracle.

But this time they could not. The Arabian hordes were too much—and probably would have been too much for Gideon, Deborah, and even Samson or King David: the old solutions would not work.

Then he must have asked the priests, "What can you do to help me?" They had nothing to offer. No known solution would bring salvation. Jehoshaphat was really in trouble this time, and he knew it.

America needs to know that Jehoshaphat's God in general is being ignored. America has become an experiment in futility. The positive liberal state simply has not worked. We have tried to buy our way out of trouble; we have tried to fight our way out of trouble. And it is not working.

Jehoshaphat tried a creative solution: he did nothing—except praise God. He assembled all the nation into the outer court of the temple, raised his hands, and praised God. He cried. He screamed. He pleaded. And God answered. But not in the way that Jehoshaphat wanted and expected. He would send no Moses or David or Samson. No, God himself would go before the people and would bring deliverance.

Can you imagine? Thousands of men, women, and children, crying, all at once, asking God to deliver them. Can you imagine what will happen if thousands of us gather at the Graham Crusade and do the same? They called God by all of his names: Adonai, Elohim, Yahweh. The Hebrew word for "praise" means "clarity." Their hue and cry sounded like anything but clarity. Their enemies were overwhelming and fast approaching, solutions were muddled or nonexistent, resources were inadequate, and their faith was ambivalent. The enemies seemed so real and God so far away.

When our world is crumbling, we tend to grasp for the familiar and the simple. At the end of his life, Karl Barth, the great German theologian whose dogmatics changed twentieth-century theology, was asked for the essentials of the Christian faith. He quietly and quickly responded, "Jesus loves me, this I know, for the Bible tells me so."

Jehoshaphat's community was in trouble, and they needed clarity. Judah's circumstances were muddled, their resources were inadequate, their enemies were overwhelming them, and their faith was at best ambivalent. But God was alive and real and uncompromised. And God was crystal clear about his relationship with Jehoshaphat and Judah: They were God's chosen people.

Likewise, the church is the property of Yahweh God, and the world had better keep its hands off! In a real sense, we are the "only show" in town, so the rest of societal institutions (e.g., social, economic, and political) need to take notice.

As Jehoshaphat's world crumbled, he grasped for the only real thing left (other than the Arabians!): his historical, reliable, faith in God. As his world fell apart, Jehoshaphat raised his hands, reaching for the only clarity he had left. In childlike openness, he cried out to God.

Our resources may dwindle, we may flow from anxiety to depression and then back; yet whatever our life situation may be, our Lord will never change. He is always there for us. And, I hope, before the Arabians overwhelm us in whatever life situation we may find ourselves, that we will reach for that very same God who has been there for us time and time again. The God of our fathers and mothers, the God who saved us.

The cross, with all its challenges and sacrifice, is still the only clarity we have. The love of God in Christ is the only thing that makes sense during hard times.

How do Jehoshaphat and the nation of Judah praise God? Using the most honorific title they know, they address him in a respectful manner, "O God of our Fathers," and they do so at their most holy of places, the temple. Reminding their covenanted God of his love and promises, the assembly respectfully asks God a battery of rhetorical questions. God is not upset by our hard questions. Then they mention past triumphs, but do not embrace them in harmful nostalgia, because they are most concerned about who God is, not about what God does. Praise takes us into God's presence, and we no longer need to linger around the outer court. True praise is adoration of the character of God, not a mere recital of past favors.

Finally, Jehoshaphat's prayer ends as it begins: with an open admission of dependency. Not exactly a revelation considering Jehoshaphat's predicament—and our own!—but nonetheless an important point. When we are in trouble, it is a good ideal unambiguously to place ourselves squarely at God's feet. Then a moment of potential destruction can become an unclenched moment of victory.

So, as the Arabians approach, Jehoshaphat does not go to the army, nor to the religious authorities: He goes straight to the Boss. "Then the Spirit of the LORD came upon Jahaziel," and he said, "Do not be afraid or discouraged because . . . the battle is not yours but God's!"

This last statement should be a watershed for our life decisions. We understand, finally, that the battle is not ours: it is God's! And perhaps now we understand Paul's contention that "we are more than conquerors with Christ Jesus; . . . who dares to stand against the people of God?" (cf. Romans 8:37–39).

Finally, the rest is rather anticlimactic. Jehoshaphat sends the priest before the nation and, the enemies of Judah were annihilated.

I am no naive person. I know there is much hard work left. Nehemiah did not rebuild the walls of Jerusalem in one lifetime. But let us begin by praising God! And one day the next generation will say about us: They may not have done this or that, but they knew how to praise God!

## Journal Question

What impossible obstacles do you face in your life? Try a Jehoshaphat solution!

# Lesson 1
## Evidence-Based Reading and Writing

### Literary Choice

Helen Adams Keller was an author, humanitarian, political activist, and lecturer. She was the first deaf-blind person to earn a bachelor of arts degree. Charles Dickens was a prolific and popular nineteenth-century British author.

### Passage 1

1  It is with a kind of fear that I begin to write the history of my life. I have, as it were, a superstitious hesitation in
2  lifting the veil that clings about my childhood like a golden mist. The task of writing an autobiography is a difficult
3  one. When I try to classify my earliest impressions, I find that fact and fancy look alike across the years that link the
4  past with the present. The woman paints the child's experiences in her own fantasy. A few impressions stand out
5  vividly from the first years of my life; but "the shadows of the prison-house are on the rest." Besides, many of the
6  joys and sorrows of childhood have lost their poignancy; and many incidents of vital importance in my early
7  education have been forgotten in the excitement of great discoveries. In order, therefore, not to be tedious I shall try
8  to present in a series of sketches only the episodes that seem to me to be the most interesting and important.
9  　　　I was born on June 27, 1880, in Tuscumbia, a little town of northern Alabama.
10 　　　The family on my father's side is descended from Caspar Keller, a native of Switzerland, who settled in
11 Maryland. One of my Swiss ancestors was the first teacher of the deaf in Zurich and wrote a book on the subject of
12 their education—rather a singular coincidence; though it is true that there is no king who has not had a slave among
13 his ancestors, and no slave who has not had a king among his.
14 　　　My grandfather, Caspar Keller's son, "entered" large tracts of land in Alabama and finally settled there. I
15 have been told that once a year he went from Tuscumbia to Philadelphia on horseback to purchase supplies for the
16 plantation, and my aunt has in her possession many of the letters to his family, which give charming and vivid
17 accounts of these trips.
18 　　　My Grandmother Keller was a daughter of one of Lafayette's aides, Alexander Moore, and granddaughter
19 of Alexander Spotswood, an early Colonial Governor of Virginia. She was also second cousin to Robert E. Lee.
20 　　　My father, Arthur H. Keller, was a captain in the Confederate Army, and my mother, Kate Adams, was his
21 second wife and many years younger. Her grandfather, Benjamin Adams, married Susanna E. Goodhue, and lived in
22 Newbury, Massachusetts, for many years. Their son, Charles Adams, was born in Newburyport, Massachusetts, and
23 moved to Helena, Arkansas. When the Civil War broke out, he fought on the side of the South and became a
24 brigadier-general. He married Lucy Helen Everett, who belonged to the same family of Everetts as Edward Everett
25 and Dr. Edward Everett Hale. After the war was over the family moved to Memphis, Tennessee.
26 　　　I lived, up to the time of the illness that deprived me of my sight and hearing, in a tiny house consisting of a
27 large square room and a small one, in which the servant slept. It is a custom in the South to build a small house near
28 the homestead as an annex to be used on occasion. Such a house my father built after the Civil War, and when he
29 married my mother they went to live in it. It was completely covered with vines, climbing roses and honeysuckles.
30 From the garden it looked like an arbour. The little porch was hidden from view by a screen of yellow roses and
31 Southern smilax. It was the favourite haunt of humming-birds and bees.
32 　　　The Keller homestead, where the family lived, was a few steps from our little rose-bower. It was called
33 "Ivy Green" because the house and the surrounding trees and fences were covered with beautiful English ivy. Its
34 old-fashioned garden was the paradise of my childhood.
35 　　　Even in the days before my teacher came, I used to feel along the square stiff boxwood hedges, and, guided
36 by the sense of smell would find the first violets and lilies. There, too, after a fit of temper, I went to find comfort
37 and to hide my hot face in the cool leaves and grass. What joy it was to lose myself in that garden of flowers, to
38 wander happily from spot to spot, until, coming suddenly upon a beautiful vine, I recognized it by its leaves and
39 blossoms, and knew it was the vine which covered the tumble-down summer-house at the farther end of the garden!
40 Here, also, were trailing clematis, drooping jessamine, and some rare sweet flowers called butterfly lilies, because
41 their fragile petals resemble butterflies' wings. But the roses—they were loveliest of all. Never have I found in the
42 greenhouses of the North such heart-satisfying roses as the climbing roses of my southern home. They used to hang
43 in long festoons from our porch, filling the whole air with their fragrance, untainted by any earthy smell; and in the
44 early morning, washed in the dew, they felt so soft, so pure, I could not help wondering if they did not resemble the
45 asphodels of God's garden.

46　　　The beginning of my life was simple and much like every other little life. I came, I saw, I conquered, as the
47　first baby in the family always does. There was the usual amount of discussion as to a name for me. The first baby in
48　the family was not to be lightly named, every one was emphatic about that. My father suggested the name of
49　Mildred Campbell, an ancestor whom he highly esteemed, and he declined to take any further part in the discussion.
50　My mother solved the problem by giving it as her wish that I should be called after her mother, whose maiden name
51　was Helen Everett. But in the excitement of carrying me to church my father lost the name on the way, very
52　naturally, since it was one in which he had declined to have a part. When the minister asked him for it, he just
53　remembered that it had been decided to call me after my grandmother, and he gave her name as Helen Adams.

54　　　I am told that while I was still in long dresses I showed many signs of an eager, self-asserting disposition.
55　Everything that I saw other people do I insisted upon imitating. At six months I could pipe out "How d'ye," and one
56　day I attracted every one's attention by saying "Tea, tea, tea" quite plainly. Even after my illness I remembered one
57　of the words I had learned in these early months. It was the word "water," and I continued to make some sound for
58　that word after all other speech was lost. I ceased making the sound "wah-wah" only when I learned to spell the
59　word.

60　　　They tell me I walked the day I was a year old. My mother had just taken me out of the bath-tub and was
61　holding me in her lap, when I was suddenly attracted by the flickering shadows of leaves that danced in the sunlight
62　on the smooth floor. I slipped from my mother's lap and almost ran toward them. The impulse gone, I fell down and
63　cried for her to take me up in her arms.

64　　　These happy days did not last long. One brief spring, musical with the song of robin and mocking-bird, one
65　summer rich in fruit and roses, one autumn of gold and crimson sped by and left their gifts at the feet of an eager,
66　delighted child. Then, in the dreary month of February, came the illness which closed my eyes and ears and plunged
67　me into the unconsciousness of a new-born baby. They called it acute congestion of the stomach and brain. The
68　doctor thought I could not live. Early one morning, however, the fever left me as suddenly and mysteriously as it
69　had come. There was great rejoicing in the family that morning, but no one, not even the doctor, knew that I should
70　never see or hear again.

71　　　I fancy I still have confused recollections of that illness. I especially remember the tenderness with which
72　my mother tried to soothe me in my waling hours of fret and pain, and the agony and bewilderment with which I
73　awoke after a tossing half sleep, and turned my eyes, so dry and hot, to the wall away from the once-loved light,
74　which came to me dim and yet more dim each day. But, except for these fleeting memories, if, indeed, they be
75　memories, it all seems very unreal, like a nightmare. Gradually I got used to the silence and darkness that
76　surrounded me and forgot that it had ever been different, until she came—my teacher—who was to set my spirit
77　free. But during the first nineteen months of my life I had caught glimpses of broad, green fields, a luminous sky,
78　trees and flowers which the darkness that followed could not wholly blot out. If we have once seen, "the day is ours,
79　and what the day has shown."

(Helen Keller, *The Story of My Life*,
http://www.gutenberg.org/files/2397/2397-h/2397-h.htm#link2HCH0001)

## Close Reading

1. Why is the author in Passage 1 hesitant to write her autobiography?
   A. She does not want to appear to be too proud.
   B. She does not remember her youth.
   C. It is hard to be a deaf-blind person and write an autobiography.
   D. She wants to recall the important things, but she is not sure that she will be able to separate the important events from the unimportant events.

2. Which of the following statements is true about Passage 1?
   A. Helen was born blind and deaf.
   B. Her father wished he had had a son.
   C. Helen was ill about age one and lost her sight and hearing.
   D. Helen was born outside Boston, Massachusetts.

3. What was an early sensory memory?
   A. Ice cream on her front porch
   B. Violets and lilies
   C. Burning barns as General Sherman marched through Alabama
   D. Baked corn bread and turnip greens

4. What would be a logical next step in this autobiography in Passage 1?

A. Helen will struggle with her disability.

B. Helen will be sent to live with her aunt.

C. The disability will have no affect on her.

D. Helen does not remember anything after that moment.

5. What behaviors indicate that Helen is a very intelligent child/person?

A. She rides a bike when she is two.

B. She is reading and writing when she is three.

C. She is coordinated and has a vivid memory, a memory that she can record on paper.

D. She is affectionate to everyone.

## Passage 2

1  Whether I shall turn out to be the hero of my own life, or whether that station will be held by anybody else, these
2  pages must show. To begin my life with the beginning of my life, I record that I was born (as I have been informed
3  and believe) on a Friday, at twelve o'clock at night. It was remarked that the clock began to strike, and I began to
4  cry, simultaneously.

5  In consideration of the day and hour of my birth, it was declared by the nurse, and by some sage women in
6  the neighbourhood who had taken a lively interest in me several months before there was any possibility of our
7  becoming personally acquainted, first, that I was destined to be unlucky in life; and secondly, that I was privileged
8  to see ghosts and spirits; both these gifts inevitably attaching, as they believed, to all unlucky infants of either
9  gender, born towards the small hours on a Friday night.

10  I need say nothing here, on the first head, because nothing can show better than my history whether that
11  prediction was verified or falsified by the result. On the second branch of the question, I will only remark, that
12  unless I ran through that part of my inheritance while I was still a baby, I have not come into it yet. But I do not at
13  all complain of having been kept out of this property; and if anybody else should be in the present enjoyment of it,
14  he is heartily welcome to keep it.

15  I was born with a caul, which was advertised for sale, in the newspapers, at the low price of fifteen guineas.
16  Whether sea-going people were short of money about that time, or were short of faith and preferred cork jackets, I
17  don't know; all I know is, that there was but one solitary bidding, and that was from an attorney connected with the
18  bill-broking business, who offered two pounds in cash, and the balance in sherry, but declined to be guaranteed from
19  drowning on any higher bargain. Consequently the advertisement was withdrawn at a dead loss—for as to sherry,
20  my poor dear mother's own sherry was in the market then—and ten years afterwards, the caul was put up in a raffle
21  down in our part of the country, to fifty members at half-a-crown a head, the winner to spend five shillings. I was
22  present myself, and I remember to have felt quite uncomfortable and confused, at a part of myself being disposed of
23  in that way. The caul was won, I recollect, by an old lady with a hand-basket, who, very reluctantly, produced from
24  it the stipulated five shillings, all in halfpence, and twopence halfpenny short—as it took an immense time and a
25  great waste of arithmetic, to endeavour without any effect to prove to her. It is a fact which will be long remembered
26  as remarkable down there, that she was never drowned, but died triumphantly in bed, at ninety-two. I have
27  understood that it was, to the last, her proudest boast, that she never had been on the water in her life, except upon a
28  bridge; and that over her tea (to which she was extremely partial) she, to the last, expressed her indignation at the
29  impiety of mariners and others, who had the presumption to go "meandering" about the world. It was in vain to
30  represent to her that some conveniences, tea perhaps included, resulted from this objectionable practice. She always
31  returned, with greater emphasis and with an instinctive knowledge of the strength of her objection, "Let us have no
32  meandering."

(Charles Dickens, *David Copperfield*, chap. 1,

http://www.gutenberg.org/files/766/766-h/766-h.htm#link2HCH0001).

## Close Reading

1. These two passages are similar in what ways?
   I.   Both are autobiographical.
   II.  Both begin at birth.
   III. Both had terrible childhoods.

   A. I                    C. III                    E. II and III
   B. II                   D. I and II

2. How are these two passages are different?

   I.   The second passage is concerned more about the historical importance of his beginning.
   II.  The second passage occurs in England.
   III. The second narrator is from a poorer family than the first narrator.

   A. I                    C. III
   B. II                   D. All

## Source Analysis

1. Based on Passage 1, the reader can make the following assumptions about the author:

   I.   The author loved and was loved by her parents.
   II.  The author will never amount to anything.
   III. The author will triumph over all adversity someday.

   A. I                        D. I and III
   B. I and II                 E. NONE of Above
   C. III

2. What is a plausible prediction based on the second passage?

   I.   Something catastrophic will occur.
   II.  After a long ordeal the narrator will succeed in life.
   III. The narrator will no doubt fail in whatever he does.

   A. I                        C. III
   B. II                       D. I and III

# Lesson 2
## Critical Reading and Writing

### Command of Evidence

Read the following passage and answer accompanying questions:

**A Book Review of Geoffrey Parker's *The Global Crisis***

1  What is the cause of global warming? What potential crises will it cause? What is ahead? Can it be avoided? The
2  world at the current time is involved in a passionate love/hate relationship with the earth's climate that began with
3  the release of Al Gore's robust if not completely accurate *An Inconvenient Truth*, a video aimed at increasing the
4  awareness of global warming. Since then, with the "go green" movement and climate awareness included in many
5  schools' curriculum, climate change is at the forefront of everyone's mind. In 2013 in the midst of continuing
6  climate-change rage, Geoffrey Parker, a recipient of the Heineken Prize for History and a European history
7  professor, wrote *The Global Crisis* in hopes that "this study will help inform the current debate on the consequences
8  for human society of sudden climatic change" (Department of History, Ohio State University). In *The Global Crisis*,
9  Geoffrey Parker moves away from the worst-case scenario approach to climate change reminiscent of Rachel
10 Carson's *Silent Spring*, and instead focuses on climate change in relation to how it has historically affected societies.
11        "Currently, most attempts to predict the consequences of climate change extrapolate from recent trends; but
12 another methodology exists. Instead of hitting 'fast forward,' we can 'rewind the tape of History' and study the
13 genesis, impact, and consequences of past catastrophes." (Parker, Location 407). Geoffrey Parker does this by
14 focusing on a period of extremes in the climate and social structures, spanning the years of 1618–80 and dubbed by
15 historians as "The General Crisis" (Location 438). Parker focuses on the years of 1640–50 since these were the years
16 of the "Little Ice Age," a time when the earth's temperatures dropped dramatically, causing an imbalance in the
17 environment that resulted in a bizarre increase of natural disasters. "Abnormal climatic conditions lasted from the
18 1640s until the 1690s—the longest as well as the most severe episode of global cooling recorded in the entire
19 Holocene Era—leading climatologists to dub this period 'The Little Ice Age'" (Locations 457–58). As a historian
20 first and foremost, Parker tirelessly shows the correlations between the climate complications and consequential
21 political upheavals. A grossly simplified version of Parker's argument is given by Hugh Macdonald, writing for the
22 Scottish branch of *The Herald*: "The link between weather conditions and revolutions is gently teased out but,
23 bluntly, it can be explained thus: the fall of the Ming dynasty was because of banditry. The rise of banditry was
24 because of famine. The famine was caused by bad weather, whether extreme cold or heavy rain or no rain at all.
25 These are my words. Parker is never this inelegant. Rather, he is patient, deliberate and scientific" (Geoffrey Parker,
26 *Global Crisis: War, Climate Change and Catastrophe in the Seventeenth Century* (New Haven: Yale University
27 Press, 2013).
28        Patient, deliberate, and scientific are the three best adjectives to describe this work. Parker takes no
29 shortcuts: in a 700-page narrative he makes his case and then presents the evidence. His citations contain an
30 exhaustive and varied collection of quotes from books, pamphlets, and journals of historians, scientists, clergymen,
31 laymen, and serfs as well as artwork from around the world that testifies to the certainty of the global crisis of the
32 1600s.
33        "Thus a Seville shopkeeper lamented that during the first six months of 1649 'the sun did not shine once,
34 . . . and if it came out it was pale and yellow, or else much too red, which caused great fear.' Thousands of miles to
35 the east, Korea's royal astronomers reported darkened skies during the daytime on 38 occasions during the
36 seventeenth century" (Location 1026).
37        *The Global Crisis* is inundated with examples such as this one; after every assertion Parker makes, he
38 quickly backs it up, filling the following pages with copious examples from historical data, thus giving himself very
39 strong credibility. Credibility is in fact the strongest trait of this book. *The Global Crisis* rests completely on "two
40 distinct categories of proxy data: a 'natural archive' and a 'human archive'" (Location 407). In the very beginning of
41 the book, Parker, ever the patient writer, breaks down both archives, showing exactly what he is using to compose
42 his research, which further shows that his findings are scientifically solid. Parker also gains credibility in another
43 way; he is extremely qualified to speak on the subject by nature of his extensive study of history. Parker, a native of
44 Britain, earned his BA, PhD, and LittD in history at Christ's College, Cambridge. He has taught at numerous well-
45 known universities such as Cambridge, St. Andrews, and Yale, to name a few. He specializes in social, political, and

46  military history of Europe from 1500 to 1650 and has written numerous books on this subject, his best-known being
47  *The Military Revolution*, which won two book prizes (Department of History, OSU). Geoffrey Parker then is no
48  stranger to the process of historical research and medieval history and comes to *The Global Crisis* fully prepared and
49  fully accredited.

50  Because of this, *The Global Crisis* has received a warm response from critiques. On *The Wall Street
51  Journal*, Brendan Simms writes, "This is a grim story, but Mr. Parker tells it with verve. His 700 pages of densely
52  printed text require stamina, but the reading is eased by enlivening narrative snapshots and a global cast of
53  remarkable characters" (Simms, "When Winter Came for Kings," May 31, 2013). The *Yale University Press* joins in
54  the praise with these words: "Parker's demonstration of the link between climate change and worldwide catastrophe
55  350 years ago stands as an extraordinary historical achievement. And the contemporary implications of his study are
56  equally important: are we at all prepared today for the catastrophes that climate change could bring tomorrow?" The
57  universal praise for this book is testimony of Parker's remarkable ability as a historian to serve the facts without a
58  heavy dressing of his opinions. This keeps his credibility high and the praise high.

59  For most of *The Global Crisis*, Parker does not present a particular argument unless it is that the global
60  crisis did occur, but even then by the second chapter even the most skeptical Montaigne becomes a global crisis
61  believer due to Parker's systematic, overwhelming evidence that simply dares to be defied. Still, this writer finds
62  this book to be an extremely enlightening read, not because of the obvious content but because of the subtext which
63  is the implications of Parker's research. There are two major implications of Parker's work that can be applied to the
64  modern discussion of global warming. The first implication is found in the final chapter of Parker's work, in which
65  he writes, "Societies can either 'pay to prepare,' and commit substantial resources now to avoid far greater costs
66  later, or else 'learn to live with increased' risks" (Location 17831). What Parker is saying is that climate change has
67  occurred in the past, and climate change will occur again in the future; the only thing that is up to humans is how we
68  will respond and whether or not a climate change will destroy us; thus our choices are to "be prepared" or "live with
69  the risks." The modern world leaders have decided to be prepared via geoengineering. According to the Oxford
70  Geoengineering Programme, geoengineering can be described as "the deliberate large-scale intervention in the
71  Earth's natural systems to counteract climate change." Experimentation with geoengineering is not a result of
72  Parker's book, but it follows the same train of thought exhibited in *The Global Crisis*. The Oxford Geoengineering
73  Programme describes the two methods for controlling the environment: solar radiation management (SRM) and
74  carbon dioxide removal (CDR). Due to the fact that the details of geoengineering are far too complex for an in-depth
75  discussion in this essay and this writer lacks knowledge of the technicality of geoengineering, this writer will not
76  attempt to explain how geoengineering is carried out; instead she would like to direct the reader's attention to how
77  geoengineering is the conclusion of the premises found in *The Global Crisis*. The argument is as follows: since the
78  climate is changing and since humans have phenomenal scientific abilities, why not use those abilities to control the
79  climate so that climate change does not become a crisis? While geoengineering is carried out in political good faith,
80  ironically, it has the potential to be another global crisis in itself. Graeme Wood describes this precarious
81  undertaking in an article titled "Reengineering the Earth," in *The Atlantic*:
82
83  Raymond Pierrehumbert, a geophysicist at the University of Chicago, imagines another possibility in which
84  sun-blocking technology works but has unforeseen consequences, such as rapid ozone destruction. If a
85  future generation discovered that a geo-engineering program had such a disastrous side effect, it couldn't
86  easily shut things down. He notes that sulfur-aerosol injection, like many geo-engineering ideas, would be
87  easy to implement. But if it failed, he says, it would fail horribly. "It's scary because it actually could be
88  done," he says. "And it's like taking aspirin for cancer." (July 1, 2009)
89
90  Ian Sample, *The Guardian's* science correspondent, further describes the danger:
91
92  Met Office researchers have called for global oversight of the radical schemes after studies showed they
93  could have huge and unintended impacts on some of the world's most vulnerable people. . . . The dangers
94  arose in projects that cooled the planet unevenly. In some cases these caused devastating droughts across
95  Africa; in others they increased rainfall in the region but left huge areas of Brazil parched. (*The Guardian*,
96  "Earth-cooling Schemes Need Global Sign-off, Researchers Say," May 31, 2013)
97

98  Thus, Michael Specter of *The New Yorker* writes, "There is only one reason to consider deploying a scheme
99  with even a tiny chance of causing such a catastrophe: if the risks of not deploying it were clearly higher. No one is
100 yet prepared to make such a calculation, but researchers are moving in that direction" (*The New Yorker*, "Climate
101 Fixer," May 14, 2012).

102       When researchers are considering the benefits and dangers of a geoengineering plan, the benefits are not
103 just that another global crisis might be avoided, but there are very political benefits involved in the geoengineering.
104 David Suzuki, a dedicated environmentalists testifies of this fact: "Doing all we can to combat climate change
105 comes with numerous benefits, from reducing pollution and associated health care costs to strengthening and
106 diversifying the economy by shifting to renewable energy, among other measures." David Rockefeller, an American
107 billionaire, said, "We are on the verge of a global transformation. All we need is the right major crisis." What these
108 men and many others like them are saying is that a global crisis can be a predecessor to a complete transformation in
109 the way government is done globally. If a political agenda is wanted, a global crisis is the time to push for it because
110 that is when the "commoners" will be most vulnerable. This way of thinking coupled with the ability to manipulate
111 the climate presents a fearful duo. This is the second implication of Geoffrey Parker's *Global Crisis*. "Admittedly,
112 the turmoil produced winner as well as losers," writes Parker. (Location 17184) He then goes on to give examples of
113 the small group that benefited from the global crisis, a group made up of aristocracy and individuals who became
114 wealthy through political alliances. The most telling example comes from Russia, "In Russia, the boyars and their
115 descendants who in 1649 won control over their serfs through the *Ulozhenie*, maintained their advantage for over
116 two centuries" (Location 17197). This writer is not suggesting that a return to serfdom is coming; rather, she is
117 making the point that Geoffrey Parker is making: in a time of crisis, the world is ripe for political conquests that can
118 forever alter the way life is done on earth. "It [global crisis] also led many governments to switch resources from
119 warfare to welfare, fostering economic regeneration" (Location 698). In this case the change was good, but it is not
120 certain that another drastic change of this nature would have equally beneficial results. When geoengineering and
121 private interests are taken in account in the global warming debate, Parker's words become even more important:
122 "Societies can either 'pay to prepare,' and commit substantial resources now to avoid far greater costs later, or else
123 'learn to live with increased' risks" (Location 17831).
124       Alexis de Tocqueville, that well-known commentator on American culture, once said, "History is a gallery
125 of pictures in which there are few originals and many copies." Tocqueville's meaning is simple: history has an
126 unfortunate habit of repeating itself. In this same line of thinking, Edmund Burke said, "Those who don't know
127 history are destined to repeat it." What Geoffrey Park does in *The Global Crisis* is present the history of the effects
128 of drastic climate change in the 1600s, so that as we look at climate change in the twenty-first century, we
129 understand the effects of a harsh climate change on an unprepared society. Christopher Booker from *The Spectator*
130 sums up *The Global Crisis* perfectly: "By exploring the impact of those extreme weather events which accompanied
131 the Little Ice Age—and by the remarkable industry of his researches (his bibliography and list of sources run to
132 nearly 150 pages)—he has added a whole new dimension to our understanding of that near-universal 'time of
133 crisis'" (*The Spectator*, June 1, 2013). (Daphnide)

## Close Reading

    1. What best describes the structure in the first paragraph?
      A. The author begins with a generalization about the book and then moves to more specific comments.
      B. The author states the thesis and then offers some evidence.
      C. The author offers a counterargument and then the thesis.
      D. The author begins the first paragraph with a series of rhetorical questions, continues with a quote from the
          book, and ends the author's argument.

    2. The author of this book review clearly thinks it is a well-argued book because
      A. The author agrees with the thesis of the book.
      B. The author lived through the events described.
      C. The author believes that the book's thesis is clearly stated and well defended.
      D. The author of the book went to Harvard University.

    3. The thesis of the reviewed book is found in
      A. Lines 1–5                           C. Lines 131–33
      B. Lines 8–10                        D. Lines 134–36

    4. Why does the author quote Tocqueville?
      A. The author respects Tocqueville.
      B. The author quotes Tocqueville to remind the reader that history repeats itself.
      C. The author is convinced that the weather in the 1830s is being repeated today.
      D. The author prefers French sociologists to American sociologists

5. What is the solution to the ecological disaster looming?
    A. A global crisis must be a predecessor to a complete transformation in the way government is done globally.
    B. There is no global crisis.
    C. A global crisis will bring needed balance to government excesses.
    D. The world is ending, and there is nothing anyone can do.

6. Geoengineering most likely means
    A. Using geography to solve climate problems.
    B. Encouraging more people to buy electric cars.
    C. Engineering the environment is a prime directive of all political and social policy.
    D. A return of expensive gasoline prices.

## Words in Context

1. What is the meaning of *extrapolate* (Line 11)?
    A. Guess
    B. Lie
    C. Deduce
    D. Estimate

2. What is the meaning of *inundated* (Line 37)?
    A. Immersed
    B. Befriended
    C. Painted
    D. Avoided

# Lesson 3

## SAT Essay

*Prompt:* As you read the passage below, consider how the author uses

- A. Evidence, such as facts or examples, to support claims.
- B. Reasoning to develop ideas and to connect claims and evidence.
- C. Stylistic or persuasive elements, such as word choice or appeals to emotion, to add power to the ideas expressed.

Read the following short story by Leo Tolstoy. In the story the protagonist discovers the power of forgiveness. But should we forgive all those who offend us? Are there some things that cannot be forgiven?

### God Sees the Truth but Waits

1     In the town of Vladimir lived a young merchant named Ivan Dmitrich Aksionov. He had two shops and a
2 house of his own.
3     Aksionov was a handsome, fair-haired, curly-headed fellow, full of fun, and very fond of singing. When
4 quite a young man he had been given to drink, and was riotous when he had had too much; but after he married he
5 gave up drinking, except now and then.
6     One summer Aksionov was going to the Nizhny Fair, and as he bade good-bye to his family, his wife said
7 to him, "Ivan Dmitrich, do not start to-day; I have had a bad dream about you."
8     Aksionov laughed, and said, "You are afraid that when I get to the fair I shall go on a spree."
9     His wife replied: "I do not know what I am afraid of; all I know is that I had a bad dream. I dreamt you
10 returned from the town, and when you took off your cap I saw that your hair was quite grey."
11     Aksionov laughed. "That's a lucky sign," said he. "See if I don't sell out all my goods, and bring you some
12 presents from the fair."
13     So he said good-bye to his family, and drove away.
14     When he had travelled half-way, he met a merchant whom he knew, and they put up at the same inn for the
15 night. They had some tea together, and then went to bed in adjoining rooms.
16     It was not Aksionov's habit to sleep late, and, wishing to travel while it was still cool, he aroused his driver
17 before dawn, and told him to put in the horses.
18     Then he made his way across to the landlord of the inn (who lived in a cottage at the back), paid his bill,
19 and continued his journey.
20     When he had gone about twenty-five miles, he stopped for the horses to be fed. Aksionov rested awhile in
21 the passage of the inn, then he stepped out into the porch, and, ordering a samovar to be heated, got out his guitar
22 and began to play.
23     Suddenly a troika drove up with tinkling bells and an official alighted, followed by two soldiers. He came
24 to Aksionov and began to question him, asking him who he was and whence he came. Aksionov answered him fully,
25 and said, "Won't you have some tea with me?" But the official went on cross-questioning him and asking him,
26 "Where did you spend last night? Were you alone, or with a fellow-merchant? Did you see the other merchant this
27 morning? Why did you leave the inn before dawn?"
28     Aksionov wondered why he was asked all these questions, but he described all that had happened, and then
29 added, "Why do you cross-question me as if I were a thief or a robber? I am travelling on business of my own, and
30 there is no need to question me."
31     Then the official, calling the soldiers, said, "I am the police-officer of this district, and I question you
32 because the merchant with whom you spent last night has been found with his throat cut. We must search your
33 things."
34     They entered the house. The soldiers and the police-officer unstrapped Aksionov's luggage and searched it.
35 Suddenly the officer drew a knife out of a bag, crying, "Whose knife is this?"
36     Aksionov looked, and seeing a blood-stained knife taken from his bag, he was frightened.
37     "How is it there is blood on this knife?"
38     Aksionov tried to answer, but could hardly utter a word, and only stammered: "I—don't know—not mine."
39 Then the police-officer said: "This morning the merchant was found in bed with his throat cut. You are the only
40 person who could have done it. The house was locked from inside, and no one else was there. Here is this blood-

41  stained knife in your bag and your face and manner betray you! Tell me how you killed him, and how much money
42  you stole?"

43      Aksionov swore he had not done it; that he had not seen the merchant after they had had tea together; that
44  he had no money except eight thousand rubles of his own, and that the knife was not his. But his voice was broken,
45  his face pale, and he trembled with fear as though he went guilty.

46      The police-officer ordered the soldiers to bind Aksionov and to put him in the cart. As they tied his feet
47  together and flung him into the cart, Aksionov crossed himself and wept. His money and goods were taken from
48  him, and he was sent to the nearest town and imprisoned there. Enquiries as to his character were made in Vladimir.
49  The merchants and other inhabitants of that town said that in former days he used to drink and waste his time, but
50  that he was a good man. Then the trial came on: he was charged with murdering a merchant from Ryazan, and
51  robbing him of twenty thousand rubles.

52      His wife was in despair, and did not know what to believe. Her children were all quite small; one was a
53  baby at her breast. Taking them all with her, she went to the town where her husband was in jail. At first she was not
54  allowed to see him; but after much begging, she obtained permission from the officials, and was taken to him. When
55  she saw her husband in prison-dress and in chains, shut up with thieves and criminals, she fell down, and did not
56  come to her senses for a long time. Then she drew her children to her, and sat down near him. She told him of things
57  at home, and asked about what had happened to him. He told her all, and she asked, "What can we do now?"

58      "We must petition the Czar not to let an innocent man perish."

59      His wife told him that she had sent a petition to the Czar, but it had not been accepted.

60      Aksionov did not reply, but only looked downcast.

61      Then his wife said, "It was not for nothing I dreamt your hair had turned grey. You remember? You should
62  not have started that day." And passing her fingers through his hair, she said: "Vanya dearest, tell your wife the
63  truth; was it not you who did it?"

64      "So you, too, suspect me!" said Aksionov, and, hiding his face in his hands, he began to weep. Then a
65  soldier came to say that the wife and children must go away; and Aksionov said good-bye to his family for the last
66  time.

67      When they were gone, Aksionov recalled what had been said, and when he remembered that his wife also
68  had suspected him, he said to himself, "It seems that only God can know the truth; it is to Him alone we must
69  appeal, and from Him alone expect mercy."

70      And Aksionov wrote no more petitions; gave up all hope, and only prayed to God.

71      Aksionov was condemned to be flogged and sent to the mines. So he was flogged with a knot, and when
72  the wounds made by the knot were healed, he was driven to Siberia with other convicts.

73      For twenty-six years Aksionov lived as a convict in Siberia. His hair turned white as snow, and his beard
74  grew long, thin, and grey. All his mirth went; he stooped; he walked slowly, spoke little, and never laughed, but he
75  often prayed.

76      In prison Aksionov learnt to make boots, and earned a little money, with which he bought *The Lives of the
77  Saints*. He read this book when there was light enough in the prison; and on Sundays in the prison-church he read
78  the lessons and sang in the choir; for his voice was still good.

79      The prison authorities liked Aksionov for his meekness, and his fellow-prisoners respected him: they called
80  him "Grandfather," and "The Saint." When they wanted to petition the prison authorities about anything, they
81  always made Aksionov their spokesman, and when there were quarrels among the prisoners they came to him to put
82  things right, and to judge the matter.

83      No news reached Aksionov from his home, and he did not even know if his wife and children were still
84  alive.

85      One day a fresh gang of convicts came to the prison. In the evening the old prisoners collected round the
86  new ones and asked them what towns or villages they came from, and what they were sentenced for. Among the rest
87  Aksionov sat down near the newcomers, and listened with downcast air to what was said.

88      One of the new convicts, a tall, strong man of sixty, with a closely-cropped grey beard, was telling the
89  others what he had been arrested for.

90      "Well, friends," he said, "I only took a horse that was tied to a sledge, and I was arrested and accused of
91  stealing. I said I had only taken it to get home quicker, and had then let it go; besides, the driver was a personal
92  friend of mine. So I said, 'It's all right.' 'No,' said they, 'you stole it.' But how or where I stole it they could not say.
93  I once really did something wrong, and ought by rights to have come here long ago, but that time I was not found
94  out. Now I have been sent here for nothing at all. . . . Eh, but it's lies I'm telling you; I've been to Siberia before, but
95  I did not stay long."

96      "Where are you from?" asked some one.

97      "From Vladimir. My family are of that town. My name is Makar, and they also call me Semyonich."

98    Aksionov raised his head and said: "Tell me, Semyonich, do you know anything of the merchants
99  Aksionov of Vladimir? Are they still alive?"

100    "Know them? Of course I do. The Aksionovs are rich, though their father is in Siberia: a sinner like
101  ourselves, it seems! As for you, Gran'dad, how did you come here?"

102    Aksionov did not like to speak of his misfortune. He only sighed, and said, "For my sins I have been in
103  prison these twenty-six years."

104    "What sins?" asked Makar Semyonich.

105    But Aksionov only said, "Well, well—I must have deserved it!" He would have said no more, but his
106  companions told the newcomers how Aksionov came to be in Siberia; how some one had killed a merchant, and had
107  put the knife among Aksionov's things, and Aksionov had been unjustly condemned.

108    When Makar Semyonich heard this, he looked at Aksionov, slapped his own knee, and exclaimed, "Well,
109  this is wonderful! Really wonderful! But how old you've grown, Gran'dad!"

110    The others asked him why he was so surprised, and where he had seen Aksionov before; but Makar
111  Semyonich did not reply. He only said:

112    "It's wonderful that we should meet here, lads!"

113    These words made Aksionov wonder whether this man knew who had killed the merchant; so he said,
114  "Perhaps, Semyonich, you have heard of that affair, or maybe you've seen me before?"

115    "How could I help hearing? The world's full of rumours. But it's a long time ago, and I've forgotten what I
116  heard."

117    "Perhaps you heard who killed the merchant?" asked Aksionov.

118    Makar Semyonich laughed, and replied: "It must have been him in whose bag the knife was found! If some
119  one else hid the knife there, 'He's not a thief till he's caught,' as the saying is. How could any one put a knife into
120  your bag while it was under your head? It would surely have woke you up."

121    When Aksionov heard these words, he felt sure this was the man who had killed the merchant. He rose and
122  went away. All that night Aksionov lay awake. He felt terribly unhappy, and all sorts of images rose in his mind.
123  There was the image of his wife as she was when he parted from her to go to the fair. He saw her as if she were
124  present; her face and her eyes rose before him; he heard her speak and laugh. Then he saw his children, quite little,
125  as they were at that time: one with a little cloak on, another at his mother's breast. And then he remembered himself
126  as he used to be—young and merry. He remembered how he sat playing the guitar in the porch of the inn where he
127  was arrested, and how free from care he had been. He saw, in his mind, the place where he was flogged, the
128  executioner, and the people standing around; the chains, the convicts, all the twenty-six years of his prison life, and
129  his premature old age. The thought of it all made him so wretched that he was ready to kill himself.

130    "And it's all that villain's doing!" thought Aksionov. And his anger was so great against Makar Semyonich
131  that he longed for vengeance, even if he himself should perish for it. He kept repeating prayers all night, but could
132  get no peace. During the day he did not go near Makar Semyonich, nor even look at him.

133    A fortnight passed in this way. Aksionov could not sleep at night, and was so miserable that he did not
134  know what to do.

135    One night as he was walking about the prison he noticed some earth that came rolling out from under one
136  of the shelves on which the prisoners slept. He stopped to see what it was. Suddenly Makar Semyonich crept out
137  from under the shelf, and looked up at Aksionov with frightened face. Aksionov tried to pass without looking at
138  him, but Makar seized his hand and told him that he had dug a hole under the wall, getting rid of the earth by putting
139  it into his high-boots, and emptying it out every day on the road when the prisoners were driven to their work.

140    "Just you keep quiet, old man, and you shall get out too. If you blab, they'll flog the life out of me, but I
141  will kill you first."

142    Aksionov trembled with anger as he looked at his enemy. He drew his hand away, saying, "I have no wish
143  to escape, and you have no need to kill me; you killed me long ago! As to telling of you—I may do so or not, as God
144  shall direct."

145    Next day, when the convicts were led out to work, the convoy soldiers noticed that one or other of the
146  prisoners emptied some earth out of his boots. The prison was searched and the tunnel found. The Governor came
147  and questioned all the prisoners to find out who had dug the hole. They all denied any knowledge of it. Those who
148  knew would not betray Makar Semyonich, knowing he would be flogged almost to death. At last the Governor
149  turned to Aksionov whom he knew to be a just man, and said:

150    "You are a truthful old man; tell me, before God, who dug the hole?"

151    Makar Semyonich stood as if he were quite unconcerned, looking at the Governor and not so much as
152  glancing at Aksionov. Aksionov's lips and hands trembled, and for a long time he could not utter a word. He
153  thought, "Why should I screen him who ruined my life? Let him pay for what I have suffered. But if I tell, they will
154  probably flog the life out of him, and maybe I suspect him wrongly. And, after all, what good would it be to me?"

155    "Well, old man," repeated the Governor, "tell me the truth: who has been digging under the wall?"

156    Aksionov glanced at Makar Semyonich, and said, "I cannot say, your honour. It is not God's will that I

157    should tell! Do what you like with me; I am in your hands."

158    However much the Governor tried, Aksionov would say no more, and so the matter had to be left.

159    That night, when Aksionov was lying on his bed and just beginning to doze, some one came quietly and sat

160    down on his bed. He peered through the darkness and recognised Makar.

161    "What more do you want of me?" asked Aksionov. "Why have you come here?"

162    Makar Semyonich was silent. So Aksionov sat up and said, "What do you want? Go away, or I will call the

163    guard!"

164    Makar Semyonich bent close over Aksionov, and whispered, "Ivan Dmitrich, forgive me!"

165    "What for?" asked Aksionov.

166    "It was I who killed the merchant and hid the knife among your things. I meant to kill you too, but I heard a

167    noise outside, so I hid the knife in your bag and escaped out of the window."

168    Aksionov was silent, and did not know what to say. Makar Semyonich slid off the bed-shelf and knelt upon

169    the ground. "Ivan Dmitrich," said he, "forgive me! For the love of God, forgive me! I will confess that it was I who

170    killed the merchant, and you will be released and can go to your home."

171    "It is easy for you to talk," said Aksionov, "but I have suffered for you these twenty-six years. Where could

172    I go to now? . . . My wife is dead, and my children have forgotten me. I have nowhere to go. . . ."

173    Makar Semyonich did not rise, but beat his head on the floor. "Ivan Dmitrich, forgive me!" he cried.

174    "When they flogged me with the knot it was not so hard to bear as it is to see you now; . . . yet you had pity on me,

175    and did not tell. For Christ's sake forgive me, wretch that I am!" And he began to sob.

176    When Aksionov heard him sobbing he, too, began to weep. "God will forgive you!" said he. "Maybe I am a

177    hundred times worse than you." And at these words his heart grew light, and the longing for home left him. He no

178    longer had any desire to leave the prison, but only hoped for his last hour to come.

179    In spite of what Aksionov had said, Makar Semyonich confessed his guilt. But when the order for his

180    release came, Aksionov was already dead.

    (Leo Tolstoy, "God Sees the Truth but Waits," in *Best Russian Short Stories*, ed. Thomas Seltzer,

http://www.gutenberg.org/cache/epub/13437/pg13437.html)

## Student Response

### Forgiveness Is True Freedom

1    According to the Noah Webster dictionary, the definition of "Truth" is as follows: "conformity to fact or reality;

2    exact accordance with that which is, or has been, or shall be." Also, the definition of "Authority" is "legal power, or

3    a right to command or act. Power, rule, sway." Lastly, the definition of "Freedom" is "a state of exemption from the

4    power or control of another; liberty; exemption from slavery, servitude or confinement. Freedom is personal, civil,

5    political, and religious." The way these terms relate to each other can be confusing. If there is no truth, can there be

6    any sense of authority? Can a person survive if there is no authority? If there is no truth, can there be freedom? But

7    if there is no freedom, can one arrive at the truth? Ultimately, the goal is to understand how one relates to God based

8    on these three things working together. Dmitrich Aksionov in Leo Tolstoy's short story "God Sees the Truth but

9    Waits" finds the truth, and it sets him free.

10    A golem, perhaps the best known of the Jewish legends, is an automaton, typically human and male,

11    created as the result of an intense, mystical meditation. The word *golem* means (or implies) something unformed and

12    imperfect, or a body without a soul. According to the Babylonian Talmud, God first created Adam as a golem, and

13    only made him an actual human after twelve hours. The interesting thing about a golem is that it is known for being

14    somewhat stupid and yet a very holy being that is close to God. The usual legend is that a golem has the word

15    "truth" engraved on its forehead; almost as if it was a living, breathing testament to a being, fully reliant on its God,

16    and so close to that ultimate truth (http://old.templesanjose.org/JudaismInfo/tradition/Golem.htm).

17    Leo Tolstoy, a late nineteenth-century Russian author, penned the simple short story "God Sees the Truth

18    but Waits." The story belongs to a man named Ivan Dmitrich Aksionov, wrongfully accused and convicted of a

19    murder, and banished to a prison in Siberia for the rest of his life. Resigning himself to his fate, Ivan dedicates his

20    life to God, spending his time in prayer. One day some new prisoners, one of them being Makar Semyonich, are sent

21    to the prison. After overhearing several conversations, Ivan is convinced that Semyonich is the man who committed

22    the murder for which he was blamed. Eventually he confronts Semyonich, but he denies committing the murder.

23    One day the guards find a tunnel. Ivan had found out earlier that it was Semyonich who was digging the hole, but

24    when questioned by the police, Ivan refuses to say he knows anything about it. Completely haunted by this,

25  Semyonich approaches Ivan later that day weeping, confessing that it was indeed he that committed the murder, and
26  begs for forgiveness. "When Ivan heard him sobbing, he too, began to weep. "God will forgive you!" said he.
27  "Maybe I am a hundred times worse than you." And at these words his heart grew light, and the longing for home
28  left him. He no longer had any desire to leave the prison, but only hoped for his last hour to come." Through this
29  story, Tolstoy brings truth down to reality, manifesting that through our trust in the one real truth, God is good.
30      In the Old Testament, God uses his servant Moses to lead his people to his promised land:
31
32      When the LORD saw that he had gone over to look, God called to him from within the bush, "Moses!
33      Moses!"
34          And Moses said, "Here I am."
35          "Do not come any closer," God said. "Take off your sandals, for the place where you are standing is
36      holy ground." Then he said, "I am the God of your father, the God of Abraham, the God of Isaac and the
37      God of Jacob." At this, Moses hid his face, because he was afraid to look at God.
38          The Lord said, "I have indeed seen the misery of my people in Egypt. I have heard them crying out
39      because of their slave drivers, and I am concerned about their suffering. So I have come down to rescue
40      them from the hand of the Egyptians and to bring them up out of that land into a good and spacious land, a
41      land flowing with milk and honey—the home of the Canaanites, Hittites, Amorites, Perizzites, Hivites and
42      Jebusites. And now the cry of the Israelites has reached me, and I have seen the way the Egyptians are
43      oppressing them. So now, go. I am sending you to Pharaoh to bring my people the Israelites out of Egypt."
44      (Exodus 3:4–10)
45
46  Although God called him then, it would be many more years until Moses was ready. First, God gave him a wife and
47  children. Next he became a shepherd. Through all of these things, the "I AM," the supreme authority, was shaping
48  his heart, giving him the humility to be a leader.
49      C. S. Lewis, in his book *The Lion, the Witch, and the Wardrobe*, presents a very real life example of a
50  figure in total authority, in complete submission. This character is Aslan. Near the beginning of the book, Aslan is
51  referenced to as "He's the King. He's the Lord of the whole wood. He's the son of the great Emperor-beyond-the-
52  Sea. The great Lion." Even with all his supremacy in being the Lord of everything, there comes a time in the book
53  when he places himself wholly under the power of the White Witch. Edmund had been a traitor, and the deep magic
54  before the dawn of time needed appeasement before the White Witch would let Edmund go. Blood needed to be
55  spilled. And in the place of Edmund, Aslan himself bowed his head and submitted. "The fool!" the White Witch
56  called him, "The fool has come. Bind him fast." And later just before she killed him, "And now, who has won? Fool,
57  did you think that by all this you would save the human traitor? Now I will kill you instead of him as our pact was
58  and so the deep magic will be appeased. Understand that you have given me Narnia forever, you have lost your own
59  life and you have not saved his. In that knowledge, despair and die." The beautiful thing about this story is that the
60  death of Aslan was not the end. "When a willing victim who had committed no treachery was killed in a traitor's
61  stead, the Table would crack and Death itself would start working backward." Thus, through his submission, there
62  was a resurrection.
63      A few weeks ago, my dad shared a story with me, which I grew to love. In Africa the natives have a special
64  way of catching a monkey. First of all, they find a coconut. Then making a small hole in it, they pour out all of the
65  coconut milk. Taking the milk, they make a sweet, irresistible dish by mixing it with rice. Next they put most of this
66  sweet rice back into the coconut. They then hang the coconut from the branch of a tree, spreading the leftover rice
67  on the ground below the coconut. Soon a monkey smells the sweet rice and comes beginning to eat all of the rice on
68  the ground. Once that rice is gone, the monkey climbs into the tree, ready to devour what's inside the coconut. So
69  sticking its hand into the hole, the monkey grabs a huge handful. But once his hand is in a fist shape, he can't get it
70  out. From the perspective of the monkey, the rice is good! He needs it to survive! But if he would merely let go, he
71  would be free. As it is in absolute denial, the monkey refuses to let go and is caught.
72      In the Gospel of Luke, Jesus shares the parable of the Prodigal Son and his older brother. In this story, the
73  wayward son begs for his freedom:
74
75      "Father, give me *my* share of the estate." So he divided his property between them.
76          Not long after that, the younger son got together all he had, set off for a distant country and there
77      squandered his wealth in wild living. After he had spent everything, there was a severe famine in that
78      whole country, and he began to be in need. So he went and hired himself out to a citizen of that country,
79      who sent him to his fields to feed pigs. He longed to fill his stomach with the pods that the pigs were
80      eating, but no one gave him *anything*.

81  When he came to his senses, he said, "How many of my father's hired servants have food to spare, and
82  here I am starving to death! I will set out and go back to my father and say to him: Father, I have sinned
83  against heaven and against you. I am no longer worthy to be called your son; make me like one of your
84  hired servants." So he got up and went to his father.
85  But while he was still a long way off, his father saw him and was filled with compassion for him; he
86  ran to his son, threw his arms around him and kissed him.
87  "The son said to him, "Father, I have sinned against heaven and against you. I am no longer worthy to
88  be called your son."
89  But the father said to his servants, "Quick! Bring the best robe and put it on him. Put a ring on his
90  finger and sandals on his feet. Bring the fattened calf and kill it. Let's have a feast and celebrate. For this
91  son of mine was dead and is alive again; he was lost and is found." So they began to celebrate. (Luke
92  15:11–24)
93
94  Freedom has many common misconceptions wrapped around it. When someone mentions freedom, the
95  ideas that come to mind are much like the younger son as he begs for his inheritance, freedom, and then leaves,
96  signifying his absolute denial of following his Father. The side of freedom that gets completely overlooked is our
97  ability to be free in a whole different way. Instead of the freedom to choose the wrong, we have the absolute
98  freedom to choose the right. The prodigal son exercised the exact same freedom by choosing to return to his Father,
99  as he did when he chose to leave.
100  In the end what is revealed is that the brightest, best, and only complete truth is found in Christ our Savior.
101  He is reality. Christ alone is perfect. The rest of us are forgiven. To refuse to forgive someone, even an unrepentant
102  "someone," is to ignore God's grace.
103  The true authority is also found in Christ, the only one with the complete right to command:
104
105  All creatures look to you
106      to give them their food at the proper time.
107  When you give it to them,
108      they gather it up;
109  when you open your hand,
110      they are satisfied with good things.
111  When you hide your face,
112      they are terrified;
113  when you take away their breath,
114      they die and return to the dust.
115  When you send your Spirit,
116      they are created,
117      and you renew the face of the ground. (Psalm 119:30) (Anna Grace)

## Close Reading

1. The protagonist, Aksionov, experiences a series of injustices. Here are a few:
   I.   He is unjustly accused of stealing silver from a merchant.
   II.  He is framed for a crime he did not commit.
   III. He loses his family and is thrown into prison.

        A. I                       D. I and II
        B. II                     E. II and III
        C. III

2. What is the main plot action in the reading passage?
   A. An innocent man comes to grips with the fact that his life was ruined by unjust fate.
   B. A sick, dying man is taking last rites.
   C. Aksionov finally gets his revenge.
   D. Aksionov's wife is reconciled to him.

3. Explain this statement: "When Aksionov heard him sobbing he [Makar], too, began to weep. 'God will forgive you!'"
   A. Aksionov was delighted to hear that this evil, guilty man was finally suffering for his sins.
   B. Aksionov too was dying of a similar disease.
   C. Aksionov was remembering his deceased wife.
   D. Aksionov understood that all were in need of forgiveness, and God gave it freely to all.
   E. Aksionov's iconic comment was retribution for all the wrongs he had endured.

4. What is the author's purpose in using so much dialogue?
   A. To advance the plot and invite the reader to experience the action without the impediment of narrative intrusion.
   B. It is necessary in a good plot.
   C. The author wants to add reason to his short story.
   D. The author tries to add a "Russian" flavor.

5. What is the narrator in the reading passage?
   A. Omniscient
   B. Limited omniscient
   C. Third-person objective
   D. First person

6. Why is the ending so full of irony?
   A. Aksionov dies before he is officially exonerated.
   B. Makar is freed when Aksionov should have been.
   C. Aksionov finally is freed, but he is too old to enjoy life.
   D. Aksionov taunts Makar for his bad choices.

7. What is the author's main point in the reading passage?
   A. Judgment belongs to God along.
   B. Bad things eventually happen to bad people.
   C. Forgiveness is a God-inspired reaction and has its own rewards.
   D. People do the dumbest things.

8. What is the main point of the Student Response?
   A. Lines 1–3
   B. Lines 30–31
   C. Lines 88–90
   D. Lines 94–99

9. The student is clearly a
   A. Moslem
   B. Buddhist
   C. Taoist
   D. Conservative Christian

10. After a background summary and recapitulation of short-story lines, what is the next step in the argument?
    A. The student offers a stern warning to readers.
    B. The student offers an inspiring Christian hymn.
    C. The student offers more theological rumination and a story about her father.
    D. The student ties the essay back to the text.

11. What is the purpose using an example from a C. S. Lewis novel in the Student Response?
    I. To offer a little levity in an otherwise serious discussion.
    II. To offer an English flavor to this discussion.
    III. To offer another example of God's benevolent but firm demand that humans submit to God.

    A. I
    B. II
    C. III
    D. I and II
    E. II and III

12. What section of the student response probably should be removed?
    A. Lines 1–9
    B. Lines 10–16
    C. Lines 17–29
    D. Lines 30–43

13. What is the most plausible explanation for the above choice?
    A. The paragraph is interesting but clearly off topic and tangential to the main purpose of the essay.
    B. The paragraph is too religious.
    C. The paragraph is too opinionated.
    D. The information in the paragraph is repeated elsewhere.

14. What score would the student response receive? __

# Lesson 4
## Reading: Document-Based Analysis

*Marbury v. Madison*
**Supreme Court of the United States (5 U.S. 137)**
**(February 24, 1803)**

1    At the December Term, 1801, William Marbury, Dennis Ramsay, Robert Townsend Hooe, and William Harper, by
2    their counsel, severally moved the court for a rule to James Madison, Secretary of State of the United States, to show
3    cause why a mandamus should not issue commanding him to cause to be delivered to them respectively their several
4    commissions as justices of the peace in the District of Columbia. This motion was supported by affidavits of the
5    following facts: that notice of this motion had been given to Mr. Madison; that Mr. Adams, the late President of the
6    United States, nominated the applicants to the Senate for their advice and consent to be appointed justices of the
7    peace of the District of Columbia; that the Senate advised and consented to the appointments; that commissions in
8    due form were signed by the said President appointing them justices, &c., and that the seal of the United States was
9    in due form affixed to the said commissions by the Secretary of State; that the applicants have requested Mr.
10    Madison to deliver them their said commissions, who has not complied with that request. . . .
11        Mr. Chief Justice MARSHALL delivered the opinion of the Court: . . .
12        It is therefore decidedly the opinion of the Court that, when a commission has been signed by the President,
13    the appointment is made, and that the commission is complete when the seal of the United States has been affixed to
14    it by the Secretary of State. . . .
15        Mr. Marbury, then, since his commission was signed by the President and sealed by the Secretary of State,
16    was appointed, and as the law creating the office gave the officer a right to hold for five years independent of the
17    Executive, the appointment was not revocable, but vested in the officer legal rights which are protected by the laws
18    of his country.
19        To withhold the commission, therefore, is an act deemed by the Court not warranted by law, but violative
20    of a vested legal right.
21        This brings us to the second inquiry, which is:
22        2. If he has a right, and that right has been violated, do the laws of his country afford him a remedy?
23        The very essence of civil liberty certainly consists in the right of every individual to claim the protection of
24    the laws whenever he receives an injury. One of the first duties of government is to afford that protection. In Great
25    Britain, the King himself is sued in the respectful form of a petition, and he never fails to comply with the judgment
26    of his court. . . .
27        The Government of the United States has been emphatically termed a government of laws, and not of men.
28    It will certainly cease to deserve this high appellation if the laws furnish no remedy for the violation of a vested legal
29    right.
30        If this obloquy is to be cast on the jurisprudence of our country, it must arise from the peculiar character of
31    the case.
32        It behooves us, then, to inquire whether there be in its composition any ingredient which shall exempt from
33    legal investigation or exclude the injured party from legal redress. . . .
34        Is the act of delivering or withholding a commission to be considered as a mere political act belonging to
35    the Executive department alone, for the performance of which entire confidence is placed by our Constitution in the
36    Supreme Executive, and for any misconduct respecting which the injured individual has no remedy?
37        That there may be such cases is not to be questioned. But that every act of duty to be performed in any of
38    the great departments of government constitutes such a case is not to be admitted. . . .
39        It follows, then, that the question whether the legality of an act of the head of a department be examinable
40    in a court of justice or not must always depend on the nature of that act.
41        If some acts be examinable and others not, there must be some rule of law to guide the Court in the exercise
42    of its jurisdiction.
43        In some instances, there may be difficulty in applying the rule to particular cases; but there cannot, it is
44    believed, be much difficulty in laying down the rule.
45        By the Constitution of the United States, the President is invested with certain important political powers,
46    in the exercise of which he is to use his own discretion, and is accountable only to his country in his political

47 character and to his own conscience. To aid him in the performance of these duties, he is authorized to appoint
48 certain officers, who act by his authority and in conformity with his orders.

49      In such cases, their acts are his acts; and whatever opinion may be entertained of the manner in which
50 executive discretion may be used, still there exists, and can exist, no power to control that discretion. The subjects
51 are political. They respect the nation, not individual rights, and, being entrusted to the Executive, the decision of the
52 Executive is conclusive. The application of this remark will be perceived by adverting to the act of Congress for
53 establishing the Department of Foreign Affairs. This officer, as his duties were prescribed by that act, is to conform
54 precisely to the will of the President. He is the mere organ by whom that will is communicated. The acts of such an
55 officer, as an officer, can never be examinable by the Courts.

56      But when the Legislature proceeds to impose on that officer other duties; when he is directed peremptorily
57 to perform certain acts; when the rights of individuals are dependent on the performance of those acts; he is so far
58 the officer of the law, is amenable to the laws for his conduct, and cannot at his discretion, sport away the vested
59 rights of others.

60      The conclusion from this reasoning is that, where the heads of departments are the political or confidential
61 agents of the Executive, merely to execute the will of the President, or rather to act in cases in which the Executive
62 possesses a constitutional or legal discretion, nothing can be more perfectly clear than that their acts are only
63 politically examinable. But where a specific duty is assigned by law, and individual rights depend upon the
64 performance of that duty, it seems equally clear that the individual who considers himself injured has a right to
65 resort to the laws of his country for a remedy. . . .

66      The question whether a right has vested or not is, in its nature, judicial, and must be tried by the judicial
67 authority. If, for example, Mr. Marbury had taken the oaths of a magistrate and proceeded to act as one, in
68 consequence of which a suit had been instituted against him in which his defense had depended on his being a
69 magistrate; the validity of his appointment must have been determined by judicial authority.

70      So, if he conceives that, by virtue of his appointment, he has a legal right either to the commission which
71 has been made out for him or to a copy of that commission, it is equally a question examinable in a court, and the
72 decision of the Court upon it must depend on the opinion entertained of his appointment.

73      That question has been discussed, and the opinion is that the latest point of time which can be taken as that
74 at which the appointment was complete and evidenced was when, after the signature of the President, the seal of the
75 United States was affixed to the commission.

76      It is then the opinion of the Court:

77      That, by signing the commission of Mr. Marbury, the President of the United States appointed him a justice
78 of peace for the County of Washington in the District of Columbia, and that the seal of the United States, affixed
79 thereto by the Secretary of State, is conclusive testimony of the verity of the signature, and of the completion of the
80 appointment, and that the appointment conferred on him a legal right to the office for the space of five years.

81      That, having this legal title to the office, he has a consequent right to the commission, a refusal to deliver
82 which is a plain violation of that right, for which the laws of his country afford him a remedy.

(http://www.law.cornell.edu/supct/html/historics/USSC_CR_0005_0137_ZO.html)

1. What is the most significance outcome of this court case?
   A. This landmark Supreme Court case originated over a controversy regarding Presidential appointments, but ultimately focused on the constitutionality of an act of Congress.
   B. The separation between the executive and legislative branches was affirmed.
   C. Chief Justice John Marshall confirmed that the Federal Judiciary has the authority to exercise what has come to be known as judicial review.
   D. Separate but equal in public education was upheld.

2. What compelling reason does Chief Justice Marshall give that Marbury had been duly appointed as an officer of the United States?
   A. Lines 15–18                          C. Lines 28–30
   B. Lines 24–27                          D. Lines 35–37

3. Why does Marshall question the act of Congress giving the Supreme Court authority to issue writs of mandamus (that is, to compel certain actions by the government)?
   A. Lines 20–21                          C. Lines 45–48
   B. Lines 24–27                          D. Lines 67–70

4. Which of the following arguments would be an example of judicial review:

  I.  The legality of the election of George Bush.

  II.  The legality of *Brown v. the Board of Education*, Topeka, Kansas

 III.  The case *Roe v. Wade*

|  |  |
|---|---|
| A. I and II | C. III |
| B. II and III | D. I and III |

## Words in Context

1.  What is the meaning of *obloquy* in Line 30?

|  |  |
|---|---|
| A.  Unhappiness | C.  Opprobrium |
| B.  Uniqueness | D.  Magnanimity |

2.  What is the meaning of *discretion* in Line 50?

|  |  |
|---|---|
| A.  Carefulness | C.  Approbation |
| B.  Probity | D.  Lucidity |

3.  What is the meaning of *vested* in Line 66?

|  |  |
|---|---|
| A.  Preferred | C.  Implied |
| B.  Inherited | D.  Conferred |

# Lesson 5

## Math: Algebra, Arithmetic Problem Solving and Data Analysis, and Passport to Advanced Math

### Data Analysis

1. What is true about this line?

| A | B | C | D |

I. Of any three points situated on a straight line, there is always one and only one which lies between the other two.
II. Any four points A, B, C, D of a straight line can always be so arranged that B shall lie between A and C and also between A and D, and, furthermore, that C shall lie between A and D and also between B and D.
III. If A and C are two points of a straight line, then there exists at least one point B lying between A and C and at least one point D so situated that C lies between A and D.
IV. If A and C are two points of a straight line, then there exists at least one point D lying between A and C and at least one point B so situated that C lies between A and D.

A. I                             D. I and II
B. II                            E. NONE
C. III and IV

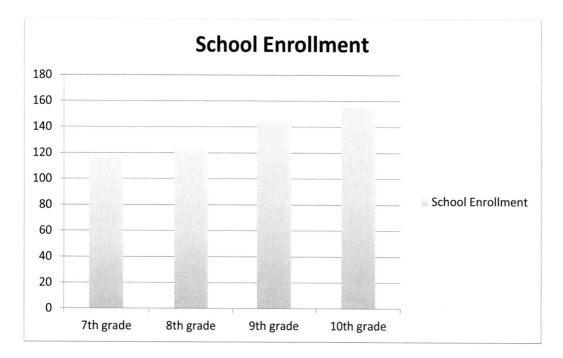

2. Based on this chart estimate the mean of these four grades:
   A. 120                        C. 131
   B. 124                        D. 138

# Algebra

1. What are three consecutive numbers, $x$, $x + 1$, and $x + 2$, whose sum is 78?

   A. 18, 19, 20          C. 25, 26, 27
   B. 21, 22, 23          D. 28, 29, 30

2. Find five consecutive numbers whose sum is 35.

   A. 5, 6, 7, 8, 9       C. 7, 8, 9, 10, 11
   B. 6, 7, 8, 9, 10      D. 8, 9, 10, 11, 12

3. The sum of the ages of A and B is 40 years, and 10 years later A will be twice as old as B. Find their present ages.

   A. A is 40, B is 20    C. A is 50, B is 30
   B. A is 30, B is 10    D. A is 60, B is 40

4. A father is four times as old as his son, and in 5 years he will be only three times as old. Find their present ages.

   A. Father is 30, Son is 10    C. Father is 60, Son is 30
   B. Father is 50, Son is 20    D. Father is 40, Son is 10

5. One man is 60 years old, and another man is 50 years. How many years ago was the first man twice as old as the second?

   A. 40                  C. 50
   B. 45                  D. 55

6. A man 50 years old has a son 10 years old. In how many years will the father be three times as old as the son?

   A. 20                  C. 10
   B. 30                  D. 40

7. A has $100, and B has $20. How much must A give B in order that they may each have the same sum?

   A. $50                 C. $40
   B. $30                 D. $60

8. If $X > 0$ and $Y < 0$, which of the following is always negative?

   A. $1X + 2Y$           D. $4XY$
   B. $2X - 1Y$           E. $X(Y + 17)$
   C. $3X2 + 3Y2$

9. What is the value of $18(2 - 8)^2 - 896$?

   A. -248                D. -716
   B. -680                E. -854
   C. 720

# Chapter 9   A Life Fully Lived and Loved 1 John 2

> *Memory Verse:* My dear children, I write this to you so that you will not sin. But if anybody does sin, we have an advocate with the Father—Jesus Christ, the Righteous One. He is the atoning sacrifice for our sins, and not only for ours but also for the sins of the whole world. —1 John 2:1–2

A therapist tells a story that amuses and stuns me. One of her patients in psychotherapy, a woman in her midtwenties, "complained that she had become nervous and fretful because her life had grown so hectic—too many big weekends, too many discos, too many late hours, too much talk, too much . . . , too much. . . ."

The therapist asked her gently, "Why don't you just stop?"

The patient stared blankly for a moment, and then her face brightened. "You mean I really don't have to do what I want to do?" (*Pulpit Digest*, May–April, 1983, 62).

The truth of 1 John, and all of Christianity, is that we do not have to do what the world says we want/have to do. Life can be different.

First John, while it is indeed a letter, has no greeting nor closing farewell as do the letters of Paul and the letters we might write today. And yet, as we read it, we cannot help but feel its intensely personal character. John had in mind a definite people in a definite time. In fact, we are fairly certain that 1 John was written in Ephesus a little after AD 100 to an early church in great transition.

By AD 100, several things had happened in the early Church (this discussion is influenced by "1 John" in Barclay's *Study Bible*). While churches still did not own property and met in homes, persecution was declining and the church was entering a new crisis, needing stability.

At the turn of the last century, the American writer Theodore Dreiser wrote a novel about a young woman named Carrie who leaves her small hometown in Wisconsin and travels to Chicago to find fame and fortune. She succeeds. But in the process, she severs all ties with home and family. Now, at the end of her life, Carrie sits alone in an exclusive hotel room, longing for the day when she will have what she always wanted: "O Carrie, . . . for you is neither surfeit nor content. In your rocking chair all alone, by your window dreaming, . . . you will dream happiness you will never find."

Separated from its roots, the early church was in grave danger of losing its soul. Or, as my professor friend Dr. Sandra Brown warns, "Do not forget to be religious." We must not become so compromised by easy times that we lose the fervency and integrity of our faith.

In the first days of Christianity, there was glory, martyrdom, and struggle. By the early second century, there was habit, tradition, and stability. Many Christians were third- and fourth-generation believers. John was writing at a time when, at least for some, the first thrill was gone and the flame of devotion had died to a flicker.

Perhaps the most common thread that runs through all late biblical writings is the decline of morality among new Christians. Hence I argue that the real theme of 1 John is sin, not love. It is with sin that John is primarily concerned, and obviously he thinks that we are all sinners (without Christ as Savior) and in need of the expiation, "the covering over" of sin afforded by the cross of Christ (P. Achtemeier and E. Achtemeier, *Proclamation 4: Aids for Interpreting the Lessons of the Church Year*).

Many new converts found the stands that Christianity demanded to be wearisome and old fashioned. They no longer wanted to be holy in the New Testament sense of the word. "Holy" in Greek means "separated" and "different." Jesus says in John 15:19, "If you belonged to the world, it would love you as its own. As it is, you do not belong to the world, but I have chosen you out of the world. That is why the world hates you." The world just did not hate Christians anymore. And that was good, . . . and that was bad.

Christian living presupposes an ethical demand, an absolute sense of what is right and wrong. But once the thrill of commitment wanes, so does the need for absolutes. Things become gray instead of black and white.

Without knowing it, many early Christians had begun to ignore the power of sin. They had slipped into fellowship, as it were, without properly committing their lives to Christ as their grandparents had done. As if standing in a garage makes one a car!

In America today, and I suspect in the church in particular, we have tended to dodge the word *sin*, which is the opposite of holiness.

But this is a cop-out. In the last century, Dr. Karl Menninger, a leader in American psychiatry, wrote a book titled *Whatever Became of Sin?* Menninger contends that mental health and moral health are identical, and that only the recognition of the reality of sin offers the suffering, struggling, anxious, sinful world real hope of being freed from bondage to destructive behavior.

Paul, in writing to the Romans, leaves no doubt about our universal involvement in sin: "All have sinned and fall short of the glory of God" (3:23). And, lest we think we are an exception, or saintly Aunt Sally is an exception, we read 1 John 1:8, 10: "If we claim to be without sin, we deceive ourselves and the truth is not in us. . . . If we claim we have not sinned, we make him [God] out to be a liar and his word is not in us."

John knows that sin is terribly destructive when working in a human life: it tends to push everything out toward the periphery. Bits and pieces go flying off until only the core is left. Eventually the core of life itself falls apart. "The wages of sin is death," is the way that Paul puts it (Romans 6:23).

So, clearly persecution was not the problem in 1 John. Seduction, complacency, and a disregard of sin was tempting believers. In a real way, I repeat, 1 John is not so much about love as it is about sin: John is concerned that his community no longer takes sin seriously enough. And obviously, John thinks that we all are sinful and in need of salvation.

At that time the peril for the early church was not persecution but seduction. The trouble that 1 John seeks to combat did not come from men out to destroy the Christian faith but from people who sought to improve it. They sought to make Christianity socially acceptable. They knew the intellectual tendencies and currents of the day and felt that the time had come for Christianity to come to terms with secular philosophy and contemporary thought.

In C. S. Lewis' imaginary conversations between the devil and his nephew (in *The Screwtape Letters*), the devil says, "The best way to destroy the Church is to get people to embrace a moderated religion. A moderated religion is as good as no religion at all."

This lukewarm religion, as it were, got this community of faith into trouble of two types: morality and theology.

In William Shakespeare's play *The Tempest* we see a society destroyed by a compromised moral and theological structure. It is a society that has turned its back on its fundamental ethic and faith. *The Tempest is* a romantic story, set on a lonely island, which for some is magical, for others a horror. Most of the cast of players eventually leave the island to which they were once banished. The island then sinks back into the sea. As the new generation assumed control of the church, the church was in danger of slipping into the ocean.

What, then, was this contemporary thought and philosophy with which the false prophets and mistaken teachers wished to align the Christian faith? The main problem was Gnosticism, a philosophy arguing that spirit alone is good. Matter and flesh are all bad, claimed gnostics. The main goal of religion is to liberate humankind. The human spirit, after all, is all good. And if left free to roam, it would lead us all into a better world. This is the spirit, I fear, on which the United States of America was founded: a belief that humankind is essentially good: if allowed to develop potential, we can solve any problem. This was the spirit, for example, behind Roosevelt's New Deal, Johnson's Great Society, Bush's Thousand Points of Light, and Clinton's New Endeavor. Every one of these plans betrays a firm belief in humankind's basic goodness. But the message of 1 John is that we must take seriously the notion that humankind is basically sinful. We therefore cannot build enough housing projects, offer enough food stamps, fund enough health clinics to change a person's heart: only God can do that. In his own way, John is standing up to the spirit of the day. John understands that we all are sinners in constant need of the expiation, or "covering over," of sins afforded us by the cross of Jesus Christ. The cure for human wrongdoing, therefore, will not lie in psychotherapy, or in education, or in changing the environment, or in engineering the genetic code. If we remove God from the picture, human responsibility to God is never considered, and we expect human beings, by their own cleverness, to eliminate evil from the world. As if we can refuse to believe in gravity! If we jump from a second-story roof, even if we do not believe in gravity, we will still certainly break our leg.

In summary, John gives several important insights to the early church. First, to claim that we have no sin and yet to destroy the bonds between human beings, as we all do, is to lie and to walk in darkness. God is light, and those who walk in his light maintain the ties of human love and fellowship (1 John 1:6–7). Second, if we say we have not sinned, we make God a liar, because God has offered Jesus Christ on the cross, to atone for our sins and for the sins of the whole world (1:10; 2:2). Third, however—and this is the good news—if we will confess our sins, God will forgive them. Not only has Christ offered the expiation for our sins on the cross (2:2), but he is also a righteous advocate for us. And because of that advocacy, God will not only forgive our evil past, but also cleanse us and make us whole, sanctifying us in our present and future lives (1:9). It is only when we know we are forgiven that we can confess that we are sinful, for then we know that we will not be eternally lost because of our sins.

So 1 John ends with good news indeed. What about those in his community who have sinned? Who have strayed? Who have embraced philosophies that are unbiblical? Who have lived immoral lives?

John understood that those who are in the church, who call themselves Christians, if they have sinned, must be disciplined. Of course, ideally, a believer will recognize one's own sin and privately repent. But occasionally, in John's church, there were those who did not repent. John wants us to know that discipline in the church is not optional: it is mandatory. In fact, it is absolutely necessary if we are to be obedient to Scripture. Matthew 18, for instance, reminds us that we are to counsel a sinning brother or sister privately, and then in a small group if they refuse to repent, and even publicly as a last resort to reclaim them. The church must purify itself by recognizing that we all need help, and discipline is a way John's church could bring new life to many believers who had fallen into sin. In spite of our hesitation to follow a similar pattern, the church today should also follow a scriptural pattern of discipline.

First John 2 is an address to the new church. It is also an address to the old church—you and me! It warns us that we should be careful not to be too soft in our faith, not to be captured by heretical philosophies that predominate in our world. Philosophies such as "You only live once, so grab the world with all the gusto you have." Or, "You have come a long way, baby." Or, "If it feels good, then do it." And so on. I am sure you can add many to this list. And the trouble is, many of the people we respect, and with whom we live day in and day out, embrace these doctrines. Sin has become passé. We no longer know what it means to fail, even though we fail fairly often, because the world rejects the notion of failure—which is what worldlings must do unless they know that one can be forgiven in Christ! First John, while it is about the problem of sin, ultimately ends in a hopeful discussion of love. John's community, soft and compromising, can begin anew as the church extends caring discipline that leads to repentance. And so can we! In Christ we can have a life fully lived and fully loved.

## Journal Question
Imagine your life in twenty years.

# Lesson 1
## Evidence-Based Reading and Writing
### Literary Choice

*Mansfield Park* (1814) is a well-written novel by Jane Austin, with rich characters, nonetheless followed a typical early nineteenth-century rags-to-riches theme. Here is chapter 1:

1      About thirty years ago Miss Maria Ward, of Huntingdon, with only seven thousand pounds, had the good
2  luck to captivate Sir Thomas Bertram, of Mansfield Park, in the county of Northampton, and to be thereby raised to
3  the rank of a baronet's lady, with all the comforts and consequences of an handsome house and large income. All
4  Huntingdon exclaimed on the greatness of the match, and her uncle, the lawyer, himself, allowed her to be at least
5  three thousand pounds short of any equitable claim to it. She had two sisters to be benefited by her elevation; and
6  such of their acquaintance as thought Miss Ward and Miss Frances quite as handsome as Miss Maria, did not scruple
7  to predict their marrying with almost equal advantage. But there certainly are not so many men of large fortune in
8  the world as there are pretty women to deserve them. Miss Ward, at the end of half a dozen years, found herself
9  obliged to be attached to the Rev. Mr. Norris, a friend of her brother-in-law, with scarcely any private fortune, and
10  Miss Frances fared yet worse. Miss Ward's match, indeed, when it came to the point, was not contemptible: Sir
11  Thomas being happily able to give his friend an income in the living of Mansfield; and Mr. and Mrs. Norris began
12  their career of conjugal felicity with very little less than a thousand a year. But Miss Frances married, in the
13  common phrase, to disoblige her family, and by fixing on a lieutenant of marines, without education, fortune, or
14  connexions, did it very thoroughly. She could hardly have made a more untoward choice. Sir Thomas Bertram had
15  interest, which, from principle as well as pride—from a general wish of doing right, and a desire of seeing all that
16  were connected with him in situations of respectability, he would have been glad to exert for the advantage of Lady
17  Bertram's sister; but her husband's profession was such as no interest could reach; and before he had time to devise
18  any other method of assisting them, an absolute breach between the sisters had taken place. It was the natural result
19  of the conduct of each party, and such as a very imprudent marriage almost always produces. To save herself from
20  useless remonstrance, Mrs. Price never wrote to her family on the subject till actually married. Lady Bertram, who
21  was a woman of very tranquil feelings, and a temper remarkably easy and indolent, would have contented herself
22  with merely giving up her sister, and thinking no more of the matter; but Mrs. Norris had a spirit of activity, which
23  could not be satisfied till she had written a long and angry letter to Fanny, to point out the folly of her conduct, and
24  threaten her with all its possible ill consequences. Mrs. Price, in her turn, was injured and angry; and an answer,
25  which comprehended each sister in its bitterness, and bestowed such very disrespectful reflections on the pride of Sir
26  Thomas as Mrs. Norris could not possibly keep to herself, put an end to all intercourse between them for a
27  considerable period.
28      Their homes were so distant, and the circles in which they moved so distinct, as almost to preclude the
29  means of ever hearing of each other's existence during the eleven following years, or, at least, to make it very
30  wonderful to Sir Thomas that Mrs. Norris should ever have it in her power to tell them, as she now and then did, in
31  an angry voice, that Fanny had got another child. By the end of eleven years, however, Mrs. Price could no longer
32  afford to cherish pride or resentment, or to lose one connexion that might possibly assist her. A large and still
33  increasing family, an husband disabled for active service, but not the less equal to company and good liquor, and a
34  very small income to supply their wants, made her eager to regain the friends she had so carelessly sacrificed; and
35  she addressed Lady Bertram in a letter which spoke so much contrition and despondence, such a superfluity of
36  children, and such a want of almost everything else, as could not but dispose them all to a reconciliation. She was
37  preparing for her ninth lying-in; and after bewailing the circumstance, and imploring their countenance as sponsors
38  to the expected child, she could not conceal how important she felt they might be to the future maintenance of the
39  eight already in being. Her eldest was a boy of ten years old, a fine spirited fellow, who longed to be out in the
40  world; but what could she do? Was there any chance of his being hereafter useful to Sir Thomas in the concerns of
41  his West Indian property? No situation would be beneath him; or what did Sir Thomas think of Woolwich? or how
42  could a boy be sent out to the East?
43      The letter was not unproductive. It re-established peace and kindness. Sir Thomas sent friendly advice and
44  professions, Lady Bertram dispatched money and baby-linen, and Mrs. Norris wrote the letters.
45      Such were its immediate effects, and within a twelvemonth a more important advantage to Mrs. Price
46  resulted from it. Mrs. Norris was often observing to the others that she could not get her poor sister and her family
47  out of her head, and that, much as they had all done for her, she seemed to be wanting to do more; and at length she
48  could not but own it to be her wish that poor Mrs. Price should be relieved from the charge and expense of one child
49  entirely out of her great number. "What if they were among them to undertake the care of her eldest daughter, a girl

50 now nine years old, of an age to require more attention than her poor mother could possibly give? The trouble and
51 expense of it to them would be nothing, compared with the benevolence of the action." Lady Bertram agreed with
52 her instantly. "I think we cannot do better," said she; "let us send for the child."
53     Sir Thomas could not give so instantaneous and unqualified a consent. He debated and hesitated;—it was a
54 serious charge;—a girl so brought up must be adequately provided for, or there would be cruelty instead of kindness
55 in taking her from her family. He thought of his own four children, of his two sons, of cousins in love, etc.;—but no
56 sooner had he deliberately begun to state his objections, than Mrs. Norris interrupted him with a reply to them all,
57 whether stated or not.
58     "My dear Sir Thomas, I perfectly comprehend you, and do justice to the generosity and delicacy of your
59 notions, which indeed are quite of a piece with your general conduct; and I entirely agree with you in the main as to
60 the propriety of doing everything one could by way of providing for a child one had in a manner taken into one's
61 own hands; and I am sure I should be the last person in the world to withhold my mite upon such an occasion.
62 Having no children of my own, who should I look to in any little matter I may ever have to bestow, but the children
63 of my sisters?—and I am sure Mr. Norris is too just—but you know I am a woman of few words and professions.
64 Do not let us be frightened from a good deed by a trifle. Give a girl an education, and introduce her properly into the
65 world, and ten to one but she has the means of settling well, without farther expense to anybody. A niece of ours, Sir
66 Thomas, I may say, or at least of yours, would not grow up in this neighborhood without many advantages. I don't
67 say she would be so handsome as her cousins. I dare say she would not; but she would be introduced into the society
68 of this country under such very favorable circumstances as, in all human probability, would get her a creditable
69 establishment. You are thinking of your sons—but do not you know that, of all things upon earth, that is the least
70 likely to happen, brought up as they would be, always together like brothers and sisters? It is morally impossible. I
71 never knew an instance of it. It is, in fact, the only sure way of providing against the connexion. Suppose her a pretty
72 girl, and seen by Tom or Edmund for the first time seven years hence, and I dare say there would be mischief. The
73 very idea of her having been suffered to grow up at a distance from us all in poverty and neglect, would be enough
74 to make either of the dear, sweet-tempered boys in love with her. But breed her up with them from this time, and
75 suppose her even to have the beauty of an angel, and she will never be more to either than a sister."
76     "There is a great deal of truth in what you say," replied Sir Thomas, "and far be it from me to throw any
77 fanciful impediment in the way of a plan which would be so consistent with the relative situations of each. I only
78 meant to observe that it ought not to be lightly engaged in, and that to make it really serviceable to Mrs. Price, and
79 creditable to ourselves, we must secure to the child, or consider ourselves engaged to secure to her hereafter, as
80 circumstances may arise, the provision of a gentlewoman, if no such establishment should offer as you are so
81 sanguine in expecting."
82     "I thoroughly understand you," cried Mrs. Norris, "you are everything that is generous and considerate, and
83 I am sure we shall never disagree on this point. Whatever I can do, as you well know, I am always ready enough to
84 do for the good of those I love; and, though I could never feel for this little girl the hundredth part of the regard I
85 bear your own dear children, nor consider her, in any respect, so much my own, I should hate myself if I were
86 capable of neglecting her. Is not she a sister's child? and could I bear to see her want while I had a bit of bread to
87 give her? My dear Sir Thomas, with all my faults I have a warm heart; and, poor as I am, would rather deny myself
88 the necessaries of life than do an ungenerous thing. So, if you are not against it, I will write to my poor sister
89 tomorrow, and make the proposal; and, as soon as matters are settled, I will engage to get the child to Mansfield;
90 you shall have no trouble about it. My own trouble, you know, I never regard. I will send Nanny to London on
91 purpose, and she may have a bed at her cousin the saddler's, and the child be appointed to meet her there. They may
92 easily get her from Portsmouth to town by the coach, under the care of any creditable person that may chance to be
93 going. I dare say there is always some reputable tradesman's wife or other going up."
94     Except to the attack on Nanny's cousin, Sir Thomas no longer made any objection, and a more respectable,
95 though less economical rendezvous being accordingly substituted, everything was considered as settled, and the
96 pleasures of so benevolent a scheme were already enjoyed. The division of gratifying sensations ought not, in strict
97 justice, to have been equal; for Sir Thomas was fully resolved to be the real and consistent patron of the selected
98 child, and Mrs. Norris had not the least intention of being at any expense whatever in her maintenance. As far as
99 walking, talking, and contriving reached, she was thoroughly benevolent, and nobody knew better how to dictate
100 liberality to others; but her love of money was equal to her love of directing, and she knew quite as well how to save
101 her own as to spend that of her friends. Having married on a narrower income than she had been used to look
102 forward to, she had, from the first, fancied a very strict line of economy necessary; and what was begun as a matter
103 of prudence, soon grew into a matter of choice, as an object of that needful solicitude which there were no children
104 to supply. Had there been a family to provide for, Mrs. Norris might never have saved her money; but having no
105 care of that kind, there was nothing to impede her frugality, or lessen the comfort of making a yearly addition to an
106 income which they had never lived up to. Under this infatuating principle, counteracted by no real affection for her

107 sister, it was impossible for her to aim at more than the credit of projecting and arranging so expensive a charity;
108 though perhaps she might so little know herself as to walk home to the Parsonage, after this conversation, in the
109 happy belief of being the most liberal-minded sister and aunt in the world.
110     When the subject was brought forward again, her views were more fully explained; and, in reply to Lady
111 Bertram's calm inquiry of "Where shall the child come to first, sister, to you or to us?" Sir Thomas heard with some
112 surprise that it would be totally out of Mrs. Norris's power to take any share in the personal charge of her. He had
113 been considering her as a particularly welcome addition at the Parsonage, as a desirable companion to an aunt who
114 had no children of her own; but he found himself wholly mistaken. Mrs. Norris was sorry to say that the little girl's
115 staying with them, at least as things then were, was quite out of the question. Poor Mr. Norris's indifferent state of
116 health made it an impossibility: he could no more bear the noise of a child than he could fly; if, indeed, he should
117 ever get well of his gouty complaints, it would be a different matter: she should then be glad to take her turn, and
118 think nothing of the inconvenience; but just now, poor Mr. Norris took up every moment of her time, and the very
119 mention of such a thing she was sure would distract him.
120     "Then she had better come to us," said Lady Bertram, with the utmost composure. After a short pause Sir
121 Thomas added with dignity, "Yes, let her home be in this house. We will endeavour to do our duty by her, and she
122 will, at least, have the advantage of companions of her own age, and of a regular instructress."
123     "Very true," cried Mrs. Norris, "which are both very important considerations; and it will be just the same
124 to Miss Lee whether she has three girls to teach, or only two—there can be no difference. I only wish I could be
125 more useful; but you see I do all in my power. I am not one of those that spare their own trouble; and Nanny shall
126 fetch her, however it may put me to inconvenience to have my chief counsellor away for three days. I suppose,
127 sister, you will put the child in the little white attic, near the old nurseries. It will be much the best place for her, so
128 near Miss Lee, and not far from the girls, and close by the housemaids, who could either of them help to dress her,
129 you know, and take care of her clothes, for I suppose you would not think it fair to expect Ellis to wait on her as well
130 as the others. Indeed, I do not see that you could possibly place her anywhere else."
131     Lady Bertram made no opposition.
132     "I hope she will prove a well-disposed girl," continued Mrs. Norris, "and be sensible of her uncommon
133 good fortune in having such friends."
134     "Should her disposition be really bad," said Sir Thomas, "we must not, for our own children's sake,
135 continue her in the family; but there is no reason to expect so great an evil. We shall probably see much to wish
136 altered in her, and must prepare ourselves for gross ignorance, some meanness of opinions, and very distressing
137 vulgarity of manner; but these are not incurable faults; nor, I trust, can they be dangerous for her associates. Had my
138 daughters been younger than herself, I should have considered the introduction of such a companion as a matter of
139 very serious moment; but, as it is, I hope there can be nothing to fear for them, and everything to hope for her, from
140 the association."
141     "That is exactly what I think," cried Mrs. Norris, "and what I was saying to my husband this morning. It
142 will be an education for the child, said I, only being with her cousins; if Miss Lee taught her nothing, she would
143 learn to be good and clever from *them*."
144     "I hope she will not tease my poor pug," said Lady Bertram; "I have but just got Julia to leave it alone."
145     "There will be some difficulty in our way, Mrs. Norris," observed Sir Thomas, "as to the distinction proper
146 to be made between the girls as they grow up: how to preserve in the minds of my daughters the consciousness of
147 what they are, without making them think too lowly of their cousin; and how, without depressing her spirits too far,
148 to make her remember that she is not a *Miss Bertram*. I should wish to see them very good friends, and would, on no
149 account, authorize in my girls the smallest degree of arrogance towards their relation; but still they cannot be equals.
150 Their rank, fortune, rights, and expectations will always be different. It is a point of great delicacy, and you must
151 assist us in our endeavours to choose exactly the right line of conduct."
152     Mrs. Norris was quite at his service; and though she perfectly agreed with him as to its being a most
153 difficult thing, encouraged him to hope that between them it would be easily managed.
154     It will be readily believed that Mrs. Norris did not write to her sister in vain. Mrs. Price seemed rather
155 surprised that a girl should be fixed on, when she had so many fine boys, but accepted the offer most thankfully,
156 assuring them of her daughter's being a very well-disposed, good-humored girl, and trusting they would never have
157 cause to throw her off. She spoke of her farther as somewhat delicate and puny, but was sanguine in the hope of her
158 being materially better for change of air. Poor woman! she probably thought change of air might agree with many of
159 her children.

(http://www.gutenberg.org/files/141/141-pdf.pdf)

## Close Reading

1. Who is the protagonist in this novel?
   A. Sir Thomas Bertram
   B. Lady Bertram
   C. Fanny Price
   D. Miss Maria Ward

2. The plot generally is about
   A. A young woman trying to find her place in the social order.
   B. The end of the Bertram dynasty.
   C. The rise of a new family dynasty.
   D. A romance of a young woman and a rich suitor

3. Which of the following statements is true about this passage?
   A. Fanny Price's aunt married a clergyperson.
   B. Fanny Price's father was a naval officer.
   C. Lord Bertram and his wife decide to send Fanny Price to a boarding school.
   D. Fanny Price lived in an orphanage.

4. Mrs. Norris has an important role in this novel.
   A. She raises Fanny Price.
   B. She is the moral conscience of the Bertrams.
   C. She is a busybody who also injects comic relief into the novel.
   D. She is an insensitive, cruel spinster who lives next door.

5. What is a central crisis emerging in the plot?
   A. Where will the Bertrams go to dinner?
   B. Where will Mrs. Harris live?
   C. What will happen to Lady Bertram?
   D. What will happen to poor Fanny?

6. What would be a logical next development in the passage??
   A. The Bertrams will lose all their money.
   B. Fanny arrives to live with the Bertrams.
   C. Fanny's dad changes.
   D. Fanny dies of typhoid fever.

## Source Analysis

1. This passage lacks initial suspense. What are possible reasons why Austen writes this way?
   A. Austin detests suspense.
   B. Suspense belongs to mystery novels, not to this sort of novel.
   C. Austen needs time to develop her characters and plot before there can be a crisis.
   D. How much suspense can a character like Lord Bertram generate?

2. What can we know about this author?
   I.   The author loved and was loved by her parents.
   II.  The author will never amount to anything.
   III. The author has a penchant for romantic novels.

   A. I
   B. I and II
   C. III
   D. I and III
   E. NONE of Above

3. What is a plausible prediction for this novel?
   I.   Something catastrophic will occur.
   II.  After a long ordeal Fanny will succeed in life.
   III. Fanny will no doubt fall in love.

   A. I
   B. II
   C. III
   D. I and III
   E. All

4. Which of the following passages is from *Mansfield Park*?

    A.  Not all that Mrs. Bennet, however, with the assistance of her five daughters, could ask on the subject was sufficient to draw from her husband any satisfactory description of Mr. Bingley. They attacked him in various ways; with barefaced questions, ingenious suppositions, and distant surmises; but he eluded the skill of them all; and they were at last obliged to accept the second-hand intelligence of their neighbour Lady Lucas. Her report was highly favourable. Sir William had been delighted with him. He was quite young, wonderfully handsome, extremely agreeable, and to crown the whole, he meant to be at the next assembly with a large party. Nothing could be more delightful! To be fond of dancing was a certain step towards falling in love; and very lively hopes of Mr. Bingley's heart were entertained.

    B.  Mrs. John Dashwood now installed herself mistress of Norland; and her mother and sisters-in-law were degraded to the condition of visitors. As such, however, they were treated by her with quiet civility; and by her husband with as much kindness as he could feel towards anybody beyond himself, his wife, and their child. He really pressed them, with some earnestness, to consider Norland as their home; and, as no plan appeared so eligible to Mrs. Dashwood as remaining there till she could accommodate herself with a house in the neighbourhood, his invitation was accepted.

    C.  The little girl performed her long journey in safety; and at Northampton was met by Mrs. Norris, who thus regaled in the credit of being foremost to welcome her, and in the importance of leading her in to the others, and recommending her to their kindness.

    D.  She was the youngest of the two daughters of a most affectionate, indulgent father; and had, in consequence of her sister's marriage, been mistress of his house from a very early period. Her mother had died too long ago for her to have more than an indistinct remembrance of her caresses; and her place had been supplied by an excellent woman as governess, who had fallen little short of a mother in affection.

# Lesson 2
## Critical Reading and Writing

### Command of Evidence

Read the following passages and answer accompanying questions:

### Passage 1

1  According to the *Oxford American Dictionary*, "a job" is "a paid position of regular employment." Career is defined
2  as "an occupation undertaken for a significant period of a person's life and with opportunities for progress."
3  Although these definitions seem to successfully delineate the distinction between the terms "job" and "career," there
4  are exceptions. Usually, a job can be transformed into a career, and a career can be turned into a job. It seems as if
5  the distinction between these terms is not merely whether or not there are "opportunities for progress" or "regular
6  employment," but rather how an individual treats the occupation. Sometimes the distinction lies in the worker's
7  hands.
8      Consider an attorney who devotes his life to serving the public. He goes above and beyond his "job"
9  requirements and truly cares about his clients. This attorney labors long hours ensuring that he pleases his clients
10  and serves them to the best of his ability. He considers his practicing law as an important part of his life and
11  consequently as an end in and of itself.
12      Now consider a lawyer who also devotes his life to his practice. He works past office hours and surpasses
13  his "job" requirements. He also wants to fully satisfy his clients. This lawyer, however, does not see his occupation
14  as an end. His desire to please his clients is only to ensure his income. Essentially he sees the practice of law as a
15  means to an end: amassing great wealth and fame. Clearly these examples illustrate the difference between a job and
16  a career.
17      Although the worker's attitude and propensity can determine whether an occupation is a job or a career,
18  sometimes the occupation itself, not the individual, inevitably makes this determination. Barbara Ehnreich, a best-
19  selling author, illustrates in her book *Nickel and Dimed* that sometimes a job cannot, in any stretch of the
20  imagination, be considered or made into a career. The individual may have no choice. One either has to treat an
21  occupation as a job, a means to making money, or decline into dire poverty. In the chapter "Serving in Florida,"
22  Ehnreich shares her experience of working in a minimum-wage environment. Jerry's, the restaurant where she was
23  employed, was "a fat person's hell." "Sinks are clogged with scraps of lettuce, decomposing lemon wedges, water-
24  logged toast crusts. Put your hand down on any counter and you risk being stuck to it by the film of ancient syrup
25  spills." The management is equally unpleasant. The assistant manager, B. J., yells from the counter, mandating
26  orders; and Joy's moods "change dramatically from shift to shift." Break time at Jerry's is nonexistent, and many of
27  the customers are rude and demanding. Workers at Jerry's, and minimum-wage workers in general, do not dare
28  leave or quit their jobs. They need the money. They have families. They are poor. They cannot make their jobs into
29  careers no matter what their attitudes or propensities. The hard cold fact is that some, in fact many, have to use their
30  work as a means to achieve an end.
31      Although it is very hard to turn a job into a career, it is equally easy to turn a career into a job. Dave Rahm,
32  a famous stunt pilot, clearly had a career. His flying shows were his life. He performed for the audience and also for
33  himself. He lived for flying and even died for it. Because stunt-piloting was such a part of Rahm's life, he excelled
34  above all others. Annie Dillard in her book *The Writing Life* said about Rahm's flying, "Like any fine artist, he
35  controlled the tension of the audience's longing. You desired, unwittingly, a certain kind of roll or climb, or a return
36  to a certain portion of the air." The occupation of this stunt pilot epitomizes a career. However, even though stunt-
37  piloting was an exemplary career for Rahm, this career, like all others, could have been easily turned into a job.
38  Rahm could have started to fly only for money or fame. He could have used his career as a step stool for himself.
39  Instead, Rahm stayed an unassuming taciturn man who loved to perform. It was his dream, his life.
40      Clearly, many factors differentiate a job from a career. Yet many times the individuals, not their
41  environment or situation, are the ones who ultimately ask themselves, "Is my occupation a means for an end or an
42  end in and of itself?" (Sarah)

## Passage 2

1 Philosophers throughout the centuries have attempted to determine the ultimate end of humans and the means to
2 achieving that end. Many times these philosophers did not come to the same conclusion. For example, Aristotle
3 believed that the end of man was happiness. Augustine believed the end of man was faith. Augustus Caesar believed
4 the end of man was honor. Emerson believed the end of man was self-reliance. Thoreau believed the end of man was
5 self-sufficiency. Abraham Maslow believed the end of human beings was self-actualization.

6 Maslow believed that self-actualization could be achieved through certain stages and, consequently,
7 invented a triangle that clearly and concisely laid out these steps. This hierarchy-of-needs triangle suggests that a
8 human must satisfy four needs—physiological, security, love, and self-esteem—before self-actualization can be
9 satisfied. These needs, Maslow claimed, should be satisfied from the most basic to the successively complicated. It
10 requires one's life in totality to fulfill these needs. A part of life, such as work, cannot meet all the needs included in
11 this needs triangle. Although the triangle is not comprehensively fulfilled by one's occupation alone, work can
12 satisfy at least one stage of the needs triangle, if not more. Many times the status of one's occupation greatly affects
13 how many stages of the triangle are fulfilled through work alone.

14 The first stage of the triangle, the Physiological stage, can almost always be attained through work. Barbara
15 Ehrenreich, in her book *Nickel and Dimed*, found that even working at Jerry's restaurant, a minimum-wage job,
16 could fulfill her basic needs. Though not dining on gourmet food or nutritious food, Barbara still survived. Although
17 she could not eat on the job or take a work break, she was still able to "pick up a Wendy's spicy chicken sandwich
18 [and] gobble it down in the car." Because of her income, Barbara had to live in a run-down trailer park and work late
19 into the night; however, she was still able to catch some sleep and have a bite to eat.

20 Ehrenreich had her basic needs satisfied by working at Jerry's, but she found that her minimum-wage job
21 really only fulfilled her bare essentials. She and her coworkers were in a constant stretch for money. They did not
22 have a feeling of safety, the second stage of the needs triangle. Her coworker Gail could not enjoy a state of security
23 nor constancy. She slept in her truck in a parking lot. Barbara and her coworkers were also constantly in danger of
24 losing their jobs and not meeting their expenses. For example, George, a nineteen-year-old Czech immigrant busboy
25 at Jerry's, was fired on ungrounded claims. This highlighted the sense of job insecurity that Barbara and her
26 coworkers already felt. They saw how precarious their own jobs were and how easily they could be swept from the
27 little security that they had. Of course, as a work's status increases, the sense of the worker's security increases.
28 However, even in high-paying jobs, there is still the insecurity of becoming laid off or fired.

29 Even though the second stage of the needs triangle was not fulfilled by working at Jerry's, Barbara saw that
30 friendship and belonging, the third stage of the triangle, did develop there. "I make friends, over time, with the other
31 girls. . . . We form a reliable mutual-support group." All workers, no matter what the work status, tend to bond.
32 Consequently, many times the Love/belonging stage of the needs triangle can be partly if not completely fulfilled
33 through work. Whether work fulfills the fourth stage, esteem, relies largely on the work's status. It is very hard to
34 develop self-esteem, confidence, and a sense of achievement in a minimum-wage or menial job. Barbara
35 experienced this at Jerry's. Customers "look at me disapprovingly no matter what I do," and her employers treated
36 her and her coworkers like criminals. B. J., the assistant manager, even "replaced the whipped-cream squirt cans
37 with big plastic whipped-cream baggies . . . because, reportedly, she saw or thought she saw employees trying to
38 inhale the propellant gas from the squirt cans, in the hope that it may be nitrous oxide." Clearly, customers and
39 managers did not help workers at Jerry's achieve the Esteem and achievement stage of the needs hierarchy. Of
40 course, sometimes a job can be very successful in boosting a worker's self-esteem and confidence. For example, a
41 successful businessman is usually very confident, satisfied, and full of self-esteem. The fulfillment of the Esteem
42 stage undoubtedly relies on the status of the work.

43 It is very hard, if not impossible, for a job to fulfill the self-actualization stage of the needs hierarchy. In
44 fact, Thomas Carlyle, one of the preeminent figures of Victorian England, believed that self-actualization is elusive
45 and unattainable. He says in his essay "From Labour," "Think it not thy business, this of knowing thyself; thou art
46 an unknowable individual: know that what thou canst work at; work at it, like a Hercules! That will be thy better
47 plan." Clearly, Carlyle would not have agreed with the last stage of Maslow's hierarchy of needs. He believed that
48 trying to fulfill the self-actualization stage was impossible. Carlyle claimed that work does not achieve self-
49 actualization but rather replaces that need with self-fulfillment and "self-perfection."

50 Clearly, work can satisfy some of Maslow's hierarchy of needs, though not all. Work usually satisfies basic
51 needs such as food and sleep; however, jobs can never completely ensure security in a worker. The esteem stage
52 may or may not be satisfied through work, depending on the work's status, and self-actualization, according to
53 Carlyle, cannot be attained through work, or even through life, for that matter. (Sarah)

1. What best describes the structure in the first paragraph of Passage 1?
   A. The author sets the tone of the essay with a clarification of "job" and "career."
   B. The author states that there really is no difference between a job and a career.
   C. The author reminds the reader that a dictionary definition is fine, but in real life, something is quite different.
   D. The author begins the first paragraph with a series of rhetorical questions, continues with a quote from the book, and ends with the author's argument.

2. Passage 1, Lines 11–14 explain
   A. The cause of so much unhappiness in the workplace/
   B. The beginning of most workers' retirement.
   C. The difference between a job and a career.
   D. A typical day in the life of a lawyer.

3. According to Passage 1, the purpose of giving the example from the novel *Nickel and Dimed* is to show that
   A. The minimum wage is too low.
   B. Many workers are in a survival mode and do not have the luxury to create a career.
   C. Many bosses are heartless.
   D. People need to work more and worry less.

4. The thesis of Passage 1 is found in
   A. Lines 1–7          C. Lines 12–15
   B. Lines 8–11         D. Lines 37-39

5. In Passage 1, what is the author's point in using the example from Dillard's *The Writing Life*?
   A. The author likes skydiving.
   B. The author's favorite author is Annie Dillard.
   C. The author is making a point that a career is pursued with a passion that infects the audience and the worker.
   D. The author argues that a vocation is not a job.

6. Where is the thesis in Passage 2?
   A. Lines 1–5          C. Lines 20–28
   B. Lines 6–13         D. Lines 50–53

7. In Passage 2, Carlyle disagreed with Maslow because
   A. The final stage of Maslow's hierarchy will never be attained.
   B. Self-actualization is irrelevant.
   C. Job productivity is central to every job description.
   D. Maslow's Hierarchy puts too much emphasis on happiness.

8. What is the best evidence to support the above statement?
   A. Lines 1–5          C. Lines 43–49
   B. Lines 6–13         D. Lines 50–53

9. The basic structure in Passage 2 can best be described in what way?
   A. The author begins with an introduction and then refutes Maslow's hierarchy.
   B. The author introduces her arguments, defines Maslow's hierarchy, and then shows its inadequacy.
   C. The author describes how Maslow's hierarchy is a good explanation of work.
   D. The author rejects Thomas Carlyle's views on work.

10. Both passages agree that

    I.   Work is not a job, not a career.
   II.   Ehrenreich will never be satisfied at her job.
  III.   Self-esteem and self-actualization are ultimately separate from a job.

        A. I                    C. III                    E. All
        B. II                   D. I and III

11. What is a common thesis that both passages reject?

    I.   Working in a fast-food restaurant is a bad idea.
   II.   Work is not a job, and a job is not a career.
  III.   Nothing that one does, not even a job, fully satisfies everything a person needs.

        A. I                    C. III                    E. II and III
        B. II                   D. I and II

# Lesson 3

## SAT Essay

*Prompt:* As you read the passage below, consider how the author uses

- A. Evidence, such as facts or examples, to support claims.
- B. Reasoning, to develop ideas and to connect claims and evidence.
- C. Stylistic or persuasive elements, such as word choice or appeals to emotion, to add power to the ideas expressed.

Describe the impact of new technologies, including transportation and communication systems, on American business and agriculture.

### America and Technology

1  **During the Industrial Revolution, America was the last Western power to join it, due to the lack of capital**
2  **investment and availability of land, as well as Britain's industrial superiority** (David M. Kennedy and Lizabeth
3  Cohen, *The American Pageant*, 15th ed. [Boston: Cengage Learning, 2014], 315). When America did industrialize,
4  the technology in America made amazing leaps. The advances in American technology caused changes in America's
5  agriculture and business.
6      When machines were first introduced by Samuel Slater, America finally had the methods to produce goods
7  (Kennedy and Cohen, 318). But there still was the problem of raw materials, especially cotton. This problem was
8  quickly solved by Eli Whitney's cotton gin. Invented in 1793, this machine was fifty times more effective than
9  picking cotton and made cotton growing profitable. The South also became the "Cotton Kingdom" with cotton
10 planting now able to spread throughout the South. In fact, the South shipped more than 400 million pounds of cotton
11 to New England alone (319). Other inventions helped agriculture increase. John Deere produced a steel plow that
12 was strong enough to break the American West's thickly matted soil, yet light enough to be pulled by horses (327–
13 28). Another invention was Cyrus McCormick's mechanical mower-reaper, which allowed one man driving a team
14 of horses to do the work of five men. These inventions allowed farmers to produce vast amounts of food. But there
15 was still the problem of shipping.
16     Inventions in transportation fixed that problem. Canals improved water transportation in the Northeast; the
17 cost of shipping a ton of grain from Buffalo to New York City was reduced to one-twentieth the original price as
18 well as reducing the number of days (Kennedy and Cohen, 330). Steamboats, invented by Robert Fulton, were even
19 faster and allowed both Southern and Western farmers to ship their goods faster and cheaper along the Mississippi
20 and other rivers that marked the land (329). The invention of the turnpike also helped overland shipping, with the
21 first turnpike being so successful that the government decided to build one from Maryland to Illinois, enriching
22 Western farmers (328). The steam-powered iron horses were able to completely ignore terrain and weather and
23 move fast (331). By the 1850s, railroads crisscrossed America, leading to and making big cites as well as ports. This
24 allowed Western farmers to ship food cheaply to Northern and Southern mouths and Southern plantation owners to
25 send huge bales of cotton to Northern mills or ports to send to Britain. With inventions in agricultural machinery and
26 transportation, American farmers were able to profit hugely, as did American businessmen.
27     Advances in technology brought numerous inventions that boosted the manufacturing business. For
28 example, after inventing the cotton gin, Eli Whitney invented firearms with interchangeable parts (Kennedy and
29 Cohen, 320). This concept was later expanded to other manufactured goods, revolutionizing manufacturing. Another
30 major invention was the sewing machine, invented by Edward Howe and perfected by Isaac Singer (321). This gave
31 another boost to businesses, allowing clothes to be manufactured cheaply and in huge amounts. More new machines
32 kept being invented as time went on, with the decade ending 1860 seeing a total of 28,000 inventions. One invention
33 in particular had large impact, the telegraph. In 1844, Samuel Morse ushered in the age of the telegraph, allowing
34 people to instantly communicate over large distances. With it, businesses could now expand to greater levels and
35 communicate without any disruption. These inventions and many more led to new styles of business.
36     With technologies creating huge profits, investing now played larger roles in creating businesses. The
37 Boston Associates, one the earliest investment capital companies, dominated the textile, railroad, banking, and
38 insurance business of Massachusetts, demonstrating the effectiveness of new business methods (Kennedy and
39 Cohen, 321). The Lancaster Turnpike's success was marked by the 15 percent annual dividends returned to its
40 stockholders (328). Investing was such a key to business that the legal principle of limited liability was invented to

41 protect individual investors from losing more than their share of money when the company they invested in goes
42 bankrupt (321). **In order to allow free trade, laws were passed in New York allowing individuals to create**
43 **corporations without applying for individual charters.** With business booming and technology being invented,
44 investing became more common and important.
45    By comparison with Britain, technology in America had an increased impact, due to the number of
46 inventions. In addition to impacts in farming and business, some technology impacted history and future events.
47 Whitney's cotton gin revived slavery in the South, possibly ensuring that the Civil War would happen (Kennedy and
48 Cohen, 318).
49

1. According to this essay, the following are true:
   I.   The Industrial Revolution came late to the United States.
   II.  The United States surpassed Great Britain in industrial production.
   III. Abundant natural resources impeded industrialization.

      A. I                              D. I and III
      B. II                             E. II and III
      C. III

2. What is an example of a paragraph transition?
      A. Line 1                         C. Line 16
      B. Line 21                    D. Line 41

3. Why is the final sentence a poor conclusion?
   A. It should have been mentioned earlier.
   B. This is an entirely new line of thought and should not be introduced at the end of an essay.
   C. It is not true.
   D. It is the main point of the essay.

4. The next step in the student-response argument might be that
   A. The student offers a stern warning to readers.
   B. The student offers a summary statement.
   C. The student predicts the results of his thesis.
   D. The student offers an evaluation of the outcome of his thesis without introducing a new argument.

5. What is the purpose of mentioning the invention of the cotton gin?
   I.   To develop a cause of the American Civil War
   II.  To discuss the advantages of Yankee ingenuity
   III. To show how an invention, an advancement in technology, can greatly impact an industry

      A. I               C. III                    E. II and III
      B. II               D. I and II

## Grammar and Usage

1. Choose the best grammar/usage form in bold sentence(s).
    2. Lines 1–2
        A. NONE
        B. Because of the lack of capital investment and the abundance of land, as well as Britain's industrial superiority, America was the last Western power to join the Industrial Revolution.
        C. During the Industrial Revolution, America, due to the lack of capital investment and availability of land, as well as Britain's industrial superiority, was the last to join.
        D. America was the last Western power to join to join the Industrial Revolution, due to the lack of capital investment and availability of land, as well as Britain's industrial superiority.

    3. Lines 42–43
        A. NONE
        B. In order to increase free trade, laws were passed in New York allowing individuals to create corporations without applying for individual charters.
        C. In order to allow free trade, without applying for individual charters, laws were passed in New York allowing individuals to create corporations.
        D. In order to assure free trade, New York State made it legal for individuals to create corporations without applying for individual charters.

# Lesson 4

## Reading: Document-Based Analysis

### The Paris Peace Treaty (September 3, 1783)

1     In the name of the most holy and undivided Trinity.

2         It having pleased the Divine Providence to dispose the hearts of the most serene and most potent Prince
3   George the Third, by the grace of God, king of Great Britain, France, and Ireland, defender of the faith, duke of
4   Brunswick and Lunebourg, arch-treasurer and prince elector of the Holy Roman Empire, etc., and of the United
5   States of America, to forget all past misunderstandings and differences that have unhappily interrupted the good
6   correspondence and friendship which they mutually wish to restore, and to establish such a beneficial and
7   satisfactory intercourse, between the two countries upon the ground of reciprocal advantages and mutual
8   convenience as may promote and secure to both perpetual peace and harmony; and having for this desirable end
9   already laid the foundation of peace and reconciliation by the Provisional Articles signed at Paris on the 30th of
10  November 1782, by the commissioners empowered on each part, which articles were agreed to be inserted in and
11  constitute the Treaty of Peace proposed to be concluded between the Crown of Great Britain and the said United
12  States, but which treaty was not to be concluded until terms of peace should be agreed upon between Great Britain
13  and France and his Britannic Majesty should be ready to conclude such treaty accordingly; and the treaty between
14  Great Britain and France having since been concluded, his Britannic Majesty and the United States of America, in
15  order to carry into full effect the Provisional Articles above mentioned, according to the tenor thereof, have
16  constituted and appointed, that is to say his Britannic Majesty on his part, David Hartley, Esqr., member of the
17  Parliament of Great Britain, and the said United States on their part, John Adams, Esqr., late a commissioner of the
18  United States of America at the court of Versailles, late delegate in Congress from the state of Massachusetts, and
19  chief justice of the said state, and minister plenipotentiary of the said United States to their high mightinesses the
20  States General of the United Netherlands; Benjamin Franklin, Esqr., late delegate in Congress from the state of
21  Pennsylvania, president of the convention of the said state, and minister plenipotentiary from the United States of
22  America at the court of Versailles; John Jay, Esqr., late president of Congress and chief justice of the state of New
23  York, and minister plenipotentiary from the said United States at the court of Madrid; to be plenipotentiaries for the
24  concluding and signing the present definitive treaty; who after having reciprocally communicated their respective
25  full powers have agreed upon and confirmed the following articles.

26        Article 1:

27         His Britannic Majesty acknowledges the said United States, viz., New Hampshire, Massachusetts Bay,
28  Rhode Island and Providence Plantations, Connecticut, New York, New Jersey, Pennsylvania, Maryland, Virginia,
29  North Carolina, South Carolina and Georgia, to be free sovereign and independent states, that he treats with them as
30  such, and for himself, his heirs, and successors, relinquishes all claims to the government, propriety, and territorial
31  rights of the same and every part thereof.

32        Article 2:

33         And that all disputes which might arise in future on the subject of the boundaries of the said United States
34  may be prevented, it is hereby agreed and declared, that the following are and shall be their boundaries, viz.; from
35  the northwest angle of Nova Scotia, viz., that angle which is formed by a line drawn due north from the source of St.
36  Croix River to the highlands; along the said highlands which divide those rivers that empty themselves into the river
37  St. Lawrence, from those which fall into the Atlantic Ocean, to the northwesternmost head of Connecticut River;
38  thence down along the middle of that river to the forty-fifth degree of north latitude; from thence by a line due west
39  on said latitude until it strikes the river Iroquois or Cataraquy; thence along the middle of said river into Lake
40  Ontario; through the middle of said lake until it strikes the communication by water between that lake and Lake
41  Erie; thence along the middle of said communication into Lake Erie, through the middle of said lake until it arrives
42  at the water communication between that lake and Lake Huron; thence along the middle of said water
43  communication into Lake Huron, thence through the middle of said lake to the water communication between that
44  lake and Lake Superior; thence through Lake Superior northward of the Isles Royal and Phelipeaux to the Long
45  Lake; thence through the middle of said Long Lake and the water communication between it and the Lake of the

46 Woods, to the said Lake of the Woods; thence through the said lake to the most northwesternmost point thereof, and
47 from thence on a due west course to the river Mississippi; thence by a line to be drawn along the middle of the said
48 river Mississippi until it shall intersect the northernmost part of the thirty-first degree of north latitude, South, by a
49 line to be drawn due east from the determination of the line last mentioned in the latitude of thirty-one degrees of the
50 equator, to the middle of the river Apalachicola or Catahouche; thence along the middle thereof to its junction with
51 the Flint River, thence straight to the head of Saint Mary's River; and thence down along the middle of Saint Mary's
52 River to the Atlantic Ocean; east, by a line to be drawn along the middle of the river Saint Croix, from its mouth in
53 the Bay of Fundy to its source, and from its source directly north to the aforesaid highlands which divide the rivers
54 that fall into the Atlantic Ocean from those which fall into the river Saint Lawrence; comprehending all islands
55 within twenty leagues of any part of the shores of the United States, and lying between lines to be drawn due east
56 from the points where the aforesaid boundaries between Nova Scotia on the one part and East Florida on the other
57 shall, respectively, touch the Bay of Fundy and the Atlantic Ocean, excepting such islands as now are or heretofore
58 have been within the limits of the said province of Nova Scotia.

59     Article 3:

60     It is agreed that the people of the United States shall continue to enjoy unmolested the right to take fish of
61 every kind on the Grand Bank and on all the other banks of Newfoundland, also in the Gulf of Saint Lawrence and
62 at all other places in the sea, where the inhabitants of both countries used at any time heretofore to fish. And also
63 that the inhabitants of the United States shall have liberty to take fish of every kind on such part of the coast of
64 Newfoundland as British fishermen shall use, (but not to dry or cure the same on that island) and also on the coasts,
65 bays and creeks of all other of his Britannic Majesty's dominions in America; and that the American fishermen shall
66 have liberty to dry and cure fish in any of the unsettled bays, harbors, and creeks of Nova Scotia, Magdalen Islands,
67 and Labrador, so long as the same shall remain unsettled, but so soon as the same or either of them shall be settled, it
68 shall not be lawful for the said fishermen to dry or cure fish at such settlement without a previous agreement for that
69 purpose with the inhabitants, proprietors, or possessors of the ground.

70     Article 4:

71     It is agreed that creditors on either side shall meet with no lawful impediment to the recovery of the full
72 value in sterling money of all bona fide debts heretofore contracted.

73     Article 5:

74     It is agreed that Congress shall earnestly recommend it to the legislatures of the respective states to provide
75 for the restitution of all estates, rights, and properties, which have been confiscated belonging to real British
76 subjects; and also of the estates, rights, and properties of persons resident in districts in the possession on his
77 Majesty's arms and who have not borne arms against the said United States. And that persons of any other
78 description shall have free liberty to go to any part or parts of any of the thirteen United States and therein to remain
79 twelve months unmolested in their endeavors to obtain the restitution of such of their estates, rights, and properties
80 as may have been confiscated; and that Congress shall also earnestly recommend to the several states a
81 reconsideration and revision of all acts or laws regarding the premises, so as to render the said laws or acts perfectly
82 consistent not only with justice and equity but with that spirit of conciliation which on the return of the blessings of
83 peace should universally prevail. And that Congress shall also earnestly recommend to the several states that the
84 estates, rights, and properties, of such last mentioned persons shall be restored to them, they refunding to any
85 persons who may be now in possession the bona fide price (where any has been given) which such persons may
86 have paid on purchasing any of the said lands, rights, or properties since the confiscation.

87     And it is agreed that all persons who have any interest in confiscated lands, either by debts, marriage
88 settlements, or otherwise, shall meet with no lawful impediment in the prosecution of their just rights.

89     Article 6:

90     That there shall be no future confiscations made nor any prosecutions commenced against any person or
91 persons for, or by reason of, the part which he or they may have taken in the present war, and that no person shall on
92 that account suffer any future loss or damage, either in his person, liberty, or property; and that those who may be in
93 confinement on such charges at the time of the ratification of the treaty in America shall be immediately set at
94 liberty, and the prosecutions so commenced be discontinued.

95     Article 7:

96   There shall be a firm and perpetual peace between his Britannic Majesty and the said states, and between
97   the subjects of the one and the citizens of the other, wherefore all hostilities both by sea and land shall from
98   henceforth cease. All prisoners on both sides shall be set at liberty, and his Britannic Majesty shall with all
99   convenient speed, and without causing any destruction, or carrying away any Negroes or other property of the
100  American inhabitants, withdraw all his armies, garrisons, and fleets from the said United States, and from every
101  post, place, and harbor within the same; leaving in all fortifications, the American artillery that may be therein; and
102  shall also order and cause all archives, records, deeds, and papers belonging to any of the said states, or their
103  citizens, which in the course of the war may have fallen into the hands of his officers, to be forthwith restored and
104  delivered to the proper states and persons to whom they belong.

105  Article 8:

106  The navigation of the river Mississippi, from its source to the ocean, shall forever remain free and open to
107  the subjects of Great Britain and the citizens of the United States.

108  Article 9:

109  In case it should so happen that any place or territory belonging to Great Britain or to the United States
110  should have been conquered by the arms of either from the other before the arrival of the said Provisional Articles in
111  America, it is agreed that the same shall be restored without difficulty and without requiring any compensation.

112  Article 10:

113  The solemn ratifications of the present treaty expedited in good and due form shall be exchanged between
114  the contracting parties in the space of six months or sooner, if possible, to be computed from the day of the
115  signatures of the present treaty. In witness whereof we the undersigned, their ministers plenipotentiary, have in their
116  name and in virtue of our full powers, signed with our hands the present definitive treaty and caused the seals of our
117  arms to be affixed thereto.

118  Done at Paris, this third day of September in the year of our Lord, one thousand seven hundred and eighty-three.
(http://memory.loc.gov/cgi-bin/ampage?collId=llsl&fileName=008/llsl008.db&recNum=93)
(http://education.nationalgeographic.com/photo/treaty-1783/)

## Student Response 1

1   At the end of the American Revolution, treaties had to be made like after any other war. The Continental Congress
2   sent its diplomats, Benjamin Franklin, John Adams, and John Jay, to negotiate and ordered them to consult with
3   their French allies at all stages of the negotiations and make no separate peace (David Kennedy and Lizabeth Cohen,
4   *The American Pageant*, 15th ed. [Boston: Cengage Learning, 2014], 166–67). However, John Jay, who was
5   suspicious of France's goals for the new nation, secretly negotiated a treaty with Britain, exactly what Congress did
6   not authorize him to do (167). Britain leaped at the opportunity and negotiated a treaty that would become the Treaty
7   of Paris.
8        According to the Treaty of Paris, Britain would formally recognize the independence of the new United
9   States of America (Kennedy and Cohen, 167). This would put an end to the Revolutionary War, which had
10  continued after the Battle of Yorktown, especially in the South (166). It also meant that Britain had finally admitted
11  defeat and saw regaining the colonies as a lost cause. Britain also agreed to give the new nation all the land east of
12  the Mississippi River and south of the Great Lakes (167). This land provided America growing room to satisfy
13  colonists' demands for land, and ensure that future conflicts concerning land would not happen. Britain also agreed
14  to let the Yankees keep a share in Newfoundland's rich fisheries, much to the displeasure of the Canadians. Britain's
15  motive for doing so was to draw America away from its French allies (167). However, the treaty was not one-sided.
16  America had to promise to cease persecution of Loyalists and recommend the restoration of their property that state
17  legislation had confiscated (167). The terms also helped start peace in America, as American Loyalists now could
18  move back to England or to Canada in peace. The states also had to vow not to put any lawful obstacles in the way
19  of collecting debts owed to British creditors (167). This also ensured that America would have to pay Britain, who
20  had lost a massive amount of money during the war, whether it was a colony or not (166). The manner of carrying
21  out such agreements in America, however, was not what London had hoped for, disrupting future harmony (167).
22  All in all, the Treaty of Paris was a major diplomatic victory and a uniquely American victory that ensured
23  independence and growth for America.

24 The Treaty of Paris was a major diplomatic victory for the newborn nation. The reasons why American
25 diplomats were able to achieve this because of one diplomat's reaction to Old World intrigue. John Jay, one of the
26 diplomats sent by Congress, arrived in Paris, vigilant of the centuries-old intrigue and rivalries that were
27 commonplace in European politics (Kennedy and Cohen, 166–67). He was rightly so, for America's European ally,
28 France, was caught between two interests. France had managed to get Spain involved in the Revolutionary War,
29 partially by promising the delivery of British-controlled Gibraltar (167). However, a combined Spanish and French
30 assault failed to fulfill this request, so France was willing to give Spain the immense land beyond the Allegheny
31 Mountains in order protect its interests with Spain. France had invested a lot of men and money in America's
32 independence, and it wanted its money's worth from America. France also wanted an America that was independent
33 in the abstract, in order to make it easier to manage in promoting France's interests and policy. France planned on
34 doing this by restricting America to the east of the Alleghenies, making America strong enough to serve France's
35 interests, but weak enough to not kick back (167). Jay, however, recognized the willingness of France to betray
36 America's interests and secretly negotiated with the British, which turned out to be a brilliant move (167). Britain
37 leaped at the opportunity to patch up relationships with its former colony, realizing that if America could not be its
38 colony, it could be its ally. It helped that a Whig ministry, favorable to the Americans, was in charge, improving
39 relationships (166). Thus America was able to curry favor of two rival European powers, despite the fact that it
40 fought against both powers in previous wars. Through this, America was able to pull off a diplomatic victory.
41 John Jay's suspicions about France and his response provided a pro-American outcome of the war. While
42 other nations lost money, manpower, or stability after the Revolution, America had its hard-fought freedom, as well
43 as new land to help it start down the path of nationhood. (Robinson)

## Student Response 2

1 The peace treaty signed in Paris in 1783 by Britain and America at the conclusion of the Revolutionary War gave
2 America liberal boundaries "stretching majestically to the Mississippi on the west, to the Great Lakes on the north,
3 and to the Spanish Florida in the South" (Kennedy and Cohen, *The American Pageant*). Furthermore, very little was
4 required on America's side, making the Treaty of Paris a sweeping diplomatic victory for the Americans. However,
5 this victory was not based on America's might, but rather the long-term interests of the British.
6 The peace treaty negotiations began in 1782 with Benjamin Franklin, John Adams, and John Jay
7 representing the Americans and Richard Oswald representing the British. Thomas Jefferson and Henry Laurens were
8 also on the American team but for various reasons did not actively participate in the negotiations. With the Treaty of
9 Paris, Britain acknowledged America's independence and gave it liberal boundaries, which doubled the size of
10 America, and also gave it a share in the lucrative fisheries of Newfoundland. Americans were required to halt all
11 further prosecutions of Loyalists, and Congress was to suggest that the confiscated Loyalists' property be returned.
12 Both sides agreed not to stand in the way of creditors desiring to collect their debts. The online branch of the *History
13 Channel* writes that "the final treaty was signed on September 3, 1783, and ratified by the Continental Congress
14 early in 1784" (www.History.com, "Treaty of Paris").
15 These terms for the Americans were extremely liberal, more liberal than America's economy and military
16 strength warranted. The reason for this can be found in Britain's long-term vision- to reopen trade routes, prevent
17 future wars in the Appalachian region, and lure America away from Britain's archenemy, the French. Trade with
18 America had made Britain wealthy; therefore, in order to keep the trade going, they needed a good relationship with
19 America. As for the large amounts of land Britain gave up to America, knowing how land-hungry the Americans
20 were, Britain did not want to leave undefined land boundaries since that might turn into armed conflict later. But
21 perhaps even more than this, Britain did not want America in a close relationship with France because such a
22 relationship would disrupt Britain and America's trade and also strain Britain and America's relationship. The
23 French were a serious threat; they had come alongside the Americas in the Revolutionary War, fighting as much for
24 America's rights as to help destroy an old enemy. The French on their part wanted control over America in return
25 for their military favor. "It [France] therefore schemed to keep the new Republic cooped up east of the Allegheny
26 Mountains. A weak America—like a horse sturdy enough to plow but not vigorous enough to kick—would be easier
27 to manage in promoting French interest and policy," write Kennedy and Cohen in *The American Pageant*. Britain
28 was willing to concede land to America, in exchange for trade, unhampered by French interests.
29 In the Treaty of Paris, Britain was considering its long-term interests and spurred on by the threat of French
30 involvement with the Americans; so Britain gave up lands and possessions with the hopes that the wounds between
31 America and Britain would be healed and British interests in America secured. Kennedy and Cohen write this of the
32 Americans: "Snatching their independence from the furnace of world conflict, they began their national career with
33 a splendid territorial birthright and a priceless heritage of freedom. Seldom, if ever, have any people been so
34 favored." (Daphnide)

1. Student Responses 1 and 2 agree that
  I.   The Treaty of Paris was beneficial to France.
  II.  America received far more liberal terms than its military victories sustained.
  III. England wanted to protect loyalist's rights in America.

    A. I and II                             C. III
    B. II                                       D. I and III

2. Britain's main purpose of the Treaty of Paris was
  A. To boost trade with the Native Americans.
  B. To maintain close ties with Americans and turn them against the French.
  C. To encourage Americans to free their slaves.
  D. To persuade America to join a growing number of British Commonwealth nations.

3. Student Response 1 mentions a primary reason the Treaty of Paris was so favorable to American interests:
  A. British fears of French encroachment
  B. The skillful negotiating of John Jay
  C. Native American Wars on the frontier
  D. British fear of an American invasion of Canada

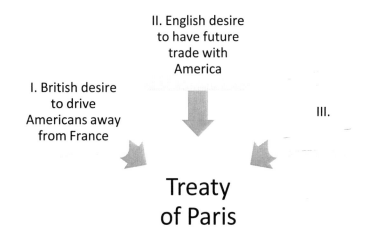

4. Based on Student Response 2, the best reason for I (in graphic above)?
  A. Skillful maneuvering of John Jay        C. Loyalist rights
  B. Cooperation in subduing Spain          D. Military victory

5. According to Student Response 1, what was the aim of French diplomacy?
  I.   To isolate and defeat Great Britain
  II.  To regain some of the land and money it lost in the French and Indian War
  III. To assure claims to New Orleans

    A. I and II                             C. III
    B. II                                       D. I and III

6. What is the purpose of "weak enough to not kick back" in Student Response 1?
  A. A hyperbole to make a point
  B. A metaphor to show French enthusiasm
  C. A colloquial expression to emphasize French intentions
  D. Personification of French response

## Data Analysis

### War Casualties

| | |
|---|---|
| American Revolution | 25,000 |
| American Civil War | 750,000 |
| World War I | 116,516 |

1. The American Civil War had significantly more casualties than all the other two wars combined. What is the best reason?
   A. Tactics in the American Civil War made weaponry more effective.
   B. Civil War medicine was antiquated and ineffective.
   C. Casualties in the American Civil War included Northerners and Southerners—both Americans!
   D. Poison gas was used in World War I.

2. Is there any correlation between the length of these three wars and increased casualties?
   A. Yes
   B. No

3. Is it plausible to assume that an American Civil War soldier had a greater chance of being injured or killed than an American soldier in World War I?
   A. Yes, that makes sense.
   B. No, it depends upon how many soldiers were involved.

4. There were far more deaths per wounded soldier in the American Civil War than in World War I. What are plausible reason(s)?
   A. Tactics in the American Civil War made weaponry more devastating.
   B. Medical practices were more effective in the Civil War.
   C. Weapons were more accurate.
   D. Military leadership used infantry in assaults more than cavalry.

## Words in Context (Paris of Treaty)

1. What is the meaning of *reconciliation* in Line 9?
   A. Understanding
   B. Forgiveness
   C. Peace
   D. Consciousness

2. What is the meaning of *plenipotentiary* in Line 19?
   A. Detractor
   B. Partner
   C. Ambassador
   D. Enemy

3. What is the meaning of *relinquishes* in Line 30?
   A. Abandons
   B. Embraces
   C. Selects
   D. Understands

4. What is the meaning of *unmolested* in Line 79?
   A. Abandoned
   B. Treated Well
   C. Sustained
   D. Bullied

5. What is the meaning of *confiscations* in Line 90?
   A. Purchases
   B. Booty
   C. Possessions
   D. Seizures

6. What is the meaning of *perpetual* in Line 96?
   A. Periodic
   B. Transient
   C. Uninterrupted
   D. Permanent

# Lesson 5
## Math: Algebra, Arithmetic Problem Solving and Data Analysis, and Passport to Advanced Math

### Passport to Advanced Math

1. What is the minimum value of the function graphed on the XY plane below?

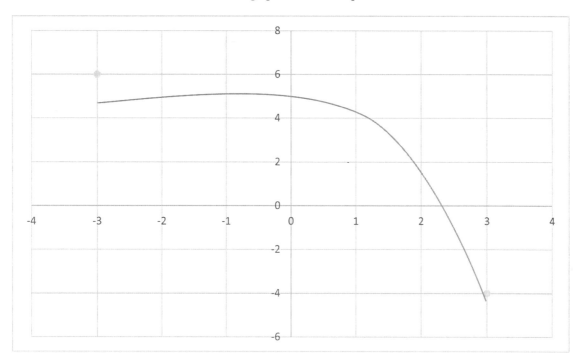

A. - 2   C. 0
B. - 4   D. 4

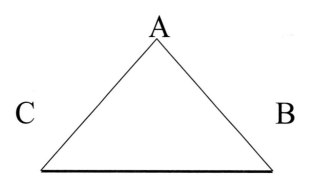

2. What is necessarily true about this triangle (above)?
  I.  Two sides are larger than any one side.
  II.  AC = AB
  III.  Angle CAB is 90

    A. I                      C. III
    B. II                   D. I and III

# Algebra

1. What is the sum of the roots?

   A. 21                    C. 6

   B. 9                     D. 3

2. What is the product of the roots?

   A. 21                    C. 6

   B. 9                     D. 3

3. What is the sum of the roots?

   A. 4/3                   C.

   B. 5/2                   D. 17/3

4. What is the product of the roots?

   A. 17/4                  C. – 12/4

   B. – 21/3                D. – 17/4

# Chapter 10   Fires of Sorrow
# Lamentations 3:22–24

> *Memory Verses:* Because of the Lord's great love we are not consumed, for his compassions never fail. They are new every morning; great is your faithfulness.
> I say to myself, "The Lord is my portion; therefore I will wait for him."
> —Lamentations 3:22–24

In his book *Night*, Elie Wiesel laments, " I lost my faith in the shadow of the gas chambers." Wiesel, a survivor of a Nazi concentration camp, was not an agnostic nor an atheist; he was a believer who decided to stop believing because God seemed to be cruel and unloving. The compassionate God Wiesel had known in youth seemed to have turned into a vindictive, destructive, vengeful creature. Wiesel echoed the words of Aeschylus in his Greek tragedy *Agamemnon* (lines 183–84), "From the gods who sit in grandeur / grace comes somehow violent." In the midst of tragedy, Jeremiah, the author of Lamentations, honestly began to question if God really loved Israel, if God would ever show them grace. And worse than that, while Israel floundered, while Jerusalem lay in ruins, sinful, heathen adjacent nations prospered. Jeremiah complained, "All my enemies have heard of my distress; they rejoice at what you have done" (Lamentations 1:21).

Have *you* lost your faith? Are you questioning whether God really cares? Jeremiah, in Lamentations, then asks questions we have all asked. At one time or another, surely we have wondered if there really is a loving God up there. And if God is there, why doesn't he leave us alone! We are believers, but we simply have stopped believing in a loving God. Quite early in our Christian lives we begin to ask, "Where is the happy ending?" William Howden, a professor at Princeton Theological Seminary, tells a story that illustrates my point well. He saw a Peanuts comic strip with Snoopy sitting on top of his doghouse. With his typewriter (no computers then) he is writing a novel. The first words are, "It was a dark and stormy night." In Lucy's characteristic forceful manner, she sees what is on the page and gives Snoopy some advice. "You stupid idiot! That's the dumbest thing I've ever read. Whoever heard of such a silly way to begin a story? Don't you know that all the good stories begin, "Once upon a time"? Snoopy, taking her advice, began his novel, "Once upon a time, it was a dark and stormy night."

If that were our lives, would it begin the same way? It seems that our lives, which begin so promising, always end in dark and stormy nights. Our fairy godmother never appears, and we never wear glass slippers.

Other people seem to have it so easy—especially wicked people! A survivor of the Lodz Ghetto, a Jewish internment camp in Poland during World War II, describes how devastating it was to look through barbed wire at laughing, fat, healthy sons and daughters of his Nazi captors playing on a merry-go-round while the Lodz emaciated children had to work from dawn to dark. The protagonist in *Fiddler on The Roof* shakes a half-cynical fist at God in the wake of another Russian pogrom: "And you call us the chosen people!"

This is the spirit of Lamentations. Written after the fall of Jerusalem and the subsequent deportation to Babylon, Jeremiah is asking God some hard questions. He is echoing the questions of suffering people spoken over centuries of disappointments, defeats, and regrets. Jeremiah had no good choices to make. Like Sophie in *Sophie's Choice* who had to make the heartrending decision between choosing life for her son or for her daughter outside the gates of a concentration camp, Jeremiah could only choose death or exile, both a form of death. Sophie had to choose to let one of her children die, the SS Colonel told her: the forced choice made her life even more unbearable.

At times we have no good choices to make: a loved one dies; we make a bad business decision; we say something that we regret; all our alternatives resulting from our tragedy are bad. Period. We have no good choices.

Or so we think. There is always another choice: trust in God. This is the flip side of Lamentations. Another message of this small book is that the Lord is afflicted when his people die; he suffers when they suffer. Thus God told Moses, "I am concerned about their suffering" (Exodus 3:7). "His compassions never fail," Jeremiah writes in Lamentations. "They are new every morning: great is your faithfulness (3:22–23)." A strange verse amid so much misery . . . or is it? "An average view of the Christian life is that it means deliverance *from* trouble. Yet it is really deliverance *in* trouble (2 Corinthians 4). It is in the fires of sorrow that we find a rock on which to stand.

Jeremiah kept his eye on the bigger picture. Even though he would never live to see it, he knew that God would deliver his people someday. He knew that "justice so moves that only those learn who suffer" (*Agamemnon*). Jeremiah was willing to suffer to see the kingdom come upon this earth. In his book *Blue Highways*, William Least

Heat Moon describes a couple who had been working on a boat for over eight years. In spite of many failures, not once in eight years did this couple lose sight of the finished product. Because they never lost the vision, they are as excited today as they were eight years ago. The boat remains unfinished.

We must keep our eye on the finished product, on the end result of our Christian walk. We must maintain our vision, and then we must trust in God's faithfulness to finish the work that he began in us. We must flow down the river. There will be stones in our path, but we must not lose sight of God's purpose for our lives; we must not even waste precious time looking when we should be flowing.

"Where does the power come to make the race to the end?" Erich Little asks in *Chariots of Fire.* "From within you!" he quickly answers his own question. From within each one of us is a reservoir of faithfulness that God has nurtured and grown over the last few years. During hard times it is appropriate for us to dip into his strength and remember who is in control of our lives. We read in Psalm 34:18, "The Lord is close to the brokenhearted and saves those who are crushed in spirit." Draw very close to this God!

Ultimately, though, Jeremiah in his book Lamentations reminds us that we must walk in tentative faith. Faith grounded in our God, not in what he does for us, and not even in what will be someday. But like the preacher in the book *How Green Was My Valley*, we confess "The truth is beyond us; . . . we go in faith." Somewhere in these fires of sorrow, even when the truth is beyond us, we find strength and clarity and hope. We discover that our God is Lord of the stormy days as well as the sunny days. We no longer care so much about how our story will end, because we have discovered that our Father will be with us no matter how the conclusion is written. The fires of sorrow turn mourning into dancing, lamentations into shouts of joy. The good news of Lamentations is that we are growing, flowing, becoming all that God has called us to be, . . . in spite of hard times.

Several years ago, it was my privilege to visit two former parishioners in New Jersey, Bill and Marion, who were moving to Hawaii. Into their living room I walked—a room that, if it were not for a draped couch, would not have remotely resembled a living room at all. Piled all over the room were items gathered for a rummage sale. It was a pitiful sight. Although the paraphernalia was invaluable to Bill and Marion, it was obvious to me that most people simply had no use for a set of 1958 children's encyclopedias or a seashell-covered ashtray lovingly made by her son on a forgotten Mother's Day decades ago. Marion and Bill were not naive. They knew that their stuff was not particularly valuable. They were quite prepared to give it up to the trash men, who would dispassionately dispose of it within the next day or two. But it was not the money or the selling that mattered: it was the sharing that mattered. With tears in their eyes and faith in their hearts, they were courageously moving to a location over three thousand miles away. In the midst of their transitory life, they simply wanted to share some of their valuables—some of the good things they had collected over the years with their world. Whether or not their world appreciated them was immaterial. For over twenty years they had lived in this home, and now they had to move on. It was an uncomfortable process at best, but now that Bill had cancer, it was made even more unappetizing. But they faced the future with hope and grace; no regrets, no vindictiveness— only faith in a God who had never failed them in Clark, New Jersey, so they had no reason to believe that God would fail them in Honolulu.

Do I need to remind you that life is that way? As we move through life, the fires of sorrow remind us that God loves us wherever we are, whatever happens to us. We only must continue to share those things we have found precious in our lives; we must continue to risk loving, no matter how hard it may be; we must continue to have faith, even though we cannot even see the horizon. If we can, we will find that the fires of sorrow burn in our souls a dawn of new hope. "Great is thy faithfulness," we keep singing.

## Journal Question

What fires of sorrow have you known? How was God faithful?

# Lesson 1
## Evidence-Based Reading and Writing

### Literary Choice

*A Doll's House* (1879) is a three-act play in prose by Henrik Ibsen. The play exhibits a critical attitude toward nineteenth-century marriage norms. It aroused great controversy at the time since it concludes with the protagonist, Nora, leaving her husband and children because she wants to discover herself.

### The End of Act 3

1    HELMER [*sadly*]. I see, I see. An abyss has opened between us—there is no denying it. But, Nora, would it not be
2        possible to fill it up?
3    NORA. As I am now, I am no wife for you.
4    HELMER. I have it in me to become a different man.
5    NORA. Perhaps—if your doll is taken away from you.
6    HELMER. But to part!—to part from you! No, no, Nora, I can't understand that idea.
7    NORA [*going out to the right*]. That makes it all the more certain that it must be done. [*She comes back with her
8        cloak and hat and a small bag, which she puts on a chair by the table.*]
9    HELMER. Nora, Nora, not now! Wait until tomorrow.
10   NORA [*putting on her cloak*]. I cannot spend the night in a strange man's room.
11   HELMER. But can't we live here like brother and sister—?
12   NORA [*putting on her hat*]. You know very well that would not last long. [*Puts the shawl round her.*] Good-bye,
13       Torvald. I won't see the little ones. I know they are in better hands than mine. As I am now, I can be of no use
14       to them.
15   HELMER. But some day, Nora—some day?
16   NORA. How can I tell? I have no idea what is going to become of me.
17   HELMER. But you are my wife, whatever becomes of you.
18   NORA. Listen, Torvald. I have heard that when a wife deserts her husband's house, as I am doing now, he is legally
19       freed from all obligations towards her. In any case, I set you free from all your obligations. You are not to feel
20       yourself bound in the slightest way, any more than I shall. There must be perfect freedom on both sides. See,
21       here is your ring back. Give me mine.
22   HELMER. That too?
23   NORA. That too.
24   HELMER. Here it is.
25   NORA. That's right. Now it is all over. I have put the keys here. The maids know all about everything in the house—
26       better than I do. Tomorrow, after I have left her, Christine will come here and pack up my own things that I
27       brought with me from home. I will have them sent after me.
28   HELMER. All over! All over!—Nora, shall you never think of me again?
29   NORA. I know I shall often think of you, the children, and this house.
30   HELMER. May I write to you, Nora?
31   NORA. No—never. You must not do that.
32   HELMER. But at least let me send you—
33   NORA. Nothing—nothing—
34   HELMER. Let me help you if you are in want.
35   NORA. No. I can receive nothing from a stranger.
36   HELMER. Nora—can I never be anything more than a stranger to you?
37   NORA [*taking her bag*]. Ah, Torvald, the most wonderful thing of all would have to happen.
38   HELMER. Tell me what that would be!
39   NORA. Both you and I would have to be so changed that—. Oh, Torvald, I don't believe any longer in wonderful
40       things happening.
41   HELMER. But I will believe in it. Tell me! So changed that—?
42   NORA. That our life together would be a real wedlock. Good-bye. [*She goes out through the hall.*]
43   HELMER [*sinks down on a chair at the door and buries his face in his hands*]. Nora! Nora! [*Looks round, and rises.*]
44       Empty. She is gone. [*A hope flashes across his mind.*] The most wonderful thing of all—?
45   [*The sound of a door shutting is heard from below.*]        (http://www.gutenberg.org/files/2542/2542-h/2542-h.htm)

## Student Response

1  "NORA: Yes, Torvald, we may be a wee bit more reckless now, mayn't we? Just a tiny wee bit!" Nora, protagonist
2  of Henrik Ibsen's iconoclastic play *A Doll's House*, stands apart from other literary figures of her era. As Nora steps
3  through the door at the beginning of the play, so the modern woman walks through the door of literature. Nora's
4  character development takes place in three stages throughout the play. First, Nora embraces discontent with her
5  current life; second, she turns to conceal her discontent; and third, she releases her discontent on her world with
6  disastrous results.
7       Nora becomes discontent with her current life and is determined no longer to remain a mere housewife.
8
9       MRS. LINDE. But where did you get it from, then?
10      NORA: [*humming and smiling with an air of mystery*]. Hm, hm! Aha!
11      MRS. LINDE: Because you couldn't have borrowed it.
12      NORA: Couldn't I? Why not?
13      MRS. LINDE: No, a wife cannot borrow without her husband's consent.
14      NORA: [*tossing her head*]. Oh, if it is a wife who has any head for business—a wife who has the wit to be a
15           little bit clever—
16      MRS. LINDE: I don't understand it at all, Nora.
17      NORA: There is no need you should. I never said I had borrowed the money. I may have got it some other
18           way. [*Lies back on the sofa.*] Perhaps I got it from some other admirer. When anyone is as attractive as
19           I am . . .
20
21      With a sense of urgency, Nora tells her friend that her borrowing money for a trip to Italy was necessary for
22  her husband's health. The reader feels that it was Nora who needed the change, that Nora was suffering from a
23  nervous complaint. The reader feels tension building as Nora appears to glory in her deception. Nora becomes a
24  second Madame Bovary, turning to wrongdoing in order to prove her strength.
25      Next, Nora attempts to conceal her discontent under a forefront of wit. Her borrowing of money becomes
26  her "little secret."
27
28      HELMER: Not—not happy!
29      NORA: No, only merry. And you have always been so kind to me. But our home has been nothing but a
30           playroom. I have been your doll-wife, just as at home I was papa's doll-child; and here the children
31           have been my dolls. I thought it great fun when you played with me, just as they thought it great fun
32           when I played with them. That is what our marriage has been, Torvald.
33
34      In the final scene, when Nora determines to leave Torvald, he is shocked that she could have kept such a
35  secret. But Nora reveals the key to her secrecy: to her, married life was nothing but a game. Nora's *demise* into
36  suicidal thoughts and depression occurs when she realizes that she can no longer play her game. She is forced to face
37  reality, and she is left with nothing, not even a sense of who she is.
38      Finally, Nora releases her discontent on her world:
39
40      NORA. I have other duties just as sacred.
41      HELMER: That you have not. What duties could those be?
42      NORA: Duties to myself.
43      HELMER: Before all else, you are a wife and a mother.
44      NORA: I don't believe that any longer. I believe that before all else I am a reasonable human being, just as
45           you are—or, at all events, that I must try and become one. I know quite well, Torvald, that most people
46           would think you right, and that views of that kind are to be found in books; but I can no longer content
47           myself with what most people say, or with what is found in books. I must think over things for myself
48           and get to understand them.
49
50      Nora's discontent is released upon her responsibility with disastrous results. Her brewing contempt for a
51  life as a wife and mother leaves her callous to the effects of her desertion of husband and children. Nora places
52  identity above God and above the people she is called to love. Ibsen's portrait of a woman who has no love other
53  than for herself is embraced by the culture as the "modern woman" admired by contemporaries such as Gustav
54  Flaubert and Simone de Beauvoir. (Alouette)

## Close Reading

1. Who is the protagonist in this scene?
   A. Nora
   B. Helmer
   C. Dr. Rank
   D. Ibsen

2. The plot generally is about a mother/wife
   A. Dying of cancer.
   B. Abandoning her family to find herself
   C. Caught in adultery
   D. Going to jail for stealing money

3. Which of the following statements is true about this passage?
   A. The protagonist dies.
   B. The protagonist leaves to go on vacation.
   C. The protagonist leaves her family.
   D. The protagonist's husband storms out of the room.

4. What is the motivation of the protagonist at the end of the play?
   A. She no longer wishes to assume a role of mother/wife that once sustained her.
   B. She is terminally ill and does not want to burden her family.
   C. She is unable to face the prospect of another childbirth.
   D. She wants to follow her dreams and be a dancer.

5. What is a central crisis emerging at the end of the play?
   A. The husband struggles to understand why his wife is leaving.
   B. A married couple deals with the death of a son.
   C. A mother abandons her family to find herself.
   D. The husband cannot decide to leave with his mistress or to stay with his family.

6. What are logical outcomes of the protagonist's departure from her family?
   I. The protagonist returns and apologizes for her independent spirit.
   II. The protagonist returns and assumes her role as parent but with a new identity.
   III. The protagonist dies in misery in a slum.

   A. I
   B. II
   C. III
   D. I and II

7. What is the tone of this excerpt?
   A. Whimsical
   B. Humorous
   C. Satirical
   D. Serious

## Command of Evidence

1. What is the thesis of the Student Response?
   A. Lines 1–6
   B. Lines 15–18
   C. Lines 21–24
   D. Lines 34–37

2. According to the Student Response, Nora changes from
   A. Phlegmatic to choleric
   B. Sanguine to phlegmatic
   C. Sanguine to choleric
   D. Choleric to phlegmatic

3. The author of the Student Response is probably in favor of
   A. A traditional, monogamous marriage
   B. An open marriage
   C. Feminist views
   D. Polygamy

4. How does the Student Response develop its argument?
   A. Begins with a quote and then analyzes the last act
   B. Begins with a clear, thoroughly developed statement about how Nora changes
   C. Begins with a general statement and moves to specific outcomes
   D. Begins with a humorous anecdote and ends with a summary

5. An alternative view of Nora might be what?
   I. Nora is justified in her departure from a burdensome, dehumanizing marriage.
   II. Nora is selfish and self-serving because she decides to abandon her family.
   III. Nora is a typical nineteenth-century woman searching for her identity.

   A. I                    C. III
   B. II                   D. All

## Words in Context

1. What is the meaning of *discontent* in the Student Response in Line 50?
   A. Angst                C. Umbrage
   B. Disgruntlement       D. Pleasure

2. What is the meaning of *demise* in the Student Response Line 35?
   A. Expiration           C. Reinvention
   B. Growth               D. Increase

# Lesson 2
## Critical Reading and Writing

### Command of Evidence

Read the following passages concerning Aristotle's *Poetics* and answer accompanying questions:

### Passage 1

1 Plato and Aristotle, though both Greek philosophers, have markedly different opinions on the purpose of poetry (and
2 indeed, their opinions on poetry extend to the whole realm of art). Aristotle, who cannot be concerned with the
3 figments of the metaphysical world, believes that poetry springs out of man's natural desire for imitation, and that
4 the more skillful the imitation, the finer the art. Plato, on the other hand, believes that the metaphysical world is of
5 more consequence than the material world, and to him, the highest calling of art is to capture the quintessential
6 essence of a material phenomonon—its form. To Aristotle, an artist should imitate the physical, while to Plato, an
7 artist should reach for the metaphysical.

8     In Aristotle's *Poetics*, he considers the genesis of man's instinct to create art and poetry. Aristotle believes
9 that poetry flows from man's natural desire for imitation: "Poetry in general seems to have sprung from two causes,
10 each of them lying deep in our nature. First, the instinct of imitation is implanted in man from childhood, one
11 difference between him and other animals being that he is the most imitative of living creatures, and through
12 imitation learns his earliest lessons; and no less universal is the pleasure felt in things imitated" (chap. 4).

13     The "pleasure felt in things imitated," the motivation that Aristotle proposes for poetry, increases as the
14 imitation becomes more accurate. Therefore, to Aristotle, the purpose of art is to correctly and precisely imitate that
15 which already exists in nature. By doing so the artist gives himself and others pleasure from the quality of his
16 imitation.

17     Plato, on the other hand, believed that imitating nature is foolhardy; after all, since nature is flawed, why
18 should an artist imitate it? Instead, Plato believed that an artist should imitate the form, or essence, of an object. If an
19 artist is trying to paint a circle, he does not try to paint a pond—an obviously imperfect circle. Instead, he attempts
20 to paint a true, perfect circle, not one of the lopsided ponds found in nature. The degree to which this artist's
21 painting comes to a true circle would, in Plato's philosophy, determine the quality of his art. Plato extended this
22 belief to all art, not just painting. True art, he believed, strives to reach beyond Aristotle's imitations of natural
23 objects, and instead attempts to encapsulate the form of an object—which is truly beautiful.

24     Plato and Aristotle, though both commensurate Greek philosophers, had radically different views on art.
25 Aristotle, the materialist, believed that art's purpose was to skillfully imitate nature. To Aristotle, the greater the
26 degree of skill in imitation, the greater the art. On the other hand, Plato believed that art was a means of reaching for
27 an object's form, or essence. Imitating nature would shortchange the listener such a natural object is flawed and
28 imperfect. Instead, Plato believed that poetry should reach for the perfection of the metaphysical world. (Daniel)

### Passage 2

1 Aristotle was a Greek philosopher lived from 384 to 322 BC. He was a disciple of Plato and a teacher of Alexander
2 the Great. Out of his many books, *Poetics* is one of the earliest surviving works of dramatic theory. In it Aristotle
3 offers an account of what he calls "poetry" (a term in Greek that means "making"). While writing about poetry, he
4 includes drama–comedy, tragedy, lyric poetry, epic poetry, and the dithyramb. He examines poetry's "first
5 principle" and categorizes it as imitation.

6     In *Poetics*, Aristotle writes, "Imitation comes naturally to human beings from childhood, and in this they
7 differ from other animals, because they have a strong propensity to imitation and in learning their earliest lessons
8 through imitations" (chap. 4). In poetry, Aristotle points out, imitation is made of colors, shapes, flowers, and other
9 objects that are seen on a day-to-day basis. It is also used to describe the characters in a poem. "For example, Homer
10 imitates better people; Cleopon, people similar to us; Hegemon of Thasos, who invented parodies, . . . worse people"
11 (chap. 2).

12     Imitation is also used in comedy. The central figures of comedy will include and imitate lowly persons such
13 as peasants and slaves. Comic characters, even those of high status, will tend to behave badly and imitate moral
14 wrong. Here imitation is used to mock inferior people. "The laughable is an error or disgrace that does not involve
15 pain or destruction" (chap. 5). Comedy intentionally incorporates all of this error, since it aims to evoke laughter.

16       Another way that imitation is used is in epic poetry. Epic poetry imitates the good and the bad characters,
17  because its job is to narrate and imitate in verse form something that happened. Epic poetry is not limited to one day
18  or one time: it is unrestricted in time and can narrate years in just one poem. While he is talking about epic poetry,
19  Aristotle mentions Homer and how well he wrote with imitation in the *Iliad* and the *Odyssey*.
20       The last way that Aristotle writes (and goes on to talk about for a good portion of the book) is how
21  imitation is used in tragedy. More specifically, tragedy is an imitation of a certain kind of action. One constituent
22  part of tragedy is the plot, the ordered sequence of events that makes up the action being imitated. "Tragedy is an
23  imitation of an action that is admirable, complete, and possesses magnitude; in language made pleasurable, each of
24  its species separated in different parts; performed by actors, not through narration; effecting through pity and fear
25  the purifications of such emotions" (*Poetics*, chap. 6).
26       At the time when Aristotle wrote *Poetics*, it was not widely known or used. But it opened up huge windows
27  for poets to express imitation in their poetry. "From the beginning those who had the strongest natural inclination
28  toward imitation, rhythm, and melody will generate poetry" (chap. 4). (Anna Grace)

1. What best describes the structure in the first paragraph of Passage 1?
   A. The author reviews the essential components of Aristotle's *Poetics*.
   B. The author unfurls his colors, so to speak, and emphatically embraces a Platonic view of life.
   C. The author defines his terms and prepares the reader for his thesis in the second paragraph.
   D. The author clearly defines the purpose of his essay by discussing the essential differences between the Greek philosophers Plato and Aristotle.

2. Passage 1, Lines 1–7 explain
   A. The quintessential differences between Aristotelian and Platonic thought.
   B. The religious views of Plato and Aristotle.
   C. The difference between Plato's writings and Aristotle's writings.
   D. A critique of the Greek poet Homer.

3. According to Passage 1, what is the purpose of art, according to Aristotle?
   A. To entertain people                  C. To imitate nature
   B. To inspire people to do great things     D. To challenge people to do greater things

4. The evidence to answer the previous question is found in
   A. Lines 1–7.                  C. Lines 13–15
   B. Lines 8–11.                D. Lines 28–29.

5. What is the best meaning for the phrase "though both commensurate Greek philosophers"?
   A. Equal in importance            C. Dangerous in intention
   B. United in thought              D. Smooth selling

6. What is the main concept, often repeated, in Passage 2?
   A. Poetry                     C. Imitation
   B. Rhetoric                   D. Metaphysics

7. Passage 2 argues that this subject is the most important subject of the book:
   A. Poetry                     C. Tragedy
   B. Drama                     D. Prose

8. The best evidence to support the above statement is in
   A. Lines 1–5                  C. Lines 20–25
   B. Lines 6–13                D. Lines 26–28

9. The basic structure in Passage 2 can best be described as
   A. The author begins with an introduction and then refutes Plato's views.
   B. The author defines poetry and then refutes it.
   C. The author defines imitation and then proceeds to show how ubiquitous it is in all of the book.
   D. The author advances the notion that art follows form.

10. Both passages agree that
    I. Imitation is the most important ingredient of all rhetoric.
    II. Plato and Socrates disagreed.
    III. *Poetics* was an important component of literary criticism.

    A. I          C. III          E. All
    B. II          D. I and III

11. What best describes the relationship between the two passages?
    A. They both compare Plato and Aristotle.
    B. Passage 1 contrasts the different views of Plato and Aristotle concerning poetry and Passage 2 is a summary of Aristotle's arguments in *Poetics* alone.
    C. Passage 1 critiques Aristotle's *Poetics* and Passage 2 critique's Plato's *The Republic*.
    D. Both passages develop the concept of "imitation of art."

# Lesson 3

## SAT Essay

### Student Response 1

*Prompt:* Think carefully about the issue presented in the following excerpt and the assignment below.

> Rules are not necessarily sacred; principles are.
>
> (Adapted from Franklin D. Roosevelt)

*Assignment:* Are there situations where it is more ethical not to follow established rules? Plan and write an essay in which you develop your point of view on this issue. Support your position with reasoning and examples taken from your reading, studies, experience, or observations. (College Board)

1  Thomas Hobbes held that inviolable rules were all that kept humanity from descending into a mire in which
2  "the life of a man is nasty, brutish, and short." Thus he advocated a principle that the most ethical position always
3  lay in obedience to the law. However, his counterpart, John Locke, posited that laws were only ethical if they
4  protected the rights of man. It follows that man does an ethically responsible thing by sometimes disobeying a law.
5  Indeed, in many cases, established rules or laws can be ethically disobeyed for higher and nobler purposes.
6      In Sophocles's work *Antigone*, we find a deviation from the norms of Western culture. After a series of
7  unfortunate events, a disenfranchised and fatherless woman by the name of Antigone is faced by the death of her
8  brothers who were vying for the throne of Athens. Her uncle assumes the position and orders that one receive a
9  proper burial but refuses the right for the other. Understandably in anguish over this, Antigone decides to disobey
10 her uncle's command and performs her brother's burial rites. Upon discovering this, her uncle angrily convenes a
11 trial. Antigone proceeds to defend her actions by appealing to a higher law, the law of the gods. This approach to
12 civil disobedience was replicated by Martin Luther King Jr., who in his short "Letter from a Birmingham Jail,"
13 criticizes white clergymen for compromising their adherence to the law of God by supporting segregation measures.
14     Gandhi was a well-known activist who is credited for bringing about the independence of India. He
15 remained peaceful and composed while he encouraged Indians to produce their own salt in violation of a British law
16 that gave monopoly rights for selling salt to English producers. Demonstrating courage in humility, he will be
17 remembered for his idealism and his assertion that all men are brothers. His reasons for civil disobedience were not
18 strictly religious but rather encapsulated the idea that colonialism dehumanizes people and that dehumanizing laws
19 must be disobeyed in the name of the dignity of humankind.
20     **In Victor Hugo's *Les Misérables*, one finds a third, fascinating appeal to civil disobedience.** Jean
21 Valjean is ruthlessly condemned to five years in jail for stealing a loaf of bread to save his sister's son. When he is
22 given his freedom, he meets a priest whom he subsequently robs. However, he is caught and is brought back to the
23 priest. Shockingly, the priest forgives him and charges him to consider the meaning of forgiveness. Thus Jean
24 Valjean decides to tear up his parole papers, which would identify him as a criminal and keep him from finding
25 decent work, and eventually he becomes a mayor of a town. He is discovered and plays a game of cat and mouse
26 with the indefatigable Inspector Javert. So stringent is Javert in his application of the law, holding that "men like you
27 [Jean Valjean] never change," but he is wrong. Here one sees how laws that continually punish criminals can
28 sometimes be unjust since they presume that once a man becomes a criminal, he will always be a criminal. Jean
29 Valjean seeks justice by disobeying the law since he has been redeemed and is living a reformed life.
30     That ethicality does not proceed from legality is clear. Antigone and Martin Luther King Jr. sought to
31 uphold a higher law by disobeying earthly ones; Gandhi called for disobedience to uphold the dignity of man and to
32 promote our interconnectedness; finally, the story of Jean Valjean reminds us that helping others while promoting
33 one's own well-being can be more ethical than obeying a lifelong parole. Hopefully, we can emulate these fictional
34 and real individuals as we seek to make the world a better and more just place. (Luke)

*Prompt:* A better understanding of other people contributes to the development of moral virtues. We shall be both kinder and fairer in our treatment of others if we understand them better. Understanding ourselves and understanding others are connected, since as human beings we all have things in common.

(Adapted from Anne Sheppard, *Aesthetics: An Introduction to the Philosophy of Art*)

*Assignment:* Do we need other people in order to understand ourselves? Plan and write an essay in which you develop your point of view on this issue. Support your position with reasoning and examples taken from your reading, studies, experience, or observations. (College Board)

## Student Response 2

1    Many people are not what they seem. But why are they not? Is a person really what they pretend to be when others
2    are around, or are they themselves behind closed doors? **The key to understanding anyone, especially yourself, is**
3    **to know what you think in your most unpretentious state. Other people are completely uninvolved in**
4    **understanding yourself and working through your thoughts.**
5         A splendid poet, Emily Dickinson is an example of a woman with a good grasp of her own self.
6    Notoriously shy, she spent her days locked away in her bedroom, writing poetry. The time alone benefited her. She
7    worked through her thoughts and understood herself. Now, Dickinson is one of the most well-known poets, with
8    poems that resound with the readers. This can be attributed to her solitary nature and understanding of her inner
9    thoughts. For Emily Dickinson, being and knowing herself was natural because she was alone.
10         Not many people would enjoy living completely alone, however. Most use alone time sparingly, and yet all
11    agree that it aids in solving personal problems. When people have decisions to make, they isolate themselves. In
12    Charles Dickens's *A Tale of Two Cities*, the hero Sydney Carton thought he knew himself. He was a wretch. But
13    when another young man was sentenced to death, Carton retreated to a quiet place for a stroll. He came to the
14    realization that he was not all bad and resolved to do a noble deed. Finally he understood himself! Finally he knew
15    what to do! It all came from being alone.
16         When people are alone, they are themselves. They can understand themselves, be themselves. Emily
17    Dickinson knew this. Sydney Carton employed it. Being around others stands in the way of knowing yourself and
18    working through your thoughts.

1. The author of Student Response 1 uses evidence from
   A. Literature, science, philosophy.
   B. Literature, philosophy, history.
   C. Literature, personal experience, history.
   D. Literature, religion, science.

2. According to Student Response 1, Antigone and Martin Luther King Jr. share
   A. A love of learning.
   B. A penchant for violence.
   C. Civil disobedience.
   D. Assassination.

3. The author of Student Response 2 uses evidence from
   A. History.
   B. Personal experience.
   C. Literature.
   D. All of the above.

4. Student Response 1 employs the following strategy:
   A. Disobeying the law is appropriate under certain conditions, such as the case with Jean Valjean.
   B. Disobeying the law is never permissible since it violates the laws of God.
   C. To violate the law is universally wrong(as in the case of Jean Valjean).
   D. Since some laws are meant to be violated, all laws are suspect.

5. Student Response 2 employs the following strategy:
   A. Isolation from the human community is necessary but never desirable, as in the case of Emily Dickinson.
   B. Isolation from the human community is necessary and even desirable, as in the case of Emily Dickinson.
   C. Isolation from the human community is sometimes necessary, as in the case of someone who is recovering from a grievous wrong.
   D. Isolation is never necessary or good for a person.

6. Student Response 2 could use the following evidence:
   A. Hector facing Achilles
   B. Billy Budd dying
   C. Captain Ahab pursuing the white whale
   D. Henry David Thoreau spending a year on Walden Pond

7. Add to this diagram of Student Response 1's evidence:

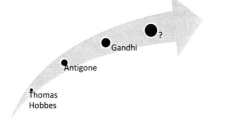

A. Thoreau              C. Valjean
B. Dickinson           D. Carton

## Grammar and Usage

Choose the best grammar/usage form in bold sentence(s).

1. Student Response 1, Line 20
   A. NONE
   B. In *Les Misérables*, one discovers a third, fascinating appeal to civil disobedience
   C. In *Les Misérables*, a person finds a third, fascinating appeal to civil disobedience
   D. Victor Hugo's nineteenth-century novel *Les Misérables* presents a legitimate, laudable example of civil disobedience

2. Student Response 2, Lines 2–4
   A. NONE
   B. Ultimately self-identity is acquired through private reflection, not by human interaction.
   C. The key to understanding anyone, especially yourself, is to know what you think in your most unpretentious state; however, other people are completely uninvolved in understanding yourself and working through your thoughts.
   D. The key to understanding anyone is to know them in their most most unpretentious state. Other people are completely uninvolved in understanding yourself and working through your thoughts.

# Lesson 4
## Reading: Document-Based Analysis

**Passage 1**

### "On the Duty of Civil Disobedience" (1849)

### Henry David Thoreau

1   I heartily accept the motto,—"That government is best which governs least"; and I should like to see it acted up to
2   more rapidly and systematically. Carried out, it finally amounts to this, which also I believe,—"That government is
3   best which governs not at all"; and when men are prepared for it, that will be the kind of government which they will
4   have. Government is at best but an expedient; but most governments are usually, and all governments are
5   sometimes, inexpedient. The objections which have been brought against a standing army, and they are many and
6   weighty, and deserve to prevail, may also at last be brought against a standing government. The standing army is
7   only an arm of the standing government. The government itself, which is only the mode which the people have
8   chosen to execute their will, is equally liable to be abused and perverted before the people can act through it.
9   Witness the present Mexican war, the work of comparatively a few individuals using the standing government as
10   their tool; for, in the outset, the people would not have consented to this measure.
11       This American government—what is it but a tradition, though a recent one, endeavoring to transmit itself
12   unimpaired to posterity, but each instant losing some of its integrity? It has not the vitality and force of a single
13   living man; for a single man can bend it to his will. It is a sort of wooden gun to the people themselves. But it is not
14   the less necessary for this; for the people must have some complicated machinery or other, and hear its din, to satisfy
15   that idea of government which they have. Governments show thus how successfully men can be imposed on, even
16   impose on themselves, for their own advantage. It is excellent, we must all allow. Yet this government never of itself
17   furthered any enterprise, but by the alacrity with which it got out of its way. It does not keep the country free. It does
18   not settle the West. It does not educate. The character inherent in the American people has done all that has been
19   accomplished; and it would have done somewhat more, if the government had not sometimes got in its way. For
20   government is an expedient by which men would fain succeed in letting one another alone; and, as has been said,
21   when it is most expedient, the governed are most let alone by it. Trade and commerce, if they were not made of
22   India rubber, would never manage to bounce over the obstacles which legislators are continually putting in their
23   way; and, if one were to judge these men wholly by the effects of their actions, and not partly by their intentions,
24   they would deserve to be classed and punished with those mischievous persons who put obstructions on the
25   railroads.
26       But, to speak practically and as a citizen, unlike those who call themselves no-government men, I ask for,
27   not at once no government, but at once a better government. Let every man make known what kind of government
28   would command his respect, and that will be one step toward obtaining it. . . . .
29       I know that most men think differently from myself; but those whose lives are by profession devoted to the
30   study of these or kindred subjects, content me as little as any. Statesmen and legislators, standing so completely
31   within the institution, never distinctly and nakedly behold it. They speak of moving society, but have no resting-
32   place without it. They may be men of a certain experience and discrimination, and have no doubt invented ingenious
33   and even useful systems, for which we sincerely thank them; but all their wit and usefulness lie within certain not
34   very wide limits. They are wont to forget that the world is not governed by policy and expediency. Webster never
35   goes behind government, and so cannot speak with authority about it. His words are wisdom to those legislators who
36   contemplate no essential reform in the existing government; but for thinkers, and those who legislate for all time, he
37   never once glances at the subject. I know of those whose serene and wise speculations on this theme would soon
38   reveal the limits of his mind's range and hospitality. Yet, compared with the cheap professions of most reformers,
39   and the still cheaper wisdom and eloquence of politicians in general, his are almost the only sensible and valuable
40   words, and we thank Heaven for him. Comparatively, he is always strong, original, and, above all, practical. Still,
41   his quality is not wisdom, but prudence. The lawyer's truth is not truth, but consistency or a consistent expediency.
42   Truth is always in harmony with herself, and is not concerned chiefly to reveal the justice that may consist with
43   wrong-doing. He well deserves to be called, as he has been called, the Defender of the Constitution. There are really
44   no blows to be given by him but defensive ones. He is not a leader, but a follower. His leaders are the men of '87. "I
45   have never made an effort," he says, "and never propose to make an effort; I have never countenanced an effort, and

46   never mean to countenance an effort, to disturb the arrangement as originally made, by which the various States
47   came into the Union." Still thinking of the sanction which the Constitution gives to slavery, he says, "Because it was
48   a part of the original compact—let it stand." Notwithstanding his special acuteness and ability, he is unable to take a
49   fact out of its merely political relations, and behold it as it lies absolutely to be disposed of by the intellect—what,
50   for instance, it behooves a man to do here in America to-day with regard to slavery, but ventures, or is driven, to
51   make some such desperate answer as the following, while professing to speak absolutely, and as a private man—
52   from which what new and singular code of social duties might be inferred? "The manner," says he, "in which the
53   governments of those States where slavery exists are to regulate it is for their own consideration, under their
54   responsibility to their constituents, to the general laws of propriety, humanity, and justice, and to God. Associations
55   formed elsewhere, springing from a feeling of humanity, or any other cause, have nothing whatever to do with it.
56   They have never received any encouragement from me, and they never will."
57        They who know of no purer sources of truth, who have traced up its stream no higher, stand, and wisely
58   stand, by the Bible and the Constitution, and drink at it there with reverence and humility; but they who behold
59   where it comes trickling into this lake or that pool, gird up their loins once more, and continue their pilgrimage
60   toward its fountain-head.
61        No man with a genius for legislation has appeared in America. They are rare in the history of the world.
62   There are orators, politicians, and eloquent men, by the thousand; but the speaker has not yet opened his mouth to
63   speak who is capable of settling the much-vexed questions of the day. We love eloquence for its own sake, and not
64   for any truth which it may utter, or any heroism it may inspire. Our legislators have not yet learned the comparative
65   value of free-trade and of freedom, of union, and of rectitude, to a nation. They have no genius or talent for
66   comparatively humble questions of taxation and finance, commerce and manufacturers and agriculture. If we were
67   left solely to the wordy wit of legislators in Congress for our guidance, uncorrected by the seasonable experience
68   and the effectual complaints of the people, America would not long retain her rank among the nations. For eighteen
69   hundred years, though perchance I have no right to say it, the New Testament has been written; yet where is the
70   legislator who has wisdom and practical talent enough to avail himself of the light which it sheds on the science of
71   legislation?
72        The authority of government, even such as I am willing to submit to—for I will cheerfully obey those who
73   know and can do better than I, and in many things even those who neither know nor can do so well—is still an
74   impure one: to be strictly just, it must have the sanction and consent of the governed. It can have no pure right over
75   my person and property but what I concede to it. The progress from an absolute to a limited monarchy, from a
76   limited monarchy to a democracy, is a progress toward a true respect for the individual. Even the Chinese
77   philosopher was wise enough to regard the individual as the basis of the empire. Is a democracy, such as we know it,
78   the last improvement possible in government? Is it not possible to take a step further towards recognizing and
79   organizing the rights of man? There will never be a really free and enlightened State until the State comes to
80   recognize the individual as a higher and independent power, from which all its own power and authority are derived,
81   and treats him accordingly. I please myself with imagining a State at least which can afford to be just to all men, and
82   to treat the individual with respect as a neighbor; which even would not think it inconsistent with its own repose if a
83   few were to live aloof from it, not meddling with it, nor embraced by it, who fulfilled all the duties of neighbors and
84   fellow-men. A State which bore this kind of fruit, and suffered it to drop off as fast as it ripened, would prepare the
85   way for a still more perfect and glorious State, which also I have imagined, but not yet anywhere seen.

(http://www.gutenberg.org/files/205/205-h/205-h.htm#linkW19)

## Student Response

1   Civil disobedience is a tricky subject. Citizens need enough power to resist government when necessary, but this
2   power should not be used or taken lightly. If citizens disobeyed the government every time they "judge for
3   themselves" (Thoreau) what is unjust or unfair, anarchy and utter chaos would soon follow. In his famous essay
4   "Civil Disobedience," Thoreau claims that men need the power to "judge for themselves" what is just and unjust,
5   and should act on this power, if need be, even if it means breaking laws and resisting the government. Thoreau
6   claims that such resistance allows a man to live according to his nature and allows a society to prepare the way for
7   "a still more perfect and glorious State, which also I have imagined, but not yet anywhere seen." Although this
8   theory seems very noble, and in the framework of Thoreau's reference may have been effective, Thoreau's theory of
9   civil disobedience is unrealistic in today's society.
10        Thoreau's theory for civil disobedience is unrealistic in today's society because today's society has fallen
11   away from believing in absolute truth. Thoreau claimed that in order for civil disobedience to work, there must be an
12   "absolute goodness" somewhere. In other words, citizens need an absolute truth and an absolute good with which to

13 compare government's laws and mandates. In the 1800s, when Thoreau wrote this essay, this absolute goodness was
14 Judeo-Christian morals. Our country was founded on these morals, and even though some citizens during Thoreau's
15 era and even during the founding of our nation were not Christian or Jewish, many still followed and believed in the
16 morals that were laid out in the Judeo-Christian religion. It is interesting to note how many times Thoreau uses the
17 word *just* in his essay. Thoreau assumes that there is a definite right and a definite wrong—a definite just and a
18 definite unjust action. While Thoreau was not a Christian, he, like most citizens up until our present day, believed
19 that our Judeo-Christian heritage and morals were the absolute goodness to which we should compare government's
20 laws and mandates. Because of our Christian-Judeo heritage, morals have been definite—up until now. Because in
21 today's society, the majority of citizens believe that truth is not absolute, but rather is relative and changing, men
22 can define their own justice. This power to define justice coupled with the power to disobey government could be
23 disastrous. Without the law to restrict citizens, citizens with no absolute goodness or truth could deem unjust
24 anything that was not convenient or pleasant to themselves, and consequently arbitrarily disobey the government.
25 This would inevitably lead to absolute anarchy and chaos.
26      Clearly, because we live in a society where "absolute goodness" does not exist in the minds of the majority,
27 civil disobedience in our society would be disastrous. The only firm goodness that holds men accountable today is
28 an artificial truth—the government's law. Without a governmental law, men would become "judges for themselves,"
29 lacking not only an artificial goodness, the law, but also an absolute goodness and truth. (Sarah)

1. In Passage 1, what does this statement mean? "They who know of no purer sources of truth, who have
   traced up its stream no higher, stand, and wisely stand, by the Bible and the Constitution, and drink at it
   there with reverence and humility; but they who behold where it comes trickling into this lake or that pool,
   gird up their loins once more, and continue their pilgrimage toward its fountain-head?" (Lines 56–59).
   A. The Bible and the Constitution have no application to civil affairs.
   B. The Bible and the Constitution are the law of the land and must be obeyed.
   C. The Bible and the Constitution, like so many traditional sources, are fine and good for hypothetical
      problems but have very little practical application.
   D. The Bible and the Constitution are pure sources of truth that are tainted with human foibles.

2. Thoreau wrote this essay on civil disobedience to explain his decision to withhold tax payments and
   thereby show his objections to the Mexican War, 1846–48. What is his main argument?
   A. Thoreau begins his essay by arguing that government derives its power from the majority because they
      are the strongest group, not because they possess the moral high ground.
   B. Government that governs best, governs least.
   C. The Mexican War is an unjust war and the government has no right to expect Americans to support it.
   D. Americans should rebel against the United States government.

3. What part of Passage 1 supports the above answer?
   A. Lines 1–2                          C. Lines 28–32
   B. Lines 11–12                        D. Lines 58–60

4. What is the main argument advanced by Passage 2?
   A. Thoreau was right.
   B. Civil disobedience violates the Bible and therefore is inappropriate.
   C. Civil disobedience is not an appropriate course of action because it presupposes a higher moral good
      that is rejected by society.
   D. Civil disobedience is a correct course of action if it is conducted peacefully.

**Data Analysis**

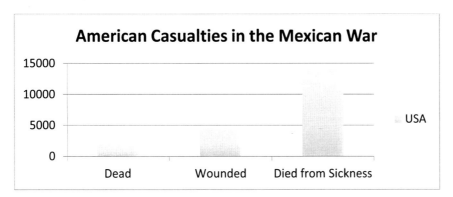

1. Which of these statements are supported by the graph?
    A. Over 20,000 soldiers died.
    B. Slightly less than double the number of soldiers were wounded compared to those who were killed.
    C. More soldiers died from sickness than from all other injuries combined.
    D. Casualties in the Mexican War were higher proportionately than any other American conflict.

2. What can be surmised from this graph?
    I.   Placing a lot of people in one place—like in an army—caused diseases to spread rapidly.
    II.  Nineteenth-century medicine was inadequate.
    III. The Mexican military forces were not very good fighters.
    IV.  Nineteenth-century American soldiers typically were unhealthy.

        A. I and II                          C. I and III
        B. II and IV                         D. II and III

3. The Mexican army suffered 25,000 deaths, due to battle and to other causes. What are plausible explanations for this larger casualty rate?
    I.   The Mexican army was larger than the American army.
    II.  American weapons and tactics were more successful.
    III. Mexican leaders did not value human life.
    IV.  A massive smallpox epidemic spread through the Mexican army.

        A. I                                 C. I and III
        B. II                                D. II and IV

# Lesson 5
## Math: Algebra, Arithmetic Problem Solving and Data Analysis, and Passport to Advanced Math

**Passport to Advanced Math**

Triangle ABC (below) is isosceles with AB = AC and BC = 48. The ratio of DE to DF is 5:7. What is the length of DC?

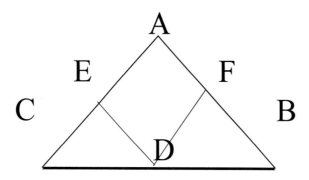

A. 10

B. 18

C. 22

D. 28

## Algebra

1.  A piece of work can be finished by 3 men in 8 days, or by 5 women in 6 days, or by 6 boys in 6 days. In what time can 2 men, 3 women, and 3 boys do the work?

    A.  3.5 days

    B.  2.85 days

    C.  3.75 days

    D.  4.25 days

2.  John, having three times as much money as Lewis, gave Lewis $2, and then had twice as much as Lewis. How much had each at first?

    A.  J., $19; L., $7

    B.  J., $17; L., $5

    C.  J., $18; L., $6

    D.  J., $20; L., $8

3.  A fish is 3 feet long; its head is equal in length to the tail, and its body is five times the length of the head and tail together. What is the length of the head?

    A.  3 inches

    B.  4 inches

    C.  6 inches

    D.  3.5 inches

4.  If 2 is subtracted from both numerator and denominator of a certain fraction, its value is 3/5; and if 1 is added to both numerator and denominator its value is 2/3. What is the fraction?

    A.  5/8

    B.  7/9

    C.  11/16

    D.  11/17

5. If 2 is added to both numerator and denominator of a certain fraction, its value is 2/3; but if 3 is subtracted from both numerator and denominator, its value is 1/2. What is the fraction?

   A. 4/7
   B. 5/6

   C. 8/13
   D. 9/11

6. If 3 is subtracted from the numerator of a certain fraction, and 3 is added to the denominator, its value will be 1/2; but if 5 is added to the numerator, and 5 is subtracted from its denominator, its value will be 2. What is the fraction?

   A. 4/9
   B. 7/12

   C. 11/13
   D. 10/11

# Chapter 11   If Christ Had Not Risen
# 1 Corinthians 15

*Memory Verses:* When the perishable has been clothed with the imperishable, and the mortal with immortality, then the saying that is written will come true: "Death has been swallowed up in victory."
  "Where, O death, is your victory?
  Where, O death, is your sting?"
The sting of death is sin, and the power of sin is the law. But thanks be to God! He gives us the victory through our Lord Jesus Christ. —1 Corinthians 15:54–57

Easter is a unique feature of Christianity. That is not because more "Christians" go to church on that Sunday, but because Easter celebrates the resurrection of Jesus Christ from the dead. The resurrection is the bedrock of our faith, the reason we can believe in the miraculous. Christianity teaches that its founder is living today! No other religion of the world makes such a startling claim. Other religions may claim that the "spirit" of their founder lives on today in his religious teachings, but Christianity claims that Jesus himself lives today—bodily! Biblical Christianity teaches that Jesus Christ really died but then arose physically (not just spiritually) from the grave and presented himself alive to many different people on many different occasions over a period of forty days (Acts 1:3; 1 Corinthians 15:3–8). Christianity further teaches that after those undeniable physical appearances, Jesus Christ bodily left this earth and promised to return physically someday (John 14:1–3; Acts 1:9–11). Although we Christians know and experience the spiritual presence of our living Lord Jesus now, we look forward to his physical return. True Christian faith holds that Jesus Christ was resurrected from the dead bodily, ascended into heaven bodily, lives today in glory bodily, and will someday return to this earth bodily.

The French skeptic and thinker Auguste Comte once told the English writer Thomas Carlyle that he was going to start a new religion that would replace Christianity. "Very good," replied Carlyle. "All you have to do is to be crucified, rise again the third day, and get the world to believe that you are still alive." "If Christ has not been raised, our preaching is useless and so is your faith," Paul argues (1 Corinthians 15:14). "If I were an enemy of Christianity, I'd aim right at the resurrection, because that's the heart of Christianity," Billy Graham writes. "I believe he rose bodily. Otherwise you'd have to throw out the Easter story, because he showed the nail prints in his hands. If Christ didn't rise, as Paul said, it all has no meaning."

From the first Easter until today, people find that their lives are changed by the historical Jesus—not merely by moral or ethical teachings.

The physical resurrection of Jesus Christ from the dead is the keystone of the Christian faith. Christianity is ultimately based not only on ethical and religious teachings (as in other world religions) but also on a historical event! The foundation of our faith is not just what Jesus taught but also what he did in history to back up his claims. You see, any self-styled religious leader can proclaim certain ethical and virtuous and noble teachings; he may even dare to say, "I am the good shepherd." Some would even go further and say, "I lay down my life for my sheep," and then actually die for "some good cause." But who can continue those statements as Jesus did (John 10:14–18) and claim a physical resurrection? "I lay down my life—only to take it up again. No one takes it from me, but I lay it down of my own accord. I have authority to lay it down and authority to take it up again." What a claim! The ethical teachings of Jesus are inseparable from his claims about himself and his power over death. If Jesus Christ did not bodily rise from the dead, then he was a deceiver (not even a good man), and Christianity is a fraud and a farce, Christians are just playing around at religious games. Christianity, then, effects history in a profound way.

Scripture teaches that such radical statements are logical conclusions, *if indeed* the resurrection of Christ did not take place. In 1 Corinthians 15:12–19 we are given several conclusions to which we must come if Christ has not risen from the dead. Without the bodily resurrection of Christ, Christianity is stripped of its basis and power. C. S. Lewis bluntly observes, "A man who was merely a man and said the sort of things Jesus said wouldn't be a great moral teacher. He'd either be a lunatic . . . or else he'd be the Devil . . . or Lord. Take your choice!" (*Mere Christianity*, book 2, chap. 3).

The apostle Paul wrote this passage to the Corinthian believers who were confused over the concept of the future physical resurrection of Christians who had already died. They did not doubt the resurrection of Christ; they believed in it wholeheartedly (1 Corinthians 15:11). But the concept of a bodily resurrection for believers was hard for them to grasp. Apparently they did not have any problem with the idea of the spirit's living on in some other world, because the immortality of the soul was certainly part of the prevalent Greek philosophy. But the resurrection of the body was a new revelation for them—a mindblower!

The apostle directed the attention of the Corinthian believers to the Lord's resurrection. If they believed in the physical resurrection of Christ, why should they find the concept of the physical resurrection of the Christian so hard to grasp (15:12)? If God raised Jesus Christ from human death, it was logical that God could raise any person from the dead. But the opposite was logically true too! If there was no such thing as the physical resurrection of persons from the dead, then even Christ could not have been raised (15:12, 16). After all, Jesus (although he was God) was a real flesh-and-blood person, and he really died. Where does that logic lead us, then? If Christ was not raised, the Christian faith has no solid foundation, and everything about it is up for grabs.

That logical conclusion is as true today as it was in Paul's day. If Christ is not risen, our preaching is empty (15:14). The nice-sounding words contain no reality. If Christ is still dead, what authority do we have for even preaching, "Love your neighbor as yourself" (Leviticus 19:18)—and still less ground for preaching the resurrection? We become humanistic preachers, with no higher authority than what the majority of the people "feel" is right—a totally subjective and relative consensus! If Jesus is not living today, the message of the Bible is void of authority and hollow: our preaching is empty!

If Christ is not risen, our faith is empty (1 Corinthians 15:14). There is no foundation for our Christian faith, if Easter is a hoax. Pinning our destiny on the teachings and claims of a man who is dead is just wishful thinking. What guarantee do we have for any hope beyond the cemetery, if the One who claimed that he could conquer death is, in reality, dead himself? Christian faith based on the teachings of a dead Christ is like a beautiful castle built on thin air.

If Christ is not risen, we are false witnesses of God (15:15). We are not just deluded religious fanatics playing church: we are downright liars! Of course, if God does not really exist, then it doesn't matter much if we're liars, since there are no absolute standards. However, if God does exist but did not raise Christ from the dead, and yet we go on celebrating Easter, then we have distorted the truth and become false witnesses against God himself (15:15). That is what we must conclude, if there is no physical resurrection from the dead (15:16).

If Christ is not risen, our faith is worthless, and we are still in our sins (15:17). Not only is our faith without foundation (15:14), but it also is useless. What good is it? Does it give us salvation? No way ! Not if the One who claimed he would take away our sins is still in a tomb near Jerusalem. If some kind of payment for the wrongs is not made, there can be no forgiving or forgetting of sins in a moral universe. If the One in whom we place our faith as Savior never triumphed over death, what proof do we have that any debt has been paid? Without the resurrection, the death penalty for our sins remains (Romans 6:23). We are still held liable for our wrongdoing. We are still in our sins: guilty! If there is no resurrection, there is no redemption and no reconciliation with God.

If Christ is not risen, those "who have fallen asleep in Christ are lost" (15:18). If Easter is a sham, then Christians who have died are forever lost. There will be no awakening from the grave. The familiar Christian epitaph, "Asleep in Jesus," is just a euphemism for "condemned to death forever." The word "perished" (15:18 NRSV) does not mean annihilation or extinction but rather loss and ruin. It is loss, not of being, but of well-being. Any so-called "light at the end of a tunnel" (reported by some near-death persons) is not necessarily the light of heaven, as many people would like to assume (see Hebrews 11:16).

If Christ is not risen, and if we have hope in Christ only for this life, we are to be pitied more than all people (1 Corinthians 15:19). Why? Because we have sacrificed and surrendered and suffered and labored and hoped for nothing but an illusion. *If* Jesus is not alive today, we are superstitious fools living in a dream world. This fantasy may give us peace of mind and hope in this life, but so what? Why all the sweat and tears if it's all a delusion? As far as the apostle Paul is concerned, if there is no resurrection, we ought to "live it up" and "do our own thing." That is exactly what he says in verse 32. Without Easter, dead Christians have perished, and living Christians are to be pitied (15:18–19).

"Every religion has its holy moments, its Easter, its holy moments, but . . . only in Christendom . . . is its faith built around miracles," writes Nancy Gibbs in *Time* magazine. That is true. But salvation is perhaps the greatest miracle: Christ died for our sins, arose from the dead, and now invites us to join him in victory. How about it? Are you ready? Will you join Christ? In order to do so, we need to confess our sins, believe that we are forgiven, and then publicly confess our faith. Think about it. If you would like to make a commitment, or to learn more about this faith, speak with a pastor or elder in the church.

But Christ has been raised from the dead (15:20)! What a glorious relief! All those previous deductions are swept away with this one great truth. The resurrection of the Lord Jesus Christ is the proof and power of Christianity. The empty tomb guarantees the Christian's hope. As the early fruit is the promise of the harvest soon to come, so the resurrection of our Lord is the guarantee that death has been conquered for every Christian. Hallelujah! He has risen indeed!

## Journal Question

Why is the resurrection so important to our faith?

# Lesson 1
## Evidence-Based Reading and Writing

### Literary Choice

*Fail-Safe* is a best-selling novel by Eugene Burdick and Harvey Wheeler. The popular and critically acclaimed novel, released in late October 1962 (during the Cuban Missile Crisis), was then adapted into a 1964 film.

### Student Response 1: *Fail-Safe* Book Review

1　The central argument of the book *Fail-Safe* is that procedures intended to prevent a disaster can actually cause the
2　disaster it sought to prevent. In the book, the military has a series of fail-safe protocols and mechanisms that are
3　designed to prevent an accidental nuclear war. One fail-safe protection is that the pilots have standing orders not to
4　go past a certain point without receiving an attack code. In the novel, a technical failure results in that exact code
5　being transmitted to a group of nuclear-armed bombers, who then fly toward Moscow. Thus the fail-safe protocols
6　cause the very thing they were intended to prevent.

7　　　Eugene Burdick and Harvey Wheeler coauthored *Fail-Safe*. Eugene was born December 12, 1918, and
8　John was born on October 17 the same year. Wheeler earned his bachelor's and master's degrees at Indiana
9　University and his PhD at Harvard, then taught at John Hopkins University. Burdick attended Stanford University
10　and Oxford University, where he earned a PhD in psychology. In addition to coauthoring *Fail-Safe* with Wheeler,
11　Burdick with William Lederer coauthored *The Ugly American*, *The Deceptive American*, and *Sarkhan: A Novel*;
12　Burdick also published *The Ninth Wave* and *The 480*, and he worked in the department of political science at the
13　University of California. Wheeler's books include *Democracy in a Revolutionary Era* and *The Virtual Library* (e-
14　book), as well as editing about a dozen others. Wheeler was also a founding editor of the *Journal of Social and
15　Biological Structures* and a longtime fellow at Center for the Study of Democratic Institutions in California. Burdick
16　died July 26, 1965, and Wheeler died September 6, 2004.

17　　　One argument of *Fail-Safe* is that humans must not rely on technology too much. The entire accidental
18　nuclear incident is caused by a small mechanical error in the machine created to ensure that no such thing would
19　happen. In fact, while the politicians and professors state that the machine should have been infallible, one scientist
20　points out that it is impossible to create such a machine: the more complex a machine becomes, the smaller the
21　mistake needs to be for a catastrophe to be created. Near the end of the book, the U.S. president and Soviet Premier
22　state that they should take care to be less dependent on technology in the future. Another argument is that events
23　cannot be plotted out to expected results. Professor Groteschele is a professor who is completely for nuclear war at
24　the time of the incident and is denounced for his theories on nuclear annihilation. He predicts that if a nuclear
25　incident happens, a full nuclear war will emerge and people will survive. He tries to convince the U.S. government
26　to launch a real nuclear attack, citing that the Soviets are Marxists, and Marxists will want to ensure that the world
27　continues. What the professor does not predict is the U.S. President offering to destroy New York City in order to
28　prevent nuclear war. So runs the novel.

29　　　One counterargument of *Failsafe* is that sometimes great sacrifices are necessary. Near the end of the book,
30　when it is clear that Moscow will be nuked, the President proposes that New York City also be bombed. This is a
31　huge sacrifice and a personal one as well, since the President's wife is currently in New York. However, it is a
32　necessary sacrifice, for the Russian military will no doubt retaliate by destroying all of America. This solution
33　shocks even the Russian premier, who exclaims, "Holy Mother of God!" But he understands that it is necessary to
34　preserve other lives.

35　　　Critics have praised the book as one of the best, if not the best, Cold War thriller. They praise it for its in-
36　depth characters and brisk, but not rushed, pace. Many critics state that the book was more exciting and meaningful
37　back during the Cold War, especially before and during the Cuban Missile Crisis. Still, it is a highly praised book.

38　　　*Fail-Safe* is a very dramatic and brisk book, in my opinion. The book provides a clear picture of the very
39　real threat of nuclear war and its repercussions. The characters are very detailed and vivid, from the young Russian
40　translator to the President to the aggressive pro-nuclear war Jewish professor. The plot is very good, especially the
41　twist near the end. All in all, it is a great book about an anxious time. (Robinson)

## Student Response 2

1 "We're not just walking wounded, we're walking dead men," says Colonel Grady in *Fail-Safe* right before his team
2 of bombers bomb Moscow and simultaneously commit suicide. Within *Fail-Safe*, human trust in technology causes
3 millions to die as an attack order is transmitted to a group of six Vindicator supersonic bombers through a technical
4 failure. *Fail-Safe* was written as a warning to humanity on the dangers of overreliance on technology. Now in the
5 year, this problem has come true. Education for an average American has fallen, health for the typical American has
6 plunged, and distractions for a regular American have soared.

7 Technology replaces knowledge. As technology improves, human learning decreases. With the Internet a
8 couple seconds away via the nearest iPhone, iPad, or Mac computer, who would actually try to learn the
9 information? Students these days have trouble spelling simple words such as *accommodate*, *ecstasy*, and *tattoo*.

10 Recently students all over the world took part in PISA (Programme for International Student Assessment),
11 a testing survey to see how each country's education compared. Out of 65 different countries, the United States
12 scored 37th in mathematics, 24th in reading, and 28th in science. Despite the U.S.'s amazing economy, they still
13 were situated under the OECD (Organization for Economic Cooperation and Development) average. The OECD
14 states, "This is most probably the cause of students in America having too much access to the Internet." All in all, as
15 a result of an improvement and increase in technology, the younger generation has become more slow-witted. Not
16 only that but also this generation will later teach the next generation and so on, in what is to be a terrible cycle in
17 human intellectual decline.

18 Health in America drops constantly as technology intrudes more and more into the average person's
19 lifestyle. More and more Americans become "couch potatoes" every day. According to the Center for Disease
20 Control and Prevention (CDC), obesity now affects 17 percent of all children and adolescents in the United States,
21 triple the rate from just one generation ago. The cause is painfully obvious. Kids are eating and drinking too many
22 calories, and they're not getting enough physical exercise. The CDC also states that children from 8 to 18 years of
23 age spend an average of 7.5 hours a day using entertainment media: TV, computers, video games, cell phones, and
24 movies. Kids themselves spend about 4.5 hours of that time watching TV. No one should be especially surprised if
25 someday everyone becomes like the tubby humans in the movie *Wall-E*.

26 Introversion is common. Too many Americans today are becoming introverts or recluses. While the
27 Internet and mobile devices have made accessing useful information easy and have exponentially increased our
28 efficiency in locating, reading, and disseminating quality information, human beings have lost their touch with the
29 present. Many people have become unable to separate themselves from technology whether for two minutes or two
30 hours. They constantly seem content to do something on their phones rather than really be present during many of
31 their daily interactions and activities. Evidence of this can be found whenever someone is driving. Next time
32 someone is at a stoplight, look around and see how many people are on their phones.

33 Technology has taken over! Education for America is in shambles, health for Americans is steadily
34 deteriorating, and distractions abound. Just as *Fail-Safe* warns, Americans are relying too much on technology; just
35 as technology cost millions of human lives in the novel *Fail-Safe*, so will technology do to America now. Chew on
36 this last statement: a recent study in Australia found that, after age 25, every hour spent watching television reduces
37 the viewer's lifespan by 21.8 minutes. Next time you sit down to watch TV, watch out! The clock is ticking.
38 (Candice)

## Close Reading

1. According to Student Response 1, why is *Fail-Safe* full of irony?
   A. Moscow is bombed.
   B. The very thing fail-safe was designed to stop, it in fact creates.
   C. The robots kill their human host.
   D. New York is bombed.

2. According to Student Response 1, the plot generally is about
   A. A fictional account of how a computer program malfunctions and causes a world catastrophe
   B. A husband and his wife and their last few days on earth
   C. An environmental catastrophe
   D. A surprise attack by Russia

3. Which of the following statements is true about Student Response 1?
   A. The novel is not well written.
   B. The novel is one of the best fictional accounts of a nuclear war in literature.
   C. The fail-safe system works after all.
   D. American missiles were able to intercept all of the bombers.

4. Why is it significant that the novel was released in October 1962?
   A. It was when John F. Kennedy was assassinated.
   B. It was during the Vietnam War.
   C. It was during the Cuban Missile Crisis.
   D. It was at the end of the fiscal year and would affect the defense budget.

5. Both Student Response 1 and Student Response 2 share a central thesis, that
   A. Modern humankind must be careful with the emerging technologies used in modern society.
   B. The Russians cannot be trusted.
   C. The Cold War is over.
   D. The United States Air Force sometimes acts rashly.

6. A central thesis of Student Response 2 can be found in
   A. Lines 1–2          C. Lines 13–14
   B. Lines 4–6          D. Lines 34–36

## Command of Evidence

1. What sort of evidence does Student Response 2 offer to support this central thesis?
   A. Technology creates laziness.
   B. Technology increases profits among social media sites.
   C. Technology has not solved problems in education and health.
   D. Technology cannot change hearts and minds.

2. Which of the following novels have a similar theme to *Fail-Safe*?
   A. *Tom Sawyer*                    C. *The Tragedy of Faust*
   B. *All Quiet on the Western Front*  D. *Frankenstein*

3. A counterargument to Student Responses 1 and 2 could be that
   A. Technology is good in the right hands.
   B. Nature should be left alone.
   C. If technology leads to problems, it is because human beings fail, not technology.
   D. Technology is easily maligned, but generally it is very necessary and good.

4. Identify the argument development in Student Response 1:

```
┌─────────────────┐   ┌─────────────────┐   ┌─────────────────┐
│   Arguments     │   │                 │   │                 │
│ Presented in the│   │ Counterargument │   │        ?        │
│      Text       │   │                 │   │                 │
└─────────────────┘   └─────────────────┘   └─────────────────┘
```

   A. Critical responses to the book
   B. State of the United States in the early 1960s
   C. History of the Cold War
   D. The Cuban Missile Crisis

# Lesson 2
## Critical Reading and Writing

### Command of Evidence

Read the following passage, from a Babcock and Wilcox book published in 1875 and still in print in new editions.

*Steam: Its Generation and Use*

1　While the time of man's first knowledge and use of the expansive force of the vapor of water is unknown, records
2　show that such knowledge existed earlier than 150 B.C. In a treatise of about that time entitled "Pneumatica," Hero,
3　of Alexander, described not only existing devices of his predecessors and contemporaries but also an invention of
4　his own which utilized the expansive force of steam for raising water above its natural level. He clearly describes
5　three methods in which steam might be used directly as a motive of power; raising water by its elasticity, elevating a
6　weight by its expansive power and producing a rotary motion by its reaction on the atmosphere. The third method,
7　which is known as "Hero's engine," is described as a hollow sphere supported over a caldron or boiler by two
8　trunnions, one of which was hollow, and connected the interior of the sphere with the steam space of the caldron.
9　Two pipes, open at the ends and bent at right angles, were inserted at opposite poles of the sphere, forming a
10　connection between the caldron and the atmosphere. Heat being applied to the caldron, the steam generated passed
11　through the hollow trunnion to the sphere and thence into the atmosphere through the two pipes. By the reaction
12　incidental to its escape through these pipes, the sphere was caused to rotate and here is the primitive steam reaction
13　turbine.
14　　　　Hero makes no suggestions as to application of any of the devices he describes to a useful purpose. From
15　the time of Hero until the late sixteenth and early seventeenth centuries, there is no record of progress, though
16　evidence is found that such devices as were described by Hero were sometimes used for trivial purposes, the
17　blowing of an organ or the turning of a skillet.
18　　　　Mathesius, the German author, in 1571; Besson, a philosopher and mathematician at Orleans; Ramelli, in
19　1588; Battista Delia Porta, a Neapolitan mathematician and philosopher, in 1601; Decause, the French engineer and
20　architect, in 1615; and Branca, an Italian architect, in 1629, all published treatises bearing on the subject of the
21　generation of steam.
22　　　　To the next contributor, Edward Somerset, second Marquis of Worcester, is apparently due the credit of
23　proposing, if not of making, the first useful steam engine. In the "Century of Scantlings and Inventions," published
24　in London in 1663, he describes devices showing that he had in mind the raising of water not only by forcing it from
25　two receivers by direct steam pressure but also for some sort of reciprocating piston actuating one end of a lever, the
26　other operating a pump. His descriptions are rather obscure and no drawings are extant so that it is difficult to say
27　whether there were any distinctly novel features to his devices aside from the double action. While there is no direct
28　authentic record that any of the devices he described were actually constructed, it is claimed by many that he really
29　built and operated a steam engine containing pistons.
30　　　　In 1675, Sir Samuel Moreland was decorated by King Charles II, for a demonstration of "a certain powerful
31　machine to raise water." Though there appears to be no record of the design of this machine, the mathematical
32　dictionary, published in 1822, credits Moreland with the first account of a steam engine, on which subject he wrote a
33　treatise that is still preserved in the British Museum.
34　　　　Dr. Denys Papin, an ingenious Frenchman, invented in 1680 "a steam digester for extracting marrowy,
35　nourishing juices from bones by enclosing them in a boiler under heavy pressure," and finding danger from
36　explosion, added a contrivance which is the first safety valve on record.
37　　　　The steam engine first became commercially successful with Thomas Savery. In 1699, Savery exhibited
38　before the Royal Society of England (Sir Isaac Newton was President at the time), a model engine which consisted
39　of two copper receivers alternately connected by a three-way hand-operated valve, with a boiler and a source of
40　water supply. When the water in one receiver had been driven out by the steam, cold water was poured over its
41　outside surface, creating a vacuum through condensation and causing it to fill again while the water in the other
42　reservoir was being forced out. A number of machines were built on this principle and placed in actual use as mine
43　pumps.
44　　　　The serious difficulty encountered in the use of Savery's engine was the fact that the height to which it
45　could lift water was limited by the pressure the boiler and vessels could bear. Before Savery's engine was entirely
46　displaced by its successor, Newcomen's, it was considerably improved by Desaguliers, who applied the Papin safety
47　valve to the boiler and substituted condensation by a jet within the vessel for Savery's surface condensation.

48       In 1690, Papin suggested that the condensation of steam should be employed to make a vacuum beneath a
49 cylinder which had previously been raised by the expansion of steam. This was the earliest cylinder and piston steam
50 engine and his plan took practical shape in Newcomen's atmospheric engine. Papin's first engine was unworkable
51 owing to the fact that he used the same vessel for both boiler and cylinder. A small quantity of water was placed in
52 the bottom of the vessel and heat was applied. When steam formed and raised the piston, the heat was withdrawn
53 and the piston did work on its down stroke under pressure of the atmosphere. After hearing of Savery's engine,
54 Papin developed an improved form. Papin's engine of 1705 consisted of a displacement chamber in which a floating
55 diaphragm or piston on top of the water kept the steam and water from direct contact. The water delivered by the
56 downward movement of the piston under pressure, to a closed tank, flowed in a continuous stream against the vanes
57 of a water wheel. When the steam in the displacement chamber had expanded, it was exhausted to the atmosphere
58 through a valve instead of being condensed. The engine was, in fact, a non-condensing, single action steam pump
59 with the steam and pump cylinders in one. A curious feature of this engine was a heater placed in the diaphragm.
60 This was a mass of heated metal for the purpose of keeping the steam dry or preventing condensation during
61 expansion. This device might be called the first superheater.
62       Among the various inventions attributed to Papin was a boiler with an internal fire box, the earliest record
63 of such construction.
64       While Papin had neglected his earlier suggestion of a steam and piston engine to work on Savery's ideas,
65 Thomas Newcomen, with his assistant, John Cawley, put into practical form Papin's suggestion of 1690. Steam
66 admitted from the boiler to a cylinder raised a piston by its expansion, assisted by a counter-weight on the other end
67 of a beam actuated by the piston. The steam valve was then shut and the steam condensed by a jet of cold water. The
68 piston was then forced downward by atmospheric pressure and did work on the pump. The condensed water in the
69 cylinder was expelled through an escapement valve by the next entry of steam. This engine used steam having
70 pressure but little, if any, above that of the atmosphere.
71       In 1711, this engine was introduced into mines for pumping purposes. Whether its action was originally
72 automatic or whether dependent upon the hand operation of the valves is a question of doubt. The story commonly
73 believed is that a boy, Humphrey Potter, in 1713, whose duty it was to open and shut such valves of an engine he
74 attended, by suitable cords and catches attached to the beam, caused the engine to automatically manipulate these
75 valves. This device was simplified in 1718 by Henry Beighton, who suspended from the bottom, a rod called the
76 plug-tree, which actuated the valve by tappets. By 1725, this engine was in common use in the collieries and was
77 changed but little for a matter of sixty or seventy years. Compared with Savery's engine, from the aspect of a
78 pumping engine, Newcomen's was a distinct advance, in that the pressure in the pumps was in no manner dependent
79 upon the steam pressure. In common with Savery's engine, the losses from the alternate heating and cooling of the
80 steam cylinder were enormous. Though obviously this engine might have been modified to serve many purposes, its
81 use seems to have been limited almost entirely to the pumping of water.
82       The rivalry between Savery and Papin appears to have stimulated attention to the question of fuel saving.
83 Dr. John Allen, in 1730, called attention to the fact that owing to the short length of time of the contact between the
84 gases and the heating surfaces of the boiler, nearly half of the heat of the fire was lost. With a view to overcoming
85 this loss at least partially, he used an internal furnace with a smoke flue winding through the water in the form of a
86 worm in a still. In order that the length of passage of the gases might not act as a damper on the fire, Dr. Allen
87 recommended the use of a pair of bellows for forcing the sluggish vapor through the flue. This is probably the first
88 suggested use of forced draft. In forming an estimate of the quantity of fuel lost up the stack, Dr. Allen probably
89 made the first boiler test.
90       Toward the end of the period of use of Newcomen's atmospheric engine, John Smeaton, who, about 1770,
91 built and installed a number of large engines of this type, greatly improved the design in its mechanical details.
92       The improvement in boiler and engine design of Smeaton, Newcomen and their contemporaries, were
93 followed by those of the great engineer, James Watt, an instrument maker of Glasgow. In 1763, while repairing a
94 model of Newcomen's engine, he was impressed by the great waste of steam to which the alternating cooling and
95 heating of the engine gave rise. His remedy was the maintaining of the cylinder as hot as the entering steam and with
96 this in view he added a vessel separate from the cylinder, into which the steam should pass from the cylinder and be
97 there condensed either by the application of cold water outside or by a jet from within. To preserve a vacuum in his
98 condenser, he added an air pump which should serve to remove the water of condensation and air brought in with
99 the injection water or due to leakage. As the cylinder no longer acted as a condenser, he could maintain it at a high
100 temperature by covering it with non-conducting material and, in particular, by the use of a steam jacket. Further and
101 with the same object in view, he covered the top of the cylinder and introduced steam above the piston to do the
102 work previously accomplished by atmospheric pressure. After several trials with an experimental apparatus based on
103 these ideas, Watt patented his improvements in 1769. Aside from their historical importance, Watt's improvements,

104 as described in his specification, are to this day a statement of the principles which guide the scientific development
105 of the steam engine.
106     The early efforts of Watt are typical of those of the poor inventor struggling with insufficient resources to
107 gain recognition and it was not until he became associated with the wealthy manufacturer, Mattheu Boulton of
108 Birmingham, that he met with the success upon which his present fame is based. In partnership with Boulton, the
109 business of the manufacture and the sale of his engines were highly successful in spite of vigorous attacks on the
110 validity of his patents.
111     It has been the object of this brief history of the early developments in the use of steam to cover such
112 developments only through the time of James Watt. The progress of the steam engine from this time through the
113 stages of higher pressures, combining of cylinders, the application of steam vehicles and steamboats, the adding of
114 third and fourth cylinders, to the invention of the turbine with its development and the accompanying development
115 of the reciprocating engine to hold its place, is one long attribute to the inventive genius of man.
116     While little is said in the biographies of Watt as to the improvement of steam boilers, all the evidence
117 indicates that Boulton and Watt introduced the first "wagon boiler," so called because of its shape. In 1785, Watt
118 took out a number of patents for variations in furnace construction, many of which contain the basic principles of
119 some of the modern smoke preventing furnaces. Until the early part of the nineteenth century, the low steam
120 pressures used caused but little attention to be given to the form of the boiler operated in connection with the
121 engines above described. About 1800, Richard Trevithick, in England, and Oliver Evans, in America, introduced
122 non-condensing, and for that time, high pressure steam engines. To the initiative of Evans may be attributed the
123 general use of high pressure steam in the United States, a feature which for many years distinguished American from
124 European practice. The demand for light weight and economy of space following the beginning of steam navigation
125 and the invention of the locomotive required boilers designed and constructed to withstand heavier pressures and
126 forced the adoption of the cylindrical form of boiler. There are in use to-day many examples of every step in the
127 development of steam boilers from the first plain cylindrical boiler to the most modern type of multi-tubular
128 locomotive boiler, which stands as the highest type of fire-tube boiler construction.

(*Steam: Its Generation and Use*, 35th ed. [New York: Babcock & Wilcox Co., 1919],
from chap. 1, http://www.gutenberg.org/files/22657/22657-h/header.html)

1. In the early development of the steam engine, the most serious problem encountered was
   A. How to build a boiler.
   B. The height to which it could lift water was limited by the pressure the boiler and vessels could bear.
   C. What sort of pulley should be used.
   D. The best energy source.

2. Most historians claim that James Watt invented the steam engine, but what is the truth?
   A. Mattheu Boulton really invented the steam engine.
   B. Savery and Papin really invented the steam engine.
   C. The invention was a collaborative effort, with Watt finally putting everything together into practical
      use.
   D. The early Greeks invented steam power

3. Evidence to support the above conclusion can be found in
   A. Lines 22–23              C. Lines 109–13
   B. Lines 34–35              D. Lines 124–28

4. Lines 106–10 explain:
   A. Like so many discoveries, they remain dormant until investment capital is available.
   B. James Watt stole someone's invention.
   C. Like so many inventions, many early mistakes were made.
   D. James Watt gave up many times in great discouragement.

5. Based upon this passage one could conclude that
   A. James Watt is a genius.
   B. Most inventions are often the culmination of decades, perhaps centuries, of scientific advancements.
   C. The press often creates a false notion of who is the "inventor."
   D. The steam engine is the most important invention since the wheel.

6. The basic structure in this passage can best be described as
   A. The author begins with an introduction to James Watt and then moves back and forward with a history of steam power.
   B. The author outlines some of the main obstacles to steam power and how they were overcome.
   C. The author gives an overview of English society in the Industrial Revolution and offers some insights to its application to steam power.
   D. The author gives a chronological overview of the invention of steam power with special attention to James Watt.

7. Which of the following passages would naturally follow from the above passage?
   A. Since the first appearance in *Steam* of the following "Requirements of a Perfect Steam Boiler," the list has been copied many times either word for word or clothed in different language and applied to some specific type of boiler design or construction.
   B. As stated in the previous chapter, the first water-tube boiler was built by John Blakey and was patented by him in 1766. Several tubes alternately inclined at opposite angles were arranged in the furnaces, the adjacent tube ends being connected by small pipes.
   C. Quite as much may be learned from the records of failures as from those of success. Where a device has been once fairly tried and found to be imperfect or impracticable, the knowledge of that trial is of advantage in further investigation.
   D. The following brief description of the Babcock and Wilcox boiler will clearly indicate the manner in which it fulfills the requirements of the perfect steam boiler already enumerated.

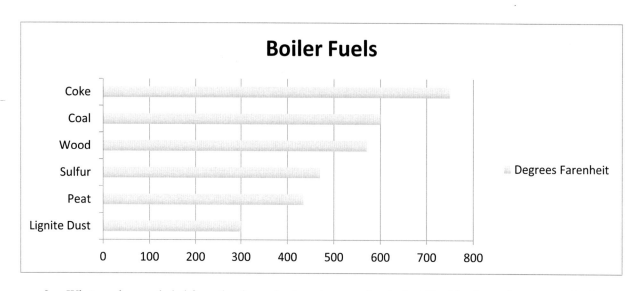

8. What can be concluded from the above chart on steam engine fuels utilized by the early steam engine?
   I. Coke burns at double the temperature of lignite dust.
   II. Coal burns at a slightly higher temperature than wood.
   III. Sulfur burns less efficiently than coal but is more abundant.
   IV. Peat is abundantly available.

   | | |
   |---|---|
   | A. I | D. IV |
   | B. II | E. I and II |
   | C. III | F. III and IV |

9. The early Glasgow to London steam engine burned peat, even though it was a relatively inefficient fuel. Why?
   A. Coal was too expensive to mine.
   B. Peat was abundantly present in the Scottish Highlands.
   C. Early steam-engine smokestacks could not handle the higher-temperature fuels.
   D. Wood was an environmental hazard.

10. Coke was the hottest-burning fuel, but it almost never was used by early steam engines. Why?
    I.   Coke, made from coal, was too expensive to produce.
    II.  Other fuels were easier to obtain.
    III. Coal, from which coke was manufactured, was imported from Germany.
    IV.  Coke was an environmental hazard.

        A. I                               C. III
        B. II                              D. I and II

## Words in Context

1.  What is the meaning of *caldron* in Line 7?
    A. A large hat                        C. A large metal pot
    B. A large barrel                   D. A stand of trees

2.  What is the meaning of *reciprocating* Line 25?
    A. Taking away                      C. Staying in line
    B. Giving back                        D. Walking beside

3.  What is the meaning of *actuating* in Line 25?
    A. Hindering                          C. Continuing
    B. Promoting                         D. Triggering

4.  What is the meaning of *ingenious* in Line 34?
    A. Dishonest                          C. Clever
    B. Nerdy                             D. Importune

# Lesson 3

## SAT Essay

### Student Response 1

*Prompt 1:* Explore and develop your opinion on the concept that success requires prior failure. Use examples from your personal experience, schoolwork, or outside reading to support your opinion.

- Failure is only the opportunity to begin again more intelligently. —*Henry Ford*
- You can't have any successes unless you can accept failure. —*George Cukor*
- I have not failed. I've just found 10,000 ways that won't work. —*Thomas Edison*

(CollegeBoard)

| | |
|---|---|
| 1 | Any great story includes challenges or failures that the hero must overcome before succeeding in the |
| 2 | chosen mission. These great stories are written by people, and people combine creativity and knowledge of the |
| 3 | world to write stories. This understanding of the world includes the knowledge that we don't always succeed the |
| 4 | first time, and we often fail several times before we succeed. To meet with success, we invariably have to fail first. I |
| 5 | will provide several examples of why this is true as taken from literature, history, and personal experience. |
| 6 | In Homer's *Iliad* the Greeks attempt to capture the city of Troy. The Greeks fight the Trojans outside the |
| 7 | city walls on a plain. The war wages for years, and thousands of men fall. The Greeks realize their effort has failed. |
| 8 | Thus they try a new approach. They make a large, hollow wooden horse and put several of their men inside. Then |
| 9 | the other Greeks leave. The Trojans come out of the city and tow the horse into their city of Troy. The Greeks in the |
| 10 | horse come out and let their returning fellow soldiers into the city, which the Greeks sack. In order to succeed, the |
| 11 | Greeks failed before realizing the better plan. |
| 12 | During the Civil War of America, Abraham Lincoln, President of the Union, attempted to capture the |
| 13 | Confederate capitol of Richmond, Virginia. He used the following generals to head his army before he came to his |
| 14 | solution: Irvin McDowell, George McClellan, John Pope, Ambrose Burnside, Joseph Hooker, and George Meade. |
| 15 | These generals all lacked what it took to capture Richmond. Their strategies failed. Finally, Lincoln found General |
| 16 | Ulysses S. Grant, who used superior forces in the right way to capture Richmond. Lincoln failed in order to succeed. |
| 17 | In my own life, I can think of when I have failed in order to succeed. I put five chickens in a coop and |
| 18 | closed the door. On a fateful night, a weasel came and killed three chickens. I identified the problem (the door had |
| 19 | not fully closed) and fixed it. I put the remaining two chickens back in the coop, and they have been free from |
| 20 | marauding weasels ever since. I failed in my attempts to protect my chickens before I found the way to succeed. |
| 21 | We, as humans, must fail in order to succeed. Failure is not a bad thing. My examples show that failure |
| 22 | actually helps us to evaluate what went wrong so we can fix it and do the thing right. (Matthew) |

### Student Response 2

*Prompt:* Is image more important than substance? The familiar saying "Don't judge a book by its cover" may be important advice, especially in our image-conscious society. Television commercials relentlessly bombard American consumers with advertisements that drive home one all-important message: image is everything. Is that true?

(College Board)

| | |
|---|---|
| 1 | When I read magazines, I normally skip right over the advertisements. Advertisements do not appeal to me. |
| 2 | This is not because I think that they are harmful, but rather because I care about reading the magazine. Rarely do I |
| 3 | become vulnerable and yield to the temptation of reading the advertisements. Even if I do so, however, it is even |
| 4 | more unlikely that I will crave the featured product. For some teenagers, though, advertisements do introduce them |
| 5 | to new products that are cool, inducing some teenagers to want them. Sometimes teenagers are harmed by |
| 6 | misleading advertisements. Though such circumstances are unfortunate, it does not mean that teenagers are harmed |
| 7 | by advertisements. |
| 8 | Advertisements are not innately malignant. Teenagers are only harmed by them if they succumb to their |
| 9 | desires and purchase the object or service advertised. Thus, advertisements themselves are not harmful to teenagers. |

10  In a well-loved Christmas movie (the name escapes me), a boy sees a Red Ryder BB gun and wants it. He
11  gets it for Christmas because he really wants it. While shooting the BB gun, he gets hurt. The boy thought the gun
12  would be safe, but counter to his wishful thinking is the aspect of danger. Although some might say he was led
13  astray by a harmful advertisement, such an argument is simply not true. The boy was not harmed by advertisements;
14  it was his own inability to perceive that even BB guns are dangerous.
15  In *The Voyage of the Dawn Treader*, a novel by C. S. Lewis, the character Edmund sees a "natural"
16  advertisement. A man fallen in a pond is turned into gold by the water. Edmund is captivated by the idea that he can
17  become wealthy by sticking things into the pond and pulling them out as gold. However, he is almost harmed by the
18  water. The blame for this is not on the "natural" advertisement, but on Edmond and his selfish, greedy desires.
19  Personal experience, movies, literature, and logic show that advertisements are not harmful to teenagers.
20  Teenagers are harmed by their selfishness and their greediness when they do not realize the danger of their actions.
21  (Matthew)
22

1.  Student Response 1 uses evidence from
    A. Literature, science, philosophy.
    B. Literature, philosophy, history.
    C. Literature, personal experience, history.
    D. Literature, religion, science.

2.  Student Response 1 effectively develops a position on the subject that is supported by appropriate examples, evidence, and reasons. What offers the best example of this?
    A. Lines 1–2
    B. Lines 12–16
    C. Lines 17–18
    D. Lines 21–22

3.  SAT graders like personal examples. Where is an example of this in Student Response 1?
    A. Lines 1–2
    B. Lines 12–16
    C. Lines 17–20
    D. Lines 21–22

4.  Student Response 1 has closure in
    A. Lines 1–2
    B. Lines 12–16
    C. Lines 17–18
    D. Lines 21–22

5.  Student Response 1 has a good variety of sentence structure. The best example of this is in
    A. Lines 1–2
    B. Lines 10–14
    C. Lines 17–18
    D. Lines 21–22

6.  What is a glaring failure in Student Response 1?
    A. The vocabulary is elementary and imprecise.
    B. No transitions are used.
    C. The essay is not well organized and focused.
    D. There are multiple grammar mistakes.

7.  Student Student Response 2 employs the following strategy:
    A. It uses almost no personal examples.
    B. It offers arguments from history and economics.
    C. It more or less develops all arguments from personal experiences.
    D. All examples are from movies and books.

8.  Evaluate Student Response 2:
    A. Well organized, with a robust introduction and conclusion.
    B. Begins with a strong introduction but ends weakly.
    C. Is too familiar with its audience and creates tension among graders.
    D. Offers no real evidence for a weak argument.

9.  What is the purpose of giving an example from a C. S. Lewis novel?
    A. To show that substance can be falsely ascertained from appearance.
    B. There are dangerous influences in the modern media.
    C. The media is the message.
    D. Nothing is more important than the actual product.

10. Criticisms of Student Response 2 might include
   I.   Some of the vocabulary choices are forced and inappropriate, such as "innately malignant" (Line 8).
   II.  Examples are stale and predictable—and emerging from personal experiences.
   III. No convincing argument is presented.
   IV.  No counterargument is offered.

   A. I
   B. II
   C. III

   D. IV
   E. I and II
   G. III and IV

11. Score Student Response 1: __

12. Score Student Response 2: __

# Lesson 4
## Reading: Document-Based Analysis

**Passage 1**

**"Farewell Address to the Army of Northern Virginia"**

**Robert E. Lee**

| | |
|---|---|
| 1 | Headquarters Army of Northern Virginia |
| 2 | Appomattox Courthouse, April 10, 1865 |
| 3 | General Order No. 9 |
| 4 | |
| 5 | Robert E. Lee |
| 6 | |
| 7 | I need not tell the survivors of so many hard fought battles who have remained steadfast to the last, that I have |
| 8 | consented to this result from no distrust of them, but feeling that valor and devotion could accomplish nothing that |
| 9 | could compensate for the loss which would have attended the continuation of the contest, I have determined to avoid |
| 10 | the useless sacrifice of those whose past services have endeared them to their countrymen. You will take with you |
| 11 | the satisfaction that proceeds from the consciousness of duty faithfully performed, and I earnestly pray that a |
| 12 | merciful God may extend to you His blessing and protection. With an increasing admiration of your constancy and |
| 13 | devotion to your country, and a grateful remembrance of your kind and generous consideration of myself, I bid you |
| 14 | an affectionate farewell. |
| 15 | |
| 16 | Robert E. Lee, General |

(National Archives, http://www.civilwar.org/education/history/primarysources/leefarewell.html)

1. In the beginning of this passage, Robert E. Lee
   A. Establishes his reluctance to surrender.
   B. Vilifies the Northern armies for their barbaric behavior.
   C. Refuses to admit defeat.
   D. Makes every effort to absolve his soldiers from all blame for this surrender.

2. General Lee speaks in the third person
   A. To maintain proper boundaries between a general officer and enlisted men but at the same time to show deference and respect.
   B. Because it was too painful for General Lee to be personal.
   C. Because General Lee felt no responsibility for this debacle.
   D. Because General Lee was irritated with his soldiers.

3. General Lee reverts to a more familiar tone. Why?
   A. He cannot be impersonal any longer.      C. He delivers a sort of "blessing" to his troops.
   B. He wishes to ask a favor.                D. He is full of pathos.

4. From this passage it is fair to conclude that
   A. General Lee does not want to surrender.  C. General Lee wants to go home.
   B. General Lee is tired.                     D. General Lee is a religious man.

5. How does General Lee finish his address?
   A. With a short summation
   B. With a heartfelt expression of amicability and a candid moment of vulnerability
   C. With a mildly sarcastic swipe at General Ulysses S. Grant
   D. With an angry outburst

# Lesson 5

## Math: Algebra, Arithmetic Problem Solving and Data Analysis, and Passport to Advanced Math

### Arithmetic Problem Solving

1. The sum of two numbers divided by 2 is 43, and their difference divided by 2 is 19. What are the numbers?

   A. 26; 64
   B. 32; 64

   C. 48; 124
   D. 24; 62

2. The sum of two numbers divided by 3 gives as a quotient 30, and their difference divided by 9 gives 4. What are the numbers?

   A. 30; 60
   B. 27; 63

   C. 32; 63
   D. 27; 62

3. Seven years ago John was one-half as old as Henry, but five years hence he will be three-quarters as old. How old is each?

   A. J., 13 yrs.; H., 19 yrs.
   B. J., 14 yrs.; H., 20 yrs.

   C. J., 13 yrs.; H., 20 yrs.
   D. J., 12 yrs.; H., 18 yrs.

4. A and B own herds of cows. If A should sell 6 cows, and B should buy 6, they would have the same number; if B should sell 4 cows to A, he would have only half as many as A. How many cows are in each herd now?

   A. A, 32 cows; B, 22 cows
   B. A, 40 cows; B, 20 cows

   C. A, 34 cows; B, 26 cows
   D. A, 36 cows; B, 24 cows

5. In 1910, the cost of 5 pounds of tea and 7 pounds of coffee was $4.94; the cost of 3 pounds of tea and 6 pounds of coffee was $3.54. What was the cost of the tea and coffee per pound?

   A. Tea, 50¢; coffee, 28¢
   B. Tea, 54¢; coffee, 32¢

   C. Tea, 52¢; coffee, 30¢
   D. Tea, 60¢; coffee, 32¢

6. What is the price of corn and oats when 4 bushels of corn with 6 bushels of oats cost $4.66, and 5 bushels of corn with 9 bushels of oats cost $6.38?

   A. Corn, 62¢; oats, 38¢
   B. Corn, 58¢; oats, 36¢

   C. Corn, 61¢; oats, 37¢
   D. Corn, 60¢; oats, 37¢

7. In 1889, a merchant mixes tea which cost him 87 cents a pound with tea which cost him 29 cents a pound. The cost of the mixture is $17.98. He sells the mixture at 55 cents a pound and gains $2.92. How many pounds of each did he put into the mixture?

   A. 12 lbs. of 86¢ kind; 26 lbs. of 29¢ kind
   B. 12 lbs. of 85¢ kind; 26 lbs. of 29¢ kind

   C. 12 lbs. of 87¢ kind; 26 lbs. of 29¢ kind
   D. 12 lbs. of 84¢ kind; 26 lbs. of 29¢ kind

## Data Analysis

### Army of Northern Virginia

| | |
|---|---|
| Slaveholders | 44.4 percent |
| Nonslaveholders | 55.6 percent |

### Southern Society at Large

| | |
|---|---|
| Slaveholders | 25 percent |
| Nonslaveholders | 75 percent |

1. What can one conclude from the charts?
    I. There were substantially more slaveholders than nonslaveholders in southern society.
    II. Proportionately there were nearly double the number of nonslaveholders in southern society than in the Army of Northern Virginia.
    III. Soldiers were richer than the general population.

   A. I          C. III
   B. II        D. I and II

2. What can you conclude about the Army of Northern Virginia?
    I. There were proportionately more slaveholders than in southern society generally.
    II. Soldiers were richer than the normal southerner.
    III. Soldiers were pro-slavery.
    IV. The Army of Northern Virginia freed many of its slaves before the Civil War ended.

   A. I          C. III
   B. II        D. IV

### Soldiers in the Army of Northern Virginia

| | |
|---|---|
| 1862 | 55,633 to 92,000 |
| 1863 | 75,000 to 50,000 |
| 1864–65 | 83,000 to 62,000 |
| 1865 (end) | 50,000 |

3. What can be surmised by the above chart?
    I. The Army of Northern Virginia reached its peak in 1862.
    II. The Confederacy reached its high tide in 1862.
    III. Fewer soldiers were available for volunteers and conscripts in 1865.

   A. I          C. III
   B. II        D. I and III

# Chapter 12   Healed by Remembrances
# Luke 24:13–35

> *Memory Verses:* When he was at the table with them, he took bread, gave thanks, broke it and began to give it to them. Then their eyes were opened and they recognized him, and he disappeared from their sight. They asked each other, "Were not our hearts burning within us while he talked with us on the road and opened the Scriptures to us?" —Luke 24:30–32

"It is the third day since all this [the crucifixion] took place. In addition, some of our women amazed us. They went to the tomb early this morning but didn't find his body. They came and told us that they had seen a vision of angels, who said he was alive" (24:21–23).

This extraordinary rendition of a conversation by Luke is a marvelous insight to the confusion that occurred on that first Easter afternoon.

How does the church in our day, and in Luke's day, encounter and know the risen Christ? Or more pointedly, why do we not know Christ? Why are we right in our assessments of our life situations, but terribly wrong in our conclusions? How can we be right and blind at the same time?

"Are you the only person staying in Jerusalem not to know what has happened there in the last few days?" Cleopas and an unidentified disciple sarcastically ask this stranger. However, in spite of this stranger's obviously sheltered life, or stupidity, the disciples were desperate to tell someone—anyone!—about their plight. "Jesus is dead!" they cried. "And we had hoped that he . . . was going to redeem Israel" (24:21).

Cleopas and his friend (wife?) were on a trip to Emmaus. They just had to get away from Jerusalem. From those crazy women and their sensationalistic rumors. From Peter, who denied the Lord and who was now confessing a cock-and-bull story about a resurrection.

No, Jesus was dead. They had seen it with their own eyes. He was dead. Dead as a doornail. Finished. Oh, they had once hoped. In the exciting days when he was performing miracle after miracle. But all that had ended on the previous Friday. No, Jesus was dead. And, while they did not believe two crazy women, a fair-weather friend (Peter), and a young disciple prone to exaggeration (John), they certainly understood the pain they felt in their hearts. They certainly believed in many things. They believed the picture of Christ's hands bleeding profusely upon the garbage lying on Golgotha hill. They believed in the sounds of Christ gasping for breath as he painfully pushed up on his pain-ridden feet, trying to survive in the hell that was a crucifixion. Oh, yes, they knew what to believe. They knew that they were in trouble: no doubt Caiaphas and his henchmen would be rounding up all the disciples of Christ they could find.

In his poem "The Hollow Men," T. S. Eliot writes, "Between the idea / And the reality / Between the motion / And the act / Falls the shadow." Cleopas and his friend (wife?) had run into the shadow. Theology and ideas and abstractions belong to others. They had no dreams left. Only a Roman Empire and a Jewish state that wanted their blood.

In Hal Borland's *When the Legends Die*, the protagonist, a Native American who had lost his home, "stood among the ashes and whispered his sorrow chant, not even saying it aloud. For small griefs you shout, but for big griefs you whisper or say nothing. The big griefs must be borne alone, inside." Or so these two travelers thought, anyway. They resented the stranger's ignorance, but like a survivor of a terrible accident or ordeal, they were grateful for the chance to tell him their story.

Yet the stranger was unflappable. He compounded their bewilderment by brilliantly expounding Scripture to them. Nothing impresses a religious person more than a thorough knowledge of their sacred literature. Furthermore, and this was quite disconcerting, this stranger was speaking as if he were present in the aforementioned events. He presumed to know their motivations and their minds! Did he dare suggest that they misunderstood the mission of their Lord?

Nonetheless, this stranger intrigued them enough that they invited him to supper. Mellowed somewhat, they asked the stranger to give the blessing. In a Galilean accent, he recites the Hallel. Suddenly, in the candlelight, as this stranger breaks the bread, they see that he has nail-scarred hands, a thorn-scarred brow. He is the Christ!

The meal was not finished before they ran seven miles back to Jerusalem. Bursting in to see the disciples, they excitedly proclaimed what everyone else already knew: He is indeed risen!

What amazes me about this story is not that Christ ate with them, nor that they recognized him at this point. What truly bothers me is why they did not recognize him from the beginning. We are given no indication in the text that the stranger did not look like Jesus. In fact, the implication is that the stranger looked like Jesus from the very beginning—after all he should since he was Jesus! Why did they not recognize him? How often do we miss Jesus' presence in our lives? On the road to Emmaus, we may be right and blind at the same time.

Doubt can lead us down a road of confusion and blindness. The Emmaus travelers were heavy with the bad news of life, true, but their reaction to that news blinded them to their Savior, who walked with them on that road in those same bad times. He was there and they did not know it.

We only can see what we imagine to be true. And what is happening, admittedly, is very new. A resurrection! Christ, too, did not evolve out of history: He created a new history.

This is a theme orchestrated by earlier Jewish writers, notably Jeremiah and Isaiah. In Isaiah 42, for instance, we see the nation of Israel being liberated from bondage in Babylon. After years of slavery, the remnant nation is going home. Going home! And God has some very exciting news for this beleaguered people: "I have called you by name, you are mine. / When you pass through the waters, I will be with you; / and through the rivers, / they shall not overwhelm you" (Isaiah 43:1–2 NRSV). God is bringing his people home; he will sweep clean the record. The sins of their fathers and mothers are forgiven. The captivity is over. They are free. And not only will the future be different, but so will the past. God has rewritten their history. What was meant to be bad for them now has become good.

That is the incredibly good news: the Jesus whom the Emmaus travelers could not see. Their despairing doubt had blinded them to the truth.

Doubt, by the way, is not all bad. As the theologian Fred Buechner suggests, doubt is "the ants in the pants of faith" (from *Wishful Thinking*). But their doubt was depressing: it was a doubt based on angry disappointment. Time and time again, they had been hurt, so much, in fact, that they could not imagine that it was now ending.

I am truly shocked at how much despair there is in America. The theologian Walter Bruggemann, in his book *Hope within History* (80), argues that "failure to hope—hopelessness—happens among the affluent, the prosperous, the successful, the employable, the competent for whom the present system works so well. We are the ones who are likely to be seduced into taking the present political, economic, intellectual system too seriously and to equating it with reality." This false complacency ill prepares us for the exigencies of life—a death, divorce, unemployment—so that we easily lose hope. Indeed, in the "you only go around once" generation, hopelessness is epidemic. We have benefited so well from the Great Society that we falsely think it is the only game in town. And when we run into a Good Friday, we are devastated. We doubt the very existence of God, much less a miraculous intervention like the resurrection.

Hope emerges among those who publicly articulate and process their grief over their suffering (Bruggemann), not among those who flee to Emmaus. No wonder Mary Magdala and Peter were so ready to believe. Failure had redefined their perimeters of rationality. It was irrational to be forgiven for their sins, but they were broken people. And broken people see more miracles than put-together people because they simply need more miracles.

At the end of World War II, many still-living victims of Nazi atrocities would not leave the concentration camps. In spite of horrible conditions and terrible memories, the victims preferred the familiarity of bondage rather than to be free. The same is true in Numbers 11. Israel rebelled against Moses because they missed onions and spices of Egypt. Again, they preferred the familiarity of bondage to the uncertainty of freedom. But the good news of the resurrection and of Isaiah 42, is that we can be healed by our remembrances.

Fred Buechner, in his autobiography *The Sacred Journey*, argues that theology (i.e., the human study of God) is informed by our own lives and ultimately becomes our autobiography. God speaks to us in a myriad of different ways at every moment of every day. In that sense we discover the transforming power of memory as we recall his hand on our lives. Specifically, we remember those people who have loved us and the people we have loved. In that sense, "each life is not just a journey through time, but a sacred journey."

Thus these Emmaus road travelers have a real crisis on their hands: the one whom they loved and by whom they were loved has deeply disappointed them. Thus, as we see above, they do not see Jesus even when he is right before their eyes.

In effect, their theology has failed them. Based on their own sacred journeys, based on their experiences, they drew conclusions from Scripture. They found a way, as it were, to justify a belief in a dead Savior. And incredibly they were therefore not able to see the live one right in front of them.

What sort of theologies do we have? Are we walking around with our own maudlin theories of God? Based on years and years of the unmiraculous, the disappointments? The theology of the Emmaus travelers was divorced from the Word (of their Lord) because their experience demanded the selfsame response. Their high views of Scripture ended on Friday afternoon. From that point on, they sort of made things up as they went along.

How many of us found truth in Sunday School as a child and now reject it? Life was so hard on us that we simply gave up believing.

I met such a man at Harvard Divinity School several years ago. Although he was a brilliant man, one of the greatest American church historians alive today, he had no faith. He had Bible knowledge, but no faith. He stopped believing in God's Word when his retarded younger brother was born to his parents. As he watched his brother struggle, and finally die when he was five, this professor—in spite of his great knowledge of the Bible—had no Scripture. Bible as the Word of God ceased to exist the day they put his brother in that cold grave.

Yet in spite of Jesus' skillful explanation of Scripture, they still did not recognize him. True, their hearts were on fire, Luke says, but exegesis—no matter how inspired—will not remove our doubt. It will not lead us into correct relationship with God. No, the heart has its reasons which reason does not know (Pascal). They did not recognize Christ until they had a meal with him, until they were reacquainted with him on a personal basis.

With unwavering accuracy, Jesus pinpoints for them their greatest blind spot: their inability to grasp the value and role of suffering.

The Jews had a long tradition of persecution and suffering (Albert Nolan, *Jesus before Christianity*, 112–13). Theoretically, the righteous man always suffered on account of his righteousness, and every faithful Jew was willing to die rather than disobey the Law. But they thought that Christ was going to deliver them from the Romans. He did not. They thought that he would never die. He died.

Ironically, the one thing Jesus was determined to destroy was suffering, the sufferings of the sick and the poor and the oppressed. But the only way to destroy suffering is to give up all worldly values and suffer the consequences. Compassion destroys suffering by suffering with, and on behalf of, those who suffer.

These travelers were in great pain. They needed relief. They were blinded by their pain because they interpreted their special suffering as God's absence. That was a terrible miscalculation.

In his seminal work *The Wounded Healer*, the deceased theologian Henri Nouwen makes some bold assertions: he argues that being wounded is not a sign of weakness. "We live in a society in which loneliness has become one of the most painful human wounds," he argues. "The growing competition and rivalry which pervade our lives . . . have created in us an acute awareness of our isolation." Therefore we Christians should not be afraid of brokenness. It makes us useful for the kingdom. It helps us speak with legitimacy to the deep loneliness and pain so prevalent in our world.

Nouwen continues by suggesting that we are called upon to recognize the sufferings of our time in our own hearts and make that recognition the starting point of our service. This leads to great risk that the Emmaus Road travelers, as well as you and I, find quite threatening. We must learn to live with the same wounds and sufferings as others do, and nobody likes that. Having to do without food and sleeping on the ground, as well as persecution by the Pharisees, was one thing with Christ alive; facing the same things now that Jesus was dead was another thing altogether. The thought was unthinkable.

In our grief, we sometimes neglect our scriptural heritage. In suffering love, we see the restoration of sight to the blind and freedom to those imprisoned (Isa. 53:10; 61:1–2). Barrenness, I'm happy to say, is not a sign of God's absence. No, in the midst of their travail, Christ is very much alive.

Jesus joins their meal and enters their histories. As they again experience his touch, as they understand their suffering, as their theologies are balanced with personal experiences, he who on the way seemed to be a stranger becomes the Lord of their lives. The one who has been invited as a guest becomes for them the host.

Jesus takes bread, blesses it, and breaks it. He gives them the bread of life and much more. He gives them hope. He gives them a reason to live and, if necessary, a reason to die.

Nevertheless, in the moment of recognition, he vanishes. But not really. They rush back to Jerusalem, healed in their remembrances, knowing that he will never die. He is risen! He is risen indeed!

## Journal Question:

Imagine a world without the resurrected Jesus Christ.

# Lesson 1
## Evidence-Based Reading and Writing

### Literary Choice

Scout Master Robert Shaler wrote a series of popular but, by all accounts, mediocre fictional novellas concerning scouting in pre-World War I England.

### Robert Shaler, *The Boy Scouts for City Improvement*

#### A Friend in Need (chap. 2)

1　They were not long in discovering the cause of all that commotion. A yellow dog of no particular breed but of the
2　kind generally denominated "cur," came tearing around the corner of the street. He had an old rusty tin pan tied to
3　his tail, and as this struck him at every jump, he was yelping like mad and trying every way possible to outrun the
4　strange thing that rattled and banged at his heels.
5　　　People thrust their heads out of windows and doors. Most of them smiled or laughed outright at the
6　spectacle. It was a time-honored custom, and naturally all stray curs must expect to be treated this way on occasion,
7　to make a holiday for thoughtless boys.
8　　　Around the corner several half-grown lads came into view, evidently those who had been the cause of the
9　wretched dog's dilemma. They were apparently enjoying the sight of the poor creature's fright and antics about as
10　much as was possible. Several of them nearly doubled up with the excess of their hilarity.
11　　　There is an old fable about what great fun boys have stoning frogs, but as a moral it is hinted that what is
12　"sport to them is death to the frogs."
13　　　In this instance, the wretched cur, thinking that his escape was cut off by the appearance of the two boys
14　just in front of him, ran into a fence corner and began to lick his wounds.
15　　　Billy Worth had a big heart. He was always ready to take the part of the oppressed, whether it chanced to
16　be a weak boy being set upon by a bully or a miserable dog abused by its tormentors. So he immediately advanced
17　toward the fence corner, followed by Hugh, who was anxious to see what his tender-hearted chum meant to do.
18　　　Billy snapped his fingers and spoke gently as he advanced. The boys near the corner hooted *derisively*, and
19　then watched, half expecting that Billy might be only intending to get within striking distance and then to throw off
20　the mask and give the wretched dog a sudden kick in order to start him running afresh.
21　　　The dog himself possibly doubted the sincerity of the approaching lad. He had received little save kicks
22　from human kind in times past, and must have come to look with more or less suspicion on such apparently friendly
23　overtures that might only hide further ill-treatment.
24　　　The poor little beast raised a pair of brown eyes *beseechingly* toward Billy. He even vainly tried to wag his
25　tail, though this proved to be a physical impossibility so long as a piece of cord kept the tin pan hitched in place.
26　　　Billy had his hand extended. The yellow cur winced as he felt a touch on his head, and then proceeded to
27　lick Billy's hand. This act quite completed the conquest of the boy's heart.
28　　　"You poor little runt," said Billy tenderly, as he continued to stroke the badgered beast's quivering head,
29　"it's a shame the way they've chased you just because you're nobody's dog. I've got a good mind to adopt you right
30　now. Look at his face, Hugh, and tell me if you ever saw a more intelligent one? And his eyes are soft and brim full
31　of friendliness. Yes, I'll do it! We lost our dog last month, and an empty kennel is something I don't like to see
32　around."
33　　　As he spoke Billy took out his knife. The dog possibly feared that some new torture was in store for him,
34　because he continued to lick Billy's hand, as though hoping in that mute fashion to plead with the boy not to hurt
35　him.
36　　　One slash of the sharp blade severed the torturing rope and the tin pan fell away. Immediately the dog
37　started to jump about joyfully, evidently trying to prove how grateful he felt. He did not attempt to run away, and
38　when Billy held out his hand and spoke to him, he acted as though fairly wild with delight.
39　　　"Say, do you really believe the little critter ever had a kind word said to him before?" Billy asked, as he
40　kept on patting the head of the yellow cur. "Just remember that you're *my* doggie now. You want to trail along close
41　to my heels till we get home, when I'll find a good bone for you, all right. And I'd like to see anybody try to abuse
42　you after this, that's what."
43　　　He even took the little beast up in his arms, and the next thing he knew it was trying to lick his face to show
44　its gratitude.

45  From the boys around the corner a series of loud jeers broke forth. They even began to throw stones and
46  such things toward the two scouts, as though resenting this interference with their "fun."

47  Billy, although a scout, could get angry at times, and he was apt to forget some of the rules to which he had
48  agreed to conform at the time he joined the patrol.

49  "For two cents," he said angrily, when a stone bounded up and struck him on the shin, "I'd be willing to go
50  back there and offer to lick the coward who threw that rock."

51  "I don't believe that would mend matters any," Hugh remarked, as he picked up the rusty old tin pan and
52  tossed it carefully into one of the scrap cans that happened to stand close by. "There are three of them there besides
53  Lige, and we'd only get into a fuss that might reflect on the scouts. We're in uniform, remember. Let it pass; you
54  can afford to. The dog thanks you anyhow; just see him frisk about as though he might be trying to jump out of his
55  skin with gratitude for a kind act and a pleasant word. It would be hard to chase him away from you now, Billy.
56  What'll you call him—Bruno, as your other dog was named?"

57  "Well, that would hardly do for such a shrimp. Frisk sounds better to me. Hey, how do you like that for a
58  name, eh, Frisk?" And he snapped his fingers at the little animal that was leaping at his side and barking joyously,
59  something perhaps that he had seldom dared to do for fear of attracting attention and having a brick shied at him for
60  his temerity.

61  "Looks to me as if any name would answer with him, if only there was a square meal tagged on at the end
62  of it," laughed Hugh. "His sides seem to be caving in. I guess he hasn't found very fat pickings lately in skirmishing
63  around town, though you'd think differently from the trash that's lying everywhere."

64  "Here's our butcher's place, so wait for me a minute while I beg some scraps of meat for my new dog. I'd
65  like to let him know he's met a real friend at last. Look at his eyes, will you, Hugh? Did you ever see such an
66  appealing pair in any common dog? I'm glad I ran across Frisk, for I'm going to like him first rate."

67  "The affection is mutual, then," said Hugh, as Billy darted past the screen door of the butcher shop, and the
68  cur, as though divining what was in the wind, sniffed at the barrier, whimpered, and wagged his tail expectantly
69  while waiting for his new master to appear again.

70  When Billy came forth he had a paper in his hand, from which he took some scraps of meat and held them
71  for the dog to jump after. It was comical to see the antics of the little animal. He tried to wag his tail so furiously
72  between leaps that it almost seemed as though he must shake it off.

73  "Did you notice how most of the men who watched the circus when that tin pan was rattling and the dog
74  yelping like a crazy thing, only laughed as if they thought it a good joke?" Hugh asked, as they walked along the
75  street heading for the home of Billy.

76  "Yes, and I guess that's about the way it used to be when they were boys," replied the other reflectively.
77  "They didn't have the scouts in those days to show boys how to have oceans of good times without being mean and
78  cruel. Times have changed some, I reckon, Hugh, since our fathers were young. That's what my dad declares when
79  he hears of something we've been and done. And say, I rather think he believes boys have got a better chance to do
80  things to-day than they used to."

81  "But did you see a single woman or girl laughing?" continued Hugh. "Every one I noticed seemed to be
82  shocked and pained, and I heard several crying 'Shame,'—just as though that would make any difference with such
83  boys as Lige Corbley and his gang!"

84  "Well, now that you mention it, I did notice Susie Collins and Mazie Tucker talking to that bunch of sneaks
85  near the corner, and I guess they must have been telling 'em what a low opinion they had of boys that could treat a
86  poor dog as they were doing. Girls aren't ever up to the same tricks as boys, and they don't like the same things.
87  They don't see any fun in going fishing or hunting. And I reckon it's as it should be, because we don't like lots of
88  things they dote on. The men thought it was a good joke. Not a single one but the minister called out, 'Shame,' did
89  they, Hugh?"

90  "Not that you could notice," Hugh answered. "And if you stop to think about it, Billy, perhaps we would
91  have laughed, too, if this had happened before we joined the scouts. Things look different to a boy after he has had
92  his eyes opened, in a good many ways."

93  (Scout Master Robert Shaler, *The Boy Scouts for City Improvement* [New York: Hurst & Co., 1914],
94  http://www.gutenberg.org/ebooks/49338)

## Close Reading

1.  What is the literary purpose of presenting a dog in this chapter?
    A.  To advance animal rights.           C.  Comic relief
    B.  To develop the character Billy       D.  Dramatic irony

2. When Billy was hit by a rock he experienced
   A. Internal conflict.
   B. Moral turpitude.
   C. Uncontrollable anger.
   D. Grief.

3. This passage implies that scouts
   A. Take care of themselves.
   B. Are selfish and self-serving.
   C. Are kind and generous.
   D. Love dogs.

4. What would be a logical next step in this story?
   A. Billy gives in to his anger.
   B. The scouts meet the girls speaking to the hoodlums.
   C. The scouts have future adventures.
   D. The scouts go to the circus.

5. Hugh functions as
   A. An antagonist.
   B. A foil who adversely affects Billy.
   C. A type-character.
   D. A foil who functions as Billy's conscience.

6. What is the narrative technique?
   A. Second person
   B. Third-person objective
   C. Omniscient narration
   D. First-person narration

7. Why?
   A. This narrative technique joins the reader to the protagonist.
   B. This narrative technique allows the author to give insights into all the characters.
   C. This narrative technique builds suspense.
   D. This narrative technique advances the theme.

## Source Analysis

1. Based on Passage 1, the reader can make the following assumptions about the author's view of women:
   A. Women are unreasonable.
   B. Women are tough.
   C. Women are frail and generally sensitive.
   D. Women are equal in intellect to men.

2. What is a plausible prediction based on the second passage?
   I. Something catastrophic will occur.
   II. After a long ordeal Billy will succeed in life.
   III. The boys will encounter new crises and experiences that will mature them.

   A. I
   B. II
   C. III
   D. I and III
   E. NONE of the above

## Words in Context

1. What is the meaning of *commotion* in Line 1?
   A. Discord
   B. Distance
   C. Turmoil
   D. Momentum

2. What is the meaning of *derisively* in Line 18?
   A. Sardonically
   B. Happily
   C. Hopefully
   D. Dangerously

3. What is the meaning of *beseechingly* in Line 24?
   A. Haltingly
   B. Convincingly
   C. Suppliantly
   D. Openly

# Lesson 2
## Critical Reading and Writing

**Command of Evidence**

Read the following passages and answer accompanying questions:

### Passage 1

**Aristotle's Definition of Rhetoric**

1     An American journalist, Pete Hamill, once wrote, "He steps on stage and draws the sword of rhetoric, and when he
2     is through, someone is lying wounded and thousands of others are either angry or consoled." Indeed, rhetoric is a
3     powerful tool, and rhetoricians wield a great amount of influence. In ancient Greece, rhetoricians were commonly
4     hated because they could speak so well that they were able to convince juries to absolve guilty people of crimes.
5     One of the most famous of these Greek rhetoric teachers is Aristotle. Aristotle defined rhetoric as "the ability, in
6     each particular case, to see the available means of persuasion" (*Rhetoric* [New York: Barnes & Noble, 2005], 105
7     [book 1, chap. 2]). *However*, this definition begs the question "What are the available means of persuasion?" In his
8     famous book, *Rhetoric*, Aristotle claims that there are three "means of persuasion": "ethos," "pathos," and "logos."
9         "Persuasion must in every case be effected either by giving them the right impression of the speaker's
10     character, by working on the emotions of the judges themselves, or by proving the truth of the statements made"
11     (*Rhetoric*, 397 [3.1]) "Ethos" is the Greek word from which the English word "ethics" is derived. A person's "ethos"
12     in ancient Greece was one's moral character. This concept of ethics is exactly what Aristotle intended to convey
13     when he wrote, "Persuasion must . . . be effected . . . by giving them the right impression of the speaker's character."
14     **According to Aristotle, to be persuasive, speakers must convince the audience that they are of upright moral**
15     **character.** Included in this point is the idea that speakers must convince the audience that they are a legitimate
16     source of information on the topic on which they are speaking. After all, if a listener is not confident that the speaker
17     knows the talked-about issue, then the listener may not judge the speaker to be reliable.
18         Next Aristotle declares that "persuasion must . . . be effected . . . by working on the emotions of the judges
19     themselves." This, in Greek, is "pathos." "Pathos" is where the English word "pathetic," which means evoking
20     emotion, is derived from. To use "pathos" in a speech is what many would call an "emotional appeal." Even though
21     emotions are sometimes used in a manipulative manner, such appeals definitely add to the persuasiveness of a
22     speech. An orator may use perfect logic and convince the audience that the speaker is a legitimate source of
23     information on a topic, but if the speech is given coldly and without emotion, many will find it unconvincing.
24     However, if the speaker is able to appeal to the listener's emotions, then the speech will become many times more
25     compelling. A powerful appeal to emotions is exemplified in Samuel Adams's speech "American Independence":
26     "We have no other alternative than independence, or the most ignominious and galling servitude. The legions of our
27     enemies thicken on our plains; desolation and death mark their bloody career; whilst the mangled corpses of our
28     countrymen seem to cry out to us as a voice from heaven." Instead of merely stating, "We must fight for freedom, or
29     succumb to slavery," Samuel Adams uses emotionally charged phrases such as "mangled corpses of our
30     countrymen." "Pathos," an appeal to emotions, is the second side of a well-ordered argument, according to Aristotle.
31         The third side of the rhetorical "triangle" is "logos," the term from which "logic" is derived. "Persuasion
32     must . . . be effected . . . by proving the truth of the statements made." The "logos" of an argument is the logical
33     soundness of the case. This aspect is extremely important in, for example, the Lincoln-Douglas debates and
34     courtroom cases. **This is the aspect of an argument that will be used to convince an audience in a case where**
35     **there are two speakers with close to equal "ethos" and "pathos."** If two presenters appear to be equally
36     legitimate sources of information, and if these two speakers both appeal to the emotions effectively, then it will be
37     by whose argument is more logical that an audience will decide which orator to believe above the other. "Logos"
38     may be broken down into informal and formal logic. Informal logical fallacies include problems such as *post hoc*
39     *ergo propter hoc*, which translates as "after this, therefore because of this." This logical fallacy, like all other
40     informal fallacies, is an argument that is obviously problematic, but it cannot be broken down into its components to
41     reveal the error. Formal logical fallacies include issues where an argument may be broken down into its elements to
42     show why it is incorrect. For example, any argument that may be broken down to "If A, then B. Therefore, if B, then

43   A," is fallible. To exemplify the falsity of this form, take the argument "If it is a cat, then it is a mammal. Therefore,
44   if it is a mammal, then it is a cat." Since, the conclusion does not necessarily follow from the true premise, and since
45   this last argument was constructed in the original form, any argument in this form commits a formal logical fallacy.
46   Informal and formal logic are the two components of "logos" which is the last element of rhetoric, according to
47   Aristotle.
48         Thus Aristotle argues that there are three components to rhetoric: ethos, pathos, and logos. *Ethos*, the Greek
49   word for "ethics," is how the speaker convinces the audience of one's own upright moral character. *Pathos*, the
50   Greek word for "passion," is how the speaker manipulates the listeners' emotions to agree with the speaker. *Logos*,
51   the Greek word for "logic," is how the speaker appeals to the common sense of the audience. Learning how to use
52   each of these three aspects of rhetoric, according to Aristotle, will equip a person to become an expert rhetorician.
53   "He steps on stage and draws the sword of rhetoric, and when he is through, someone is lying wounded and
54   thousands of others are either angry or consoled." All thanks to the trident of rhetoric. (John)

## Close Reading

1. Why did the author begin with a quote from Pete Hamill?
   A. He wished to show how powerful rhetoric can be.
   B. He showed how out of date Aristotle is.
   C. He was introducing a new syntax.
   D. He was emphasizing the impact of literary analysis.

2. What organizational plan does the author employ?
   A. He defines "rhetoric" and then elaborates on its nuances.
   B. He defines "poetry" and shows how to write it.
   C. He introduces ethos, logos, and pathos and defines and illustrates each.
   D. He compares rhetoric to life.

3. What example does the author offer to illustrate logos?
   A. Presidential debates
   B. Closing statements in court
   C. A campaign speech
   D. The Lincoln-Douglas debates

4. The author finishes his essay with
   A. A summary statement.
   B. A new conclusion.
   C. A distracting comment
   D. A happy thought

## Grammar and Usage

Choose the best grammar/usage form in bold sentence(s).

1. Lines 14–15
   A. NONE
   B. Aristotle argues that a persuasive speaker must convince the audience that he/she is of upright moral character.
   C. Aristotle, to be persuasive, argues that a speaker must convince his/her audience that he/she is of upright moral character.
   D. According to Aristotle a speaker must convince his/her audience that he/she is of upright moral character.

2. Lines 34-35
   A. NONE
   B. This is the aspect of an argument which will be used to convince an audience where there are two speakers with close to equal "ethos" and "pathos."
   C. This argument convinces an audience where there are two speakers with close to equal "ethos" and "pathos."
   D. This will convince an audience where there are two speakers with close to equal "ethos" and "pathos."

## Words in Context

1. What is the meaning of *wield* in Line 3?
   A. Exhibit
   B. Overcome
   C. Brandish
   D. Remove

2. What is the meaning of *desolation* in Line 27?
   A. Barrenness
   B. Happiness
   C. Incidence
   D. Hopelessness

3. What is the meaning of *trident* in Line 54?
   A. A submarine
   B. Three-pronged spear
   C. A jet fighter
   D. A type of sandwich

# Lesson 3
## SAT Essay

*Prompt:* Major Anderson viewed his Charleston assignment with justifiable concern. He realized that his slightest misstep or miscalculation could touch off a civil war between the North and the South. But Anderson had to act. On the evening of December 26, 1860, he ordered his men to secretly move from vulnerable Fort Moultrie to the more easily defended Fort Sumter. Anderson's move to Fort Sumter was condemned throughout the South as aggression. At the same time, Northerners praised the major for defying the disloyal Southerners. Unwittingly, Anderson had made Fort Sumter the final cause and the first objective of an unavoidable war. History and human experience both illustrate the fact that decisions are never easy. Good choices can sometimes be costly. Write an essay to support your opinion on this idea. Use examples from your personal experience, schoolwork, or outside reading to support your opinion. (CollegeBoard)

### Student Response 1

1  Battlefields are the places where leaders succeed or fail. The battlefield shows the strategies that make great
2  leaders great. The Trojan war and the American Civil War are two conflicts that demonstrate how leaders succeed.
3  These instances give strong credence to and bolster the idea that strong leaders are flexible.
4  In the Trojan War, the Greeks fight a battle on the plains of Troy for a long time. Many soldiers die in years
5  of bloodshed. The Greek leaders are strong, flexible, and decide to fake a retreat and leave some men in a hollow
6  wooden horse. The Greeks leave and the Trojans come out and drag the horse into their city. The Greeks spring
7  from the horse and open the city gates to let the other Greeks into the city. This strategy wins the battle. By being
8  flexible, the leaders of the Greeks win and become strong leaders.
9  **In the American Civil War, Ambrose Burnside, commander of the Union forces, makes a poor**
10  **leader. His inflexibility caused the Union forces to lose to the numerically disadvantaged Confederate forces**
11  **at the Battle of Fredericksburg by attacking head-on against the entrenched enemy.** Inflexibility by leaders
12  leads to defeat, making them weak.
13  Another Civil War general, George B. McClellan, is popular with his troops. He is known for not wasting
14  their lives. He changes his plans based on intelligence reports, and his troops all love him as a result of his
15  flexibility.
16  Great leaders are flexible. Leaders who are terrible are inflexible. Flexibility is the mark of a good leader.
17  Whether the scene is the battlefield, the government, or business, great leaders will be flexible. They will recognize
18  their mistakes and seek to correct them. If they are hard-headed, like General Burnside, they will not acknowledge
19  their mistakes, however, and will lead their charges into defeat and failure. To be a great leader, be flexible. (Matt)

### Student Response 2
"The gem cannot be polished without friction, nor man perfected without trials." This ancient Chinese proverb
poetically expresses the belief that hardship and adversity are necessary to help us develop strength of character.

*Assignment:* Can we develop strength of character without facing hardship and adversity? Write an essay to support your opinion on this idea. Use examples from personal experience, observation, or reading.

1  The old woman was an example to her community. She had strength of character few others possessed. All
2  the parents in her community attempted to steer their kids into gaining the character of this woman. Few were
3  successful. For this community was one where nothing ever went wrong. **This old lady, however, came from a**
4  **place where everything went wrong and to her; there was nothing as desperate as the place she came from**
5  **and where she now lived. It was her background that gave her strength of character.** Being hardened by
6  hardship and adversity, she developed strength of character. To develop strength of character, we must face hardship
7  and adversity.
8  The American Civil War lasted a long time. The men who fought it went through hard times. Shortages of
9  food and clothing were prevalent. Battlefield casualty rates were high, and wounded men suffered greatly in
10  hospitals. Strength of character developed in these American soldiers. After the war, the strength of character the

11    southern soldiers developed enabled them to survive Reconstruction and helped them to rebuild the war-ravaged
12    American south.
13          Odysseus, the hero of Homer's *Odyssey*, went through hardships on the battlefield at Troy. These hardships
14    gave him strength of character. On his way back to his homeland, Odysseus encountered myriad dangers and trials.
15    All the men with him perished. Only Odysseus survived. After many years Odysseus made it home. His strength of
16    character, developed in the refining fire of battle, gave him the perseverance to make it home.
17          In my life, I have faced hardships. I have toiled under the hot southern summer sun to build fences on my
18    farm. I have heaved large fleece-covered sheep on the ground to shear them. I have stacked hay bales one on top of
19    the other to the ceiling. These hardships have given me strength of character. Through many situations, I can now go
20    with resolute perseverance that springs from working on a farm.
21          Personal experience, history, and literature show that character strength comes from adversity and hardship.
22    When struggling through life, remember that it gives you strength of character. (Matt)

1.   In Student Response 1, the author
    A.  Argues that flexibility is impossible.
    B.  Argues that the South should have won the Civil War if they were more flexible.
    C.  Uses a series of examples from history to show the importance of flexibility.
    D.  Concedes that flexibility can lead to equivocation.

2.   In Student Response 2 the author organizes his essay
    A.  By evoking the memory of Odysseus.
    B.  By offering a series of anecdotes.
    C.  By refusing to give in to impossible odds.
    D.  By a series of bullet points.

3.   Explain this statement: "Through many situations, I can now go with resolute perseverance that springs
    from working on a farm." (Student Response 2)
    A.  After struggling through many difficult farm situations, I have developed perseverance.
    B.  The North benefited from the Civil War.
    C.  Odysseus showed perseverance.
    D.  Nothing is more difficult than working on a farm.

4.   A recurring problem in both responses is that
    A.  The thesis is not mentioned until the second paragraph.
    B.  Transitions are weak.
    C.  There are too many personal examples.
    D.  The examples are too arcane.

5. Based upon examples in both passages, it is logical to assume that
    I.   The student loves Greek philosophy.
   II.  The student knows a great deal about the Civil War
 III.  The student is a southerner.
 IV.  The student might be in a World Literature class that is reading Greek literature.

        A. I                         D. I, II, III
        B. II                       E. II, III, IV
        C. III

6. Where is the main point of the Student Response 1?
    A. Lines 2–3                 C. Lines 12–14
    B. Lines 5–6                 D. Lines 15–18

7. Where is the main point of the Student Response 2?
    A. Lines 1–3                 C. Lines 15–16
    B. Lines 5–6                 D. Lines 20–21

8. Which part of Student Response 1 becomes a polemic?
    A. Line 1                                    C. Line 14
    B. Line 10                                 D. Line 18

9. What is the most plausible explanation for the above choice?
    A. An imperative sentence is aused.
    B. The sentence is religious.
    C. The sentence is opinionated.
    D. The information in the paragraph is repeated elsewhere.

10. What score would the student responses receive? Each of the essays receives __.

# Grammar and Usage

Choose the best grammar/usage form in bold sentence(s).

1. Student Response 1, Lines 9–12
    A. NONE
    B. In the American Civil War, Ambrose Burnside, commander of the Union forces, makes a poor leader. His inflexibility causes the Union forces to lose to the numerically disadvantaged Confederate forces at the Battle of Fredericksburg by attacking head-on against the entrenched enemy.
    C. In the American Civil War, Union commander General Ambrose Burnside, by inflexibly attacking head-on against the entrenched enemy, causes the Union forces to lose to the numerically disadvantaged Confederate forces at the Battle of Fredericksburg.
    D. In the American Civil War, Ambrose Burnside, commander of the Union forces proves to be a poor leader. His inflexibility caused the Union forces to lose to the numerically disadvantaged Confederate forces at the Battle of Fredericksburg by attacking head-on against the entrenched enemy.

2. Student Response 2, Lines 3–5
    A. NONE
    B. This old lady, however, came from a place where everything went wrong and to her, there was nothing as desperate as the place she came from. It was her background that gave her strength of character.
    C. This old lady, however, came from a place where everything went wrong and to her, there was nothing as desperate as the place where she now lived. It was her background that gave her strength of character.
    D. It was her background that gave this old lady, whose desperate background was not mitigated by her present circumstances, strength of character.

# Lesson 4
## Reading: Document-Based Analysis

### Manifest Destiny (1839)

In 1845, John L. O'Sullivan (1813–95), editor of the *Democratic Review*, referred in his magazine to America's "manifest destiny to overspread the continent allotted by Providence for the free development of our yearly multiplying millions."

1   The American people having derived their origin from many other nations, and the Declaration of National
2   Independence being entirely based on the great principle of human equality, these facts demonstrate at once our
3   disconnected position as regards any other nation; that we have, in reality, but little connection with the past history
4   of any of them, and still less with all antiquity, its glories, or its crimes. On the contrary, our national birth was the
5   beginning of a new history, the formation and progress of an untried political system, which separates us from the
6   past and connects us with the future only; and so far as regards the entire development of the natural rights of man,
7   in moral, political, and national life, we may confidently assume that our country is destined to be the great nation of
8   futurity.
9       It is so destined, because the principle upon which a nation is organized fixes its destiny, and that of
10  equality is perfect, is universal. It presides in all the operations of the physical world, and it is also the conscious law
11  of the soul—the self-evident dictates of morality, which accurately defines the duty of man to man, and
12  consequently man's rights as man. Besides, the truthful annals of any nation furnish abundant evidence, that its
13  happiness, its greatness, its duration, were always proportionate to the democratic equality in its system of
14  government. . . .
15      What friend of human liberty, civilization, and refinement, can cast his view over the past history of the
16  monarchies and aristocracies of antiquity, and not deplore that they ever existed? What philanthropist can
17  contemplate the oppressions, the cruelties, and injustice inflicted by them on the masses of mankind, and not turn
18  with moral horror from the retrospect?
19      America is destined for better deeds. It is our unparalleled glory that we have no reminiscences of battle
20  fields, but in defense of humanity, of the oppressed of all nations, of the rights of conscience, the rights of personal
21  enfranchisement. Our annals describe no scenes of horrid carnage, where men were led on by hundreds of thousands
22  to slay one another, dupes and victims to emperors, kings, nobles, demons in the human form called heroes. We
23  have had patriots to defend our homes, our liberties, but no aspirants to crowns or thrones; nor have the American
24  people ever suffered themselves to be led on by wicked ambition to depopulate the land, to spread desolation far and
25  wide, that a human being might be placed on a seat of supremacy.
26      We have no interest in the scenes of antiquity, only as lessons of avoidance of nearly all their examples.
27  The expansive future is our arena, and for our history. We are entering on its untrodden space, with the truths of God
28  in our minds, beneficent objects in our hearts, and with a clear conscience unsullied by the past. We are the nation of
29  human progress, and who will, what can, set limits to our onward march? Providence is with us, and no earthly
30  power can. We point to the everlasting truth on the first page of our national declaration, and we proclaim to the
31  millions of other lands, that "the gates of hell"—the powers of aristocracy and monarchy—"shall not prevail against
32  it."
33      The far-reaching, the boundless future will be the era of American greatness. In its magnificent domain of
34  space and time, the nation of many nations is destined to manifest to mankind the excellence of divine principles; to
35  establish on earth the noblest temple ever dedicated to the worship of the Most High—the Sacred and the True. Its
36  floor shall be a hemisphere—its roof the firmament of the star-studded heavens, and its congregation an Union of
37  many Republics, comprising hundreds of happy millions, calling, owning no man master, but governed by God's
38  natural and moral law of equality, the law of brotherhood—of "peace and good will amongst men." . . .
39      Yes, we are the nation of progress, of individual freedom, of universal enfranchisement. Equality of rights
40  is the cynosure of our union of States, the grand exemplar of the correlative equality of individuals; and while truth
41  sheds its effulgence, we cannot retrograde, without dissolving the one and subverting the other. We must onward to
42  the fulfillment of our mission—to the entire development of the principle of our organization—freedom of
43  conscience, freedom of person, freedom of trade and business pursuits, universality of freedom and equality. This is
44  our high destiny, and in nature's eternal, inevitable decree of cause and effect we must accomplish it. All this will be
45  our future history, to establish on earth the moral dignity and salvation of man—the immutable truth and

46 beneficence of God. For this blessed mission to the nations of the world, which are shut out from the life-giving
47 light of truth, has America been chosen; and her high example shall smite unto death the tyranny of kings, hierarchs,
48 and oligarchs, and carry the glad tidings of peace and good will where myriads now endure an existence scarcely
49 more enviable than that of beasts of the field. Who, then, can doubt that our country is destined to be the great nation
50 of futurity?

(http://www.digitalhistory.uh.edu/disp_textbook.cfm?smtID=3&psid=362)

1.  What is the chief argument of this document?
    A. America is one among many nations.
    B. America is unique among nations and destined to be great.
    C. Native Americans unfortunately must be destroyed to make way for progress.
    D. Americans have a divine right to govern the Western hemisphere.

2. What technique does the author employ in lines 15–18?
    A. Analogy                                      C. Rhetorical Question
    B. Hyperbole                                    D. Simile

3.  The United States has a "manifest destiny" for the following reasons:
    I.   It is a Christian nation.
    II.  It is a nation of immigrants.
    III. It has treated the Native Americans well.
    IV.  It is a noble merging of liberty and virtue.

        A. I                                        D. IV
        B. II                                       E. All
        C. III

4.  Which of the following policy decisions would be an example of manifest destiny?
    I.   Emancipation of slavery
    II.  The annexation of Hawaii
    III. Participation in the Mexican War
    IV.  American entrance into World War I

        A. I                                        C. III and IV
        B. II                                       D. II and III

5.  With which of the following slogans would the author agree?
    I.   America—love it or leave it
    II.  America—right or wrong—it is my home
    III. America—the greatest and the best nation on earth
    IV.  America—the home of the brave

        A. I                                        D. IV
        B. II                                       E. All
        C. III

6. In what ways does this painting capture the theme of the passage?

(1873 Library of Congress Digital Collection, http://cdn.loc.gov/service/pnp/ppmsca/09800/09855v.jpg)

A. The print shows a loving God watching over settlers as they move to their new homes.
B. The print shows an allegorical female figure of America leading hopeful pioneers westward, as they travel on foot, in a stagecoach, Conestoga wagon, and by railroads, where they encounter Native Americans and herds of bison.
C. Persistent settlers will not be deterred by storms, Native Americans, or herds of bison.
D. Inevitable progress—represented by a railroad engine—will ensure that America will triumph.

7. What is true about this print?
  I. Everyone is looking toward the West.
 II. All are engaged in some activity—no one is standing idle.
III. Slaves and Native Americans join in the inexorable progress of American hegemony.

A. I                          D. I and II
B. II                         E. II and III
C. III

# Words in Context

1.  What is the meaning of *futurity* in Line 8?
    A.  The unexpected
    B.  The possibility of anything
    C.  Pertaining to the future
    D.  The decline of all

2.  What is the meaning of *antiquity* in Line 16?
    A.  Ancient times
    B.  Out of date
    C.  Irrelevant
    D.  Irreverent

3.  What is the meaning of *enfranchisement* in Line 21?
    A.  Abortion
    B.  Homecoming
    C.  Officeholder
    D.  Suffrage

4.  What is the meaning of *cynosure* in Line 40?
    A.  Dilettante
    B.  Novice
    C.  Leader
    D.  Follower

5.  What is the meaning of *exemplar* in Line 40?
    A.  Archetype
    B.  Exception
    C.  Momentum
    D.  Monitor

6.  What is the meaning of *beneficence* in Line 46?
    A.  Exuberance
    B.  Caution
    C.  Magnanimity
    D.  Generosity

# Lesson 5

## Math: Algebra, Arithmetic Problem Solving and Data Analysis, and Passport to Advanced Math

**Passport to Advanced Math**

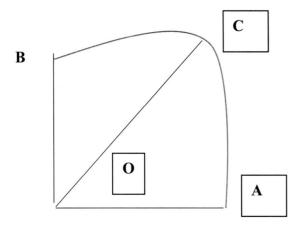

1. Which of the following statements is true?

   I.   The angle subtended at the center of a circle by an arc equal to the radius is the same for all circles.
   II.  For if AC be the arc equal to the radius, and AB the arc subtending a right angle, then AOC : AOB :: AC : AB.
   III. BO is equal to AO
   IV.  CO is equal to AO

       A. I, II, III                 C. I, II                  E. All
       B. II, III                  D. I, III

2. What is true about this sphere?

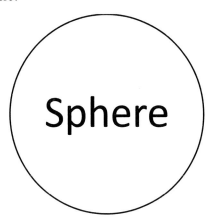

I.   A sphere is a solid bounded by a surface every point of which is equally distant from a fixed point which is called the center of the sphere.
II.  The straight line which joins any point of the surface with the center is called a diameter.
III. The section of the surface of a sphere made by any plane is a circle.
IV.  A pole of a circle is equally distant from every point of the radius of the circle.

A. I, II                     C. I, III                    E. All
B. III, IV                   D. II, IV

## Arithmetic Problem Solving

1.  There are three numbers whose sum is 96; the second is three times the first, and the third is four times the first. What are the numbers?

    A.  3, 9, 27                    C.  12, 36, 48.
    B.  7, 14, 49                   D.  6, 12, 24

2.  Divide the number 126 into two parts such that one part is 8 more than the other.

    A.  59, 67                      C.  36, 43
    B.  63, 71                      D.  58, 66

3.  The sum of two numbers is 25, and the larger is 3 less than three times the smaller. What are the numbers?

    A.  7, 18                       C.  8, 19
    B.  6, 17                       D.  9, 20

4.  Arthur bought some apples and twice as many oranges for 78 cents. The apples cost 3 cents apiece, and the oranges 5 cents apiece. How many of each did he buy?

    A.  4 apples, 8 oranges         C.  5 apples, 10 oranges
    B.  6 apples, 12 oranges        D.  7 apples, 14 oranges

# Chapter 13   The Unseen World in Which We Live
# 1 Samuel 1:21–28

> *Memory Verses:* "I prayed for this child, and the LORD has granted me what I asked of him. So now I give him to the LORD. For his whole life he will be given over to the LORD." And he worshiped the LORD there. —1 Samuel 1:27–28

In spite of the fact that Mother's day is not a religious holiday, you will never find this pastor ignoring it. Besides the fact that I have a profound respect for all mothers, I can also painfully remember the Mother's Day that I foolishly ignored. When I was ten, my mother magnanimously announced, "I do not want any gifts for Mother's Day; no flowers, candy, no cards—just be nice to me."

So we honored her request. I can tell by the smirks on your faces that you think I was pretty dumb--but, hey, we were very nice to her!

My mother cried all day, and for two weeks we had navy beans and corn bread—or whatever else my poor father could cook.

Mother's Day, though, has some religious roots. It was begun in 1908 by a small town Sunday school superintendent and proclaimed by President Woodrow Wilson in 1914 as an official civic holiday. Every year Hallmark Corporation and FTD make a mint as we do penance for our gross advantage-taking of our long-suffering mothers.

After Wilson, others tried to make this day "Family Day." But who is kidding whom? Mothers do more counseling than all the ministers and therapists combined. They do more doctoring than all the doctors. Economists estimate that a mother provides the equivalent of $60,000 worth of free services every year. A fact that I have learned in over a decade of pastoral ministry is "Show me a strong and vital mother, and I will show you a strong and vital family."

So, this day, above all days, deservedly belongs to our mothers. You deserve it, Mom, because you are special. In a world that says to take and to take and to take, you continually give and give and give. As Glen Campbell sang eons ago, a mother is someone "who gave up the good life for me."

If I may take a personal digression—I am especially appreciative of my wife, Karen. I appreciate her dedication to duty. Her sacrifices. With no complaints, my magna cum laude college graduate coaxes English peas into all our mouths, wipes tears from disappointed children's faces, and patiently teaches us to wash our hands before meals. Thank you, Karen!

Another mother who deserves credit is Hannah.

Hannah, as mothers go, deserves to be in the "mother's hall of fame." Hannah lived with her husband, Elkanah, in Ephraim (Israel). Elkanah was a character. A pragmatist, a guy to keep the peace at any cost, Elkanah was committed to the stability of his family.

But in spite of Elkanah's normal, if not always solicitous, attention, Hannah was very unhappy. First, Hannah had no children. For a Jewish woman at this time, to be barren was disgraceful. A woman's value was directly related to how many sons she provided for her husband. Remember, in this pre-social welfare society, children were the only hope most people had in their old age (see the book of Ruth).

In addition to this personal tragedy, Hannah had to bear Peninnah's taunting. Peninnah, Elkanah's second wife, was producing one son after another for Elkanah. And Peninnah loved to gloat about her good fortune. The fact is, Hannah's future was in great jeopardy. Because of her barrenness, Elkanah had every legal right to give Hannah back to her parents, or even worse, to force her out of her house into the street.

Yes, Hannah had no reason to rejoice when Elkanah's family traveled to Shiloh, the chief pre-Jerusalem shrine of Judaism. At Shiloh everyone enjoyed the joyous Feast of Tabernacles (today it is called Succoth), a celebration of the founding of the Mosaic tabernacle. But 1 Samuel 1:1–5 reminds us that there was no joy in Hannah's heart. She wept.

As you know, when others rejoice and you are hurting, it can be salt in your wounds. It was almost too much for Hannah. In recognition of God's bountiful blessings, a sacrifice was offered on the altar. Everyone shouted praises and thanksgivings! Hands were raised in unabashed joy! The priests sacrificed an unblemished lamb on the altar, and everyone joyfully partook of this special sacrifice in a festive family celebration. Elkanah, Peninnah, and their many children ate together. Poor Hannah, though, ate alone.

Hannah felt betrayed and broken. Even her loving Father God seemed to have abandoned her. Not only had he closed her womb (1 Samuel 1:6), but whenever she went to the synagogue to worship, she was reminded again and again of her worthlessness. She was a subhuman, a person captured in "marginality"—a concept coined by Dr. Sang Lee, a professor at Princeton Theological Seminary. Dr. Lee suggests that some of us, because of circumstances or handicaps, are treated by others, and ourselves, as marginal persons, with little or no value. In 1 Samuel 1:10 we read these pathetic words: "In her deep anguish Hannah prayed to the LORD, weeping bitterly." Hannah had reached the end of her rope.

Perhaps some of you today have reached the end of your rope. Perhaps you are captured in circumstances, of which you are the victim, not the perpetrator. Perhaps you feel that God is dead. Or at least that you have been ignored. And when God does not ignore you, it seems that he merely sends more catastrophes your way. What hope do we have? We will see.

Yet to her credit, Hannah did not lose hope. Hannah respectfully ignored her well-intentioned but stupid husband, who asks, "Hannah, why are you weeping? Why don't you eat? Why are you downhearted? Don't I mean more to you than ten sons?" What empathy!

Hannah correctly saw God as the solution to her problems. Hannah slipped quietly away to the tabernacle and silently prayed: "LORD Almighty, if you will only look on your servant's misery and remember me, and not forget your servant but give her a son, then I will give him to the LORD for all the days of his life, and no razor will ever be used on his head" (1:11). Hannah promised that if God would give her a son, she would dedicate him to the service of God, that she would bring him up as a Nazirite in token of his complete dedication to God (Numbers 6:1–8). Hannah's fervent prayers were finally answered, and God gave her Samuel.

A mother should be a prophet. A prophet's task, according to the theologian Walter Bruggemann, "is to nurture, nourish, and evoke a consciousness and perception alternative to the consciousness and perception of the dominant culture around us." The mother "is an iconoclast, challenging the apparently holy, revered, and awesome" (Heschel, *The Prophets*, vol. 1). A mom, indeed, any godly parent, invites their children to accept a way of life—a life centered on Christ—that is different from the world. Do you want your children and grandchildren to reject the world's values and accept Christ as an authority? Increasingly parents are called to be counterrevolutionaries!

In spite of so much stress and anxiety, brokenness and hopelessness, Hannah had an assurance and peacefulness that only comes from deeply held faith. She was not manipulating God with her emotions nor playing games of "positive faith." No, Hannah employed no gimmicks to get Samuel. He was a gift of God. As Thomas Merton explains, "All these finally permeate our being with love in-so-far as our living faith tells us we are in the presence of God, that we live in Christ, that in the Spirit of God we 'see' God our Father without 'seeing': we know Him in 'unknowing' (*Contemplative Prayer*, 34)." With no fanfare, with no bands playing, with more than a little "unknowing," Hannah dreamed, believed, prayed, and hoped little Samuel into being.

Mothers need to believe, to pray, and to dream when no one else can.

Although John Wesley emphasized the sinfulness of his preconversion life, he was raised in a Christian home (Mulder, *Conversions*, 54). His father was a preacher. His mother, though, was most important to John Wesley's spiritual development. His mother, Susanna, was an extraordinary woman of beauty, learning, efficiency, and piety. She gave birth to nineteen children, but only nine lived. She homeschooled all her children. She disciplined them. She was there for them. She believed in them when no one else would. Finally, John and his brother Charles started the Methodist Church. There are over ten million Methodists today.

I conducted the funeral for Karen's grandmother. As I looked around the room, I counted over fifty people who were on fire for the Lord because of this faithful woman. Fifty! What a testimony to a mother's faithfulness!

It takes great sacrifice. Later, in 1 Samuel 2, we see poor Hannah giving her little baby boy away to Eli. But a good mother keeps her word. A good mother knows that she has to give up her children some day.

In the movie *Elena*, a Greek family has been captured by communist revolutionaries. They are held in a prison. But Elena, an industrious mother, helps her children escape. She remains so that the authorities will not chase her children.

For her crime, Elena is shot the next day. As the soldiers raise their rifles to shoot her, Elena raises her hands and cries, "My Children!"

## Journal Question

Discuss how your mom, or another significant adult, affected your walk with God.

# Lesson 1
## Evidence-Based Reading and Writing

### Literary Choice

After meeting at Harvard University some years ago, Jim and Karen Stobaugh were married and have four home-educated adult children. Jim's education includes: BA, cum laude, Vanderbilt University; M A, Rutgers University; MDiv, Princeton Theological Seminary; Charles E. Merrill Fellow, Harvard University, DMin, Gordon-Conwell Theological Seminary. In 2014, Harvard Square Editions published his first critically acclaimed and Amazon bestselling novel, *Growing Up White*. His most recent book is *Life to Bitter Souls*. Finally, Dr. Stobaugh is the pastor of Covenant Presbyterian Church, Boswell, Pennsylvania.

### James P. Stobaugh, *Life to the Bitter Soul* (chap. 17)

1 Jake Stevens was a transplanted southerner. The city was as foreign to him as it was to Tony and to Margaret.

2     Jake grew up in Pedlam, Arkansas, during the troubled Civil Rights era. Jake never intended to live in the
3 city, much less pastor an urban church. Not that he was opposed to doing it, he merely did not think about it. His
4 naïveté and nascent optimism blinded him to the exigencies of sociology, though, and he was unprepared for the
5 adjustment that urban life drew from his psyche.

6     Jake was afflicted with Plato's tripartite soul. He approached his new calling logically, high-spirited, and
7 with strong desires. He loved his God, and he was coming to love his new city, and to Jake, this was all logical. The
8 whole city corresponded to his own soul. It was wrapped up in and absorbed into his soul. In fact, his soul and
9 Pittsburgh were becoming one. At first, the state of the whole fulfilled its function without attempting to interfere in
10 the functions of the other. But before long, the city and Jake's soul began to merge. Or if they did not exactly merge,
11 they intermingled and produced something new. Or something very, very, old that neither had known for a while.

12     In any event, in Jake and in Pittsburgh, injustice was the contrary state of the whole, and while it was
13 abundantly available everywhere, this in no way mitigated both the city's and Jake's consternation with its
14 existence. Thus homelessness, crime, poverty, and other perfidies existed everywhere; their inevitable existence in
15 no way mitigated Jake's need to try to ameliorate all. Jake did not yell curses to the early morning as Frank did,
16 although he thought about doing so, but he did attack nefarious systemic evil everywhere he found it. In other
17 words, Jake did not merely observe. He lived the life with vigilant warring hope as he lived among ruined urbanity
18 of the 1980s.

19     His experience in the southern Arkansas Delta and at Vanderbilt University fashioned his views of
20 everything southern and indirectly everything northern.

21     The Southern Agrarians dominated the English department at Vanderbilt when he attended in the early
22 1970s. Agrarians (pro-southern conservatives who celebrated everything southern rural and vilified everything
23 northern urban) were major contributors to the revival of southern literature in the Southern Renaissance. No
24 English faculty in the world could boast such talent and articulateness. Jake's professors bemoaned the increasing
25 loss of southern identity and culture to northern industrialization. They believed that the southern agrarian cultural
26 roots of the United States were superior to the emerging simplistic and materialistic northern industrialism.

27     Vanderbilt English professors like John Aden and Walter Sullivan scorned the dilettante. There were no
28 creative writing courses at Vanderbilt. No one had earned the right to write creatively. They taught students to
29 revere the masters of rhetoric—William Shakespeare, Allen Tate, Leo Tolstoi (the faculty always spelled "Tolstoy"
30 as "Tolstoi"), William Faulkner, Robert Penn Warren, Eudora Welty, T. S. Eliot, and Kathryn Anne Porter—without
31 presuming that Jake was of the same genus or species.

32     His professors, too, were not reticent to be snobbish about their choices. Charles Dickens and Henry
33 Wadsworth Longfellow, both beloved by generations of Americans, were crucified with the sobriquet "pedestrian."

34     Similarly, O. Henry was summarily executed with the appellation "predictable." And of course, nothing of
35 worth had been written by northern authors since Nathaniel Hawthorne died. T. S. Eliot would have been an
36 exception, but he had migrated to England.

37     Vanderbilt English majors knew their place in the universe: a few, a very few, would someday write fiction
38 and enter the Halls of Valhalla, but not before they were fifty-five and only if they lived somewhere south of the
39 Mason-Dixon Line. Vanderbilt English majors drank Crown Royal Bourbon and smirked as they proclaimed,
40 "Harper Lee's *To Kill a Mockingbird* is a blatant example of the American public's penchant for mediocrity. If the
41 public had any taste at all, it would prefer William Faulkner's *Intruder in the Dust*."

42  Jake loved writing, and later in life that was to be his primary livelihood, but for now he was "called" to the
43  pastoral ministry.

44  He had been called, in fact, since he was a freshman at Vanderbilt. Jake made a commitment to Christ and
45  to the ministry when he was seventeen and living in Pedlam, Arkansas, an ordinary southeast Arkansas Delta
46  community. In that cauldron of racial discord, Jake met his Savior, and he never looked back.

47  In spite of the fact that he was a conservative evangelical, he chose the liberal, Unitarian Harvard Divinity
48  School. He risked the challenging theology because he wished to be near his older brother, Little Martin, who was
49  attending Harvard Business School.

50  The trip from his family farm outside Pedlam, Arkansas, to Cambridge, Massachusetts, would take a year.

51  Jake began his trip to Harvard on a particularly warm, hopeful Southeast Arkansas September day. The
52  Delta fall, as usual, was conflicted by tepid, late summer afternoons and frosty winter mornings. Jake was conflicted
53  too. He was driving alone in his red 1974 Fiat 128 across the country to Boston. He had never been farther north
54  than Nashville, and honestly, he was afraid. All his life he had heard about Yankees, and in his estimation they were
55  only a step lower than the demons that afflicted demoniacs in biblical narratives.

56  His northward trip began on Arkansas State Route 1, a rather boring road that wound through white cotton
57  fields and one-grocery-store towns.

58  He drove by Bo's old farm one last time to look at the aging willow tree that still intruded in his
59  remembrances. In his youth, his friend Bo had been stripped naked, tied to that willow tree, and skinned alive by
60  Jake's Sunday school teacher.

61  He stopped at the Spirit of St. Louis Lion Gas Station to buy an RC Cola and a Moon Pie.

62  Before he finished his moon pie and RC Cola, Jake fell asleep, and his little red Fiat 128 curved to the
63  right, made a 45-degree turn, and hit a concrete bridge. Under ordinary circumstances, this was an unexciting bridge;
64  besides having an occasional thoughtless Dairy Queen cup thrown over its side, this little fourteen-foot structure,
65  built by the WPA, had never known any excitement. Against its rain-washed side, his poor Fiat 128 crumbled like a
66  cheap, flimsy pop can.

67  Jake's seat belt saved his life. Nonetheless, almost immediately Jake knew he was in big trouble. He
68  smelled the odor of pungent burning rubber and sweet warm blood. Raisin bran cereal that had burst on impact fell
69  from the ceiling of the car like snowflakes. It fell on Jake's face and in his blood, forming a carpet of rusty brown
70  trails all over the interior of his Fiat.

71  Before that day was to end, Jake experienced horror, as he had never known. This was his attack up
72  Cemetery Ridge, his landing on Normandy. Like a soldier veteran, he would survive physically, but he would never
73  be the same mentally or spiritually.

74  Jake broke his hand in two places and severed his right foot. His right femur jutted from his right thigh. His
75  hip was cracked. For the first three days, Jake faded in and out of consciousness. For the first time in Arkansas, a
76  physician performed reconstructive microsurgery and placed Jake's foot back on his stub. It worked! But for the
77  next four months, Jake despaired in a windowless hospital room.

78  The handicap casualty he always retained, along with a limp that grew more pronounced as he aged, was a
79  hyperalertness. He gained a thousand-yard stare. In fact, he could look at the most ordinary object and see far
80  beyond the material composing the object into the atomic structure and beyond, to infinitude itself. He saw God;
81  indeed, he touched the face of God. Like soldiers returning from horrible battle, he bore the mark of a warrior who
82  had been struggling with fate itself.

83  Jake, like a New World explorer, encountered heretofore-unknown lands.

84  Suddenly the big things no long made sense to Jake. Only small things made sense. He tried to do those
85  small things, and he tried to make them into big things. He considered making money and experimenting with
86  substances heretofore not a temptation. He justified these things by explaining to himself that God did not really
87  exist, or if he did, he did not really love Jake.

88  But Jake could not escape the tender, loving touch of a God who had been so good and so kind for so long.
89  That wistful memory crowded out the present doubts.

90  It was God's love, then, that drew Jake home and, ultimately, to all things good in his life.

91  In other ways, though, this disaster became a memorable event in his life. Jake reached out to God with a
92  broken body, and he learned an important lesson: God will only bless a broken people, a people limp from
93  struggling. Jake concluded that no people who seriously pursued God would or could escape brokenness.

94  This would be an important insight that would help him survive future conflicts with his family and friends
95  over his controversial life choices.

96  Jake's namesake, Jacob in the book of Genesis, was broken—and then blessed. Jacob was a conniving,
97  selfish scoundrel. He cheated his brother out of his birthright; he tricked his aging father in order to get the paternal
98  blessing. Then he had no alternative except to flee the inevitable, justifiable wrath of his brother.

99    Jacob went to the land of his mother's relatives. It was ironic that Laban, a relative, tortured and broke
100   Jacob for over twenty years. Jacob had met his match! But God had other adventures in store for his selfish saint. In
101   Genesis 32, as Jacob was on the way toward home, he received word that his brother, Esau, was planning to meet
102   him with four hundred men. Jacob was justifiably scared. He therefore divided his party into two companies for
103   safety, and then he sent most of them ahead with gifts of appeasement. He even put his family in front of himself,
104   coward that he was, so that they, too, might be a part of the buffer between him and his cheated brother. The still-
105   crafty Jacob planned to run and save his own skin if he saw that Esau was not in good humor. Jacob was still playing
106   with a loaded deck.

107       But Jacob "the supplanter" was about to run out of tricks. While Jacob waited alone that last night before
108   he was finally to meet Esau, a man came into his campsite and began to wrestle with him. The stranger was an angel
109   of God. Jake Stevens wrestled with God for four months at Jefferson Memorial Hospital. Jake had reached the end
110   of his human rope, and a cosmic explosion erupted. A new life, a new flowering of spirituality, would grow out of
111   the resulting crater.

112       In that hospital room, there was something of fury, something of evil, in the intense struggling. All of
113   Jacob's ample trickery, all of his pseudospirituality, was struggling with the Perfect God. The wrestlers groaned,
114   gasped for breath, and cried as each push led to even greater efforts. Silhouetted against the rising moon, at times the
115   two figures lost all temporal location. For a moment, generations upon generations of Christians were standing on
116   that hill, struggling, for all they are worth, with Almighty God and Jake. Paul, the Pharisee, snickered as Stephen
117   screamed in mortal pain, and then God struck him blind on the road to Damascus. Peter denied Jesus Christ three
118   times and then became the leader of the early church. Martin Luther struggled with God all night and then nailed his
119   95 theses on the door of the Wittenberg Castle Church. John Wesley was consumed with despair until his heart was
120   strangely warmed. No, Jake Stevens was not alone in Jefferson Memorial Hospital. He was surrounded with a crowd
121   of witnesses. The baton was passed to him. He touched his tag-team partner, and the procession moved forward.

122       Jake collapsed—permanently, eternally broken. He was a new man; he was Israel, a man who had touched
123   the face of God. Jake was no victor. He could only cling to his adversary. As the sun rose, Jacob held and grasped,
124   in hopefulness and for all he was worth, God, whom he now knew so well, who destroyed and resurrected him both
125   at once.

126       His dad sat next to him for many days as Jake struggled in and out of consciousness. At one point Jake was
127   dying. Fatty embolisms disconnected from his maimed body and flowed malevolently toward his heart. His dad,
128   sitting next to Jake and nervously eating cucumbers, willed that Jake live. And he did. But Jake was never the same.

129       Jake again met his older brother, Little Martin, the boy with whom he had spent his youth. His quiet but
130   fun-loving little brother Henry brought some of that optimism back into broken Jacob's life. His mother adroitly
131   orchestrated all, and in time Jake recovered. But never fully. He was to carry with him the horror of that moment all
132   his life.

133       Next year, Jake continued on his journey to Harvard, broken but blessed. His divine adversary was his
134   friend, and he was holding Jake up. It felt good! Jacob moved forward but with humble chariness. Now he trusted
135   God alone for his future.

## Close Reading

1.  What is the narrative technique of this passage?
    A.  First person
    B.  Limited omniscient
    C.  Omniscient
    D.  Third-person objective

2.  While this passage is clearly partly autobiographical, why would the author use this narrative technique?
    A.  To force an objective edge to his protagonist
    B.  To increase credibility
    C.  To criticize this protagonist
    D.  To offer insights into the setting

3.  The main character (protagonist) is round (well-developed). How does the author develop him?
    A.  Internal conflict
    B.  External conflict
    C.  Thematic turmoil
    D.  Setting changes

4.  This passage implies that God
    A.  Never allows bad things to happen to good people.
    B.  Is uninterested in the daily affairs of humankind.
    C.  Advises against long trips.
    D.  Breaks whom he loves.

5.  What would be a logical next step in this story?
    A.  The author commits suicide.
    B.  The author becomes an agnostic.
    C.  The author continues in his life while "limping."
    D.  The author dies of cancer.

6.  The biblical story of Jacob functions as
    A.  The namesake of the protagonist who was "broken and then blessed."
    B.  A foil who adversely affects the protagonist.
    C.  A character type.
    D.  A moral tale.

# Lesson 2

## Critical Reading and Writing

### Command of Evidence (Student Response)

1  "There is an element of truth in each position which becomes falsehood, precisely when it is carried through too
2  consistently." These words from Reinhold Niebuhr, a theologian and political writer in the 1950s, was in reference to
3  American idealism, "Yankeeism," an ironic blend of Christian principles and a thirst for prosperity held together by the
4  stout assertion of America's innocence. It was this innocence that Niebuhr viewed as the "element of truth" that had
5  become a falsehood in America because it had been acted upon too consistently. Niebuhr dedicated his book *The Irony*
6  *of American History* (New York: Scribner, 1952) to expounding this idea, warning of the detrimental consequences of
7  acting upon this idea, and finally, proposing a remedy for the consequential problems that arise: a realization of man's
8  inherent sin nature.
9      As its name implies, the focus of Niebuhr's books is the ironic incongruities of American history in relation to
10  American idealism. Niebuhr breaks up the book in to eight sections. He emphasizes how the atomic bomb at Hiroshima
11  and the Cold War were the catalysts for revealing the incongruities hidden in "Yankeeism." "Our dreams of a pure
12  virtue are dissolved in a situation in which it is possible to exercise the virtue of responsibility toward a community of
13  nations only by courting the prospective guilt of the atomic bomb" (*Irony*) To Niebuhr, America was using unjust
14  means for a just end, and this was a delusion of our innocence. However, while America was losing her innocence, she
15  was too blinded by her imperialistic idea of indestructibility to see any incongruities in her philosophy. Thus, while it
16  was true that America had an innocent genesis, her dogmatic belief in her innocence was the "element of truth" that had
17  quickly become a "falsehood." The irony is further developed in the fact that the fight against communism was taking
18  America to a place where ultimate victory meant world power, but as William Pitt, one of Britain's prime ministers,
19  said, "Unlimited power is apt to corrupt the minds of those who possess it": this is what was happening to America,
20  warned Niebuhr. "Though we are quickly acquiring the pride of power which always accompanies its possession, . . .
21  we have been so diluted by the concept of our innocency that we are ill prepared to deal with the temptations of power
22  which now assail us" (*Irony*). Because of this combination of unlimited power and erroneous innocence, Niebuhr
23  warned that America was essentially no different than communism, since communism also held a contorted image of
24  itself. Niebuhr defends this bold statement by showing that both communism and American Jeffersonianism are based
25  on the same three principles: historical management, man's perfectibility, and that economics is the sole dictator of
26  happiness. "In the liberal world the evils in human nature and history were ascribed to social institutions . . . or to some
27  other manageable defect in human nature or environment"(*Irony*). Both communism and America believe that the
28  problems of humans and history arise from a mismanagement of environmental factors, and that perfectibility in
29  humanity is achieved when the perfect environment is achieved. So while America believes property to be "the
30  instrument of justice" and communism believes it is "the source of all evil," they both believe that property
31  (economics) is the great determining force of history (*Irony*). "Both creeds miss the truth about property. Since
32  property is a form of power, it cannot be unambiguously a source of social peace and justice" (*Irony*). Niebuhr observes
33  that the only reason the American creed has not led to such atrocities as the communist's creed has exhibited is
34  because, ironically, America does not follow her own creed consistently. "One has an uneasy feeling that some of our
35  dreams of managing history might have resulted in similar cruelties if they had flowered into action"( *Irony*).
36      Niebuhr's remedy for the situation is for America to return to one of the most basic tenets of orthodox
37  Christianity: human beings are inherently sinfully and consequently finite. Niebuhr once said this of original sin:
38  "Original sin is that thing about man which makes him capable of conceiving of his own perfection and incapable of
39  achieving it." Regarding America's delusion of achieving perfection, he writes:
40
41      Yet we cannot deny the indictment that we seek a solution for practically every problem of life in quantitative
42      terms; and are not fully aware of the limits of this approach. . . . No national culture has been as assiduous as
43      our own in trying to press the wisdom of the social and political sciences, indeed of all the humanities, into the
44      limits of the natural sciences. . . . The result is frequently a preoccupation with the minutiae which obscures
45      the grand and tragic outlines of contemporary history, and offers vapid solutions for profound problems.
46      (*Irony*).
47
48  America cannot attempt to be the judge of the world while standing on the moral high ground of American
49  exceptionalism, for that (exceptionalism) is in itself a falsehood. However, Niebuhr laments that "modern man lacks

50  the humility to accept the fact that the whole drama of history is enacted in a frame of meaning too large for human
51  comprehension or management" (*Irony*).
52          Niebuhr's theologically influenced answer to the problem of America's inordinate sense of her infallibility is a
53  good reflection of him as a man. *The Irony of American History* in itself sums up Niebuhr, the man, in that it is a
54  combination of political treatise and Christian theology, two subjects that characterized Niebuhr's life. Born to German
55  Evangelical parents, Niebuhr grew up in a deeply religious family; after attending seminary, he followed in the
56  footsteps of his father and became a preacher. Later he became vice president of Union Theological Seminary in New
57  York, a post he held for over thirty years. At the beginning of his life, Niebuhr was heavily involved with the Socialist
58  party while rejecting Marx's teachings, first preaching the Social Gospel in the 1920s; however, it seems that he later
59  moved away from socialism, instead founding a liberal lobbying party, Americans for Democratic Action. Politically,
60  he was anti-communism, anti-nuclear weapons, anti-discrimination, and a pacifist originally, although later he
61  supported both World War II and the Cold War, in hopes that war would bring peace. Niebuhr was both a preacher and
62  an involved citizen, and yet he was so much more. He was a thinker, a truth seeker, delving into the mysteries of the
63  balance between man's inherent sin nature and moral responsibility to do justice in such books as *Moral Man and*
64  *Immoral Society*, *The Children of Light and the Children of Darkness*, and *The Nature and Destiny of Man: A*
65  *Christian Interpretation*. Ryan Prior wrote this for *The American Conservative*: "To read Niebuhr is to relish these
66  tensions, to grip the fundamental balance of the moral universe. 'Man's capacity for justice makes democracy
67  possible,' he wrote. 'But man's inclination to injustice makes democracy necessary. . . . Goodness, armed with power,
68  is corrupted, . . . [but] pure love without power is destroyed.' Much of Niebuhr's worldview depends on these
69  balances." Niebuhr's strong grasp on reality and the metaphysical, revealed through his numerous works, has captured
70  the attention of many.
71          In an interview with Niebuhr on the ABC Television Network, Mike Wallace said of Niebuhr, "No man has
72  had as much influence as a preacher in this generation, and no preacher has had as much influence outside of the
73  church" (interview, April 27, 1958). Although not everyone agreed with Niebuhr during his life, almost everyone
74  respected him for the intellectual giant that he was. The *Times* magazine posthumously wrote of him that he was "pre-
75  eminent in his field, the greatest Protestant theologian in America since Jonathan Edwards." Arthur Schlesinger Jr., a
76  historian and contemporary of Niebuhr, writing for the *New York Times* in 1992, says this about Niebuhr's influence:
77
78          He persuaded me and many of my contemporaries that original sin provides a far stronger foundation for
79          freedom and self-government than illusions about human perfectibility. Niebuhr's analysis was grounded in
80          the Christianity of Augustine and Calvin, but he had, nonetheless, a special affinity with secular circles. . . .
81          We cannot play the role of God to history, and we must strive as best we can to attain decency, clarity, and
82          proximate justice in an ambiguous world." ("Reinhold Niebuhr's Long Shadow," June 22)
83
84          In the more recent past, politicians such as Jimmy Carter, Hilary Clinton, John McCain, Mitt Romney, and
85  President Barack Obama, as well as many others, have praised Niebuhr for his foreign affairs ideas as laid out in *The*
86  *Irony of American History*, creating an unprecedented renewal of interest in Niebuhr. Surprisingly, Niebuhr gathers
87  admirers from both liberals and conservatives; it is a testament to his ability to speak transcending truth. However,
88  despite the efforts of both parties, Niebuhr cannot be pinned down to one extreme: doing so would remove a crucial
89  element of his message.
90          Niebuhr's ultimate purpose in *The Irony of American History* is to find a happy medium in the sphere of
91  politics by introducing a critical missing component to the picture: original sin. Niebuhr wrote, "Modern man's
92  confidence in his virtue caused an equally unequivocal rejection of the Christian idea of the ambiguity of human virtue"
93  (*Irony*). Without this component, Niebuhr argues that when power is used in conjunction with an unchallenged belief in
94  the essential goodness of man or a country, disaster will inevitable ensue. He does not favor inaction but rather, as
95  Arthur Schlesinger Jr. put it, "Humility, he believed, must temper, not sever, the nerve of action" ("Long Shadow").
96  Niebuhr wrote *The Irony of American History* to reveal the incongruities in American thinking, fueled by the fear that
97  "American power in the service of American idealism could create a situation in which we would be too impotent to
98  correct you when you are wrong and you would be too idealistic to correct yourself" (*Irony*). (Daphnide)

## Close Reading

1. How does the author begin her essay?
   A. A provocative counterargument
   B. A quote from Niebuhr and a statement of her thesis.
   C. The historical background of the Cold War
   D. A rhetorical question

2. What is the primary purpose of this essay?
   A. A polemic against McCarthyism
   B. A summary of historical revision
   C. A book review
   D. A political speech

3. Why does the author mention Jimmy Carter and Hillary Clinton (Lines 84–86)?
   A. To show how anti-establishment Niebuhr was
   B. To criticize the Democratic Party
   C. To show how influential this book is
   D. To clarify the author's position on historical studies

4. The author finishes her essay with
   A. A summary statement.
   C. A new conclusion.
   B. A distracting comment.
   D. A happy thought.

# Lesson 3

## SAT Essay

*Prompt:* As you read the passage below, consider how the author uses

    A. Evidence, such as facts or examples, to support claims.
    B. Reasoning to develop ideas and to connect claims and evidence.
    C. Stylistic or persuasive elements, such as word choice or appeals to emotion, to add power to the ideas expressed.

### Student Response 1

*Prompt:* "The price of greatness is responsibility." Winston Churchill. Do we expect too much from our public figures? (CollegeBoard)

1       "With great power comes great responsibility," we all know the superhero quote, but it holds a remarkable
2    insight into how we view the world. In a position of leadership, perhaps a military commander, millions of lives are in
3    your hands. Naturally we would expect a commander's decisions to be calculated and well planned. **We do not expect**
4    **too much from our public figures, they have a responsibility not only to take care of themselves but also to take**
5    **care of others.**
6       Chester A. Arthur was a corrupted politician. When he became president, however, his changed his ways.
7    Instead of giving out jobs to anyone who favored him, he championed the civil service system, attempting to create
8    equality. When he was a minor politician no one expected him to necessarily act in a responsible way; however, as
9    soon as he became president, millions of people across America decided that he need to step up his game. This
10   expectation was justified because of the enormous responsibility he had.
11   When Dwight D. Eisenhower was planning D Day he worked all day and night trying to perfect the plan. He knew that
12   millions of lives were in his hands and that his decisions would decide the fate of Europe and perhaps even the world.
13   Eisenhower wrote out an apology letter before launching the attack in case of failure. In it he accepted full
14   responsibility for any mishaps that might happen to jeopardize the troops. All of the Allies expected Eisenhower to take
15   this caution and they were right. If Eisenhower were just playing around with toy soldiers, or just commanding men in
16   a video game, no one would have thought twice about his decisions. His position of leadership; however, elevated him
17   to a position where he was responsible for countless men. Thus, he needed to have this expectation to sober his
18   decisions.
19       Chester A. Arthur and Dwight D. Eisenhower were put in positions of leadership and power and both of them
20   received justified expectations and responsibility from the public. They wielded such power that they needed this
21   responsibility to help sober their decisions. Those in authority make decisions that are no game. They take upon
22   themselves great responsibility. When responsible for thousands of people expectation is a given. Because we all know
23   that, "With great power comes great responsibility (David)."

### Student Response 2

"The gem cannot be polished without friction, nor man perfected without trials." This ancient Chinese proverb
poetically expresses the belief that hardship and adversity are necessary to help us develop strength of character.

*Prompt:* "That which we obtain too easily, we esteem too lightly. It is dearness only which gives everything its value." (CollegeBoard)

1       Many times those who have everything seem to not care. Billionaires such as Bill Gates believe that they have
2    too much money and begin to give some away, while those in poverty cling on the little spare cash they have. It seems
3    odd that those with the most could care the least. This is because we do not value things that we have not worked for.

4       I learned this concept first hand with my own money. When I was younger, my parents would buy clothes for
5  me and give me an allowance. This allowance money was often laid on my desk and forgotten, or I would carelessly
6  place where it would be lost. However, when my parents stopped this and decided to pay us four dollars an hour for
7  mowing the lawn, I learned the true importance of money. I saved up first to buy a watch, then a cell phone, and finally
8  an ipod.

9       This is also clearly seen in the movie *Captain Courageous*, where a young boy finds being forced to work for
10  his living on a ship instead of being lazy all day. When he is finally given his measly pay check for his three months of
11  labor, he spends it carefully and reverently because of the work he spent achieving it.

12       This principle is especially true with those who have natural talent. The movie *Rudy* focuses on a boy whose
13  dream is to play sports, but he cannot do well because of his weak body and lack of natural talent. When he does finally
14  achieve some of his goals, it is easy to say that he is more satisfied and happy than many other players who did well
15  because of their natural talents.

16       It is amazing that those who have the most often care the least. People who have money squander it while
17  children are starving in the streets. **There is only value in things that we strive for and achieve and were not just**
18  **given to us** (Marci).

1. In Student Response 1 the author:
   A. Argues that we should indeed expect much from our public officials.
   B. Argues that public officials are only human and we should not expect too much from them.
   C. Argues that the quote from Winston Churchill is irrelevant.
   D. Concedes that perfection is impossible, but leaders should reach for it anyway.

2. In Student Response 2 the author argues:
   A. Most people do not appreciate hard work.
   B.. Men work harder than women.
   C. There is only value in things that we strive for and achieve and were not just given to us.
   D. We should never take a free handout.

3. In Student Response 1 the author organizes his essay
   A. By discussing two politicians who failed to rise to greatness.
   B. By offering two historical illustrations.
   C. By two colorful metaphors.
   D. By a series of bullet points.

4. In Student Response 2 the author organizes her essay
   A. By offering a counterargument.
   B. By offering two historical illustrations.
   C. By two colorful metaphors.
   D. By giving four examples: a businessman, herself, and two movies.

5. Explain this statement: "They wielded such power that they needed this responsibility to help sober their decisions."
   A. Many successful people are alcoholics
   B. Responsibility is necessary to add clarity to decisions.
   C. Power corrupts absolutely.
   D. No one can be right all the time.

6. A recurring problem in both responses:
   A. The thesis is mentioned early but not repeated enough through the essay.
   B. Transitions are weak
   C. There are too many personal examples
   D. The examples are too arcane

7. What score would the student responses receive? Each of the essays receive __.

## Grammar and Usage

Choose the best grammar/usage form in bold sentence(s).

1. Student Response 1, Lines 3–5
   A. NONE.
   B. We do not expect too much from our public figures and they have a responsibility not only to take care of themselves but also to take care of others.
   C. We do not expect too much from our public figures, but they have a responsibility not only to take care of themselves but also to take care of others.
   D. We do not expect too much from our public figures but they have a responsibility not only to take care of themselves but also to take care of others.

2. Student Response 2, Lines 17–18
   A. NONE
   B. There is only value in things that we strive for and achieve and was not just given to us.
   C. There is only value in things for which we strive and were free.
   D. There is only value in things for which we work hard to achieve.

# Lesson 4

## Reading: Document-Based Analysis

### Emancipation Proclamation (January 1, 1863)

The nation was embroiled in the American Civil War when President Abraham Lincoln delivered the Emancipation Proclamation on January 1, 1863.

1　By the President of the United States of America:

2　A Proclamation.

3　　　Whereas, on the twenty-second day of September, in the year of our Lord one thousand eight hundred and
4　sixty-two, a proclamation was issued by the President of the United States, containing, among other things, the
5　following, to wit:

6　　　That on the first day of January, in the year of our Lord one thousand eight hundred and sixty-three, all
7　persons held as slaves within any State or designated part of a State, the people whereof shall then be in rebellion
8　against the United States, shall be then, thenceforward, and forever free; and the Executive Government of the United
9　States, including the military and naval authority thereof, will recognize and maintain the freedom of such persons, and
10　will do no act or acts to repress such persons, or any of them, in any efforts they may make for their actual freedom.

11　　　That the Executive will, on the first day of January aforesaid, by proclamation, designate the States and parts
12　of States, if any, in which the people thereof, respectively, shall then be in rebellion against the United States; and the
13　fact that any State, or the people thereof, shall on that day be, in good faith, represented in the Congress of the United
14　States by members chosen thereto at elections wherein a majority of the qualified voters of such State shall have
15　participated, shall, in the absence of strong countervailing testimony, be deemed conclusive evidence that such State,
16　and the people thereof, are not then in rebellion against the United States." Now, therefore I, Abraham Lincoln,
17　President of the United States, by virtue of the power in me vested as Commander-in-Chief, of the Army and Navy of
18　the United States in time of actual armed rebellion against the authority and government of the United States, and as a
19　fit and necessary war measure for suppressing said rebellion, do, on this first day of January, in the year of our Lord
20　one thousand eight hundred and sixty-three, and in accordance with my purpose so to do publicly proclaimed for the
21　full period of one hundred days, from the day first above mentioned, order and designate as the States and parts of
22　States wherein the people thereof respectively, are this day in rebellion against the United States, the following, to wit:

23　　　Arkansas, Texas, Louisiana, (except the Parishes of St. Bernard, Plaquemines, Jefferson, St. John, St. Charles,
24　St. James Ascension, Assumption, Terrebonne, Lafourche, St. Mary, St. Martin, and Orleans, including the City of
25　New Orleans) Mississippi, Alabama, Florida, Georgia, South Carolina, North Carolina, and Virginia, (except the forty-
26　eight counties designated as West Virginia, and also the counties of Berkley, Accomack, Northampton, Elizabeth City,
27　York, Princess Ann, and Norfolk, including the cities of Norfolk and Portsmouth), and which excepted parts, are for the
28　present, left precisely as if this proclamation were not issued.

29　　　And by virtue of the power, and for the purpose aforesaid, I do order and declare that all persons held as
30　slaves within said designated States, and parts of States, are, and henceforward shall be free; and that the Executive
31　government of the United States, including the military and naval authorities thereof, will recognize and maintain the
32　freedom of said persons.

33　　　And I hereby enjoin upon the people so declared to be free to abstain from all violence, unless in necessary
34　self-defense; and I recommend to them that, in all cases when allowed, they labor faithfully for reasonable wages.

35　　　And I further declare and make known, that such persons of suitable condition, will be received into the armed
36　service of the United States to garrison forts, positions, stations, and other places, and to man vessels of all sorts in said
37　service.

38　　　And upon this act, sincerely believed to be an act of justice, warranted by the Constitution, upon military
39　necessity, I invoke the considerate judgment of mankind, and the gracious favor of Almighty God.

40　　　In witness whereof, I have hereunto set my hand and caused the seal of the United States to be affixed.

41　　　Done at the City of Washington, this first day of January, in the year of our Lord one thousand eight hundred
42　and sixty three, and of the Independence of the United States of America the eighty-seventh.

43　　　By the President: ABRAHAM LINCOLN WILLIAM H. SEWARD, Secretary of State.

1. A logical purpose of this document might be?
   A. To help the Union win the war.
   B. To raise money for troops.
   C. To satisfy abolitionists in Kentucky.
   D. To free slaves everywhere.

2. What is true about this document?
   A. While the Proclamation did not instantly liberate a single slave, it did allow black men to serve in the Union Army and Navy.
   B. Slavery was forbidden in the entire United States.
   C. Slavery was forbidden in the South.
   D. Confederate slaveholders were declared to be criminals.

3. Although the wording of the Proclamation resounded liberation for slaves, it was actually quite restricted in meaning. In what way?
   I. Only male slaves were freed.
   II. Slaves were free after they served in the Union army.
   III. It only pertained to those states that had seceded from the Union.
   IV. It excluded Confederate areas the North already controlled.
   V. Slaves' freedom was dependent on a Union victory.

   A. I & II                    C. III, IV, & V
   B. I, II, & III              D. None

4. What would be a logical outcome of this proclamation?
   A. England would support the Confederacy.      D. Thousands of freed slaves would join the Union
   B. The South would win the war.                   army.
   C. Women would now want more rights.

5. Which of the following policy decisions would be an example of the Emancipation Proclamation (Executive Orders):
   I. The Bill of Rights
   II. The Lousiana Purchase
   III. The Gulf of Tonkin Resolution
   IV. The Declaration of War against Japan

   A. I                         C. III and IV
   B. II                        D. II and III

6. With which of the following statements would the author agree?
   A. All men are created equal.                  C. Americans must unite against France's invasion of
   B. States' rights are paramount.                  Mexico
                                                   D. Low tariffs

7. Part of Confederate President Jefferson Davis's response to the Emancipation Proclamation included, "We may well leave it to the instincts of that common humanity which a beneficent Creator has implanted in the breasts of our fellow men of all countries to pass judgment on a measure by which several millions of human beings of an inferior race, peaceful and contented laborers in their sphere, are doomed to extermination." (Address to the Confederate Congress, January 12, 1863, in *Official Records*, Series 4, vol. 2:336–50.)
   What is true about this portion of Davis's response?
   I. The slaves, according to Davis, were happy and content.
   II. Davis wondered why Lincoln encouraged slaves to kill their masters.
   III. Davis felt that common sense dictated that the whole thing was absurd.
   IV. Davis was sure God would severely punish Lincoln on the judgment day.

   A. I & II                    C. II & III
   B. II & IV                   D. I & IV

# Lesson 5

## Math: Algebra, Arithmetic Problem Solving and Data Analysis, and Passport to Advanced Math

### Arithmetic Problem Solving

1.  Divide the number 56 into two parts, such that one part is three-fifths of the other.
    A. 20; 36
    B. 22; 35
    C. 35; 21
    D. 22; 34

2.  If the sum of two numbers is 42, and one is three-fourths of the other, what are the numbers?
    A. 26; 20
    B. 24; 18
    C. 22; 16
    D. 26; 24

3.  The village of Cork is situated directly between two cities 72 miles apart, in such a way that it is five-sevenths as far from one city as from the other. How far is it from each city?
    A. 40; 28 miles
    B. 41; 27 miles
    C. 42; 30 miles.
    D. 44; 32 miles

4.  A son is five-ninths as old as his father. If the sum of their ages is 84 years, how old is each?
    A. 30; 54 yrs.
    B. 24; 60 yrs.
    C. 28; 56 yrs.
    D. 32; 52 yrs.

5.  Two boys picked 26 boxes of strawberries. If John picked five-eighths as many as Henry, how many boxes did each pick?
    A. J, 8 boxes; H, 14 boxes
    B. J, 6 boxes; H, 12 boxes
    C. J, 12 boxes; H, 18 boxes
    D. J, 10 boxes; H, 16 boxes.

6.  In a school containing 420 pupils, there are three-fourths as many boys as girls. How many are there of each?
    A. 240 boys; 180 girls
    B. 240 girls; 180 boys
    C. 260 girls; 200 boys
    D. 200 boys; 260 girls

7.  A man bought a lot of lemons for $5; for one-third he paid 4 cents apiece, and for the rest 3 cents apiece. How many lemons did he buy?
    A. 150
    B. 144
    C. 122
    D. 160

### Algebra

Expand this expression: $(x^2y - mn^3)^2$

A. $2x^4y^2 - 2x^2ymn^3 + 2m^2n^4$

B. $x4y^2 - 2x\ 2ymn^2 + m^2n^6$

C. $x^4y^2 - 2x^2ymn^3 + m^2n^6$

D. $x^4y^2 - 2x^2ymn^3 + m^2n^6$

# Chapter 14   A Man under a Word
# 1 Kings 17:1–8

> *Memory Verse:* The Word of the LORD came to [Elijah]. —1 Kings 17:8

Even a cursory reading of 1 Kings shows us that the main focus to this book of the Bible is not kings, but prophets! In fact, 1 Kings is not very impressed with kings at all. They are extras, secondary characters: the real story is about the prophets. The kings are incidental public points of reference who simply provide a context for the really important people—the people whom the theologian Walter Brueggemann calls "history makers." Kings may be convenient for schoolchildren to memorize, but the real action is with the men and women of God: people under a Word.

Elijah appears abruptly. That is how God's Word comes into the royal arena. And he immediately begins to irritate people, especially royal-type people who *think* that they are in control of things.

They think they are in control because it is clear to us (the readers) that in fact God and his designated spokesperson are in control.

Like Ahab, we are scarcely ready for Elijah. His name means "Yahweh is my God." And from the beginning, Elijah lets us know who is in charge: God. *We* want to be in charge; we think we are in charge, but no, Elijah reminds us, God is in control. Period.

In our Scripture passage (1 Kings 17), Israel is facing an energy crisis. This is a particularly embarrassing turn of event to an oriental monarch who claims authority over the elements.

Ahab in particular is irritated. He is syncretistic, a compromiser: he worships several gods. And why not? Why not cover all the bases? Perchance something will bring prosperity.

Ahab, like most modernists, is like a Hegelian. Hegel believed strongly in the dialectic. He starts with a *thesis* (a position put forward for argument). Opposed to this is a contradictory statement, an *antithesis*. Out of their opposition comes a *synthesis* that embraces both. But since the truth lies only in the whole system, this first synthesis is not yet the truth of the matter, but becomes a new thesis, with its corresponding antithesis and synthesis. And so on. Truth, then, is not absolute and is always open to interpretation. Truth lies in the "search" in the "system."

Ahab's wicked wife Jezebel, who worshiped various Palestinian and Phoenician gods and goddesses, made it easier for Ahab to be apostate. But with all that open-mindedness, Ahab seemed to be more powerless than ever! How embarrassing!

Ahab is a modern man. Paul Johnson in *Modern Times* (48) describes men like Ahab. Ahab and Jezebel sought the decline and ultimately the collapse of the religious impulse that seeks the true God. It would leave a huge vacuum. In large measure, the history of modern times is the history of how that vacuum is filled. The German Nietzsche [whom I call postmodern] rightly perceived that the most likely candidate would be what he called the "Will to Power," which offered a far more comprehensive and in the end more plausible explanation of human behavior than either Marx or Freud. In place of religious belief, there would be secular ideology. Those who once filled the ranks of the totalitarian clergy would become totalitarian politicians. And above all, the Will to Power would produce a new kind of messiah, uninhibited by any religious sanctions whatever, and with an unappeasable appetite for controlling humanity. The end of the old order, with an unguided world adrift in a relativistic universe, was a summons for such gangster-statesmen to emerge. In Johnson's day they were Tojo, Hitler, and Mussolini. They were not slow to make their appearance in Johnson's world nor in Elijah's.

Ahab, on the other hand, was under a Word—the Word of God. A God who never changed, never equivocated and meant business.

Yet for Elijah, God is not some distant "scary" figure. In the theology of Carl F. H. Henry, God is understood as the God who stands (who eternally exists), who stoops (who creates and who redeems his fallen creation), and who stays (who preserves, renews, and consummates his creation).

In Elijah's life, God's Word was definitive. For Ahab, immediate experience was the operative factor.

And so, experience and reasoning and accommodation and open-mindedness have brought a drought to Israel. Let's see what the Word of God will bring.

Elijah reminds Ahab that there is no rain because God wants Ahab to know that God is God and to know what a chump Ahab is. He wants Ahab and Jezebel to know what he thinks about their good ideals and good reasoning when they contradict the Word of God. Such arrogance brings death, hard times, destruction, and sterility.

Elijah reminds us all that kings are really silly when they are compared to God. That their ideals are quite stupid when they are compared to the Word of God. That things do not after all have to be like the kings say they will be. Thus, Elijah is a subversive. His message hints of a way around royal administration. It hints of a God who is more powerful than all the mighty people in the whole world.

Yes, Elijah is a man under a Word. He knows that he must do things, irrational things, compelled by God's command, even though it seems a little foolish. This is the same foolishness of which Paul speaks in 1 Corinthians 1:25. The foolishness of man is the wisdom of God.

Elijah is commanded to be fed by ravens and to drink only from the brook. He is to shun all the regular supplies of food that are guaranteed by conventional administration. He is to become utterly vulnerable and rely only on what God gives (see Matthew 6:25–33). The command of God sends us all into high-risk situations.

The command of God, in fact, is shown to be utterly reliable. The ravens do as the heavenly Father promised. The brook does provide water, not forever but until the promise has been kept. God's promises are sure and can be trusted. The text offers a juxtaposition of human vulnerability and divine power. Perhaps only promises made to vulnerable are kept. Certainly Ahab, who liked to cover all his bases, resisted being vulnerable and never knew any promises from God except for "disaster" (1 Kings 21:21).

This passage in 1 Kings 17 invites us to remember ancient times, clear back to the miracle of manna (Exodus 16). That old story is now reenacted. We are called to be vulnerable. To take risks. To be under a Word. Are you ready? Are you willing?

## Journal Question

Like Elijah, Christians are called to be different from the world. However, the problem is that some Christians are different in "insignificant ways." In what ways can you be significantly different from the world?

# Lesson 1
## Evidence-Based Reading and Writing

### Literary Choice

"My Captain! My Captain!" is part of a series of post-Civil War poems written by the American poet Walt Whitman. Walter Whitman, along with Emily Dickinson, is among the most influential modern poets in the American canon, often called the father of free verse.

### O Captain! My Captain!

*(The Patriotic Poems of Walt Whitman* [New York: Doubleday, 1918], 16.)

1   O Captain! my Captain! our fearful trip is done,
2   The ship has weather'd every rack, the prize we sought is won,
3   The port is near, the bells I hear, the people all exulting,
4   While follow eyes the steady keel, the vessel grim and daring;
5       But O heart! heart! heart!
6       O the bleeding drops of red,
7       Where on the deck my Captain lies,
8       Fallen cold and dead.
9
10  O Captain! my Captain! rise up and hear the bells;
11  Rise up—for you the flag is flung—for you the bugle trills,
12  For you bouquets and ribbon'd wreaths—for you the shores a-crowding,
13  For you they call, the swaying mass, their eager faces turning;
14      Here Captain! dear father!
15      This arm beneath your head!
16      It is some dream that on the deck,
17      You've fallen cold and dead.
18
19  My Captain does not answer, his lips are pale and still,
20  My father does not feel my arm, he has no pulse nor will,
21  The ship is anchor'd safe and sound, its voyage closed and done,
22  From fearful trip the victor ship comes in with object won;
23      Exult O shores, and ring O bells!
24      But I with mournful tread,
25      Walk the deck my Captain lies,
26      Fallen cold and dead.

(http://catalog.hathitrust.org/Record/007675868)

### Student Response

#### Into the Mist: Lincoln and Whitman

1   On Friday, April 14, 1865, Abraham Lincoln was shot at Ford's Theatre, 10th Street, Washington, D.C. It is a
2   popular tale that Lincoln foresaw this event. Lincoln's dream regarding the ghost in his looking glass is indeed
3   truthful, but it occurred long before his assassination (around the time of his reelection in 1864) and was not the only
4   dream in which Lincoln prophesied his own death. Mere days before his assassination, Lincoln dreamed that he was
5   sailing on a ship toward an indefinite shore. This dream recalls the extended metaphor in Walt Whitman's famous
6   poem written in honor of Lincoln's death. Whitman's poem "O Captain! My Captain!" completes the unresolved
7   dream that haunted Lincoln during the Civil War.
8           On Wednesday, April 13, 1865, Abraham Lincoln had a dream: he was traveling as captain of a speeding
9   ship into a mist that shrouded the final destination from view. The next day, Lincoln shared his dream with his
10  cabinet, and Gideon Welles, Lincoln's Secretary of the Navy, recorded the president's account in his diary. While

11  waiting for news of a recent battle, "The President remarked [that the news] would, he had no doubt, . . . come
12  favorable, for he had last night the usual dream which he had preceding nearly every great and important event of
13  the War. Generally the news had been favorable which succeeded this dream, and the dream itself was always the
14  same." When Welles inquired into the nature of this dream, Lincoln said that it took place on a ship, "and that he
15  was moving with great rapidity toward an indefinite shore; that he had this dream preceding Sumter, Bull Run,
16  Antietam, Gettysburg, Stone River, Vicksburg, Wilmington, etc." Lincoln continued, "I had . . . this strange dream
17  again last night, and we shall, judging from the past, have great news very soon. I think it must be from Sherman.
18  My thoughts are in that direction, as are most of yours." Little did Lincoln know that the "great news" would not
19  come from Sherman. Welles finished this passage in his own words: "I write this conversation three days after it
20  occurred, in consequence of what took place Friday night, and but for which the mention of this dream would
21  probably have never been noted. Great events did, indeed, follow, for within a few hours the good and gentle, as
22  well as truly great, man who narrated his dream closed forever his earthly career." The story is profound, but
23  Lincoln's dream appears to have presented a prophetic metaphor.
24       What Lincoln saw in foresight Walt Whitman addressed in hindsight. Whitman's poem "O Captain! My
25  Captain!" utilizes the metaphor that permeated Lincoln's prophetic dream and extends it to reveal the mysterious
26  ship's final destination. "O Captain! my Captain! our fearful trip is done; / The ship has weather'd every rack, the
27  prize we sought is won; / The port is near, the bells I hear, the people all exulting, / While follow eyes the steady
28  keel, the vessel grim and daring." Lincoln's ship had arrived at victory and celebration, but just as Lincoln never
29  knew the end to his dream, Whitman's captain is not alive to witness his journey's successful conclusion. "My
30  Captain does not answer, his lips are pale and still; / My father does not feel my arm, he has no pulse nor will."
31       "O Captain! My Captain!" provides the resolution to Lincoln's misty dream, which eluded him during his
32  lifetime. Lincoln never beheld his ship's final destination because death hung as a mist that cut off his sight of the
33  shore. "Exult, O shores, and ring, O bells! / But I, with mournful tread, / Walk the deck my Captain lies, / Fallen
34  cold and dead."(John)


## Close Reading

1. What is the central metaphor in this scene?
   A. A sunrise on the ocean
   B. A ship returning to port without its captain
   C. A senseless war casualty
   D. A stormy night

2. The plot concerns
   A. The assassination of Abraham Lincoln.
   B. Civil War dead.
   C. The surrender at Appomattox Courthouse.
   D. Union victory at sea.

3. Which of the following statements is true about this passage?
   A. The captain dies.
   B. The captain leaves to go on vacation.
   C. The captain barely survives a storm.
   D. The crew saves the captain.

4. What is the central irony of this poem?
   A. The captain is the victor.
   B. The Civil War is over.
   C. The conflict is almost over.
   D. The captain has brought the ship home to port, only to die in the process.

5. The tone of the poem?
   A. Triumphant
   B. Sanguine
   C. Sad
   D. Choleric

6. The poet creates the tone by
   A. Hyperbole
   B. Repeating words like "cold and dead"
   C. Analogy
   D. Onomatopoeia

7.  What can the reader surmise about Walt Whitman by reading this poem?
    I.   Whitman admired Abraham Lincoln.
    II.  Whitman despised classical poetry.
    III. Whitman was glad the Civil War had ended.
    IV.  Whitman hated the South.

    A. I and II            C. I and III
    B. III and IV          D. All

## Command of Evidence

1.  Where is the thesis of the Student Response?
    A. Lines 2–3           C. Lines 25–28
    B. Lines 5–7           D. Lines 32–34

2.  According to the Student Response, the central metaphor in "O Captain! My Captain!"?
    A. A vision of the Confederate surrender to General Sherman
    B. A dream that Mrs. Lincoln had
    C. A prophetic message received at church
    D. A recurring dream that Lincoln had

3.  How does the Student Response develop its argument?
    A. It first authenticates the dream by offering witnesses and then applies it to the poem.
    B. It quotes lines from the poem to support its argument.
    C. It exonerates Gideon Welles from any wrongdoing.
    D. It invites the reader to put more credibility in dreams.

4.  What is an assumption that the Student Response makes?
    I.   The dream was prophetic.
    II.  Lincoln misunderstood the dream.
    III. Lincoln had a death wish.

    A. I           C. III          E. All
    B. II          D. I and II

## Words in Context

1.  What is the meaning of *profound* in Student Response in Line 22?
    A. Superficial         C. Thoughtful
    B. Magnanimous         D. Caustic

2.  What is the meaning of *foresight* in Student Response in Line 24?
    A. Discernment         C. Sagacity
    B. Luck                D. Happiness

3.  What is the meaning of *hindsight* in Student Response in Line 24?
    A. Reasoning           C. Focusing
    B. Yearning            D. Retrospection

4.  What is the meaning of *permeated* in Student Response in Line 25?
    A. Overcoming          C. Dancing
    B. Pervading           D. Confronting

# Lesson 2
## Critical Reading and Writing

### Command of Evidence

Read the following passages and answer accompanying questions:

### Passage 1

1  "The game had never been fair, the dice were loaded. They were swindlers and thieves of pennies and dimes, and
2  they had been trapped and put out of the way by the swindlers and thieves of millions of dollars," wrote Upton
3  Sinclair in his book *The Jungle*, decrying the workers' fate in the industrial revolution. Sinclair reflects the view of a
4  growing number of people in the 1800s and 1900s who traced the workers' suffering to the system of capitalism,
5  arguing that capitalisms inherently produce exploitation. The most influential voice against capitalism was that of
6  Karl Marx, a German philosopher, who created the strongest alternative to capitalism: communism. While the ideas
7  of socialists like Sinclair and communists like Marx are very controversial, both men turned to their philosophies,
8  which were based on legitimate side effects of the industrial revolution.
9      The industrial revolution began in the early 1800s. At the time when the first steam engines were used in
10  Europe, Europe's population numbered 188 million; fifty years later it was 266 million. A good number of Europe's
11  poor, mostly from the countryside (by 1813 industrialization had replaced agriculture as the dominant trade in
12  Britain, the center of the industrial revolution), crowded in the big cities, seeking work in the factories. These cities
13  were not prepared for such a huge influx of people; consequentially, they lived in horrible, insanitary conditions.
14  Work in the factories was also dangerous, and oftentimes workers were underpaid. These workers were mostly
15  whole families, with children as young as five working anywhere from eleven to fifteen hours each day. Accidents
16  from the machinery were common. The factories were often dark and dank. The British government sent out
17  commissioners in the 1830s and 1840s to investigate the conditions of the factories, in order to see what legislation
18  needed to be enacted for the protection of the workers. One group of medical commissioners described what they
19  saw: "Children have been worked a most unreasonable and cruel length of time daily, and . . . even adults have been
20  expected to do a certain quantity of labor which scarcely any human being is able to endure" (*Second Report, with
21  Minutes of Evidence and Reports by the Medical Commissioners*, vol. 5, Session 29 January–20 August 1833; cf.
22  http://lhswildcats.org/files/lhs/docs/n2284/indurrevdocactivity008.pdf). These dire conditions led Friedrich Engels, a
23  close friend of Karl Marx, to comment, "The ways in which the vast mass of the poor are treated by modern society
24  is truly scandalous" (*The Conditions of the Working Class in England*). This scandal was the socialists' and
25  communists' strongest ally when advancing their philosophies.
26      There is great debate surrounding how much the industrial revolution improved the lives of the poorer
27  class. On the one hand, they were pushed out of the outdated agricultural economy into the progress of the industrial
28  revolution, but yet these new opportunities did not eliminate their poverty; however, there is no debate that lives of
29  the upper classes, and particularly the middle class, were greatly improved. Many owners of factories were poor or
30  middle-class entrepreneurs such as Andrew Carnegie, who began as a factory worker at age thirteen. Some middle
31  class leaders worked for the improvement of workers' lives; others viewed poverty as a sign of laziness, were
32  committed to the idea of self-help that "Heaven helps those who help themselves," and did little to improve the lives
33  of the poor. This led socialists to believe that there was a class conspiracy, that the bourgeoisie was purposefully
34  oppressing the worker class in order to retain power. "Not only are they slaves of the bourgeois class, and of the
35  bourgeois state; they are daily and hourly enslaved by the machine, by the over-looker, and, above all, by the
36  individual bourgeois manufacturer himself," wrote Karl Marx in his *Communist Manifesto* (1848). The world was in
37  such turmoil because of capitalism, which bred exploitation and greed, argued Marx and his supporters; the only
38  remedy they saw was to exchange capitalism for socialism.
39      In Upton Sinclair's book *The Jungle* (1906), Sinclair tells the story of a young immigrant who works in
40  Chicago's stockyards, butchering pigs. In one scene, Sinclair describes the brutality the unwary pigs faced, making a
41  comparison between them and the working class. "One could not stand and watch very long without being
42  philosophical, without beginning to deal in symbols and similes and to hear the hog-squeal of the universe." **Just as
43  Fate threw the pigs to death, so too, Sinclair argued, the industrial revolution had thrown the workers to
44  their deaths in the stockyards and factories of the middle class.** (Daphnide)

1. What would be the best title of this essay?
   A. The Rise of the Cold War
   B. The Russian Revolution
   C. The Rise of Marxism
   D. Naturalistic Novels

2. Why did the author begin with a quote from an Upton Sinclair novel?
   A. To show the negative side of the Industrial Revolution
   B. To offer an example of an early twentieth-century novel
   C. To criticize meat-packing plants
   D. To vilify Karl Marx

3. What organizational plan does the author employ?
   A. Defines "Marxism" and then gives examples.
   B. Ties the rise of Marxism to naturalism.
   C. Offers examples of the impact of the industrial revolution.
   D. Using the rhetoric of Sinclair's novel, she weaves emerging Marxism into the fabric of the industrial revolution

4. What example does the author offer to illustrate logos?
   A. A quote from Engels
   B. Criticism of Sinclair
   C. A popular song
   D. A personal comment

5. The author finishes her essay with
   A. A summary statement
   B. A new conclusion
   C. A distracting comment
   D. The way she began—an image from Sinclair's *The Jungle*

# Passage 2

1  William Shakespeare said of humor, "In jest there is truth." The cartoon has been a form of jest for centuries, and it
2  has helped illuminate the truths of society for just as long. Bill Watterson employs the medium of the cartoon to do
3  exactly this in his work *The Essential Calvin and Hobbes.* Calvin, a precocious six-year-old boy, and his imaginary
4  friend Hobbes, a stuffed tiger, are the main characters of the comic strip. They allow the reader to laugh at the
5  nuggets of truth Watterson presents and to see some of the trends in late twentieth-century American society.
6      Calvin and Hobbes was a daily comic strip that ran from 1985 to 1995. It was created and drawn by Bill
7  Watterson. Calvin is a first-grader endowed by Watterson with vocabulary and wit beyond his years. Calvin enjoys
8  making all manner of mischief and avoiding his homework whenever possible. His constant companion is his
9  stuffed tiger, Hobbes; who in Calvin's imagination is a fully animated individual capable of all human powers,
10 including speech and thought. Hobbes shares in Calvin's adventures, and although he sometimes disagrees with
11 Calvin, he is Calvin's best friend.
12     Although Calvin and Hobbes spend a great deal of time outdoors, they are entranced by television.
13 Watterson uses them to criticize the effects of television on America's youth. This is exemplified in several cartoons
14 in the Calvin and Hobbes series. In one cartoon, the first panel shows Calvin reading from a book: "It says here that
15 'Religion is the opiate of the masses.' . . . What do you suppose that means?'' The next panel shows a television
16 with a thought bubble which reads: "It means Karl Marx hadn't seen anything yet." Calvin and Hobbes go on to
17 discuss the poor quality of television programming. Then they become enthralled by a program and sit down in front
18 of the TV to watch. Just as Karl Marx believed that religion was a useless comfort to the masses, Watterson
19 advances the idea that television fulfills a similar need on an industrial scale. Watterson expresses concern about the
20 amount of time children spend watching TV. He depicts Calvin and Hobbes spending an entire Sunday morning
21 watching cartoons. In another cartoon, Calvin's father tells them to go outside to play and enjoy the fresh air. Calvin
22 and Hobbes immediately proceed to Susie's house, where they watch her TV. It is clear that Watterson was
23 concerned about TV's grasp on young Americans.
24     Watterson uses Calvin and Hobbes to comment on the American educational system. **In several cartoons**
25 **he pokes fun at the ineffective methods of the school system.** In one cartoon, Calvin and his classmate, Susie, are
26 sent to the principal's office for passing notes. They are hysterical because they think they're going to be spanked,
27 and Susie believes that her academic career will be ruined. Watterson makes fun of the expectations placed on

28 children from their early years. He also takes a shot at the school system's methods of teaching. Watterson
29 accomplishes this with a cartoon in which Calvin regurgitates information for a test and comments cynically that he
30 has figured out the system.
31     Watterson tackles many issues of the day. He mocks sexism with Calvin's refusal to allow Susie into the tree
32 house. He comments on voter attitudes with Calvin's plea for suffrage. When Hobbes asks Calvin why he desires
33 this privilege, Calvin answers that he "want[s] a bigger piece of the pie." Watterson is advancing the opinion that
34 American voters are greedy and more interested in their own welfare than that of the country. Calvin and Hobbes
35 also touch on urban decay. They discuss where they will go in the afterlife. Hobbes suggests "Pittsburgh?" Calvin
36 asks, "If we're good or if we're bad?" This is a reference to the decline of American cities. Watterson also ridicules
37 pop culture and its influence on children. Calvin is trying to increase his "sex appeal" by drinking a certain brand of
38 soda. Hobbes tries out ridiculous clothes, and Calvin makes fun of him for not being cool. It is apparent that
39 Watterson does not appreciate advertising's sway over children.
40     Watterson also criticizes the spoiled attitudes of children. For example, Calvin and Hobbes go to the beach
41 and are unhappy and sit in the car because the water is too cold and the sand is too hot. In another strip, Calvin and
42 Hobbes don't know what to do with the fish they caught and decide to eat cheese sandwiches, instead of cleaning the
43 fish. Rather than walking on a nice day, Calvin tries to get his mom to drive him to a friend's house.
44     Watterson used Calvin and Hobbes to entertain a decade of readers and beyond. The comic strip elicited
45 laughter through their endearing relationship and sophisticated satire. Through this laughter Watterson offers a
46 glimpse of society's imperfections. The jest makes the truth at its core a pleasure for the readers to discover. (Joe)

1. What would be the best title of this essay?
   A. Comics in the Newspapers
   B. Calvin and Hobbes as a Lens into American Society
   C. An Angry Tiger
   D. A Precocious Child

2. Why did the author begin with a quote from Shakespeare?
   A. To tie his thesis to British literature
   B. To offer an example of early seventeenth-century literature
   C. To show the impact of humor on society
   D. To honor Calvin's perspicuity

3. What organizational plan does the author employ?
   A. To establish the scope of Calvin and Hobbes and then give examples of its impact
   B. To tie this cartoon to daily American life
   C. To illustrate its impact on modern America
   D. To draw the reader step by step into his argument

4. What example does the author offer to illustrate logos?
   A. Lines 6–7
   B. Lines 13–15
   C. Lines 24–26
   D. D. Lines 41–44

5. The author finishes his essay with
   A. A summary statement.
   B. A new conclusion.
   C. A distracting comment.
   D. A final criticism of Watterson.

## Grammar and Usage

Choose the best grammar/usage form in bold sentence(s).:

1. Passage 1, Lines 42–44
   A. NONE
   B. Just as Fate has thrown the pigs to death, so too, Sinclair argued, the industrial revolution had thrown the workers to their deaths in the stockyards and factories of the middle class.
   C. Just as Fate threw the pigs to death, so too, Sinclair argued, the industrial revolution threw the workers to their deaths in the stockyards and factories of the middle class.
   D. Just like Fate threw the pigs to death, so too, Sinclair argued, the industrial revolution sacrificed the workers to their deaths in the stockyards and factories of the middle class.

2. Passage 2, Lines 24–25
   A. NONE
   B. In several cartoons, he pokes fun at the ineffective methods of the school system.
   C. He pokes fun at the ineffective methods of the school system.
   D. A cartoon even pokes fun at the ineffective methods of the school system.

# Lesson 3
## SAT Essay

### Student Response 1

*Prompt:* In what way is failure a good thing?

1     Failure is not necessarily a bad thing. For some, finding their college thesis stolen would mean the end of a
2 career. For others, like my friend Ryan Fattman, the loss of a college thesis ended up resulting in a successful
3 political career: he recently unseated a forty-four-year incumbent state senator. Romans 8:28 says that all things
4 work together for the good of those who love God; as a Christian, I believe that God uses failure in our lives to
5 either bring us closer to himself or teach us something about either ourselves or God that we did not know before.
6 Men like Thomas Edison, credited with the invention of the electric lightbulb, tried again and again to find a way
7 that worked. As Edison said, "I have not failed. I've just found 10,000 ways that won't work." Beyond finding
8 "10,000 ways that won't work," failure also teaches valuable lessons that could not be learned any other way.
9 Whenever I don't do the work required for an assignment, I receive a low grade and fail. Failure is not always evil;
10 rather, "failure is only the opportunity to begin again more intelligently," Henry Ford said. But Henry Ford himself
11 had problems.
12     Ford is a prime example of someone who never let failure get him down. **His wife repeatedly told him to**
13 **get his inventions out of her kitchen, and many of his friends believed the "horseless carriage" would never**
14 **become a commodity that every American would desire.** He never let this discourage him, however, and he
15 eventually realized his dream as he persevered through his failures. "You can't have any successes unless you can
16 accept failure," George Cukor writes. How true! Those who dwell on their past failures never look up to see the
17 bright sun of the future. Pip from Charles Dickens's *Great Expectations* believed that becoming a gentleman meant
18 fancy clothes and polished speech, but what he actually discovered is that those who persevere through their failures
19 and discouragements are the true gentlemen. Failure is not always evil, and much success can be gained by learning
20 from our mistakes and putting that acquired knowledge to work as we strive toward the ultimate goal of success.
21 (Benjamin)

### Student Response 2
*Prompt:* What is more important: character or accomplishments?

1     Character is a tricky thing to define. Like most parts of the nonphysical human person, character, like the
2 "soul" or "conscience," is not something palpable like an arm or a leg. Character can be seen and felt only when
3 perfected by adversity.
4     Frank Thomas, portrayed by Viggo Mortensen in the movie *Hidalgo*, was an American who competed in
5 many grueling cross-country races with his horse, Hidalgo. Ultimately his character is pushed to the limit when he
6 enters the trans-Arabian desert race, and sandstorms and locust lunches test his endurance. In the end, his character
7 is fully formed, and he is a different man by the race's end.
8     Racing is not the only thing that builds character. School builds character as well. Even though, as Winston
9 Churchill described it, "school was an unending spell of worries that did not then seem pretty, of toil uncheered by
10 fruition, . . . a time of discomfort, restriction, and purposeless monotony." Yet many of our most valuable lessons
11 are learned in the classroom. Sitting through hours of boring lectures does have a purpose, and the knowledge
12 gained will help us in our journey through life.
13     Along that journey, we encounter diverse people as well. Every human being has a story, like the young
14 man from a Brooklyn school who confessed that his principal "told each of us that we matter." His story made
15 national news, and his school received enough money to send his class on a field trip to Harvard. **Before her**
16 **mention on TV, this principal felt as though her countless hours of time invested in her students had gone to**
17 **waste.** However, as her students revealed, that time was anything but wasted: her own character was also built when
18 she was mentoring her students.
19     Character is never built in vain. In the classic stories of *Frog and Toad* by Arnold Lobel, Toad makes a
20 batch of cookies, which he and Frog proceed to eat. They find they cannot stop eating them and try many ways to
21 stop. Finally Frog builds their "willpower" by throwing the cookies to the birds. Although Toad sullenly walks
22 home, declaring that he would bake a cake, Frog benefited from the endeavor, and his character was strengthened.

23      Determination is also a prime factor in character building. Charging ahead among all obstacles is
24 something our culture greatly esteems. When I walked outside, shovel in hand, to try to make a dent in the wall of
25 snow covering the walkway, it seemed as though I'd never finish. By persevering, though, I was able to accomplish
26 the task and earn a "well done" from my father.
27      "The gem cannot be polished without friction," the Chinese proverb quips, "nor man perfected without
28 trials." Trials are not things to avoid; rather, we should actively seek them out and use them to grow our character. If
29 this seems ridiculous, observe the spike of athletes and hipsters flocking to "endurance races" and other challenging
30 events. They are stupid!
31      Recently, two men attempted to free-climb the El Capitan cliff in Yosemite National Park. With ropes only
32 there to catch them when they fell (which was often), these two men persisted amid their trials and finally succeeded
33 in reaching the summit, to the joy of their wives and loyal followers on social media. Now that they have free
34 climbed El Capitan, how hard is it for them to take out the trash for their wives, or move the bookcase to a different
35 spot in the living room? Adversity not only builds up character; it also prepares us to face the difficulties of
36 everyday life.
37      Gold is only refined by fire. Without the fiery testing, there would be no gold jewelry or coins. In the same
38 way, hardships refine us and equip us to work as hard as we can to do the right thing. In Alexandre Dumas's *The*
39 *Count of Monte Cristo*, Edmond Dantès endures unimaginable hardships during his fourteen years in prison. After
40 the trial is ended, however, he ends up making his fortune from buried treasure.
41      While character is not always palpable, it is always being formed, even in the most unlikely circumstances.
42 Trials build us up.

## Close Reading

1. In Student Response 1 the author
   - A. Argues that failure can be a good thing.
   - B. Calls failure a necessary evil.
   - C. Says that failure must be avoided at all costs.
   - D. Concedes that failure is a bad thing.

2. In Student Response 2 the author organizes his essay
   - A. By using evoking the memory of someone who had character.
   - B. By offering a series of anecdotes.
   - C. By refusing to give in to impossible odds.
   - D. By a series of bullet points.

3. Explain this statement: "Adversity not only builds up character; it also prepares us to face the difficulties of everyday life" (Student Response 2, Lines 35–36).
   - A. After struggling through many difficult farm situations, one develops perseverance.
   - B. Adversity will prepare us to overcome the most difficult problems.
   - C. Adversity will make other obstacles seem small.
   - D. Nothing is more difficult than climbing problems.

4. A recurring problem in both responses is that
   - A. The thesis is not mentioned until the second paragraph.
   - B. Transitions are weak.
   - C. There are too many personal examples.
   - D. The examples are too arcane.

5. What is the main point of Student Response 1?
   - A. Lines 2–3      C. Lines 15–16
   - B. Lines 5–6      D. Lines 18–19

6. What is the main point of the Student Response 2?
   - A. Lines 1–3      C. Lines 15–16
   - B. Lines 5–6      D. Lines 40–41

7. The student?
   A. An athlete
   B. A born-again Christian
   C. A history lover
   D. A race-car driver

8. Evidence can be found in Student Response 1:
   A. Lines 1–2
   B. Lines 3–5
   C. Lines 12–14
   D. Lines 16–18

9. What section of Student Response 1 probably should be removed?
   A. Lines 1–2
   B. Line 10
   C. Lines 15–16
   D. Lines 19–19

10. What is the most plausible explanation for the above choice?
    A. People are not stupid.
    B. The sentence is too religious.
    C. The sentence is too opinionated and not supported by evidence.
    D. The information in the paragraph is repeated elsewhere.

11. What score would the student responses receive?
    Student Response 1: __. Student Response 2: __.

## Grammar and Usage

Choose the best grammar/usage form in bold sentence(s).:

1. Student Response 1, Lines 11–13
   A. NONE
   B. His wife repeatedly told him to get his inventions out of her kitchen, and many friends believed the "horseless carriage" would never amount to a thing.
   C. His wife repeatedly told him to get his inventions out of her kitchen, and many friends believed the "horseless carriage" would never become a commodity that every American would desire.
   D. His wife repeatedly told him to get his inventions out of her kitchen, and many friends believed the "horseless carriage" would never attract a market.

2. Student Response 2, Lines 15–16
   A. NONE
   B. Prior to her mention on TV, this principal felt as though countless hours of invested time in her students had gone to waste.
   C. At first the principal felt as though her countless hours of invested time in her students had gone to waste.
   D. Before the mention of the principal's school on TV, she was certain that her countless hours of time invested in her students had gone to waste.

# Lesson 4
## Reading: Document-Based Analysis

### "Farewell Letter to the American People," by George W. Harkins

The "Farewell Letter to the American People" (1832) denounced the removal of the Choctaw Nation to Oklahoma. This letter, by the chief of the Choctaw tribe, also marked the beginning of a large process removed Native Americans living East of Mississippi, known as the Trail of Tears.

1 To the American People:
2
3 It is with considerable diffidence that I attempt to address the American people, knowing and feeling sensibly my
4 incompetency; and believing that your highly and well-improved minds would not be well entertained by the
5 address of a Choctaw. But having determined to emigrate west of the Mississippi River this fall, I have thought
6 proper in bidding you farewell to make a few remarks expressive of my views, and the feelings that actuate me on
7 the subject of our removal.
8     Believing that our all is at stake and knowing that you readily sympathize with the distressed of every
9 country, I confidently throw myself upon your indulgence and ask you to listen patiently. I do not arrogate to myself
10 the prerogative of deciding upon the expediency of the late treaty, yet I feel bound as a Choctaw, to give a distinct
11 expression of my feelings on that interesting, (and to the Choctaws), all important subject.
12     We were hedged in by two evils, and we chose that which we thought the least. Yet we could not recognize
13 the right that the state of Mississippi had assumed, to legislate for us. —Although the legislature of the state were
14 qualified to make laws for their own citizens, that did not qualify them to become law makers to a people that were
15 so dissimilar in manners and customs as the Choctaws are to the Mississippians. Admitting that they understood the
16 people, could they remove that mountain of prejudice that has ever obstructed the streams of justice, and prevent
17 their salutary influence from reaching my devoted countrymen[?] We as Choctaws rather chose to suffer and be free,
18 than live under the degrading influence of laws, which our voice could not be heard in their formation.
19     Much as the state of Mississippi has wronged us, I cannot find in my heart any other sentiment than an
20 ardent wish for her prosperity and happiness.
21     I could cheerfully hope, that those of another age and generation may not feel the effects of those
22 oppressive measures that have been so illiberally dealt out to us; and that peace and happiness may be their reward.
23 Amid the gloom and horrors of the present separation, we are cheered with a hope that ere long we shall reach our
24 destined land, and that nothing short of the basest acts of treachery will ever be able to wrest it from us, and that we
25 may live free. Although your ancestors won freedom on the field of danger and glory, our ancestors owned it as their
26 birthright, and we have had to purchase it from you as the vilest slaves buy their freedom.
27     Yet it is said that our present movements are our own voluntary acts—such is not the case. We found
28 ourselves like a benighted stranger, following false guides, until he was surrounded on every side, with fire and
29 water. The fire was certain destruction, and a feeble hope was left him of escaping by water. A distant view of the
30 opposite shore encourages the hope; to remain would be inevitable annihilation. Who would hesitate, or who would
31 say that his plunging into the water was his own voluntary act? Painful in the extreme is the mandate of our
32 expulsion. We regret that it should proceed from the mouth of our professed friend, for whom our blood was co-
33 mingled with that of his bravest warriors, on the field of danger and death.
34     But such is the instability of professions. The man who said that he would plant a stake and draw a line
35 around us, that never should be passed, was the first to say he could not guard the lines, and drew up the stake and
36 wiped out all traces of the line. I will not conceal from you my fears, that the present grounds may be removed. I
37 have my foreboding; who of us can tell after witnessing what has already been done, what the next force may be[?]
38     I ask you in the name of justice, for repose for myself and for my injured people. Let us alone—we will not
39 harm you, we want rest. We hope, in the name of justice, that another outrage may never be committed against us,
40 and that we may for the future be cared for as children, and not driven about as beasts, which are benefited by a
41 change of pasture.
42     Taking an example from the American government, and knowing the happiness which its citizens enjoy
43 under the influence of mild republican institutions, it is the intention of our countrymen to form a government
44 assimilated to that of our white brethren in the United States, as nearly as their condition will permit.

45        We know that in order to protect the rights and secure the liberties of the people, no government
46 approximates so nearly to perfection as the one to which we have alluded. As east of the Mississippi we have been
47 friends, so west we will cherish the same feelings with additional fervor; and although we may be removed to the
48 desert, still we shall look with fond regard, upon those who have promised us their protection. Let that feeling be
49 reciprocated. . . .

(http://www.ushistory.org/documents/harkins.htm)

1. The chief argument of this document is what?
   I.   To regain Choctaw land lost to the United States
  II.   To express outrage at unjust actions by the United States government
  III.   To explain Choctaw rights and to offer some sort of closure to the forced immigration of Harkin's people

      A. I               B. I and II             C. III              D. All

2. What technique does the author employ in lines 8–9?
  A. Analogy                             C. Irony
  B. Hyperbole                       D. Simile

3. Lines 19–20 show an example of
  A. Magnanimity                     C. Retribution
  B. Hyperbole                       D. Subjugation

4. What is the main fear that Harkin expresses in this passage?
  A. That the Choctaw Nation will not get a fair deal
  B. That his people will die of starvation
  C. That his people will not be allowed to live in Oklahoma
  D. That his people will not be left alone in Oklahoma, and further perfidies will be committed against them

5. With which of the following statements would the author agree?
   I.   The United States is a bad country.
  II.   The United States is making a mistake moving his people to Oklahoma
  III.   The Choctaw Nation is no threat to the United States
  IV.   The Choctaw Nation should be moved back to the State of Mississippi.

      A. I and II            C. III and IV            E. All
      B. II and III          D. IV

## Words in Context

1.   What is the meaning of *actuate* in Line 6?
    A.   Neutralize                   C.   Reciprocate
    B.   Stimulate                    D.   Desensitize

2.   What is the meaning of *indulgence* in Line 9?
    A.   Forbearance                 C.   Impunity
    B.   Impatience                 D.   Extravagance

3.   What is the meaning of *expediency* in Line 10?
    A.   Morbidity                    C.   Sentiment
    B.   Peculiarity                D.   Feasibility

4.   What is the meaning of *benighted* in Line 28?
    A.   Enlightened                C.   Brazen
    B.   Unenlightened            D.   Forlorn

# Lesson 5

## Math: Algebra, Arithmetic Problem Solving and Data Analysis, and Passport to Advanced Math

**Analyzing Data**

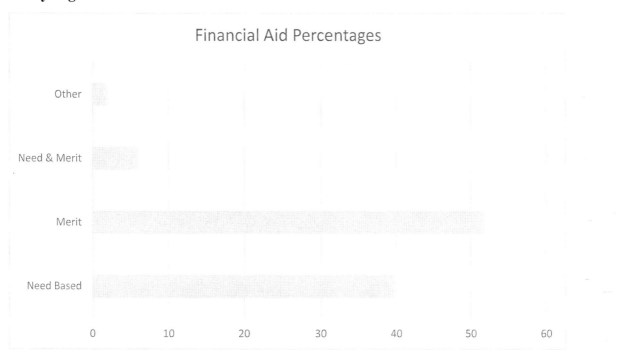

1. Which of the following statements are true?

    I. The majority of students receive some sort of financial aid.
   II. Merit awards are more often awarded than any other category
  III. Racial minorities dominate the need based categories.
   IV. More men than women receive aid.

       A. I                       C. I and II                  E. All
       B. II                      D. III and IV

2. From this data one can conclude that

    A. Need is the primary criteria for aid determination
    B. Southern students get more aid than northern students.
    C. Good grades and high college admission test scores will help students receive more aid.
    D. Students usually receive need and merit scholarships

## Arithmetic Problem Solving

1. Charles and Henry together have 49 marbles, and Charles has twice as many as Henry and 4 more. How many marbles has each?

   A. Carl, 34; Henry, 15
   B. Henry, 34; Carl, 15

   C. Henry, 32; Carl, 13
   D. Henry, 36; Carl, 16

2. In an orchard containing 33 trees, the number of pear trees is 5 more than three times the number of apple trees. How many are there of each kind?

   A. 22 pear; 4 apple
   B. 26 pear; 6 apple

   C. 26 pear; 7 apple
   D. 24 pear; 6 apple

3. John and Mary gathered 23 quarts of nuts. John gathered 2 quarts more than twice as many as Mary. How many quarts did each gather?

   A. John, 16 qts.; Mary, 7 qts.
   B. John, 16 qts.; Mary, 6 qts.

   C. John, 7 qts.; Mary, 16 qts.
   D. John, 14 qts.; Mary, 8 qts.

4. To the double of a number I add 17 and obtain as a result 147. What is the number?

   A. 62
   B. 65

   C. 66
   D. 64

# Chapter 15 Grieving for Lost Heroes
# 2 Samuel 1:17–27

> *Memory Verse:* A gazelle lies slain on your heights, Israel.
> How the mighty have fallen! –2 Samuel 1:19

I can still remember sitting in Advanced Math class (in 1970) when I heard the news. My friend, Curly Mays, was dead. Killed a few miles from the DMZ, Curly's position had survived the first onslaught of the NVA (North Vietnamese Army), but not the second one. And Curly, Lance Corporal, USMC, was dead.

I loved Curly. We were on the same baseball team, Western Auto. He had, yes, curly blond hair. Every Fourth of July his dad, E. G., and my dad stayed up all night smoking pork ribs, chicken legs, raccoon, and rattlesnake.

His dad was the town barber. Not a very good one, I might add. But my dad took me there, once every month on a Saturday morning. By this time other boys were going to a hair stylist. But not my dad. He was a loyal person. Once a month we went to Mr. May's barbershop and heard all the scores and all the fishing stories.

Mr. Mays cried when he heard the news. And so did I. Right in math class.

And I nearly did again when I read *In Retrospect* by former Defense Department Chairman Robert S. McNamara. A mistake. Curly died for a mistake. And I nearly cried again.

"I want Americans to understand why we made the mistakes we did," Mr. McNamara says in his new book. "That is the only way our nation can ever hope to leave the past behind. The ancient Greek dramatist Aeschylus wrote, 'The reward of suffering is experience.'"

I fear, Mr. McNamara, that I do not understand your point. Why did you send Curly into a war that had no meaning? That could not be won? I fear we learned very little from this "suffering." And I imagine Americans were feeling a lot of pain years ago when his book was published.

Today we hear another cry of pain. David's cry of pain. And we grieve with David. The lesson from 2 Samuel is a scream of pain, and David will not be quieted, he will not be comforted, and he will not be ignored.

A messenger has come to David with the news that King Saul and Jonathan, who is Saul's son and David's best friend, have been killed while fighting the Philistines on Mount Gilboa. The messenger clearly believes that he is bringing good news to David. For years Saul has been a threat to David. Now, with the deaths of Saul the king and Jonathan, the heir to the throne, the obstacles that prevented David from becoming king have been cleared. David is now free to be who he is meant to be. It is time for rejoicing. . . . But David does not rejoice. From somewhere deep within him, something boils up inside him. David aches with loss:

> Your glory, O Israel, lies slain upon your high places!
> How the mighty have fallen!
> Tell it not in Gath,
> proclaim it not in the streets of Ashkelon;
> or the daughters of the Philistines will rejoice. (1:19–20 NRSV)

Don't let your enemies see you cry. Don't tell it in Gath, a great Philistine city. They would not understand. They would see it as weakness. Their god is not big enough to handle their pain. In Gath they have a theology that deflects pain. In Ashkelon they worship a great, great god—a god who dwells high above every defeat, a god who knows not at all of death.

Among ourselves, and in our community, weep as we remember all that has been and that will be no more. Remember the glory that was Saul's kingdom and the prosperity and happiness it brought you. Grieve also for broken hopes and lost dreams.

> Tell it not in Gath,
> proclaim it not in the streets of Ashkelon;
> or the daughters of the Philistines will rejoice. . . .
> [But] O daughters of Israel, weep over Saul,
> who clothed you with crimson in luxury. (1:20, 24 NRSV)

Among yourselves, and in the community of the faithful, weep as you remember all that has been and that will be no more. Remember the glory that was Saul's kingdom and the prosperity and happiness it brought you: the clothes of expensive crimson, the golden ornaments, all the beauty of it. Grieve also for the broken hopes and lost dreams you cherished.

Cry for Jonathan. Innocent Jonathan! Who stood by his father even when he was evil and disobedient. David's good friend.

David has become King David. Undisputed. His first act as king, his first command, is that they should learn to grieve properly. Write this down and teach it to the people, so that they will know how to speak of their pain.

Pain can silence us. We can lose so much that no words can be found to speak of it. It is important for us to find the sons and symbols by which we can articulate our hurt. That is the reason we have Memorial Day. To remember their sacrifice. To say little; to feel much.

David commands that all the people learn to sing the song of lament. Many would object, saying that the past is best forgotten and put behind us. We cannot live in the past, after all. Certainly David will not make his home in the past. David is the future for Israel, but David wisely recognizes that the way to the future does not go around Mount Gilboa. He goes right up to the top alone and laments:

> You mountains of Gilboa,
>> let there be no dew or rain upon you, nor bounteous fields.
>> [Let the land be scourged.]
> For there the shield of the mighty was defiled,
>> the shield of Saul, anointed with oil no more. (1:21 NRSV)

The shield that was also our own defense and our security. After each battle it was washed with oil to keep it in readiness for the next battle, but now it lies on Gilboa, abandoned, defeated, "defiled, . . . anointed with oil no more." We face the future without the shield we knew and trusted for so long.

Look! See! The bodies of Saul and Jonathan. David summons us to see it all, not to turn our faces aside. Remember their beauty and their strength, now gone, and grieve for all that is lost to us. The king commands us to learn to tell of the pain and the loss. "How the mighty have fallen in the midst of the battle!"

David howls his anguish aloud on the heights of Gilboa. He screams out his loss and pain to whoever will hear. Everyone must hear and everyone must learn of this pain. David's song is a lament, however, primarily directed to God. Thus the theologian Walter Brueggemann writes:

> The laments are addressed to someone! And precisely in the presence of God . . . is where the hurtful issues must be dealt with. Nowhere but with [God] does Israel vent her greatest doubt, her bitterest resentments, her deepest anger. Israel knows that one need not fake it alone. In the dialogue [with God], Israel expects to understand what is happening and even to have it changed.

Articulating our pain, we muster hope that the bitter present may be transformed by God's future. By speaking our wounds, we hope for healing. Write down this lament, orders King David, and teach it to the people so they may know how to speak their hurt. There are not many places where we can speak of painful things and lost things. Too much in our society would comfort us with the false comfort of the world's answers. But David commands us to go to Mount Gilboa and to speak with God. Cry to God. Give up the false comfort of the world.

David reminds us that there is a place where our pains and losses are respected and treasured, even also as our joys and triumphs are valued. That is the place of the Lord. The shield of Saul lies defiled on Mount Gilboa and will no longer protect us, but in crying out our anguish, we address ourselves to the One who will be our shield and security for the future.

So cry loudly today and remember all that we have lost . . . and what God will do in the future. Those who dwell in the Philistine cities of Gath and Ashkelon will misunderstand and will think we are weak. The Philistines will mock, "Where is your God?" But we know that Christ's words on the cross—"My God, my God, why have you forsaken me?"—are sublime and presage an age of honesty and of victory. Today we among the tattered dreams on Mount Gilboa. I call you to serve the only God who really matters. The God who is with us in sadness and in happiness. Grieve with David. Remember! And then conquer your world!

## Journal Question:

What failure or grief do you carry in your heart? Can you place it on the cross at Calvary?

# Lesson 1
## Evidence-Based Reading and Writing

### Literary Choice

To avoid interference from Tory Lieutenant-Governor Dunmore, the Second Virginia Continental Convention met March 20, 1775 at St. John's Church, Richmond, Virginia. Fiery Patrick Henry presented resolutions to raise a militia. Henry's opponents urged caution and patience until the crown replied to Congress's latest petition for reconciliation. On the 23rd, Henry presented a proposal to organize a volunteer company of patriot cavalry and infantry in every Virginia county. By custom, Henry addressed himself to the Convention's president, Peyton Randolph of Williamsburg, and ended with the rousing slogan "Give me liberty or give me death!"

St. John's Church, Richmond, Virginia
March 23, 1775

1  Mr. President: No man thinks more highly than I do of the patriotism, as well as abilities, of the very worthy
2  gentlemen who have just addressed the House. But different men often see the same subject in different lights; and,
3  therefore, I hope it will not be thought disrespectful to those gentlemen if, entertaining as I do, opinions of a
4  character very opposite to theirs, I shall speak forth my sentiments freely, and without reserve. This is no time for
5  ceremony. The question before the House is one of awful moment to this country. For my own part, I consider it as
6  nothing less than a question of freedom or slavery; and in proportion to the magnitude of the subject ought to be the
7  freedom of the debate. It is only in this way that we can hope to arrive at truth, and fulfill the great responsibility
8  which we hold to God and our country. Should I keep back my opinions at such a time, through fear of giving
9  offence, I should consider myself as guilty of treason towards my country, and of an act of disloyalty toward the
10  majesty of heaven, which I revere above all earthly kings.
11      Mr. President, it is natural to man to indulge in the illusions of hope. We are apt to shut our eyes against a
12  painful truth, and listen to the song of that siren till she transforms us into beasts. Is this the part of wise men,
13  engaged in a great and arduous struggle for liberty? Are we disposed to be of the number of those who, having eyes,
14  see not, and, having ears, hear not, the things which so nearly concern their temporal salvation? For my part,
15  whatever anguish of spirit it may cost, I am willing to know the whole truth; to know the worst, and to provide for it.
16      I have but one lamp by which my feet are guided; and that is the lamp of experience. I know of no way of
17  judging of the future but by the past. And judging by the past, I wish to know what there has been in the conduct of
18  the British ministry for the last ten years, to justify those hopes with which gentlemen have been pleased to solace
19  themselves, and the House? Is it that insidious smile with which our petition has been lately received? Trust it not,
20  sir; it will prove a snare to your feet. Suffer not yourselves to be betrayed with a kiss. Ask yourselves how this
21  gracious reception of our petition comports with these war-like preparations which cover our waters and darken our
22  land. Are fleets and armies necessary to a work of love and reconciliation? Have we shown ourselves so unwilling to
23  be reconciled, that force must be called in to win back our love? Let us not deceive ourselves, sir. These are the
24  implements of war and subjugation; the last arguments to which kings resort. I ask, gentlemen, sir, what means this
25  martial array, if its purpose be not to force us to submission? Can gentlemen assign any other possible motive for it?
26  Has Great Britain any enemy, in this quarter of the world, to call for all this accumulation of navies and armies? No,
27  sir, she has *none*. They are meant for us; they can be meant for no other. They are sent over to bind and rivet upon us
28  those chains which the British ministry have been so long forging. And what have we to oppose to them? Shall we
29  try argument? Sir, we have been trying that for the last ten years. Have we anything new to offer upon the subject?
30  Nothing. We have held the subject up in every light of which it is capable; but it has been all in vain. Shall we resort
31  to entreaty and humble supplication? What terms shall we find which have not been already exhausted? Let us not, I
32  beseech you, sir, deceive ourselves. Sir, we have done everything that could be done, to avert the storm which is
33  now coming on. We have petitioned; we have remonstrated; we have supplicated; we have prostrated ourselves
34  before the throne, and have implored its interposition to arrest the tyrannical hands of the ministry and Parliament.
35  Our petitions have been slighted; our remonstrances have produced additional violence and insult; our supplications
36  have been disregarded; and we have been spurned, with contempt, from the foot of the throne. In vain, after these
37  things, may we indulge the fond hope of peace and reconciliation. There is no longer any room for hope. If we wish
38  to be free, if we mean to preserve inviolate those inestimable privileges for which we have been so long contending,
39  if we mean not basely to abandon the noble struggle in which we have been so long engaged, and which we have

40  pledged ourselves never to abandon until the glorious object of our contest shall be obtained, we must fight! I repeat
41  it, sir, we must fight! An appeal to arms and to the God of Hosts is all that is left us!
42      They tell us, sir, that we are weak; unable to cope with so formidable an adversary. But when shall we be
43  stronger? Will it be the next week, or the next year? Will it be when we are totally disarmed, and when a British
44  guard shall be stationed in every house? Shall we gather strength by irresolution and inaction? Shall we acquire the
45  means of effectual resistance, by lying supinely on our backs, and hugging the delusive phantom of hope, until our
46  enemies shall have bound us hand and foot? Sir, we are not weak if we make a proper use of those means which the
47  God of nature hath placed in our power. Three millions of people, armed in the holy cause of liberty, and in such a
48  country as that which we possess, are invincible by any force which our enemy can send against us. Besides, sir, we
49  shall not fight our battles alone. There is a just God who presides over the destinies of nations; and who will raise up
50  friends to fight our battles for us. The battle, sir, is not to the strong alone; it is to the vigilant, the active, the brave.
51  Besides, sir, we have no election. If we were base enough to desire it, it is now too late to retire from the contest.
52  There is no retreat but in submission and slavery! Our chains are forged! Their clanking may be heard on the plains
53  of Boston! The war is inevitable, and let it come! I repeat it, sir, let it come.
54      It is in vain, sir, to extenuate the matter. Gentlemen may cry, Peace, Peace, but there is no peace. The war is
55  actually begun! The next gale that sweeps from the north will bring to our ears the clash of resounding arms! Our
56  brethren are already in the field! Why stand we here idle? What is it that gentlemen wish? What would they have? Is
57  life so dear, or peace so sweet, as to be purchased at the price of chains and slavery? Forbid it, Almighty God! I
58  know not what course others may take; but as for me, give me liberty or give me death!
59                                          (http://www.history.org/almanack/life/politics/giveme.cfm)


## Student Response

### Patrick Henry's Use of Rhetorical Devices

1   On March 23, 1775, as Americans were debating whether or not to go to war against Great Britain, Patrick Henry
2   delivered his famous speech, "Give Me Liberty or Give Me Death." Throughout the oration, he utilizes three
3   rhetorical devices to emphasize his arguments. The first is rhetorical questioning, asking his fellow Americans
4   questions to which they already know the answer. Second, he uses repetition to accentuate his points even more.
5   Third, he reminds the men of recent events and facts regarding England's dealings with America. This is another
6   technique used to stress the need for action. **The powerful truth that emerges from this great speech is**
7   **augmented by his use of questions, repetition, and recent events and facts.**
8       Throughout this address, Patrick Henry asks rhetorical questions. He realizes that the answer to every
9   question is obvious. As he asks the questions, his main argument can be found in the expected answer. When he
10  addresses Britain's recent movement of troops to America, he asks, "Are fleets and armies necessary to a work of
11  love and reconciliation? . . . What means this martial array, if its purpose be not to force us to submission? . . . Has
12  Great Britain any enemy, in this quarter of the world, to call for all this accumulation of navies and armies?" He then
13  proceeds to ask what America has to respond with. "And what have we to oppose to them? Shall we try argument?
14  . . . What terms shall we find which have not been already exhausted?" Later in the speech, he presents another line
15  of rhetorical questions: "When shall we be stronger? Will it be the next week, or the next year? Will it be when we
16  are totally disarmed, and when a British guard shall be stationed in every house? Shall we gather strength but
17  irresolution and inaction? Shall we acquire the means of effectual resistance by lying supinely on our backs and
18  hugging the delusive phantom of hope, until our enemies shall have bound us hand and foot?" At the end of the
19  speech, he offers his last question. "Is life so dear, or peace so sweet, as to be purchased at the price of chains and
20  slavery?" This question is perhaps one of the greatest and most famous questions asked in America's history.
21      Another rhetorical device that Henry employs is repetition. He repeats points and phrases throughout the
22  speech. In one section of his speech, he uses anaphora, repeating the beginning of a phrase. "We have petitioned; we
23  have remonstrated; we have supplicated; we have prostrated ourselves before the throne." He proceeds to explain
24  what happened after they did these things. "Our petitions have been slighted; our remonstrances have produced
25  additional violence and insult; our supplications have been disregarded; and we have been spurned, with contempt,
26  from the foot of the throne!" Later in the speech, Henry states that he will repeat certain things because he believes
27  they are so important. "We must fight! I repeat it, sir, we must fight!" "The war is inevitable, and let it come! I
28  repeat it, sir, let it come."
29      **Referring to recent events and facts is a third rhetorical device used by Patrick Henry to convince his**
30  **audience of the need to go to war.** He testifies that the only guide he has is that of experience and the past. "I have
31  but one lamp by which my feet are guided; and that is the lamp of experience. I know of no way of judging the

32　future but by the past." He reminds the House of recent events and actions by the British. In one statement, he shows
33　his familiarity with the British ministry and their actions over the past ten years. "And judging by the past, I wish to
34　know what there has been in the conduct of the British ministry for the last ten years to justify those hopes with
35　which gentlemen have been pleased to solace themselves and the House." Further in the oration, he reminds the
36　audience of the basics of war and how they are evident in recent British actions. "Ask yourselves how this gracious
37　reception of our petition comports with those warlike preparations which cover our waters and darken our land. . . .
38　These are the implements of war and subjugation; the last arguments to which kings resort." Not only does he
39　remind the House of British actions, but also the actions of fellow colonists to the north. "The next gale that sweeps
40　from the north will bring to our ears the clash of resounding arms! Our brethren are already in the field!" His
41　knowledge of the events throughout America and Britain and the basics of warfare serve Henry well in emphasizing
42　the need for war.
43　　　　This speech is perhaps most famous for its last sentence: "I know not what course others may take; but as
44　for me, give me liberty or give me death!" However, this premise is elevated by the preceding arguments presented
45　by Henry throughout. The arguments are accentuated by the three rhetorical devices of questions, repetition, and
46　knowledge of current events and facts. These three devices are used to persuade his audience to acknowledge the
47　powerful truth, that the American colonists must declare war against Britain. (Claire)

## Close Reading (Speech)

1. Patrick Henry utilizes the following literary device several times
   A. Simile
   B. Onomatopoeia
   C. Allusion
   D. Rhetorical Question

2. The reference to "sirens" refers to what book?
   A. *The Vicar of Wakefield*
   B. *Iliad*
   C. *Odyssey*
   D. *Pilgrim's Progress*

3. Which of the following statements is true about this passage?
   A. Patrick Henry argues that waiting any longer to form a militia is foolish and bordering on cowardice.
   B. Patrick Henry reluctantly desires to leave the mother country.
   C. Patrick Henry wants to command this militia.
   D. Patrick Henry wants to abolish slavery.

4. What is a central fallacy in Patrick Henry's speech?
   A. A straw-man fallacy
   B. A syllogism fallacy
   C. A redundancy fallacy
   D. An exaggeration fallacy

5. What is the tone of the speech?
   A. Tentative
   B. Sanguine
   C. Sad
   D. Choleric

6. What can the reader surmise about Patrick Henry by reading this speech?
   I. Patrick Henry is a patriot radical.
   II. Patrick Henry is in favor of a compromise with England.
   III. Patrick Henry wants to go to war with England.
   IV. Patrick Henry speaks indirectly to potential allies (e.g., France).

   A. I and II
   B. III and IV
   C. I and III
   D. All

## Command of Evidence (Student Response)

1. The thesis is first presented in
   A. Lines 2–3
   B. Lines 6–7
   C. Lines 25–28
   D. Lines 45–46

2. What is a favorite form of evidence used in the Student Response?
   A. History from the conflict
   B. Acts of Parliament
   C. Quotes from the speech
   D. British newspapers

3. How does the Student Response develop its argument?
   A. It outlines the three salient components aspects of the rhetorical response and then develops these more in subsequent paragraphs.
   B. It chronologically outlines the growing conflict and fits the speech into the crisis.
   C. It analyzes the speech, line by line.
   D. It states a thesis and then offers alternative interpretations.

4. What is an assumption that the Student Response makes?
   I. The speech was effective.
   II. Patrick Henry was a wealthy planter.
   III. The American Revolution was inevitable.

   A. I
   B. II
   C. III
   D. I and II
   E. All

## Words in Context

1. What is the meaning of *magnitude* in Line 6 of Patrick Henry's speech?
   A. Measurement
   B. Plenitude
   C. Enormity
   D. Remarkableness

2. What is the meaning of *illusions* in Line 11 of Patrick Henry's speech?
   A. Delusions
   B. Caricatures
   C. Images
   D. Moments

3. What is the meaning of *temporal* in Line 14 of Patrick Henry's speech?
   A. Sequential
   B. Random
   C. Momentary
   D. Earthly

4. What is the meaning of *anguish* in Line 15 of Patrick Henry's speech?
   A. Distress
   B. Angst
   C. Remorse
   D. Fatigue

5. What is the meaning of *solace* in Line 18 of Patrick Henry's speech?
   A. Fatigue
   B. Unhappiness
   C. Succor
   D. Disease

6. What is the meaning of *insidious* in Line 19, Patrick Henry's speech?
   A. Cantankerous
   B. Smooth
   C. Treacherous
   D. Remorse

7. What is the meaning of *remonstrances* in Line 35, Patrick Henry's speech?
   A. Delusion
   B. Remark
   C. Supplication
   D. Protest

8. What is the meaning of *extenuate* in line 54, Patrick Henry's Speech?
   A. Mitigate
   B. Palliate
   C. Remove
   D. Pretend

## Grammar and Usage

Choose the best grammar/usage form in bold sentence(s).,

1. Student Response, Lines 6–7
   A. NONE
   B. The powerful truth that emerges from this great speech is augmented by his use of questions, repetition, and facts.
   C. The powerful truth is augmented by his use of questions, repetitions, and and facts.
   D. Questions, repetition, and facts augment the powerful emerging truths of this great speech.

2. Student Response, Lines 20–30
   A. NONE
   B. Third, Patrick Henry uses recent events and facts to persuade his audience to go to war.
   C. Referring to recent events and facts is a third rhetorical device used by Patrick Henry.
   D. Referring to recent events and facts is a third rhetorical device used by Patrick Henry to convince his audience of going to war.

# Lesson 2
## Critical Reading and Writing

### Command of Evidence

Read the following passages and answer accompanying questions:

### Passage 1

As a nation of immigrants and diversity, the sole factor uniting an otherwise opposite people is language. Unlike other countries, America does not share the common bond of ethnicity, religion, race, or native language as unification. Therefore it is essential that something bond this mass of immigrants. The common English language is this missing link. Furthermore, this assertion confronts bilingual education. According to a variety of sources, it appears that bilingual education in the long term is not a viable alternative to conducting classes in standard American English.

S. I. Hayakawa argued that English is "the cornerstone of our democratic government" because it "enables us to discuss our views and allows us to maintain a well-informed electorate." The basic success of any American largely depends on their ability to speak, read, and understand English, as Greg Lewis suggested. These sources reveal the simple importance of English to our nation. English is the mode of communication for government, education, recreation, and entertainment. Its importance in society is invaluable. S. I. Hayakawa went on to say, "By agreeing to learn and use a single, universally spoken language, we have been able to forge a unified people from an incredibly diverse population."

Now with regard to those who speak an alternative first language (such as Spanish or Chinese), enforcing "English as an official language" may sound unconstitutional. After all, the constitution does not demand English to be a requirement of a citizen of America. However, trying to live in a state that enforces two official languages has proved to be chaotic, as evident in California. How much more chaos would ensue if two languages were enforced nationally? In fact, if English and Spanish are established as "official" languages of the United States, what's not to say that every other language represented somewhere in the country will want the same status? This is clearly an unattainable feat. Early in time, language confusion resulted at the Tower of Babel, and now it continues in places such as Belgium, where incompatible languages (Dutch and French) have contributed to political instability.

In this dilemma the happy medium seems to be the institution known as bilingual education: the educating of students in normal studies by means of their native language. However, there are some foundational flaws with this idea. First off, bilingualism is costly. Canada, for example, spends nearly $400 million per year on this program. Second, the government feels it must accommodate for the immigrants who make America their home rather than the opposite. If a family considers the move to a foreign nation, a language change should be factored into their decision making. Because of this misunderstanding, bilingual education in other countries has changed the whole goal behind this institution. Rather than using a child's native language to introduce them to English early in their education, bilingualism has turned into preserving the child's native language. This leads me to the third flaw in bilingual education. By essentially segregating immigrant students from the English language through bilingualism, the educational system has hindered their learning of English rather than fostering it. **Keeping children with foreign languages out of an English environment will nurture their native tongue rather than promote the language of the larger society.**

Although there are flaws, bilingual education would not be completely faulty if it actually employed the child's native language to help them understand English. If bilingual education did not stray from this basic intention, then I would argue that it is a viable option for learning English. However, due to government misrepresentation toward immigrants and due to basic bureaucracy, the current implementation of bilingual education is not a worthwhile option to continue to pursue. (Callie)

## Close Reading

1. What would be the best title of this essay?
   A. The Importance of a Common Language
   B. The Importance of Cultural Diversity
   C. Bilingual Education
   D. Citizenship for All

2. What is the importance of the S. I. Hayakawa quote?
   A. To criticize Ebonics
   B. To advocate Japanese culture
   C. To offer an authority stating that standard English is important
   D. To support a one-nation, one-government theory

3. What organizational plan does the author employ?
   A. She offers an alternative option at first and then argues the opposite.
   B. She defines the perimeters of her argument and then argues against opposite positions.
   C. She invites readers to consider a nation without standard English.
   D. She strongly supports bilingual education.

4. What example does the author offer to illustrate her argument?
   A. Belgium, where, she claims, is discord
   B. The chaos existing in the border states
   C. Spanish fairy tales
   D. Opposite examples

5. The author finishes her essay with
   A. A summary statement
   B. A new conclusion
   C. A distracting comment
   D. The way she began

6. Identify a weakness in the conclusion:
   A. She introduces a new argument.
   B. She contradicts herself.
   C. She does not finisher her thoughts.
   D. She exaggerates some claims.

## Passage 2

1  America has been a breeding ground for communities that have gone on to impact more than a small geographical
2  area. These communities are found in schools, churches, neighborhoods, businesses, and even government. More
3  often than not, these communities—whether "based on geography, ethnicity, race, religion, marital status,
4  occupation, class, economic status, gender, political affiliation, shared interest, or even language" (Shea, 259)—have
5  impacted those around them for good,. However, the small percentage of communities that are part of a not-good
6  impact seem to influence society in a counterproductive way. Think about Germany and the Nazi ideals during the
7  era of the World Wars. They were definitely a community, but not beneficial to society. Think about the Ku Klux
8  Klan in America. They were (and still are) a community, a group demanding radical segregation.
9        Yet another controversial community has slowly and silently crept into the limelight of social issues. So
10 long unspoken and unheard of, this group felt a glimmer of hope and courage after well-known megastars advocated
11 on their behalf. The homosexual community is now an openly embraced idea of our culture. Is there really
12 something inherently wrong with same-sex marriage? Can the ideals of this community really impact culture in a
13 negative way? Closer examination reveals how counterintuitive this lifestyle is.
14        In the early 1900s homosexuality was unheard of. Girls danced with boys, and boys brought girls out on
15 dates. Period. Nowadays it seems that everywhere we turn, there are signs of this lifestyle. At the park the other day,
16 an obviously homosexual couple walked with arms interlocked. It was clear that those who passed by this couple
17 were noticeably uncomfortable with the situation. They just didn't know how to react. What has so radically
18 changed in society?
19        Popular performer Lady Gaga wrote a song with which the community of homosexuals so identified that
20 they used it as some sort of slogan. It sings, "No matter gay, straight, or bi / Lesbian, transgendered life / I'm on the
21 right track baby / I was born to survive." The chorus suggests they were born this way: "Oh—there ain't no other
22 way / Baby, I was born this way."
23        Other famous faces, especially talk-show host and comedian Ellen DeGeneres, have brought the
24 homosexual movement to the forefront of social issues. Same-sex marriage was debated in many states, legalized in
25 some states, and ruled a constitutional right by the U.S. Supreme Court in June 2015. This community strives for
26 equality and acceptance amid a prejudice toward their beliefs about sexual inclination.

27       Some research has identified the purpose behind this community. Besides wanting to fulfill their own
28 individual desires (claimed to be in their genetic code) about relationships (and marriage), Toby Johnson, who calls
29 himself a "gay spiritual writer," said that homosexuality is an "evolutionary variation that has resulted in life."
30 Furthermore, Johnson suggested that humans have "evolved" the same way some animal species have evolved in
31 sexuality. As a spokesperson for the homosexual community, Johnson argued homosexuality is "a possible
32 reproductive strategy for controlling population." What other purpose than controlling population does this
33 increasing identification have? Johnson suggested, "Gay people may exist primarily to be teachers and guides."

34       Is this controversial community really counterproductive to society? For one thing, marriage has been
35 completely redefined through the prominent presence of this society. Marriage no longer means the sole covenant
36 between a man and a woman. It has been redefined to mean any promise between whomever you wish. If it is part of
37 your "genetics," how can we "limit your freedom" by imposing traditional marriage on your lifestyle?

38       However, William Lane Craig, a research professor of philosophy at Talbot School of Theology, argues,
39 "Just because you're genetically disposed to some behavior doesn't mean that behavior is morally right. To give an
40 example, some researchers suspect there may be a gene which predisposes some people to alcoholism. Does that
41 mean that it's all right for someone with such predisposition to go ahead and drink to his heart's content and become
42 an alcoholic?" The same applies to homosexuality. Just because a person may feel an attraction to another of the
43 same sex, it does not mean it is morally right. Just because I may believe with all my heart that stealing for myself is
44 right, it doesn't justify my actions. The facts (and courts) tell us that stealing is wrong. Regarding what you believe
45 to be fact is one way homosexuals try to rationalize their behavior.

46       According to our moral code, homosexual acts are "unequivocally condemned." Homosexuality is a sexual
47 sin, just like adultery or lust. It is unnatural for this type of behavior. Homosexuality is against the design of
48 marriage, which clearly states it is a union between a man and a woman. Besides the inherent moral problems with
49 this community of people, it is not a viable lifestyle to support ongoing human life. Same-sex marriage provides no
50 way of reproduction of the human species. Yes, Toby Johnson said homosexuality is a viable lifestyle to curb
51 overpopulation pressures. However, what happens when the population is curbed too far? Will we devolve
52 (according to Johnson) once the population is controlled? After all, one purpose of homosexuality is the next
53 evolutionary step for humans. Yet "being fruitful" or "multiplying" is just one of the purposes behind marriage.
54 Homosexual practice cannot fulfill this goal.

55       In addition, homosexual behavior is physically harmful. According to Timothy J. Dailey, a senior fellow at
56 the Center for Marriage and Family Studies, "Homosexual activists attempt to portray their lifestyle as normal and
57 healthy, and insist that homosexual relationships are the equivalent in every way to their heterosexual counterparts.
58 Hollywood and the media relentlessly propagate the image of the fit, healthy, and well-adjusted homosexual. The
59 reality is quite opposite to this caricature." Homosexual relationships are at a higher risk of many diseases than is the
60 traditional couple. Some of the many diseases include HPV, hepatitis, gonorrhea, syphilis, gay bowel syndrome,
61 HIV/AIDS, STDs, and various cancers. **In addition, research has proved that homosexuals have a greater risk**
62 **for suicide and a shorter life span than others do.**

63       The homosexual community may argue that they are an "evolutionary step" for humankind. Toby Johnson
64 argues, "In modern human society, gay people demonstrate that (1) people don't have to reproduce and raise
65 children to lead fulfilled and contributing lives, and (2) the blending of masculine and feminine traits results in more
66 pleasing personalities and cooperative characteristics in humans than the division of traits." However,
67 homosexuality has serious moral implications. It is an unnatural way of life that not only causes physical disease but
68 also clearly goes against the design of marriage. (Callie)

**Sources**

Chappell, Bill. "Supreme Court Declares Same-Sex Marriage Legal in All 50 States." The Two-Way, NPR. 2015.
    http://www.npr.org/sections/thetwo-way/2015/06/26/417717613.
Craig, William Lane [research professor of philosophy at Talbot School of Theology]. "A Christian Perspective on
    Homosexuality." A chapter in *Hard Questions, Real Answers*, 129–44. Wheaton, IL: Crossway Books, 2003.
    http://www.reasonablefaith.org/a-christian-perspective-on-homosexuality.
Dailey, Timothy J. [PhD, senior fellow at the Center for Marriage and Family Studies of the Family Research
    Council]. "The Negative Health Effects of Homosexuality." 2007.
    http://www.battlefortruth.org/ArticlesDetail.asp?id=235.
Johnson, Toby [PhD, gay spiritual writer]. "The Purpose of Homosexuality." 2013.
    http://www.tobyjohnson.com/purpose.html.

## Close Reading

1.  What would be the best title of this essay?
    A.  The Biblical View of Same-Sex Marriage
    B.  The Rise of the Ku Klux Klan
    C.  What Is a Healthy, Productive Community?
    D.  The End of Innocence

2.  Why did the author begin with a quote from Shea?
    A.  To emphasize the plurality of American culture
    B.  To celebrate diversity
    C.  To emphasize the need for tolerance
    D.  To warn about divergent groups like the Nazis

3.  What organizational plan does the author employ?
    A.  To celebrate diversity
    B.  To define the problem and discuss positive and negative groups
    C.  To illustrate cultural diversity's impact on modern America
    D.   To draw the reader step by step into the argument

4.  The author finishes the essay with
    A.  A summary statement
    B.  A new conclusion
    C.  A distracting comment
    D.  A final criticism of unhealthy communities (i.e., the homosexual community)

## Grammar and Usage

Choose the best grammar/usage form in bold sentence(s).:

1.  Passage 1, Lines 30–33
    A.  NONE
    B.  Teaching native children their own language rather than English will discourage assimilation into American society.
    C.  Keeping children out of an English environment will nurture their native tongue but not promote the language of society.
    D.  Keeping children out of an English environment will promote their native tongue and hinder the promotion of the language of society.

2.  Passage 2, Lines 61–62
    A.  NONE
    B.  In addition, research has proven that homosexuals have a greater risk for suicide and a shorter life span in general compared to those who are not.
    C.  In addition, research proves that homosexuals commit suicide more often and live a shorter life span than those who are heterosexual.
    D.  In addition, research has proven that homosexuals have a greater risk for suicide and a shorter life span than those who reject the truth.

# Lesson 3
## SAT Essay

### Student Response 1

*Prompt:* Is humor a way to escape a problem or to deal with it?

1     "Laughter is the best form of medicine." Often this quote is recited when an individual is faced with an
2   unbearable task or challenge; some, likewise, find comfort in laughing at trials or troublesome individuals, in order
3   to prevent tension or bitterness from remaining locked—like a raging lion—in a cage. Humor, in the midst of trial,
4   certainly relieves, restores, and renews the soul of a tarnished fighter.
5     In her famous novel *The Hiding Place*, Corrie Ten Boon, a great figure of the Holocaust era, recounted her
6   difficult task of hiding twelve Jews in her tiny home. Although she might have sought to run from the turbulent task
7   set before her, she faced it with the might of a true hero. As circumstances became more serious, however, she
8   would attempt to calm both herself and her friends by joking about the food rationings. At one point she found great
9   laughter in feeding one of her most devoted Jews roast pork (which he loved!).
10     My aunt likewise used humor to help me persevere while working at her law office. As we began the
11   dreaded job of filing numerous cases, she would occasionally joke about the stress, the importance of a lawyer's
12   suit, why manicured nails drew in clients, and so forth. Such silliness certainly aided in soothing my nerves.
13     Laughter is the greatest stress reliever in the history of medicine. While some might consider humor
14   running from problems, it instead is an energy booster, to give the strength to carry on—victoriously. Do you know
15   what I mean? (Christy).

### Student Response 2

*Prompt:* What is more important: character or accomplishments?

1     A middle school girl is finally accepted into the group of "cool" kids. She had been trying to be noticed by
2   them for almost a year now, and she will have to try hard to stay in the group. This meant dressing differently,
3   talking differently, and even giving up some of her old friends. Is being in this group really the best thing for her?
4   No. She is conforming to the ways of the group and no longer thinking, acting, or being herself. Being part of a
5   group restrains you from making your own thoughts and decisions.
6     In George Orwell's *Animal Farm*, all of the farm animals begin to follow the pigs. This is fine at first, but
7   the pigs start to make rules and tell the other animals how it is. No longer thinking for themselves, the animals
8   follow the pigs into destruction. Groups will overpower you and become more of an influence than even yourself.
9   They will hinder your ability to think for yourself and develop your own opinions.
10     Albert Einstein was the odd one out. Growing up, he had very few friends and was never really part of a
11   group. So he imagined, he thought, he came up with original ideas that were all his own. Not being part of a group
12   enabled him to think and come up with his own ideas. Who really knows?
13     Giving both George Orwell's group of animals and Albert Einstein's lack of a group, it is plain to see that
14   being in a group is bad. A group will smother your own thoughts and push their own ideas upon you. Being in a
15   group does not allow you your freedom to think and have ideas of your own. (Marty)

   1. In Student Response 1 the author
      A. Argues that laughter is a good thing.       C. Argues that humor is disrespectful.
      B. Argues that laughter is a form of escape.   D. Concedes that laughter is a necessary evil.

   2. In Student Response 2 the author organizes the essay
      A. By evoking the memory of someone who had character.
      B. By offering a series of anecdotes.
      C. By stating a thesis and offering a couple of examples.
      D. By a series of bullet points.

3. What is a recurring problem in both responses?
    I. The thesis is not mentioned until the second paragraph.
    II. Transitions are weak.
    III. There are too many personal examples.
    IV. The essays are too short.

        A. I and II                  C. I, II, and III                E. All
        B. III and IV               D. I and IV

4. What is the main point of Student Response 1?
    A. Lines 3–4          B. Lines 5–6          C. Lines 15–16         D. Lines 18–19

5. The main point of the Student Response 2?
    A. Lines 3–5          B. Lines 8–9          C. Lines 12–13         D. Lines 14–15

6. What is a significant stylistic problem in both essays?
    A. First person is used.
    B. Second-person pronouns are used.
    C. There are too many misplaced modifiers.
    D. There are agreement problems.

7. Evidence can be found in Student Response 1:
    A. Lines 1–2          B. Lines 3–4          C. Lines 5–9         D. Lines 11–5

8. Evidence can be found in Student Response 2:
    A. Lines 1–2          B. Lines 3–5          C. Lines 6–9         D. Lines 14–15

9. What section of the Student Response 1 probably should be removed?
    A. Lines 1–2          B. Lines 10–11         C. Lines 28–30        D. Lines 14–15

10. What section of the Student Response 2 probably should be removed?
    A. Line 2          B. Line 7          C. Line 9         D. Line 12

11. What is the most plausible explanation for the above choice in Student Response 1?
    A. The statement is colloquial.
    B. The sentence is too religious.
    C. The sentence is too opinionated.
    D. The information in the paragraph is repeated elsewhere.

12. What is the most plausible explanation for the above choice in Student Response 2?
    A. The statement is colloquial.
    B. The sentence is too religious.
    C. The sentence is too opinionated.
    D. The information in the paragraph is repeated elsewhere.

13. What score would the student responses receive?
    Student Response 1 receives __. Student Response 2 receives __.

# Lesson 4
## Reading: Document-Based Analysis

**Declaration of Sentiments and Resolutions (1848)**
**Woman's Rights Convention, via Elizabeth Cady Stanton**
**(Seneca Falls, N.Y., July 19–20)**

1   When, in the course of human events, it becomes necessary for one portion of the family of man to assume among
2   the people of the earth a position different from that which they have hitherto occupied, but one to which the laws of
3   nature and of nature's God entitle them, a decent respect to the opinions of mankind requires that they should
4   declare the causes that impel them to such a course.
5       We hold these truths to be self-evident: that all men and women are created equal; that they are endowed by
6   their Creator with certain inalienable rights; that among these are life, liberty, and the pursuit of happiness; that to
7   secure these rights governments are instituted, deriving their just powers from the consent of the governed.
8   Whenever any form of government becomes destructive of these ends, it is the right of those who suffer from it to
9   refuse allegiance to it, and to insist upon the institution of a new government, laying its foundation on such
10   principles, and organizing its powers in such form, as to them shall seem most likely to effect their safety and
11   happiness. Prudence, indeed, will dictate that governments long established should not be changed for light and
12   transient causes; and accordingly all experience hath shown that mankind are more disposed to suffer, while evils
13   are sufferable, than to right themselves by abolishing the forms to which they are accustomed. But when a long train
14   of abuses and usurpations, pursuing invariably the same object, evinces a design to reduce them under absolute
15   despotism, it is their duty to throw off such government, and to provide new guards for their future security. Such
16   has been the patient sufferance of the women under this government, and such is now the necessity which constrains
17   them to demand the equal station to which they are entitled. The history of mankind is a history of repeated injuries
18   and usurpations on the part of man toward woman, having in direct object the establishment of an absolute tyranny
19   over her. To prove this, let facts be submitted to a candid world.
20       He has never permitted her to exercise her inalienable right to the elective franchise.
21       He has compelled her to submit to laws, in the formation of which she had no voice.
22       He has withheld from her rights which are given to the most ignorant and degraded men—both natives and
23   foreigners.
24       Having deprived her of this first right of a citizen, the elective franchise, thereby leaving her without
25   representation in the halls of legislation, he has oppressed her on all sides.
26       He has made her, if married, in the eye of the law, civilly dead. He has taken from her all right in property,
27   even to the wages she earns.
28       He has made her, morally, an irresponsible being, as she can commit many crimes with impunity, provided
29   they be done in the presence of her husband.
30       In the covenant of marriage, she is compelled to promise obedience to her husband, he becoming, to all
31   intents and purposes, her master—the law giving him power to deprive her of her liberty. and to administer
32   chastisement.
33       He has so framed the laws of divorce, as to what shall be the proper causes, and in case of separation, to
34   whom the guardianship of the children shall be given, as to be wholly regardless of the happiness of women—the
35   law, in all cases, going upon a false supposition of the supremacy of man, and giving all power into his hands.
36       After depriving her of all rights as a married woman, if single, and the owner of property, he has taxed her
37   to support a government which recognizes her only when her property can be made profitable to it.
38       He has monopolized nearly all the profitable employments, and from those she is permitted to follow, she
39   receives but a scanty remuneration. He closes against her all the avenues to wealth and distinction which he
40   considers most honorable to himself. As a teacher of theology, medicine, or law, she is not known.
41       He has denied her the facilities for obtaining a thorough education, all colleges being closed against her.
42       He allows her in Church, as well as State, but a subordinate position, claiming Apostolic authority for her
43   exclusion from the ministry, and, with some exceptions, from any public participation in the affairs of the Church.
44       He has created a false public sentiment by giving to the world a different code of morals for men and
45   women, by which moral delinquencies which exclude women from society, are not only tolerated, but deemed of
46   little account in man.

47  He has usurped the prerogative of Jehovah himself, claiming it as his right to assign for her a sphere of
48  action, when that belongs to her conscience and to her God.

49  He has endeavored, in every way that he could, to destroy her confidence in her own powers, to lessen her
50  self-respect and to make her willing to lead a dependent and abject life.

51  Now, in view of this entire disfranchisement of one-half the people of this country, their social and
52  religious degradation in view of the unjust laws above mentioned, and because women do feel themselves
53  aggrieved, oppressed, and fraudulently deprived of their most sacred rights, we insist that they have immediate
54  admission to all the rights and privileges which belong to them as citizens of the United States.

55  In entering upon the great work before us, we anticipate no small amount of misconception,
56  misrepresentation, and ridicule; but we shall use every instrumentality within our power to effect our object. We
57  shall employ agents, circulate tracts, petition the State and National legislatures, and endeavor to enlist the pulpit
58  and the press in our behalf. We hope this Convention will be followed by a series of Conventions embracing every
59  part of the country.
60

61  RESOLUTIONS
62  *Whereas*, The great precept of nature is conceded to be, that "man shall pursue his own true and substantial
63  happiness." Blackstone in his Commentaries remarks, that this law of Nature being coeval with mankind, and
64  dictated by God himself, is of course superior in obligation to any other. It is binding over all the globe, in all
65  countries and at all times; no human laws are of any validity if contrary to this, and such of them as are valid, derive
66  all their force, and all their validity, and all their authority, mediately and immediately, from this original; therefore,

67  *Resolved*, That such laws as conflict, in any way with the true and substantial happiness of woman, are
68  contrary to the great precept of nature and of no validity, for this is "superior in obligation to any other."

69  *Resolved*, That all laws which prevent woman from occupying such a station in society as her conscience
70  shall dictate, or which place her in a position inferior to that of man, are contrary to the great precept of nature, and
71  therefore of no force or authority.

72  *Resolved*, That woman is man's equal—was intended to be so by the Creator, and the highest good of the
73  race demands that she should be recognized as such.

74  *Resolved*, That the women of this country ought to be enlightened in regard to the laws under which they
75  live, that they may no longer publish their degradation by declaring themselves satisfied with their present position,
76  nor their ignorance, by asserting that they have all the rights they want.

77  *Resolved*, That inasmuch as man, while claiming for himself intellectual superiority, does accord to woman
78  moral superiority, it is pre-eminently his duty to encourage her to speak and teach, as she has an opportunity, in all
79  religious assemblies.

80  *Resolved*, That the same amount of virtue, delicacy, and refinement of behavior that is required of woman
81  in the social state, should also be required of man, and the same transgressions should be visited with equal severity
82  on both man and woman.

83  *Resolved*, That the objection of indelicacy and impropriety, which is so often brought against woman when
84  she addresses a public audience, comes with a very ill-grace from those who encourage, by their attendance, her
85  appearance on the stage, in the concert. Or in feats of the circus.

86  *Resolved*, That woman has too long rested satisfied in the circumscribed limits which corrupt customs and a
87  perverted application of the Scriptures have marked out for her, and that it is time she should move in the enlarged
88  sphere which her great Creator has assigned her.

89  *Resolved*, That it is the duty of the women of this country to secure to themselves their sacred right to the
90  elective franchise.

91  *Resolved*, That the equality of human rights results necessarily from the fact of the identity of the race in
92  capabilities and responsibilities.

93  *Resolved*, therefore, That, being invested by the Creator with the same capabilities, and the same
94  consciousness of responsibility for their exercise, it is demonstrably the right and duty of woman, equally with man,
95  to promote every righteous cause by every righteous means; and especially in regard to the great subjects of morals
96  and religion, it is self-evidently her right to participate with her brother in teaching them, both in private and in
97  public, by writing and by speaking, by any instrumentalities proper to be used, and in any assemblies proper to be
98  held; and this being a self-evident truth growing out of the divinely implanted principles of human nature, any
99  custom or authority adverse to it, whether modern or wearing the hoary sanction of antiquity, is to be regarded as a
100 self-evident falsehood, and at war with mankind.

101 *Resolved*, That the speedy success of our cause depends upon the zealous and untiring efforts of both men
102 and women, for the overthrow of the monopoly of the pulpit, and for the securing to women an equal participation
103 with men in the various trades, professions, and commerce. (http://ecssba.rutgers.edu/docs/seneca.html)

1. What is the chief argument of this document?
   I.   To protest the prison system
  II.   To demand more rights for children
 III.   To demand more rights for women

        A. I                           C. III
        B. I and II                  D. All

2. The beginning of the Declaration comes from the
     A. Declaration of Independence.       C. United States Constitution.
     B. Virginia Declaration of Rights.     D. Gettysburg Address.

3. This Declaration of Woman's Rights has three parts:
     A. Introduction, Body, and Conclusion    C. Argument, Evidence, Solution
     B. Preamble, Grievances, Resolutions    D. Thesis, Counterargument, Conclusion

4. The Preamble ends with
     A. Line 2                        C. Line 19
     B. Line 6                        D. Line 22

5. With which of the following statements would the author agree?
    I.   Men have too many rights.
   II.   Men have unjustly subjugated women.
  III.   Liquor is the cause of all evil.
  IV.   Men and women have the same abilities.

        A. I and II        C. III and IV               E. All
        B. II and III      D. II and IV

## Words in Context

1.   What is the meaning of *inalienable* in Line 20?
     A.  Foreign                      C.  Incontrovertible
     B.  Implicit                    D.  Irrevocable

2.   What is the meaning of *remuneration* in Line 39?
     A.  Numerology                C.  Compensation
     B.  Anachronism             D.  Oratory

# Lesson 5

## Math: Algebra, Arithmetic Problem Solving and Data Analysis, and Passport to Advanced Math

**Passport to Advanced Math**

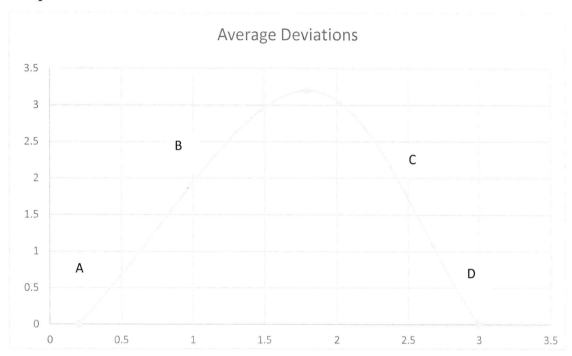

1. The nature of an average supposes deviations from it. Deviations from an average, or "errors," are assumed to conform to the law that the greater errors are less frequent than the smaller, so that most events approximate to the average; and that errors have no "bias," but are equally frequent and equally great in both directions from the mean, so that they are scattered symmetrically. If the Y (vertical) axis represents the degree of deviation, and the X (horizontal) axis determines frequency of deviation, what is true about the above chart?

   I. As the deviations grow greater, the number of them grows less.
   II. Deviations occur more frequently in the beginning.
   III. Greater in degree deviations occur at the end.
   IV. The smallest degree of deviation occurs between 1.5 to 2.

   A. I                    C. III                    E. All
   B. II                   D. IV

2. Assuming that X on the above diagram is a measurement of average colds yearly afflicting Americans, with Y being the most frequent number of colds with the severest effect, what is true about this chart?
   I. A has less severe colds less frequently than B.
   II. B has less severe colds more frequently than D.
   III. C has more severe colds more frequently than B.
   IV. D has more severe colds more frequently than B.

   A. I                    B. II                    C. I and III                    D. II and IV

# Arithmetic Problem Solving

1. To four times a number, I add 23 and obtain 95. What is the number?

   A. 14
   B. 16

   C. 17
   D. 18

2. From three times a number, I take 25 and obtain 47. What is the number?

   A. 22
   B. 24

   C. 26
   D. 28

3. Find a number that being multiplied by 5 and having 14 added to the product will equal 69.

   A. 12
   B. 11

   C. 14
   D. 13

4. Mary bought some tea and coffee for $10.39. If she paid for the tea 61 cents more than five times as much as for the coffee, how much did she pay for each?

   A. Tea, $8.76; coffee, $1.63
   B. Tea, $8.36; coffee, $1.50

   C. Tea, $8.75; coffee, $1.63
   D. Tea, $1.63; coffee, $8.76

5. Two houses together contain 48 rooms. If the second house has 3 more than twice as many rooms as the first, how many rooms has each house?

   A. 12 first house; 25 second house
   B. 16 first house; 33 second house

   C. 15 first house; 33 second house
   D. 11 first house; 22 second house

# Chapter 16   When We Walked by Faith Alone

# Deuteronomy 8

---

*Memory Verses:* Remember how the LORD your God led you all the way in the wilderness these forty years, to humble and test you in order to know what was in your heart, whether or not you would keep his commands. —Deuteronomy 8:2

---

Shortly before my maternal grandmother died—I called her Big Momma (not mother!)—she recorded on paper her earliest memories. Besides making the best cream gravy and biscuits in Desha County, Arkansas, Big Mamma's memory was strong and clear.

Surprisingly, her favorite memory was not graduation from high school, or attending college, not even her wedding day. No, her favorite memory was a visit to her own grandmother.

Big Mamma's grandmother lived in a two-room, unpainted pre-Huey P. Long poor North Louisiana clapboard house.

"The good old days," she began, "were when beans and hash tasted good."

"On top of the stove sat a black iron three-legged pot," she began. "Sometimes it overflowed with chicken and dumplin's, or enticed me with homemade vegetable soup, or—even better—appetizing whole squirrels bouncing around in boiling gray stew water."

At that point I felt the same way you do!

Boiled squirrel. Yuk! While I am an enthusiastic fan of those furry critters, my ardor does not lead me to the soup pot!

But what attracted my grandmother to the squirrel stew was not the squirrel stew itself: it was her own grandmother. She loved her. Her grandmother Kolb (Big Mamma's maiden name) was an affirming presence in her life. Even in her memory, my grandmother still enjoyed Great-Great-Grandmother Kolb.

As we gather around the Lord's Table at church, let us pause, remember, and then give thanks.

The Lord's Supper is, after all, a time of remembering and giving thanks. In fact, our faith is based on memory. Memories full of who God is and what God has done in our corporate (i.e., church) and private lives. Our faith is placed in and understood in the faithfulness of God. History is not just part of our past: we are actually part of an unfolding drama, a production, if you will, that has been occurring since time began.

This communion, at least, began with the Last Supper before the Jesus' crucifixion. But that first communion, after all, was part of a larger production: the Passover.

"Let every person in every generation think of himself as a former slave, free from bondage," the oldest continuous meal in history begins (i.e., the Jewish Passover).

So much of our understanding of the Last Supper, a Passover meal, is informed by Leonardo da Vinci's painting *The Last Supper* (http://www.davincilife.com/lastsupper.html). Great art, lousy history. All the details in the painting are historically and scripturally inaccurate. The painting depicts daylight outside the window, whereas the actual Last Supper took place at night (Mark 14:17). The figures are seated about the table on benches, but benches were not invented until the Middle Ages (Jesus and his disciples reclined on mats or cushions; John 13:23). Da Vinci portrays the meal as consisting of fish and ordinary leavened bread; but if the Last Supper was a Passover meal, it had to consist of unleavened bread, roast lamb, and bitter herbs. Finally, in da Vinci's painting Jesus is alone with the twelve apostles, whereas the Synoptic Gospels record that the disciples prepared the Supper during the day, and that it was evening when Jesus arrived with the twelve apostles and their families. Women and children were *never* omitted from the Seder meal. To do so would have been a violation of Jewish Law (Exodus 12).

Passover was, and remains, the most important and the most popular feast of the year for Jews. Passover was already an ancient feast by the time it was celebrated by Jesus and his disciples. No one knows really how far back it dates. Passover is a memorial of the exodus from Egypt (Exodus 12:14), but it contains recollections from throughout Jewish history. There are memories from the days of the patriarchs, the judges, the kings, the exile, and being ruled by the Greeks. Bad memories, good memories, they are all recollected in the communion event.

It is customary for a people being delivered to celebrate their freedom. The quirky nature of the exodus story is that it is surrounded by two such celebrative meals: this one, the fast-food version of Passover, eaten hurriedly, was the forerunner of a more elaborate Passover ritual still celebrated today.

This first meal was to be eaten on the night of the last plague (the death of the Egyptian firstborn). While eating the meal, the men were to hold their walking sticks in hand, and everyone at the table was to have shoes on, as though in preparation to leave. The bread that accompanied the meal was to be unleavened, emphasizing the urgency of what was about to happen. This first ritual meal was to celebrate the Lord's Passover.

As directed, the ritual meal was perpetuated, and the story of deliverance was woven into the fabric of this celebration. The Passover following the deliverance of Israel from the house of bondage is more elaborate. There is less urgency: the family members recline on cushions instead of sitting as if to make a run for it. Perhaps we recall times when table fellowship in our own families was important.

Do you recall the movie *Babette's Feast* (1987)? It is a beautiful film in which a poor French cook finds herself on a desolate peninsula. The townsfolk have been greatly influenced by their minister, who died some years before Babette's arrival.

Babette has been buying lottery tickets with the little money she makes—something that I most emphatically do not recommend—and eventually word gets back to her that she has won the lottery, some ten thousand francs! The anniversary of the minister's death is about to be celebrated, and his daughters plan the celebration, which would have been a drab affair. However, Babette steps in and asks if she can fix the food for the feast.

Until then, she was forced to make the minister's prescribed menu for the community: hard, crusty brown bread and fish soup. Now Babette is going to fix a culinary masterpiece. She sends off for ingredients: turtles, all manner of edible fowl, vegetables, and specialty items that the villagers have long ago forgotten or have never seen.

Babette goes to work, and many of the townsfolk think she must be some sort of witch, with all the pots and kettles going. They decide that they will not enjoy the food of the feast. But Babette's cooking transforms the villagers. Never before have they tasted anything like what they eat. Their entire lives are changed by the meal. They will remember it for the rest of their lives!

Imagine what Passover must have been like when Jesus took the bread and cup of this ritual feast and changed their meaning for all who follow him. The unleavened bread that reminded them of the manna in the wilderness was not the true food of eternal life.

"Take, eat. This is my body, which is for you. Do this in remembrance of me."

Imagine the wondering eyes of the disciples as Jesus might well have taken up the cup of wine reserved for the prophet Elijah during the Passover celebration, changing its meaning as well: "Take, drink. This cup is the new covenant in my blood, which is shed for you and others for the forgiveness of sins. Do this, as often as you drink it, in remembrance of me."

Why is this meal different from all the others? It is because in it we remember how Jesus really has passed over from death to life and how he has given us this life, too.

*Remembrance* is the essence of the Passover. Peter and James and John and the rest of the Twelve were remembering that night; they remembered other meals that they had had with their friend: the God-anointed rabbi, whom some confessed to be the Messiah, who called them from their fishing boats (Mark 1; Acts 10:38). They were remembering all the way.

Most of their meals had been simple fare. When they were lucky, there was a piece of dried fish, but usually only dried dates and unleavened bread. Some of them remembered the wedding at Cana. Now that was a spread! Wine, food, partying—what a day!

But now, shadows, thick and dark clouds, seemed to gather around Jesus' head. He would die the next afternoon.

In its early history, the Lord's Supper was celebrated every time the church gathered. The central event was not the preaching or the anthem. It was the Lord's Supper! "Food is not feed," the social anthropologist Mary Douglas reminds us. Eating, especially at the Lord's Supper, is a human occasion. It was an iconoclastic meal. An alternative offering to the culture of their day.

By AD 45, Middle Eastern/Roman/Hellenistic culture, including Judaism, could no longer sustain life the way it once could. Violence was common; corruption at the highest levels an everyday occurrence. As Peter Berger, a Christian sociologist explains, every religious worldview depends upon a social basis for its continuing existence. So long as social and cultural arrangements remain essentially unchanged, the religious ideas that are used to legitimate them retain their plausibility. But when the social environment alters drastically, so that the arrangements with the religious beliefs are now threatened, the beliefs no longer appear plausible.

The Communion meal, ergo, was a subversive activity of the early church. It offered an alternative to the message of death and corruption so prevalent in first-century society. Central to the early church revival was the notion of "individual conversion." Every believer had to have a very personal conversion experience. At the same time, this experience was tempered and sharpened by the community at the Communion celebration.

In Deuteronomy 8, the Israelites are told to remember God's blessings. For more than forty years, the Lord miraculously and faithfully fed, clothed, and protected his chosen, if stubborn, people. God has been so good to us, too, in the church. Remember and give thanks.

We are to remember our chastisement too (Deuteronomy 8:5). Sometimes God's discipline has not been understood, a sickness not comprehended. But we remember, and we give thanks anyhow. Because we love God and we know that God loves us. After all, God sent his only begotten Son to die for us.

In 1976, Craig Masback missed qualifying for the Olympics by one-tenth of a second. In 1980, he was ready and sure that he would win. He probably would have, too, but the Olympics were canceled. In 1984, poor Craig, now the fastest human being in the world, was sick with the flu during the Olympic Games. Craig never won an Olympic medal.

But Craig will win the race of life. For Christ is the Lord and Savior of his life. When interviewed, Craig Masback, a child of the living God, said, "There was certainly sadness in my life, but I enjoyed the struggle of trying!"

Ah, in the struggle we give thanks too. Only in the darkness will we discover a sustaining God. The Trappist monk Thomas Merton writes in *New Seeds of Contemplation*, "When the time comes to enter the darkness in which we are helpless and alone; in which we feel the insufficiency of our greatest strength and the hollowness of our strongest virtues, . . . and there is nothing in the world to guide us or to give us light—then we find out whether or not we live by faith." Let us remember the times we walked by faith alone. When we were lost in a problem or situation and God came through for us.

I remember my beginnings, and I sincerely give thanks. In Deuteronomy 8:14, Moses reminds the Israelites to remember their deliverance from slavery in Egypt. They were to remember from whence they came so that they would be prepared to go into the future. I can remember when Communion meant nothing to me. I then remember accepting Jesus Christ as my Lord and Savior. Do you? Remember and give thanks—or, please, do not leave this worship service without giving Christ your life and your whole heart. Remember your sins, and then give them to Christ. Watch how your life will change!

Of course, Communion is about Christ. And he is the center of our focus. But we give thanks for the hundreds, thousands of people who have sacrificed on our behalf. Who prayed for us. Who taught us. Who gave us this building and this tradition of mission giving. We give thanks. We remember.

In Ernest Hemingway's book *For Whom the Bell Tolls* (the title quoting a poem by John Donne), we meet Robert Jordan. Jordan, an American expatriate who volunteered to fight Spanish fascists in the Spanish Civil War, 1936–39, is mortally wounded. As he lies near death, Jordan whispers to his beloved fiancée, "Now you will go for us both; . . . we go together in thee. . . . Now you must go for us both."

When Christ died on the cross, he gave his life for us all. Now we who serve Christ can celebrate that sacrifice and accept it for our lives again. We are reminded at Communion that Jesus Christ is in us, and as we go we carry Christ with us.

So . . . the tradition that is passing on to you goes right back to the Lord. Through Hayes, Rutledge, Guthre, Peter—and now through us. Remember. And give thanks.

Let us pray. O God, our Father, we thank you for this sacrament. For all who down the centuries at this table have found the light that never fades, the joy that no one took away from them, the forgiveness of their sins, the presence of your Son, our Lord Jesus Christ. And so we come. Again. Expecting, knowing that you are here. Thank you for the memories! Amen.

## Journal Question

Describe what the Lord's Supper means to you.

# Lesson 1
## Evidence-Based Reading and Writing

### Literary Choice

Wilfred Owen was a World War I English poet. His shocking, realistic war poetry on the horrors of warfare stood in stark contrast to the popular and heroic perception of war at the time. Owen was killed one week before the Armistice.

### Greater Love

| | |
|---|---|
| 1 | Red lips are not so red |
| 2 | As the stained stones kissed by the English dead. |
| 3 | Kindness of wooed and wooer |
| 4 | Seems shame to their love pure. |
| 5 | O Love, your eyes lose lure |
| 6 | When I behold eyes blinded in my stead! |
| 7 | |
| 8 | Your slender attitude |
| 9 | Trembles not exquisite like limbs knife-skewed, |
| 10 | Rolling and rolling there |
| 11 | Where God seems not to care: |
| 12 | Till the fierce love they bear |
| 13 | Cramps them in death's extreme decrepitude. |
| 14 | |
| 15 | Your voice sings not so soft,— |
| 16 | Though even as wind murmuring through raftered loft,— |
| 17 | Your dear voice is not dear, |
| 18 | Gentle, and evening clear, |
| 19 | As theirs whom *none* now hear, |
| 20 | Now earth has stopped their piteous mouths that coughed. |
| 21 | |
| 22 | Heart, you were never hot |
| 23 | Nor large, nor full like hearts made great with shot; |
| 24 | And though your hand be pale, |
| 25 | Paler are all which trail |
| 26 | Your cross through flame and hail: |
| 27 | Weep, you may weep, for you may touch them not. |

### Student Response

### The War on Love

1      "There's a grief that can't be spoken / There's a pain goes on and on / Empty chairs at empty tables / Now
2  my friends are dead and gone." The ravages of war and the devastating effects of armed conflict find their way into
3  a wide array of novels, stories, and poems.. One of the many poets who witnessed action on the front lines of World
4  War I was Wilfred Edward Salter Owen. His poem *Greater Love* contrasts the sacrificial love shown by soldiers on
5  the battlefield to the comparatively shallow love of romantic affection. The brutality of World War I was, to Wilfred
6  Owen at least, a horror that overcame even love itself.
7      This idea may most obviously be seen in the imagery of the poem "Red lips are not so red / As the stained
8  stones kissed by the English dead." In these first two lines of his poem, Owen immediately contrasts the sight of
9  romance with the sight of war. The image of the battlefield remains ever more vivid. "Heart, you were never hot /

10 Nor large, nor full like hearts made great with shot." In these lines, Owen argues that a heart swelled with romantic
11 love is not nearly as meaningful as the heart which has sacrificed itself for a greater cause. Wilfred Owen asserts that
12 after seeing the horrifying sights of a battlefield, the sight of beauty is meaningless.
13      Second, the title of Owen's poem is itself a part of his message. In a letter to a friend on May 1917, Owen
14 quotes the Christian Bible as he writes, "Greater love hath no man than this, that a man lay down his life for a friend.
15 Is it spoken in English only and French? I do not believe so." This letter perhaps reveals the ultimate purpose of
16 "Greater Love": men who die for love of their country and their home are the ones who show true love. This is a
17 greater love than romance, for it is more sacrificial. Indeed, according to Owen, greater is the love which stains the
18 stones of England than the love which lures the eyes.
19      Finally, Owen's choice to pen his thoughts in the form of a poem is itself an emphasis of the predominant
20 theme in "Greater Love." "Your voice sings not so soft / Though even as wind murmuring through raftered loft / . . .
21 / As theirs whom *none* now hear. / Now earth has stopped their piteous mouths that coughed." These powerful lines
22 point out that those who die on the battlefield do not experience the glorified end of poetic heroes. This war, into
23 which Europe had largely rushed with enthusiasm, was not the epic romanticized experience that the world had
24 expected. Owen believes that the poetry of love is meaningless when faced with the lack of poetry on the battlefield.
25 After viewing the brutality of armed conflict, Owen will never again feel the beauty of a romantic poem.
26      In "Greater Love" Wilfred Owen speaks of the shallowness of romance when faced with the horrors of war.
27 The sheer violence of armed conflict removes the blissful illusion of romantic affection. The love of soldiers for
28 what they defend is far greater than the love of a man for a woman. "Phantom faces at the windows / Phantom
29 shadows on the floor / Empty chairs at empty tables / Where my friends will meet no more." (John)

## Close Reading (Poem)

1. Owen employs what vivid literary device in the first line?
   A. Simile
   B. Onomatopoeia
   C. Metaphor
   D. Hyperbole

2. The "red lips" image contrasts
   A. Romantic love with the love among World War I comrades.
   B. The sacrifice of soldiers with romantic lovers.
   C. The folly of romantic love with wartime carnage.
   D. The timeless love of war sacrifice with romantic love.

3. Lines 22–27 employs what literary device?
   A. Simile
   B. Analogy
   C. Hyperbole
   D. Personification

4. What is the tone of the poem?
   A. Tentative
   B. Sanguine
   C. Moribund
   D. Serious

5. The poet creates the tone by
   A. Hyperbole.
   B. Connotation of morbid words.
   C. War scenes.
   D. Repetition.

6. What can the reader surmise about the poet?
   I. The poet was a thoughtful soldier.
   II. The poet hated war.
   III. The poet loved his comrades
   IV. The poet was anti-British

   A. I and II
   B. III and IV
   C. I, II, and III
   D. All

## Command of Evidence (Student Response)

1. The thesis is first presented in
   A. Lines 1–2.
   B. Lines 3–5
   
   C. Lines 16–19.
   D. Lines 24–29.

2. What is a favorite form of evidence used in the Student Response?
   A. Romantic novels
   B. Popular songs
   
   C. Quotes from the poem
   D. Other poems

3. How does the Student Response develop its argument?
   A. It uses a quote from another literary work to illustrate the theme of the poem and then goes through the poem line by line.
   B. It summarizes the poem and then makes a relevant point at the end.
   C. It analyzes the poem, line by line.
   D. It states a thesis and then offers alternative interpretations.

4. What is an assumption that the Student Response makes?

   I. The poem was effective.
   II. The poem was ungenerous in its assessment of romantic love.
   III. The poet was brave.

   A. I
   B. II
   
   C. III
   D. I and III

5. The Student Essay failed to observe this important component of the poem:
   A. The poet hated war.
   B. Romantic love, legitimate and wholesome, paled in the light of comrade devotion and sacrifice.
   C. The poet was in love with a woman
   D. The poet was a coward

6. The title "Greater Love" comes from
   A. The Koran
   B. A Shakespeare Play
   C. A Homeric Epic
   D. The Bible

7. Owen's allusion of "Greater Love" refers to what character?
   A. Mohammed
   B. Othello
   C. Achilles
   D. Jesus Christ

## Words in Context

1. What is the meaning of *decrepitude* in Line 13 in "Greater Love"?
   A. Strength
   B. Beauty
   
   C. Debility
   D. Felicity

2. What is the meaning of *piteous* in Line 20 in "Greater Love"?
   A. Distressing
   B. Remorseful
   
   C. Ungrateful
   D. Unhappy

# Lesson 2
## Critical Reading and Writing

**Command of Evidence**

Read the following passages and answer accompanying questions:

### Passage 1

1     In 1919, the Eighteenth Amendment to the Constitution was ratified, banning alcohol in the United States (David M.
2     Kennedy and Lizabeth Cohen, *The American Pageant*, 15th ed. [Boston: Cengage Learning, 2014], A34). Success
3     was finally achieved, and the Prohibition crusade had won. However, the Prohibitionists were incredibly naive to
4     think that thousands of years of drinking alcohol would just stop after one law was made. **Slavery had taken**
5     **decades of eventual phasing out in the European world and in half the United States, and even then it**
6     **required America's bloodiest war to wipe it out in its most prevalent area.** Although the Prohibition movement
7     was strong, its opposition was also very strong and common: immigrants.
8         When immigrants came to America, they brought their customs and traditions with them. This included
9     alcoholic beverages. Immigrants were used to socializing in pubs, taverns, bars, and any place that served alcohol.
10    Two of the most prevalent groups of immigrants were the Irish and Germans, who brought with them beer and
11    whiskey, something that Native Americans hated them for doing (*Pageant*, 314). After all, the stereotypical Irish is
12    drunk, and Germans are also well known for their drinking. Both these groups were large in America: over eight
13    million people with German ancestry and more than four and a half million with Irish blood (*Pageant*, 739). Like
14    most immigrants, they were concentrated in the most influential area of the United States, Northeastern cities such
15    as New York and Chicago. The South and West, on the other hand, had few immigrants and were more supportive
16    of Prohibition (*Pageant*, 775). But despite their numbers, the immigrants were unable to stop the Eighteenth
17    Amendment, so they took what was supposed to be their last drinks before the law came into effect. But they had no
18    idea that alcohol would soon become so profitable and violent due to the criminal underworld taking over.
19        When a business becomes illegal, the criminal element moves in and makes it all the more brutal. The
20    Prohibitionists were remarkably shortsighted to think that they could make criminal something everyone never
21    previously regarded as illegal and use federal agents to enforce a law the majority did not want, all this in a country
22    with a weak government and independent people. If the agencies, both federal and state, had been stronger,
23    Prohibition might have been enforceable. But both types of government agencies were understaffed, and their agents
24    were underpaid, making them susceptible to bribery (*Pageant*, 778–79). While Prohibition is known for its
25    "dryness," it was also known as a time of gangsters. With a business as profitable as alcohol now illegal, the
26    criminals moved in to corner the market on the manufacturing of illegal alcohol, also known as "moonshine" or
27    "bootleg" (*Pageant*, 778). Moonshiners had always existed in America, but since all other forms of liquor were
28    made unavailable, they were now the sole suppliers of the thousands of "speakeasies" that popped up (*Pageant*,
29    775). Seeing huge profit, gangsters moved in to organize and make money. With money to bribe officers of the law
30    and using business tactics, they netted huge profits. By 1930, the annual "take" of organized crime was estimated to
31    be from $12 to $18 billion, an income several times what the central government at Washington took in (*Pageant*,
32    780). The gangsters' method for dealing with competition was murder. Al "Scarface" Capone, the most infamous
33    mob boss of bootlegging, waged a bloody gang war from 1925 to 1931, which netted him millions of blood dollars
34    and massacred seven unarmed rival gang members on Valentine's Day 1929 (*Pageant*, 779). These murders were
35    often done during a gang war, with gangsters using their iconic sawed-off shotguns and machine guns; gang warfare
36    in Chicago alone claimed over 500 lives of gangsters (*Pageant*, 779). And that record does not include bystanders or
37    people who were never found. Clearly, Prohibition inflicted too much collateral damage via gangsters and was
38    repealed by the Twenty-First Amendment in 1933 (*Pageant*, 718). But by then, criminals had learned from the
39    Prohibition, restructuring organized crime and expanding to other areas such as prostitution, narcotics, and
40    gambling. Racketeering began during the Prohibition, when gangsters started demanding "protection money" from
41    honest merchants and racketeers invaded organizations such as labor unions (*Pageant*, 780). So ironically, the
42    movement to criminalize alcohol caused crime to improve.

43　　　To say that Prohibition was naive is an understatement. It tried to criminalize something that had been legal
44　since the colonists first arrived here without an eventual phasing out. It expected the understaffed and underpaid
45　federal authorities to enforce a law that the majority of Americans opposed, something they had never done before.
46　Prohibition caused hundreds of lives to be lost in the wars between rival gangs of bootleggers. It only made crime
47　worse. The only good thing that Prohibition did was to teach people that they should be careful in lawmaking, since
48　laws proposed and enacted could have unforeseen consequences. (Robinson)


## Close Reading

　　1. What would be the best title for this essay?
　　　　A. The American Experience　　　　　　　　C. The Effect of Prohibition
　　　　B. The Roaring Twenties　　　　　　　　　　D. Between the Wars


　　2. The essay begins with
　　　　A. A discussion of immigration.
　　　　B. A comparison of slavery emancipation to Prohibition.
　　　　C. A discussion of slavery.
　　　　D. Support for a one-nation, one-government theory.


　　3. What is a weakness in the introduction?
　　　　I.　 Slavery is not like drinking alcohol.
　　　　II.　Blame for the failure of a movement on one group (i.e., immigrants) is spurious.
　　　III.　Prohibition was the result of crime, not the cause.

　　　　　　A. I　　　　　　　　　　　　　　　　　C. I and II
　　　　　　B. II and III　　　　　　　　　　　　　D. All


　　4. What organizational plan does the author employ?
　　　　A. The essay is two essays: a discussion of immigration as a cause for Prohibition and then violence
　　　　　　generated by Prohibition.
　　　　B. An argument and then copious evidence
　　　　C. A chronological account of Prohibition
　　　　D. A thematic approach to immigration


　　5. The author finishes the essay with
　　　　A. A summary statement.　　　　　　　　　C. A distracting comment.
　　　　B. A new conclusion.　　　　　　　　　　　D. The way it began.


　　6. What is a weakness in the conclusion?
　　　　A. It is too general.　　　　　　　　　　　C. It does not finish the thoughts.
　　　　B. It fails to return to its thesis.　　　　　　D. It exaggerates some claims.


## Passage 2

1　In the essay "Best in Class," Margaret Talbot talks about the tradition of valedictorians, more specifically its use in
2　high schools and the student competition for the title (http://www.newyorker.com/magazine/2005/06/06/best-in-
3　class). In the essay, Talbot identifies how the student drive can produce fierce feuds and arguments while competing
4　for the title of valedictorian and explains how many schools respond to them. In the essay, Talbot relies on pathos,
5　emotion, and logos to connect with her audience, but she relies more heavily on pathos.
6　　　　For the beginning of the paper, Talbot describes Daniel Kennedy, the principal of Sarasota High School
7　during the entire valedictorian institute. She also explains the setting, in order to grab the audience's attention. Then
8　Talbot writes about how the conflict started between two students, one of whom took an easy extra-credit course in
9　order to win the title and a rival's furious response. She provides interviews with the students some years later, as
10　well as with the parents, to explain the thoughts of those involved; she seeks to humanize the scene and provide
11　emotional information about the incident, thereby connecting with the audience's emotions.

12 Talbot then describes the severity of the conflict within the school. She describes the tensions as people
13 took sides for or against the student who earned the title through the extra credit. She cites that tensions were so high
14 that "some Teachers considered boycotting graduation; students talked of booing Davies [the valedictorian winner]
15 when he walked out onstage." Talbot even reports an incident where a teacher called the parent of Davies's rival
16 because she was "a pressure cooker . . . about to burst." She documents the escalating struggle through Kennedy's
17 quotes as he is trying to make sure the school does not erupt into total war. Talbot describes the escalating conflict
18 so dramatically that it evokes strong disbelief in the audience about the incident. Talbot then reports the compromise
19 proposed by the principal and the abolishing of the valedictorian title, not only in Sarasota, but in other school
20 districts as well. She ends the section with a quote from Kennedy, who advises principals never to have a
21 valedictorian, highlighting his exhaustion about the event.

22 Next Talbot describes the current effort to get the title valedictorian to explain why this conflict is so
23 frequent today. Then she gives other stories of students who went to great measures to earn the title, some even
24 going as far as suing the school they went to. Again, Talbot is highlighting the conflict in order to evoke disbelief in
25 the reader. **Talbot then describes the history of the title and what it means for the students after they earn the**
26 **title, as well as the dishonesty that is involved.** She then contemplates the good and bad of getting rid of the
27 valedictorian title in order to provoke the audience to take a side. Talbot ends with describing the mother of the
28 would-be valedictorian who started it all and her opinion on the abolition of the title, to provide a perspective from
29 someone who unwittingly engineered the removal of something their child dearly wanted.

30 Margret Talbot uses emotion to connect to the audience, specifically the emotion of disbelief. She does this
31 by telling the history of the title *valedictorian* and its phasing out. Using this method, Talbot relies more heavily on
32 pathos over logos to connect with the readers. (Robinson)

## Close Reading

1. What would be the best title for this essay?
   A. Valedictorians
   B. The Futility of Class Rank
   C. The Use of Pathos
   D. The End of Innocence

2. What organizational plan does the author employ?
   A. He vilifies class rank and offer supportive evidence.
   B. He describes Talbot's arguments and then offers textual evidence.
   C. He discusses the advantages of using pathos in essays.
   D. He draws the reader step by step into his argument.

3. The author finishes his essay with
   A. A summary statement
   B. A new conclusion
   C. A distracting comment
   D. A final criticism of Talbot

## Grammar and Usage

Choose the best grammar/usage form in bold sentence(s).:

1. Passage 1, Lines 4–6

    A. NONE
    B. Slavery required decades of eventual phasing out in the European world and in half the United States and even then required America's bloodiest war to wipe it out in its most prevalent area.
    C. Slavery had taken decades to end in the European world and in half the country and even then required America's bloodiest war to wipe it out in its most prevalent area.
    D. Slavery ended slowly in the old world and required a bloody civil war to be fought in America for it to end here.

2. Passage 2, Lines 25–26

    A. NONE
    B. Talbot then contemplates the end of the valedictorian title in order to provoke the audience to take a side.
    C. Talbot then proposes the ending of the valedictorian title in order to provoke the audience to take a side.
    D. Talbot then contemplates getting rid of the valedictorian title in order to provoke the audience to take a side.

# Lesson 3
## SAT Essay

Examine the following picture and answer the questions:

Edmund Duffy. From Ever Darkening Clouds, ca. 1944. Published in the *Baltimore Sun*. Crayon, ink brush, and opaque white over graphite underdrawing. Art Wood Collection of Cartoon and Caricature, Prints and Photographs Division, Library of Congress LC-DIG-ppmsca-07517.

1. A purpose of this photograph/poster could be
   I.   To sell war bonds.
   II.  To recruit more Army Air Corps volunteers.
   III. To belittle Adolf Hitler.

|            |            |         |
|------------|------------|---------|
| A. I       | C. III     | E. All  |
| B. II      | D. I and II|         |

2. Which group (s) might find this photograph objectionable?
   A. American soldiers        C. German Americans
   B. Moms of Army Air Corps soldiers      D. NONE

3. Which of the following strategies does the photographer employ to influence his audience?
   I.   A hand of death reaches from the skies to destroy the Nazi war effort.
   II.  A hand of death warns the viewer that the war is not over and will require more sacrifice.
   III. A hand of death via the Army Air Corps is seeking Adolf Hitler.
   IV.  Death will come to many German fighter pilots.
   V.   A hand of death is reaching down to kill many German civilians.

|                    |                      |         |
|--------------------|----------------------|---------|
| A. I and III       | C. IV and V          | E. All  |
| B. I, II, and III  | D. I, II, III, and V |         |

## Student Response

*Prompt:* As you read the passage below, consider how the author uses

    A.  Evidence, such as facts or examples, to support claims.
    B.  Reasoning to develop ideas and to connect claims and evidence.
    C.  Stylistic or persuasive elements, such as word choice or appeals to emotion, to add power to the ideas expressed.

Discuss literary works where the setting is critical.

1        In Jack London's *Call of the Wild*, Stephen Crane's *The Red Badge of Courage*, and Ernest Hemingway's
2  *A Farewell to Arms*, the setting plays a vital role in the story. In the spirit of the naturalist literary movement, the
3  setting is used to develop the protagonist; however, each author does this a little bit differently.
4        The setting is used most directly to develop the protagonist in *Call of the Wild*. "Buck lived at a big house
5  in the sun-kissed Santa Clara Valley," writes London in the beginning of *The Call of the Wild* (15). London follows
6  the journey of Buck, the canine protagonist, that transports Buck from a mild setting to a harsh setting in the
7  Klondike region of Canada, where a gold rush is happening in 1897. Once in this environment, Buck changes from a
8  friendly, gentle dog to a fierce fighter—killing first another dog and then a man. "He was aware of a great pride in
9  himself—a pride greater than any he had yet experienced. He had killed man, the noblest game of all, and he had
10  killed in the face of the law of club and fang" (103). Among the three novels, *The Call of the Wild* is the most
11  dramatic use of the setting; Buck is a complete product of his environment. Unlike Hemingway and Crane's
12  protagonists, Buck has no inherent ideas of civilized behavior; he is civilized because in his first environment, he is
13  trained to be civilized. Once in a harsher environment, he reverts back to a primordial beast. "The dominant
14  primordial beast was strong in Buck, and under the fierce conditions of trail life it grew and grew" (28) Again, when
15  Buck comes into the possession of another kind master, John Thornton, in a kinder environment, he softens a bit.
16  When Thornton dies, Buck once again returns to the "dominant primordial beast" in full blow. "It was the call, the
17  many-noted call, sounding more luringly and compellingly than ever before. And as never before, he was ready to
18  obey. John Thornton was dead. The last tie was broken" (104). Hence, the setting defines Buck's character.
19        In *The Red Badge of Courage*, Crane's protagonist, Henry Fleming, begins with a lot of presuppositions
20  about honor and bravery in wartime. So, unlike Buck, he is not a complete product of his setting. "He had, of course,
21  dreamed of battles all his life—of vague and bloody conflicts that had thrilled him with their sweep and fire. . . . He
22  had imagined peoples secure in the shadow of his eagle-eyed prowess" (2). The setting does not define him, but
23  rather develops him. The setting is the Civil War, and through this war setting, Henry is forced to come face-to-face
24  with his own weaknesses and erroneous daydreams about glorious war. The war reveals Henry's doubts about how
25  he measures up to his ideal of courage. "But here he was confronted with a thing of moment. It had suddenly
26  appeared to him that he might run. He was forced to admit that as far as war was concerned, he knew nothing of
27  himself"(6). Hence, when his fear and the terrible reality of combat drowned his ideals, he deserted his regiment. "A
28  lad whose face had borne an expression of exalted courage, the majesty of he who dares give his life, was, at an
29  instant, smitten abject. . . . There was a revelation. He, too, threw down his gun and fled. There was no shame in his
30  face. He ran like a rabbit" (34). For the rest of the book, Henry struggles to justify his cowardice, searching for
31  redemption. His redemption comes because of the setting. Returning to his regiment, Henry, fueled by his pride,
32  finds courage to remain fighting and because of his unwarranted bravery receives a medal. In the war setting,
33  Henry's cowardice is brought to light, and a chance for redemption is provided; the setting develops him from a boy
34  to a man. "He felt a quiet manhood, nonassertive but of sturdy and strong blood. . . . He had been to touch the great
35  death, and found that, after all, it was but the great death. He was a man" (116).
36        The setting of war is also used in Ernest Hemingway's World War I novel *A Farewell to Arms*. The
37  protagonist is Frederic Henry, an American ambulance driver for the Italian army. Unlike Henry Fleming, Frederic
38  Henry does not struggle with abstract ideas such as courage and duty, but faces war with cool stoicism; hence, the
39  war setting does not develop him psychologically like it does Henry Fleming. Instead, the war setting provides the
40  logical reasons behind the events of the plot line, much in the same way that *The Call of the Wild* was set in the year
41  of the Klondike gold rush and thus gives a logical reason for Buck's abduction.
42        Unique to Hemingway, is the use of weather and different specific settings to develop the protagonist by
43  providing a parallel between what was occurring psychologically in the protagonist. The most common setting is
44  rain, which appears in all the important events of the book. "At the start of the winter came the permanent rain and
45  with the rain came the cholera. But it was checked and in the end only seven thousand died of it in the army"

46 (*Farewell*, 4) The writers at *LitCharts* explain, "Whenever Henry makes a significant nighttime transition from one
47 place to another—the night that he leaves Milan to return to the front, the night of the large-scale Italian retreat, and
48 the night that he and Catherine row across the lake from Italy to Switzerland—it is pouring rain." And finally, the
49 night Catherine, Henry's lover, dies in childbirth, it is again raining. "It was like saying good-bye to a statue. After a
50 while I went out and left the hospital and walked back to the hotel in the rain." The raining is the physical parallel of
51 Henry's attempt to outrun death. No matter how much he tries, how much he hopes, death overtakes him. "I'm
52 afraid of the rain because sometimes I see me dead in it," says Catherine. More specific settings include the contrast
53 between the fast-paced cities Henry frequented before meeting Catherine and his willingness to live in a slow-paced
54 town in Switzerland for the sake of love. The setting in *A Farewell to Arms* is used symbolically to develop the
55 protagonist, by giving a tangible manifestation of the inner dynamism of the protagonist.
56       **Working in a naturalist frame of mind, which emphasizes the role of the environment in the shaping**
57 **of people, all three authors use strong settings as the catalyst for the dynamism of the protagonists.** Because of
58 the frigid and cruel environment, Buck, in Jack London's *Call of the Wild*, changes from a civilized, well-behaved
59 dog into a wild, primitive dog. Ernest Hemingway uses the rainy setting in a symbolic way to develop his
60 protagonist, Frederic Henry. For Stephen Crane's Henry Fleming, the Civil War battle scene first reveals his
61 shortcomings and then develops him as a person. (Daphnide)

1. The following are examples of evidence, such as facts or examples, to support claims:
    I.   Lines 1–2                                III.  Lines 36–38
    II.  Lines 4–5                                IV.  Lines 57–59

        A. I                                     D. II and III
        B. II                                  E. IV
        C. I, II, and III                     F. NONE

2. Which of the above lines (in question 1) show reasoning (without examples) to develop ideas and to connect claims and evidence?
        A. I                                     D. II and III
        B. II                                  E. IV
        C. I, II, and III                     F. NONE

3. Which of the above lines (in question 1) show stylistic or persuasive elements, such as word choice or appeals to emotion, to add power to the ideas expressed?
        A. I                                     D. II and III
        B. II                                  E. IV
        C. I, II, and III                     F. NONE

4. The author is probably
        A. A born-again Christian.                     C. Someone who loves television.
        B. A well-read student.                       D. NONE.

5. What organizational strategy does the essay employ?
        A. The introduction presents three examples, and the rest of the essay develops these three examples.
        B. A contradictory theory is introduced and then destroyed.
        C. Anecdotal selections from three novels are developed.
        D. A summary of the lives of Hemingway, Fleming, and London is provided.

6. An example of the literary device juxtaposition is in
        A. Lines 1–2
        B. Lines 4–5
        C. Lines 19–20
        D. Lines 37–41

7. What score would this essay receive? __

## Grammar and Usage

Choose the best grammar/usage form in bold sentence(s).

Lines 56–57
A. NONE
B. Working in a naturalist frame of mind which emphasizes the role of the environment in shaping people; all three authors employ strong settings that are the catalyst for the dynamism of the protagonists.
C. All three naturalist authors use the setting to develop all key characters.
D. All three authors use strong naturalists settings that are the catalyst for the dynamism of the protagonists.

# Lesson 4
## Reading: Document-Based Analysis

### The Declaration of Independence (July 4, 1776)

1     When in the Course of human events, it becomes necessary for one people to dissolve the political bands which have
2 connected them with another, and to assume among the powers of the earth, the separate and equal station to which
3 the Laws of Nature and of Nature's God entitle them, a decent respect to the opinions of mankind requires that they
4 should declare the causes which impel them to the separation.
5     We hold these truths to be self-evident, that all men are created equal, that they are endowed by their
6 Creator with certain unalienable Rights, that among these are Life, Liberty and the pursuit of Happiness. —That to
7 secure these rights, Governments are instituted among Men, deriving their just powers from the consent of the
8 governed, —That whenever any Form of Government becomes destructive of these ends, it is the Right of the
9 People to alter or to abolish it, and to institute new Government, laying its foundation on such principles and
10 organizing its powers in such form, as to them shall seem most likely to effect their Safety and Happiness. Prudence,
11 indeed, will dictate that Governments long established should not be changed for light and transient causes; and
12 accordingly all experience hath shewn, that mankind are more disposed to suffer, while evils are sufferable, than to
13 right themselves by abolishing the forms to which they are accustomed. But when a long train of abuses and
14 usurpations, pursuing invariably the same Object evinces a design to reduce them under absolute Despotism, it is
15 their right, it is their duty, to throw off such Government, and to provide new Guards for their future security. —
16 Such has been the patient sufferance of these Colonies; and such is now the necessity which constrains them to alter
17 their former Systems of Government. The history of the present King of Great Britain is a history of repeated
18 injuries and usurpations, all having in direct object the establishment of an absolute Tyranny over these States. To
19 prove this, let Facts be submitted to a candid world.
20     He has refused his Assent to Laws, the most wholesome and necessary for the public good.
21     He has forbidden his Governors to pass Laws of immediate and pressing importance, unless suspended in
22 their operation till his Assent should be obtained; and when so suspended, he has utterly neglected them.
23     He has refused to pass other Laws for the accommodation of large districts of people, unless those people
24 would relinquish the right of Representation in the Legislature, a right inestimable to them and formidable to
25 tyrants only.
26     He has called together legislative bodies at places unusual, uncomfortable, and distant from the depository
27 of their public Records, for the sole purpose of fatiguing them into compliance with his measures.
28     He has dissolved Representative Houses repeatedly, for opposing with manly firmness his invasions on the
29 rights of the people.
30     He has refused for a long time, after such dissolutions, to cause others to be elected; whereby the
31 Legislative powers, incapable of Annihilation, have returned to the People at large for their exercise; the State
32 remaining in the mean time exposed to all the dangers of invasion from without, and convulsions within.
33     He has endeavoured to prevent the population of these States; for that purpose obstructing the Laws for
34 Naturalization of Foreigners; refusing to pass others to encourage their migrations hither, and raising the
35 conditions of new Appropriations of Lands.
36     He has obstructed the Administration of Justice, by refusing his Assent to Laws for establishing Judiciary
37 powers.
38     He has made Judges dependent on his Will alone, for the tenure of their offices, and the amount and
39 payment of their salaries.
40     He has erected a multitude of New Offices, and sent hither swarms of Officers to harass our people, and eat
41 out their substance.
42     He has kept among us, in times of peace, Standing Armies without the Consent of our legislatures.
43     He has affected to render the Military independent of and superior to the Civil power.
44     He has combined with others to subject us to a jurisdiction foreign to our constitution, and unacknowledged
45 by our laws; giving his Assent to their Acts of pretended Legislation:
46     For Quartering large bodies of armed troops among us:
47     For protecting them, by a mock Trial, from punishment for any Murders which they should commit on the
48 Inhabitants of these States:
49     For cutting off our Trade with all parts of the world:

50   For imposing Taxes on us without our Consent:

51   For depriving us in many cases, of the benefits of Trial by Jury:

52   For transporting us beyond Seas to be tried for pretended offences:

53   For abolishing the free System of English Laws in a neighbouring Province, establishing therein an
54   Arbitrary government, and enlarging its Boundaries so as to render it at once an example and fit instrument for
55   introducing the same absolute rule into these Colonies:

56   For taking away our Charters, abolishing our most valuable Laws, and altering fundamentally the Forms of
57   our Governments:

58   For suspending our own Legislatures, and declaring themselves invested with power to legislate for us in
59   all cases whatsoever.

60   He has abdicated Government here, by declaring us out of his Protection and waging War against us.

61   He has plundered our seas, ravaged our Coasts, burnt our towns, and destroyed the lives of our people.

62   He is at this time transporting large Armies of foreign Mercenaries to compleat the works of death,
63   desolation and tyranny, already begun with circumstances of Cruelty & perfidy scarcely paralleled in the most
64   barbarous ages, and totally unworthy the Head of a civilized nation.

65   He has constrained our fellow Citizens taken Captive on the high Seas to bear Arms against their Country,
66   to become the executioners of their friends and Brethren, or to fall themselves by their Hands.

67   He has excited domestic insurrections amongst us, and has endeavoured to bring on the inhabitants of our
68   frontiers, the merciless Indian Savages, whose known rule of warfare, is an undistinguished destruction of all
69   ages, sexes and conditions.

70   In every stage of these Oppressions We have Petitioned for Redress in the most humble terms: Our
71   repeated Petitions have been answered only by repeated injury. A Prince whose character is thus marked by every
72   act which may define a Tyrant, is unfit to be the ruler of a free people.

73   Nor have We been wanting in attentions to our British brethren. We have warned them from time to time of
74   attempts by their legislature to extend an unwarrantable jurisdiction over us. We have reminded them of the
75   circumstances of our emigration and settlement here. We have appealed to their native justice and magnanimity, and
76   we have conjured them by the ties of our common kindred to disavow these usurpations, which, would inevitably
77   interrupt our connections and correspondence. They too have been deaf to the voice of justice and of consanguinity.
78   We must, therefore, acquiesce in the necessity, which denounces our Separation, and hold them, as we hold the rest
79   of mankind, Enemies in War, in Peace Friends.

80   We, therefore, the Representatives of the united States of America, in General Congress, Assembled,
81   appealing to the Supreme Judge of the world for the rectitude of our intentions, do, in the Name, and by Authority of
82   the good People of these Colonies, solemnly publish and declare, That these United Colonies are, and of Right ought
83   to be Free and Independent States; that they are Absolved from all Allegiance to the British Crown, and that all
84   political connection between them and the State of Great Britain, is and ought to be totally dissolved; and that as
85   Free and Independent States, they have full Power to levy War, conclude Peace, contract Alliances, establish
86   Commerce, and to do all other Acts and Things which Independent States may of right do. And for the support of
87   this Declaration, with a firm reliance on the protection of divine Providence, we mutually pledge to each other our
88   Lives, our Fortunes and our sacred Honor.

89                                    (http://www.archives.gov/exhibits/charters/declaration_transcript.html)

## The British Response to the Declaration of Independence (October 31, 1776)

1    His Majesty's Most Gracious Speech to Both Houses of Parliament on Thursday, October 31, 1776
2
3    My Lords, and Gentlemen, Nothing could have afforded Me so much Satisfaction as to have been able to inform
4    you, at the Opening of this Session, that the Troubles, which have so long distracted My Colonies in North America,
5    were at an End; and that My unhappy People, recovered from their Delusion, had delivered themselves from the
6    Oppression of their Leaders, and returned to their Duty. But so daring and desperate is the Spirit of those Leaders,
7    whose Object has always been Dominion and Power, that they have now openly renounced all Allegiance to the
8    Crown, and all political Connection with this Country. They have rejected, with Circumstances of Indignity and
9    Insult, the Means of Conciliation held out to them under the Authority of Our Commission: and have presumed to
10    set up their rebellious Confederacies for Independent States. If their Treason be suffered to take Root, much
11    Mischief must grow from it, to the Safety of My loyal Colonies, to the Commerce of My Kingdoms, and indeed to
12    the present System of all Europe. One great Advantage, however, will be derived from the Object of the Rebels
13    being openly avowed, and clearly understood. We shall have Unanimity at Home, founded in the general Conviction
14    of the Justice and Necessity of Our Measures.
15      I am happy to Inform you, that, by the Blessing of Divine Providence on the good Conduct and Valour of
16    My Officers and Forces by Sea and Land, and on the Zeal and Bravery of the Auxiliary Troops in My Service,
17    Canada is recovered; and although, from unavoidable Delays, the Operations at New York could not begin before
18    the Month of August, the Success in that Province has been so important as to give the strongest Hopes of the most
19    decisive good Consequences. But, notwithstanding this fair Prospect, We must, at all Events, prepare for another
20    Campaign.
21      I continue to receive Assurances of Amity from the several Courts of Europe; and am using My utmost
22    Endeavours to conciliate unhappy Differences between Two neighbouring Powers; and I still hope, that all
23    Misunderstandings may be removed, and Europe continue to enjoy the inestimable Blessings of Peace. I think
24    nevertheless that, in the present Situation of Affairs, it is expedient that We should be in a respectable State of
25    Defence at Home.
26      Gentlemen of the House of Commons, I will order the Estimates for the ensuing Year to be laid before you.
27    It is [a] Matter of real Concern to Me, that the important Considerations which I have stated to you must necessarily
28    be followed by great Expence: I doubt not, however, but that My faithful Commons will readily and chearfully grant
29    Me such Supplies, as the Maintenance of the Honour of my Crown, the Vindication of the just Rights of Parliament,
30    and the Publick Welfare shall be found to require.
31      My Lords, and Gentlemen, in this arduous Contest I can have no other Object but to promote the true
32    Interests of all My Subjects. No people ever enjoyed more Happiness, or lived under a milder Government, than
33    those now revolted Provinces: the Improvements in every Art, of which they boast, declare it: their Numbers, their
34    Wealth, their Strength by Sea and Land, which they think sufficient to enable them to make Head against the whole
35    Power of the Mother Country, are irrefragable Proofs of it. My Desire is to restore to them the Blessings of Law and
36    Liberty, equally enjoyed by every British Subject, which they have fatally and desperately exchanged for all the
37    Calamities of War, and the arbitrary Tyranny of their Chiefs.
38                (http://chapin.williams.edu/exhibits/His%20Majestys%20Speech.pdf)

1.  The Declaration of Independence is a
    A. Creed.
    B. Law.

    C. List.
    D. Charter.

2.  Lines 1–4 are
    A. A Salutation.
    B. A Preamble.

    C. A Resolution.
    D. An Abdication.

3. In what order does the author develop his argument?
    I.   Therefore the American colonists are forced to rebel.
    II.  These rights have been violated by the British government.
    III. God has given humankind certain rights.

    A. I, II, and III
    B. II, I, and III

    C. III, II, and I
    D. III, I, and II

4. The Declaration of Independence is structured as
    A. Introduction, Grievances, Declaration.
    B. Grievances and Resolutions.

    C. Pleas, Plans, and Demands.
    D. Laws, Penalties, and Demands.

5. The author of the Declaration of Independence probably
    A. Was an atheist.
    B. Was a scientist.

    C. Was a Presbyterian.
    D. Believed in God.

6. The British Response
    I.   Used language similar to language used in the Declaration of Independence.
    II.  Admitted that the Americans had real grievances and wished to pursue reconciliation.
    III. Dismissed all American demands as spurious.

    A. I
    B. II and III

    C. I and III
    D. NONE

7. What is the meaning of Lines 21–25 in the British Response?
    A. Federal courts in Europe are favorably disposed toward British demands.
    B. The war between France and Germany will soon be resolved.
    C. The conflict in America might very well spread to Europe, so England must be prepared.
    D. The King is pleading to the better nature of his American colonists.

8. If the King ignores the American movement toward independence, the results would bring deleterious results in
    I.   The American colonies
    II.  Other colonies
    III. Europe

    A. I
    B. II

    C. II and III
    D. I and III

# Words in Context

## Declaration of Independence

1.  What is the meaning of *tenure* in Line 38?
    A.  Foothold
    B.  Feeling
    C.  Contract
    D.  Obligation

2.  What is the meaning of *arbitrary* in Line 54?
    A.  Unplanned
    B.  Unethical
    C.  Capricious
    D.  Forfeited

## British Response

3.  What is the meaning of *conciliate* in Line 22?
    A.  Reconcile
    B.  Resolve
    C.  Deny
    D.  Emancipate

4.  What is the meaning of *vindication* in line 29?
    A.  Examination
    B.  Renaming
    C.  Denial
    D.  Exculpation

# Lesson 5
## Math: Algebra, Arithmetic Problem Solving and Data Analysis, and Passport to Advanced Math

### Passport to Advanced Math

1. Which of the following statements are true?
   I.   Things equal to the same thing or equal things are equal to each other.
   II.  If equals be added to equals, the sums are equal.
   III. If equals be subtracted from equals, the remainders are unequal.
   IV.  If equals be multiplied by equals, the products are equal.

   A. I and II            C. I, II, and IV           E. All
   B. II and III          D. II, III, and IV

2. Which of the following statements are true?
   I.   If equals be divided by equals, the quotients are equal.
   II.  The whole is greater than any of its parts.
   III. Like powers, or like roots, of equals are equal.
   IV.  The product of two real integers is always a positive number.

   A. I, II, and III      C. I, II, and IV           E. All
   B. II and III          D. II, III, and IV

### Arithmetic Problem Solving

1. Divide the number 23 into three parts, such that the second is 1 more than the first, and the third is twice the second.
   A. 4; 5; 10        B. 3; 4; 8        C. 2; 3; 6        D. 5; 6; 12

2. Divide the number 137 into three parts, such that the second shall be 3 more than the first, and the third shall be five times the second.
   A. 16; 19; 99                      C. 18; 22; 110
   B. 17; 20; 100                     D. 15; 30; 100

3. Mr. Ames builds three houses. The first cost $2,000 more than the second, and the third twice as much as the first. If they all together cost $18,000, what was the cost of each house?
   A. $5000; $3000; $10,000           C. $5000; $4000; $12,000
   B. $4000; $2000; $8,000            D. $3000; $2000; $6,000

4. An artist, who had painted three pictures, charged $18 more for the second than the first, and three times as much for the third as the second. If he received $322 for the three, what was the price of each picture?
   A. $45; $72; $188                  C. $50; $68; $204
   B. $50; $74; $220                  D. $40; $58; $196

### Algebra

1. There are $c$ boys at play, and 5 others join them. How many boys are there in all?
   A. $c + 5$                         C. $c/5$
   B. $c(5)$                          D. $c + 5(c)$

2. What is the sum of $x + x + x +$ etc. written $d$ times?
   A. $3x + x$                        C. $dx$
   B. $d(x^2)$                        D. $d(3x)$

# Chapter 17   The Courage to Be Different John 14

> *Memory Verses:* Jesus answered, "I am the way and the truth and the life. No one comes to the Father except through me. If you really know me, you will know my Father as well. From now on, you do know him and have seen him." —John 14:6–7

In April 1956, C. S. Lewis, a famous English Christian philosopher, a confirmed bachelor, married Joy Davidman, an American poet with two children. After four brief, intensely happy years, Lewis found himself again alone, and inconsolable. His beloved Joy died of cancer. "No one ever told me that grief felt so like fear," Lewis writes. "Talk to me about the truth of religion, and I'll listen gladly. Talk to me about the duty of religion, and I'll listen submissively. But don't come talking to me about the consolations of religion, or I shall suspect that you don't understand" (from *A Grief Observed* [1961]). The cry of absence was deep in the heart of C. S. Lewis.

John 14 is a picture of Christ preparing his disciples for his imminent absence. We hear again the cries we all have expressed and heard. This is the cry of all those who have looked thoughtfully at the world into which they are thrust by no choice of their own, and the anguish they feel. This is the cry of Philip and Thomas. This is our cry too.

Paul Tillich, a famous theologian who taught at Union Seminary (N.Y.), understood John 14 to be a sermon spoken to prepare Christ's disciples for his imminent ascension. Tillich affirmed the importance of "the courage to be" as an essential resource for authentic living.

In John 14 we sense the beginnings of grief and therefore deep apprehension. Even fear. Literally, Christ is calling his disciples to be without his physical presence. In John 13:31–33, Jesus disclosed that he will be betrayed by one of his own disciples and will soon die. Jesus is trying to prepare his disciples for his death. In the face of Christ's absence, what basis for hope do we have?

Thomas was Jesus' disciple known as "the Twin." Notwithstanding his reputation, Thomas was more than a sullen skeptic. At Bethany, when Jesus announced his plans to continue to Jerusalem, Peter fussily protested, but to Thomas's credit, he said, "Let us also go, that we may die with him" (John 11:16). Even at the Last Supper, Thomas, wanting to stay with Jesus, asked how they could know the way. The crucifixion, which occurs chronologically after John 14, demolished Thomas's faith. He was absent when Christ first appeared to the disciples and was utterly unable to believe their fantastic report. Only when he was confronted by the living Lord was he able to believe. Some historians believe that Thomas went to India and founded the church there.

Certainly our passage foreshadows the Thomas who was to come. Thomas had an obsession to know.

One of the most basic human needs we humans have is the need to know the future. We spend billions trying to predict it and then to control it.

But that, of course, is rarely possible. Thomas said to Christ, "Lord, we do not know where you are going; so how can we know the way to get there?" (John 14:5). This is Thomas's request for Jesus to clarify his assurance that he is going to heaven to prepare a place for his friends (John 14:1–4). Thomas would have been very pleased if Christ had answered that question. We like to know what we face. That is the genius in the MacDonald Corporation: we might hate Big Macs, but better the known and predictable than the unknown and unpredictable. The Holiday Inns lure travelers to their motels with the promise "No surprises." Yes, we have a great need to know. However, as we study the Scriptures, we discover that Jesus never promised to tell us our future. At least not with the specificity that we want. We imagine that the first thing the disciples asked after they recovered from the initial shock of seeing their risen Lord was "Tell us all about the valley of the shadow of death!" We want to know what death will be like. We spend millions trying to know and to control our future.

But the simple truth is, Jesus never offered knowledge of death's domain. He offered hope. Instead of offering an advanced briefing, Jesus said, "Be not afraid. . . . I will be with you."

In Christian terms, our hope is never in advance information, but rather in the promise of divine companionship. Our hope is not based upon control, but on relationship with the One who controls. "Lo, I am with you always" is, pure and simple, the only thing we can grasp as life tumbles down around us. On the faithful basis of goodness and mercy following us all the rest of our life—as it has in the past—we are able to rest assured that what we need in the future will be there just like it was yesterday.

There is a spirit of the age that values knowledge above everything. Where are the cathedrals in Johnstown? The banks? Hospitals? Universities? Pittsburgh even has a Cathedral of Learning! But knowledge is not the basis of our hope—Christ is.

C. S. Lewis writes:

> Meanwhile, where is God? This is one of the most disquieting symptoms. When you are happy, so happy that you have no sense of needing Him, so happy that you are tempted to feel His claims upon you as an interruption, if you remember yourself and turn to Him with gratitude and praises, you will be—or so it feels—welcomed with open arms. But go to Him when your need is desperate, when all other help is vain, and what do you find? A door slammed in your face, and a sound of bolting and double bolting on the inside. After that, silence. You may as well turn away. The longer you wait, the more emphatic the silence will become. There are no lights in the windows. It might be an empty house. Was it ever inhabited? It seemed so once. And that seemingly was as strong as this. What can this mean? Why is He so present a commander in our time of prosperity; and so very absent a help in time of trouble? (*A Grief Observed*, 4–5)

This quote from Lewis captures the feeling we always have when we experience change: abandonment.

Philip was a heavyweight disciple. The fourth disciple to follow Christ, he brought his close friend Nathanael to Christ too. A practical man, Philip had already figured out the cost of feeding the multitude before Jesus asked about the extent of the disciples' food supply. Apparently he kept his "come and see" attitude when he invited Greek-speaking Jews to Christ. But Philip too was a modern man. He wanted to know too much.

Philip asked, "Lord, show us the Father and that will be enough for us" (John 14:8). Ignoring Jesus' answer, Philip continued along Thomas's line of conversation. But in Philip's answer I sense great fear: a fear of abandonment.

Philip is experiencing what the theologian Martin Marty calls a "winter in the heart." Have you ever felt that God has abandoned you? Using half of the Psalms as examples, Marty describes the Christian life, at times, as being a dark night of the soul, the cloud of unknowing, the negative way to God.

Elisabeth Kübler-Ross in her classic book *On Death and Dying* (1969) describes death as "a fearful frightening happening, and the fear of death is a universal fear even if we think we have mastered it on many levels. . . . It is inconceivable for our unconscious to imagine an actual ending of our own life here on earth, and if this life of ours has to end, the ending is always attributed to a malicious intervention from the outside by someone else." If Kübler-Ross is correct, then perhaps we understand better Philip's rather violent reaction to Christ's statement that he is leaving them. Philip is, in other words, angry. He feels abandoned. He wants to blame someone.

Remember Peter's reaction that Christ will die? "No, Lord!" he exclaimed. And remember the reactions of the disciples to Christ's statement at the Last Supper that he was to die the next day? Incredulity! They could not believe it was true. Or, to use Kübler-Ross's terminology, they were experiencing denial.

Confronting and solving problems is a painful process that we would rather avoid. But the very avoidance results in greater pain, though, and we find ourselves unable to grow spiritually. Philip, for his own good, needed to accept reality—no matter how painful. The Christian psychiatrist Scott Peck in his book *The Road Less Traveled* (1978) suggests that healthy peope accept reality at all costs. Philip and Thomas, and all of us, must accept the realities of life—even if at times they are distasteful.

The fact is that Philip and Thomas were learning an important truth: Life is difficult. Christ wants them to see this truth, because, once they see it, he wants them to transcend it. Life is in fact a series of problems. Christ is presenting Philip with his first one. What will Philip do?

Where then, when we feel abandoned, is the courage we need to go on? Simply put, we learn in John 14 that it is not what we know but whom we know that counts. Faith is trust, not exact knowledge. Thomas wants to know more, and so do we. Philip wants to know more too and feels abandoned when he realizes that Christ will be leaving them. But Christ is leaving the Holy Spirit with them to comfort them—small comfort until they meet the Holy Spirit at Pentecost. But for now Christ is asking for a personal response, not a theological one. And so today, we are asked for the same. If we want to have a life that grows out of a deep share of God's love, then we need to have faith in Christ, and in him alone.

"Show us the Father," Philip blurts out; "Why doesn't God say something, do something?" another asks. Jesus' answer is that in his life, as God's only Son, God has shown something and done something. This is good news that needs telling and retelling. That is where we come in; however, the task is not ours alone, and that is where the Holy Spirit comes in.

And yet, the "Holy Spirit" is an unknown quantity. The Jewish mind had a very rudimentary concept of the Holy Spirit. Christ's promise, therefore, that the Spirit is coming is an invitation of faith. An invitation, again, to relate to God as a being rather than as information.

The invitation to you, and to me, is a deep share of faith, hope, and love. An invitation to trust in God without anything but a profound and abiding belief in God's love.

## Journal Question

If you were alive during biblical times, what one question would you ask Jesus?

# Lesson 1
## Evidence-Based Reading and Writing

### Literary Choice

Edwin Arlington Robinson (1869–1935) was a gifted but eccentric poet, who championed naturalistic themes with realistic style.

**Luke Havergal**

| | |
|---|---|
| 1 | Go to the western gate, Luke Havergal, |
| 2 | There where the vines cling crimson on the wall, |
| 3 | And in the twilight wait for what will come. |
| 4 | The leaves will whisper there of her, and some, |
| 5 | Like flying words, will strike you as they fall; |
| 6 | But go, and if you listen she will call. |
| 7 | Go to the western gate, Luke Havergal— |
| 8 | Luke Havergal. |
| 9 | |
| 10 | No, there is not a dawn in eastern skies |
| 11 | To rift the fiery night that's in your eyes; |
| 12 | But there, where western glooms are gathering, |
| 13 | The dark will end the dark, if anything: |
| 14 | God slays Himself with every leaf that flies, |
| 15 | And hell is more than half of paradise. |
| 16 | No, there is not a dawn in eastern skies— |
| 17 | In eastern skies. |
| 18 | |
| 19 | Out of a grave I come to tell you this, |
| 20 | Out of a grave I come to quench the kiss |
| 21 | That flames upon your forehead with a glow |
| 22 | That blinds you to the way that you must go. |
| 23 | Yes, there is yet one way to where she is, |
| 24 | Bitter, but one that faith may never miss. |
| 25 | Out of a grave I come to tell you this— |
| 26 | To tell you this. |
| 27 | |
| 28 | There is the western gate, Luke Havergal, |
| 29 | There are the crimson leaves upon the wall. |
| 30 | Go, for the winds are tearing them away,— |
| 31 | Nor think to riddle the dead words they say, |
| 32 | Nor any more to feel them as they fall; |
| 33 | But go, and if you trust her she will call. |
| 34 | There is the western gate, Luke Havergal— |
| 35 | Luke Havergal. |

## Student Response

### Analysis of "Luke Havergal"

1  Born in 1869, one of the greatest American poets of all time was Edwin Arlington Robinson. His life was full of
2  troubles, which had a huge influence on his life, poetry, and writings. **He was the first major American poet of the**
3  **twentieth century, dedicating his life solely to poetry, his wages being living with absolutely nothing.** One of
4  the best pieces of poetry that he wrote is "Luke Havergal." Although it is widely read and loved, it is the most
5  complicated and least understood of all his work.
6      "Luke Havergal" is in the form of an address from the speaker, whose identity is somewhat shaded, to Luke
7  himself. What is known is that Luke has lost a woman. By what means is not entirely clear, but several allusions
8  suggest that she committed suicide. The very first command given to Luke is to "Go to the western gate." The rest of
9  the poem presents a series of arguments, beseeching Luke through images, trying to convince him of the need for
10  him to commit suicide so that he can join his loved one and be with her in hell.
11      The western gate is a symbol of death. In the west the sun sets, ending the day, ending life. The speaker
12  commands Luke, "in the twilight wait for what will come," for, "No, there is not a dawn in the eastern skies." "The
13  dark will end the dark." Also by the western gate, dead leaves fall. "The leaves will whisper some—whisper of her,
14  and strike you as they fall."
15      In the next stanza Robinson writes, "God slays Himself with every leaf that flies." If God created, not only
16  the leaves, but also created Luke, in his very own image; how could God not be slain as his creation, with a piece of
17  the Creator in himself, turns his face from his God?
18      But yet again in the last stanza the speaker urges, "Go to the western gate, Luke Havergal, / There are the
19  crimson leaves upon the wall. / Go—for the winds are tearing them away— / Nor think to riddle the dead words
20  they say, / Nor anymore to feel them as they fall; / But go! And if you trust her she will call." Here the speaker tries
21  to hurry Luke by telling him the leaves are being torn away, longing for him to act before he might think of what he
22  was actually doing. Also appealed to, is his sense of loyalty to his woman because of the word "trust."
23      In this poem, Robinson uses two genius techniques to draw in the reader and increase the imagery. The first
24  of these is the rhythm of his stanzas. Each of the four stanzas has seven lines and an eighth line, which repeats the
25  end of the seventh line. The seventh line is also a repetition of the first line. This gives the poem a singular drive.
26
27      Go to the western gate, Luke Havergal—
28      Luke Havergal.
29      No, there is not a dawn in eastern skies—
30      In eastern skies.
31      Out of a grave I come to tell you this—
32      To tell you this.
33      There is the western gate, Luke Havergal—
34      Luke Havergal.
35
36      **The other technique used, is Robinson's delicate wash of red, which holds the poem together.** First it
37  is described in the vines: "There where the vines cling crimson on the wall." Next in Luke's eyes: "To rift the fiery
38  night in your eyes," "In the eastern skies," "The kiss that flames upon your forehead," and "The crimson leaves."
39  Last, although it is not mentioned in the actual poem, the red that holds all of these reds together is the suicidal red
40  of blood.
41      "Luke Havergal" is an incredible work. Wrapped up in imagery and verse, Robinson writes of a man caught in a
42  breathless crisis. As he wrote in another poem, "Give him the darkest inch your shelf allows, / Hide him in lonely
43  garrets, if you will,— / But his hard, human pulse is throbbing still / With the sure strength that fearless truth
44  endows." (Anna)

## Close Reading (Poem)

1. What literary device does Robinson employ in the first stanza?
   A. Assonance
   B. Onomatopoeia
   C. Metaphor
   D. Alliteration

2. The "western gate" represents
   A. A new beginning.
   B. Death.
   C. Broken promises.
   D. Hope eternal.

3. What is the tone of the poem?
   A. Tentative
   B. Sanguine
   C. Choleric
   D. Serious

4. The poet creates the tone by
   A. Images and language.
   B. Rhyme.
   C. Rhythm.
   D. Alliteration.

5. This poem is an example of
   A. Romanticism.
   B. Existentialism.
   C. Naturalism.
   D. Absurdism.

6. The author probably is
   A. An agnostic.
   B. An atheist.
   C. A fervent believer.
   D. A secularist.

7. One credible explanation of this poem might be
   A. Havergal is heading west.
   B. Havergal is committing suicide.
   C. Havergal is lost.
   D. Havergal is a gardener.

## Command of Evidence (Student Response)

1. A good summary would be
   A. Lines 2–3
   B. Lines 17–18
   C. Lines 27–30
   D. Lines 40–42

2. What is a favorite form of evidence used?
   A. Quotes from movies
   B. Literary devices
   C. Quotes from the poem
   D. Other poems

3. How does the Student Response develop its argument?
   A. It uses a quote from another literary work to illustrate the theme of the poem and then goes through the poem line by line.
   B. It summarizes the poem and then makes a relevant point at the end.
   C. It analyzes the speech, line by line.
   D. It states a thesis and then offers alternative interpretations.

4. An assumption that the Student Response makes?
   I. The poem was well-written.
   II. The poem was about death.
   III. The poet died young.

   A. I
   B. II
   C. III
   D. I and II

5. A weakness in the essay is the unsubstantiated generalizations it makes in
   A. Lines 4–5.
   B. Lines 10–12.
   C. Lines 24–25.
   D. Lines 38–39.

## Grammar and Usage

Choose the best grammar/usage form in bold sentence(s).

1.  Student Response, Lines 2–3
    A.  NONE
    B.  He was the first major 20th-century American poet, dedicating his life solely to poetry, and his wages being living with absolutely nothing.
    C.  Dedicating his life solely to poetry, the talented Robinson lived in poverty yet was the first major American poet of the twentieth century.
    D.  Dedicating his life solely to poetry, he was the first major American poet of the twentieth century, his wages being living with absolutely nothing.

2.  Student Response, Line 36
    A.  NONE
    B.  Robinson holds his poem together with a delicate wash of red.
    C.  The other technique used, is Robinson's delicate wash of red holding the poem together.
    D.  The other technique used, is Robinson's delicate wash of red.

# Lesson 2
## Critical Reading and Writing

### Command of Evidence

Read the following passages and answer accompanying questions:

### Passage 1

1 Samuel Johnson described metaphysical poets as "men of learning, and, to show their learning was their whole
2 endeavor." Puritan Edward Taylor (1642–1729) is not a metaphysical poet, but much of his poetry mirrors its
3 writing style. Taylor varied poetic devices and writing techniques inspired by the metaphysical poets, such as
4 Quixotic nature metaphors like "Spinning wheels, bowling balls, excrement and insects to give ingenious and often
5 grotesque expression to his intense emotions" (George McMichael et al., *Anthology of American Literature*, 9th, ed.,
6 1:109), as well as using personification. In "Huswifery," Taylor metaphorically characterizes housewives as a
7 "Loom" being used by God to weave the yarn of life, similar to Donne's method of personification in "Death Be Not
8 Proud," in which he degrades and diminishes the power of death, as though it were a meek, inconsequential
9 doorway. The metaphysical poets, such as the revered John Donne or Andrew Marvell, influenced Taylor through
10 the use of farfetched conceits, hyperbole, and detailed nature and animal imagery, though they differed in their
11 approach to God; Taylor's relationship was personal and infinite, while metaphysical poets largely remained distant
12 from God, relying on their God-given intellect instead.
13     The eminent metaphysical poet John Donne (1572–1631) revealed bold imagery, imaginative plots,
14 abstract conceits, hyperbole, and specific descriptions of nature in his writing. In Donne's early, preconversion
15 seduction poem "The Flea," similar to Andrew Marvell's "To his Coy Mistress," the speaker is a playful courtier
16 trying to woo a virginal, modest lady of the court. He audaciously makes the absurd assertion that because a flea has
17 bitten both of them, and their blood has intermingled within its insect body, surely they must already have made a
18 physical connection, and she is "ruined" from the commingling, and therefore they must be wed. In line 3 the
19 speaker claims, "It sucked me first, and now sucks thee, / And in this flea our two bloods mingled be" (Donne),
20 trying to convince the lady through scientific terms that they are bound together in inevitable love. The poet
21 demonstrates his position as a man of learning of the natural world and also with his skill for detailed, unusual
22 metaphors. Donne's ham-handed speaker uses a hyperbolic command when he entreats the lady not to murder the
23 flea in line 10: "Oh stay, three lives in one flea spare; / Where we almost, nay more than married are" (Donne),
24 stretching the societal assumption that because their blood has mixed inside this bug, the interior of the insect is now
25 a holy vessel containing three God-blessed lives: the flea's, his own, and the lady's. Inside an invertebrate wedding
26 chamber they lie and consecrate a marriage bed surrounded by "walls of jet," which disturbingly are the inner lining
27 of the flea, which the reader would envision as an engorged tick, symbolizing pregnancy. Donne's speaker portrays
28 a wishful picture of their hypothetical union in order to goad his audience—the virgin—to accept his love, which
29 ironically drives her to the enraged, "cruel and sudden" killing of the bug. The histrionic courtier purports that
30 because her impetuous crime of triple "murder" is such a heinous sin, she should give up morals and sacrifice her
31 virginity, or else be a hypocrite.
32     Edward Taylor similarly bends his reader's imagination, but where he differs is the presence and role he
33 ascribes to God. Taylor was a Puritan devoted to the Protestant cause, whereas Donne's preconversion writing had a
34 deistic view, believing that God set the world on its course and let it go, not intervening, so Donne fulfills God's
35 purpose through the honing of his intellect. Ironically, the protagonist in his poem uses his intellect in a devilish
36 pursuit, twisting facts, drawing preposterous conclusions, and using his prey's religious superstitions against her
37 own mind. While Taylor used many similar conceits and imagery, his poems were more Christian and didactic.
38     Edward Taylor came to America in 1668 after religious persecution in England: the state-controlled
39 Anglican Church oppressed his dissenting Puritan convictions and forced him out of teaching. In New England he
40 spent three years at Harvard College, where "[his life] was busy and rigorous with recitations, disputations, and
41 lectures carried on in Latin; with studies in Greek, Hebrew, logic, metaphysics, rhetoric, and astronomy; and with
42 daily morning and evening prayers" (Poetry Foundation). Taylor displays his acuity for science and religious
43 devotion in his works, like "Upon a Spider Catching a Fly," in which he scientifically describes nuances of a
44 spider's predatory maneuvers based on empirical observations to compare how a spider catches his prey to how
45 Satan tempts and seduces sinners. Taylor writes, "I saw a pettish wasp / Fall foule therein: / Whom yet thy Whorle

46 pins did not clasp / Lest he should fling / His sting (Lines 6–10). The spider is leery of an insect capable of
47 defending itself—metaphorically illustrating Satan's difficulty in subduing one who is armed with the power of
48 God. Taylor then contrasts his findings of how a spider treats a wasp with the alternative, a fly, which is symbolic of
49 the enfeebled, defenseless state of man without God. Mockingly, the speaker says, "Whereas the silly Fly, / Caught
50 by its leg / Thou by the throate tookst hastily / And 'hinde the head / Bite Dead" (Lines 21–25). Taylor likens
51 humanity to the fly and the spider to Satan, proclaiming in lines 41–45, "But mighty, Gracious Lord / Communicate
52 / Thy Grace to breake the Corde, afford / Us Glories Gate / And State." Taylor calls out to God to "breake the
53 Corde" that holds us in sinful bondage leading to death, unequivocally invoking the power of God to redeem man, as
54 opposed to Donne's early worldview, in which a distant God does not intervene or interact with people.
55      **Taylor emulated the metaphysical poets, using literary devices such as complex or unusual conceits,**
56 **hyperbole, and close observations of nature, but he differed in regard to the role of God's involvement in the**
57 **world, and he reflects this in his writing**. As a clergyman, Taylor feared that some of his writings were too sensual
58 to publish in his lifetime—only a couple short stanzas were printed before his death in 1729. A secret rebel from the
59 square, stodgy, preacher stereotype, he was expressive, artistic, and drew from the sophisticated writing techniques,
60 poetic devices, and liberality of metaphysical poets using the same extent of nature imagery, though the conceits he
61 crafted are more decidedly ones to instruct, explore, and perpetuate the Christian faith.

## Close Reading

1. What would be the best title for this essay?
   A. Men of God
   B. Taylor, Donne, and Marvell: Metaphysical Poets
   C. John Donne: The Renegade
   D. Edward Taylor and Metaphysical Poets

2. How did the essay begin?
   A. A differentiation of Taylor from other Metaphysical Poets
   B. A denunciation of Metaphysical Poetry
   C. A discussion of slavery
   D. An analysis of Edward Taylor's poetry

3. What organizational plan does the author employ?
   A. A series of anecdotes thoroughly explained
   B. A contrast of 17th-and 18th-century British poets
   C. A contrast of Taylor and other Metaphysical poets, with substantial textual differences included
   D. A vindication of the poetry of Marvell and Donne

4. The thesis of this essay?
   A. Taylor's poetry is similar in worldview but different in style from other Metaphysical Poets.
   B. Taylor's poetry is similar in style but different in worldview from other Metaphysical Poets.
   C. Taylor's influence on Puritanism is unlike anything that happened in British history.
   D. Taylor hated women, and his poetry showed it.

5. The author finishes his essay with
   A. A summary statement.                    C. A distracting comment.
   B. A new conclusion.                       D. The way he began.

6. It is fair to conclude that the author
   A. Is an atheist.
   B. Does not like Baptists.
   C. Is a homeschooler.
   D. Favors the Judeo Christian view of the world.

## Passage 2

World War I had important consequences for African-Americans, Women, and Labor. For African Americans, a new sense of pride emerged as evidenced by the Harlem Renaissance. Women saw new empowerment manifested in gaining the right to vote in 1920 and more females entering the workforce. Labor in this era ballooned with the new urban industries and compulsory labor laws to support the war effort. These developments permanently affected each, with African Americans forming the foundation that allowed them to ascend the social ladder and assert themselves during the civil rights movement in the 1960s, the feminist movement growing and gaining influence, and the country's economic muscle shifting to primarily reside within the urban sphere.

Following World War I, African Americans felt entitled to equal rights, and rightfully so, after their involvement and sacrifice in the conflict. The military operated in segregated units, and while white soldiers did receive undue disdain after the messy conflict, upon returning home African American soldiers received even less recognition for their efforts despite having undergone the same experiences. This contributed to a new cultural and intellectual movement: the Harlem Renaissance formed the intellectual backbone for the civil rights movement, which would come about in the 1960s. An important writer in the Harlem Renaissance was poet Langston Hughes, who in his work, "I Too, Sing America," describes the injustices of prejudice still present in American culture: "I am the darker brother. / They send me to eat in the kitchen / When company comes. . . . Tomorrow, / I'll be at the table / When company comes. . . . They'll see how beautiful I am / And be ashamed"—thereby foreshadowing the reform of the 1960s. In his poem, Hughes demonstrates not only the rising force of African American intellectualism, but also the justness of their push to equality. The role of African Americans in World War II would push civil rights leaders to boldly actualize Hughes's vision of equality.

**During the war, women throughout America increasingly contributed toward the war effort in roles that earlier were typically occupied almost exclusively by men, giving the female populace newfound self-recognition and desire for legal equality.** "The First World War created many new job opportunities for women. . . . Women were encouraged to enter industry and also agriculture, . . . spurred on by the slogan 'Labor Will Win the War'" (Bailey and Kennedy, *The American Pageant*, 727), creating an environment where no matter how strong the traditional patriarchy, intellectual honesty could not disallow women the same rights after functioning in the same capacity as men, and contributing significantly to the war effort. Realizing this, President Woodrow Wilson declared woman suffrage "a vitally necessary war measure" (*Pageant*, 727). In clear and undeniable triumph, women therefore gained the right to vote with the Nineteenth Amendment in 1920, having received the final thrust of World War I adding to nearly a century of struggle for women's rights.

While drawing women into the work place more and more, World War I also required more of men. A global war of this scale had never been known, and in 1918 the United States government issued a "'work or fight' rule, requiring all able-bodied males to be regularly employed in some useful occupation" (*Pageant*, 727). Although wages increased, so did inflation. Due to this compulsory labor law, "during the conflict there were some six thousand strikes" (728). (Zach)

## Close Reading

1. What would be the best title of this essay?
   A. World War I
   B. The Futility of Class Rank
   C. The Effect of World War I on African Americans, Women, and Labor
   D. American Minorities

2. What organizational plan does the author employ?
   A. He discusses World War I.
   B. He celebrates the end of World War I.
   C. He hints at how African Americans, women, and labor were affected by World War I and offers examples.
   D. He laments the adverse effect of racism on African Americans.

3. The author finishes his essay with
   A. A summary statement.                     C. A distracting comment on labor.
   B. A new conclusion.                         D. A final criticism of Germany.

## Grammar and Usage

Choose the best grammar/usage form in bold sentence(s).

1. Passage 1, Lines 54–56

    A. NONE
    B. Differing in regard to the role of God's involvement in the world and reflects this in his writing, nonetheless, Taylor emulated the metaphysical poets using literary devices such as complex or unusual conceits, hyperbole, and close observations of nature.
    C. While Edward Taylor differed from other Metaphysical Poets in the way he felt toward God, nonetheless Taylor emulated the metaphysical poets with literary devices such as complex or unusual conceits, hyperbole, and close nature observations.
    D. Taylor emulated the metaphysical poets with literary devices such as complex or unusual conceits, hyperbole, and close observations of nature, but differed in regard to the role of God's involvement in the world and reflects this in his writing.

2. Passage 2, Lines 20–22

    A. NONE
    B. During the war, American women increasingly contributed toward the war effort in roles that in the past were typically occupied almost exclusively by men, giving the female populace newfound self-recognition and desire for legal equality.
    C. During the war, women throughout America increasingly contributed toward the war effort in roles that were typically occupied almost exclusively by men, giving the female populace newfound self-recognition and desire for legal equality.
    D. During the war, assuming roles heretofore reserved for men, American women gained new confidence and desires for more legal rights.

# Lesson 3
## SAT Essay

### Student Essay 1

*Prompt:* Do you think that ease does not challenge us and that we need adversity to help us discover who we are?

1 "I seed de beginin and de end," says Dilsey in *The Sound and the Fury*, a novel on the fall of the United States
2 South. She perseveres through these trials, and adversity makes her stronger. Trials are what define us. There are
3 two examples that come to mind: My first debate, and Jane Eyre's life.
4 **In my first debate, my body became sweaty, and my hand shook terribly; I could feel all the eyes of**
5 **my classmates and their parents upon me.** I did terribly, and this terrible experience is unpleasant to think about.
6 However, since I persevered, I was able to do excellently in several debates after that. I am now planning to
7 participate in tournaments. If I had never stood with my sweaty forehead and clammy hands, I would never have
8 discovered the great fun and benefits that debate brings.
9 Jane Eyre grew up as a neglected, abused child. She was forced to live with her cruel aunt after the death of
10 both her parents. Her malicious cousin often hit her, with no repercussions from his parents to control him. Poor
11 Jane was then sent to a terrible school, where children were given very little to eat. Sadly, her best friend died from
12 lack of proper care. Jane, however, emerged as a phoenix does from fire: Stronger and more beautiful on the inside.
13 The examples of my disastrous speech and Jane Eyre's mistreatment show that trials and adversity help us
14 to discover who we are. It is amidst the flames that we realize our phoenix qualities. As a phoenix, we can emerge
15 stronger. (Christy)

### Close Reading

1. What is the purpose of the quote from *Sound and the Fury*?
   A. An illustration of the importance of failure
   B. A summary statement of persevering through adversity to the end
   C. There is no real purpose.
   D. A celebration of adversity

2. Two illustrations include
   A. A William Faulkner character and Jane Eyre.
   B. A southern family and a debate competition failure.
   C. Jane Eyre and Dilsey.
   D. A debate competition failure and Jane Eyre.

3. Which of the following strategies does the essay employ?
   A. A statement of purpose with two examples
   B. A couple of anecdotes
   C. A contradictory position and then the true argument
   D. Three rhetorical questions

4. The essay finishes with
   A. A summary statement.
   B. A rhetorical question.
   C. An image of a mythological creature emerging from fire.
   D. A tangential excursion.

5. Where is the best example of a stylistic or persuasive element, such as word choice or appeals to emotion, to add power to the ideas expressed?
   A. Lines 2–3
   B. Lines 9–10
   C. Lines 11–12
   D. Lines 14–15

6. What score would this essay receive? __

## Student Essay 2

*Prompt:* Is a strong moral character the most important qualification for a leader? Plan and write an essay in which you develop your point of view on this issue. Support you position with reasoning and examples taken from your reading, studies, experience, or observations.

1  Morality, the foundation of a successful society, remains the most important qualification of a leader.
2  While many individuals imagine a "moral" leader as a ruthless, stubborn, stoic character such as Javier, in *Les*
3  *Misérables*, or Frodo, a church leader in *The Hunchback of Notre Dame*, a true moral leader respects human life and
4  defends it. A man who defends the helpless presents himself as a greater leader than he who fights brilliant battles,
5  gives gifts to the people, but does not truly care for their welfare.
6  Respect for human life is perhaps one of the most important values that makes a moral leader superior to a
7  superficial one. In *Les Misérables*, Jean Valjean displayed a sense of morality in his respect for the lives of his
8  fellow countrymen, regardless of their social status. He involved himself in their affairs and attempted to improve
9  their lives if possible. At one point in the novel, he helped a prostitute by promising her, on her deathbed, to care for
10 her child as his own. His dedication to aiding the lowliest citizens revealed him to be a great leader—a moral one.
11 Similarly, the Count of Monte Cristo displayed a sense of, sometimes, harsh morality in his role as a
12 wealthy patron of the city. **Although he was not an actual leader, he used his elevated status to bless those who**
13 **aided his father before his imprisonment and to punish those who used the misery of others to become**
14 **wealthy.** Though his judgment was slightly harsh, his morality drove him to display goodness to those in need.
15 Napoleon and Alexander the Great, although mighty leaders, did not achieve true greatness because they
16 lacked a sense of true morality. A real leader is not one who dresses finely and speaks well, but one who loves the
17 lowliest. A man of compassion, a man of honor. (Sophia)

1.  How is the essay structured?
    A. A rhetorical question is advanced, answered.
    B. A thesis and then illustrations to support the thesis are given.
    C. A series of anecdotes support a thesis presented at the end.
    D. A spurious argument is advanced and then refuted.

2.  The following are examples of the thesis:
    I.   John Valjean
    II.  Mother Teresa
    III. Count of Monte Cristo
    IV.  Napoleon

    A. I
    B. II and IV
    C. I, II, and III
    D. I and III

3.  What organizational strategy does the essay employ?
    A. The introduction with a thesis and several examples.
    B. A contradictory theory is introduced and then destroyed.
    C. Anecdotal selections from three novels are developed.
    D. A summary of the lives of Napoleon and Alexander the Great.

4.  What is a major flaw in this essay?
    A. Spelling errors.
    B. Poor transitions.
    C. Undeveloped thought.
    D. Undeveloped examples are given in the introduction.

5.  What score would this essay receive? __ .

# Grammar and Usage

Choose the best grammar/usage form in bold sentence(s).

1. Student Essay 1, Lines 4–5
   A. NONE
   B. During my first debate, with the eyes of my classmates and their parents peering at me, my body sweated and my hands shook.
   C. In my first debate, my body sweat, and my hands shook, I could feel all the eyes of my classmates and their parents upon me.
   D. In my first debate, with my body shaking and sweating, I could feel all the eyes of my classmates and their parents upon me.

2. Student Essay 2, Lines 12–13
   A. NONE
   B. Although he was not a leader, he used his elevated status to bless those who aided his father before his imprisonment and punish those who used the misery of others to become wealthy.
   C. He used his elevated status to bless those who aided his father before his imprisonment and punish those who used the misery of others to become wealthy.
   D. His leadership was questionable because he used his elevated status to bless those who aided his father and punish those who used the misfortune of others to become wealthy.

# Lesson 4
## Reading: Document-Based Analysis

### Federalist Paper No. 67 (March 11, 1788)

1     To the People of the State of New York:

2     THE constitution of the executive department of the proposed government, claims next our attention. There is hardly
3     any part of the system which could have been attended with greater difficulty in the arrangement of it than this; and
4     there is, perhaps, none which has been inveighed against with less candor or criticized with less judgment. Here the
5     writers against the Constitution seem to have taken pains to signalize their talent of misrepresentation. Calculating
6     upon the aversion of the people to monarchy, they have endeavored to enlist all their jealousies and apprehensions in
7     opposition to the intended President of the United States; not merely as the embryo, but as the full-grown progeny,
8     of that detested parent. To establish the pretended affinity, they have not scrupled to draw resources even from the
9     regions of fiction. The authorities of a magistrate, in few instances greater, in some instances less, than those of a
10     governor of New York, have been magnified into more than royal prerogatives. He has been decorated with
11     attributes superior in dignity and splendor to those of a king of Great Britain. He has been shown to us with the
12     diadem sparkling on his brow and the imperial purple flowing in his train. He has been seated on a throne
13     surrounded with minions and mistresses, giving audience to the envoys of foreign potentates, in all the supercilious
14     pomp of majesty. The images of Asiatic despotism and voluptuousness have scarcely been wanting to crown the
15     exaggerated scene. We have been taught to tremble at the terrific visages of murdering janizaries, and to blush at the
16     unveiled mysteries of a future seraglio.
17         Attempts so extravagant as these to disfigure or, it might rather be said, to metamorphose the object, render
18     it necessary to take an accurate view of its real nature and form: in order as well to ascertain its true aspect and
19     genuine appearance, as to unmask the disingenuity and expose the fallacy of the counterfeit resemblances which
20     have been so insidiously, as well as industriously, propagated.
21         In the execution of this task, there is no man who would not find it an arduous effort either to behold with
22     moderation, or to treat with seriousness, the devices, not less weak than wicked, which have been contrived to
23     pervert the public opinion in relation to the subject. They so far exceed the usual though unjustifiable licenses of
24     party artifice, that even in a disposition the most candid and tolerant, they must force the sentiments which favor an
25     indulgent construction of the conduct of political adversaries to give place to a voluntary and unreserved
26     indignation. It is impossible not to bestow the imputation of deliberate imposture and deception upon the gross
27     pretense of a similitude between a king of Great Britain and a magistrate of the character marked out for that of the
28     President of the United States. It is still more impossible to withhold that imputation from the rash and barefaced
29     expedients which have been employed to give success to the attempted imposition.
30         In one instance, which I cite as a sample of the general spirit, the temerity has proceeded so far as to ascribe
31     to the President of the United States a power which by the instrument reported is EXPRESSLY allotted to the
32     Executives of the individual States. I mean the power of filling casual vacancies in the Senate.
33         This bold experiment upon the discernment of his countrymen has been hazarded by a writer who
34     (whatever may be his real merit) has had no inconsiderable share in the applauses of his party; and who, upon this
35     false and unfounded suggestion, has built a series of observations equally false and unfounded. Let him now be
36     confronted with the evidence of the fact, and let him, if he be able, justify or extenuate the shameful outrage he has
37     offered to the dictates of truth and to the rules of fair dealing.
38         The second clause of the second section of the second article empowers the President of the United States
39     "to nominate, and by and with the advice and consent of the Senate, to appoint ambassadors, other public ministers
40     and consuls, judges of the Supreme Court, and all other OFFICERS of United States whose appointments are NOT
41     in the Constitution OTHERWISE PROVIDED FOR, and WHICH SHALL BE ESTABLISHED BY LAW."
42     Immediately after this clause follows another in these words: "The President shall have power to fill up ??
43     VACANCIES that may happen DURING THE RECESS OF THE SENATE, by granting commissions which shall
44     EXPIRE AT THE END OF THEIR NEXT SESSION." It is from this last provision that the pretended power of the
45     President to fill vacancies in the Senate has been deduced. A slight attention to the connection of the clauses, and to
46     the obvious meaning of the terms, will satisfy us that the deduction is not even colorable.

47     The first of these two clauses, it is clear, only provides a mode for appointing such officers, "whose
48 appointments are NOT OTHERWISE PROVIDED FOR in the Constitution, and which SHALL BE
49 ESTABLISHED BY LAW"; of course it cannot extend to the appointments of senators, whose appointments are
50 OTHERWISE PROVIDED FOR in the Constitution, and who are ESTABLISHED BY THE CONSTITUTION, and
51 will not require a future establishment by law. This position will hardly be contested.
52     The last of these two clauses, it is equally clear, cannot be understood to comprehend the power of filling
53 vacancies in the Senate, for the following reasons: First. The relation in which that clause stands to the other, which
54 declares the general mode of appointing officers of the United States, denotes it to be nothing more than a
55 supplement to the other, for the purpose of establishing an auxiliary method of appointment, in cases to which the
56 general method was inadequate. The ordinary power of appointment is confined to the President and Senate
57 JOINTLY, and can therefore only be exercised during the session of the Senate; but as it would have been improper
58 to oblige this body to be continually in session for the appointment of officers and as vacancies might happen IN
59 THEIR RECESS, which it might be necessary for the public service to fill without delay, the succeeding clause is
60 evidently intended to authorize the President, SINGLY, to make temporary appointments "during the recess of the
61 Senate, by granting commissions which shall expire at the end of their next session." Secondly. If this clause is to be
62 considered as supplementary to the one which precedes, the VACANCIES of which it speaks must be construed to
63 relate to the "officers" described in the preceding one; and this, we have seen, excludes from its description the
64 members of the Senate. Thirdly. The time within which the power is to operate, "during the recess of the Senate,"
65 and the duration of the appointments, "to the end of the next session" of that body, conspire to elucidate the sense of
66 the provision, which, if it had been intended to comprehend senators, would naturally have referred the temporary
67 power of filling vacancies to the recess of the State legislatures, who are to make the permanent appointments, and
68 not to the recess of the national Senate, who are to have no concern in those appointments; and would have extended
69 the duration in office of the temporary senators to the next session of the legislature of the State, in whose
70 representation the vacancies had happened, instead of making it to expire at the end of the ensuing session of the
71 national Senate. The circumstances of the body authorized to make the permanent appointments would, of course,
72 have governed the modification of a power which related to the temporary appointments; and as the national Senate
73 is the body, whose situation is alone contemplated in the clause upon which the suggestion under examination has
74 been founded, the vacancies to which it alludes can only be deemed to respect those officers in whose appointment
75 that body has a concurrent agency with the President. But lastly, the first and second clauses of the third section of
76 the first article, not only obviate all possibility of doubt, but destroy the pretext of misconception. The former
77 provides, that "the Senate of the United States shall be composed of two Senators from each State, chosen BY THE
78 LEGISLATURE THEREOF for six years"; and the latter directs, that, "if vacancies in that body should happen by
79 resignation or otherwise, DURING THE RECESS OF THE LEGISLATURE OF ANY STATE, the Executive
80 THEREOF may make temporary appointments until the NEXT MEETING OF THE LEGISLATURE, which shall
81 then fill such vacancies." Here is an express power given, in clear and unambiguous terms, to the State Executives,
82 to fill casual vacancies in the Senate, by temporary appointments; which not only invalidates the supposition, that
83 the clause before considered could have been intended to confer that power upon the President of the United States,
84 but proves that this supposition, destitute as it is even of the merit of plausibility, must have originated in an
85 intention to deceive the people, too palpable to be obscured by sophistry, too atrocious to be palliated by hypocrisy.
86     I have taken the pains to select this instance of misrepresentation, and to place it in a clear and strong light,
87 as an unequivocal proof of the unwarrantable arts which are practiced to prevent a fair and impartial judgment of the
88 real merits of the Constitution submitted to the consideration of the people. Nor have I scrupled, in so flagrant a
89 case, to allow myself a severity of animadversion little congenial with the general spirit of these papers. I hesitate
90 not to submit it to the decision of any candid and honest adversary of the proposed government, whether language
91 can furnish epithets of too much asperity, for so shameless and so prostitute an attempt to impose on the citizens of
92 America.
93     PUBLIUS [Alexander Hamilton].                (http://www.foundingfathers.info/federalistpapers/)

## Anti-Federalist Paper No. 1 (November 26, 1787)

1 I am pleased to see a spirit of inquiry burst the band of constraint upon the subject of the NEW PLAN for
2 consolidating the governments of the United States, as recommended by the late Convention. If it is suitable to the
3 GENIUS and HABITS of the citizens of these states, it will bear the strictest scrutiny. The PEOPLE are the grand
4 inquest who have a RIGHT to judge of its merits.
5     The hideous daemon of Aristocracy has hitherto had so much influence as to bar the channels of
6 investigation, preclude the people from inquiry and extinguish every spark of liberal information of its qualities. At
7 length the luminary of intelligence begins to beam its effulgent rays upon this important production; the deceptive

8    mists cast before the eyes of the people by the delusive machinations of its INTERESTED advocates begins to
9    dissipate, as darkness flies before the burning taper; and I dare venture to predict, that in spite of those mercenary
10   dectaimers, the plan will have a candid and complete examination.

11        Those furious zealots who are for cramming it down the throats of the people, without allowing them either
12   time or opportunity to scan or weigh it in the balance of their understandings, bear the same marks in their features
13   as those who have been long wishing to erect an aristocracy in THIS COMMONWEALTH [of Massachusetts].
14   Their menacing cry is for a RIGID government, it matters little to them of what kind, provided it answers THAT
15   description. As the plan now offered comes something near their wishes, and is the most consonant to their views of
16   any they can hope for, they come boldly forward and DEMAND its adoption.

17        They brand with infamy every man who is not as determined and zealous in its favor as themselves. They
18   cry aloud the whole must be swallowed or NONE at all, thinking thereby to preclude any amendment; they are
19   afraid of having it abated of its present RIGID aspect. They have strived to overawe or seduce printers to stifle and
20   obstruct a free discussion, and have endeavored to hasten it to a decision before the people can duly reflect upon its
21   properties. In order to deceive them, they incessantly declare that NONE can discover any defect in the system but
22   bankrupts who wish no government, and officers of the present government who fear to lose a part of their power.
23   These zealous partisans may injure their own cause, and endanger the public tranquility by impeding a proper
24   inquiry; the people may suspect the WHOLE to be a dangerous plan, from such COVERED and DESIGNING
25   schemes to enforce it upon them.

26        Compulsive or treacherous measures to establish any government whatever, will always excite jealousy
27   among a free people: better remain single and alone, than blindly adopt whatever a few individuals shall demand, be
28   they ever so wise. I had rather be a free citizen of the small republic of Massachusetts, than an oppressed subject of
29   the great American empire. Let all act understandingly or not at all. If we can confederate upon terms that wilt
30   secure to us our liberties, it is an object highly desirable, because of its additional security to the whole. If the
31   proposed plan proves such an one, I hope it will be adopted, but if it will endanger our liberties as it stands, let it be
32   amended; in order to which it must and ought to be open to inspection and free inquiry.

33        The inundation of abuse that has been thrown out upon the heads of those who have had any doubts of its
34   universal good qualities, have been so redundant, that it may not be improper to scan the characters of its most
35   strenuous advocates. It will first be allowed that many undesigning citizens may wish its adoption from the best
36   motives, but these are modest and silent, when compared to the greater number, who endeavor to suppress all
37   attempts for investigation. These violent partisans are for having the people gulp down the gilded pill blindfolded,
38   whole, and without any qualification whatever.

39        These consist generally, of the NOBLE order of C[incinnatu]s, holders of public securities, men of great
40   wealth and expectations of public office, Bankers and Lawyers: these with their train of dependents form the
41   Aristocratick combination. The Lawyers in particular, keep up an incessant declamation for its adoption; like greedy
42   gudgeons they long to satiate their voracious stomachs with the golden bait. The numerous tribunals to be erected by
43   the new plan of consolidated empire, will find employment for ten times their present numbers; these are the
44   LOAVES AND FISHES for which they hunger. They will probably find it suited to THEIR HABITS, if not to the
45   HABITS OF THE PEOPLE. There may be reasons for having but few of them in the State Convention, lest THEIR
46   OWN INTEREST should be too strongly considered. The time draws near for the choice of Delegates. I hope my
47   fellow-citizens will look well to the characters of their preference, and remember the Old Patriots of 75; they have
48   never led them astray, nor need they fear to try them on this momentous occasion.
49
50   A Federalist

          (http://www.thefederalistpapers.org/anti-federalist-papers/antifederalist-paper)

## Close Reading

   1.   Passages 1 and 2 share what?
       A. Both argue that a strong executive branch is necessary.
       B. Both attack the motivation of their opponents.
       C. Both agree that slavery is a knotty issue.
       D. Neither group wishes to have an allowance with England.

2.  Inflammatory lines include what lines?
    I.    Passage 1, Lines 17–20
    II.   Passage 2, Lines 11–16
    III.  Passage 1, Lines 81–85

    A. I                    C. I and III
    B. II                   D. All

3.  How do the passages develop their arguments?
    A. Each passage systematically refutes its opponent's arguments.
    B. Each passage makes an argument and offers supporting anecdotes.
    C. Each passage asks a rhetorical question.
    D. Each passage restates the problem in a new way.

## Words in Context

### Passage 1

1.  What is the meaning of *inveighed* in Line 4?
    A.  Implied              C.  Fulminated
    B.  Denied              D.  Chosen

2.  What is the meaning of *aversion* in Line 6?
    A.  Dislike             C.  Admire
    B.  Disgust            D.  Fortify

3.  What is the meaning of *potentates* in Line 13?
    A.  Followers          C.  Emperors
    B.  Rascals           D.  Senators

4.  What is the meaning of *imputation* in Line 26?
    A.  Plea               C.  Acquittal
    B.  Adjudication      D.  Accusation

5.  What is the meaning of *sophistry* in Line 84?
    A.  Impurity          C.  Fortune
    B.  Fallaciousness   D.  Undesirability

6.  What is the meaning of *palliated* in Line 85?
    A.  Alleviate         C.  Increase
    B.  Diminish         D.  Militate

### Passage 2

1.  What is the meaning of *luminary* in Line 7?
    A.  Rogue             C.  Celebrity
    B.  Rascal           D.  Denizen

2.  What is the meaning of *satiate* in Line 42?
    A.  Retard            C.  Assuage
    B.  Stimulate        D.  Remove

3.  What is the meaning of *voracious* in Line 42?
    A.  Greedy            C.  Improper
    B.  Inconsolable     D.  Rapacious

# Lesson 5

## Math: Algebra, Arithmetic Problem Solving and Data Analysis, and Passport to Advanced Math

### Passport to Advanced Math

What is true about these two lines?

I. Through a given point an indefinite number of lines can be drawn in a plane.
II. Neither one will cut a given line in the plane.
III. The lines shall continue, right and left, into infinity.
IV. The two lines will intersect again at some point.

A. I and II                   C. I, II, and III              E. All
B. II and IV                  D. IV

### Arithmetic Problem Solving

1. Three persons, A, B, and C, invest $47,000 in business. B puts in $500 more than twice as much as A, and C puts in three times as much as B. How many dollars does each put into the business?
   A.  A. $5000; B, $10,500; C. $31,500        C.  A. $2500; B. $500; C. $30,500
   B.  A. $3500; B. $7000; C. $28,500          D.  A. $5000; B. $15,000; C. $35,000

2. In three lots of land there are 80,750 square feet. The second lot contains 250 square feet more than three times as much as the first lot, and the third lot contains twice as much as the second. What is the size of each lot in square feet?
   A.  6,000; 12,125; 32,500                   C.  4,000; 18,250; 48,500
   B.  8,000; 24,250; 48,500                   D.  12,000; 32,250; 56,500

3. By his will a man leaves $225,000 to be divided as follows: his son to receive $10,000 less than twice as much as the daughter, and the widow four times as much as the son. What was the share of each?
   A.  Daughter, $15,000; son, $30,000; widow, $150,000
   B.  Daughter, $35,000; son, $50,000; widow, $200,000
   C.  Daughter, $25,000; son, $50,000; widow, $170,000
   D.  Daughter, $25,000; son, $40,000; widow, $160,000

4. A man and his two sons picked 25 quarts of berries. The older son picked 5 quarts less than three times as many as the younger son, and the father picked twice as many as the older son. How many quarts did each pick?
   A.  Father, 12 qts.; older son, 6 qts.; younger son, 4 qts.
   B.  Father, 14 qts.; older son, 7 qts.; younger son, 4 qts.
   C.  Father, 16 qts.; older son, 8 qts.; younger son, 2 qts.
   D.  Father, 15 qts.; older son, 5 qts.; younger son, 5 qts.

# Chapter 18    Walk by Faith
# Philippians 3:4–14

> *Memory Verses:* But whatever were gains to me I now consider loss for the sake of Christ. What is more, I consider everything a loss because of the surpassing worth of knowing Christ Jesus my Lord, for whose sake I have lost all things. I consider them garbage, that I may gain Christ and be found in him, not having a righteousness of my own that comes from the law, but that which is through faith in Christ—the righteousness that comes from God on the basis of faith. I want to know Christ—yes, to know the power of his resurrection and participation in his sufferings, becoming like him in his death, and so, somehow, attaining to the resurrection from the dead. —Philippians 3:7–11

One of my favorite books is *War and Peace*, by Leo Tolstoy. I like it so much because it celebrates the triumph of love and goodness.

Pierre, "shy, observant and natural looking," was distinguished by no particular gift of intelligence, good looks, or moral courage. And, while his physical appearance never changed, his character did. And he became a hero of epic proportions. He selfishly put himself in harm's way numerous times and eventually married the beautiful and equally heroic Natasha. Somehow the love between Natasha and Pierre mitigated all the horrible pain that the Napoleonic invasion of Russia had wrought on their generation.

Everything—face, gait, eyes, voice—everything was at once transformed in her. To her own surprise, the force of life and hopes of happiness floated to the surface and demanded satisfaction. From that first evening Natasha seemed to have forgotten all that had happened to her. From that time she never once complained of her position; she said not one word about the past, and was not afraid of already making lighthearted plans for the future (Edmund Fuller's version, 503).

Natasha and Pierre looked back on their past, noted its impact, and then went boldly into the future.

Likewise, while in prison, Paul is assessing all the reasons he has to boast: great education, privileged birth, and advantageous citizenship (but not good looks! 2 Corinthians 10:10). Yet he decides it is all meaningless when compared to the value that salvation has brought to his life. It is difficult to communicate to persons with present-day understandings that establishing a relationship with Jesus Christ is the most important thing that can happen to them in their lives. The empirical mind-set of many twentieth-century people looks for facts that can be measured, seen, and touched.

Cynics or skeptics, when considering such a proposition, may ask, "How can you have a relationship with Someone who is dead and gone?" (Or if they have enough faith to believe in the resurrection, "Someone who is gone?") Others may query, "Wealth is power and influence in today's world, so how can the mystical idea of a Savior be more important than the security of money, possessions, and power?"

In this time of some danger, Paul is undertaking a time-honored existential journey into serious reflection upon what is ultimately important in the faith journey. He is offering one understanding of the way that Christ and culture impact one another. The great theologian Reinhold Niebuhr has suggested categories for understanding the relationship of Christianity and culture:

- Christ against culture
- Christ and culture
- Christ of culture
- Christ—the transformer of culture

Paul is speaking of ultimate things, what really matters. What are the abiding qualities of biblical Christianity that transcend time, place, and culture? And this is a critical question for Paul's community, which is undergoing persecution and other threats, and ourselves, who are constantly fighting against assimilation and compromise with the world. Collapsing culture can only be rebuilt on the framework of biblical Christianity. This is my personal premise and the heart of New Evangelicalism.

Nothing I am or have compares with knowing Christ. Wow! Do you see how incredibly threatening this statement is? If Paul really means it, his jailers, his accusers, and his world have no control over him. Only God does. And Paul is privileged to live under the wing of Romans 8: nothing can separate us from the love of Christ Jesus. This knowledge takes Paul to where he wants to go: to a new understanding of his value as a person to God and to others.

Paul understands that theology cannot be reduced to the sociology of knowledge. We can use the sociology of knowledge as a critical tool for helping us understand truth. But biblical truth is always transcendent.

Consider these two truths that Paul presents: First, *we are saved only by grace*. We can say that with our lips and write that in our doctrine, but are we living as if we believe it? Read again what Paul says in today's text: "I regard *everything as loss* because of the surpassing value of knowing Christ Jesus my Lord. For his sake I have suffered the loss of all things, and I regard them as rubbish, in order that I may gain Christ and be found in him, not having a righteousness of my own that comes from the law, but one that comes through faith in Christ, *the righteousness from God based on faith*" (Philippians 3:8–9 NRSV, emphasis added).

We are not saved by the church we attend, the money we tithe, or the persons we have invited to worship. We are saved only by grace through faith in Christ!

God's grace is not "cheap grace," as Dietrich Bonhoeffer so well describes in his book *The Cost of Discipleship*. Our response to God's grace is a life of Christian service. Good works, however noble, are still only a response to what God has done.

When on some final day we are called before our Maker, it will not be our good works that save us. What ultimately will save us will be God's mercy. It is all grace! Are you ready?

Second, *Jesus Christ is the ultimate truth*. Knowing the God revealed through Christ brings meaning, purpose, and fulfillment to our lives. When we know whose we are, we have a new perspective on who we are and how special and sacred life is (Philippians 3:10–14).

Theologically, I am what some call a "Neo-Augustinian." I have a strategy for how the church should respond in our culture: focusing on doctrine, discipline, church and society, and eschatology. Just like me, Augustine was living as a Christian while a civilization was coming apart at the seams.

I believe that the church needs to be clear about truth—about doctrine and theology. I believe there is cognitive and moral truth that transcends culture.

I believe that Christians need to be people of discipline: the recovery of church discipline at the church and family levels is crucial. How does the church relate to society? Augustine did not take a rejectionist posture toward a dying society. I want to take the best that society offers and incorporate it into a Christian vision. I want to retain good aspects of the Enlightenment. Augustine had an ultimately optimistic view of history. He was able to look beyond his own time, to look for *The City of God*.

Paul believed very strongly in the Judeo-Christian notion that the existence of God is the basis for absolutes in truth and morals. Yet today, scientism often is our ultimate truth. Because of the disestablishment of Christianity, Western society has been wrestling with epistemology for the past several hundred years. If materialism is your metaphysics, then scientism becomes your dominant epistemology. Science becomes the way to know anything that is to be known.

As Paul writes this letter to the Philippian church, he admittedly has a different heresy with which to deal: tendencies toward Gnosticism (the worship of knowledge). Yet on further study, one begins to see that the enemy is about the same as our worship of scientific knowledge. Carl Sagan has become our high priest.

Religion to Paul is the only proper path to knowledge and will eventually wither away if people replace it with scientifically based truth. For instance, it is one thing to celebrate America's advances in computer technology. It is quite another thing to say that the only truth is to be found at Harvard or MIT.

When does loss become gain? When we surrender our control and our search for security in tangible things; when we discover that trusting in God and God's design is ultimately more satisfying. As a historian I understand and firmly believe that human history is always reconstructed; it is never created. When someone gives me a theory of history, including his own, I ask, "What evidence can you marshal to build your case?" History is always reconstructed from evidence.

But what Paul is declaring is that salvation comes from beyond history. It is really something new. Something is created that was not here. A new birth. And that is worth more than all the knowledge, money, or prestige in the whole world.

## Journal Question

Give an example of cheap grace.

# Lesson 1
## Evidence-Based Reading and Writing

**Literary Choice**

Lord Byron was a leading figure of the Romantic Movement in early nineteenth-century England. The notoriety of his iconic lifestyle is surpassed only by the brilliance of his writings. Appropriately, Byron died at a young age in Greece, pursuing romantic adventures of heroism.

### The Prisoner of Chillon

| | |
|---|---|
| 1 | My hair is grey, but not with years, |
| 2 | Nor grew it white |
| 3 | In a single night, |
| 4 | As men's have grown from sudden fears: |
| 5 | My limbs are bow'd, though not with toil, |
| 6 | But rusted with a vile repose, |
| 7 | For they have been a dungeon's spoil, |
| 8 | And mine has been the fate of those |
| 9 | To whom the goodly earth and air |
| 10 | Are bann'd, and barr'd—forbidden fare; |
| 11 | But this was for my father's faith |
| 12 | I suffer'd chains and courted death; |
| 13 | That father perish'd at the stake |
| 14 | For tenets he would not forsake; |
| 15 | And for the same his lineal race |
| 16 | In darkness found a dwelling place; |
| 17 | We were seven—who now are one, |
| 18 | Six in youth, and one in age, |
| 19 | Finish'd as they had begun, |
| 20 | Proud of Persecution's rage; |
| 21 | One in fire, and two in field, |
| 22 | Their belief with blood have seal'd, |
| 23 | Dying as their father died, |
| 24 | For the God their foes denied;— |
| 25 | Three were in a dungeon cast, |
| 26 | Of whom this wreck is left the last. |
| 27 | |
| 28 | There are seven pillars of Gothic mould, |
| 29 | In Chillon's dungeons deep and old, |
| 30 | There are seven columns, massy and grey, |
| 31 | Dim with a dull imprison'd ray, |
| 32 | A sunbeam which hath lost its way, |
| 33 | And through the crevice and the cleft |
| 34 | Of the thick wall is fallen and left; |
| 35 | Creeping o'er the floor so damp, |
| 36 | Like a marsh's meteor lamp: |
| 37 | And in each pillar there is a ring, |
| 38 | And in each ring there is a chain; |
| 39 | That iron is a cankering thing, |
| 40 | For in these limbs its teeth remain, |
| 41 | With marks that will not wear away, |
| 42 | Till I have done with this new day, |
| 43 | Which now is painful to these eyes, |
| 44 | Which have not seen the sun so rise |

| | |
|---|---|
| 45 | For years—I cannot count them o'er, |
| 46 | I lost their long and heavy score |
| 47 | When my last brother droop'd and died, |
| 48 | And I lay living by his side. |
| 49 | |
| 50 | They chain'd us each to a column stone, |
| 51 | And we were three—yet, each alone; |
| 52 | We could not move a single pace, |
| 53 | We could not see each other's face, |
| 54 | But with that pale and livid light |
| 55 | That made us strangers in our sight: |
| 56 | And thus together—yet apart, |
| 57 | Fetter'd in hand, but join'd in heart, |
| 58 | 'Twas still some solace in the dearth |
| 59 | Of the pure elements of earth, |
| 60 | To hearken to each other's speech, |
| 61 | And each turn comforter to each |
| 62 | With some new hope, or legend old, |
| 63 | Or song heroically bold; |
| 64 | But even these at length grew cold. |
| 65 | Our voices took a dreary tone, |
| 66 | An echo of the dungeon stone, |
| 67 | A grating sound, not full and free, |
| 68 | As they of yore were wont to be: |
| 69 | It might be fancy—but to me |
| 70 | They never sounded like our own. |
| 71 | |
| 72 | I was the eldest of the three |
| 73 | And to uphold and cheer the rest |
| 74 | I ought to do—and did my best— |
| 75 | And each did well in his degree. |
| 76 | The youngest, whom my father loved, |
| 77 | Because our mother's brow was given |
| 78 | To him, with eyes as blue as heaven— |
| 79 | For him my soul was sorely moved: |
| 80 | And truly might it be distress'd |
| 81 | To see such bird in such a nest; |
| 82 | For he was beautiful as day— |
| 83 | (When day was beautiful to me |
| 84 | As to young eagles, being free)— |
| 85 | A polar day, which will not see |
| 86 | A sunset till its summer's gone, |
| 87 | Its sleepless summer of long light, |
| 88 | The snow-clad offspring of the sun: |

| 89 | And thus he was as pure and bright, |
|----|-------------------------------------|
| 90 | And in his natural spirit gay, |
| 91 | With tears for nought but others' ills, |
| 92 | And then they flow'd like mountain rills, |
| 93 | Unless he could assuage the woe |
| 94 | Which he abhorr'd to view below. |
| 95 | |
| 96 | The other was as pure of mind, |
| 97 | But form'd to combat with his kind; |
| 98 | Strong in his frame, and of a mood |
| 99 | Which 'gainst the world in war had stood, |
| 100 | And perish'd in the foremost rank |
| 101 | With joy:—but not in chains to pine: |
| 102 | His spirit wither'd with their clank, |
| 103 | I saw it silently decline— |
| 104 | And so perchance in sooth did mine: |
| 105 | But yet I forced it on to cheer |
| 106 | Those relics of a home so dear. |
| 107 | He was a hunter of the hills, |
| 108 | Had followed there the deer and wolf; |
| 109 | To him this dungeon was a gulf, |
| 110 | And fetter'd feet the worst of ills. |
| 111 | |
| 112 | Lake Leman lies by Chillon's walls: |
| 113 | A thousand feet in depth below |
| 114 | Its massy waters meet and flow; |
| 115 | Thus much the fathom-line was sent |
| 116 | From Chillon's snow-white battlement, |
| 117 | Which round about the wave inthralls: |
| 118 | A double dungeon wall and wave |
| 119 | Have made—and like a living grave |
| 120 | Below the surface of the lake |
| 121 | The dark vault lies wherein we lay: |
| 122 | We heard it ripple night and day; |
| 123 | Sounding o'er our heads it knock'd; |
| 124 | And I have felt the winter's spray |
| 125 | Wash through the bars when winds were high |
| 126 | And wanton in the happy sky; |
| 127 | And then the very rock hath rock'd, |
| 128 | And I have felt it shake, unshock'd, |
| 129 | Because I could have smiled to see |
| 130 | The death that would have set me free. |
| 131 | |
| 132 | I said my nearer brother pined, |
| 133 | I said his mighty heart declined, |
| 134 | He loathed and put away his food; |
| 135 | It was not that 'twas coarse and rude, |
| 136 | For we were used to hunter's fare, |
| 137 | And for the like had little care: |
| 138 | The milk drawn from the mountain goat |
| 139 | Was changed for water from the moat, |
| 140 | Our bread was such as captives' tears |
| 141 | Have moisten'd many a thousand years, |
| 142 | Since man first pent his fellow men |
| 143 | Like brutes within an iron den; |
| 144 | But what were these to us or him? |
| 145 | These wasted not his heart or limb; |

| 146 | My brother's soul was of that mould |
|-----|-------------------------------------|
| 147 | Which in a palace had grown cold, |
| 148 | Had his free breathing been denied |
| 149 | The range of the steep mountain's side; |
| 150 | But why delay the truth?—he died. |
| 151 | I saw, and could not hold his head, |
| 152 | Nor reach his dying hand—nor dead,— |
| 153 | Though hard I strove, but strove in vain, |
| 154 | To rend and gnash my bonds in twain. |
| 155 | He died—and they unlock'd his chain, |
| 156 | And scoop'd for him a shallow grave |
| 157 | Even from the cold earth of our cave. |
| 158 | I begg'd them, as a boon, to lay |
| 159 | His corse in dust whereon the day |
| 160 | Might shine—it was a foolish thought, |
| 161 | But then within my brain it wrought, |
| 162 | That even in death his freeborn breast |
| 163 | In such a dungeon could not rest. |
| 164 | I might have spared my idle prayer— |
| 165 | They coldly laugh'd—and laid him there: |
| 166 | The flat and turfless earth above |
| 167 | The being we so much did love; |
| 168 | His empty chain above it leant, |
| 169 | Such Murder's fitting monument! |
| 170 | |
| 171 | But he, the favourite and the flower, |
| 172 | Most cherish'd since his natal hour, |
| 173 | His mother's image in fair face |
| 174 | The infant love of all his race |
| 175 | His martyr'd father's dearest thought, |
| 176 | My latest care, for whom I sought |
| 177 | To hoard my life, that his might be |
| 178 | Less wretched now, and one day free; |
| 179 | He, too, who yet had held untired |
| 180 | A spirit natural or inspired— |
| 181 | He, too, was struck, and day by day |
| 182 | Was wither'd on the stalk away. |
| 183 | Oh, God! it is a fearful thing |
| 184 | To see the human soul take wing |
| 185 | In any shape, in any mood: |
| 186 | I've seen it rushing forth in blood, |
| 187 | I've seen it on the breaking ocean |
| 188 | Strive with a swoln convulsive motion, |
| 189 | I've seen the sick and ghastly bed |
| 190 | Of Sin delirious with its dread: |
| 191 | But these were horrors—this was woe |
| 192 | Unmix'd with such—but sure and slow: |
| 193 | He faded, and so calm and meek, |
| 194 | So softly worn, so sweetly weak, |
| 195 | So tearless, yet so tender—kind, |
| 196 | And grieved for those he left behind; |
| 197 | With all the while a cheek whose bloom |
| 198 | Was as a mockery of the tomb |
| 199 | Whose tints as gently sunk away |
| 200 | As a departing rainbow's ray; |
| 201 | An eye of most transparent light, |
| 202 | That almost made the dungeon bright; |

203 And not a word of murmur—not
204 A groan o'er his untimely lot,—
205 A little talk of better days,
206 A little hope my own to raise,
207 For I was sunk in silence—lost
208 In this last loss, of all the most;
209 And then the sighs he would suppress
210 Of fainting Nature's feebleness,
211 More slowly drawn, grew less and less:
212 I listen'd, but I could not hear;
213 I call'd, for I was wild with fear;
214 I knew 'twas hopeless, but my dread
215 Would not be thus admonishèd;
216 I call'd, and thought I heard a sound—
217 I burst my chain with one strong bound,
218 And rushed to him:—I found him not,
219 *I* only stirred in this black spot,
220 *I* only lived, *I* only drew
221 The accursed breath of dungeon-dew;
222 The last, the sole, the dearest link
223 Between me and the eternal brink,
224 Which bound me to my failing race
225 Was broken in this fatal place.
226 One on the earth, and one beneath—
227 My brothers—both had ceased to breathe:
228 I took that hand which lay so still,
229 Alas! my own was full as chill;
230 I had not strength to stir, or strive,
231 But felt that I was still alive—
232 A frantic feeling, when we know
233 That what we love shall ne'er be so.
234      I know not why
235      I could not die,
236 I had no earthly hope—but faith,
237 And that forbade a selfish death.
238
239      What next befell me then and there
240      I know not well—I never knew—
241 First came the loss of light, and air,
242      And then of darkness too:
243 I had no thought, no feeling—none—
244 Among the stones I stood a stone,
245 And was, scarce conscious what I wist,
246 As shrubless crags within the mist;
247 For all was blank, and bleak, and grey;
248 It was not night—it was not day;
249 It was not even the dungeon-light,
250 So hateful to my heavy sight,
251 But vacancy absorbing space,
252 And fixedness—without a place;
253 There were no stars, no earth, no time,
254 No check, no change, no good, no crime
255 But silence, and a stirless breath
256 Which neither was of life nor death;
257 A sea of stagnant idleness,
258 Blind, boundless, mute, and motionless!
259 A light broke in upon my brain,—

260      It was the carol of a bird;
261 It ceased, and then it came again,
262      The sweetest song ear ever heard,
263 And mine was thankful till my eyes
264 Ran over with the glad surprise,
265 And they that moment could not see
266 I was the mate of misery;
267 But then by dull degrees came back
268 My senses to their wonted track;
269 I saw the dungeon walls and floor
270 Close slowly round me as before,
271 I saw the glimmer of the sun
272 Creeping as it before had done,
273 But through the crevice where it came
274 That bird was perch'd, as fond and tame,
275      And tamer than upon the tree;
276 A lovely bird, with azure wings,
277 And song that said a thousand things,
278      And seemed to say them all for me!
279 I never saw its like before,
280 I ne'er shall see its likeness more:
281 It seem'd like me to want a mate,
282 But was not half so desolate,
283 And it was come to love me when
284 None lived to love me so again,
285 And cheering from my dungeon's brink,
286 Had brought me back to feel and think.
287 I know not if it late were free,
288      Or broke its cage to perch on mine,
289 But knowing well captivity,
290      Sweet bird! I could not wish for thine!
291 Or if it were, in wingèd guise,
292 A visitant from Paradise;
293 For—Heaven forgive that thought! the while
294 Which made me both to weep and smile—
295 I sometimes deem'd that it might be
296 My brother's soul come down to me;
297 But then at last away it flew,
298 And then 'twas mortal well I knew,
299 For he would never thus have flown—
300 And left me twice so doubly lone,—
301 Lone as the corse within its shroud,
302 Lone as a solitary cloud,
303      A single cloud on a sunny day,
304 While all the rest of heaven is clear,
305 A frown upon the atmosphere,
306 That hath no business to appear
307      When skies are blue, and earth is gay.
308
309      A kind of change came in my fate,
310 My keepers grew compassionate;
311 I know not what had made them so,
312 They were inured to sights of woe,
313 But so it was:—my broken chain
314 With links unfasten'd did remain,
315 And it was liberty to stride
316 Along my cell from side to side,

317 And up and down, and then athwart,
318 And tread it over every part;
319 And round the pillars one by one,
320 Returning where my walk begun,
321 Avoiding only, as I trod,
322 My brothers' graves without a sod;
323 For if I thought with heedless tread
324 My step profaned their lowly bed,
325 My breath came gaspingly and thick,
326 And my crush'd heart felt blind and sick.
327 I made a footing in the wall,
328     It was not therefrom to escape,
329 For I had buried one and all,
330     Who loved me in a human shape;
331 And the whole earth would henceforth be
332 A wider prison unto me:
333 No child, no sire, no kin had I,
334 No partner in my misery;
335 I thought of this, and I was glad,
336 For thought of them had made me mad;
337 But I was curious to ascend
338 To my barr'd windows, and to bend
339 Once more, upon the mountains high,
340 The quiet of a loving eye.
341
342     I saw them—and they were the same,
343 They were not changed like me in frame;
344 I saw their thousand years of snow
345 On high—their wide long lake below,
346 And the blue Rhone in fullest flow;
347 I heard the torrents leap and gush
348 O'er channell'd rock and broken bush;
349 I saw the white-wall'd distant town,
350 And whiter sails go skimming down;
351 And then there was a little isle,
352 Which in my very face did smile,
353     The only one in view;
354 A small green isle, it seem'd no more,
355 Scarce broader than my dungeon floor,
356 But in it there were three tall trees,
357 And o'er it blew the mountain breeze,
358 And by it there were waters flowing,
359 And on it there were young flowers growing,
360     Of gentle breath and hue.

361 The fish swam by the castle wall,
362 And they seem'd joyous each and all;
363 The eagle rode the rising blast,
364 Methought he never flew so fast
365 As then to me he seem'd to fly;
366 And then new tears came in my eye,
367 And I felt troubled—and would fain
368 I had not left my recent chain;
369 And when I did descend again,
370 The darkness of my dim abode
371 Fell on me as a heavy load;
372 It was as is a new-dug grave,
373 Closing o'er one we sought to save,—
374 And yet my glance, too much opprest,
375 Had almost need of such a rest.
376
377     It might be months, or years, or days—
378     I kept no count, I took no note—
379 I had no hope my eyes to raise,
380     And clear them of their dreary mote;
381 At last men came to set me free;
382     I ask'd not why, and reck'd not where;
383 It was at length the same to me,
384 Fetter'd or fetterless to be,
385     I learn'd to love despair.
386 And thus when they appear'd at last,
387 And all my bonds aside were cast,
388 These heavy walls to me had grown
389 A hermitage—and all my own!
390 And half I felt as they were come
391 To tear me from a second home:
392 With spiders I had friendship made
393 And watch'd them in their sullen trade,
394 Had seen the mice by moonlight play,
395 And why should I feel less than they?
396 We were all inmates of one place,
397 And I, the monarch of each race,
398 Had power to kill—yet, strange to tell!
399 In quiet we had learn'd to dwell;
400 My very chains and I grew friends,
401 So much a long communion tends
402 To make us what we are:—even I
403 Regain'd my freedom with a sigh.
404 (http://www.poetryfoundation.org/poem/173098)
405

## Student Response

### Analysis

1 "Mine has been the fate of those / To whom the goodly earth and air / Are bann'd, and barr'd—forbidden fare,"
2 laments the prisoner of Chillon in Lord Byron's poem. The "Prisoner of Chillon" was written by Lord Byron, the
3 famed English Romantic poet. Inspired by the tale of the imprisonment of a priest in the Castle of Chillon in
4 Switzerland, Byron discusses the hardships of imprisonment and makes a case for the plight of those persecuted for
5 religious views.
6     Byron was inspired to write this poem after visiting, with fellow poet Shelley, the Chillon Castle in
7 Switzerland where a certain priest, François Bonivard, was imprisoned for preaching a message that was not in line
8 with the government's philosophy. Hence the "Prisoner of Chillon" is essentially a historical poem since it is based
9 on the story of a real person. However, Bonivard's experiences as described and romanticized by Byron transcend

10 the immediate setting and serve as an outlet for a more general discussion of hope, despair, and loneliness as well as
11 human cruelty. "Finish'd as they had begun / Proud of Persecution's rage / One in fire, and two in field / Their belief
12 with blood have seal'd / Dying as their father died / For the God their foes denied."

13    Byron writes the poem in first-person narrative, giving the story the feel of a testimony. This is especially
14 effective for drawing the reader into the text and bringing to life the agony of the prisoner, as the reader is taken into
15 his thoughts through stream of consciousness. "I was the eldest of the three / And to uphold and cheer the rest / I
16 ought to do—and did my best." The story line traces the prisoner's heartbreaking story in chronological order and
17 follows the death of his brothers. This poem overflows with pathos as Byron employs piteous terms to describe the
18 agony and conditions of imprisonment. Such pathos is most seen in the death of Bonivard's youngest brother, "the
19 favorite and the flower / Most cherish'd since his natal hour." "A frantic feeling, when we know / That what we love
20 shall ne'er be so. / I know not why / I could not die, / I had no earthly hope—but faith, / And that forbade a selfish
21 death." After the death of his brothers, Byron spends the rest of the poem in stream of consciousness as the prisoner
22 is alone with his thoughts. "There were no stars, no earth, no time, / No check, no change, no good, no crime / But
23 silence, and a stirless breath / Which neither was of life nor death; / a sea of stagnant idleness, / Blind, boundless,
24 mute, and motionless!"

25    There a few themes in this poem that Byron capitalizes on: the fragility of humanity, the effect of hope, and
26 the cruelty of religious persecution. Byron begins the poem with a tragic description of the prisoner: "My hair is
27 grey, but not with years. . . . / My limbs are bow'd, though not with toil, / But rusted with a vile repose." As the
28 poem progresses, the narrator attributes his physical weakness to his prison cell, showing the fragility of his
29 humanity. Byron explores this theme most fully through the accounts of the narrator's two brothers. In a before and
30 after style, Byron shows how the men's strength and vitality had become "a dungeon's spoil." "He was a hunter of
31 the hills, / Had followed there the deer and wolf, / To him this dungeon was a gulf, / And fetter'd feet the worst of
32 ills." Here a man who once "against the world in war had stood" now capitulated to the chains of a stone cell. This is
33 a general theme that runs through the first part of the poem, but is interrupted with another theme, the theme of hope
34 in the latter end. "It was the carol of a bird. . . . / A lovely bird, with azure wings, / And song that said a thousand
35 things." Byron personifies hope as a bird, and it is this bird that saves the prisoner from following in the path of his
36 brothers. "It was come to love me when / None lived to love me so again, / And cheering from my dungeon's brink,
37 / Had brought me back to feel and think." As a representation of the plight of all the imprisoned, Byron makes the
38 point that hope is the only thing that saves the imprisoned person from utterly despairing. And yet these people
39 should not be imprisoned for their peaceful faith: this is the main theme of Byron's poem, the cruelty of unjust
40 imprisonment. From the descriptions of the prisoner's physical deterioration to the mental agony of hearing one's
41 brother's pain and unable to alleviate them, Byron makes a clear condemnation of unjust imprisonment. Using
42 pathos and a tragic story line arouses deep pity from the reader and trumpets the plight of the unjustly accused.

43    The "Prisoner of Chillon" is both the story of one man's imprisonment and the story of all those who have
44 been unjustly imprisoned for religious belief. By romanticizing the story in true Byron style, this poet is able to
45 denounce unjust imprisonment while exploring the themes of fragility, hope, and cruelty. (Daphnide)


## *Growing Up White* (Excerpt)
### James P. Stobaugh


1    Mr. Hugh Huckleberry, Gertrude's husband, owned a bakery, and Big Daddy worked in that shop.
2    For the rest of his too-short adolescence, he lived with Uncle Hugh and Aunt Gertrude and indulged himself in
3 heretofore unknown and exotic fare such as donuts fried in Crisco. He was too old to be adopted, but in the postwar
4 Southern pantheon, he found repose and succor in Auntie's cheap frame unpainted house nestled between the locust-
5 humming Ouachita River Delta and the hog-infested Northern Louisiana Pine Barrens. Big Daddy felt the red sandy
6 loam and dared again to venture home.
7    He put on weight and met his future wife, Mary Lou Huckleberry, whose father, Nehemiah Huckleberry, was
8 Hugh's brother.
9    Gertrude, whom Big Daddy called Auntie, read him poetry, history, drama, prose fiction, and even a few
10 nonfiction speeches and essays. She gifted illiterate Big Daddy with a love for literature that he gave his daughter,
11 my mom, and thereby bequeathed along the line to me.
12    Auntie loved the British Romantics. Goethe, she felt was obscene; Thoreau and Emerson, supercilious; Poe,
13 talented but weird. But Wordsworth, Shelley, and especially Byron were exquisite! Their grasp of the unassailable
14 was a sublime escape from Auntie's harsh life.

15      Her favorite poem was Byron's "The Prisoner of Chillon." It is the story of a man who spends most of his adult
16 life unjustly *sequestered* in a mountain prison. The young man grows old but is able to maintain his romantic beliefs
17 in justice, freedom, and goodness. Only at the end of his life, when ironically the prisoner is released, does he lose
18 his hope.
19      Now that was something that Big Daddy could understand—being in prison. But he could not quite grasp the
20 notion of believing in a cause, in an abstract ideology. Yet Byron taught Big Daddy how to love. He inspired him
21 once again to risk that inferno emotion that had been quenched by neglect and abuse so many years before. In this
22 face of facileness and superficiality that Big Daddy had so thoroughly grasped into his soul, Lord Byron enticed him
23 again into the burning noonday heat.
24      Ultimately, though, this troubling poem is about disillusionment and failure; the point was not lost on Big
25 Daddy. Lord Byron's poetic work explores the struggle between a person's ending his suffering by accepting it
26 rather than holding on to the hope of freedom:
27
28      My hair is gray, but not with years,
29         Nor grew it white
30         In a single night,
31      As men's have grown from sudden fears;
32      My limbs are bow'd, though not with toil,
33      But rusted with a vile repose,
34      For they have been a dungeon's spoil,
35      And mine has been the fate of those
36      To whom the goodly earth and air
37      Are bann'd, and barr'd—forbidden fare.
38
39      In the dusty evenings of northern Louisiana, while Auntie Gertrude read Byron, Big Daddy discovered again the
40 seductive companion of hope. Just as the prisoner of Chillon hears the singing of a bird outside his window, and it
41 reminds him that there are beauty and hope in the world—so also Big Daddy remembers a love he had once, a love
42 freely given him by Little Tommy and his mom, a gentle minuet whose tune he had long forgotten.
43      Unfortunately, though, the prisoner of Chillon survives but loses his ability to believe in the transcendent, to
44 believe in God. When he regains his freedom, it is too late:
45
46      In quiet we had learn'd to dwell—
47      My very chains and I grew friends,
48      So much a long communion ends
49      To make us what we are: —even I
50      Regain'd my freedom with a sigh.
51
52      As Oedipus cried in the Greek tragedy *Oedipus Rex*:
53
54      Is there a man more agonized?
55      More wed to pain and frenzy?
56      Not a man on earth,
57      the joy of your life ground down to nothing,
58      O Oedipus, name for the ages—
59
60      Big Daddy knew that Byron and Sophocles captured his past, but he earnestly hoped that they did not prophesy
61 his future. He had new hope, though, and a later religious experience added to his optimism.

            (James P. Stobaugh, *Growing Up White* [New York: Harvard Square Editions, 2014])

## Close Reading (Poem)

1. What is the narrative technique in the poem?
   A. Third-person Objective      C. First person
   B. Second person      D. Omniscient

2. This narrative strategy offers the following advantages:
   I.   The reader is drawn into the action.
   II.  The poet can explore the interior life of the narrator.
   III. The poet can easily make social statements.

        A. I      C. II and III
        B. I and II      D. All

3. The narrator is credible because he
   A. Vilifies his enemies.      C. Willingly admits flaws and inhibitions.
   B. Offers vague details.      D. Offers theological insights.

4. Lines 275–290
   A. Offer an example of an uncaged bird who is beautiful and free but does not change the prisoner's hopeless condition.
   B. Lament that a simple bird is free and he is not.
   C. Curse a teasing bird.
   D. Thank God for the simple pleasure of seeing a bird.

5. What is the tone of the poem?
   A. Tentative      C. Reflective
   B. Sanguine      D. Serious

6. The poet creates the tone by
   A. Hyperbole.      C. Internal thought and reflection.
   B. Connotation of morbid words.      D. Repetition.

7. The whole poem is
   A. A frame story      C. Magic Realism
   B. A flashback      D. Stream of Consciousness

## Command of Evidence (Student Response)

1. The Student Response argues that the poem is
   A. A parody.      C. A lighthearted criticism of incarceration.
   B. A criticism of religious imprisonment.      D. A celebration of prison freedom.

2. The thesis is first presented in
   A. Lines 1–2.      C. Lines 13–14
   B. Lines 3–5.      D. Lines 25–26

3. What is a favorite form of evidence used?
   A. Romantic novels      C. Quotes from the poem
   B. Popular songs      D. Other poems

4. How does the Student Response develop its argument?
   A. It uses a quote from another literary work to illustrate the theme of the poem and then goes through the poem line by line.
   B. It summarizes the poem and then makes a relevant point at the end.
   C. It makes an argument and then offers supportive textual evidence.
   D. It states a thesis and then offers alternative interpretations.

5. What is an assumption that the Student Response makes?
   I.   The poem was both a testimony and a social statement.
   II.  The poem was propaganda.
   III. The poet was full of hyperbole.

   A. I                B. II                C. III                D. I and III

6. What is an example of irony?
   A. The poet hated the Swiss.
   B. The poet was happy to be released but now too old and broken to enjoy his freedom.
   C. The poet was in love with a woman.
   D. The poet was making a social statement about tyrannical regimes.

7. How is the excerpt from *Growing Up White* different from the Student Response?
   I.   *GUW* is a narrative; the Student Response is a critical analysis.
   II.  *GUW* is negative about the poem; the Student Response is not.
   III. *GUW* offers a fictional account of events surrounding the poet's incarceration. The Student Response is merely a critical analysis.

   A. I                B. II and III                C. III                D. All

8. The *GUW* excerpt uses the poem "Prisoner of Chillon"
   A. To show how Big Daddy has become bitter and unforgiving.
   B. To show the hopelessness of Big Daddy's situation.
   C. To show the redemption of Big Daddy through literature.
   D. To criticize the organized church.

9. The *GUW* excerpt uses the quote from Sophocles's *Oedipus Rex* to illustrate
   A. Big Daddy's love of Greek drama.
   B. How hopeless Big Daddy once was.
   C. The horror that Big Daddy experienced as a youth.
   D. The fact that Big Daddy created his own problems.

10. In the *GUW* excerpt, Big Daddy is also changed by
    A. The love of his adopted parents.          C. A religious conversion experience.
    B. Western literature.                        D. The march of time.

11. The evidence for the above answer can be found in
    A. Lines 1–5.        B. Lines 24–30.        C. Lines 45–50.        D. Lines 60–61.

12. In the *GUW* excerpt, the logical next scene would be
    A. Big Daddy having a conversion experience.      C. Big Daddy joining the U.S. Army.
    B. Big Daddy marrying Big Momma.                  D. Big Daddy dying of a snakebite.

## Words in Context

1. What is the meaning of *pantheon* in *GUW* Line 4?
   A. Five structures                C. A place of worship
   B. Six armies                     D. Another word for "hell"

2. What is the meaning of *unassailable* in *GUW* Line 13?
   A. Squandered        B. Forgotten        C. Unknown        D. Undeniable

3. What is the meaning of *sequestered* in *GUW* Line 16?
   A. Impounded                      C. Remembered
   B. Stolen                         D. Denied

# Lesson 2
## Critical Reading and Writing

### Command of Evidence

Read the following passages and answer accompanying questions:

**Passage 1**

### Remarks on the 20th Anniversary of Voice of America
### President John F. Kennedy (February 26, 1962)

1    Occupying as I do a rather secondary status these days, I am very appreciative to you all for waiting. I think that this
2    meeting is tied up with the common American interest in Colonel Glenn, and I feel that in addition to being dry, we
3    are also contributing a little to telling the story of which he is a great part—as are Alan Shepard and the others.
4        I was most anxious to come here personally today, because I put such great importance in the work that you
5    are doing. The Voice of America occupies, I believe, a key part in the story of American life. What we do here in
6    this country, and what we are, what we want to be, represents really a great experiment in a most difficult kind of
7    self-discipline, and that is the organization and maintenance and development of the progress of free government.
8    And it is your task, as the executives and participants in the Voice of America, to tell that story around the world.
9        This is an extremely difficult and sensitive task. On the one hand you are an arm of the Government and
10   therefore an arm of the Nation, and it is your task to bring our story around the world in a way which serves to
11   represent democracy and the United States in its most favorable light. But on the other hand, as part of the cause of
12   freedom, and the arm of freedom, you are obliged to tell our story in a truthful way, to tell it, as Oliver Cromwell
13   said about his portrait, "Paint us with all our blemishes and warts, all those things about us that may not be so
14   immediately attractive."
15       We compete with other means of communication, of those who are our adversaries who tell only the good
16   stories. But the things that go bad in America, you must tell that also. And we hope that the bad and the good is
17   sifted together by people of judgment and discretion and taste and discrimination, that they will realize what we are
18   trying to do here.
19       This presents to you an almost impossible challenge, and it is a source of satisfaction to me that in the last
20   20 years you have met that challenge so well. I know that there are those who are always critical of the Voice, but I
21   believe that over the years, faced with this very difficult challenge, far more difficult than that of an American editor
22   or a newspaperman, or a commentator on an American radio or television station, you have been able to tell our
23   story in a way which makes it believable and credible. And that is what I hope you will continue to do in the future.
24       The first words that the Voice of America spoke were 20 years ago. They said, "The Voice of America
25   speaks. Today America has been at war for 79 days. Daily at this time we shall speak to you about America and the
26   war, and the news may be good or bad. We shall tell you the truth." And so you have, for 20 years—and so you shall
27   for 20 years more.
28       In 1946 the United Nations General Assembly passed a resolution reading in part, "Freedom of information
29   is a fundamental human right, and the touchstone of all the freedoms to which the United Nations is consecrated."
30   This is our touchstone as well. This is the code of the Voice of America. We welcome the views of others. We seek
31   a free flow of information across national boundaries and oceans, across iron curtains and stone walls. We are not
32   afraid to entrust the American people with unpleasant facts, foreign ideas, alien philosophies, and competitive
33   values. For a nation that is afraid to let its people judge the truth and falsehood in an open market is a nation that is
34   afraid of its people.
35       The Voice of America thus carries a heavy responsibility. Its burden of truth is not easy to bear. It must
36   explain to a curious and suspicious world what we are. It must tell them of our basic beliefs. It must tell them of a
37   country which is in some ways a rather old country—certainly old as republics go. And yet it must make our ideas
38   alive and new and vital in the high competition which goes on around the world since the end of World War II.
39       In the last 20 years the Voice of America and its parent organization have grown in strength and in stature,
40   but in the next 20 years our opportunities to tell our story will expand beyond belief. The advent of the
41   communications satellite, the modernization of education of less-developed nations, the new wonders of electronics
42   and technology, all these and other developments will give our generation an unprecedented opportunity to tell our
43   story. And we must not only be equal to the opportunity, but to the challenge as well.

44      For in the next 20 years your problem and ours as a country, in telling our story, will grow more complex.
45 The choices we present to the world will be more difficult, and for some the future will seem even more empty of
46 hope and progress. The barrage upon truth will grow more constant, and some people cannot bear the responsibility
47 of a free choice which goes with self-government. And finally, shrinking from choice, they turn to those who
48 prevent them from choosing, and thus find in a kind of prison, a kind of security.
49      We believe that people are capable of standing the burdens and the pressures which choice places upon
50 them, and it is because of this strong conviction that this organization functions, and it is because there is this
51 commitment to this view that you continue to serve in it.
52      None of you are interested in serving in an agency which merely reflects a line which the Government from
53 time to time may set down. You serve in it—and you all could serve in different agencies or in different parts of
54 life—because you believe, I am sure, that this is a vital part of telling our story around the world.
55      And as you tell it, it spreads. And as it spreads, not only is the security of the United States assisted, but the
56 cause of freedom.
57      So I salute you on your 20th birthday and say that in the next 20 years when these choices will become
58 more vital to us, I believe that the Voice of America will be fulfilling its function, as it did that first day when it
59 committed itself to truth.
60      Thank you.

(Kennedy Library, http://www.presidency.ucsb.edu/ws/?pid=9075)

## Close Reading

1. Why is President Kennedy pleased to present this speech?
   - A. The honorarium is huge.
   - B. He needs the publicity.
   - C. He believes the VOA is important to democracy.
   - D. He has nothing else to do.

2. The speech begins with
   - A. A few personal comments.
   - B. A denunciation of Russia.
   - C. A celebration of free speech.
   - D. A thank-you to Mrs. Kennedy.

3. What organizational plan does the author employ?
   - A. A series of anecdotes thoroughly explained
   - B. A historical review of circumstances and a look to the future
   - C. A series of rhetorical questions
   - D. A statement of appreciation plus important reasons why the VOA is important to the future

4. Which lines present the thesis of this speech?
   - A. Lines 1–2
   - B. Lines 5–8
   - C. Lines 27–28
   - D. Lines 58–59

5. The author finishes his speech
   - A. With a summary statement.
   - B. With a new conclusion.
   - C. With another accolade.
   - D. The way he began.

6. It is fair to conclude that the author
   - A. Feels that America has the best form of government in the world.
   - B. Believes in equality for women.
   - C. Is a homeschooler.
   - D. Favors the Judeo-Christian view of the world.

7. Lines 51–53 provide a rhetorical example of
   - A. Ethos.    B. Logos.    C. Pathos.    D. NONE

8. Lines 27–33 present a rhetorical example of
   - A. Ethos.    B. Logos.    C. Pathos.    D. NONE

## Passage 2

## Analysis of the Kennedy Speech

1　John F. Kennedy once said, "We are not afraid to entrust the American people with unpleasant facts, foreign ideas,
2　alien philosophies, and competitive values. For a nation that is afraid to let its people judge the truth and falsehood
3　in an open market is a nation that is afraid of its people." With this statement, J. F. K. created an interesting paradox
4　by claiming to trust the American people with "foreign ideas" and "alien philosophies" while in the midst of a
5　communist scare. There is truth in J. F. K.'s words: a nation afraid to trust its people with the truth is a nation afraid
6　of its people. But sadly, America is not exempt from that truth. Perhaps no government in history was ever truly "not
7　afraid to entrust" its citizens with strange conceptions, disgusting truths, and intoxicating new philosophies.

8　　　　Kennedy begins his statement by saying, "We are not afraid," and it stands to reason that he is speaking
9　about the American government, more specifically, the American government under the Kennedy Administration. It
10　is interesting that he would make such a claim so publicly when his own term of office had been so wrought with
11　fear of a "foreign idea." Communism came to America and hid under America's bed like a giant spectral monster.
12　And like children afraid of the dark, the American public saw communism as an imminent threat to their safety,
13　happiness, and the future of their nation.

14　　　　The Kennedy Administration and the preceding administration were far from entrusting the American
15　people with this foreign concept. In fact, they were determined to eliminate any threat this new philosophy posed. In
16　the late 1940s and far into the 1950s, the Red Scare, or Communist Scare, started years before Kennedy took office.
17　According to the History Channel Network, "Federal employees were analyzed to determine whether they were
18　sufficiently loyal to the government, and the House Un-American Activities Committee, as well as U.S. Senator
19　Joseph R. McCarthy, investigated allegations of subversive elements in the government and the Hollywood film
20　industry." It was a period characterized by a "climate of fear and repression."

21　　　　Such historic figures as Harry Truman, J. Edgar Hoover, and Joseph McCarthy worked tirelessly to
22　terrorize the American citizens into the belief that communism was too lethal an idea to allow into the American
23　mind. For one, "McCarthy used hearsay and intimidation to establish himself as a powerful and feared figure in
24　American politics. He leveled charges of disloyalty at celebrities, intellectuals, and anyone who disagreed with his
25　political views, costing many of his victims their reputations and jobs." The article continues by saying, "The
26　advances of communism around the world convinced many U.S. citizens that there was a real danger of 'Reds'
27　taking over their own country. Figures such as McCarthy and Hoover fanned the flames of fear by wildly
28　exaggerating that possibility." Such tactics as these arose, not from entrusting the American people with ideas, but
29　from fear. The American government was afraid of communism and afraid of the American people's reaction to it,
30　so they waged a war of terror on the American public so no American would dare become communist or accepting
31　of communists. Americans were not allowed to "judge the truth or falsehood in an open market," and this restriction
32　was perpetuated by Kennedy himself.

33　　　　Just two years after Kennedy made this statement about trusting the American people and other
34　governments being afraid of their citizens, America entered into the Vietnam War and, four years after that, a
35　terrible lie was told. On March 16, 1968, American soldiers entered the village of My Lai. The Charlie Company,
36　containing about 140 men, came to My Lai ready to face the 48th Vietcong infantry battalion, but when they arrived,
37　the enemy was nowhere to be seen. As reported by PBS.org, "According to sworn testimony, Captain Medina told
38　the soldiers that there would be no civilians, or 'innocents' in the village on March 16, and anyone who was present
39　was an enemy or enemy sympathizer. But that information was based on faulty intelligence; the Vietcong were 150
40　miles away, on the other side of the Province." The soldiers came in firing, only to find elderly old men, children,
41　and women present in the village. But instead of leaving them in peace, the Charlie Company rounded them up,
42　made them stand in a ditch, and then fired down on them in a hail of bullets. "By the end of the day, they had shot
43　and killed between 300 and 507 unarmed and unresisting men, women, and children, none of them apparently
44　members of the enemy forces. Most of the survivors hid under the dead bodies of their families and neighbors."

45　　　　The events at My Lai, later known as the My Lai Massacre, "would only come to light more than a year
46　later." According to many sources, the My Lai Massacre was hushed up by the government for as long as possible
47　before the story was revealed by a newscaster who spoke with one of the members of the Charlie Company. Far
48　from trusting the American people with the "unpleasant facts," the government ordered a quiet military investigation
49　that resulted in charges against only twenty men, all of whom were later acquitted or never convicted at all. To
50　further their wrongs, the government released the leaders of the My Lai Massacre, Lieutenant William Calley and
51　Captain Medina, for fear of the American people. "Public sentiment overwhelmed the White House, and President
52　Nixon ordered Calley released and confined to his quarters pending a review of his conviction. In total, he ended up
53　serving four and a half months in a military prison. Captain Medina was acquitted, having denied that he gave any

54 orders for the massacre." These were men who had been convicted of mass premeditated murder and were then
55 acquitted due to the government's fear of their people. First, they lied; then they gave into pressures from public
56 sentiment. America is truly "a nation that is afraid to let its people judge the truth and falsehood in an open market,
57 . . . [a nation] that is afraid of its people." (Alyssa)

## Close Reading

1. What would be the best title of this essay?
   A. McCarthyism
   B. The Kennedy Doctrine
   C. The Failure of the Voice of America
   D. The Cold War

2. What organizational plan does the author employ?
   A. She vilifies American involvement in the Vietnam War.
   B. She questions J. F. Kennedy's morality.
   C. She contradicts Kennedy's speech.
   D. After quoting Kennedy, she exposes American xenophobia.

3. The author finishes her essay with
   A. A summary statement.
   B. A new conclusion.
   C. An anecdote.
   D. A final criticism of Kennedy.

4. A legitimate criticism of the argument might be that
   I. It is a spurious argument to tie the My Lai Massacre to John F. Kennedy's administration.
   II. Harry S. Truman was not part of the Joseph McCarthy Red Scare Trials.
   III. World War II caused most of American angst toward foreigners.

   A. I
   B. II
   C. I and II
   D. II and III

# Lesson 3
## SAT Essay

### Student Essay 1

*Prompt:* Do you think that things attain more value if we need to work for them?

1　In today's culture, we have great deal of things. We tend to hoard "stuff," keeping it for some future necessity that
2　we know in our hearts will never occur. Then there are those things that really matter to us. So, are those things only
3　that which we strived for, or can they be other, more easily acquired keepsakes? I submit that the things we value are
4　things we worked hard to get.
5　　　　Starting with perhaps the item with most generic value, money, I can say with certainty that it is most
6　useful to those who worked for it. Recently a sad yet oft-repeated story was shared in an article on the Yahoo home
7　page, telling about a book that traced the spending habits of lottery winners. Interestingly, most blew all of their
8　speedily gained cash on worthless investments, drugs, or simply poorly planned, exorbitant spending. The money
9　didn't really matter to the winner; it was a quick thrill, but their discernment was so poor that they lost it almost as
10　soon as it was in their hands.
11　　　　On the other hand, those who worked hard to earn their fortune tend to use it far more judiciously. They
12　invest wisely, spend on important things, and still have plenty left for pleasure and relaxation. Bill Gates is a good
13　example. He and other rich entrepreneurs struggled for their wealth, and it matters more to them because of this fact.
14　　　　Even smaller, more "real" items like hobby equipment or wedding rings gain intrinsic value when earned.
15　**A wedding ring matters to a spouse because they've earned their marriage, not with money, but with time**
16　**spent in building the relationship.** Divorced couples care not so much, because the physical manifestation of
17　commitment (the ring) doesn't matter.
18　　　　People's opinions definitely have a key part in determining an item's intrinsic value. If struggle has
19　occurred to get it, it matters more. The object becomes a symbol of triumph over adversity, and it is encouraging.
20　(Tyler)

### Close Reading

1.　The essay begins with
　　A.　Restating the essay's purpose and illustrating the importance of hard work.
　　B.　A summary statement of persevering through adversity to the end.
　　C.　Declaring no real purpose.
　　D.　A celebration of hard work.

2.　One illustrations includes
　　A.　The effect of free money on welfare recipients.
　　B.　Effect of wedding rings.
　　C.　The cause of divorce.
　　D.　Easy money's effect on lottery winners.

3.　Which of the following strategies does the essay employ?
　　A.　A statement of purpose with several examples
　　B.　A couple of anecdotes
　　C.　A contradictory position and then the true argument
　　D.　Three rhetorical questions

4.　The essay finishes with
　　A.　A summary statement.　　　　　　　C.　A restatement of the thesis.
　　B.　A rhetorical question.　　　　　　　D.　A tangential excursion.

5.　"On the other hand" in Line 11 is
　　A.　A Metaphor　　　　B.　A Simile　　　　C.　A Transition　　　　D.　A Paradox

6.    What score would this essay receive? __.


## Student Essay 2

*Prompt:* Discuss decision making: Do good decisions come easily? Or do they require much consideration? (CollegeBoard)

1    Flexibility is the sign of a strong and wise leader. Inflexibility leads to disaster in my life while flexibility leads to
2    victory and triumph. In literature, inflexibility hurts when it manifests itself in leaders, but when flexibility comes, it
3    brings help and aid to a wounded cause. Studying history proves the same point. Flexibility shows through in
4    powerful, sage-like leaders.
5         I play capture-the-flag a lot. I can think of two examples when I was the leader where my flexibility or lack
6    thereof either helped my team or hurt it. In one instance, I was flexible and adopted a previously untried strategy. I
7    told my subordinates not to charge until we had captured most of the enemy. Once this feat was accomplished, my
8    team charged the remaining enemy and took the flag. Another time, I applied the same strategy modified a little. I
9    tried to get the best of the enemies in jail before charging, which I did. Instead of being flexible and switching my
10   team into offensive mode for the charge, I held back, and someone on the other team charged and freed the high-
11   profile prisoners. Flexibility allowed me to win; inflexibility caused me to lose.
12        In Homer's *Iliad*, the Greek leaders fight many years in a deadlock with the enemy on the plains of Troy.
13   These leaders were inflexible as they sought to win with the same strategy. However, these leaders gained wisdom
14   and attacked using a different strategy that led them to victory. When they became wise, the Greek leaders became
15   flexible. A wise and strong leader shows flexibility
16        At the Battle of Gettysburg, General Lee of the Confederate forces used an attack strategy for three days.
17   His strategy led to the loss of almost 30,000 men as well as the loss of the battle. His inflexibility as a leader did not
18   reflect wisdom. When Adolf Hitler attacked Russia, he used the blitzkrieg strategy that had worked so well for him
19   everywhere else. His strategy, however, was no match for large Russia and its cold winters; thus Hitler lost the
20   campaign because of inflexibility.
21        Inflexibility is only fine for a leader in one circumstance. In *Uncle Tom's Cabin*, Tom's character is
22   steadfast and inflexible. People acknowledge him as a strong leader because of that adherence to virtue.
23        Personal experience, literature, and history show that good leaders adopt tactics that are flexible. However,
24   literature also shows that leaders must hold fast to character. (Matthew)


## Close Reading

1.    How is the essay structured?
      A. A rhetorical question is advanced and then answered.
      B. A thesis is stated and then illustrations to support the thesis.
      C. A series of anecdotes support a thesis presented at the end.
      D. A spurious argument is advanced and then refuted.

2.    The following are examples of the thesis:
      I.    The Battle of Gettysburg
      II.   The German invasion of the Soviet Union
      III.  The Greek Trojan horse
      IV.   Charles Lindberg's flight to Paris

          A. I and IV                              C. I, II, and III
          B. II                                    D. I and III

3.    What organization strategy does the essay employ?
      A. The introduction with a thesis and several examples.
      B. A contradictory theory is introduced and then destroyed.
      C. Anecdotal selections from three novels are developed.
      D. A summary of the lives of Napoleon and Alexander the Great.

4. How does the essay end?
   A. An anecdote
   B. A rhetorical question
   C. A restatement of the argument with evidence
   D. A tangential issue

5. What score would this essay receive? __.

## Grammar and Usage

Choose the best grammar/usage form in bold sentence(s).

Student Essay 1, Lines 14–16

    A. NONE
    B. A wedding ring matters to a spouse because they've earned their marriage, not with money, but with time.
    C. A wedding ring matters to a married couple because they've earned their marriage, not with money, but with time spent in building the relationship.
    D. A wedding ring matters to a spouse because he has earned his marriage, not with money, but with time building the relationship.

# Lesson 4
## Reading: Document-Based Analysis

### City on a Hill
### John Winthrop (1630)

1  From the former Considerations arise these Conclusions. —1. First, This loue among Christians is a reall thing, not
2  imaginarie. 2ly. This loue is as absolutely necessary to the being of the body of Christ, as the sinews and other
3  ligaments of a naturall body are to the being of that body. 3ly. This loue is a divine, spirituall, nature; free, active,
4  strong, couragious, permanent; undervaluing all things beneathe its propper object and of all the graces, this makes
5  us nearer to resemble the virtues of our heavenly father. 4thly. It rests in the loue and wellfare of its beloued. For the
6  full certain knowledge of those truthes concerning the nature, use, and excellency of this grace, that which the holy
7  ghost hath left recorded, 1 Cor. 13, may give full satisfaction, which is needful for every true member of this louely
8  body of the Lord Jesus, to worke upon theire heartes by prayer, meditation continuall exercise at least of the speciall
9  [influence] of this grace, till Christ be formed in them and they in him, all in eache other, knitt together by this bond
10 of loue.
11     It rests now to make some application of this discourse, by the present designe, which gaue the occasion of
12 writing of it. Herein are 4 things to be propounded; first the persons, 2ly the worke, 3ly the end, 4thly the meanes.
13 1. For the persons. Wee are a company professing ourselves fellow members of Christ, in which respect onely
14 though wee were absent from each other many miles, and had our imployments as farre distant, yet wee ought to
15 account ourselves knitt together by this bond of loue, and, live in the exercise of it, if wee would have comforte of
16 our being in Christ. This was notorious in the practise of the Christians in former times; as is testified of the
17 Waldenses, from the mouth of one of the adversaries Aeneas Sylvius "mutuo ament pere antequam norunt," they use
18 to loue any of theire owne religion even before they were acquainted with them. 2nly for the worke wee have in
19 hand. It is by a mutuall consent, through a speciall overvaluing providence and a more than an ordinary approbation
20 of the Churches of Christ, to seeke out a place of cohabitation and Consorteshipp under a due forme of Government
21 both ciuill and ecclesiasticall. In such cases as this, the care of the publique must oversway all private respects, by
22 which, not only conscience, but meare civill pollicy, dothe binde us. For it is a true rule that particular Estates cannot
23 subsist in the ruin of the publique. 3ly The end is to improve our lives to doe more service to the Lord; the comforte
24 and encrease of the body of Christe, whereof we are members; that ourselves and posterity may be the better
25 preserved from the common corruptions of this evill world, to serve the Lord and worke out our Salvation under the
26 power and purity of his holy ordinances. 4thly for the meanes whereby this must be effected. They are twofold, a
27 conformity with the worke and end wee aime at. These wee see are extraordinary, therefore wee must not content
28 ourselves with usuall ordinary meanes. Whatsoever wee did, or ought to have, done, when wee liued in England, the
29 same must wee doe, and more allsoe, where wee goe. That which the most in theire churches mainetaine as truthe in
30 profession onely, wee must bring into familiar and constant practise; as in this duty of loue, wee must loue brotherly
31 without dissimulation, wee must loue one another with a pure hearte fervently. Wee must beare one anothers
32 burthens. We must not looke onely on our owne things, but allsoe on the things of our brethren. Neither must wee
33 thinke that the Lord will beare with such faileings at our hands as he dothe from those among whome wee have
34 lived; and that for these 3 Reasons; 1. In regard of the more neare bond of mariage between him and us, wherein hee
35 hath taken us to be his, after a most strickt and peculiar manner, which will make them the more jealous of our loue
36 and obedience. Soe he tells the people of Israell, you onely have I knowne of all the families of the Earthe, therefore
37 will I punishe you for your Transgressions. 2ly, because the Lord will be sanctified in them that come neare him. We
38 know that there were many that corrupted the service of the Lord; some setting upp altars before his owne; others
39 offering both strange fire and strange sacrifices allsoe; yet there came noe fire from heaven, or other sudden
40 judgement upon them, as did upon Nadab and Abihu, whoe yet wee may think did not sinne presumptuously. 3ly
41 When God gives a speciall commission he lookes to have it strictly observed in every article; When he gave Saule a
42 commission to destroy Amaleck, Hee indented with him upon certain articles, and because hee failed in one of the
43 least, and that upon a faire pretense, it lost him the kingdom, which should have beene his reward, if hee had
44 observed his commission. Thus stands the cause betweene God and us. We are entered into Covenant with Him for
45 this worke. Wee haue taken out a commission. The Lord hath given us leave to drawe our own articles. Wee haue
46 professed to enterprise these and those accounts, upon these and those ends. Wee have hereupon besought Him of
47 favour and blessing. Now if the Lord shall please to heare us, and bring us in peace to the place we desire, then hath
48 hee ratified this covenant and sealed our Commission, and will expect a strict performance of the articles contained

49 in it; but if wee shall neglect the observation of these articles which are the ends wee have propounded, and,
50 dissembling with our God, shall fall to embrace this present world and prosecute our carnall intentions, seeking
51 great things for ourselves and our posterity, the Lord will surely breake out in wrathe against us; be revenged of
52 such a [sinful] people and make us knowe the price of the breache of such a covenant.
53         Now the onely way to avoyde this shipwracke, and to provide for our posterity, is to followe the counsell of
54 Micah, to doe justly, to love mercy, to walk humbly with our God. For this end, wee must be knitt together, in this
55 worke, as one man. Wee must entertaine each other in brotherly affection. Wee must be willing to abridge ourselves
56 of our superfluities, for the supply of other's necessities. Wee must uphold a familiar commerce together in all
57 meekeness, gentlenes, patience and liberality. Wee must delight in eache other; make other's conditions our oune;
58 rcjoicc together, mourne together, labour and suffer together, allwayes haueving before our eyes our commission
59 and community in the worke, as members of the same body. Soe shall wee keepe the unitie of the spirit in the bond
60 of peace. The Lord will be our God, and delight to dwell among us, as his oune people, and will command a blessing
61 upon us in all our wayes. Soe that wee shall see much more of his wisdome, power, goodness and truthe, than
62 formerly wee haue been acquainted with. Wee shall finde that the God of Israell is among us, when ten of us shall be
63 able to resist a thousand of our enemies; when hee shall make us a prayse and glory that men shall say of succeeding
64 plantations, "the Lord make it likely that of New England." For wee must consider that wee shall be as *a citty upon*
65 *a hill.* The eies of all people are uppon us. Soe that if wee shall deale falsely with our God in this worke wee haue
66 undertaken, and soe cause him to withdrawe his present help from us, wee shall be made a story and a by-word
67 through the world. Wee shall open the mouthes of enemies to speake evill of the wayes of God, and all professors
68 for God's sake. Wee shall shame the faces of many of God's worthy servants, and cause theire prayers to be turned
69 into curses upon us till wee be consumed out of the good land whither wee are a goeing.
70         I shall shutt upp this discourse with that exhortation of Moses, that faithfull servant of the Lord, in his last
71 farewell to Israell, Deut. 30. Beloued there is now sett before us life and good, Death and evill, in that wee are
72 commanded this day to loue the Lord our God, and to loue one another, to walke in his wayes and to keepe his
73 Commandements and his Ordinance and his lawes, and the articles of our Covenant with him, that wee may liue and
74 be multiplied, and that the Lord our God may blesse us in the land whither wee goe to possesse it. But if our heartes
75 shall turne away, soe that wee will not obey, but shall be seduced, and worshipp and serue other Gods, our pleasure
76 and proffitts, and serue them; it is propounded unto us this day, wee shall surely perishe out of the good land whither
77 wee passe over this vast sea to possesse it;

78
79                     Therefore lett us choose life
80                       that wee, and our seede
81                       may liue, by obeyeing His
82                   voyce and cleaveing to Him,
83                        for Hee is our life and
84                         our prosperity.

(https://history.hanover.edu/texts/winthmod.html)

## Close Reading

1.  This passage argues that
    A.  Winthrop's community must build in high places.
    B.  Native Americans will guide the community to high places.
    C.  Like the Greeks, who conquered all, Winthrop's community will be a city on a hill.
    D.  Winthrop's community was to be an example for the rest of the world in rightful living.

2.  This passage most seems like a
    A.  Sermon
    B.  Speech
    C.  Song
    D.  Essay

3.  What metaphor does Winthrop use for the relationship between his community and God?
    A.  A flock
    B.  A partnership
    C.  A marriage
    D.  A team

4.  How does Winthrop develop his argument?
    A.  He pleads with his community to repent.
    B.  He establishes humankind's relationship with God and applies that to circumstances.
    C.  He reminisces about times in England.
    D.  He misses his wife.

5.  It is probable that Winthrop is
    A.  A pious Christian.
    B.  Anti-Semitic.
    C.  Roman Catholic.
    D.  An agnostic.

6.  What assumptions can be inferred from this passage?
    I.    Freedom of religion
    II.   The eradication of Native Americans
    III.  Equal rights for women
    IV.   God is sovereign.

    A. I and II
    B. II and III
    C. III and IV
    D. IV

# Lesson 5

## Math: Algebra, Arithmetic Problem Solving and Data Analysis, and Passport to Advanced Math

### Passport to Advanced Math

1. Which of the following statements are true?

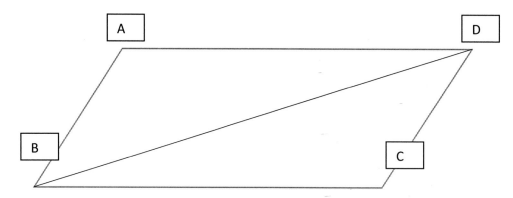

    I. If a ball, B, is struck a blow which if acting alone would drive the ball to A, and a blow which alone would drive it to C, and both blows are delivered at once, the ball takes the direction BD, the diagonal of the parallelogram of BA and BC, and the force is just sufficient to drive the ball to D. BD is the resultant of the two forces.

   II. If a third force, represented by some line BE, operates simultaneously with those represented by BA and BC, then the diagonal of the parallelogram of BD and BE is the resultant of the three forces.

 III. Hence the resultant of forces is always more than the sum of the forces unless the forces act in the same direction.

 IV. The more nearly their lines of action approach each other, the more nearly does their resultant approach their sum.

      A. I and II           C. I, II, and III          E. All
      B. II and IV         D. I, II, and IV

### Arithmetic Problem Solving

1. Three brothers have 574 stamps. John has 15 less than Henry, and Thomas has 4 more than John. How many has each?
   A. H, 100 stamps; J, 85 stamps; T, 170 stamps
   B. H, 180 stamps; J, 180 stamps; T, 179 stamps
   C. H, 200 stamps; J, 185 stamps; T, 189 stamps
   D. H, 205 stamps; J, 190 stamps; T, 195 stamps

2. If one person is just a year older than another, what is the ratio of the age of the younger to that of the older, at successive birthdays?
   A.  1/1, 2/2, 3/3, 4/4          C.  2/3, 4/6, 8/12, 16/23
   B.  0/1, 1/2, 2/3, 3/4          D.  NONE

3. A merchant bought $a$ barrels of sugar and $p$ barrels of molasses. How many barrels in all did he buy?
   A.  a(p)         B.  $2a + p$.        C.  $a + 3p$.        D.  $a + p$.

## Data Analysis

The above chart records the death rate at three colonial settlements: Jamestown, Plymouth, and Boston.

1. The following is true:
   I. In Year 1 Jamestown's death rate was double the death rate of Boston.
   II. More people died in Jamestown than in any other settlement.
   III. In Year 15, the death rate in all three settlements was less than half the death rate in Year 1.

   A. I                    C. III
   B. II and III           D. All

2. What assumptions can be drawn from Year 5?
   A. The death rate decreased from Year 1 in all settlements.
   B. Sickness or some other catastrophe struck the Boston settlement.
   C. The birth rate increased.
   D. Native Americans attacked all three settlements.

3. Based on these statistics the following facts might be inferred:
   I. Many settlers were unprepared for the first year in the colonies.
   II. Native American attacks were more numerous.
   III. There was a shortage of women.
   IV. Gold was discovered.

   A. I and II             C. III
   B. III and IV           D. All

## Algebra

1. Charles walked $x$ miles and rode 9 miles. How far did he go?
   D. $x + 9$              F. $2x + 9$
   E. $2(x)$               G. $2x + 9(x)$

2. A person bought a silk dress for $m$ dollars, a muff for 20 dollars, a shawl for $v$ dollars, and a pair of gloves for $c$ dollars. What was the entire cost?
   A. $20m + v + c$
   B. $m + 20v + c$
   C. $m + 20 + v + c$
   D. $m + 20 + v(c)$

# Chapter 19   Make Me a Blessing
# Genesis 12

---

*Memory Verses:* The LORD had said to Abram, "Go from your country, your people and your father's household to the land I will show you. I will make you into a great nation, and I will bless you; I will make your name great, and you will be a blessing. I will bless those who bless you, and whoever curses you I will curse; and all peoples on earth will be blessed through you." —Genesis 12:1–3

---

"O God," I complained rather than prayed, "Jimmy."

Jimmy, one of our "adopted" street people, sat in a corner of my tired inner-city Pittsburgh church basement. Unshaven, polluting the room with his pungent body odor, he pulled his moth-eaten (but nonetheless impressive) Harris Tweed jacket around his shoulders.

Jimmy was the last person I wanted to meet this early December morning. I had come to my office to grab a few quiet moments, but I had been greeted by light leaking from beneath our poorly insulated basement door. Exorbitant light bills demanded that I investigate.

I found Jimmy, who had managed, somehow, to enter the church last night.

Jimmy was the kind of person who would disappoint even the most dedicated humanitarian. "I need two bucks," he would plead. "Pay you back next week," he lied.

It was not the money or the lying that bothered me; it was his persistent, unmitigated gall. While the rest of us lived within limits, Jimmy—by lying, stealing, and conning others—managed to exceed the limits.

Like the time he lived in a hotel by telling the Red Cross his house had burned down. The truth was, for almost thirty years now, he had never lived in a house, only in doorways, abandoned buildings, and shelters. But Jimmy had enjoyed his hotel accommodations while they lasted. Jimmy always enjoyed the fruits of his sins! Maybe that irritated me a little too .Jimmy had never joined my church, but he had not missed a service in more than a year. Of course not! Church services were an entrepreneurial venture for Jimmy! He worked the north door during Sunday school, the basement door between services (to catch recalcitrant smokers who were more than willing to do penance for their nasty sin), and brazenly worked the front door (sometimes standing a few yards from me!) after church services. When he was seriously conning people, Jimmy could make $40 an hour! While preparing our budget, my former church officers jokingly thought of making Jimmy a separate budget line item.

Now Jimmy had decided to camp in our church basement. He wheezed, and as he moved, a urine bag peeked from beneath his Harris Tweed. Then it hit me: Jimmy's not here to sleep, eat, or con anyone. His colon cancer has finally caught up with him. He's come here to die. He was part of our family—we had adopted him. He had come home to his family to die. I am no longer a sentimentalist. I have had to learn, usually the hard way, to think quickly, to act decisively. The urban world is merciless. And right then, despite Jimmy's predicament, I had had enough of lingering death and problems and Jimmys. I wonder why he couldn't die in somebody else's church. But I knew, too, the importance our church offered urban dwellers, especially homeless ones: a destination, a home.

"Did you hear that the Pirates took the Expos last night?" Jimmy asked me. He knew I was caught. He had never read Matthew, but he still knew I had to help him. What else could I do? If I could not help a man die in dignity, what meaning did any of this ministry stuff have?

Coming home for Christmas. Jimmy had come home for Christmas—to die. And he knew that home is the place where you go when you have to go there and a place where they have to take you in. He was our family.

"The sense of being lost, displaced, and homeless is pervasive in contemporary culture. ... We have everything but possess nothing." When we have God as our Abba, Father, then we have everything. There is a basic need for human beings to be "named." We need to be known, to be loved, to have an identity. To lose what Brueggemann calls "lostness" and Barth calls "otherness." We need to find a home. To cease to be a Kafkaesque stranger. One of the great ironies of American culture is that, though shaped by a great emphasis on our vast physical environment, we are not encouraged to put down roots into that environment.

Professor Sang Lee, of Princeton Theological Seminary, reminds us that there is an opportunity for American churches "to acknowledge their own non-intimacy and to embark upon a search for Home which, when found, could be the true Home for all people of all races." Americans make their homes in the strangest places. Pico Iyer in *Harper's Magazine* (August 1995) writes, "Airports are the new epicenters and paradigms of our dawning post-national age—

not just the bus terminals of the global village but the prototypes, in some sense, for polyglot, multicolored, user-friendly future." Airports are like MacDonald's—they have no national origin or allegiance. They never go to bed. Never stop producing a product. Go on and on and on. No beginning. No ending. Self-contained cities with restaurants, showers, theatres, etc. But, if they produce a product, satisfy a need, they still are not and will never be home. They are only a place we go and come from but never live in."

In Genesis 12, Abraham is homeless. He no longer lives in Ur, but he does not yet really live anywhere else. Haran was just a stopover. Yet he still has much: the promises of God.

God's covenant with Abram, which became the basis for future covenants with Israel and with Christians, was essentially a promise to bless Abram so that Abram and his descendants might bless the world. All future covenants between the Lord and his chosen people carried this purpose. God blesses a people in order to make them a blessing to others.

Abram/Abraham was promised a place to dwell, a place of promise, a home, the promised land. He was to possess the land. He never really made it his home. He was always a sojourner there, but he was a man always looking for a city, "whose architect and builder is God" (Hebrews 11:10).The actual possession of the land came hundreds of years later, when Joshua led Israel into Canaan. Christians have the promise of a home, whose architect and builder is the Lord Jesus Christ (John 14:1–6). Our homes on earth are given by God and cherished deeply, but our ultimate home, the home of promise, is heaven.

The West Indian slave community treasured a story called "Turtle Knows Your Name." The tale goes like this. Once there was a little boy, and he had a very long name: Upsilimana Tumpalera. He lived with his grandmother. It took this child a long time to learn to say his name. But finally he managed to do it right, and his grandmother was delighted. The granny told her son to teach his name to his playmates. He did.

Later the granny challenged her grandson to speak her own name. The turtle told him: Mapaseedo Jackalindy Eye Pie Tackarindy. Do you know *your* name? The greatest fear of us all is not that we will starve, or be powerless, but that we have no name. That we will have no history. Abram's (or Abraham's) name became and remains great because of an enormous progeny both physically and spiritually. He became the father of descendants as numerous as the stars. The name of Christian becomes great through our "new name" (Revelation 2:17). The new person in Jesus Christ is represented by the "new name." Also, there is a parallel in our covenant promise to the great nation promised Abram. The 144,000 people of Revelation 14:1 represent an awesome complete number of folks who have the names of the Lamb and his Father written on their foreheads.

Again and again God protected Abraham, Isaac, and Jacob from their foes. Later God delivered Israel from slavery in Egypt, protected and provided for them in the wilderness, and eventually led them to conquest of as much of Canaan as they were willing to take. Throughout the period of the judges and the reigns of Saul, David, and Solomon, God protected his people when they remained loyal to the covenant. They were, then, free. Free people. Free in the assurance of their salvation. Freedom, like privacy, is often thought of in spatial terms. To be free is to be unencumbered and able to move without hindrance. When problems arise, freedom means that one can move on, to a new city, a new job. Because going is as important as arriving, the temptation is always present to confuse movement with progress. Movement has become merely linear: Movement takes the place of progress, which has a definite direction, a good direction, and is a force that controls human beings. Progress was what the old revolutions were evidence of. Movement Has none of this naive, moralistic nonsense in it. Motion rather than fixity is our condition—but motion without any content or goal not imposed on it by human will. Somewhere in the middle of the twentieth century, America lost its way. Progress lost its meaning. Everyone began to confuse "movement" and "progress."

We, though, know what real progress is: true progress is to be used by the Lord. The August 31 meditation by Oswald Chambers in *My Utmost for His Highest* reminds us that God does not create fat juicy grapes to just sit and look pretty. He produces fat juicy grapes that will be crushed for his glory. We Christians will be home when we are in God's hand and being used by God. Christians are given the security of eternal life in Jesus Christ. Jesus has promised to keep us in his hand (John 10:27–28). Furthermore, we have the promise of the church's triumph over evil. Jesus declared that "the gates of Hades will not prevail against it" (Matthew 16:18 NRSV). God blesses his people according to his promises. God always has and he always will. May we be loyal and keep our promises to God so that his blessings in our lives will in turn make us blessings to others.

## Journal Question

Where is your home? What is your name?

# Lesson 1
## Evidence-Based Reading and Writing

### Literary Choice

Mark Twain, the reluctant writer—he always preferred the life of a river pilot—was arguably the greatest nineteenth-century author that America produced. *The Adventures of Huckleberry Finn*, in particular, is one of the greatest novels in all time, and the first American example of realism.

### Chapter: The Last

1    The first time I catched Tom private I asked him what was his idea, time of the evasion? —what it was he'd planned
2    to do if the evasion worked all right and he managed to set a n---- free that was already free before? And he said,
3    what he had planned in his head from the start, if we got Jim out all safe, was for us to run him down the river on the
4    raft, and have adventures plumb to the mouth of the river, and then tell him about his being free, and take him back
5    up home on a steamboat, in style, and pay him for his lost time, and write word ahead and get out all the n----s
6    around, and have them waltz him into town with a torchlight procession and a brass-band, and then he would be a
7    hero, and so would we. But I reckoned it was about as well the way it was.
8        We had Jim out of the chains in no time, and when Aunt Polly and Uncle Silas and Aunt Sally found out
9    how good he helped the doctor nurse Tom, they made a heap of fuss over him, and fixed him up prime, and give him
10   all he wanted to eat, and a good time, and nothing to do. And we had him up to the sick-room, and had a high talk;
11   and Tom give Jim forty dollars for being prisoner for us so patient, and doing it up so good, and Jim was pleased
12   most to death, and busted out, and says:
13       "Dah, now, Huck, what I tell you? —what I tell you up dah on Jackson islan'? I tole you I got a hairy
14   breas', en what's de sign un it; en I tole you I ben rich wunst, en gwineter to be rich agin en it's come true; en heah
15   she is! Dah, now! doan' talk to me— signs is signs, mine I tell you; en I knowed jis' 's well 'at I 'uz gwineter be
16   rich agin as I's a-stannin' heah dis minute!"
17       And then Tom he talked along and talked along, and says, le's all three slide out of here one of these nights
18   and get an outfit, and go for howling adventures amongst the Injuns, over in the Territory, for a couple of weeks or
19   two; and I says, all right, that suits me, but I ain't got no money for to buy the outfit, and I reckon I couldn't get
20   none from home, because it's likely pap's been back before now, and got it all away from Judge Thatcher and drunk
21   it up.
22       "No, he hain't," Tom says; "it's all there yet—six thousand dollars and more; and your pap hain't ever been
23   back since. Hadn't when I come away, anyhow."
24       Jim says, kind of solemn:
25       "He ain't a-comin' back no mo', Huck."
26       I says:
27       "Why, Jim?"
28       "Nemmine why, Huck—but he ain't comin' back no mo."
29       But I kept at him; so at last he says:
30       "Doan' you 'member de house dat was float'n down de river, en dey wuz a man in dah, kivered up, en I
31   went in en unkivered him and didn' let you come in? Well, den, you kin git yo' money when you wants it, kase dat
32   wuz him."
33       Tom's most well now, and got his bullet around his neck on a watch-guard for a watch, and is always
34   seeing what time it is, and so there ain't nothing more to write about, and I am rotten glad of it, because if I'd a
35   knowed what a trouble it was to make a book I wouldn't a tackled it, and ain't a-going to no more. But I reckon I got
36   to light out for the Territory ahead of the rest, because Aunt Sally she's going to adopt me and sivilize me, and I
37   can't stand it. I been there before.

## Student Response

### The Ending of *The Adventures of Huckleberry Finn*

1   **Literary critics have debated over the ending of *The Adventures of Huckleberry Finn*, arguing whether or not**
2   **it is disappointing or if it is in keeping with the rest of the work.** It is this writer's opinion that the ending is not
3   at all disappointing. Instead, the conclusion to this classic is consistent with the rest of the story, allowing humor to
4   define the outcome. Also, it is not a letdown because it is simply logical. In both *The Adventures of Tom Sawyer* and
5   *The Adventures of Huckleberry Finn*, Mark Twain makes it very clear that while both Tom and Huck have great
6   adventures, they are still young boys who have guardians to take care of them. If Huck had not ended up at the
7   Phelps home with Tom, he may never have returned to the Widow Douglass, his caretaker. Because the ending is
8   both humorous and logical, this writer holds that it is in fact an appropriate ending.

9       The ending is a hilarious description of Tom's and Huck's efforts to rescue Jim. Critics argue that this
10  simply deteriorates the plot that has built up to this point. This writer, however, believes that their humorous
11  escapades are in keeping with the long line of comical events in the book. In the beginning of the book, when Huck
12  is still living with the Widow Douglass, he joins a secret club led by Tom Sawyer. In their oath, the boys make
13  several dramatic claims that the reader understands are completely fictitious. "'Now we'll start this band of robbers
14  and call it Tom Sawyer's Gang. Everybody that wants to join has got to take an oath, and write his name in blood.
15  . . . If anybody done anything to any boy in the band, whichever boy was ordered to kill that person and his family
16  must do it, and he mustn't eat and he mustn't sleep till he had killed them and hacked a cross in their breasts, which
17  was the sign of the band.'" This graphic oath is made so disturbing that the reader recognizes that the boys are not
18  serious. Instead, Tom orates a humorous speech for the reader. Later in the novel, as Jim and Huck make their way
19  down the Mississippi River, they meet two con artists. These two men trick Jim and Huck into believing that they
20  are royalty from Europe. " 'Bilgewater, I am the late Dauphin!' . . . 'You are what?' 'Yes, my friend, it is too true—
21  your eyes are lookin' at this very moment on the pore disappeared Dauphin, Looy the Seventeen, son of Looy the
22  Sixteen and Marry Antonette.'" Mark Twain incorporates both slapstick and dry humor throughout the novel. This is
23  partially why Tom's plans to rescue Jim in the ending, which include pix-axes, blood, spoons, and a moat, do not
24  deviate from the plot.

25      Another reason this conclusion is plausible is that Huck really is just a young boy who needs someone to
26  look after him. Mark Twain, when developing the characters of both Huck and Tom, ensures that they have a loving
27  guardian to look after them, even if their own parents are not there to help. In the preceding literary work, *The*
28  *Adventures of Tom Sawyer*, Twain gives Tom his aunt Polly to care for him. For Huck Finn, he lives with the
29  Widow Douglass, as his father is not fit to take care of him. "The Widow Douglass, she took me for her son, and
30  allowed she would sivilize me; but it was rough living in the house all the time, considering how dismal regular and
31  decent the widow was in all her ways." As well, at the ending, Twain again presents another opportunity for Huck to
32  have a real home. "But I reckon I got to light out for the Territory ahead of the rest, because Aunt Sally she's going
33  to adopt me and sivilize me and I can't stand it." While Huck believes he can escape being 'civilized,' the reader
34  recognizes that he'll most likely have to go back home and attend school again. The plot leading up to the ending
35  makes this possible.

36      **While arguments have emerged that the ending of *The Adventures of Huckleberry Finn* is**
37  **disappointing and not in keeping with the plot, it is this writer's contention that it is indeed in keeping with**
38  **the plot and is fitting based on two points.** First, the humorous parts of the ending are simply a reflection of the
39  many comical moments throughout the book. Second, Mark Twain understands that Huck must return to the
40  Widow's home to become 'civilized.' Therefore, it is imperative that he be found by such a family as the Phelps.

## Close Reading

1.  Twain employs colloquial language to
    I.   Add realism to his protagonist.
    II.  Add humor.
    III. Identify this literary piece as a juvenile novel.

    A. I                B. I and II              C. II and III              D. All

2.  What is the narrative technique?
    A. Omniscient                          C. First person
    B. Limited omniscient                  D. Third-person objective

3. What is the tone of most of the novel?
   A. Tentative
   B. Sanguine
   C. Choleric
   D. Humorous

4. The author creates the tone by
   A. Humorous scenes and language.
   B. Alliteration.
   C. Internal conflict.
   D. Antagonistic characters.

5. This novel is an example of
   A. Romanticism.
   B. Existentialism.
   C. Naturalism.
   D. Realism.

6. Tom Sawyer is a
   A. Protagonist.
   B. Foil.
   C. Antagonist.
   D. Enemy.

7. The author is probably
   A. An agnostic.
   B. An atheist.
   C. A fervent believer.
   D. A secularist.

## Command of Evidence (Student Response)

1. The beginning of the Student Response (Line 1) is inadequate because
   A. The student should always begin with a generalization.
   B. The student should always begin with name of the literary piece.
   C. The student should not begin with unnamed sources (literary critics).
   D. The student is not credentialed to be a critic and needs to admit it.

2. A good summary of the student argument would be
   A. Lines 7–8.
   B. Lines 17–18.
   C. Lines 27–30.
   D. Lines 39–40.

3. What is a favorite strategy of argumentation used?
   A. Arguments and then counterarguments
   B. Arguments and then supportive textual quotes
   C. Arguments with supporting anecdotes
   D. Arguments with quotes from critics

4. "Another reason" is an example of
   A. Onomatopoeia
   B. Dialecticism
   C. Syllogism
   D. Transitions

5. The conclusion
   A. Offers a new tangent.
   B. Summarizes the argument.
   C. Contradicts the thesis.
   D. Restates the question.

6. Line 10, "This writer, however, believes," is poor syntax because it is
   A. Irrelevant.
   B. Tangential.
   C. Redundant.
   D. Trite.

7. The reason for the above answer?
   A. Twain simply does not like adults.
   B. Twain should not use substandard English in a formal novel.
   C. To say "The writer believes" is self-evident.
   D. Some words are misspelled.

## Grammar and Usage

Choose the best grammar/usage form in bold sentence(s).

1. Student Response, Lines 1–2

   A. NONE
   B. Literary critics, believing that the plot shifts in the last few chapters are alien to Twain's plot scheme, have fervently criticized the ending of *The Adventures of Huckleberry Finn*.
   C. Literary critics, criticizing the end of *The Adventures of Huckleberry Finn*, believe the last few chapters are alien to Twain's intent.
   D. Literary critics often argue over the ending of *The Adventures of Huckleberry Finn*, arguing whether or not it is disappointing or if it is in keeping with the rest of the work.

2. Student Response, Lines 34–36

   A. NONE
   B. While arguments have emerged that the ending of *The Adventures of Huckleberry Finn* disappoints and not in keeping with the plot, it is this writer's contention that it is indeed keeping with the plot and is fitting based on two points.
   C. While arguments that the ending of *The Adventures of Huckleberry Finn* is disappointing and not in keeping with the plot, it is this writer's contention that it is indeed keeping with the plot and is fitting based on two points.
   D. In spite of criticism to the contrary, the ending is in concert with the rest of the plot in two ways.

# Lesson 2
## Critical Reading and Writing

### Command of Evidence

Read the following passages and answer accompanying questions:

### Passage 1

1　In her book *Nickel and Dimed*, Barbara Ehrenreich went to great lengths to produce a firsthand account of the trials
2　endured by the lower classes. Ehrenreich's experiences have given her readers a clearer picture of the emotional and
3　physical strain that has become a reality for all too many Americans. Ehrenreich's story is very insightful and gives
4　the reader a greater appreciation of the hardships that the lower classes face, but the proposed solutions she implies
5　in *Nickel and Dimed* would be ineffective.

6　　　From the reader's perspective, Ehrenreich's purpose in writing is quite respectable and insightful. She
7　attempts to portray the desperate life and propose solutions to the challenges of many lower-class Americans.
8　Although few upper-class Americans have given up their affluence to understand the life of the "working poor,"
9　Ehrenreich humbly went undercover and did just that. She relocated to several cities, where she worked as a server,
10　maid, and salesclerk. Her firsthand account of the lower class enables the reader to better understand the intensity of
11　the workload and the emotional anguish of trying to make ends meet. *Nickel and Dimed* gives the reader an
12　insightful understanding that would be unattainable with mere facts and statistics. Not only does Ehrenreich tell
13　about her experiences, but she also looks for the roots of the problem and subtly proposes solutions.

14　　　To offer an effective solution, one must first understand the roots of the problem. In paragraph 8 of the
15　expert from *Nickel and Dimed*, Ehrenreich points out some of the problems she sees with society:
16

17　　　　　But as the days go by, my old life is beginning to look exceedingly strange. The e-mails and phone
18　　　　　messages addressed to my former self come from a distant race of people with exotic concerns and far too
19　　　　　much time on their hands. . . . When I sit down one morning in my real home to pay bills from my past life,
20　　　　　I am dazzled by the two- and three-figure sums owed to outfits like Club Body Tech and Amazon.com.
21

22　　　This passage and others like it show that Ehrenreich believes the problem with society is that the rich have
23　too much time and money and the poor have no leisure time and hardly enough money to make ends meet. She sees
24　that the problem is "our highly polarized and unequal society." However, this reader argues that the "unequal
25　society" is only a symptom of the underlying problem in the hearts of humans and in the feeble church. According to
26　the Bible, the church should be responsible for the care of the poor and needy (Proverbs 31:8–9; Galatians 2:10). Dr.
27　George Grant, a biblical historian, says history proves that when the church fulfills its proper role according to
28　Scripture, nearly all social and economic problems are resolved. Therefore, a lack of care and concern for the poor is
29　not the biggest problem, rather it is ultimately a symptom of the fault of the church.

30　　　Not only does Ehrenreich believe that the "highly polarized" society is the reason for the hardships endured
31　by lower classes, but she also suggests that the solution to this problem is to spread the wealth. She subtlety
32　advances her political agenda through a strong appeal to pathos. She plays upon the empathy of the reader to suggest
33　that everything would be better if everything were equal. This classic socialistic propaganda has several admirable
34　goals, but many untenable solutions. Despite the very subtle appearance, Ehrenreich is nonetheless advocating for
35　government-regulated redistribution of wealth: taking from the rich and giving to the poor. Although socialism
36　might sound like an effective solution, history proves that socialistic and communistic nations are ineffective
37　because productivity is not rewarded, and therefore entire nations become impoverished, as seen in the Soviet
38　Union.

39　　　In summary, this reader finds Ehrenreich's firsthand accounts respectable and insightful, but her solutions
40　to the challenges that lower-class Americans face are ineffectual. Ehrenreich is not simply telling story; she is
41　advancing a counterproductive socialistic agenda. (Jacqueline).

1. What would be the best title for this essay?
   A. Nickel and Dimed
   B. The Working Class
   C. Nickel and Dimed Socialism
   D. Waiting Tables

2. From this essay the reader might surmise that the author is a
   A. Libertarian.
   B. Socialist.
   C. Liberal.
   D. Conservative.

3. What is the purpose of Lines 16–19?
   A. The author wishes to increase readers' empathy with the poor.
   B. The author wishes to show that Ehrenreich's pithy insights are really veiled socialism.
   C. The author wishes to show how hard it is to live on minimum wages.
   D. The author implies that she is supportive of price controls.

4. What organizational plan does the author employ?
   A. She offers an alternative option at first and then argues the opposite.
   B. She defines the perimeters of her argument and then argues against opposite positions.
   C. She analyzes Ehrenreich's book and then criticizes it.
   D. She strongly supports price controls.

5. What example does the author offer to illustrate her argument?
   A. Examples from communist countries
   B. The failure of socialism in China
   C. Socioeconomic data
   D. Opposite examples

6. The author finishes her essay with
   A. A summary statement.
   B. A new conclusion.
   C. A distracting comment.
   D. The way she began.

7. What is one flaw in the author's reasoning?
   A. She generalizes too much.
   B. She supports a capitalist agenda.
   C. She dislikes working at a fast-food restaurant.
   D. She prefers to read books more than working.

8. An example?
   A. She assumes all poor people are lazy.
   B. She misrepresents communism.
   C. She assumes socialism and communism are the same.
   D. She supports unrealistic social theories.

9. It is fair to assume that the author of the essay is
   A. An agnostic
   B. A socialist
   C. A European
   D. A born-again Christian

10. The entire essay could be called a
    A. Summary.
    B. Précis.
    C. Polemic.
    D. Diatribe.

## Passage 2

1  What role does community play in modern society? What characteristics lead to a productive, successful
2  community? Throughout the ages, many sociologists and philosophers have proposed multiple answers to these
3  questions, with some advocating for extreme tribalism and others suggesting radical self-sufficiency. This writer
4  attempts display the spectrum of ideas by discussing the traditional Alvord, the moderate Howard and Etzioni, and
5  the radical Thoreau.
6      Lori Arviso Alvord, in "Walking the Path between Two Worlds" (chap. 2 in *The Scalpel and the Silver*
7  *Bear* [1999]), describes her journey from the Dinetah reservation to Dartmouth University. As she reflects on that

8  rough transition, she argues that a productive, successful community would be like her own Navajo tribe. She even
9  goes so far as to say that her tribal membership was "central to mental health, to spiritual heath, to physical health."
10  She argues that security, education, place of belonging, strong relationships, humility, cooperation, and respect for
11  elders are all vital characteristics for a healthy community because they are so important to her Navajo tribe. After
12  she moved to Dartmouth and settled down with her fellow Native American students, she realized that community is
13  not determined by bloodline because even tribes as different as the Paiutes, Sioux, Cherokees, Chippewas, Navajos,
14  and Pueblos were able to come together and "coalesce into a solid community." These Native Americans were
15  "friends, lovers, rivals, enemies," yet they came together and formed a productive and successful community. In
16  summary, Alvord argues that the world is "full of wandering singular souls," but a true community is characterized
17  by "a feeling of inclusion in something larger, of having a set place in the universe where one always belongs. It
18  provides connectedness and a blueprint for how to live."

19  In his essay titled "The New Community," Amitai Etzioni identifies two main characteristics necessary for
20  productive, successful communities. He argues that close-knit relationships are vital to communities, and when these
21  relationships are lost, the result is "isolation, lack of caring for one another, and exposure to rowdiness and crime."
22  Etzioni also believes that communities must have the "essential moral underpinnings" in order to be successful. He
23  discusses numerous historical examples like the gold rush, where weak social bonds and loose morals contributed to
24  the decline of society. Despite his strong belief in community, he clearly does not believe that America should return
25  to village tribalism. Etzioni calls for small, intimate communities within the larger society. He desires unity among
26  diversity. "We need to strengthen the communitarian elements in the urban and suburban centers, to provide the
27  social bonds that sustain the moral voice, but at the same time avoid tight networks that suppress pluralism and
28  dissent. . . . In short, we need new communities in which people have choices and readily accommodate divergent
29  subcommunities but still maintain common bands."

30  In her article titled "In Search of the Good Family," Jane Howard establishes ten characteristics that define
31  a productive and successful community, which she calls a "good family." She argues that true communities must
32  have "a chief, or heroine, or founder," have a member who keeps track of everyone else, be valued by all their
33  members, convey affection, have at least one "flamboyant eccentric," be hospitable, esteem their rituals, have a
34  sense of place, relate with their posterity, and "honor their elders." Like Etzioni, Howard seeks to combine
35  traditional philosophies with modern ideas. The first five characteristics are contemporary ideas, while the last five
36  are more traditional values. "Let that be a lesson to clans based on interest as well as to those based on genes."

37  In his essay titled "Where I Lived, and What I Lived For," Henry David Thoreau thoroughly contorts
38  Alvord's traditional ideas of community. He argues that there is no such thing as a productive, successful
39  community. Instead, the goal should be to produce independent individuals. He believes that an individual's desires
40  are incompatible with the society and that a person should seek his own dreams and aspirations without allowing
41  society to dictate his life. He argues that success for the individual can only be achieved by moving away from
42  primitive traditional communities and advancing toward modern individuality. In advocating for this sort of
43  Descartian "individualism," Thoreau suggests living independently and self-sufficiently, as he did on Walden Pond.
44  "I went to the woods because I wished to live deliberately, to front only the essential facts of life, and see if I could
45  not learn what it had to teach, and not, when I came to die, discover that I had not lived."

46  Communities are complex issues, and these four views reveal how broad the spectrum truly is. The many
47  opinions regarding what role communities have in society show the importance of this issue. Alvord, Howard,
48  Etzioni, and Thoreau present many opposing ideas, yet each offers practical insights into which characteristics
49  produce productive and successful communities. (Jacqueline)

1. What would be the best title of this essay?
   A. The Importance of Community
   B. Community: A Survey
   C. The Romantics: Thoreau and Emerson
   D. The End of all Things

2. How does the author begin her essay?
   A. Summary
   B. Argument
   C. Rhetorical questions
   D. Quotes

3. What organizational plan does the author employ?
   A. A summary statement about several views on community
   B. A diatribe
   C. A précis
   D. A polemic

# Lesson 3
## SAT Essay

### Student Response 1

*Prompt:* What is more important: genetics or environment?

1  "Why are we the way we are? Why are some Type B individuals and some Type A individuals? Why are
2  some agreeable and others disagreeable? Why are some peacemakers and others peace-breakers? These questions
3  have haunted philosophers and scientists alike for centuries. Many philosophers and scientists throughout the ages
4  have come to the conclusion that everyone is born a blank slate and individuals are solely the products of their
5  environment. Others claim that individuals are solely the products of their innate natures and genetic makeup.
6  Although both of these conclusions have flaws, both are correct to a certain extent. We are not solely the products of
7  our environment neither are we solely the products of our innate nature and genetic makeup. Rather it is a
8  combination of genetic makeup and environment that makes us the way we are?

9  Although we are not solely the product of our genetic makeup, genetic makeup does contribute to our
10  personalities, intelligence, and even happiness. According to Csikszentmihalyi, a genetic engineer, in his article,
11  "The Future of Happiness," Scientists have actually found a gene that helps determine happiness. In fact, scientists
12  studying identical twins found that, "fifty percent of happiness is inherited." Csikszentmihalyi, and other genetic
13  scientists also found that an individual's genetic makeup may also determine other behavioral characteristics.
14  Genetic engineers have come to the conclusion that, "Schizophrenia, propensity to divorce, and even political
15  beliefs" are possibly the product of genetics. Although these genetic determinants are still being examined, scientists
16  know for certain that intelligence is determined by a g gene, which determines not only the shape of our brain, but
17  also what parts of our brain are the most functional. In other words, this g gene not only determines how intelligent
18  we are, but also what kind of intelligent we are. If the g gene causes the right side of one's brain to be larger than the
19  left, that individual will be more creative than one whose g gene causes the left side of the brain to be larger than the
20  right side. Clearly, genetics does play a major role in making us the way we are.

21  Although scientists have found that genetics contribute to not only our phenotypic characteristics, but also
22  our behavioral characteristics, environment also plays a major role in making us the way we are. In the words of
23  Lewis Thomas in his article "On Cloning a Human Being," "If all you had was the genome, and no people around,
24  you'd grow a sort of vertebrate plant, nothing more." The effect an environment has on an individual can be seen by
25  the different personalities of identical twins. Identical twins have the exact same genome. They have the same genes
26  that supposedly determine "Schizophrenia, propensity to divorce, and even political beliefs" (Csikszentmihalyi),
27  however, their personalities are usually vastly different. Because identical twins have the exact same genetic
28  makeup, the difference between their personalities must be caused by the differences in their environment. If one
29  twin is carefree and outgoing whereas the other twin is studious and introverted, such personalities must have been
30  caused by the twin's different environments. Maybe one twin was bullied as a young child and consequently
31  inadvertently closed in on him/herself as to not get hurt. Maybe the other twin went to a party as a young child and
32  inadvertently decided that a party and social lifestyle was the path for him/her. Perhaps the environmental factors in
33  these twins' life were subtler, such as a small fight, or an approving eye, but either way, something in the twin's
34  environment must have determined their different personalities.

35  Clearly, we are the way we are because of both genetic and environmental factors. Genetic engineers today
36  are finding genes that are instrumental in determining our behavioral characteristics, however, genetically identical
37  twins could never be exactly the same because environmental factors also play a major role in our development and
38  personalities. (Sarah)

### Student Response 2

*Prompt:* In human relationships, do opposites attract? Or should we see out like-minded partners?

1  Conventional wisdom states that "opposites attract." Some people understand this to mean that people who
2  have differing personality traits and interests often get along best and create interesting friendships. However, in a
3  friendship both people need to think and connect in a similar fashion, while still retaining different personality traits.

4   One example of this is the relationship I had with my former debate partner. My goal was to win and to do
5   our best at the next tournament, while his was to have fun and do as little work as possible. I sent him the case we
6   would be running six weeks prior to the tournament, along with six articles about it, and asked him to read through it
7   before the tournament. He replied, saying that he had read through it and liked the case; however, at the tournament
8   he told the debate coach that he did not even know that we would be running this case. We could not get along
9   because we had different ways of thinking about debate and different goals in mind.
10  Although it is necessary for both friends to agree on certain things, it would be boring if both friends were
11  exactly the same. It is generally agreed that friends of differing personality traits get along best. For example, if two
12  friends were both melancholic, introverted, and thoughtful, they might spend an entire hour sitting together and
13  saying nothing. However, if they were both sanguine, they might be bouncing off the wall for the entire hour
14  without ever relaxing. We need friends that balance us out and have different personality traits to add while they still
15  agree with us on many things.
16  **It is important that all friends have something in common with those they are friends with so that**
17  **they can have a deep and meaningful friendship.** However, there also need to be some differing traits among
18  friends to keep things interesting while they still agree on core issues. We often get along best with those we can
19  relate to while still receiving new ideas. (Marci)

## Close Reading

1. In Student Response 1 the author
   A. Argues that the environment always trumps genetics.
   B. Argues that genetics always trumps environment.
   C. Argues that a combination of genetic makeup and environment that makes us the way we are.
   D. Argues that neither genetics nor environment determine who we are.

2. In Student Response 2 the author organizes her essay
   A. By offering a rhetorical questions.
   B. By offering a series of anecdotes.
   C. By stating a thesis and offering a couple of examples.
   D. By a series of bullet points.

3. What is a problem in Student Response Essay 2?
   I.   No specific examples are given.          III.    There are too many personal examples.
   II.  Transitions are weak.                    IV.     The essay is too short.

   A. I and II                                   C. II and III
   B. III and IV                                 D. I and IV

4. Where is the main point of the Student Response 1?
   A. Lines 3–5                                  C. Lines 21–25
   B. Lines 12–15                                D. Lines 35–38

5. Where is the main point of the Student Response 2?
   A. Lines 4–5          B. Lines 8–9            C. Lines 12–13          D. Lines 16–19

6. What is a significant stylistic problem in Student Response 2?
   A. First person is used.                      C. There are too many misplaced modifiers.
   B. Second-person pronouns are used.           D. There are agreement problems.

7. Where can evidence be found in Student Response 1?
   A. Lines 1–2         B. Lines 3–5             C. Lines 21–34          D. Lines 35–38

8. Where can evidence be found in Student Response 2?
   A. Lines 1–2         B. Lines 3–5             C. Lines 4–9            D. Lines 11–5

9. What score would the student responses receive?
   Student Response 1: __. Student Response 2: __.

## Grammar and Usage

Choose the best grammar/usage form in bold sentence(s).

Student Response 2, Lines 16–17

A. NONE
B. It is important that all friends have something in common with friends so that they can have a deep and meaningful friendship.
C. All meaningful friendships contain common interests.
D. It is important that all friends have something in common with whom they are friends with so that they can have a deep and meaningful friendship.

# Lesson 4
## Reading: Document-Based Analysis

### First Inaugural Address
### Abraham Lincoln (1861)

1    *Fellow-Citizens of the United States:*

2         In compliance with a custom as old as the Government itself, I appear before you to address you briefly and
3    to take in your presence the oath prescribed by the Constitution of the United States to be taken by the President
4    "before he enters on the execution of this office."

5         I do not consider it necessary at present for me to discuss those matters of administration about which there
6    is no special anxiety or excitement.

7         Apprehension seems to exist among the people of the Southern States that by the accession of a Republican
8    Administration their property and their peace and personal security are to be endangered. There has never been any
9    reasonable cause for such apprehension. Indeed, the most ample evidence to the contrary has all the while existed
10    and been open to their inspection. It is found in nearly all the published speeches of him who now addresses you. I
11    do but quote from one of those speeches when I declare that—

12         I have no purpose, directly or indirectly, to interfere with the institution of slavery in the States where it
13         exists. I believe I have no lawful right to do so, and I have no inclination to do so.

14         Those who nominated and elected me did so with full knowledge that I had made this and many similar
15    declarations and had never recanted them; and more than this, they placed in the platform for my acceptance, and as
16    a law to themselves and to me, the clear and emphatic resolution which I now read:

17         *Resolved,* That the maintenance inviolate of the rights of the States, and especially the right of each State to
18         order and control its own domestic institutions according to its own judgment exclusively, is essential to
19         that balance of power on which the perfection and endurance of our political fabric depend; and we
20         denounce the lawless invasion by armed force of the soil of any State or Territory, no matter what pretext,
21         as among the gravest of crimes.

22         I now reiterate these sentiments, and in doing so I only press upon the public attention the most conclusive
23    evidence of which the case is susceptible that the property, peace, and security of no section are to be in any wise
24    endangered by the now incoming Administration. I add, too, that all the protection which, consistently with the
25    Constitution and the laws, can be given will be cheerfully given to all the States when lawfully demanded, for
26    whatever cause—as cheerfully to one section as to another.

27         There is much controversy about the delivering up of fugitives from service or labor. The clause I now read
28    is as plainly written in the Constitution as any other of its provisions:

29         No person held to service or labor in one State, under the laws thereof, escaping into another, shall in
30         consequence of any law or regulation therein be discharged from such service or labor, but shall be
31         delivered up on claim of the party to whom such service or labor may be due.

32         It is scarcely questioned that this provision was intended by those who made it for the reclaiming of what
33    we call fugitive slaves; and the intention of the lawgiver is the law. All members of Congress swear their support to
34    the whole Constitution—to this provision as much as to any other. To the proposition, then, that slaves whose cases
35    come within the terms of this clause "shall be delivered up" their oaths are unanimous. Now, if they would make the
36    effort in good temper, could they not with nearly equal unanimity frame and pass a law by means of which to keep
37    good that unanimous oath?

38         There is some difference of opinion whether this clause should be enforced by national or by State
39    authority, but surely that difference is not a very material one. If the slave is to be surrendered, it can be of but little
40    consequence to him or to others by which authority it is done. And should anyone in any case be content that his
41    oath shall go unkept on a merely unsubstantial controversy as to how it shall be kept?

42         Again: In any law upon this subject ought not all the safeguards of liberty known in civilized and humane
43    jurisprudence to be introduced, so that a free man be not in any case surrendered as a slave? And might it not be well
44    at the same time to provide by law for the enforcement of that clause in the Constitution which guarantees that "the
45    citizens of each State shall be entitled to all privileges and immunities of citizens in the several States"?

46     I take the official oath to-day with no mental reservations and with no purpose to construe the Constitution
47 or laws by any hypercritical rules; and while I do not choose now to specify particular acts of Congress as proper to
48 be enforced, I do suggest that it will be much safer for all, both in official and private stations, to conform to and
49 abide by all those acts which stand unrepealed than to violate any of them trusting to find impunity in having them
50 held to be unconstitutional.

51     It is seventy-two years since the first inauguration of a President under our National Constitution. During
52 that period fifteen different and greatly distinguished citizens have in succession administered the executive branch
53 of the Government. They have conducted it through many perils, and generally with great success. Yet, with all this
54 scope of precedent, I now enter upon the same task for the brief constitutional term of four years under great and
55 peculiar difficulty. A disruption of the Federal Union, heretofore only menaced, is now formidably attempted.

56     I hold that in contemplation of universal law and of the Constitution the Union of these States is perpetual.
57 Perpetuity is implied, if not expressed, in the fundamental law of all national governments. It is safe to assert that no
58 government proper ever had a provision in its organic law for its own termination. Continue to execute all the
59 express provisions of our National Constitution, and the Union will endure forever, it being impossible to destroy it
60 except by some action not provided for in the instrument itself.

61     Again: If the United States be not a government proper, but an association of States in the nature of
62 contract merely, can it, as a contract, be peaceably unmade by less than all the parties who made it? One party to a
63 contract may violate it—break it, so to speak—but does it not require all to lawfully rescind it?

64     Descending from these general principles, we find the proposition that in legal contemplation the Union is
65 perpetual confirmed by the history of the Union itself. The Union is much older than the Constitution. It was
66 formed, in fact, by the Articles of Association in 1774. It was matured and continued by the Declaration of
67 Independence in 1776. It was further matured, and the faith of all the then thirteen States expressly plighted and
68 engaged that it should be perpetual, by the Articles of Confederation in 1778. And finally, in 1787, one of the
69 declared objects for ordaining and establishing the Constitution was "to form a more perfect Union."

70     But if destruction of the Union by one or by a part only of the States be lawfully possible, the Union is less
71 perfect than before the Constitution, having lost the vital element of perpetuity.

72     It follows from these views that no State upon its own mere motion can lawfully get out of the Union; that
73 resolves and ordinances to that effect are legally void, and that acts of violence within any State or States against the
74 authority of the United States are insurrectionary or revolutionary, according to circumstances.

75     I therefore consider that in view of the Constitution and the laws the Union is unbroken, and to the extent of
76 my ability, I shall take care, as the Constitution itself expressly enjoins upon me, that the laws of the Union be
77 faithfully executed in all the States. Doing this I deem to be only a simple duty on my part, and I shall perform it so
78 far as practicable unless my rightful masters, the American people, shall withhold the requisite means or in some
79 authoritative manner direct the contrary. I trust this will not be regarded as a menace, but only as the declared
80 purpose of the Union that it will constitutionally defend and maintain itself.

81     In doing this there needs to be no bloodshed or violence, and there shall be none unless it be forced upon
82 the national authority. The power confided to me will be used to hold, occupy, and possess the property and places
83 belonging to the Government and to collect the duties and imposts; but beyond what may be necessary for these
84 objects, there will be no invasion, no using of force against or among the people anywhere. Where hostility to the
85 United States in any interior locality shall be so great and universal as to prevent competent resident citizens from
86 holding the Federal offices, there will be no attempt to force obnoxious strangers among the people for that object.
87 While the strict legal right may exist in the Government to enforce the exercise of these offices, the attempt to do so
88 would be so irritating and so nearly impracticable withal that I deem it better to forego for the time the uses of such
89 offices.

90     The mails, unless repelled, will continue to be furnished in all parts of the Union. So far as possible the
91 people everywhere shall have that sense of perfect security which is most favorable to calm thought and reflection.
92 The course here indicated will be followed unless current events and experience shall show a modification or change
93 to be proper, and in every case and exigency my best discretion will be exercised, according to circumstances
94 actually existing and with a view and a hope of a peaceful solution of the national troubles and the restoration of
95 fraternal sympathies and affections.

96     That there are persons in one section or another who seek to destroy the Union at all events and are glad of
97 any pretext to do it I will neither affirm nor deny; but if there be such, I need address no word to them. To those,
98 however, who really love the Union may I not speak?

99     Before entering upon so grave a matter as the destruction of our national fabric, with all its benefits, its
100 memories, and its hopes, would it not be wise to ascertain precisely why we do it? Will you hazard so desperate a
101 step while there is any possibility that any portion of the ills you fly from have no real existence? Will you, while the

102	certain ills you fly to are greater than all the real ones you fly from, will you risk the commission of so fearful a
103	mistake?

104	All profess to be content in the Union if all constitutional rights can be maintained. Is it true, then, that any
105	right plainly written in the Constitution has been denied? I think not. Happily, the human mind is so constituted that
106	no party can reach to the audacity of doing this. Think, if you can, of a single instance in which a plainly written
107	provision of the Constitution has ever been denied. If by the mere force of numbers a majority should deprive a
108	minority of any clearly written constitutional right, it might in a moral point of view justify revolution; certainly
109	would if such right were a vital one. But such is not our case. All the vital rights of minorities and of individuals are
110	so plainly assured to them by affirmations and negations, guaranties and prohibitions, in the Constitution that
111	controversies never arise concerning them. But no organic law can ever be framed with a provision specifically
112	applicable to every question which may occur in practical administration. No foresight can anticipate nor any
113	document of reasonable length contain express provisions for all possible questions. Shall fugitives from labor be
114	surrendered by national or by State authority? The Constitution does not expressly say. May Congress prohibit
115	slavery in the Territories? The Constitution does not expressly say. Must Congress protect slavery in the Territories?
116	The Constitution does not expressly say.

117	From questions of this class spring all our constitutional controversies, and we divide upon them into
118	majorities and minorities. If the minority will not acquiesce, the majority must, or the Government must cease.
119	There is no other alternative, for continuing the Government is acquiescence on one side or the other. If a minority
120	in such case will secede rather than acquiesce, they make a precedent which in turn will divide and ruin them, for a
121	minority of their own will secede from them whenever a majority refuses to be controlled by such minority. For
122	instance, why may not any portion of a new confederacy a year or two hence arbitrarily secede again, precisely as
123	portions of the present Union now claim to secede from it? All who cherish disunion sentiments are now being
124	educated to the exact temper of doing this.

125	Is there such perfect identity of interests among the States to compose a new union as to produce harmony
126	only and prevent renewed secession?

127	Plainly the central idea of secession is the essence of anarchy. A majority held in restraint by constitutional
128	checks and limitations, and always changing easily with deliberate changes of popular opinions and sentiments, is
129	the only true sovereign of a free people. Whoever rejects it does of necessity fly to anarchy or to despotism.
130	Unanimity is impossible. The rule of a minority, as a permanent arrangement, is wholly inadmissible; so that,
131	rejecting the majority principle, anarchy or despotism in some form is all that is left.

132	I do not forget the position assumed by some that constitutional questions are to be decided by the Supreme
133	Court, nor do I deny that such decisions must be binding in any case upon the parties to a suit as to the object of that
134	suit, while they are also entitled to very high respect and consideration in all parallel cases by all other departments
135	of the Government. And while it is obviously possible that such decision may be erroneous in any given case, still
136	the evil effect following it, being limited to that particular case, with the chance that it may be overruled and never
137	become a precedent for other cases, can better be borne than could the evils of a different practice. At the same time,
138	the candid citizen must confess that if the policy of the Government upon vital questions affecting the whole people
139	is to be irrevocably fixed by decisions of the Supreme Court, the instant they are made in ordinary litigation between
140	parties in personal actions the people will have ceased to be their own rulers, having to that extent practically
141	resigned their Government into the hands of that eminent tribunal. Nor is there in this view any assault upon the
142	court or the judges. It is a duty from which they may not shrink to decide cases properly brought before them, and it
143	is no fault of theirs if others seek to turn their decisions to political purposes.

144	One section of our country believes slavery is right and ought to be extended, while the other believes it is
145	wrong and ought not to be extended. This is the only substantial dispute. The fugitive-slave clause of the
146	Constitution and the law for the suppression of the foreign slave trade are each as well enforced, perhaps, as any law
147	can ever be in a community where the moral sense of the people imperfectly supports the law itself. The great body
148	of the people abides by the dry legal obligation in both cases, and a few break over in each. This, I think, cannot be
149	perfectly cured, and it would be worse in both cases after the separation of the sections than before. The foreign
150	slave trade, now imperfectly suppressed, would be ultimately revived without restriction in one section, while
151	fugitive slaves, now only partially surrendered, would not be surrendered at all by the other.

152	Physically speaking, we cannot separate. We cannot remove our respective sections from each other nor
153	build an impassable wall between them. A husband and wife may be divorced and go out of the presence and
154	beyond the reach of each other, but the different parts of our country cannot do this. They cannot but remain face to
155	face, and intercourse, either amicable or hostile, must continue between them. Is it possible, then, to make that
156	intercourse more advantageous or more satisfactory after separation than before? Can aliens make treaties easier
157	than friends can make laws? Can treaties be more faithfully enforced between aliens than laws can among friends?

158  Suppose you go to war, you cannot fight always; and when, after much loss on both sides and no gain on either, you
159  cease fighting, the identical old questions, as to terms of intercourse, are again upon you.

160  This country, with its institutions, belongs to the people who inhabit it. Whenever they shall grow weary of
161  the existing Government, they can exercise their constitutional right of amending it or their revolutionary right to
162  dismember or overthrow it. I cannot be ignorant of the fact that many worthy and patriotic citizens are desirous of
163  having the National Constitution amended. While I make no recommendation of amendments, I fully recognize the
164  rightful authority of the people over the whole subject, to be exercised in either of the modes prescribed in the
165  instrument itself; and I should, under existing circumstances, favor rather than oppose a fair opportunity being
166  afforded the people to act upon it. I will venture to add that to me the convention mode seems preferable, in that it
167  allows amendments to originate with the people themselves, instead of only permitting them to take or reject
168  propositions originated by others, not especially chosen for the purpose, and which might not be precisely such as
169  they would wish to either accept or refuse. I understand a proposed amendment to the Constitution—which
170  amendment, however, I have not seen—has passed Congress, to the effect that the Federal Government shall never
171  interfere with the domestic institutions of the States, including that of persons held to service. To avoid
172  misconstruction of what I have said, I depart from my purpose not to speak of particular amendments so far as to say
173  that, holding such a provision to now be implied constitutional law, I have no objection to its being made express
174  and irrevocable.

175  The Chief Magistrate derives all his authority from the people, and they have referred none upon him to fix
176  terms for the separation of the States. The people themselves can do this if also they choose, but the Executive as
177  such has nothing to do with it. His duty is to administer the present Government as it came to his hands and to
178  transmit it unimpaired by him to his successor.

179  Why should there not be a patient confidence in the ultimate justice of the people? Is there any better or
180  equal hope in the world? In our present differences, is either party without faith of being in the right? If the
181  Almighty Ruler of Nations, with His eternal truth and justice, be on your side of the North, or on yours of the South,
182  that truth and that justice will surely prevail by the judgment of this great tribunal of the American people.

183  By the frame of the Government under which we live this same people have wisely given their public
184  servants but little power for mischief, and have with equal wisdom provided for the return of that little to their own
185  hands at very short intervals. While the people retain their virtue and vigilance no Administration by any extreme of
186  wickedness or folly can very seriously injure the Government in the short space of four years.

187  My countrymen, one and all, think calmly and *well* upon this whole subject. Nothing valuable can be lost
188  by taking time. If there be an object to *hurry* any of you in hot haste to a step which you would never take
189  *deliberately*, that object will be frustrated by taking time; but no good object can be frustrated by it. Such of you as
190  are now dissatisfied still have the old Constitution unimpaired, and, on the sensitive point, the laws of your own
191  framing under it; while the new Administration will have no immediate power, if it would, to change either. If it
192  were admitted that you who are dissatisfied hold the right side in the dispute, there still is no single good reason for
193  precipitate action. Intelligence, patriotism, Christianity, and a firm reliance on Him who has never yet forsaken this
194  favored land are still competent to adjust in the best way all our present difficulty.

195  In your hands, my dissatisfied fellow-countrymen, and not in mine, is the momentous issue of civil war.
196  The Government will not assail you. You can have no conflict without being yourselves the aggressors. You have no
197  oath registered in heaven to destroy the Government, while I shall have the most solemn one to "preserve, protect,
198  and defend it."

199  I am loath to close. We are not enemies, but friends. We must not be enemies. Though passion may have
200  strained it must not break our bonds of affection. The mystic chords of memory, stretching from every battlefield
201  and patriot grave to every living heart and hearthstone all over this broad land will yet swell the chorus of the Union,
202  when again touched, as surely they will be, by the better angels of our nature.

(http://www.bartleby.com/124/pres31.html)

## Close Reading

1. What is the chief argument of this speech?
   I. To end slavery
   II. To assuage concerns of southern dissenters
   III. To preserve the Union

   A. I                          C. II and III
   B. I and II                   D. All

2. Evidence for the above argument?
   A .Lines 1–2                  C. Lines 150–51
   B. Lines 12–13                D. Lines 200–201

3. The speech has three parts:
   A. Introduction, Body, and Conclusion        C. Argument, Evidence, Solution
   B. Preamble, Grievances, Resolutions         D. Thesis, Counterargument, Conclusion

4. With which of the following statements would the author agree?

   I. Slavery should be abolished immediately.
   II. The Union must be preserved.
   III. Rebels must be hanged.
   IV. The military draft must be instituted

   A. I                          D. II and IV
   B. II                         E. All
   C. III and IV

5. Where is one example of pathos in this speech?
   A. Lines 75–80                C. Lines 125–26
   B. Lines 99–103               D. Lines 194–20

6. The Union cannot be dissolved because

   I. It is older than the Constitution.
   II. One cannot divorce someone and live in the same area.
   III. God commands that the Union be preserved.

   A. I                          C. I and II
   B. II                         D. III

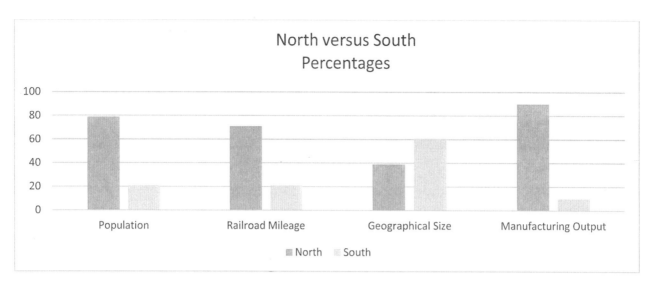

7. According to the chart (above), what is true?

    I.   The South had more churches than the North.
   II.  The North has many more manufacturing jobs.
 III.  The South is larger geographically than the North.

        A. I                                   C. II and III
        B. I and II                          D. All

8. From this chart, devise a viable southern military strategy to win the Civil War:
A. Attack quickly.
B. Use a strategic defense based on geography.
C. Invent a secret weapon.
D. Send subversive military groups north.

## Words in Context

1. What is the meaning of *inviolate* in Line 17?
    A.  Profane                         C.  Unchanged
    B.  Sacred                           D.  Redundant

2. What is the meaning of *perpetuity* in Line 57?
    A.  Remonstration                  C.  Wholeness
    B.  Eternity                         D.  Permanency

# Lesson 5

## Math: Algebra, Arithmetic Problem Solving and Data Analysis, and Passport to Advanced Math

**Data Analysis**

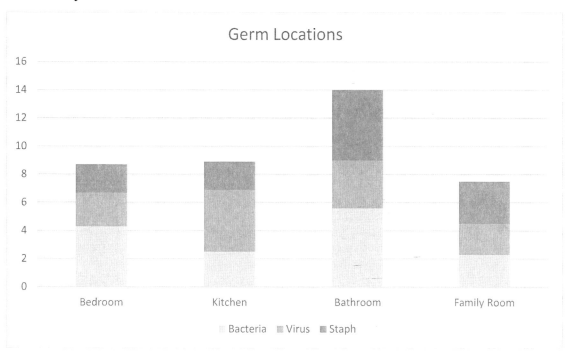

| Location | Bacteria | Virus | Staph |
|----------|----------|-------|-------|
| Bedroom | 4.3 | 2.4 | 2 |
| Kitchen | 2.5 | 4.4 | 2 |
| Bathroom | 5.6 | 3.4 | 5 |
| Family Room | 2.3 | 2.2 | 3 |

Which of the following statements are true?

I. There are more germs in the bathroom than in any other room.
II. The family room has more staph germs than the kitchen and bedroom combined.
III. The kitchen has more virus germs than the bathroom.
IV. The bathroom has more bacteria germs than the kitchen and family room combined.

    A. I and II                            C. I, III, and IV
    B. III and IV                            D. All

## Arithmetic Problem Solving

1.  Find two numbers whose sum is 74 and whose difference is 18.
    A. 27; 47                          C. 29; 45
    B. 28; 46.                         C. 30; 43

2.  It was between 12:00 and 1:00 o'clock when a man, mistaking the hour hand for the minute hand, thought that it was 55 minutes later than it really was. What time was it?

    A. 5— min. past 12:00              C. 5— min. past 12:00

    B. 5— min. past 12:00              D. 5— min. past 12:00

## Algebra

1.  What is the sum of $b + b + b + b + b + b + b + b$?

    I.   8b                            III.  $b + b + b + b + b + 2b$
    II.  4b + 4b                       IV.   16b/2

        A. I and II                        C. I, II, and IV
        B. II and III                      D. All

2.  Express the sum of $x$ and $y$.
    A. x + y                           C. xy
    B. x – y                           D. xy/2

3.  George is $x$ years old, Martin is $y$, and Morgan is $z$ years. What is the sum of their ages?
    A. x + yz                          C. xyz
    B. x y + z                         D. x + y + z

4.  What is the sum of $m$ taken $b$ times?

    I.   b + m                         III.  bm – b
    II.  bm                            IV.   mb

        A. II and IV                       C. I
        B. II and III                      D. All

# Chapter 20  Necessary Forgiveness
# Isaiah 54

> *Memory Verses:* "For a brief moment I abandoned you,
> but with deep compassion I will bring you back," . . . says
> the LORD. —Isaiah 54:7–8

Professor McMickle, one of my preaching instructors at Princeton, told a story about a prisoner in Sing Sing. This prisoner, sentenced for life, was coming up for parole. As he approached the room where the parole officers were seated, he shuffled a stack of papers. In his hands were all sorts of documents supporting his contention that he deserved parole. Letters from psychologists, reports from other prisoners, a testimony from the warden—all these documents said the same thing: they argued that this man had changed, that he had repented of his crime, and, in short, was sufficiently rehabilitated to be released. Naturally, as the prisoner opened the door, he was hopeful.

It had been almost five years since he had committed his life to Christ. He knew that this did not matter to the parole board, but it mattered to him. For he knew that he was forgiven.

Nevertheless, he very much wanted to be released. And, as he retired from the room to allow the committee to judge his case, this prisoner uttered a short prayer. "Thy will be done, Lord," he pleaded, "but please help the parole board to see that I've changed."

When he returned to the room later, he immediately knew their answer. The chairperson began, "We are impressed by the progress you have made. But your crime was so terrible that we feel that you have not suffered enough. Parole denied. Review again in 60 months."

The prisoner was distraught. "Chaplain," the prisoner later told McMickle, "God has forgiven me, but they cannot. They simply cannot accept the possibility that God has redeemed me."

In spite of the fact that this prisoner has irrefutable evidence that he has repented and has been rehabilitated, he is not forgiven by his parole board. And so it is with some of us. We all sin, but oftentimes in the courts of our friends and neighbors, we are never allowed to repent. Or at least we never are treated as if we are forgiven—even if we have repented! And worse still, more often than not, *we* are the people who cannot forgive!

My main concern now is about our responsibility to forgive one another. I do not think that I am exaggerating when I suggest that everyone holds a grudge smoldering in the heart, perhaps even against a friend, spouse, son or daughter, or parent sitting next to you, Yes, you! The wife who cannot forgive the unfaithful husband; the daughter who cannot forgive the neglectful father; the son who cannot forgive the possessive mother; the mother who cannot forgive the insensitive son. All of us need to take this appeal to heart. I see the consequences of our unforgivingness every day. An unforgiving mind-set robs us of our peace: it takes away our happiness and wrecks our lives. The last few chapters of Isaiah are a story of a nation on the other side of disaster, the story of a nation that is finally reaping the rewards of forgiveness. Very simply, Israel had sinned horribly; it deserved the punishment it received—and much more. Sent into exile in Babylonia-Persia for over seventy years, the children of Israel suffered greatly for their transgression. These were seventy lonely, painful, awful years. As the psalmist laments, "By the rivers of Babylon—there we sat down and there we wept when we remembered Zion. On the willows there we hung up our harps. . . . How could we sing the LORD's song in a foreign land?" (Psalm 137:1–2, 4 NRSV). These were terrible years for the Israelites. They felt as though God were absent from their lives; there was no joy in their nation.

Then the exile ended. People of Israel, having learned the errors of their ways, had changed. Some were willing to return to their ancestral land, which the Persians now called the province of Judah. They were ready to return to Zion, to full fellowship with God, to good health. In short, they were forgiven. "For one brief moment I left you," God said; "with deep love I will take you back. I turned away angry for only a moment, but I will show you my love forever" (cf. Isaiah 54:7–8). Sin does bring consequences: we reap what we sow (Galatians 6:7–9). Like Israel, we also must accept the consequences of our sin. But Israel must also accept its forgiveness—an equally difficult task. The wrath of God lasted a short time; but Israel's mind could have fixated on that seventy years and lost all perspective.

And so we are fascinated with our own sin, yet especially the sin of our neighbor. We sometimes are not so impressed with redemption. Israel experienced redemption. By God's *grace* (a term stressed in the New Testament), they have been redeemed. Redemption is an act of God. What right do we have to reject an act of God in another person's life?

You may argue, "You do not know what he did to me. If you did, you could not forgive him either!" Yet how can I do anything else if the Lord Almighty of the universe forgives him? The woman caught in adultery also deserved to die (John 8). In the eyes of the Jewish law, adultery was a capital offense. She should have been stoned to death. Many were. And perhaps they deserved to die. Perhaps she deserved to die. That is not the issue here. Jesus is not denying that the poor woman is guilty—no doubt she is. His point is this? "Because you are not without sin yourself, how can you stand in judgment of her? If God has forgiven her, can you not forgive her?" As with the Pharisees, our inability to forgive one another is tied to two problems: Our inability to forgive ourselves, and a more serious problem, an ego problem, our propensity to play God.

We must forgive ourselves; it is the height of arrogance not to do so. After all, if God can forgive us, why cannot we forgive ourselves? Christ ordered, "Love your neighbor as yourself." We want love, and we spend a lot of money seeking it. All we really have to learn to do is to receive it. It is a free gift from God. So also is forgiveness. It is undeserved and free. Can we open ourselves to God's love and accept the fact that God has accepted us in spite of what we are or what we have done? We must. Then it becomes possible for us to love others. That means to forgive them just as we have already been forgiven, since love cannot flow out where hatred, jealousies, and hurt feelings block the way. Once we have truly experienced God's forgiving grace, how can we possibly deny it for anyone else?

But we oftentimes do, especially for ones who are close to us—or at least we try, as if God's grace is tied to our intrinsic power! Our love flows out freely enough to people who attract us, but when we have been hurt, or when someone differs from us in their belief or injures us in some way, we freeze. Then we cannot unlock ourselves to let love flow even when it is needed and when we want it to flow.

The net result is that we are confused; we seem to lose control of our feeling. What do we do when we grow insecure? We become angry at God and one another. And in a real sense, we assume roles that are reserved for God. As a result, we short-circuit the work of grace in the lives of our family and friends. Ironically, our friends or family members may have honestly repented, even gone through a terrible ordeal. God has forgiven them; they may have forgiven themselves; they are ready to be healed. But what do we do? We see ourselves as the victim; so we stand by, reminding our poor friend of their sin. "Wait a minute," we argue, "you got off too easy. I thing you need to repent a little more." Every time our friend begins to feel better, feel wholeness, we are standing by with a snarl, reminding them that they are really not OK, that at least one person (*I*) has not forgiven that friend.

That is the height of arrogance! I don't care how hurt we were, are, or will be. We must not keep our loved one from the forgiveness of God! We can forgive our loved ones, no matter how much they hurt us. Consider the story of David and his wayward son Absalom. Absalom rebelled against his father. David had every reason to be angry, to hate Absalom. But he found the strength, integrity, and clarity of vision within himself to forgive Absalom. He forgave Absalom after he committed public disloyalty; he forgave Absalom after he had himself acclaimed as king; he even forgave Absalom when he drove David from Jerusalem. And what a poignant moment it was when David learned that one of his generals had killed his beloved son. "O Absalom, my son, my son!" David wept. "If only I had died instead of you" (2 Samuel 18:33). His tears were the tears of a father who had forgiven his unrepentant son.

One of the awful and maybe unjust aspects of unforgivingness and unforgiveness is that it consumes the guilty and innocent alike. If we do not forgive, we are strangely drawn into the web of our crime.

Bruno Bettelheim, a Jewish psychologist held in Dachau Concentration Camp during World War II, illustrates my point well. No one disagrees that the Jews were treated horribly during the War. They were unjustly brutalized and many were exterminated by the Nazi regime. But in a way, the survivors were left with an awful legacy. The Jewish survivors of the Holocaust, Bettelheim suggests, became no better than their captors. They began to emulate the cruelty of their prison guards; because of unforgivingness and its effect, many of them became as angry, hateful, and sadistic as the ones who once tried to destroy them. Because of unforgivingness, they became the evil influence.

We must forgive one another, even if the person who hurt us has not repented. Even if we are completely in the right, even if we are the victim. Christ did. As Francis B. Sayre declares, "Christ depends upon us to show others what he is truly like. It is an awesome thought. But how better can the knowledge of Christ be gained in a world of men and women imprisoned with human bodies?"

## Journal Question

Is there someone whom you cannot forgive? Why?

# Lesson 1
## Evidence-Based Reading and Writing

### Literary Choice

Jonathan Swift was one of the most talented and vituperative English satirists of all time. *Gulliver's Travels* is, then, a hilarious satire of eighteenth-century British elite society.

### Part 5, Chapter 7

*The author's great love of his native country. His master's observations upon the constitution and administration of England, as described by the author, with parallel cases and comparisons. His master's observations upon human nature.*

The reader may be disposed to wonder how I could prevail on myself to give so free a representation of my own species, among a race of mortals who are already too apt to conceive the vilest opinion of humankind, from that entire congruity between me and their *Yahoos*. But I must freely confess, that the many virtues of those excellent quadrupeds, placed in opposite view to human corruptions, had so far opened my eyes and enlarged my understanding, that I began to view the actions and passions of man in a very different light, and to think the honour of my own kind not worth managing; which, besides, it was impossible for me to do, before a person of so acute a judgment as my master, who daily convinced me of a thousand faults in myself, whereof I had not the least perception before, and which, with us, would never be numbered even among human infirmities. I had likewise learned, from his example, an utter detestation of all falsehood or disguise; and truth appeared so amiable to me, that I determined upon sacrificing everything to it.

Let me deal so candidly with the reader as to confess that there was yet a much stronger motive for the freedom I took in my representation of things. I had not yet been a year in this country before I contracted such a love and veneration for the inhabitants, that I entered on a firm resolution never to return to humankind, but to pass the rest of my life among these admirable *Houyhnhnms*, in the contemplation and practice of every virtue, where I could have no example or incitement to vice. But it was decreed by fortune, my perpetual enemy, that so great a felicity should not fall to my share. However, it is now some comfort to reflect, that in what I said of my countrymen, I extenuated their faults as much as I durst before so strict an examiner; and upon every article gave as favourable a turn as the matter would bear. For, indeed, who is there alive that will not be swayed by his bias and partiality to the place of his birth?

I have related the substance of several conversations I had with my master during the greatest part of the time I had the honour to be in his service; but have, indeed, for brevity sake, omitted much more than is here set down.

When I had answered all his questions, and his curiosity seemed to be fully satisfied, he sent for me one morning early, and commanded me to sit down at some distance (an honour which he had never before conferred upon me). He said, "he had been very seriously considering my whole story, as far as it related both to myself and my country; that he looked upon us as a sort of animals, to whose share, by what accident he could not conjecture, some small pittance of reason had fallen, whereof we made no other use, than by its assistance, to aggravate our natural corruptions, and to acquire new ones, which nature had not given us; that we disarmed ourselves of the few abilities she had bestowed; had been very successful in multiplying our original wants, and seemed to spend our whole lives in vain endeavours to supply them by our own inventions; that, as to myself, it was manifest I had neither the strength nor agility of a common *Yahoo*; that I walked infirmly on my hinder feet; had found out a contrivance to make my claws of no use or defence, and to remove the hair from my chin, which was intended as a shelter from the sun and the weather: lastly, that I could neither run with speed, nor climb trees like my brethren," as he called them, "the *Yahoos* in his country.

"That our institutions of government and law were plainly owing to our gross defects in reason, and by consequence in virtue; because reason alone is sufficient to govern a rational creature; which was, therefore, a character we had no pretence to challenge, even from the account I had given of my own people; although he manifestly perceived, that, in order to favour them, I had concealed many particulars, and often said the thing which was not.

"He was the more confirmed in this opinion, because, he observed, that as I agreed in every feature of my body with other *Yahoos*, except where it was to my real disadvantage in point of strength, speed, and activity, the shortness of my claws, and some other particulars where nature had no part; so from the representation I had given him of our lives, our manners, and our actions, he found as near a resemblance in the disposition of our minds." He

47   said, "the *Yahoos* were known to hate one another, more than they did any different species of animals; and the
48   reason usually assigned was, the odiousness of their own shapes, which all could see in the rest, but not in
49   themselves. He had therefore begun to think it not unwise in us to cover our bodies, and by that invention conceal
50   many of our deformities from each other, which would else be hardly supportable. But he now found he had been
51   mistaken, and that the dissensions of those brutes in his country were owing to the same cause with ours, as I had
52   described them. For if," said he, "you throw among five *Yahoos* as much food as would be sufficient for fifty, they
53   will, instead of eating peaceably, fall together by the ears, each single one impatient to have all to itself; and
54   therefore a servant was usually employed to stand by while they were feeding abroad, and those kept at home were
55   tied at a distance from each other: that if a cow died of age or accident, before a *Houyhnhnm* could secure it for his
56   own *Yahoos*, those in the neighbourhood would come in herds to seize it, and then would ensue such a battle as I
57   had described, with terrible wounds made by their claws on both sides, although they seldom were able to kill one
58   another, for want of such convenient instruments of death as we had invented. At other times, the like battles have
59   been fought between the *Yahoos* of several neighbourhoods, without any visible cause; those of one district
60   watching all opportunities to surprise the next, before they are prepared. But if they find their project has miscarried,
61   they return home, and, for want of enemies, engage in what I call a civil war among themselves.
62       "That in some fields of his country there are certain shining stones of several colours, whereof the *Yahoos*
63   are violently fond: and when part of these stones is fixed in the earth, as it sometimes happens, they will dig with
64   their claws for whole days to get them out; then carry them away, and hide them by heaps in their kennels; but still
65   looking round with great caution, for fear their comrades should find out their treasure." My master said, "he could
66   never discover the reason of this unnatural appetite, or how these stones could be of any use to a *Yahoo*; but now he
67   believed it might proceed from the same principle of avarice which I had ascribed to mankind. That he had once, by
68   way of experiment, privately removed a heap of these stones from the place where one of his *Yahoos* had buried it;
69   whereupon the sordid animal, missing his treasure, by his loud lamenting brought the whole herd to the place, there
70   miserably howled, then fell to biting and tearing the rest, began to pine away, would neither eat, nor sleep, nor work,
71   till he ordered a servant privately to convey the stones into the same hole, and hide them as before; which, when his
72   *Yahoo* had found, he presently recovered his spirits and good humour, but took good care to remove them to a better
73   hiding place, and has ever since been a very serviceable brute."
74       My master further assured me, which I also observed myself, "that in the fields where the shining stones
75   abound, the fiercest and most frequent battles are fought, occasioned by perpetual inroads of the neighbouring
76   *Yahoos*."
77       He said, "it was common, when two *Yahoos* discovered such a stone in a field, and were contending which
78   of them should be the proprietor, a third would take the advantage, and carry it away from them both;" which my
79   master would needs contend to have some kind of resemblance with our suits at law; wherein I thought it for our
80   credit not to undeceive him; since the decision he mentioned was much more equitable than many decrees among
81   us; because the plaintiff and defendant there lost nothing beside the stone they contended for: whereas our courts of
82   equity would never have dismissed the cause, while either of them had any thing left.
83       My master, continuing his discourse, said, "there was nothing that rendered the *Yahoos* more odious, than
84   their undistinguishing appetite to devour every thing that came in their way, whether herbs, roots, berries, the
85   corrupted flesh of animals, or all mingled together: and it was peculiar in their temper, that they were fonder of what
86   they could get by rapine or stealth, at a greater distance, than much better food provided for them at home. If their
87   prey held out, they would eat till they were ready to burst; after which, nature had pointed out to them a certain root
88   that gave them a general evacuation.
89       "There was also another kind of root, very juicy, but somewhat rare and difficult to be found, which the
90   *Yahoos* sought for with much eagerness, and would suck it with great delight; it produced in them the same effects
91   that wine has upon us. It would make them sometimes hug, and sometimes tear one another; they would howl, and
92   grin, and chatter, and reel, and tumble, and then fall asleep in the mud."
93       I did indeed observe that the *Yahoos* were the only animals in this country subject to any diseases; which,
94   however, were much fewer than horses have among us, and contracted, not by any ill-treatment they meet with, but
95   by the nastiness and greediness of that sordid brute. Neither has their language any more than a general appellation
96   for those maladies, which is borrowed from the name of the beast, and called *hnea-yahoo*, or *Yahoo's evil*; and the
97   cure prescribed is a mixture of their own dung and urine, forcibly put down the *Yahoo's* throat. This I have since
98   often known to have been taken with success, and do here freely recommend it to my countrymen for the public
99   good, as an admirable specific against all diseases produced by repletion.
100      "As to learning, government, arts, manufactures, and the like," my master confessed, "he could find little or
101   no resemblance between the *Yahoos* of that country and those in ours; for he only meant to observe what parity there
102   was in our natures. He had heard, indeed, some curious *Houyhnhnms* observe, that in most herds there was a sort of
103   ruling *Yahoo* (as among us there is generally some leading or principal stag in a park), who was always more

104   deformed in body, and mischievous in disposition, than any of the rest; that this leader had usually a favourite as like
105   himself as he could get, whose employment was to lick his master's feet and posteriors, and drive the female *Yahoos*
106   to his kennel; for which he was now and then rewarded with a piece of ass's flesh. This favourite is hated by the
107   whole herd, and therefore, to protect himself, keeps always near the person of his leader. He usually continues in
108   office till a worse can be found; but the very moment he is discarded, his successor, at the head of all the *Yahoos* in
109   that district, young and old, male and female, come in a body, and discharge their excrements upon him from head
110   to foot. But how far this might be applicable to our courts, and favourites, and ministers of state, my master said I
111   could best determine."

112       I durst make no return to this malicious insinuation, which debased human understanding below the
113   sagacity of a common hound, who has judgment enough to distinguish and follow the cry of the ablest dog in the
114   pack, without being ever mistaken.

115       My master told me, "there were some qualities remarkable in the *Yahoos*, which he had not observed me to
116   mention, or at least very slightly, in the accounts I had given of humankind." He said, "those animals, like other
117   brutes, had their females in common; but in this they differed, that the she *Yahoo* would admit the males while she
118   was pregnant; and that the hes would quarrel and fight with the females, as fiercely as with each other; both which
119   practices were such degrees of infamous brutality, as no other sensitive creature ever arrived at.

120       "Another thing he wondered at in the *Yahoos*, was their strange disposition to nastiness and dirt; whereas
121   there appears to be a natural love of cleanliness in all other animals." As to the two former accusations, I was glad to
122   let them pass without any reply, because I had not a word to offer upon them in defence of my species, which
123   otherwise I certainly had done from my own inclinations. But I could have easily vindicated humankind from the
124   imputation of singularity upon the last article, if there had been any swine in that country (as unluckily for me there
125   were not), which, although it may be a sweeter quadruped than a *Yahoo*, cannot, I humbly conceive, in justice,
126   pretend to more cleanliness; and so his honour himself must have owned, if he had seen their filthy way of feeding,
127   and their custom of wallowing and sleeping in the mud.

128       My master likewise mentioned another quality which his servants had discovered in several Yahoos, and to
129   him was wholly unaccountable. He said, "a fancy would sometimes take a *Yahoo* to retire into a corner, to lie down,
130   and howl, and groan, and spurn away all that came near him, although he were young and fat, wanted neither food
131   nor water, nor did the servant imagine what could possibly ail him. And the only remedy they found was, to set him
132   to hard work, after which he would infallibly come to himself." To this I was silent out of partiality to my own kind;
133   yet here I could plainly discover the true seeds of spleen, which only seizes on the lazy, the luxurious, and the rich;
134   who, if they were forced to undergo the same regimen, I would undertake for the cure.

135       His honour had further observed, "that a female *Yahoo* would often stand behind a bank or a bush, to gaze
136   on the young males passing by, and then appear, and hide, using many antic gestures and grimaces, at which time it
137   was observed that she had a most offensive smell; and when any of the males advanced, would slowly retire, looking
138   often back, and with a counterfeit show of fear, run off into some convenient place, where she knew the male would
139   follow her.

140       "At other times, if a female stranger came among them, three or four of her own sex would get about her,
141   and stare, and chatter, and grin, and smell her all over; and then turn off with gestures, that seemed to express
142   contempt and disdain."

143       Perhaps my master might refine a little in these speculations, which he had drawn from what he observed
144   himself, or had been told him by others; however, I could not reflect without some amazement, and much sorrow,
145   that the rudiments of lewdness, coquetry, censure, and scandal, should have place by instinct in womankind.

146       I expected every moment that my master would accuse the *Yahoos* of those unnatural appetites in both
147   sexes, so common among us. But nature, it seems, has not been so expert a school-mistress; and these politer
148   pleasures are entirely the productions of art and reason on our side of the globe.

149                           (http://www.gutenberg.org/files/829/829-h/829-h.htm)

## Student Response

### Yahoos

1 "For as to those filthy *Yahoos*, although there were few greater Lovers of Mankind, at that time, than myself; yet I
2 confess I never saw any sensitive Being so detestable on all Accounts; and the more I came near them, the more
3 hateful they grew, while I stayed in that Country" (part 4, chap. 3). *Gulliver's Travels*, by Jonathan Swift, tells the
4 story of Gulliver's unusual encounters with several different cultures. In his third adventure, Gulliver meets Yahoos,
5 whom Swift characterized to symbolize the materialistic and ignorant elite of England at that time. In today's world,
6 Yahoos can be compared to self-seeking or egotistical persons.

7 **After being exiled from the miniscule Lilliputians and taken away from the gigantic**
8 **Brobdingnagians, Gulliver finally travels into a land with creatures strikingly similar to him.** "My Horror and
9 Astonishment are not to be described, when I observed, in this abominable Animal, a perfect human Figure" (part 4;
10 chap. 3). Yahoos have the physical appearance of a human, but their thinking and actions are at crude levels. They
11 live under the dominion of the Houyhnhnms, who have the physical appearance of horses but with a sound intellect.
12 The Yahoos are full of different ethnic groups, and they participate in many sexual and vulgar activities. They love
13 being filthy and dirty, and they dig through the earth to find stones. These stones have no use to them, but the
14 Yahoos hoard every one that they find. Swift greatly contrasts the Yahoos with their masters, the Houyhnhnms. In
15 the real world, people classify humans as the knowledgeable and superior breed, and horses as the ignorant and
16 inferior animals. However, Swift portrays the exact opposite in his book. The physically humanlike Yahoos live a
17 materialistic and deranged life, while the physically horselike Houyhnhnms live a rational and peaceful life. Gulliver
18 is completely disgusted at the Yahoos, yet recognizes that he too is one because of his similar appearance. Gulliver
19 represents a Yahoo by appearance but a Houyhnhnm by reason.

20 The Yahoos seem like fictional and unrealistic characters, but Jonathan Swift used them to symbolize the
21 materialistic and ignorant elite in his time. However, the Yahoos can actually be compared to any modern-day
22 person who only cares for oneself and is full of greed and lust. Gulliver draws a wonderful parallel between the
23 Yahoos and humans. In the instance when the Yahoos are searching for stones, the Yahoos are prizing and hoarding
24 something that has absolutely no value and no purpose. This seems absurd, but Gulliver reasons that this is similar to
25 human greed. "My Master said, he could never discover the Reason of this unnatural Appetite, or how these stones
26 could be of any use to a *Yahoo*; but now he believed it might proceed from the same Principle of Avarice, which I
27 had ascribed to Mankind" (part 4, chap. 7). **Modern-day reality stars often get so caught up in their popularity**
28 **that they focus only on their fame and what will get them on the headlines.** They pride themselves on some
29 things that are truly meaningless in life, and often they lose their rationality and commit capricious actions without
30 truly thinking about the consequences of such actions. They could be the modern-day Yahoos.

31 *Gulliver's Travels* by Jonathan Swift tell the story of Gulliver's unusual encounters with several different
32 cultures. In his third adventure, Gulliver meets Yahoos, whom Swift characterized to symbolize the materialistic and
33 ignorant elite of England at that time. In today's world, Yahoos can be compared to a self-seeking or egotistical
34 person. (Hanna)

## Close Reading

1. Swift creates satire through
   I. Hyperbole          II. Understatement          III. Caricature

   A. I                                    C. II and III
   B. I and II                             D. All

2. What is the narrative technique?
   A. Omniscient                           C. First person
   B. Limited omniscient                   D. Third-person objective

3. The tone of most of the novel?
   A. Tentative                            C. Choleric
   B. Sanguine                             D. Humorous

4.  The author creates the tone by
    A. Humorous scenes and language.          C. Internal conflict.
    B. Alliteration.                          D. Antagonistic characters.

5. What is the worldview of the novel?
    A. Romanticism                            C. Naturalism
    B. Theism                                 D. Existentialism

6.  Yahoos are
    I.   Vulgar.                              III.   Pretentious.
    II.  Facile.                              IV.    Intelligent.

        A. I and II                               C. I, II, and III
        B. III and IV                             D. All

7.  What work shows some similarity to *Gulliver's Travels*?
    A. *Cry, the Beloved Country.*            C. *Panchatantra.*
    B. *Frankenstein.*                        D. *Catcher in the Rye.*

8.  Why does Swift contrast the two creatures, Houynhynms and Yahoos?
    A. He wishes to exaggerate to make a point.
    B. These two are totally different, as reason and unreason, sanity and madness exist in all humankind.
    C. He wishes to ridicule the English church.
    D. He attempts to contrast different types of household pets.

## Command of Evidence (Student Response)

1.  Where is the first place the Student Response presents its thesis?
    A.  Lines 1–2                             C.  Lines 26–27
    B.  Lines 4–6                             D.  Lines 31–33

2.  The beginning of the Student Response in Line 1 is inadequate because
    A.  The student should always begin with a generalization.
    B.  The student should always begin with name of the literary piece.
    C.  The student should not begin with unnamed sources (literary critics).
    D.  The student has a quote but no subsequent supporting comments.

3.  A good summary of the student argument would be in
    A.  Lines 7–8                             C.  Lines 27–30
    B.  Lines 17–18                           D.  Lines 31–33

4.  What is a favorite strategy of argumentation used?
    A.  Quotes with restatement of argument
    B.  Arguments and then supportive textual quotes
    C.  Arguments with supporting anecdotes
    D.  Arguments with quotes from critics

5.  A legitimate criticism of the Student Response could be that
    A.  The arguments are presented too much.
    B.  The essay is too wordy and tentative.
    C.  The essay has too many quotes.
    D.  The essay is too short.

6.  According to the Student Response, a good example of a modern Yahoo is
    A.  A factory worker.                     C.  A small-town politician.
    B.  A movie star .                        D.  A pastor.

## Words in Context

The following words are from the literary excerpt:

1. What is the meaning of *detestation* in Line 12?
   A. Obeisance
   B. Abhorrence
   C. Adoration
   D. Candor

2. What is the meaning of *veneration* in Line 16?
   A. Disdain
   B. Reverence
   C. Affection
   D. Jealousy

3. What is the meaning of *contrivance* in Line 35?
   A. Intrigue
   B. Mischievousness
   C. Avoidance
   D. Contraption

## Grammar and Usage

Choose the best grammar/usage form in bold sentence(s).

1. Student Response, Lines 7–8

   A. NONE
   B. After being exiled from the miniscule Lilliputians and after being taken away from the gigantic Brobdingnagians, Gulliver finally travels into a land with creatures strikingly similar to himself.
   C. Exiled from the Lilliputians and taken away from the gigantic Brobdingnagians, Gulliver travels to a land full of creatures strikingly similar to himself.
   D. After being exiled from the miniscule Lilliputians and taken away from the gigantic Brobdingnagians, Gulliver arrives at a land with creatures strikingly similar to himself.

2. Student Response, Lines 27–28

   A. NONE
   B. Contemporary reality stars, enamored by their popularity, only selfishly focus on their fame and what will get them headlines.
   C. Modern reality stars often are full of their popularity that they only focus on their fame and what will get them on the headlines.
   D. Modern-day reality stars get caught up in their popularity that they only focus on their fame and what will make them famous.

# Lesson 2
## Critical Reading and Writing

### Command of Evidence

Read the following passages and answer accompanying questions:

### Passage 1

Ravi Zacharias, a famous theologian and philosopher once said, "I do not wish to write the laws; let me write the songs." Zacharias made this statement because he realized that music is, in a way, culture externalized. Not only does music define a culture, but it also influences that culture. This is especially true in the African American community. Music for the African American community has been a "potent form of cultural identity" since the beginning of time. Africans brought over their ancient melodies and rhythms to America, and these melodies and rhythms helped them remain a cultural entity throughout their oppression and enslavement. Because music plays such a major role in African Americans' culture, and because African Americans are an integral culture in America, it is no wonder that African music and culture has "always had a profound influence on mainstream American culture." Rap and Hip-hop were initially associated with African Americans; however, this delineation can no longer be made. In fact, the most popular rapper of this decade, Eminem, is as white as he can be. White's embracement of this African American musical genre is not a "new phenomenon." According to Dr. Cynthia Neal Spence of Spelman College, "White America has always found Black culture to be exciting, exotic, and perhaps more expressive and less restrained than what they identify as their culture." For example, "Elvis Presley admitted that much of his music was patterned after blacks." Even famous jazz-writer George Gershwin incorporated African melodies and rhythms into his pieces, which were considered the definition of American music and culture during his lifetime.

Because African American music profoundly defines their culture and influences it, and because whites have in the past and in the present accepted and integrated African music into their own styles, such acceptance and integration has inevitably shaped and influenced American culture. This cultural influence is realized even in youth clothing choices. In More Speigler's article "Marketing Street culture, Bringing Hip-Hop to the Mainstream," Speigler relates that he witnessed a teenage boy in white East Coast Massachusetts with "Baggy jeans over designed sneakers, gold hoops adorning both ears and a Tommy Hilfiger shirt on his chest." Speigler claims, "Four years ago, this teen would not have imagined wearing his clean-cut country-club peers Hilfiger clothes." But now "Smalls and other hip-hop stars have become a crucial part in Hilfiger's attempt to tap into the youth market." Clearly, the rap genre has diffused into the white world and has not failed to influence the white culture—even in everyday choices such as clothing.

**In conclusion, because whites have embraced African American music not only in the past, but also in the present, and because music is culture externalized, African American music defines African culture while it also influences American culture.** By integrating and accepting African music into American music, we are also integrating African culture into American culture. (Sarah)

1. What would be the best title of this essay?
   A. The Negro Spiritual
   B. Hip-Hop
   C. Racism Is Alive
   D. African American Music Influences

2. What is the purpose of the first quote?
   A. The author wishes to increase readers' empathy with the poor.
   B. The author believes poets are very influential.
   C. The author argues that songs have more impact on culture than laws.
   D. The author loves to dance.

3.  What organizational plan does the author employ?
    A.  She offers a thesis at first and then argues the opposite.
    B.  She defines the perimeters of her argument and then argues against opposite positions.
    C.  She admits that Hip-Hop has a deleterious effect on culture.
    D.  She understands that Hip-Hop has negative components yet has helped create a distinctive culture.

4.  Where does the author illustrate her argument?
    A.  Lines 1–5               C.  Lines 17–26
    B.  Lines 12–15             D.  Lines 26–30

5.  The author finishes her essay with
    A.  A summary statement.    C.  A distracting comment.
    B.  A new conclusion.       D.  The way she began.

## Passage 2

1   In the excerpt "Building the House," Mary Oliver draws an analogy between a handyman constructing a house and a
2   poet constructing a poem. She claims that while a handyman positively desires that "hour of interruption, of
3   hammerless quiet, in which he will sit and write down poems or stories," a poet positively desires a rest from the
4   hammerless quiet and demands action. Oliver elucidates this analogy through metaphor, concrete detail, and
5   personal observation.
6           Oliver's use of extended metaphor allows the reader to observe two realistic occupations, constructing and
7   writing, while keeping in mind the broader implications of the descriptions. The description of the handyman
8   desiring repose is an extended metaphor, which symbolizes a human's need for change and repose. The description
9   of the poet desiring action and revolution symbolizes a human's need for activity and motion. Oliver is not merely
10  speaking on behalf of the poet and the handyman in this excerpt; she is also using these concrete examples as
11  extended metaphors to show the feelings of all humankind with regard to repose and inactivity, motion and activity.
12          Because Oliver uses two specific occupations to symbolize the desires of all humankind, she is able to use
13  copious amounts of concrete detail. Concreteness allows the reader to visualize the excerpt. For example, one can
14  almost see the handyman building "a boat, a fence, kitchen cabinets, a table, a barn, a house. One can visualize the
15  handyman clambering down from his ladder to "sit and write down poems, . . . in no hurry and perfectly happy."
16  One can also visualize the poet "in the posture of deliberate or hapless inaction, . . . which sooner or later will
17  demand action!" If Oliver had merely claimed that humans sometimes desired repose and sometimes desired action,
18  the reader would have experienced only an abstract concept, with no life or vitality. It is the description of two
19  realistic occupations, amid the broader abstract implication of all human desires, which contributes concreteness to
20  the passage and brings the it to life.
21          Personal observation and anecdote also gives the work concreteness and vitality. Oliver relates that she,
22  "for many years in a place called Blackwater Woods, wrote while she walked." She claims, "That motion, hardly
23  more than a dreamy sauntering, worked for me; it kept my body happy while I scribbled." This personal anecdote
24  gives the reader a personal and real example of the human desire of motion.
25          Clearly, Mary Oliver, by using two specific occupations as symbols or extended metaphors of the broader
26  implications of all of human desires, is able to create a concrete and personal essay. Concreteness helps the reader
27  visualize the passage, while personal observation adds logos and vitality to the work. (Sarah)

1. What would be the best title for this essay?
   A. The Importance of Community
   B. The Handyman Poet
   C. Building a Poem
   D. Rock of Ages

2. How does the author begin her essay?
   A. Summary of argument
   B. Evidence
   C. Rhetorical questions
   D. Quotes

3. What organizational plan does the author employ?
   A. Argument, Evidence, Counterargument
   B. Thesis, Supporting Details, Conclusion
   C. Summary, Anecdotes
   D. Anecdotes, Commentary, Conclusion

4. The two literary techniques that she employs are
   A. Simile and metaphor.
   B. Hyperbole and allusion.
   C. Analogy and extended metaphor.
   D. Conflict and resolution.

5. What is the author's primary strategy of creating transitions?
   A. Using guide words
   B. Pausing for affect
   C. Mentioning a word or thought from the preceding paragraph
   D. Double indent

## Grammar and Usage

Choose the best grammar/usage form in bold sentence(s).

Passage 1, Lines 27–28

   A. NONE
   B. In conclusion, because people have embraced African American music not only in the past, but also in the present, and because music is in a way, culture externalized, African American music defines African culture as it also influences American culture.
   C. In conclusion, because whites have embraced African American music now and in the past, and because music is in a way, culture externalized, African American music defines African culture as it also influences American culture.
   D. In conclusion, African American music defines African culture as it also influences American culture.

# Lesson 3
## SAT Essay

### Student Response 1

*Prompt:* When is it appropriate to defy or to disobey authority?

1  In the early 1800s, African American slaves spoke out against their authorities for equal rights. They were granted
2  some, but not full equality like their white counterparts. In the 1960s, African Americans spoke out against authority
3  again and finally gained their rights. **It is always important to question the decisions and positions of authority**
4  **when a certain person feels their rights are being violated.** William Lloyd Garrison was the author of the
5  newspaper *The Liberator* in the 1800s. He denounced slavery, the decisions of the Founding Fathers to allow slavery
6  in the new "free" nation, and the principle that a slave counted as three-fifths of a person when counting population.
7  Garrison questioned and spoke against his authority, the government, and eventually gained numerous supporters.
8  They fought an extremely hard battle, which included raids, killings, and libel. Finally the government gave in to
9  their wishes and passed the Thirteenth and Fourteenth Amendments, which banned slavery and allowed for equal
10  protection of the law respectively. In this instance, the government had so much power it could pass whatever
11  legislation and bills it wanted. However, it was up to the people to change this. If the people had been quiet about
12  their feelings, slavery might still be allowed in the United States today.
13  Similarly, African Americas fought another battle in the 1960s. This time they were demanding equal rights
14  and desegregation after *Plessy v. Ferguson*'s ruling of "separate but equal" facilities. The African Americans
15  questioned their authorities by having lunch-counter sit-ins, marches to Washington, and many other nonviolent
16  demonstrations. Martin Luther King Jr.'s famous "I Have a Dream" speech in front of the Lincoln Memorial decried
17  the segregated nation and rallied the people to have Congress pass legislation to allow for equal civil rights for
18  everyone. Martin Luther King Jr. and many other people were not shy, keeping their views to themselves, but
19  instead were outspoken against their authority, the government. Their actions resulted in the passing of the Civil
20  Rights Act of 1964 and the Voting Rights Act of 1965. The government's support of segregation was attacked and
21  torn down by the people.
22  The Civil Rights Movement was only possible because of the great number of supporters present, but even
23  one person can question an authority if they feel that authority is not doing something right. Henry David Thoreau's
24  *Civil Disobedience* is a short story he wrote relating why he would not pay taxes to the government and hence was
25  put into jail. Thoreau was the only person against the government in this case, but he was not terrified. Anyone and
26  everyone should be allowed to question the authorities. If free speech and civil disobedience were not allowed, a
27  country could easily turn into Hitler's Germany before World War II. As seen in history, Hitler was a cruel dictator
28  who demanded that everything be done his way. The lack of free speech and the lack of people rising against him
29  resulted in a tyrannical government. People cannot be afraid to speak out if they want their rights and their lives
30  preserved.
31  If is sometimes necessary to challenge one's authority because authorities are not always right. Authorities
32  like the government have often blocked equality and civil rights for many groups, but because of the people's
33  protesting, these rights were finally granted to the people. Challenging one's authority can lead to a more peaceful
34  and desirable environment in the end. (Hannah)

## Student Response 2

*Prompt:* Does one focus on personal achievement, or on the greater public good?

1      Why do so many people dream of being widely popular and loved by everyone? Unfortunately, an
2 instinctive trait found in most humans is the desire to please others, rather than gain true satisfaction and
3 achievement by reaching and surpassing their own standards. First, what pleases the crowd is often not what is the
4 right thing to do, and some people just are not given the gifts that bring popularity. Second, those in history who
5 stood against the tide and aimed to reach their personal standards stand clearly apart.
6      While some have the natural ability to more easily please others, too often the world's definition of success
7 is not either morally acceptable or in the best interests of the individual. Some traits eliciting popularity, such as
8 beauty, wit, strength, or athletic ability, are inherent as well as superficial, not bringing any lasting positive affect on
9 humanity. For instance, one person might not study at all and still get grade A on a test, while another studies
10 voraciously but can only attain a B; hence comparisons only lead to pride or disappointments. In Homer's *Iliad*,
11 Achilles is held in high esteem among men, but he had a hard and wicked heart, which led him to dishonorable
12 actions. Success doesn't equal achievement.
13      Thankfully, some great people focused their lives on personal achievement, and many came to benefit.
14 These include President Harry S. Truman, who earned the respect of the American people by valiantly opposing
15 political corruption. **Despite her parents' disdain, Florence Nightingale became a hero as a war nurse.** When
16 criticized for his lack of success, Thomas Edison stuck it out and invented the lightbulb.
17      While success may seem nice, it is not a measure of true achievement since we can learn from numerous
18 historical figures. (Pam)

## Close Reading

1. Student Response 1
   A. Argues that violating authority is critical in a democracy.
   B. Argues that authority must be obeyed at all costs.
   C. Argues that free speech and civil disobedience are tied together.
   D. Concedes that excessive lawbreaking is a necessary evil.

2. In Student Response 2, the author organizes her essay
   A. By posing a rhetorical question and then developing her thesis.
   B. By offering a series of anecdotes.
   C. By stating a thesis and offering a couple of examples.
   D. By a series of bullet points.

3. A problem in Student Response Essay 2:
   I.  No specific examples are given.      III.  There are too many personal examples.
   II.  Transitions are weak.      IV.  The essay is too short.

       A. I and II              C. II and III              E. All
       B. III and IV            D. IV

4. Where is the best statement of the main point of the Student Response 1?
   A. Lines 3–4                 C. Lines 15–16
   B. Lines 8–9                 D. Lines 31–34

5. Where is the main point of the Student Response 2?
   A. Lines 1–5                 C. Lines 12–13
   B. Lines 8–9                 D. Lines 16–18

6. What is a significant stylistic problem in both essays?
   A. First person is used.
   B. Second-person pronouns are used.
   C. Transitions are weak.
   D. There are agreement problems.

7. What score would the Student Responses receive?
   Student Response 1: ___. Student Response 2: ___.

## Grammar and Usage

Choose the best grammar/usage form in bold sentence(s).

1. Student Response 1, Lines 3–4

   A. NONE
   B. One must question the decisions and positions of authority when a certain person feels their rights are being violated.
   C. One must question authority when people feel that their rights are being violated.
   D. It is always important to question the decisions and positions of authority when someone feels their rights are being violated.

2. Student Response 2, Line 15

   A. NONE
   B. Despite her parents' disdain, Florence Nightingale became a heroic war nurse.
   C. Despite her parents disdain, Florence Nightingale was a war nurse.
   D. Despite her parent's disdain, Florence Nightingale became a war nurse.

# Lesson 4
## Reading: Document-Based Analysis

### Chinese Exclusion Act (1882)

1   An Act to execute certain treaty stipulations relating to Chinese.
2
3   *Preamble.* Whereas, in the opinion of the Government of the United States the coming of Chinese laborers to this
4   country endangers the good order of certain localities within the territory thereof:
5
6   *Therefore*, Be it enacted by the Senate and House of Representatives of the United States of America in Congress
7   assembled, That from and after the expiration of ninety days next after the passage of this act, and until the
8   expiration of ten years next after the passage of this act, the coming of Chinese laborers to the United States be, and
9   the same is hereby, suspended; and during such suspension it shall not be lawful for any Chinese laborer to come, or,
10  having so come after the expiration of said ninety days, to remain within the United States.
11
12  *Sec. 2.* That the master of any vessel who shall knowingly bring within the United States on such vessel, and land or
13  permit to be landed, and Chinese laborer, from any foreign port of place, shall be deemed guilty of a misdemeanor,
14  and on conviction thereof shall be punished by a fine of not more than five hundred dollars for each and every such
15  Chinese laborer so brought, and may be also imprisoned for a term not exceeding one year.
16
17  *Sec. 3.* That the two foregoing sections shall not apply to Chinese laborers who were in the United States on the
18  seventeenth day of November, eighteen hundred and eighty, or who shall have come into the same before the
19  expiration of ninety days next after the passage of this act, and who shall produce to such master before going on
20  board such vessel, and shall produce to the collector of the port in the United States at which such vessel shall arrive,
21  the evidence hereinafter in this act required of his being one of the laborers in this section mentioned; nor shall the
22  two foregoing sections apply to the case of any master whose vessel, being bound to a port not within the United
23  States by reason of being in distress or in stress of weather, or touching at any port of the United States on its voyage
24  to any foreign port of place: Provided, That all Chinese laborers brought on such vessel shall depart with the vessel
25  on leaving port.
26
27  *Sec. 4.* That for the purpose of properly identifying Chinese laborers who were in the United States on the
28  seventeenth day of November, eighteen hundred and eighty, or who shall have come into the same before the
29  expiration of ninety days next after the passage of this act, and in order to furnish them with the proper evidence of
30  their right to go from and come to the United States of their free will and accord, as provided by the treaty between
31  the United States and China dated November seventeenth, eighteen hundred and eighty, the collector of customs of
32  the district from which any such Chinese laborer shall depart from the United States shall, in person or by deputy, go
33  on board each vessel having on board any such Chinese laborer and cleared or about to sail from his district for a
34  foreign port, and on such vessel make a list of all such Chinese laborers, which shall be entered in registry-books to
35  be kept for that purpose, in which shall be stated the name, age, occupation, last place of residence, physical marks
36  or peculiarities, and all facts necessary for the identification of each of such Chinese laborers, which books shall be
37  safely kept in the custom-house; and every such Chinese laborer so departing from the United States shall be entitled
38  to, and shall receive, free of any charge or cost upon application therefore, from the collector or his deputy, at the
39  time such list is taken, a certificate, signed by the collector or his deputy and attested by his seal of office, in such
40  form as the Secretary of the Treasury shall prescribe, which certificate shall contain a statement of the name, age,
41  occupation, last place of residence, personal description, and fact of identification of the Chinese laborer to whom
42  the certificate is issued, corresponding with the said list and registry in all particulars. In case any Chinese laborer
43  after having received such certificate shall leave such vessel before her departure he shall deliver his certificate to
44  the master of the vessel, and if such Chinese laborer shall fail to return to such vessel before her departure from port
45  the certificate shall be delivered by the master to the collector of customs for cancellation. The certificate herein
46  provided for shall entitle the Chinese laborer to whom the same is issued to return to and re-enter the United States
47  upon producing and delivering the same to the collector of customs of the district at which such Chinese laborer
48  shall seek to re-enter; and upon delivery of such certificate by such Chinese laborer to the collector of customs at the

49  time of re-entry in the United States, said collector shall cause the same to be filed in the custom house and duly
50  canceled.
51
52  *Sec. 5.* That any Chinese laborer mentioned in section four of this act being in the United States, and desiring to
53  depart from the United States by land, shall have the right to demand and receive, free of charge or cost, a certificate
54  of identification similar to that provided for in section four of this act to be issued to such Chinese laborers as may
55  desire to leave the United States by water; and it is hereby made the duty of the collector of customs of the district
56  next adjoining the foreign country to which said Chinese laborer desires to go to issue such certificate, free of charge
57  or cost, upon application by such Chinese laborer, and to enter the same upon registry-books to be kept by him for
58  the purpose, as provided for in section four of this act.
59
60  *Sec. 6.* That in order to the faithful execution of articles one and two of the treaty in this act before mentioned, every
61  Chinese person other than a laborer who may be entitled by said treaty and this act to come within the United States,
62  and who shall be about to come to the United States, shall be identified as so entitled by the Chinese Government in
63  each case, such identity to be evidenced by a certificate issued under the authority of said government, which
64  certificate shall be in the English language or (if not in the English language) accompanied by a translation into
65  English, stating such right to come, and which certificate shall state the name, title, or official rank, if any, the age,
66  height, and all physical peculiarities, former and present occupation or profession, and place of residence in China of
67  the person to whom the certificate is issued and that such person is entitled conformably to the treaty in this act
68  mentioned to come within the United States. Such certificate shall be prima-facie evidence of the fact set forth
69  therein, and shall be produced to the collector of customs, or his deputy, of the port in the district in the United
70  States at which the person named therein shall arrive.
71
72  *Sec. 7.* That any person who shall knowingly and falsely alter or substitute any name for the name written in such
73  certificate or forge any such certificate, or knowingly utter any forged or fraudulent certificate, or falsely personate
74  any person named in any such certificate, shall be deemed guilty of a misdemeanor; and upon conviction thereof
75  shall be fined in a sum not exceeding one thousand dollars, and imprisoned in a penitentiary for a term of not more
76  than five years.
77
78  *Sec. 8.* That the master of any vessel arriving in the United States from any foreign port or place shall, at the same
79  time he delivers a manifest of the cargo, and if there be no cargo, then at the time of making a report of the entry of
80  vessel pursuant to the law, in addition to the other matter required to be reported, and before landing, or permitting
81  to land, any Chinese passengers, deliver and report to the collector of customs of the district in which such vessels
82  shall have arrived a separate list of all Chinese passengers taken on board his vessel at any foreign port or place, and
83  all such passengers on board the vessel at that time. Such list shall show the names of such passengers (and if
84  accredited officers of the Chinese Government traveling on the business of that government, or their servants, with a
85  note of such facts), and the name and other particulars, as shown by their respective certificates; and such list shall
86  be sworn to by the master in the manner required by law in relation to the manifest of the cargo. Any willful refusal
87  or neglect of any such master to comply with the provisions of this section shall incur the same penalties and
88  forfeiture as are provided for a refusal or neglect to report and deliver a manifest of cargo.
89
90  *Sec. 9.* That before any Chinese passengers are landed from any such vessel, the collector, or his deputy, shall
91  proceed to examine such passengers, comparing the certificates with the list and with the passengers; and no
92  passenger shall be allowed to land in the United States from such vessel in violation of law.
93
94  *Sec. 10.* That every vessel whose master shall knowingly violate any of the provisions of this act shall be deemed
95  forfeited to the United States, and shall be liable to seizure and condemnation on any district of the United States
96  into which such vessel may enter or in which she may be found.
97
98  *Sec. 11.* That any person who shall knowingly bring into or cause to be brought into the United States by land, or
99  who shall knowingly aid or abet the same, or aid or abet the landing in the United States from any vessel of any
100 Chinese person not lawfully entitled to enter the United States, shall be deemed guilty of a misdemeanor, and shall,
101 on conviction thereof, be fined in a sum not exceeding one thousand dollars, and imprisoned for a term not
102 exceeding one year.
103
104 *Sec. 12.* That no Chinese person shall be permitted to enter the United States by land without producing to the
105 proper officer of customs the certificate in this act required of Chinese persons seeking to land from a vessel. And

106  any Chinese person found unlawfully within the United States shall be caused to be removed therefrom to the
107  country from whence he came, by direction of the United States, after being brought before some justice, judge, or
108  commissioner of a court of the United States and found to be one not lawfully entitled to be or remain in the United
109  States.
110
111  *Sec. 13.* That this act shall not apply to diplomatic and other officers of the Chinese Government traveling upon the
112  business of that government, whose credentials shall be taken as equivalent to the certificate in this act mentioned,
113  and shall exempt them and their body and household servants from the provisions of this act as to other Chinese
114  persons.
115
116  *Sec. 14.* That hereafter no State court or court of the United States shall admit Chinese to citizenship; and all laws in
117  conflict with this act are hereby repealed.
118
119  *Sec. 15.* That the words "Chinese laborers," whenever used in this act, shall be construed to mean both skilled and
120  unskilled laborers and Chinese employed in mining.
121
122  Approved, May 6, 1882.
123                                                           (http://www.ourdocuments.gov/doc.php?flash=true&doc=47&page=transcript)

## Close Reading

1.   What is the purpose of this law?
     I.   To suspended immigration of Chinese laborers for ten years.
     II.  To made Chinese residents ineligible for naturalization.
     III. To preserve European American domination of politics.

          A. I                                    C. II and III
          B. I and II                             D. All

2.   Where is evidence for the above argument?
     I.   Lines 1–2          III.  Lines 111–12          V.  Lines 116–17
     II.  Lines 6–10         IV.   Lines 113–14

          A. I and II              C. II and V
          B. III and IV            D. I and IV

3. What is true about this pie graph?
   I.   There are more Northern Europeans than all other groups combined.
   II.  Northern Europeans were the best workers.
   III. There were economic problems in Northern Europe that drove immigrants to America.
   IV.  Congress consisted of a Pro-German majority.

        A. I                            C. I, II, and III
        B. II                          D. All

4.  What are possible reasons why the Chinese Exclusion Act was ratified?
   I.   In the late nineteenth century, nations had the ability to control immigration (through better record keeping and passports).
   II.  All European and Western nations enacted similar legislation.
   III. Concern about the impact of immigration on the economic well-being of America's workforce as well as anxiety about the feasibility of assimilating immigrants of diverse ethnic and cultural origins.
   IV.  A desire to maintain a Democratic Party majority voting bloc.

        A. I and II                  C. I, II, and III
        B. III and IV               D. All

# Lesson 5

## Math: Algebra, Arithmetic Problem Solving and Data Analysis, and Passport to Advanced Math

### Passport to Advanced Math

1. Which of the following is a convergent series?
   A. 1 + 1/2 + 1/4+ 1/8
   B. 2 + 1/16 + 1/8 + 1/4
   C. 1 + 1/32 + 1/4 + 1/16
   D. 1 + 2 + 4 + 8

2. Which of the following is a divergent series?
   A. 1 + 1/2 + 1/4+ 1/8
   B. 2 + 1/16 + 1/8 + 1/4
   C. 1 + 1/32 + 1/4 + 1/16
   D. 1 + 2 + 4 + 8

### Arithmetic Problem Solving

1. How far could a man ride at the rate of 8 miles an hour so as to walk back at the rate of 4 miles an hour and be gone only 9 hours?
   A. 24 miles
   B. 21 miles
   C. 18 miles
   D. 27 miles

2. On a route, a messenger travels at the rate of 10 miles an hour. Another messenger starts 4 hours later on the same route and travels at the rate of 12 miles an hour. How long will it take the second to overtake the first?
   A. 18 hrs.
   B. 20 hrs.
   C. 24 hrs.
   D. 27 hrs.

### Algebra

1. If $d$ is a whole number, what is the next larger number?
   A. d + 1
   B. d – 1
   C. d(1)
   D. d + d

2. A boy bought a pound of butter for $y$ dollars, a pound of meat for $z$ dollars, and a bunch of lettuce for $s$ dollars. How much did they cost altogether?
   A. y(z)(s)
   B. y(z) + s
   C. y + z + s
   D. 0 + z + y

3. A merchant sold $x$ barrels of flour one week, 40 barrels the next week, and $y$ barrel(s) the following week. How many barrels did he sell?
   A. x – 40 – y
   B. x + 40 + y
   C. 40x + y
   D. 40 – x + y

4. At what time between 11:00 and 12:00 o'clock are the hands two minutes apart?
   A. 54— min.
   B. 56— min.
   C. 55— min.
   D. 57— min.

# Chapter 21  Are We Different?

# Isaiah 58

*Memory Verses.* Is not this the kind of fasting I have chosen: to loose the chains of injustice and untie the cords of the yoke, to set the oppressed free and break every yoke? Is it not to share your food with the hungry and to provide the poor wanderer with shelter—when you see the naked, to clothe them, and not to turn away from your own flesh and blood? Then your light will break forth like the dawn, and your healing will quickly appear: then your righteousness will go before you, and the glory of the LORD will be your rear guard. —Isaiah 58:6–8

During the summer of 1978 I was privileged to work with Dr. George Gallup Sr. and the Princeton Religious Research Center. Dr. Gallup compiled statistics concerning religious America and, in a seminal research poll, compared two population groups: One population group was comprised of Americans who attended church at least twice a month. Another group never attended church. He recorded divorce rates, criminal rates, child abuse rates, and so forth. Guess what he found? There was no measurable difference between people who went to church and those who did not. Recently another study was completed, and the results were similar. Are we practicing Christians really any different from the rest of the world? Does faith in Christ make a difference?

Isaiah is presenting a few of these demands to a faithless Judean community, who wonders why their worship does not make them righteous in God's eyes and restore them to fellowship with him. The occasion described in this chapter—so close to the heart of the religious Isaiah—is a communal fast day, with its ritual practices of repentance. But religious ritual profits nothing when it does not reflect the heart. Isaiah's community learned that they could not pursue business as usual on the fast day, oppressing their workers (58:3) and quarreling in their usual fashion (58:4). Worship that is pleasing to God is a sincere seeking after his will and then obedience to him. Good intentions are not enough. We must do something with our faith.

Specifically, in the early Corinthian church, and in the church today, that means working in the community to loose the bonds of every servitude that binds human beings: hunger for food and spiritual things, homelessness, nakedness. Sincerity and obedience allow Christians to be merciful, but only if the two act together. And finally, Isaiah 58 teaches us that this is the only way of pleasing God, and it is a manner of life different from that of the surrounding world.

In 1988 I had served my Pittsburgh urban church for over five years. I had grown tired of the world's answers to our problems. It was evident to me, as to many eminent economists, that the social welfare system was not working. As Dr. William J. Wilson writes in his important book *The Truly Disadvantaged* (1987; 2nd ed., 2012), "The American social welfare system has done a terrible disservice to the poor." In spite of our best intentions, our welfare system has bred contempt, dependency, and injustice throughout America. While I was reading Isaiah 58, I realized that God wanted the church to do more.

So, my small church purchased a small house and rented it to homeless people. We made the rent very low and allowed the tenants to work for us if they could not afford the rent. We called it our Isaiah 58 House. It returned dignity and justice to our community. It was our way of living out our faith. We were willing to obey God at all costs.

Good intentions may carry a lot of weight in the secular world, but in the Christian world they have very little credibility unless they are factored into obedience to God. We do not have to succeed. But we must obey God. Period.

A true servant of God has a knowledge of God different from the world's knowledge. The world speculates about God and draws its thoughts from its own wisdom and experience. Christians know God in their heart and have his Word. We see God in his Son, and we have his wisdom. We know his hidden plan—that is, to save the whole world. What a wonderful and terrible knowledge, bringing a burden and a liberating feeling all at once! This special insight should guide us in our lifestyle decisions, in our community decisions. Paul is encouraging the Corinthian community to move beyond petty differences and make God's wisdom a reality (1 Corinthians 1–4).

Wisdom is a tricky thing. I asked some kids what wisdom is, and they responded, "Oh, yeah, that thing that Mr. Miyagi in the *Karate Kid* has." But the wisdom of which Paul writes is far beyond the wisdom of this world: "When I came to you, brothers and sisters, I did not come proclaiming to you the testimony of God in lofty words or wisdom. For I decided to know nothing among you except Jesus Christ, and him crucified. And I came to you in weakness and in fear and in much trembling. My speech and my proclamation were not with plausible words of wisdom, but with a demonstration of the Spirit and of power, so that your faith might not rest on human wisdom but on the power of God" (1 Corinthians 2:1–5 NRSV).

Do we really embrace the wisdom of God? In the summer of 1989 the Maine Seacoast Mission, a Christian ministry in which I am enrolled as a mission pastor, invited my family to go to remote Matinicus Island, twenty-five miles off the coast of Maine. This community desperately needed to hear the gospel, and we did the best we could. But while the spiritual life of most of the island was in a shamble, the physical beauty of the island was breathtaking. I had never been in such a beautiful place!

Later that summer we were privileged to witness a total lunar eclipse. It is impossible to describe how it felt to look out on the Atlantic Ocean and watch the moon disappear before our eyes! But as we returned to the parsonage later that night, I noticed that most people on the island had missed the entire eclipse. They continued to watch TV or accomplish other inside activities. As the writer E. B. White reflects, "Most people prefer the image over the reality." Instead of stepping outside to see the actual event taking place, they kept their eyes on the small screen.

God is calling us to be different, to commit our lives to something that really matters.

In Matthew we see that true followers of God have a value in God's eyes, a value of which the world knows nothing. Our true worth is given us, not by society's judgments of us, not by our own self-estimates, but by our God, who has enlisted us in his purpose. In fact, we may seem unimportant to our friends and useless to the world, but in God's eyes we are the salt of the earth—that precious commodity in Jesus' time that not only preserved and flavored but was sometimes even used for money. Similarly, we are shinning lights for the world, giving guidance and comfort to all. Brothers and sisters, we have a worth, not in ourselves, and not granted by society, but given us by our Lord. And God will not share us with other gods! We are totally his—or we are not.

We are not seeking to be at peace with our world. Peace is not détente, and that is what we often mean by peace. To live in détente would be to live in a state of unawareness and of false harmony, in a passivity of mere existence, toleration, and denial. We would be subject to and live in fear of inexplicable and unpredictable eruptions from within.

Dr. Robert Kopp, one of the best preachers I know, and an old friend, laments that there is a profound belief gap in our church today. He is convinced that the Presbyterian Church is politically dominated by people who don't believe Jesus is who he said he is and who our constitution and confessions say he is. He is convinced that our biggest problem is unconverted clergy and unconvinced laity. As someone once said in describing the problem with too many churches, "Walking into a MacDonald's does not make us a Big Mac." As the great preacher Lloyd Ogilvie reflects, "You can't give away what you ain't got for yourself." We will be different when we truly believe and faithfully live the gospel!

## Journal Question

Do you have a cause worth dying for? What is it?

# Lesson 1
## Evidence-Based Reading and Writing

### Literary Choice

No one really knows who Homer was, but he was unquestionably one of the most important Western authors of all time. In particular, the *Iliad* has inspired generations with its stories of glory and greed, bravery and trickery.

**The Death of Hector**

| | |
|---|---|
| 1 | "At last is Hector stretch'd upon the plain, |
| 2 | Who fear'd no vengeance for Patroclus slain: |
| 3 | Then, prince! you should have fear'd, what now you feel; |
| 4 | Achilles absent was Achilles still: |
| 5 | Yet a short space the great avenger stayed, |
| 6 | Then low in dust thy strength and glory laid. |
| 7 | Peaceful he sleeps, with all our rites adorn'd, |
| 8 | For ever honour'd, and for ever mourn'd: |
| 9 | While cast to all the rage of hostile power, |
| 10 | Thee birds shall mangle, and the gods devour." |
| 11 | Then Hector, fainting at the approach of death: |
| 12 | "By thy own soul! by those who gave thee breath! |
| 13 | By all the sacred prevalence of prayer; |
| 14 | Ah, leave me not for Grecian dogs to tear! |
| 15 | The common rites of sepulture bestow, |
| 16 | To soothe a father's and a mother's woe: |
| 17 | Let their large gifts procure an urn at least, |
| 18 | And Hector's ashes in his country rest." |
| 19 | "No, wretch accursed! relentless he replies; |
| 20 | (Flames, as he spoke, shot flashing from his eyes;) |
| 21 | Not those who gave me breath should bid me spare, |
| 22 | Nor all the sacred prevalence of prayer. |
| 23 | Could I myself the bloody banquet join! |
| 24 | No—to the dogs that carcase I resign. |
| 25 | Should Troy, to bribe me, bring forth all her store, |
| 26 | And giving thousands, offer thousands more; |
| 27 | Should Dardan Priam, and his weeping dame, |
| 28 | Drain their whole realm to buy one funeral flame: |
| 29 | Their Hector on the pile they should not see, |
| 30 | Nor rob the vultures of one limb of thee." |
| 31 | Then thus the chief his dying accents drew: |
| 32 | "Thy rage, implacable! too well I knew: |
| 33 | The Furies that relentless breast have steel'd, |
| 34 | And cursed thee with a heart that cannot yield. |
| 35 | Yet think, a day will come, when fate's decree |
| 36 | And angry gods shall wreak this wrong on thee; |
| 37 | Phoebus and Paris shall avenge my fate, |
| 38 | And stretch thee here before the Scaean gate." |
| 39 | He ceased. The Fates suppress'd his labouring breath, |
| 40 | And his eyes stiffen'd at the hand of death; |
| 41 | To the dark realm the spirit wings its way, |
| 42 | (The manly body left a load of clay,) |
| 43 | And plaintive glides along the dreary coast, |
| 44 | A naked, wandering, melancholy ghost! |

(Homer, *Iliad* 22.414–58, http://www.bartleby.com/203/189.html)

## Student Response

### Hector

1   The *Iliad* (or Song of Ilion) is an epic poem traditionally attributed to Homer. Set in the Trojan War, it tells of the
2   battles and events during a few weeks in the final year of the war. Along with the *Odyssey*, also attributed to Homer,
3   the *Iliad* is among the oldest extant works of Western literature, and its written version is usually dated to around the
4   eighth century BC. Among the many heroes on the Greek side and on the Trojan side, Hector, leader of the Trojan
5   army, is undeniably one of the greatest.

6   Hector demonstrates himself as a brave, authoritative, courageous, and formidable warrior, who will fight
7   to the death for the sake of his people. Once while talking to his wife he says, "But I would die of shame to face the
8   men of Troy, . . . if I would shrink back from battle now, a coward. I've learned it all too well. To stand up bravely,
9   always to fight in the front ranks of Trojan soldiers, winning my father great glory." He also demonstrates his strong
10  character by his love for his family, when he mightily and nobly proclaims to his wife, "No, no, let the earth coming
11  piling over my dead body before I hear your cries, I hear you dragged away!" Thus it is shown that Hector fights in
12  order to protect his family. Hector is also favored by the gods, and many times does it say, "Victory was now
13  vouchsafed to Hector."

14  But standing on the outskirts of the battle, there were two men who changed the minds of the gods and the
15  fate and destiny of Hector. These men were Achilles and Patroclus. Near the end of the battle, Patroclus could stand
16  watching no longer, and begged Achilles to be allowed to defend the ships. Achilles relented and lent Patroclus his
17  armor, sending him off with a stern admonition not to pursue the Trojans, lest he take Achilles's glory. But
18  Patroclus, ignoring Achilles's command, pursues and reaches the gates of Troy, where he is killed by Hector.

19  After that Hector is referred to and called "a murderer," just because one man, out of the hundreds that
20  Hector had killed, happened to be Achilles's favorite. From then on, the victory vouchsafed to Hector is taken away,
21  and the inconsistent gods begin to give the victory to Achilles, and Hector's fate is inevitable.

22  Despite all of this, Hector is still determined to protect his city and his family to the death. When his entire
23  army flees to safety inside the city of Troy, Hector is left standing outside to fight Achilles. Then as Hector throws
24  his spear and misses his target, he says, "Alas! the gods have lured me on to my destruction. . . . Death is now
25  indeed exceedingly near at hand, and there is no way out of it—for so Zeus and his son Apollo the far-darter have
26  willed it, though heretofore they have been ever ready to protect me. But now, my doom has come upon me."

27  The inconsistency of the gods determined many things in the war, such as the deaths of Patroclus and
28  Hector. But the one thing that it didn't determine was the character of each individual warrior. The greatness of
29  Hector is seen in the unity of his character. He is the only character that, in the face of immense adversity, showed
30  himself as a complete man. (Anna)

## Close Reading

1.  Alexander Pope's translation is
    A.  Drama.
    B.  Poetry.
    C.  Prose.
    D.  Song.

2.  What is the narrative technique?
    A.  Omniscient
    B.  Limited Omniscient
    C.  First person
    D.  Third-person objective

3.  What is the tone of most of the narrative?
    A.  Serious
    B.  Sanguine
    C.  Choleric
    D.  Humorous

4.  The author creates the tone by
    A.  Humorous scenes and language.
    B.  Alliteration.
    C.  Tense interpersonal rivalries.
    D.  Antagonistic characters.

5.  Identify the worldview of the novel.
    A.  Romanticism
    B.  Theism
    C.  Naturalism
    D.  Existentialism

6. Achilles is seeking revenge for
   A. A disparaging remark about his courage.
   B. The kidnapping of Helen.
   C. The death of Patroclus.
   D. A lost battle.

7. Hector's wife is a
   A. Foil.
   B. Antagonist.
   C. Companion.
   D. Goddess.

8. What is a persistent theme in the *Iliad*?
   A. Hope
   B. Valor
   C. Fate
   D. Grace

## Command of Evidence (Student Response)

1. Where is the first place the Student Response presents its thesis?
   A. Lines 1–2
   B. Lines 5–6
   C. Lines 26–27
   D. Lines 29–30

2. What general strategy does the essay employ?
   A. The greatness of Hector is pronounced in the beginning but not fully developed until the end.
   B. The end of poor Hector is foreshadowed.
   C. The unpredictability of the gods is described.
   D. The Trojans are presented as worthy opponents.

## Words in Context

The following words are from the literary excerpt:

1. What is the meaning of *implacable* in Line 32?
   A. Deleterious
   B. Perfunctory
   C. Pitiless
   D. Remorseful

2. What is the meaning of *plaintive* in Line 43?
   A. Silly
   B. Nostalgic
   C. Uncaring
   D. Sentimental

# Lesson 2
## Critical Reading and Writing

### Command of Evidence

Read the following passages and answer accompanying questions:

### Passage 1

1    Have you ever had to remind your father to beat the eggs properly for lemon meringue pie? Or have you ever had to
2    warn your dad not to burn the chicken roast? Most likely not. This is because women have generally occupied the
3    role of cooking in the household. However, the roles of men and women are shifting in today's society, including
4    this stereotype of cooking. Traditionally men have been viewed as the breadwinners and women the homemakers.
5    However, now society has moved to a more equal playing ground. While there is still a distinction about who is
6    responsible for cooking, this stereotype is beginning to unravel.
7            Women grew up being told that they must learn to cook, to be the good housewife. They were told: "If you
8    want to catch a husband, you'd better know how to cook" or "Don't you want to be able to cook for your family and
9    your husband?" (*FB*). Cooking, cleaning, and being the good housewife were even seen as fulfillment for many
10   women. It is understandable, then, that women were often stereotyped as the family cooks. Men, on the other hand,
11   were taught to work hard and make a living for their family. A man's attitude toward the kitchen is described by
12   Dave Barry in "Lost in the Kitchen": "I would no more enter that kitchen than I would attempt to park a nuclear
13   aircraft carrier, but my wife, who runs her own business, glides in very casually and picks up exactly the right
14   kitchen implement and starts doing the exactly right thing without receiving instructions whatsoever." This basic
15   distinction is where the cooking stereotype originated.
16           This stereotype was initiated by the basic differences between men and women. Gender differences have
17   been "programmed" into our personalities. Men and women were designed to be different. I have heard, more often
18   than not, the differences between men and women as comedy acts. Why do we find this comparison so amusing?
19   Because we acknowledge how different we really are from the opposite sex. We can laugh about it because we
20   know it to be true: men and women are neurologically different. It is part of their nature. Physically they are
21   different. Therefore, they need to be approached differently.
22           Another origin of this stereotype, not surprisingly, is the media. The television was a huge promoter of the
23   cooking stereotype. Other media like advertising, magazines, and graphics all contributed to this label. One British
24   study examined the connections between biology and cognition. In their study on men and women, they found that
25   "perhaps men and women were socialized to respond differently." They found that women "were more likely to
26   reject absolute answers in favor of the 'somewhat,'" while men "were far more likely to assert that the objects were
27   completely in or out of a particular category." Their conclusion stated that "men saw the world in black and white,
28   whereas women saw more grey" (Wallace). Even studies admit to the differences between men and women on the
29   neurological level. Together they were designed to be an independent team. "One partner, the male, would be
30   focused on purposes, and the other, the woman, would be focused on relationships" (Eckman). This, many would
31   argue, would explain women mood swings. They are wired for it.        There is strong evidence to suggest that men
32   and women are designed differently.
33           However, this does not mean that they must be stereotyped to specific jobs. They must be approached
34   differently but certainly not be limited to a field simply because a society has dictated so. Widespread culture has
35   already broken this stereotype. Popular cooking shows are not limited to women chefs. Rather, there is an
36   abundance of men, creating a gender balance in the kitchen. Media and advertising specifically target men in the
37   kitchen through "manly" meals like barbeque, meat, and seafood. Famous "celebrity" chefs like Alton Brown, Guy
38   Fieri, and Tyler Florence have led the way to break the "women-only-in-the-kitchen" mind-set.
39           In my own life, I see the walls of this stereotype being broken down. When I was little, I always remember
40   my mom cooking the meals and teaching me things in the kitchen. As I reached my early teen years and developed a
41   passion for cooking and good food, I noticed how my dad and brothers became more involved in the kitchen. No
42   longer was my mom the only person responsible for meals in our house. Now there are days when my dad is solely
43   responsible (and he makes some pretty good food!) and days when my brothers are responsible. My dad often jokes
44   around in the kitchen that we are his soux chefs when he is cooking and he ours. My parents have not let a trifling
45   stereotype keep the family from enjoying the cooking process. Cooking is a family activity, not a sole task left for
46   mom, and we have loads of fun doing it.

47  Even outside of my family, cooking seems to be shared by husband and wife fairly equally. Dad grills and
48  experiments with bold flavors. Mom cooks more greens and is focused on home cooking, traditions, and timely
49  meals. The basic differences of men and women lead them to different cooking styles, but the task of cooking is no
50  longer stereotyped to women.
51      One could argue about who benefited from perpetuating a cooking stereotype. It might seem obvious that
52  men would benefit the most since it was generally assumed that they were unable to handle themselves in the
53  kitchen. Therefore they would have little to do with the daily meal preparation or cleanup, thus leaving someone else
54  (the women) to make their meals. On the other hand, women might have benefited for so long under such a
55  stereotype because it was assumed that women were only capable of household chores—leaving them out of the
56  demanding workforce. Regardless, as the evidence has suggested, this stereotype, this mind-set, is no longer as
57  potent as it was before. Now men take on the cooking responsibilities as much as women, debunking the myth of
58  cooking stereotypes. (Callie)

### Sources

Barry, Dave. "Lost in the Kitchen." http://teachers.sduhsd.net/jconn/Lost%20in%20the%20Kitchen%20DB.pdf.
Eckman, David [PhD, Senior Lecturer, Kesed Seminars]. "God Formed the Man and Fashioned the Woman."
    Christian Broadcasting Networks (CBN), 2014. http://www.cbn.com/family/marriage/adamneve_2.aspx.
*FB.* "Cooking & Gender: Men, Women & Stereotypes." *Fabulously Broke*, June 23, 2010.
    http://www.fabulouslybroke.com/2010/06/cooking-gender-men-women-stereotypes/.
Miller, Sharon Hodde, guest blogger. "Gender Differences All in the Brain." May 16, 2011.
    http://www.christianitytoday.com/women/2011/may/gender-differences-all-in-brain.htm
Wallace, Lane. "Why Do Women See the World in Shades of Grey?" *The Atlantic*, April 28, 2011.
    http://www.theatlantic.com/health/archive/2011/04/why-do-women-see-the-world-in-shades-of-gray/237880/.

## Close Reading

1.  What would be the best title for this essay?
    A. The Happy Cook                    C. Who Is in the Kitchen?
    B. Chef Mania                        D. Favorite Home Recipes

2.  How does the author begin her essay?
    A. Anecdote                          C. Thesis
    B. Rhetorical question               D. Paradox

3.  What is the purpose of the beginning?
    I.   The author wishes to increase readers' empathy with the topic.
    II.  The author believes women are better cooks.
    III. The author shows that stereotypes linger but are changing.
    IV.  The author loves to cook.

        A. I and II                      C. I and III
        B. II and III                    D. II and IV

4.  Where is the thesis stated?
    A. Lines 3–4                         C. Lines 44–48
    B. Lines 32–34                       D. Lines 51–57

5.  What organizational plan does the author employ?
    A. She offers a thesis at first and then argues the opposite.
    B. She defines the perimeters of her argument and then offers evidence.
    C. She admits that male chauvinism has a deleterious effect on culture.
    D. She understands the negative impact of gender prejudice.

6.  The author finishes her essay
    A. With a summary statement.         C. With a distracting comment.
    B. With a new conclusion.            D. The way she began.

## Passage 2

1   Sorely unable to socially interact with those around him, protagonist Stephen Dedalus focused his attention on rigid
2   academics, his writing, and less than honorable secretive actions in aim of a life apart from what he knew. James
3   Joyce developed his protagonist into a complex character in *A Portrait of an Artist as a Young Man* (1916) through
4   the use of foils, the plot, and the setting. Throughout Stephen's journey, the reader experiences how art becomes his
5   religion.

6       At an early age, Stephen Dedalus watched, listened, and observed. He took notes on things and people
7   around him, and he formed his own worldview in life. One way in which he was so well developed was through the
8   other characters he observed. For example, his parents progressed his character, yet not necessarily in a beneficial
9   way. Basically, Stephen learned that he did not want to be like his parents when he grew up.

10       Indeed, he did just that. He nearly broke his mother's heart when he left the ideals of family, faith
11   (Catholicism), and country. In addition, he resolved to be nothing like his father, whom he described as "a medical
12   student, an oarsman, a tenor, an amateur actor, a shouting politician, . . . a drinker, a good fellow, a story teller,
13   somebody's secretary, something in a distillery, a tax gatherer, a bankrupt, and at present a praiser of his own past."
14   These sarcastic remarks suggest that Stephen had every intention to be something apart (something more
15   meaningful) than what his parent's lived for. His intentions of such a purpose-filled life were not as effectively
16   accomplished. Obviously, these two characters developed Stephen into the opposite of themselves. Stephen was
17   unsatisfied with the condition he was in so he purposed to change it. His means, however, left him missing the mark,
18   missing the aim he intended to hit. Soon Stephen found himself in less-than-honorable activities that he justified as
19   artistic expressions.

20       In addition to his parents, various classmates throughout the years developed Stephen into the character he
21   became. These schoolmates were responsible for the constant teasing, taunting, and mocking of quiet (yet bright)
22   Stephen. Experiences like those made Stephen stronger rather than timid. Unfortunately, though, Stephen did not
23   always choose the right alternative when brushing off the harassing from his schoolmates (even through college).
24   For example, Stephen soon focused his attention on the young woman he was attracted to. Too shy to approach her,
25   Stephen resorted to fulfilling his sexual desires in secret with prostitutes.

26       Set in Dublin, Ireland, Stephen's setting suggests an equally disheartening outlook on life as Stephen felt
27   his circumstances. Due to persistent financial woes, Stephen's family moved many times throughout Ireland, from
28   the "dull phenomenon of Dublin" to the colorless city streets. Either such place reflects the same bleak
29   dissatisfaction that dwelled in Stephen's heart. The setting is critical to this story because it sets the tone for the
30   agitated and conflicted life of Stephen Dedalus.

31       The plot itself largely developed Stephen's character. His character began as a sensitive yet smart child. As
32   years passed by, this character transformed into a rather rebellious man who rejected most of his childhood roots for
33   a life of writing and fulfillment through art. The most interesting thing about his character (and the plot) is that
34   nearly everything he does is in direct contradiction to some part of himself.

35       He seems to be insecure but proud of his intelligence as well. He complains of being lonely (without
36   family, friends, or lover), yet he is too fearful to get close enough to a person to love them. Instead of forming
37   meaningful relationships, Stephen resorted to empty relationships with prostitutes to fulfill his desires. Some days
38   Stephen was a passionate romantic, dreaming of a life spent with the one he loved, Emma. Yet his own stubborn
39   intellect and attitude of realism logically concluded that no such relationship was feasible. "One Stephen is too shy
40   to kiss the young lady he yearns for. The other readily turns to prostitutes to satisfy his sexual urges. One is a timid
41   outsider bullied by his classmates. The other is courageous enough to confront and question authority. One devoutly
42   hopes to become a priest. The other cynically rejects religion."

43       Even at the end of *A Portrait of an Artist as a Young Man*, Stephen remains unsatisfied and tattered from
44   searching for a life he concludes cannot exist. As a result, art became his new addiction; his new drug. Other foils
45   used to develop Stephen include his parents and classmates. In addition, the bleak setting in Ireland developed
46   Stephen into a complicated and conflicted character. (Callie)

1.  What would be the best title of this essay?
    A.  The Weakness of Religion
    B.  The End of All Things
    C.  The Growth of an Essayist
    D.  The Development of a Protagonist

2.  How does the author begin her essay?
    A.  Summary of argument
    B.  Evidence
    C.  Rhetorical questions
    D.  Quotes

3.  What organizational plan does the author employ?
    A.  Argument, Evidence, Counterargument
    B.  Thesis, Supporting Details, Conclusion
    C.  Summary, Anecdotes
    D.  Anecdotes, Commentary, Conclusion

4.  The two literary techniques that she employs are
    A.  Simile and metaphor
    B.  Hyperbole and allusion
    C.  Analogy and extended metaphor
    D.  Internal character conflict and resolution

5.  What might be a criticism of this essay?
    A.  Too wordy
    B.  No transitions
    C.  Not enough textual evidence
    D.  Poor examples

# Lesson 3
## SAT Essay

### Student Response 1

*Prompt:* Agree or disagree with this statement: "That which we obtain too easily, we esteem too lightly. It is dearness only which gives everything its value."

1    Many times those who have everything seem to not care. Billionaires such as Bill Gates believe that they
2    have too much money and begin to give some away, while those in poverty cling to the little spare cash they have. It
3    seems odd that those with the most could care the least. This is because we do not value things that we have not
4    worked for.
5        I learned this concept firsthand with my own money. When I was younger, my parents would buy clothes
6    for me and give me an allowance. This allowance money was often laid on my desk and forgotten, or I would
7    carelessly place it where it would be lost. However, when my parents stopped this and decided to pay us four dollars
8    an hour for mowing the lawn, I learned the true importance of money. I saved up first to buy a watch, then a cell
9    phone, and finally an iPod.
10       This is also clearly seen in the movie *Captain Courageous*, where a young boy finds himself being forced
11   to work for his living on a ship instead of being lazy all day. When he is finally given his measly paycheck for his
12   three months of labor, he spends it carefully and reverently because of the work he spent achieving it.
13       This principle is especially true with those who have natural talent. **The movie *Rudy* focuses on a boy**
14   **whose dream is to play sports, but he cannot do well because of his weak body and lack of natural talent.**
15   When he does finally achieve some of his goals, it is easy to say that he is more satisfied and happy than many other
16   players who did well because of their natural talents.
17       It is amazing that those who have the most often care the least. People who have money squander it while
18   children are starving in the streets. There is only value in things that we strive for and achieve and were not just
19   given to us. (Marci)

### Student Response 2

*Prompt:* How are problems solved? On the lowest level? Or on a global scale?

1    "A house divided cannot stand" is the famous quote by Abraham Lincoln during the early processes of
2    setting up America's government. As Lincoln said, each component of a greater group must agree and cooperate
3    with the others in order for the group to succeed as a whole in the end. People should take more responsibility for
4    solving problems that affect their communities over solving problems that affect the nation in general.
5        The United States of America is composed of fifty independent states that cooperate together to form a
6    collective nation. The ratio of an individual to the people of the entire nation would be one to several million.
7    However, the ratio of an individual to the people of a state would be one to several ten thousand. Because
8    communities are small, the voice of a certain person has a higher chance of being heard. When all the individual
9    communities are successful, the nation will be successful.
10       In a simpler form, an out-of-tune piano can only be fixed back in tune if the tuner works on every string
11   individually. A tuner cannot retune the piano in one try, but instead must listen to every key and make sure each one
12   sounds exactly right. This piano analogy can be applied to communities and a nation. The communities are like the
13   strings of the piano, and when one is off pitch, the entire nation does not run properly. The only way to fix the
14   nation's problems is to work on the communities individually.
15       In our current government, the total debt is over thirteen trillion dollars. That is an extremely large amount and
16   an accumulation of debts from many past years. It would be nearly impossible, if not completely impossible, to
17   tackle this national problem at once. A better way reduce the national debt is to reduce the state debts first.
18   California is one of the states with a huge financial problem, however this debt of California is still less than that of
19   the national government. If the people of California took responsibility in solving California's debt, the national debt
20   may seem easier to conquer.

21      **If the people in every state were to eliminate their debts, the nation in general would have a lower debt**
22      **too.** It is the easiest to tackle a problem by taking small bites. If each person in a community takes responsibility for
23      solving the problems in that particular community first, the nation as a whole would advance faster.
24          Solving a nation's problems can be overwhelming because they are often so large and diverse people do not
25      know where to start. However, if individuals focus on solving the problems of communities first, like checking each
26      string of an out-of-tune piano, the whole nation will be affected in a positive way (Hannah).

## Close Reading

1. Student Response 1
   A. Argues that everyone wants to be rich.
   B. Argues that working hard only counts if it leads to prosperity.
   C. Argues that hard work and satisfaction are disconnected.
   D. Argues that working hard for something does increase appreciation.

2. Student Response 2
   A. Argues that problems are solved at the lowest level.
   B. Argues that everyone should play the piano.
   C. Argues that Rudy was happy because he was able to play football.
   D. Argues that some problems can never be solved.

3. What is the purpose of the initial quote in Student Response 2?
   A. Nothing can be solved if people are disagreeing.
   B. The biggest problems are solved as people cooperate on the smallest level.
   C. The Union won the Civil War by cooperating.
   D. The national debt will be decreased one dollar at a time.

4. In Response 2 the author organizes her essay
   A. By offering rhetorical questions and then developing her thesis.
   B. By offering an argument and a series of supporting anecdotes.
   C. By stating a thesis and offering a counterargument.
   D. By a series of bullet points.

5. A problem in Student Response Essay 2 is that
   I.  No specific examples are given.      III.    There are too many personal examples.
   II.  Transitions are weak.           IV.    The essay is too short.

         A. I and II                   C. II
         B. III and IV               D. IV

6. Where is the best statement of the main point in Student Response 1?
   A. Lines 1–4               C. Lines 12–13
   B. Lines 8–9               D. Lines 15–16

7. Where is the best statement of the main point in Student Response 2?
   A. Lines 2–3               C. Lines 12–13
   B. Lines 8–9               D. Lines 24–26

8. What score would the student responses receive?
   Student Response 1 receives ___. Student Response 2 receives ___.

## Grammar and Usage

Choose the best grammar/usage form in bold sentence(s).

1. Student Response 1, Lines 13–14

    A. NONE
    B. The movie *Rudy* is about a boy whose dream is to play sports, but he cannot do well because of his weak body and lack of natural talent.
    C. The movie *Rudy* focuses on a boy whose dream is to play sports, but he fails because of his weak body and lack of natural talent.
    D. The movie *Rudy* focuses on a weak, ordinary boy whose dream is to play sports.

2. Student Response 2, Lines 21–22

    A. NONE
    B. If the people in every state eliminated their debts, the nation in general would have a lower debt too.
    C. If all persons eliminated their own debts, the nation in general would have a lower debt too.
    D. If the people in every state were to eliminate their debts, the nation would have a lower debt too.

# Lesson 4
## Reading: Document-Based Analysis

**Peace without Victory**

**Woodrow Wilson (January 22, 1917)**

1   Gentlemen of the Senate:
2
3     On the 18th of December last, I addressed an identical note to the governments of the nations now at war
4   requesting them to state, more definitely than they had yet been stated by either group of belligerents, the terms upon
5   which they would deem it possible to make peace. I spoke on behalf of humanity and of the rights of all neutral
6   nations like our own, many of whose most vital interests the war puts in constant jeopardy.
7     The Central Powers united in a reply which stated merely that they were ready to meet their antagonists in
8   conference to discuss terms of peace. The Entente Powers have replied much more definitely and have stated, in
9   general terms, indeed, but with sufficient definiteness to imply details, the arrangements, guarantees, and acts of
10   reparation which they deem to be indispensable conditions of a satisfactory settlement. We are that much nearer a
11   definite discussion of the peace which shall end the present war. We are that much nearer the discussion of the
12   international concert which must thereafter hold the world at peace.
13     In every discussion of the peace that must end this war, it is taken for granted that that peace must be
14   followed by some definite concert of power which will make it virtually impossible that any such catastrophe should
15   ever overwhelm us again. Every lover of mankind, every sane and thoughtful man must take that for granted.
16     I have sought this opportunity to address you because I thought that I owed it to you, as the council
17   associated with me in the final determination of our international obligations, to disclose to you without reserve the
18   thought and purpose that have been taking form in my mind in regard to the duty of our government in the days to
19   come, when it will be necessary to lay afresh and upon a new plan the foundations of peace among the nations.
20     It is inconceivable that the people of the United States should play no part in that great enterprise. To take
21   part in such a service will be the opportunity for which they have sought to prepare themselves by the very
22   principles and purposes of their polity and the approved practices of their government ever since the days when they
23   set up a new nation in the high and honorable hope that it might, in all that it was and did, show mankind the way to
24   liberty.
25     They cannot in honor withhold the service to which they are now about to be challenged. They do not wish
26   to withhold it. But they owe it to themselves and to the other nations of the world to state the conditions under which
27   they will feel free to render it.
28     That service is nothing less than this, to add their authority and their power to the authority and force of
29   other nations to guarantee peace and justice throughout the world. Such a settlement cannot now be long postponed.
30   It is right that before it comes, this government should frankly formulate the conditions upon which it would feel
31   justified in asking our people to approve its formal and solemn adherence to a League for Peace. I am here to
32   attempt to state those conditions.
33     The present war must first be ended; but we owe it to candor and to a just regard for the opinion of
34   mankind to say that, so far as our participation in guarantees of future peace is concerned, it makes a great deal of
35   difference in what way and upon what terms it is ended. The treaties and agreements which bring it to an end must
36   embody terms which will create a peace that is worth guaranteeing and preserving, a peace that will win the
37   approval of mankind, not merely a peace that will serve the several interests and immediate aims of the nations
38   engaged. We shall have no voice in determining what those terms shall be, but we shall, I feel sure, have a voice in
39   determining whether they shall be made lasting or not by the guarantees of a universal covenant; and our judgment
40   upon what is fundamental and essential as a condition precedent to permanency should be spoken now, not
41   afterwards when it may be too late.
42     No covenant of cooperative peace that does not include the peoples of the New World can suffice to keep
43   the future safe against war; and yet there is only one sort of peace that the peoples of America could join in
44   guaranteeing. The elements of that peace must be elements that engage the confidence and satisfy the principles of
45   the American governments, elements consistent with their political faith and with the practical convictions which the
46   peoples of America have once for all embraced and undertaken to defend.

47    I do not mean to say that any American government would throw any obstacle in the way of any terms of
48  peace the governments now at war might agree upon or seek to upset them when made, whatever they might be. I
49  only take it for granted that mere terms of peace between the belligerents will not satisfy even the belligerents
50  themselves. Mere agreements may not make peace secure. It will be absolutely necessary that a force be created as a
51  guarantor of the permanency of the settlement so much greater than the force of any nation now engaged, or any
52  alliance hitherto formed or projected, that no nation, no probable combination of nations, could face or withstand it.
53  If the peace presently to be made is to endure, it must be a peace made secure by the organized major force of
54  mankind.

55    The terms of the immediate peace agreed upon will determine whether it is a peace for which such a
56  guarantee can be secured. The question upon which the whole future peace and policy of the world depends is this?
57  Is the present war a struggle for a just and secure peace, or only for a new balance of power? If it be only a struggle
58  for a new balance of power, who will guarantee, who can guarantee the stable equilibrium of the new arrangement?
59  Only a tranquil Europe can be a stable Europe. There must be, not a balance of power, but a community of power;
60  not organized rivalries, but an organized common peace.

61    Fortunately we have received very explicit assurances on this point. The statesmen of both of the groups of
62  nations now arrayed against one another have said, in terms that could not be misinterpreted, that it was no part of
63  the purpose they had in mind to crush their antagonists. But the implications of these assurances may not be equally
64  to all—may not be the same on both sides of the water. I think it will be serviceable if I attempt to set forth what we
65  understand them to be.

66    They imply, first of all, that it must be a *peace without victory*. It is not pleasant to say this. I beg that I may
67  be permitted to put my own interpretation upon it and that it may be understood that no other interpretation was in
68  my thought. I am seeking only to face realities and to face them without soft concealments. Victory would mean
69  peace forced upon the loser, a victor's terms imposed upon the vanquished. It would be accepted in humiliation,
70  under duress, at an intolerable sacrifice, and would leave a sting, a resentment, a bitter memory upon which terms of
71  peace would rest, not permanently but only as upon quicksand. Only a peace between equals can last. Only a peace
72  the very principle of which is equality and a common participation in a common benefit. The right state of mind, the
73  right feeling between nations, is as necessary for a lasting peace as is the just settlement of vexed questions of
74  territory or of racial and national allegiance.

75    The equality of nations upon which peace must be founded if it is to last must be an equality of rights; the
76  guarantees exchanged must neither recognize nor imply a difference between big nations and small, between those
77  that are powerful and those that are weak. Right must be based upon the common strength, not upon the individual
78  strength, of the nations upon whose concert peace will depend. Equality of territory or of resources there of course
79  cannot be; nor any other sort of equality not gained in the ordinary peaceful and legitimate development of the
80  peoples themselves. But no one asks or expects anything more than an equality of rights. Mankind is looking now
81  for freedom of life, not for equipoise of power.

82    And there is a deeper thing involved than even equality of right among organized nations. No peace can
83  last, or ought to last, which does not recognize and accept the principle that governments derive all their just powers
84  from the consent of the governed, and that no right anywhere exists to hand peoples about from sovereignty to
85  sovereignty as if they were property. I take it for granted, for instance, if I may venture upon a single example, that
86  statesmen everywhere are agreed that there should be a united, independent, and autonomous Poland, and that,
87  henceforth, inviolable security of life, of worship, and of industrial and social development should be guaranteed to
88  all peoples who have lived hitherto under the power of governments devoted to a faith and purpose hostile to their
89  own.

90    I speak of this, not because of any desire to exalt an abstract political principle which has always been held
91  very dear by those who have sought to build up liberty in America but for the same reason that I have spoken of the
92  other conditions of peace which seem to me clearly indispensable because I wish frankly to uncover realities. Any
93  peace which does not recognize and accept this principle will inevitably be upset. It will not rest upon the affections
94  or the convictions of mankind. The ferment of spirit of whole populations will fight subtly and constantly against it,
95  and all the world will sympathize. The world can be at peace only if its life is stable, and there can be no stability
96  where the will is in rebellion, where there is not tranquility of spirit and a sense of justice, of freedom, and of right.

97    So far as practicable, moreover, every great people now struggling toward a full development of its
98  resources and of its powers should be assured a direct outlet to the great highways of the sea. Where this cannot be
99  done by the cession of territory, it can no doubt be done by the neutralization of direct rights of way under the
100 general guarantee which will assure the peace itself. With a right comity of arrangement, no nation need be shut
101 away from free access to the open paths of the world's commerce.

102   And the paths of the sea must alike in law and in fact be free. The freedom of the seas is the sine qua non of
103 peace, equality, and cooperation. No doubt a somewhat radical reconsideration of many of the rules of international

104 practice hitherto thought to be established may be necessary in order to make the seas indeed free and common in
105 practically all circumstances for the use of mankind, but the motive for such changes is convincing and compelling.
106 There can be no trust or intimacy between the peoples of the world without them. The free, constant, unthreatened
107 intercourse of nations is an essential part of the process of peace and of development. It need not be difficult either
108 to define or to secure the freedom of the seas if the governments of the world sincerely desire to come to an
109 agreement concerning it.

110 It is a problem closely connected with the limitation of naval armaments and the cooperation of the navies
111 of the world in keeping the seas at once free and safe. And the question of limiting naval armaments opens the wider
112 and perhaps more difficult question of the limitation of armies and of all programs of military preparation. Difficult
113 and delicate as these questions are, they must be faced with the utmost candor and decided in a spirit of real
114 accommodation if peace is to come with healing in its wings, and come to stay.

115 Peace cannot be had without concession and sacrifice. There can be no sense of safety and equality among
116 the nations if great preponderating armaments are henceforth to continue here and there to be built up and
117 maintained. The statesmen of the world must plan for peace, and nations must adjust and accommodate their policy
118 to it as they have planned for war and made ready for pitiless contest and rivalry. The question of armaments,
119 whether on land or sea, is the most immediately and intensely practical question connected with the future fortunes
120 of nations and of mankind.

121 I have spoken upon these great matters without reserve and with the utmost explicitness because it has
122 seemed to me to be necessary if the world's yearning desire for peace was anywhere to find free voice and utterance.
123 Perhaps I am the only person in high authority among all the peoples of the world who is at liberty to speak and hold
124 nothing back. I am speaking as an individual, and yet I am speaking also, of course, as the responsible head of a
125 great government, and I feel confident that I have said what the people of the United States would wish me to say.

126 May I not add that I hope and believe that I am in effect speaking for liberals and friends of humanity in
127 every nation and of every program of liberty? I would fain believe that I am speaking for the silent mass of mankind
128 everywhere who have as yet had no place or opportunity to speak their real hearts out concerning the death and ruin
129 they see to have come already upon the persons and the homes they hold most dear.

130 And in holding out the expectation that the people and government of the United States will join the other
131 civilized nations of the world in guaranteeing the permanence of peace upon such terms as I have named I speak
132 with the greater boldness and confidence because it is clear to every man who can think that there is in this promise
133 no breach in either our traditions or our policy as a nation, but a fulfillment, rather, of all that we have professed or
134 striven for.

135 I am proposing, as it were, that the nations should with one accord adopt the doctrine of President Monroe
136 as the doctrine of the world: that no nation should seek to extend its polity over any other nation or people, but that
137 every people should be left free to determine its own polity, its own way of development, unhindered, unthreatened,
138 unafraid, the little along with the great and powerful.

139 I am proposing that all nations henceforth avoid entangling alliances which would draw them into
140 competitions of power, catch them in a net of intrigue and selfish rivalry, and disturb their own affairs with
141 influences intruded from without. There is no entangling alliance in a concert of power. When all unite to act in the
142 same sense and with the same purpose, all act in the common interest and are free to live their own lives under a
143 common protection.

144 I am proposing government by the consent of the governed; that freedom of the seas which in international
145 conference after conference representatives of the United States have urged with the eloquence of those who are the
146 convinced disciples of liberty; and that moderation of armaments which makes of armies and navies a power for
147 order merely, not an instrument of aggression or of selfish violence.

148 These are American principles, American policies. We could stand for no others. And they are also the
149 principles and policies of forward-looking men and women everywhere, of every modern nation, of every
150 enlightened community. They are the principles of mankind and must prevail.
151 (http://www.firstworldwar.com/source/peacewithoutvictory.htm)

## Close Reading

1. What is the purpose of this speech?
    I.   To appeal for a "peace without victory"
    II.  To warn belligerents about unrestricted submarine warfare
    III. To set the stage for the League of Nations

        A. I                            C. I and III
        B. I and II                     D. All

2. Evidence for the above argument?

    I.   Lines 52–57        III. Line 72–78
    II.  Lines 63–71        IV.  Lines 98–105

        A. I and II                     C. III and V
        B. II                           D. IV

3. Lines 13–15 refer to
    A. The Armistice                    C. The Concordant
    B. The League of Nations            D. The Allies

4. What are possible reasons why Wilson made this speech in 1917?
    I.   World War I made American neutrality increasingly difficult to maintain.
    II.  Wilson was afraid he would lose the 1918 election.
    III. The distress engendered by the sinking of the *Lusitania*.
    IV.  To set the stage for the creation of a League of Nations after the war ended.

        A. I and II                     C. I, II, and III
        B. I and IV                     D. All

5. Why would this speech offend both the Allies and the Central Powers?
    A. It was pro-English.
    B. It made threats.
    C. It was "meddling" by a neutral power (i.e, the USA).
    D. It caused the price of wheat to double.

## Words in Context

1. What is the meaning of *equipoise* in Line 81?
    A. Status quo                       C. Obduracy
    B. Discord                          D. Resiliency

2. What is the meaning of *sovereignty* in Line 85?
    A. Freedom                          C. Dominion
    B. Independence                     D. Eradication

3. What is the meaning of *candor* in Line 113?
    A. Collusion                        C. Redundancy
    B. Forthrightness                   D. Peacefulness

# Lesson 5
## Math: Algebra, Arithmetic Problem Solving and Data Analysis, and Passport to Advanced Math

### Passport to Advanced Math

Find the value of $x$ in the following equations:

1. $5x^2 - 12 = 33$.
   A. $x = \pm 2$
   B. $x = \pm 4$
   C. $x = \pm 3$
   D. $x = \pm 5$

2. $3x^2 + 4 = 16$.
   A. $x = \pm 2$
   B. $x = \pm 4$
   C. $x = \pm 3$
   D. $x = \pm 5$

3. $4x^2 + 11 = 136 - x^2$.
   A. $x = \pm 2$
   B. $x = \pm 4$
   C. $x = \pm 3$
   D. $x = \pm 5$

4. $5(3x^2 - 1) = 11(x^2 + 1)$.
   A. $x = \pm 2$
   B. $x = \pm 4$
   C. $x = \pm 3$
   D. $x = \pm 5$

### Arithmetic Problem Solving

1. A courier who travels at the rate of 19 miles per 4 hours is followed, 8 hours later, by another who travels at the rate of 19 miles per 3 hours. *How long* will it take the second to overtake the first? *How far* will the first have gone before he is overtaken?
   A. 22 hrs.; 150 miles
   B. 20 hrs.; 148 miles
   C. 24 hrs.; 152 miles
   D. 18 hrs.; 160 miles

2. A train going at the rate of 20 miles per hour is followed, on a parallel track, 4 hours later, by an express train. The express overtakes the first train in 5– hours. What is the speed of the express train?
   A. 35 miles per hour
   B. 45 miles per hour
   C. 25 miles per hour
   D. 40 miles per hour

3. A messenger started for Washington at the rate of 6– miles an hour. Six hours later a second messenger followed and in 4– hours overtook the first just as he was entering the city. At what rate did the second messenger go? How far was it to Washington?
   A. 15 miles; 71 miles
   B. 14– miles; 70 miles
   C. 16 miles; 72 miles
   D. 14– miles; 70— miles

## Algebra

1.  A rectangle whose length is 4 ft. more than its width would have its area increased 56 sq. ft. if its length and width were each made 2 ft. more. What are its dimensions?

    A.  10 ft. by 14 ft.
    B.  11 ft. by 15 ft.

    C.  16 ft. by 20 ft.
    D.  8 ft. by 12 ft.

2.  The length of a room is double its width. If the length were 3 ft. less and the width 3 ft. more, the area would be increased 27 sq. ft. Find the dimensions of the room.

    A.  12 ft. by 24 ft.
    B.  10 ft. by 22 ft.

    C.  7 ft. by 21 ft.
    D.  9 ft. by 27 ft.

3.  A floor is two-thirds as wide as it is long. If the width were 2 ft. more and the length 4 ft. less, the area would be diminished 22 sq. ft. What are its dimensions?

    A.  12 ft. by 18 ft.
    B.  12 ft. by 24 ft.

    C.  14 ft. by 21 ft.
    D.  16 ft. by 32 ft.

# Chapter 22   Greater Demands
# Matthew 5

> *Memory Verses:* You are the light of the world. A town built on a hill cannot be hidden. Neither do people light a lamp and put it under a bowl. Instead they put it on its stand, and it gives light to everyone in the house. In the same way, let your light shine before others, that they may see your good deeds and glorify your Father in heaven. —Matthew 5:14–16

Some Christians seem to feel that because they have been redeemed by Christ, they have no other demands laid upon them by God. But I believe that God never wants what we have: God wants much more. I doubt that this thought occurred to my good friend Dr. David Hall, MIT graduate, adjunct professor at the University of Pittsburgh Medical School, and board-certified family practice physician. Some years ago David and several other Christian medical professors established a clinic that was housed in a basement of a church, and they offered medical services on the basis of people's ability to pay. This was quality care, mind you. I and hundreds like us went to David, and we paid full price. We went because it was the best medical care in town. But thousands went because it was all they could afford. David could have been a millionaire. He is not. David and his wife, Susie, and their family (five children!) live in a modest house in one of the worst parts of town. But David is called to this place. And he knows that God demands more. More than anyone and anything. He therefore quietly does his work. Day after day. Quietly obeying God. Do you?

This was the call to Corinthian Christians nearly two thousand years ago, and it is the call to the church today. Typical first-century Corinthians had a lot of work ahead of them, too. Normally a prosperous, modern, well-educated entrepreneurial church (cf. 2 Corinthians 8), there was very little they could not create with their own hands or buy with their money. Thus this new message of Apollos and Paul and others was initially both intriguing for its novelty and later attractive for its life-changing power. But to the chagrin of every red-blooded capitalist, hardworking, and modern "Corinthian," the gospel was never, is never, and will never be, bought, controlled, or owned by any single person. Ponder, then, how the Corinthians dealt with the concept of grace.

Look at the prophet Amos's nation. Amos castigates his religious culture for forgetting the moral and ethical side of their religion, which demands a radical lifestyle. The spirit of modernity remains unconnected to all place or time. Like sin, it lodges itself in the soul of humankind and drives us from God. It does not have to do so. Not if we remember the concept of grace. God's grace in Christ can call us back to God anywhere, anytime. But in an age when consumerism, self-sufficiency, and self-centeredness have become so attractive, grace is difficult to conceptualize, much less believe and apply to one's life. After all, there is no such thing as "unmerited favor." Everyone knows that one never receives something for nothing. We discard grace from our minds as quickly as we discard the *Reader's Digest* Clearing House Sweepstakes entry form when it arrives in the mail. We do not even read it.

Paul's "followers," likely not fully aware of what they were doing, also took license with this concept and entered into a good old carnal quarrel with followers of Apollos. In other churches, like Galatia, believers interpreted salvation through grace (i.e., unmerited favor) to be license to commit whatever felt good, including licentiousness (Galatians 5:19). Although there was a little immorality among the Corinthian saints and some of them were not above a little rationalism here and there, by and large, the greatest problem in Corinth was not the unbridled body but the unbridled mind and tongue.

But Paul comes down on them like lightning: He chides them for behaving like ordinary men and women, for being "of the flesh," that is, of the old life, and not of the new life of the Spirit (1 Corinthians 3:3, 16).

Moses, approaching death, hurting with physical pain and with knowledge that he will never touch the Promised Land, sets before his people a choice between life and death, good and evil, blessing and curse (Deuteronomy 27–28). Furthermore, Moses insists that his nation make a choice and that they choose life—the way of the Law, Torah, the way of God, eternal life. Every day of our lives we are forced to make similar decisions. Whom will we serve? Where will we work? How much will we work? What will we do with our money? How many children will we have? Whom will we serve? The question haunts all of biblical history. Elijah echoes the same words on Mount Carmel: "If God be God, worship him! If Baal be god, then worship him!" (cf. 1 Kings 18). And Joshua, Samuel, David, the prophets, Jesus, and all the apostles—didn't they all ask us to make good choices?

As Paul declares in several other letters, our ignorance—once an excuse—no longer exists, and we need to choose. After wandering in the wilderness for forty years, we have suddenly seen the Promised Land. After living in blessed nihilistic, humanistic ignorance all our Corinthian lives, suddenly we know the truth. "See, I set before you today life and prosperity." But we need to make those decisions. Do you choose life? Do you choose Jesus Christ?

In retrospect, the book of Deuteronomy must have seemed rather strong stuff to Paul's crowd in Corinth. They wouldn't have had a prayer! And remember that Paul is writing 1 Corinthians to his friends! Think of what he would have said to his enemies (cf. Galatians 5:12)!

Paul's friends who belonged to Apollos pledged allegiance to their popular leader. Now this is not merely a matter of giving glory to God—it is more a matter of control. Who is in control? The Corinthians (and ourselves?) hate to say that God is in control, because he is not one of us. But ah, if Larry or Jim, or someone else is given the credit, then ultimately we want a little credit. Giving honor and glory to someone we cannot control means losing our own control. But this is a greater demand on the Christian.

Jesus argues that he alone satisfies the wishes of God. In him is a righteousness that exceeds that of the scribes and Pharisees (Matthew 5). In him alone is found that perfect obedience that fulfills all the requirements of God (and they are great). Wow! In the Sermon on the Mount we find some of the most revolutionary teachings in the Bible. With prophetic cogency, Jesus speaks out against the very essence of Judaic holiness: Pharisaism. The Pharisees were a lay group who historically stood in opposition to the Jewish priestly class. The name *Pharisee* means "separate"; by their fanaticism for ritual and law, the Pharisees had set themselves apart from the rest of society. In their isolation, their attitude became one of comparison and inflated superiority. Ahem . . . any Pharisees present today?

Adherence to the law and tradition became an obsession. Ironically, the law became a barrier to God. Instead of losing control to God, which is the path to new life, the Pharisees grasped more control. And, not merely satisfied in being captured by their own hypocrisy, they sought to spread their bad news to others (Matthew 23:15).

But in that revolutionary statement, the Sermon on the Mount, Jesus restores the very heart of Judaism and fulfills it with a Christian message. He is the only way. And to reach Jesus Christ, we must go through the cross. And as we go through the cross, we lose control. Each believer must enter the depths of their own heart, discover what external structures demand their allegiance, and then move beyond those and give God everything. What is it that is holding us back? Fear of family rejection? You cannot follow Christ unless you give up your mom and dad. Fear of losing our jobs? Is there anything more valuable than eternal life? Fear of being a fool? What is it?

Granted, this may take time. But salvation begins the moment we begin the journey. The moment we accept Jesus Christ as Lord of our lives, his free gift of salvation, we begin to let him control our lives. We confuse the spiritual with the material. There is a tendency to satisfy our spiritual needs by materialistic means. But it cannot be done. While product advertisements promise us happiness and fulfillment, they will not deliver that. Coca-Cola may promote itself as the "real thing" and may want to teach the world to sing in perfect harmony, but it won't happen until the world learns to trust Jesus Christ as their Savior and live accordingly.

The issue before us is timeless. It is the same issue that confronted Corinthian believers: Will we accept the greater demands of being a believer? Or will we play at it? Will we go into the Promised Land? Will we dare to give God alone the glory? And finally, will we abdicate the throne of our lives and let God reign? No doubt about it: the Christian life has greater demands!

## Journal Question

What major life choices do you face?

# Lesson 1
## Evidence-Based Reading and Writing

### Literary Choice

In a time in which women had virtually no rights, publicly supporting independent thought and actions in women was seen as potentially transgressive. Yet in that sense, in early modern England (1613), Elizabeth Cary wrote a subversive play. Cary tells the story of Mariam, the second wife of Herod the Great, King of Judea from 39 to 4 BC. In 29 BC, Herod is thought dead at the hand of Octavian (later called Emperor Augustus), and Mariam faces her ambivalent feelings about her husband; Herod had loved her, but he had also murdered her grandfather and brother. In act 4, however, Herod returns, dispelling the false report of his death. Herod's evil sister Salome falsely convinces Herod that his wife has been unfaithful in his absence, which results in Herod ordering Mariam's execution.

### *The Tragedy of Mariam*
### Act 1, Scene 2

[MARIAM. ALEXANDRA.]

1 ALEXANDRA.
2 What means these tears? My Mariam doth mistake,
3 The news we heard did tell the tyrant's end:
4 What weep'st thou for thy brother's murd'rer's
5 sake?
6 Will ever wight a tear for Herod spend?
7 My curse pursue his breathless trunk and spirit,
8 Base Edomite, the damnèd Esau's heir:
9 Must he ere Jacob's child the crown inherit?
10 Must he, vile wretch, be set in David's chair?
11 No, David's soul, within the bosom placed
12 Of our forefather Abram, was ashamed:
13 To see his seat with such a toad disgraced,
14 That seat that hath by Judah's race been famed.
15 Thou fatal enemy to royal blood,
16 Did not the murder of my boy suffice,
17 To stop thy cruel mouth that gaping stood,
18 But must thou dim the mild Hircanus' eyes?
19 My gracious father, whose too ready hand
20 Did lift this Idumean from the dust:
21 And he, ungrateful caitiff, did withstand
22 The man that did in him most friendly trust.
23 What kingdom's right could cruel Herod claim,
24 Was he not Esau's issue, heir of hell?
25 Then what succession can he have but shame?
26 Did not his ancestor his birth-right sell?
27 Oh yes, he doth from Edom's name derive,
28 His cruel nature which with blood is fed:
29 That made him me of sire and son deprive,
30 He ever thirsts for blood, and blood is red.
31 Weep'st thou because his love to thee was bent,
32 And read'st thou love in crimson characters?
33 Slew he thy friends to work thy heart's content?
34 No: hate may justly call that action hers.
35 He gave the sacred priesthood for thy sake
36 To Aristobulus, yet doomed him dead:
37 Before his back the ephod warm could make,

38 And ere the miter settled on his head:
39 Oh, had he given my boy no less than right,
40 The double oil should to his forehead bring
41 A double honor, shining doubly bright;
42 His birth anointed him both priest and king.
43 And say my father and my son he slew
44 To royalize by right your prince-born breath:
45 Was love the cause, can Mariam deem it true,
46 That Mariam gave commandment for her death?
47 I know by fits he showed some signs of love,
48 And yet not love, but raging lunacy:
49 And this his hate to thee may justly prove,
50 That sure he hates Hircanus' family.
51 Who knows if he, unconstant wavering lord,
52 His love to Doris had renewed again?
53 And that he might his bed to her afford,
54 Perchance he wished that Mariam might be slain.
55
56 MARIAM.
57 Doris! Alas, her time of love was past,
58 Those coals were raked in embers long ago
59 In Mariam's love and she was now disgraced
60 Nor did I glory in her overthrow.
61 He not a whit his first-born son esteemed,
62 Because as well as his he was not mine:
63 My children only for his own he deemed,
64 These boys that did descend from royal line
65 These did he style his heirs to David's throne;
66 My Alexander, if he live, shall sit
67 In the majestic seat of Solomon;
68 To will it so, did Herod think it fit.
69
70 ALEXANDRA.
71 Why, who can claim from Alexander's brood
72 That gold-adornèd lion-guarded chair?
73 Was Alexander not of David's blood?
74 And was not Mariam Alexander's heir?

| | | | |
|---|---|---|---|
| 75 | What more than right could Herod then bestow, | 107 | The boy's large forehead first did fairest seem, |
| 76 | And who will think except for more than right | 108 | Then glanced his eye upon my Mariam's cheek: |
| 77 | He did not raise them, for they were not low, | 109 | And that without comparison did deem, |
| 78 | But born to wear the crown in his despite: | 110 | What was in either but he most did like. |
| 79 | Then send those tears away that are not sent | 111 | And, thus distracted, either's beauty's might |
| 80 | To thee by reason, but by passion's power: | 112 | Within the other's excellence was drowned: |
| 81 | Thine eyes to cheer, thy cheeks to smiles be bent, | 113 | Too much delight did bare him from delight, |
| 82 | And entertain with joy this happy hour. | 114 | For either's love the other's did confound. |
| 83 | Felicity, if when she comes, she finds | 115 | Where if thy portraiture had only gone, |
| 84 | A mourning habit, and a cheerless look, | 116 | His life from Herod, Anthony had taken: |
| 85 | Will think she is not welcome to thy mind, | 117 | He would have lovèd thee, and thee alone, |
| 86 | And so perchance her lodging will not brook. | 118 | And left the brown Egyptian clean forsaken, |
| 87 | Oh, keep her whilst thou hast her; if she go, | 119 | And Cleopatra then to seek had been |
| 88 | She will not easily return again: | 120 | So firm a lover of her wanèd face: |
| 89 | Full many a year have I endured in woe, | 121 | Then great Anthonius' fall we had not seen, |
| 90 | Yet still have sued her presence to obtain: | 122 | By her that fled to have him hold the chase. |
| 91 | And did not I to her as presents send | 123 | Then Mariam in a Roman's chariot set, |
| 92 | A table, that best art did beautify, | 124 | In place of Cleopatra might have shown: |
| 93 | Of two, to whom Heaven did best feature lend, | 125 | A mart of beauties in her visage met, |
| 94 | To woo her love by winning Anthony? | 126 | And part in this, that they were all her own |
| 95 | For when a prince's favor we do crave, | 127 | |
| 96 | We first their minions' loves do seek to win: | 128 | MARIAM. |
| 97 | So I, that sought Felicity to have, | 129 | Not to be empress of aspiring Rome, |
| 98 | Did with her minion Anthony begin | 130 | Would Mariam like to Cleopatra live: |
| 99 | With double sleight I sought to captivate | 131 | With purest body will I press my tomb, |
| 100 | The warlike lover, but I did not right: | 132 | And wish no favors Anthony could give. |
| 101 | For if my gift had borne but half the rate, | 133 | |
| 102 | The Roman had been overtaken quite. | 134 | ALEXANDRA. |
| 103 | But now he farèd like a hungry guest, | 135 | Let us retire us, that we may resolve |
| 104 | That to some plenteous festival is gone; | 136 | How now to deal in this reversèd state: |
| 105 | Now this, now that, he deems to eat were best, | 137 | Great are th'affairs that we must now revolve, |
| 106 | Such choice doth make him let them all alone. | 138 | And great affairs must not be taken late. |

(https://www.wwnorton.com/college/english/nael/noa/pdf/cary_e.pdf)

## Student Response

### Herod: Antagonist or Protagonist

1   "Foul sacrilege to rob those lights so pure, from out a temple made by heav'nly skill. I am the villain that have done
2   the deed." When Herod speaks these lines in the final climactic soliloquy of Elizabeth Cary's play *The Tragedy of*
3   *Mariam*, he realizes that he has killed his beloved wife, Mariam, upon false charges. He is driven nearly to the point
4   of insanity upon this discovery, and the play ends at a point where Herod's next actions could easily involve suicide
5   or unjustified mass executions. Although, at first glance, Herod seems to be the antagonist of the obvious
6   protagonist Mariam, a deeper analysis reveals that Herod is in fact the tragic victim of the play.
7         Despite its seemingly obvious answer, one must ask, "Is Herod truly the antagonist of *The Tragedy of*
8   *Mariam*?" One example of Herod's antagonistic nature is seen in his murder of Baba's sons. However, due to the
9   nearness of the conflict between Anthony and Caesar, several powerful people in Judea made claims to the throne,
10   sometimes exercising force to support their claims. Baba's sons had been ardent supporters of one of Herod's
11   fiercest enemies, and in a world where royal bloodshed was an everyday occurrence, Herod knew he was in danger
12   if he allowed the boys to live. It was Herod's circumstances more than Herod himself that mandated the execution.
13         Another execution at the hands of Herod recounted in *The Tragedy of Mariam* is the murder of Josephus
14   (uncle of Herod; not the historian). Again, though, this murder was not based on anything that Herod could have
15   easily prevented. Herod's own sister, Salome, accuses Josephus of infidelity toward both wife (Salome) and lord
16   (Herod.) Although both charges are lies, the supposed crimes are punishable by death, so Herod is merely
17   implementing the usual punishment for the crimes that he is told have been committed.

18  The most important murder of the entire play by far is the execution of Mariam, Herod's wife. Once again,
19  the execution is justified by the charges brought against her. The only reason the murder is unjust is because the
20  accusations are lies, but Herod possesses no simple means of ascertaining the truth of Mariam's fidelity or lack
21  thereof. In reality, therefore, Herod is much less the antagonist than he is merely the tool that many powerful people
22  manipulate to exercise their wishes. Herod's circumstances, not Herod himself, collectively make up the antagonist
23  of Elizabeth Cary's *The Tragedy of Mariam*.
24      If Herod is not the antagonist, one must necessarily ask, "Is Mariam truly the protagonist then?" Although
25  Mariam is discontented with her marriage, this seems to be more Mariam's fault than Herod's. Herod's first entrance
26  in act 4, scene 1 is marked by a love soliloquy which reveals Herod's heartfelt and passionate love toward Mariam.
27  Whatever Mariam's feelings are toward her husband, Herod feels entirely fulfilled in his marriage.
28      Herod's conversation with Nuntio in act 5, scene 1, is another soliloquy, albeit a continually interrupted
29  one, in which Herod mourns in deeply moving words the death of his beloved Mariam. Although he still believes the
30  execution justified at that time, Herod is heartbroken at the loss of his wife.
31      One of the most chilling speeches of the entire play comes at the end of act 5, scene 1, when Herod laments
32  the fact that he has ordered and carried out the unjust execution of his blameless wife, Mariam.
33
34      I'll muffle up myself in endless night, and never let mine eyes behold the light. Retire thyself, vile monster,
35      worse than he that stained the virgin earth with brother's blood, still in some vault or den enclosèd be,
36      where with thy tears thou may'st beget a flood, which flood in time may drown thee. Happy day, when
37      thou at once shalt die and find a grave. A stone upon the vault, someone shall lay, which monument shall
38      an inscription have, and these shall be the words it shall contain: *Here Herod lies, that hath his Mariam*
39      *slain.*
40
41  Mariam, quietly led to her death with hardly a protest, is indeed not the protagonist of Cary's tragedy. Herod is this
42  protagonist, the tragic victim of his own inevitable circumstances.
43      In *The Tragedy of Mariam*, Elizabeth Cary develops Herod and Mariam's characters in such a way that the
44  audience questions the seemingly obvious casting of protagonist and antagonist. Through complex character
45  development, Cary eventually places Herod into Mariam's appropriate place as protagonist, and fills the vacated
46  position of antagonist with Herod's circumstances, forces that drive him ultimately to the brink of suicide. "Foul
47  sacrilege to rob those lights so pure, from out a temple made by heav'nly skill. I am the villain that have done the
48  deed." (John)

## Close Reading

1.  The play is really
    A. Syntax
    B. Poetry

    C. Prose
    D. Song

2.  Even though her husband, Herod, murdered several of Mariam's family members, she is saddened at the
    apparent death of her husband because
    I.   Herod loved her.
    II.  She has forgiven Herod.
    III. He is the father of her children.

    A. I and II
    B. II and III

    C. I and III
    D. All

3.  What is the tone of most of the drama?
    A. Serious
    B. Sanguine

    C. Choleric
    D. Humorous

4.  The author creates the tone by
    A. Humorous scenes and language.
    B. Alliteration.

    C. Insightful dialogue.
    D. Antagonistic characters.

5. What is the worldview of the drama?
   A. Romanticism
   B. Theism
   C. Naturalism
   D. Existentialism

6. Alexandra is an important
   A. Paradox.
   B. Foil.
   C. Protagonist.
   D. Antagonist.

7. The excerpt develops Mariam's character through
   I. Internal conflict.
   II. Dialogue with a foil.
   III. Stream of consciousness.

   A. I and II
   B. II and III
   C. I and III
   D. All

8. What is a persistent theme?
   A. Hope
   B. Felicity
   C. Unforgiveness
   D. Grace

## Command of Evidence (Student Response)

1. Where is the thesis?
   A. Lines 1–2
   B. Lines 5–6
   C. Lines 26–27
   D. Lines 30–34

2. The thesis is presented as a
   A. Declaration.
   B. Rhetorical question.
   C. Anecdote.
   D. Query.

3. What is a general strategy that the essay employs?
   A. State argument and offer textual evidence.
   B. Offer opposing critical analysis.
   C. Create a dialectic and then draw a conclusion.
   D. Set up a bogus argument and then refute it.

4. According to the Student Essay, who is the protagonist in this play?
   A. Salome
   B. Mariam
   C. Alexandra
   D. Herod

5. Salome is the
   A. Protagonist.
   B. Antagonist.
   C. Heroine.
   D. Confidant.

6. A similar story line is found in which Shakespeare play?
   A. *Othello*
   B. *Macbeth*
   C. *Romeo and Juliet*
   D. *King Lear*

# Lesson 2
## Critical Reading and Writing

### Command of Evidence

Read the following passages and answer accompanying questions:

### Passage 1

1  In many of Nathaniel Hawthorne's stories such as "The Birthmark," the author points out the limits of science. This
2  occurred in an era when authors like Mary Shelley, Robert Louis Stevenson, and George Gaylord Simpson argue
3  that science replaces any view of humans such as Christianity or any other belief. This asserted science as the
4  supreme source of knowledge. Hawthorne had a fear of the power of science because of this possible replacement of
5  Christianity. I agree with Hawthorne's fear because of several reasons.
6       I fear the power of science mainly because of the fallibility that science has in comparison to the Bible.
7  Although science can often be used to support the Bible through various discoveries, it can also contradict the Bible
8  by twisting biblical doctrines or flatly rejecting the Bible and accepting absurd beliefs such as evolution. The
9  problem with this belief is that humankind is elevating science, which can at times be false, to a position of
10  perfection that can never be changed or doubted when regarded as the supreme source of knowledge. Despite this
11  reasoning, there are many instances where science has failed and the Bible has succeeded. One of the most famous
12  examples deals with the earth's shape. Hundreds of years ago, influential scientists convinced the modern world that
13  the earth was flat. The Bible, however, clearly shows this view to be incorrect. Isaiah 40:22 reads, "He sits
14  enthroned above the circle of the earth, and its people are like grasshoppers. He stretches out the heavens like a
15  canopy, and spreads them out like a tent to live in." This clearly points to the circular shape of the earth,
16  contradictory to the incorrect view that top scientists held of a flat earth. This is mainly why I fear the power of
17  science.
18       I also fear the power of science because of the view humankind holds of God. In theory, science makes
19  some sense to a normal human being. **People can easily observe "science" in the natural world. The problem is**
20  **that people are seeing the wonderful world that God created and attributing it to millions of years that**
21  **developed nonlife into life.** This is because today's society has thrown God out of our culture. Our culture has
22  slowly removed God from one phrase at a time. Things like "Merry Christmas" and the Pledge of Allegiance have
23  been twisted into things like "Happy Holidays" and "One Nation . . . indivisible." Society has abandoned God by
24  removing anything related to God, including cultural and patriotic phrases. It tries to put God out of the picture
25  while still trying to preserve the celebratory or patriotic views that these phrases present. This abandonment has let
26  science creep in to replace the position of God and Christianity.
27       For these two reasons, I share Nathaniel Hawthorne's fear of the power of science. People have twisted
28  science and the Bible so far that the Bible is put down while science is ever elevated to a state at which it is the
29  ultimate, perfect source of knowledge in this world. Our society has abandoned a perfect God to follow a fallible
30  science. (Robinson).

### Close Reading

    1.  What would be the best title for this essay?
        A. Biblical Truth                    C. Reasons Why I Fear Science
        B. Rationalism versus Romanticism      D. Hawthorne's Birthmark

    2.  What is the purpose of the first example?
        A.  The author wishes to increase readers' understanding of literature.
        B.  The author believes novelists are very influential.
        C.  The author argues that novels should be read and understood.
        D.  The author warns that these literary examples capture the problems of a worldview.

3. What organizational plan does the author employ?
    A. He offers a thesis at first and then argues the opposite.
    B. He defines the perimeters of his argument and then argues against opposite positions.
    C. He defines the perimeter of his argument and then offers personal examples.
    D. He asks a series of rhetorical questions.

4. Where is the example that the author offers to illustrate his argument?
    A. Lines 1–5
    B. Lines 12–15

    C. Lines 17–18
    D. Lines 20–25

5. The author finishes his essay with
    A. A summary statement.
    B. A new conclusion.

    C. A warning.
    D. The way he began.

6. This essay can best be described as a
    A. Polemic.
    B. Creed.

    C. Analogy.
    D. Paradox.

7. What is one syntax problem?
    A. Misplaced modifiers
    B. Different-tense verbs

    C. Pronoun Agreement
    D. Punctuation of titles of literary works

# Passage 2

1   In 1968, when Arthur C. Clarke published *2001: A Space Odyssey*, complete with pesky aliens, rogue governments,
2   and pernicious robots who had become too intelligent, it was clear that Clarke's novel belonged the science-fiction
3   genre, in the same line of thought as H. G. Wells' *1984* or Aldous Huxley's *Brave New World*. However, when Kurt
4   Vonnegut published *Slaughterhouse-Five* the following year (1969), he created a complicated story where reality
5   and fiction were hopelessly intertwined, making it difficult to pinpoint his genre as strictly science fiction. However,
6   when *Slaughterhouse-Five* is compared with *2001 Space Odyssey*, it becomes apparent that through literary
7   elements both books are dealing with the same issue, but approach the subject in a different tone and reach different
8   conclusions.
9       The core issue explored in these books is the universal question "What is human life?" It is an attempt to
10  understand the meaning of life by going back to humanity's basic origins and concepts. "After three million years of
11  darkness, TMA-1 had greeted the lunar dawn" (Clarke, 99). Clarke begins his quest for the answer to "What is the
12  meaning of life?" by starting with a Darwinian evolution of humanity, proposing that the first spark of intelligence
13  was produced by a "crystal monolith" the Tycho Magnetic Anomaly-1 (TMA-1) intelligence in an inanimate crystal
14  block. The story is centered around this TMA-1 and is broken up in three parts, beginning with the evolution of man
15  approximately three million years ago, according to Clarke; the rediscovery of the TMA-1 some three million years
16  later; and the final exploration of the black box.
17      Kurt Vonnegut approaches the question in a completely different way. Drawing from his experience as a
18  POW during World War II and writing partially autobiographically and partially pure fiction, Vonnegut tries to
19  makes sense of the pain and violence of life. The protagonist is Billy Pilgrim, a mediocre man who struggles to
20  enjoy his successful life after living in the horrors of World War II. "It is so short and jumbled and jangled; . . . there
21  is nothing intelligent to say about a massacre. Everything is supposed to be very quiet after a massacre, and it always
22  is, except for the birds. And what do the birds say? All there is to say about a massacre, things like 'Poo-tee-weet?'"
23  (Vonnegut, *Slaughterhouse-Five*). In both stories by Clarke and Vonnegut, the characters are not the center of the
24  story.
25      In *2001 Space Odyssey*, the characters in the story include an ape-man, a doctor, two astronauts, and HAL,
26  an intelligent robot; however, they are never fully developed; the true focus is on the TMA-1 and its implications.
27  "The political and social implications were immense; every person of real intelligence—everyone who looked an
28  inch beyond his nose—would find his life, his values, and his philosophy, subtly changed" (Clarke, Location 1275).
29  Likewise, even though Billy Pilgrim is the protagonist, Vonnegut never leaves his themes of life and death,
30  particularly the theme of time. "And I asked myself about the present: how wide it was, how deep it was, how much
31  was mine to keep" (Vonnegut, *Slaughterhouse-Five*).
32      Although both deal with the same topic, Clarke and Vonnegut approach it with drastically different tones.
33  Clarke maintains a doomsayer tone; there is no humor in his story. Although the story is set in 2001, it still is tainted

34 with the Cold War's fearful obsession with nuclear weapons. "There before him, a glittering toy no Star-Child could
35 resist, floated the planet Earth with all its peoples. . . . Down there on that crowded globe, the alarms would be
36 flashing across the radar screens, the great tracking telescopes would be searching the skies—and history as men
37 knew it would be drawing to a close" (Clarke, 297). Along with the imminent destruction of the earth, Clarke warns
38 humans of the dangers of technology via the tragedy of Hal, the robot who kills an astronaut while in space,
39 reminiscent of Mary Shelley's *Frankenstein*. "Frank had been deliberately killed—it was so utterly irrational. It was
40 beyond all reason that Hal, who had performed flawlessly for so long, should suddenly turn assassin" (Clarke, 184).
41 Clarke writes in third-person omniscient narration with passive voice, a fact emphasizing that his focus in the story
42 is not the characters but rather the discussion of lofty ideas about existence.

43 Swinging to the other side of the pendulum is Vonnegut, who writes in a witty, almost satirical tone.
44 Vonnegut lacks the sophistication of Clarke. His wording is colloquial, and rarely does he wallow in highfalutin
45 philosophical theories. He delivers his philosophies in the language of the common person. "It is just an illusion here
46 on Earth that one moment follows another one, like beads on a string, and that once a moment is gone, it is gone
47 forever" (Vonnegut, *Slaughterhouse-Five*). Vonnegut frames his story within a framework reminiscent of
48 absurdism; his protagonist is outside of time and lives scenes in his life outside of a chronological order; without
49 warning, his protagonist is whisked away to an alien land; senseless violence occurs, such as his wife's unnecessary
50 death and his own sudden murder. The events in the plot seem to be senseless and absurd. Michael Crichton, writing
51 a review in 1969, said this of Vonnegut's book: "Vonnegut, armed with his schizophrenia, takes an absurd,
52 distorted, wildly funny framework which is ultimately anesthetic. In doing so, his science fiction heritage is clear,
53 but his purposes are very different: he is nearly always talking about the past, not the future." (*New Republic*,
54 "Michael Crichton's 1969 Review of Kurt Vonnegut's 'Slaughterhouse-Five). While Vonnegut mostly talks about
55 the past, Clarke takes about the future to talk about the past; both discuss principles that transcend time.

56 In both stories they learn the answer to their questions from aliens; however, their conclusions are different.
57 The answer giver in *2001: Space Odyssey* is the crystal monolith, the giver of life and intelligence as well as raising
58 humans to a higher consciousness, playing a similar role as George Lucas's force in his *Star Wars* saga. Clarke takes
59 a New Age approach to solve the mystery of life—to become returning to the impersonal source of life and be
60 reborn as stars that transcend worldly problems. "Even as one David Bowman ceased to exist, another became
61 immortal. . . . In an empty room, floating amid the fires of a double star twenty thousand light-years from Earth, a
62 baby opened its eyes and began to cry" (Clarke, 291). In his introduction, Clarke writes, "For every man who has
63 ever lived, in this Universe shines a star."

64 In his iconoclastic way, Vonnegut decides that life is what it is; we are all trapped in life like an a "bug in
65 amber" and ought to therefore, in the words of his wise aliens, "Ignore the awful times and concentrate on the good
66 ones." Again, like Clarke, aliens are the founts of wisdom in the plot. These aliens, the Tralfamadorians, are shaped
67 like toilet plungers, another example of Vonnegut's tongue-in-cheek style, and present a radical way of viewing life.
68 "The most important thing I learned on Tralfamadore was that when a person dies he only appears to die. He is still
69 very much alive in the past, so it is very silly for people to cry at his funeral. All moments, past, present, and future,
70 always have existed, always will exist." In both books a huge emphasis is placed on time. Vonnegut, by telling his
71 story out of chronological order and expounding on the theories of the Tralfamadore, comes to the conclusion that
72 time is an illusion. "The time would not pass. Somebody was playing with the clocks, and not only the electronic
73 clocks but the wind-up kind too. The second hand on my watch would twitch once, and a year would pass, and then
74 it would twitch again. There was nothing I could do about it. As an Earthling I had to believe whatever clocks said—
75 and calendars." Clarke tells the story in chronological order, but when David Bowman comes into contact with the
76 TMA-1, which is the higher consciousness, time as humans know it disappears. "Time flowed more and more
77 sluggishly, approaching a moment of stasis—as a swinging pendulum, at the limit of its arc, seems frozen for one
78 eternal instant, before the next cycle begins." Both authors agree that time is eternal.

79 Arthur C. Clarke and Vonnegut differ dramatically in their writing style. Clarke is formal and highfalutin,
80 strictly adhering to the science-fiction genre. Vonnegut is colloquial, with a dark kind of slapstick comedy, floating
81 around the science-fiction genre. Both authors are asking the questions that all people ask: What is the meaning of
82 life? More specifically, how do we cope in life? Clarke, through the TMA-1, finds his answers in the stars, in the
83 joining of humanity with a higher force. Vonnegut ignores the ideals of the heavens and resorts to surrendering to
84 the senseless force of Fate. (Daphnide)

1. What would be the best title for this essay?
   A. The Loss of Innocence
   B. Arthur C. Clarke versus Kurt Vonnegut Jr.
   C. Billy Pilgrim
   D. Rock of Ages

2. How does the author begin her essay?
   A. Summary of argument
   B. Introduction to the argument
   C. Rhetorical questions
   D. Quotes

3. What organizational plan does the author employ?
   A. Argument, Evidence, Counterargument
   B. Thesis, Supporting Details, Conclusion
   C. Summary, Anecdotes
   D. Anecdotes, Commentary, Conclusion

4. What techniques does she employ?
   A. Humor
   B. Hyperbole and allusion
   C. Extensive textual evidence
   D. Conflict and resolution

5. What is the author's primary strategy of creating transitions?
   I.   Using guide words like "although"
   II.  Pausing for affect
   III. Mentioning a word or thought from the preceding paragraph
   IV.  Double indent

   A. I and II
   B. III and IV
   C. I and III
   D. NONE

6. The word "highfalutin" in Line 77 is
   A. An Allusion
   B. Slang
   C. A Colloquialism
   D. A Hyperbole

## Grammar and Usage

Choose the best grammar/usage form in bold sentence(s).

Passage 1, Lines 18–20

A. NONE
B. People can easily observe "science" in the natural world; the problem is that they are seeing the wonderful world God created and attributing it to millions of years of random chance that developed nonlife into life.
C. People can easily observe "science" in the natural world but they are seeing the wonderful world God created and attributing it to millions of years that grouped nonlife into life.
D. People can easily observe "science" in the natural world, however, people are seeing the wonderful world God created and attributing it to millions of years that turned nonlife into life.

# Lesson 3
## SAT Essay

### Student Response 1

*Prompt:* What is true success?

1  It's called being chained to a desk. Big lawyers work long hours, sometimes 50 or 60 hours a week, doing
2  not very exciting business-related legal work. These lawyers are the very best out there. They have been scooped
3  from the top 10 percent of their law school's graduating class. Top lawyers typically make $145,000 or $160,000 per
4  year as soon as they start working. The longer they stay with the firm, the more they make. When these lawyers
5  become partners in the firm, they really make a lot. In some firms, they make several million dollars each year.
6  Looking at all the return from the job—high salary, benefits, and prestige—these lawyers are successful. However,
7  many of them find success to be disastrous. Their job gives them no work-life balance; it is all work, even on some
8  weekends. Many top lawyers quit their jobs after only a few years, burned out by their demanding work.
9  In F. Scott Fitzgerald's *The Great Gatsby*, Jay Gatsby pursues a married woman until he gets her to love
10  him. He achieved his goal and was successful. However, he lets the woman of his dreams drive his car, and she hits
11  and kills a lady with it. **The grieving husband of the slain woman seeks to avenge his wife's death, but instead**
12  **of shooting the woman who ran over his wife, he shot and killed Jay Gatsby before taking his own life.** For Jay
13  Gatsby, success was disastrous.
14  In volume 2 of *Civil War*, by Shelby Foote, a book I read on my own initiative, General Bragg of the
15  Confederate Army chases success and wins a battle. However, he does not pursue the beaten foe nor capture the
16  defeated Union soldiers, even though he could have done so. His foes eventually strengthen and then beat him. For
17  Bragg, success was disastrous.
18  In *Great Expectations*, by Charles Dickens, Estella, a snob, pursues a well-to-do husband, ignoring Pip,
19  who loves her. Ten years down the road, after being successful and marrying the gentleman of her dreams, she
20  realizes that her life has become not so good as she had wished it to be. For Estella, success was disastrous.
21  Literature, history, and careers show that success can be disastrous. (Matthew)

### Student Response 2
*Prompt:* Is image more important than substance?

1  Few things in life are as disappointing as bad dessert. You walk into a restaurant, and on the way to your
2  table, the waiter takes you past the cake window. In it, you see a beautiful cake slice, three layers tall, adorned with
3  chocolate on its top and sides. Foregoing dinner, you think about that wonderful cake and order it. A slice is brought
4  to your table. With heart thumping, eyes shining bright, and your table manners forgotten, you pick up the slice and
5  bite deep into it. "Ah," you ejaculate, "the icing is abominable and the substance is poor. What a terrible cook."
6  After this fulmination, you stand up and leave the restaurant, with patrons starting at you and the waiter running
7  after you to make sure you pay. In life, substance is much more important than appearance.
8  I am a history buff. I used to read about the Civil War in prodigious quantities of books. I carried with me
9  tomes that had hundreds of pages. My favorite multivolume work, by Shelby Foote, was a brilliant masterpiece of
10  scholarship combined with a novelist's eye for creativity in writing. I thoroughly enjoyed reading two of his
11  volumes (1,600 pages in all) on the intricate details of the Civil War. However, judging from appearances, few
12  people would want to read a book that on its cover says, "The Civil War: From Fort Sumter to Perryville," with a
13  few soldiers printed on the cover and little detail, thus conveying minimal vividness. Yet this series, once opened
14  and read, far outstrip the cover details.
15  Once I purchased a type of bird called a guinea. These creatures are supposed to run around, eat bugs, and
16  warn owners of strangers. However, they are not hardy. My cute, promising guinea chick died just days after I
17  acquired it. Here, too, appearances deceive.
18  In the 1930s, Hitler rose to power in Germany. The people of that country were enamored with him. They
19  thought he would make Germany a better place after all of its financial issues and the severe reparation they had to

20 pay after losing World War I. However, Hitler led Germany right into World War II, and millions of Germans (and
21 others) lost their lives and property due to the ravages of war.
22 Animals, books, and people may appear good. Once you experience them, you know whether they are good
23 or bad. Sometimes, like that cake, the substance tells far more than the appearance. (Matthew).

## Close Reading

1. In Student Response 1,
   A. Hard work will bring desired results.      C. Success is more difficult to attain than it appears.
   B. Success is impossible.                     D. Author concedes that the Civil War was terrible.

2. In Student Response 2, the author organizes the essay
   A. By stating a rhetorical questions and then developing the thesis.
   B. By offering a series of anecdotes.
   C. By stating a thesis and offering several examples.
   D. By a series of bullet points.

3. What is a problem in Student Response 1?
   I.   No specific examples are given.
   II.  Transitions are weak.
   III. There are too many personal examples.
   IV.  The essay is too short.
   V.   The thesis is not clearly stated nor tied to the topic.

   A. I and II          C. II and III
   B. III and IV        D. V

4. Identify any problem in Student Response 2:
   I.   Examples not tied closely to the thesis.      IV. Essay is too short.
   II.  Transitions are weak.                         V.  Thesis not clearly stated nor tied to the topic.
   III. Too many personal examples.

   A. I and II          C. II and III
   B. III and IV        D. I, II, IV, and V

5. Where is the main point of the Student Response 1?
   A. Lines 3–4         C. Line 18
   B. Lines 8–9         D. Line 21

6. Where is the main point of the Student Response 2?
   A. Line 3            C. Lines 12–13
   B. Lines 8–9         D. Lines 22–23

7. What is a significant stylistic problem in Student Essay 2?
   A. First person is used.              C. Transitions are weak.
   B. Second-person pronouns are used.   D. There are agreement problems.

8. Where can evidence for the preceding problem found in Student Response 2?
   A. Lines 1–2         C. Lines 12–14
   B. Lines 8–9         D. Lines 22–23

9. What score would the student responses receive?
   Student Response 1 receives __. Student Response 2 receives: __.

## Grammar and Usage

Choose the best grammar/usage form in bold sentence(s).

Student Response 1, Lines 11–12

A. NONE
B. The grieving husband of the slain woman, before he takes his own life, avenges his wife's death by killing Jay Gatsby.
C. The grieving husband of the slain woman seeks avenges his wife's death but instead of shooting the man who ran over her, he shot and killed Jay Gatsby before taking his own life.
D. The slain woman's grieving husband avenges his wife's death and instead of shooting the woman who ran over her, he shot and killed Jay Gatsby before taking his own life.

# Lesson 4
## Reading: Document-Based Analysis

**Seventh Annual Message to Congress**

**Theodore Roosevelt (December 3, 1907)**

1  *To the Senate and House of Representatives*:
2      The conservation of our natural resources and their proper use constitute the fundamental problem which
3  underlies almost every other problem of our national life. . . . As a nation we not only enjoy a wonderful measure of
4  present prosperity but if this prosperity is used aright it is an earnest of future success such as no other nation will
5  have. The reward of foresight for this nation is great and easily foretold. But there must be the look ahead, there
6  must be a realization of the fact that to waste, to destroy, our natural resources, to skin and exhaust the land instead
7  of using it so as to increase its usefulness, will result in undermining in the days of our children the very prosperity
8  which we ought by right to hand down to them amplified and developed. For the last few years, through several
9  agencies, the government has been endeavoring to get our people to look ahead and to substitute a planned and
10  orderly development of our resources in place of a haphazard striving for immediate profit. Our great river systems
11  should be developed as national water highways, the Mississippi, with its tributaries, standing first in importance,
12  and the Columbia second, although there are many others of importance on the Pacific, the Atlantic, and the Gulf
13  slopes. The National Government should undertake this work, and I hope a beginning will be made in the present
14  Congress; and the greatest of all our rivers, the Mississippi, should receive special attention. From the Great Lakes
15  to the mouth of the Mississippi there should be a deep waterway, with deep waterways leading from it to the East
16  and the West. Such a waterway would practically mean the extension of our coastline into the very heart of our
17  country. It would be of incalculable benefit to our people. If begun at once it can be carried through in time
18  appreciably to relieve the congestion of our great freight-carrying lines of railroads. The work should be
19  systematically and continuously carried forward in accordance with some well-conceived plan. The main streams
20  should be improved to the highest point of efficiency before the improvement of the branches is attempted; and the
21  work should be kept free from every taint of recklessness or jobbery. The inland waterways which lie just back of
22  the whole Eastern and Southern coasts should likewise be developed. Moreover, the development of our waterways
23  involves many other important water problems, all of which should be considered as part of the same general
24  scheme. The government dams should be used to produce hundreds of thousands of horse-power as an incident to
25  improving navigation; for the annual value of the unused water-power of the United States perhaps exceeds the
26  annual value of the products of all our mines. As an incident to creating the deep waterways down the Mississippi,
27  the government should build along its whole lower length levees which, taken together with the control of the
28  headwaters, will at once and forever put a complete stop to all threat of floods in the immensely fertile delta region.
29  The territory lying adjacent to the Mississippi along its lower course will thereby become one of the most
30  prosperous and populous, as it already is one of the most fertile, farming regions in all the world. I have appointed
31  an inland waterways commission to study and outline a comprehensive scheme of development along all the lines
32  indicated. Later I shall lay its report before the Congress.
33      Irrigation should be far more extensively developed than at present, not only in the States of the Great
34  Plains and the Rocky Mountains, but in many others, as, for instance, in large portions of the South Atlantic and
35  Gulf States, where it should go hand in hand with the reclamation of swampland. The Federal Government should
36  seriously devote itself to this task, realizing that utilization of waterways and water-power, forestry, irrigation, and
37  the reclamation of lands threatened with overflow, are all interdependent parts of the same problem. The work of the
38  Reclamation Service in developing the larger opportunities of the Western half of our country for irrigation is more
39  important than almost any other movement. The constant purpose of the government in connection with the
40  Reclamation Service has been to use the water resources of the public lands for the ultimate greatest good of the
41  greatest number; in other words, to put upon the land permanent home-makers, to use and develop it for themselves
42  and for their children and children's children. . . .
43      The effort of the government to deal with the public land has been based upon the same principle as that of
44  the Reclamation Service. The land law system which was designed to meet the needs of the fertile and well-watered
45  regions of the Middle West has largely broken down when applied to the drier regions of the Great Plains, the
46  mountains, and much of the Pacific slope, where a farm of 160 acres is inadequate for self-support. . . .Three years
47  ago a public-lands commission was appointed to scrutinize the law, and defects, and recommend a remedy. Their

48  examination specifically showed the existence of great fraud upon the public domain, and their recommendations for
49  changes in the law were made with the design of conserving the natural resources of every part of the public lands
50  by putting it to its best use. Especial attention was called to the prevention of settlement by the passage of great
51  areas of public land into the hands of a few men, and to the enormous waste caused by unrestricted grazing upon the
52  open range. The recommendations of the Public-Lands Commission are sound, for they are especially in the interest
53  of the actual home-maker; and where the small home-maker cannot at present utilize the land they provide that the
54  government shall keep control of it so that it may not be monopolized by a few men. The Congress has not yet acted
55  upon these recommendations, but they are so just and proper, so essential to our national welfare, that I feel
56  confident, if the Congress will take time to consider them, that they will ultimately be adopted.
57      Some such legislation as that proposed is essential in order to preserve the great stretches of public grazing-
58  land which are unfit for cultivation under present methods and are valuable only for the forage which they supply.
59  These stretches amount in all to some 300,000,000 acres, and are open to the free grazing of cattle, sheep, horses,
60  and goats, without restriction. Such a system, or lack of system, means that the range is not so much used as wasted
61  by abuse. As the West settles, the range becomes more and more overgrazed. Much of it cannot be used to
62  advantage unless it is fenced, for fencing is the only way by which to keep in check the owners of nomad flocks
63  which roam hither and thither, utterly destroying the pastures and leaving a waste behind so that their presence is
64  incompatible with the presence of home-makers. The existing fences are all illegal. . . . All these fences, those that
65  are hurtful and those that are beneficial, are alike illegal and must come down. But it is an outrage that the law
66  should necessitate such action on the part of the Administration. The unlawful fencing of public lands for private
67  grazing must be stopped, but the necessity which occasioned it must be provided for. The Federal Government
68  should have control of the range, whether by permit or lease, as local necessities may determine. Such control could
69  secure the great benefit of legitimate fencing, while at the same time securing and promoting the settlement of the
70  country. . . . The government should part with its title only to the actual home-maker, not to the profit-maker who
71  does not care to make a home. Our prime object is to secure the rights and guard the interests of the small ranchman,
72  the man who ploughs and pitches hay for himself. It is this small ranchman, this actual settler and home-maker, who
73  in the long run is most hurt by permitting thefts of the public land in whatever form.
74      Optimism is a good characteristic, but if carried to an excess it becomes foolishness. We are prone to speak
75  of the resources of this country as inexhaustible; this is not so. The mineral wealth of the country, the coal, iron, oil,
76  gas, and the like, does not reproduce itself, and therefore is certain to be exhausted ultimately; and wastefulness in
77  dealing with it today means that our descendants will feel the exhaustion a generation or two before they otherwise
78  would. But there are certain other forms of waste which could be entirely stopped—the waste of soil by washing, for
79  instance, which is among the most dangerous of all wastes now in progress in the United States, is easily
80  preventable, so that this present enormous loss of fertility is entirely unnecessary. The preservation or replacement
81  of the forests is one of the most important means of preventing this loss. We have made a beginning in forest
82  preservation, but . . . so rapid has been the rate of exhaustion of timber in the United States in the past, and so
83  rapidly is the remainder being exhausted, that the country is unquestionably on the verge of a timber famine which
84  will be felt in every household in the land. . . . The present annual consumption of lumber is certainly three times as
85  great as the annual growth; and if the consumption and growth continue unchanged, practically all our lumber will
86  be exhausted in another generation, while long before the limit to complete exhaustion is reached the growing
87  scarcity will make itself felt in many blighting ways upon our national welfare. About twenty per cent of our
88  forested territory is now reserved in national forests, but these do not include the most valuable timberlands, and in
89  any event the proportion is too small to expect that the reserves can accomplish more than a mitigation of the trouble
90  which is ahead for the nation. . . . We should acquire in the Appalachian and White Mountain regions all the forest-
91  lands that it is possible to acquire for the use of the nation. These lands, because they form a national asset, are as
92  emphatically national as the rivers which they feed, and which flow through so many States before they reach the
93  ocean.
94              (http://www.pbs.org/weta/thewest/resources/archives/eight/trconserv.htm)

## Close Reading

1. What is the purpose of this message?
   I.   To encourage Congress to enact legislation to preserve America's natural resources.
   II.  To raise money to buy the Yellowstone National Park area.
   III. To encourage Congress to undertake major projects (e.g., building levees) to increase American prosperity.

   A. I                          C. I and III
   B. I and II                   D. All

2. What are possible reasons why Roosevelt gave this speech?
   I.   Natural resources were in danger.
   II.  Congress had funds to spend.
   III. Roosevelt loved bald eagles.
   IV.  A desire to maintain a Republican Party majority voting bloc.

   A. I and II                   C. I, II, and III
   B. III and IV                 D. All

3. What does "Optimism is a good characteristic, but if carried to an excess it becomes foolishness," mean?
   A. The sky is the limit in America.
   B. Americans should be careful.
   C. Americans have abundant but not inexhaustible resources.
   D. Americans should wisely spend their income for laudable projects (e.g., the Panama Canal).


## Words in Context

1. What is the meaning of *congestion* in Line 18?
   A. Delineation               C. Overcrowding
   B. Confusion                 D. Indigestion

2. What is the meaning of *descendants* in Line 77?
   A. Inheritance               C. Surrogates
   B. Hooligans                 D. Posterities

# Lesson 5

## Math: Algebra, Arithmetic Problem Solving and Data Analysis, and Passport to Advanced Math

**Passport to Advanced Math**

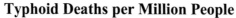

### Typhoid Deaths per Million People

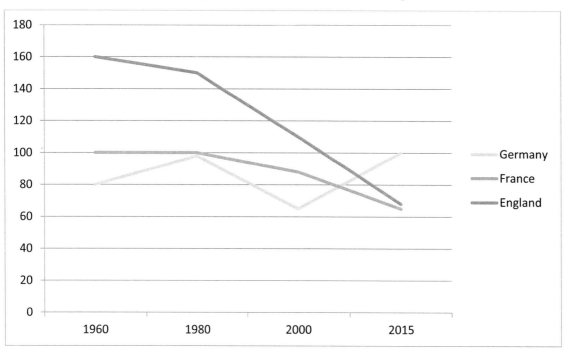

| Years | Germany | France | England |
|-------|---------|--------|---------|
| 1960 | 80 | 100 | 160 |
| 1980 | 98 | 100 | 150 |
| 2000 | 65 | 88 | 110 |
| 2015 | 100 | 65 | 68 |

1. What is true about the above chart?
   I. Typhoid deaths have declined in all three countries.
   II. All three countries had a death rate of 100 per million people in 1980 and 2015.
   III. By 2015 no nation had deaths greater than 100 per million people.

   A. I        B. I and II        C. I and III        D. All

2. What is true about the above chart?
   I. English typhoid rates dropped more than 50 percent since 1960.
   II. French typhoid rates did not drop until after 1980.
   III. Germany had a severe outbreak of typhoid between 2000 and 2015.

   A. I        B. I and II        C. I and III        D. All

## Arithmetic Problem Solving

1.  Two persons start at 10:00 AM from towns A and B, 55½ miles apart. The one starting from A walks at the rate of 4¼ miles per hour, but stops 2 hours on the way; the other walks at the rate of 3¾ miles per hour without stopping. When will they meet? How far will each have traveled?
    A. 5:00 p.m.; 20 miles from B; 24½ miles from A
    B. 7:00 p.m.; 40 miles from B; 22½ miles from A
    C. 6:00 p.m.; 30 miles from B; 25½ miles from A
    D. 4:00 p.m.; 25 miles from B; 20½ miles from A

2.  A person who runs at the rate of 12½ yards per second, starts 16 yards behind another whose rate is 11 yards per second. How soon will the first person be 8 yards ahead of the second?
    A. 8 sec.                           C. 12 sec.
    B. 10 sec.                          D. 16 sec.

3.  A rectangle has its length and width respectively 4 ft. longer and 2 ft. shorter than the side of an equivalent square. Find its area.
    A. 12 sq. ft.                       C. 14 sq. ft.
    B. 16 sq. ft.                       D. 18 sq. ft.

4.  An enclosed garden is 24 ft. greater in length than in width, and 684 sq. ft. is used for a walk 3 ft. wide extending around the garden inside the fence. What are the dimensions of the garden?
    A. 44 ft. by 68 ft.                 C. 48 ft. by 72 ft.
    B. 50 ft. by 70 ft.                 D. 64 ft. by 108 ft.

5.  From one end of a line, I cut off 5 feet less than one-fifth of it, and from the other end 4 feet more than one-fourth of it, and then there remained 34 feet. How long was the line?
    A. 60 ft.                           C. 32 ft.
    B. 48 ft.                           D. 64 ft.

6.  A can do twice as much work as B, and B can do twice as much as C; together they can complete a piece of work in 4 days. In what time can each alone complete the work?
    A. A, 7 days; B, 14 days; C, 28 days    C. A, 5 days; B, 10 days; C, 25 days
    B. A, 6 days; B, 12 days; C, 24 days    D. A, 8 days; B, 16 days; C, 32 days

7.  Separate 57 into two parts, such that one divided by the other may give 5 as a quotient, with 3 as a remainder.
    A. 7; 49                            C. 9; 48
    B. 6; 42                            D. 8; 46

8.  Divide 92 into two parts, such that one divided by the other may give 4 as a quotient, with 2 as a remainder.
    A. 16; 72                           C. 20; 80
    B. 14; 68                           D. 18; 74

9.  Fourteen persons engaged a yacht, but before sailing, four withdrew, causing the expense for each remaining yachtsperson to be increased by $4. What was paid for the yacht?
    A. $120                             C. $160
    B. $140                             D. $180

# Chapter 23   Trees and Snakes
# Genesis 3

---

*Memory Verse:* Now the serpent was more crafty than any of the wild animals the LORD God had made. He said to the woman, "Did God really say, 'You must not eat from any tree in the garden'?" —Genesis 3:1

---

In his commentary on Genesis, Walter Brueggemann argues that human beings, in their relationship with God, are characterized by three traits: vocation, permission, and prohibition. In Genesis 2:15 we read that Adam and Eve are to care for and to tend the garden. The word pair "till and keep" (NRSV) suggests a gardener or a shepherd. In either case, work belongs to the garden. From the very beginning of human destiny, God is prepared to entrust part of his work to humankind; if we do not do this assigned work, it will not be done. We are called, as it were, to a special task. This call is a central part of our identity. Its abandonment or perversion, as we shall see in a few minutes, is done so at our very profound peril.

We live in a culture that ranks our value as persons according to our jobs. We are constantly receiving materialistic messages from our culture that tell us, "You are what you do." Luther's recovery of a gospel understanding of vocation says, to the contrary, "We have worth because God is calling us."

"The place God calls you to is the place where your deep gladness and the world's deep hunger meet," declares Frederick. God is not calling you to be lawyers, schoolteachers, and so forth: God is calling you to be his child and to share the good news of his reign with others.

There is also a permission (Genesis 2:16). Everything is permitted (see Paul in 1 Corinthians 6:12; 10:23). We are given, as it were, a free will to make choices. But we are not independent beings. We are subject to God's limits.

Finally, clearly there is an element of prohibition to the human condition (Genesis 2:17). Basic to humanity is the need to do without some things. To refrain from certain behaviors, to postpone pleasure at times. These prohibitions are often given with no apology or explanation—as the prohibition to eat of the tree of the knowledge of good and evil. What actually counts is the fact of the prohibition and the authority of God, who speaks and rightfully expects humankind to obey fully.

The task, for us, in a nutshell, is to hold these three facets of divine purpose in balance. How? Church, Word, Mission. We need to be free, but at the same time we live with divine limits. And we live with freedom and limits for one expressed call: to do God's will.

Genesis 3 is an examination of how Adam and Eve—and by inference all of us—pervert God's mandated balance of permission, prohibition, and vocation. The result is sin. It is tragically ironic that one of the first times humankind is sought by God, they are hiding in the garden—full of sin and brokenness. This position is, I fear, one of the places we begin worship.

As we approach the throne in our worship, then, we need to take sin seriously. And that is what this message is about. We will examine the subtle arguments of Satan and observe Eve's responses to understand our own inherent flaws.

The snake describes God's prohibition as an option rather than a given. "Did God really say, 'You must not eat fruit from any tree in the garden'?" (Genesis 3:1). The serpent engages in a bit of sociology in order to relativize the law of God. The serpent's theological talk, which seems deferential, is not to serve God but to avoid the claims of God. This is the first example we have of situational ethics. The snake shrewdly suggests a very modern ideal: a theory that rejects moral absolutes and maintains that decision must arise spontaneously from the demands of specific situations and contexts. And as a result, there is no room for an omnipotent and omniscient God.

It is interesting that the snake speaks of God in the third person. Until now Eve has never done so. God was always present everywhere. But suddenly she speaks about God as if he is not present. In other words, perhaps God is not God after all. God is not a party to the discussion but is the involved object of the discussion. This is not speech to God or with God but about God. God is objectified. The serpent is the first in history to practice theology in place of obedience.

The matter of death has been mentioned in 2:17 by God, but it has not been a threat nor his main point. Life was/is always God's main goal. Consequence for eating of the forbidden tree is not a threat but a candid acknowledgment of a boundary of life. But the boundary is altered by the serpent into a threat. It is transformed into a terror that puts everything in question. The serpent suggests that God does not love Adam and Eve after all. It is a primary attack on the very basic nature of God. But it is the serpent, not God, who has made death into a primary human agenda. "You will not die!" (3:4 NRSV).

This is an enduring problem in the Bible: (1) David and Bathsheba (2 Samuel 11–12) step over prescribed boundaries and experience disaster with Absalom. (2) Isaiah indicts the king of Assyria who, by his own "wisdom," has removed peoples' boundaries and plundered their treasures; his "destruction" is coming (Isaiah 10). (3) The king of Tyre in Ezekiel 28 steps over the line, claims to be God, and dies. (4) Belshazzar in Daniel 5 misuses the temple artifacts from Jerusalem, blasphemes God, steps over the boundaries, and dies. (5) Other examples are Herod Agrippa I in Acts 12 and Ananias and Sapphira in Acts 5, who step over the line and are destroyed.

One simple fact the serpent conveniently forgot to mention: We do not *break* God's laws. God's laws *break us*.

In Genesis 3, the serpent repeats God's speech with just enough of a twist to miss the point. The serpent grossly misrepresents God in 3:1 ("not eat from *any* tree") and is corrected by the woman in 3:2–3, yet with her own exaggeration that God said, "You must not *touch* it." By then misquotation has raised to consciousness the possibility of an alternative to the way of God. From that point onward, things become distorted as actions follow words.

The rhetoric of trust and fidelity has given way to analysis and calculation. Control has been gained by Adam and Eve, but at great price. Now distortion and death reign. The giveness of God's rule is no longer the boundary of a safe place. No, God is now understood as a barrier to be circumvented.

"She took some and ate it, . . . and he ate it" (3:6). What a sorry conclusion to a wonderful story! What has started as a story of trust and obedience, life and hope (Genesis 2), has become an account of crime and punishment (chap. 3). Now having taken life into their own hands, the couple stands exposed beyond the safe perimeters of vocation, permission, prohibition. The prohibition of 2:17 is violated. The permission of 2:16 is perverted. The vocation of 2:15 is neglected. There is no more mention of tending and keeping, no mention of call. They have no energy for that. Their interest has focused completely on self, on their new freedom and terror that comes with it.

We see the power of sin and death in Dostoevsky's *Crime and Punishment*. There is a strange slippage between the crime and the punishment. The torture of Raskolnikov is in seeing what is not there, in hearing voices and imagining threats. The power of guilt takes on its own life. It works life's destruction. Thus the conscious nakedness of 3:7 and the hiding of 3:8 already manifest the power of death, even before the Lord of the garden takes any action. Sin has set before Adam and Eve a destiny not heretofore envisioned by anyone and never intended by a good and loving God.

Are we hiding in the garden? Have we broken the fragile balance of permission, prohibition, and vocation? Have we gained new and perhaps wanted knowledge, but suddenly find ourselves dying?

I have some good news (even though we don't deserve it!): "In Christ, God was reconciling the world to himself" and "has given us the ministry of reconciliation (2 Corinthians 5:18–19 NRSV). We who know we are lost are controlled by anxiety (as Adam and Eve are anxious in 3:10). We seek to escape our fears by sinning or circumventing the realities of God. But ultimately, even as we hide in the garden, we discover that God was right all along. He is the boundary and rediscovered center of our life (from Bonhoeffer). We discover that God after all wants us to be free—but not autonomously free. God seeks us even after we stumble and still wants us to serve him. We are called children of God, permitted to do many things, prohibited from doing others. But always, always—we are loved more than we can imagine!

## Journal Question

Do you have any unconfessed sins that you are hiding from God?

# Lesson 1
## Evidence-Based Reading and Writing

### Literary Choice

Virgil created Aeneas, a "George Washington" figure, and wrote the memorable narrative *Aeneid*, about the founding of Rome.

### Excerpt from Virgil's *Aeneid*, Book 1

| | |
|---|---|
| 1 | Arms, and the man I sing, who, forc'd by fate, |
| 2 | And haughty Juno's unrelenting hate, |
| 3 | Expell'd and exil'd, left the Trojan shore. |
| 4 | Long labors, both by sea and land, he bore, |
| 5 | And in the doubtful war, before he won |
| 6 | The Latian realm, and built the destin'd town; |
| 7 | His banish'd gods restor'd to rites divine, |
| 8 | And settled sure succession in his line, |
| 9 | From whence the race of Alban fathers come, |
| 10 | And the long glories of majestic Rome. |
| 11 | O Muse! the causes and the crimes relate; |
| 12 | What goddess was provok'd, and whence her hate; |
| 13 | For what offense the Queen of Heav'n began |
| 14 | To persecute so brave, so just a man; |
| 15 | Involv'd his anxious life in endless cares, |
| 16 | Expos'd to wants, and hurried into wars! |
| 17 | Can heav'nly minds such high resentment show, |
| 18 | Or exercise their spite in human woe? |
| 19 | Against the Tiber's mouth, but far away, |
| 20 | An ancient town was seated on the sea; |
| 21 | A Tyrian colony; the people made |
| 22 | Stout for the war, and studious of their trade: |
| 23 | Carthage the name; belov'd by Juno more |
| 24 | Than her own Argos, or the Samian shore. |
| 25 | Here stood her chariot; here, if Heav'n were kind, |
| 26 | The seat of awful empire she design'd. |
| 27 | Yet she had heard an ancient rumor fly, |
| 28 | (Long cited by the people of the sky,) |
| 29 | That times to come should see the Trojan race |
| 30 | Her Carthage ruin, and her tow'rs deface; |
| 31 | Nor thus confin'd, the yoke of sov'reign sway |
| 32 | Should on the necks of all the nations lay. |
| 33 | She ponder'd this, and fear'd it was in fate; |
| 34 | Nor could forget the war she wag'd of late |
| 35 | For conqu'ring Greece against the Trojan state. |
| 36 | Besides, long causes working in her mind, |
| 37 | And secret seeds of envy, lay behind; |
| 38 | Deep graven in her heart the doom remain'd |
| 39 | Of partial Paris, and her form disdain'd; |
| 40 | The grace bestow'd on ravish'd Ganymed, |
| 41 | Electra's glories, and her injur'd bed. |
| 42 | Each was a cause alone; and all combin'd |
| 43 | To kindle vengeance in her haughty mind. |
| 44 | For this, far distant from the Latian coast |
| 45 | She drove the remnants of the Trojan host; |

| | |
|---|---|
| 46 | And sev'n long years th' unhappy wand'ring train |
| 47 | Were toss'd by storms, and scatter'd thro' the main. |
| 48 | Such time, such toil, requir'd the Roman name, |
| 49 | Such length of labor for so vast a frame. |
| 50 | Now scarce the Trojan fleet, with sails and oars, |
| 51 | Had left behind the fair Sicilian shores, |
| 52 | Ent'ring with cheerful shouts the wat'ry reign, |
| 53 | And plowing frothy furrows in the main; |
| 54 | When, lab'ring still with endless discontent, |
| 55 | The Queen of Heav'n did thus her fury vent: |
| 56 | "Then am I vanquish'd? must I yield?" said she, |
| 57 | "And must the Trojans reign in Italy? |
| 58 | So Fate will have it, and Jove adds his force; |
| 59 | Nor can my pow'r divert their happy course. |
| 60 | Could angry Pallas, with revengeful spleen, |
| 61 | The Grecian navy burn, and drown the men? |
| 62 | She, for the fault of one offending foe, |
| 63 | The bolts of Jove himself presum'd to throw: |
| 64 | With whirlwinds from beneath she toss'd the ship, |
| 65 | And bare expos'd the bosom of the deep; |
| 66 | Then, as an eagle gripes the trembling game, |
| 67 | The wretch, yet hissing with her father's flame, |
| 68 | She strongly seiz'd, and with a burning wound |
| 69 | Transfix'd, and naked, on a rock she bound. |
| 70 | But I, who walk in awful state above, |
| 71 | The majesty of heav'n, the sister wife of Jove, |
| 72 | For length of years my fruitless force employ |
| 73 | Against the thin remains of ruin'd Troy! |
| 74 | What nations now to Juno's pow'r will pray, |
| 75 | Or off'rings on my slighted altars lay?" |
| 76 | Thus rag'd the goddess; and, with fury fraught. |
| 77 | The restless regions of the storms she sought, |
| 78 | Where, in a spacious cave of living stone, |
| 79 | The tyrant Aeolus, from his airy throne, |
| 80 | With pow'r imperial curbs the struggling winds, |
| 81 | And sounding tempests in dark prisons binds. |
| 82 | This way and that th' impatient captives tend, |
| 83 | And, pressing for release, the mountains rend. |
| 84 | High in his hall th' undaunted monarch stands, |
| 85 | And shakes his scepter, and their rage commands; |
| 86 | Which did he not, their unresisted sway |
| 87 | Would sweep the world before them in their way; |
| 88 | Earth, air, and seas thro' empty space would roll, |
| 89 | And heav'n would fly before the driving soul. |
| 90 | In fear of this, the Father of the Gods |
| 91 | Confin'd their fury to those dark abodes, |
| 92 | And lock'd 'em safe within, oppress'd with mountain loads; |
| 93 | Impos'd a king, with arbitrary sway, |
| 94 | To loose their fetters, or their force allay. |
| 95 | To whom the suppliant queen her pray'rs address'd, |
| 96 | And thus the tenor of her suit express'd. |

(http://classics.mit.edu/Virgil/aeneid.1.i.html)

## Student Response

### Themes of Virgil's *Aeneid*

1   The *Aeneid* is a true masterpiece, a saga that sings praises to the ancestors of Roman culture. It details the great
2   journey of the exiled Trojans from their native home as they lay the foundation of Rome. They are guided by the
3   great wisdom and unflagging courage of their hero Aeneas, the first Greek hero to exhibit the very human traits of
4   personal growth and change through life's trials. Through his struggles, Aeneas, like all men, comes to question his
5   beliefs yet emerges with his faith in his household gods intact. **This growth of a people into a nation and a man
6   into a great hero and man of faith are central themes in this epic story.**

7   The *Aeneid* is larger in scope than the collective stories of the characters involved; it is the history and
8   beginning of Rome, one of the greatest cities in the world. In this way it is a national epic, chronicling how a people,
9   driven from their native home by war, journeyed in a great exodus from Troy to the site of future Italy, dealing with
10  the loss of their land and loved ones along the way. "I sing of arms and of the man who first came from the coasts of
11  Troy to Italy and the Lavinian shores, exiled by fate. Much was he tossed about upon the lands and on the ocean by
12  supernal powers because of cruel Juno's sleepless wrath. Many things he also suffered in war, until he built a city,
13  and brought his gods into Latium; from which came the Latin race, the Alban sires, and walls of lofty Rome." Juno
14  favored Carthage above Troy, and her vengeful nature drove her to commit untold acts of sabotage toward the
15  Trojans. She allowed, even encouraged, the destruction of Troy by the Greeks, provoked the Trojan women to set
16  fire to the Trojan fleet, and incited Turnus to wage war upon the exiles. Despite constant interference from the
17  goddess, the Trojans were given hope for the continuity of their race with a promised land; "The land from which
18  you trace your birth and first beginnings of your race shall take you back unto its joyful breast. Go seek your ancient
19  mother, and there rest. There shall all shores Aeneas' rule obey, and a long line of sons hold sovereign sway." As
20  leader of the people, Aeneas was a hero burdened with the responsibility of guiding and protecting his estranged
21  countrymen. Though in one dimension it is a story of a people becoming a nation, in another the *Aeneid* is a tale of a
22  great warrior becoming a great leader.

23  Throughout the epic, Aeneas struggles with the loss of his country and the hardships he faces in his fight to
24  build a new nation. After his marriage to Dido, queen of the Carthaginians, Aeneas must sacrifice his own happiness
25  in favor of following his destiny to Italy. "Had fate permitted I should lead my life under my own direction, and put
26  off my burdens at my will, I should have first had care for Troy, and for the dear remains of my own people. Priam's
27  lofty roofs would have remained, and Pergamus again, rebuilt by me, take back our conquered race. But now
28  Grynaean Apollo points the way to Italy. To Italy commands the word of the Lycaean oracle. This is my love, my
29  country this. . . . Not of my own accord do I seek Italia." It is obvious that Aeneas would have chosen a different life
30  for himself had he been given the opportunity; but the choices he made to fulfill his purpose in life shaped him to
31  become a legendary leader. He endures heartache, physical discomfort, the underworld, desperate battles, and
32  numerous setbacks to accomplish his goals. The daily testing of his courage and resolve only serves to mold him
33  into a stronger, wiser man; the reader may reflect that God provides trials in order for humans to grow. Thus, fate as
34  influenced by the gods had a part in Aeneas's journey.

35  **In circumstances beyond his control, Aeneas was both supported and inhibited by the involvement of
36  gods in his life.** His goddess mother gave him advice and intervened with Juno on his behalf; on the other hand,
37  Juno misled the Trojan women into burning four of the ships in Aeneas's fleet. "Aeneas, by this grave disaster
38  shocked, turned over and over his heavy cares, in doubt whether on these Sicilian fields to stay, forgetful of the
39  fates, or try once more to reach the Italian shores." Discouraged and confused, Aeneas questioned whether he should
40  continue on against such great odds. Juno was fighting him every step of the way, and Aeneas had no control over
41  what she would do next. Faced with such obstacles, Aeneas felt that his fate was beyond his control, and he
42  questioned the gods; however, his faith in the promise of a favorable outcome gave him the confidence necessary to
43  continue the journey he had begun. This theme of man's struggle with fate gives the *Aeneid* a symbol of universal
44  relevance, because all humans feel that at some point in their life they have no control over the outcome of their
45  lives.

46  The *Aeneid* is a powerful story, filled with tragedy, love, suffering, war, and victory. It is a commendation
47  devoted to the ancestors of the Roman race. It is entirely human, never overly embellished with a hero who has
48  miraculous godlike abilities, nor manipulated to provide a simple resolution. Its roots in the mythology of Greek
49  culture provide a complicated framework for Aeneas's faith in some form of divine being to flourish. Foremost it is
50  the history of a nation, secondly a character study of an immensely influential man, and finally an inference to the
51  association that divinities have with human existence. (Ellen)

## Close Reading

1. The genre of the *Aeneid*?
   A. Drama
   B. Poetry
   C. Prose
   D. Song

2. What is the narrative technique?
   A. Omniscient
   B. Limited omniscient
   C. First person
   D. Third-person objective

3. What is the tone of most of the narrative?
   A. Serious
   B. Sanguine
   C. Choleric
   D. Humorous

4. The author creates the tone by
   A. Epic external and internal conflicts.
   B. Alliteration.
   C. Tense interpersonal rivalries.
   D. Antagonistic characters.

5. What is the worldview of the novel?
   A. Romanticism
   B. Theism
   C. Naturalism
   D. Realism

6. What is a central motif of the narrative?
   A. Unrequited Love
   B. Revenge
   C. Journey
   D. Homelessness

7. Identify a narrative with a similar motif:
   A. *Oedipus Rex*
   B. *Julius Caesar*
   C. *Plutarch's Lives*
   D. *Odyssey*

8. "Frothy Furrows" in Line 53 is an example of
   A. Alliteration
   B. Assonance
   C. Rhyme
   D. Hyperbole

9. What has a persistent presence in the *Aeneid*?
   A. Hope
   B. Valor
   C. Fate
   D. Grace

10. The narrative begins where it ends. Explain.
    A. Virgil hints that Aeneas will die.
    B. Virgil states that all the events will lead to a city on the Tiber (i.e., Rome).
    C. The narrative is a frame story, with Aeneas remembering his quest.
    D. Virgil apologizes for giving away the story line.

11. A logical book 2 of this narrative would be
    A. The fall of Troy and the beginning of Aeneas's journey.
    B. A love story.
    C. An obstacle to overcome as Aeneas begins his journey.
    D. The murder of Achilles.

## Command of Evidence (Student Response)

1. Where is the first place the Student Response presents its thesis?
   A. Lines 1–2
   B. Lines 5–6
   C. Lines 26–27
   D. Lines 48–50

2. What is a general strategy that the essay employs?
   A. Uses the maturation of the protagonist as the engine
   B. The tragic story of foils like Dido
   C. The unpredictability of the gods
   D. Episodic adventures

3. A major flow of this essay?
   A. Gross generalizations.
   B. Inadequate textual evidence.
   C. Conclusion introduces previously unmentioned themes (the thesis) of the novel.
   D. Incredulous foils.

4. An implied definition of epic is found in
   A. Lines 1–2
   B. Lines 7–9
   C. Lines 38–39
   D. Lines 49–50

5. Fate is defined as
   A. Chance.
   B. Predestination.
   C. Happenstance.
   D. The will of the gods.

6. What is a significant difference between the gods and goddesses that Aeneas encounters, and the Judeo-Christian God?
   A. The Judeo-Christian God is omnipresent.
   B. The Judeo-Christian God is omnipotent.
   C. The Judeo-Christian God is never pernicious and moody.
   D. The Judeo-Christian God is unpredictable.

## Words in Context (Literary Passage)

1. What is the meaning of *haughty* in Line 2?
   A. Umbrage
   B. Angst
   C. Hubris
   D. Reticence

2. What is the meaning of *frothy* in Line 53?
   A. Lathered
   B. Plowed
   C. Bothered
   D. Incense

3. What is the meaning of *tempests* in Line 81?
   A. Zephyrs
   B. Exaggerations
   C. Droughts
   D. Storms

4. What is the meaning of *undaunted* in Line 84?
   A. Unhappy
   B. Reluctant
   C. Impervious
   D. Repetitive

5. What is the meaning of *arbitrary* in Line 93?
   A. Capricious
   B. Predictable
   C. Magnanimous
   D. Perfunctory

6. What is the meaning of *fetters* in Line 94?
   A. Predilections
   B. Presents
   C. Restraints
   D. Angst

7. What is the meaning of *suppliant* in Line 95?
   A. Supplicatory
   B. Deceptive
   C. Beneficent
   D. Duplicitous

## Grammar and Usage

Choose the best grammar/usage form in bold sentence(s).

1. Student Response, Lines 6–7

    A. NONE
    B. This growth of a people into a nation is a central theme in this epic story.
    C. The growth of a people into a great nation, a man into a great hero, and a man into great faith are central themes in this epic drama.
    D. This growth of a people into a nation and a man into a great hero and man of faith fill this epic story.

2. Student Response, Lines 35–36

    A. NONE
    B. In circumstances beyond his control, Aeneas was both supported and inhibited by pernicious gods in his life.
    C. Aeneas, without his permission, was both supported and inhibited by the involvement of gods in his life.
    D. The gods support and inhibit Aeneas—without his knowledge, control, or permission.

# Lesson 2

## Critical Reading and Writing

### Command of Evidence

Read the following passages and answer accompanying questions:

### Passage 1

"Midway upon the journey of our life I found myself within a forest dark, for the straightforward pathway had been lost. Ah me! How hard a thing it is to say what was this forest savage, rough, and stern, which in the very thought renews the fear. So bitter is it, death is little more; but of the good to treat, which there I found, speak will I of the other things I saw there." While walking through a dark forest which in many ways reflects the Bible's "valley of the shadow of death," Dante meets the poet Virgil, who agrees to lead Dante out of the dangerous woods. However, in the epitome of "around the world to get next door," Dante first travels through Hell, Purgatory, and Heaven before returning home. In his journey through Hell, Dante witnesses the various regions of Hell and learns what sinners are condemned to the several sections and what punishments are inflicted upon them. In every case, the natures of the regions of Hell are appropriate to the vices of the sinners that are condemned thereto.

As Virgil and Dante enter through the famous gates of Hell, they first arrive at the Vestibule where those guilty of Indifference are punished. These people showed a lack of conviction in their lives, and thus pursued neither good nor evil. The neutral angels who took no side in the battle between Lucifer and God are also punished here. This region is not truly part of Hell, Purgatory, or Heaven, since those souls contained therein are neither truly sinful nor truly righteous. These people chase after an eternally spinning but blank banner, and there is no hope of ever truly catching it. This futile and meaningless effort represents their Indifference in their earthly lives.

After crossing the Vestibule, Dante and Virgil come to the river Acheron. Newly dead souls arrive in the Vestibule, and if condemned to a region of Hell, are ferried across Acheron by Charon, the famous boatman of ancient Greek and Roman mythology. This crossing of the Acheron is, in many ways, similar to the proverbial crossing of the Rubicon. Although the gate with the famous line "All hope abandon, ye who enter in!" stands at the entrance to the Vestibule, the crossing of the Acheron symbolizes the deepening loss of all hope. The souls in Vestibule have no hope of ever changing their undesirable situation, but nonetheless, they are barely separated from the temporal world. Those who have crossed the Acheron have been baptized in the waters of Hell, and have been fully separated from the land of the living.

After being ferried across Acheron, Dante and Virgil land on the shore of the first circle of Hell, Limbo. The citizens of this section led relatively moral lives on Earth, but were nonetheless Unbaptized, and thus could not be accepted into Heaven. The members of this region live what may seem like a somewhat pleasant life, especially for Hell. The reason for the relative lenience of this punishment is most likely Dante's fascination with many of the people contained in this circle. Virgil himself resides here along with Socrates, Horace, Ovid, Aeneas, and many other famous ancient poets, philosophers, and mythological characters. Dante, himself a poet and a devout follower of many of the ancient poets and philosophers, did not wish to inflict too harsh a punishment on these people, and thus created a region especially for them.

In the second circle of Hell, true punishment begins to be realized. The members of this region have been damned because they were guilty of Lust in their earthly lives. In essence, therefore, their pursuit of love was their undoing. Therefore, in Hell, they are doomed to be blown around endlessly and aimlessly by a constant wind. This aimless wind points to the fact that their pursuit of love in their earthly lives was aimless.

The third circle is home to the Gluttons. Here the connection between sin and punishment is obvious. Gluttons have overindulged their appetites in their earthly lives, and thus must lie and constantly be showered upon by a filthy rain that falls eternally upon them. This precipitation represents the excess food that they consumed temporally, and they must endure a continual shower of this "food" for eternity.

In the fourth circle, Dante and Virgil witness two groups of sinners continually pushing weights in opposite directions in a circular trench. When the two groups collide with each other, they both turn around, only to collide again on the other side of the circle. These souls are guilty of Avarice or Prodigality. The connection here seems quite vague until Virgil explains that Avarice and Prodigality have one primary aspect in common: both squander

44    what Fortune has given them. Thus, in Hell, the souls guilty of these sins are doomed to squander the only
45    possession they have left, an eternal existence.
46        The fifth circle contains those souls guilty of Wrath in their temporal lives. Just as Wrath consumed them
47    on Earth, they are now consumed by mud in Hell. Dante considered Wrath to be something that, when admitted into
48    a person's heart, would completely envelope that person until nothing else could be seen from such an individual
49    that was untainted by that Wrath. Similarly, these souls contained in the mud of the fifth circle of Hell are almost
50    unrecognizable because of how much mire covers them.
51        As Virgil and Dante are ferried across Styx by Phlegyas, they notice that some sinners are completely
52    submerged in that river. These souls are those who were Sullen in their earthly lives, and just as they constantly
53    muttered complaints on Earth, they are now doomed to gurgle mud for eternity. Styx also separates the first five
54    circles of Hell, which may all be included in the broader category of Incontinence from the lower levels of Hell
55    which include the general categories of Violence and Fraud.
56        After crossing Styx, Virgil and Dante come to the City of Dis. This city, guarded by Pater Dis,
57    encompasses the rest of Hell. Pater Dis is another name for Pluto used by writers of ancient Roman mythology, such
58    as Virgil himself. The levels of Hell contained inside the City of Dis are much more similar to the modern
59    conception of Hell than the upper levels, and also contain the more serious sins. Thus Dante, fluent in Roman
60    mythology, compared the inner levels of Hell to the Greek and Roman underworld.
61        Within the City of Dis, Virgil and Dante first come to the sixth circle, where Heretics are punished. These
62    souls dwell in tombs of glowing hot coals. This connection is one of the more vague connections between sin and
63    punishment in the Inferno, but there are three primary possibilities. First, many verses throughout the Bible—such as
64    2 Samuel 22:9; Psalm 18:8; and Proverbs 25:22—refer to God's wrath in the context of coals. Heresy being a
65    serious sin, the coals could be a manifestation of God's wrath against these sinners. Second, this punishment could
66    be a direct reference to Psalm 140:10, where it is written, "May burning coals fall upon them; may they be cast into
67    the fire, into deep pits from which they cannot rise." Third, in Isaiah 6:6–7, "One of the seraphs flew to me with a
68    burning coal in his hand, which he had taken from the altar with tongs. He touched my mouth with it and said,
69    'Behold, this has touched your lips; and your iniquity is taken away and your sin is forgiven.'" Although the
70    Heretics in Hell are not forgiven by this punishment, it is possible, since their sins proceeded primarily from their
71    mouths, that the punishment of hot coals is a reference to this verse in Isaiah.
72        The seventh circle of Hell, where Violence is punished, is divided into three different sections. First is the
73    section that punishes Violence against others. The people in this section are submerged in a river of blood
74    traditionally called Phlegethon (another allusion to Roman mythology). The more violence the person committed on
75    Earth, the deeper a part of Phlegethon the soul lies in. This connection is obvious, implying that the blood of those
76    whom one murders will return and torture one in Hell. Second is punishment for Violence against self. Both suicides
77    and squanderers reside here, eternally transformed into trees. Just as they held their life of little esteem on Earth,
78    their life is totally void of value in Hell. Third is punishment for Violence against God. These souls must bear
79    perpetual punishment by flakes of fire that fall ceaselessly from the sky. Again, this reference is likely an allusion to
80    the aforementioned biblical verses that compare God's wrath to hot coals.
81        At the edge of the third ring of the seventh circle is a deep abyss which, similar to Styx, separates one
82    general subdivision from another. Styx separates Incontinence from Violence (Heresy was considered, in a sense,
83    violence against God,) whereas the Abyss separates Violence from Fraud.
84        The eighth circle to which Virgil and Dante come, after descending the Abyss on the back of Geryon,
85    contains ten pouches. The first pouch is home to Seducers and Panderers. Both of these types of sinners took
86    advantage of other people's helplessness and used it for their advantage. Likewise, now demons take advantage of
87    the souls' naked helplessness by whipping them ceaselessly. The second pouch is home to Flatterers. Flattery is full
88    of empty, vain, and ultimately grotesque language. Similarly, the Flatterers are condemned to spend eternity in a
89    ditch of filth. The third pouch is home to Simonists, who were somewhat common in the Middle Ages and sold
90    pardons and ecclesiastical offices. These men preached about piety and yet sold pardons for those who could not live
91    up to God's standards. Therefore, their punishment places them with their "heads buried in the sand," concealing
92    their true identity. The fourth pouch is home to the Diviners. These were people who attempted to predict the future.
93    Thus their punishment is to have their heads turned backward for eternity. The fifth pouch is home to the Barterers,
94    those who took bribes. These souls are in a pool of pitch, so they must surface to breathe, but the demons rip these
95    souls' bodies whenever they surface. This is similar to bribery; once one has accepted one bribe, it leads to another
96    and another until they become unavoidable. The sixth pouch is home to the Hypocrites. These Hypocrites walk
97    continuously weighed down by lead-lined garments. Their Hypocrisy has returned to weigh them down in Hell. In
98    the seventh pouch live the Thieves. These Thieves are continually tortured by serpents. Serpents, in Christianity,
99    represent treachery, and thus they are a perfect torture for those who have practiced Thievery. The eighth pouch
100   houses the False Counselors. A few specific sinners are named in this section, all of which gave counsel that was

101 fraudulent at some point. These people are now consumed in fire, since their false counsel consumed those who took
102 their advice. The ninth pouch is home to the Schismatics. All sinners in this pouch worked, at some time or another,
103 to cause division, and thus they are continually wounded, and their flesh "divided," by devils who slash at them with
104 weapons. In the tenth and final pouch of Malebolge, the Counterfeiters spend eternity. Various types of Falsifiers
105 dwell here, and all have, in some way or another, deformed shapes. Their bodies have been changed, just as they
106 attempted to change the truth in their temporal lives.
107      **The ninth and final circle of Hell contains those guilty of treachery.** In this section, referred to as
108 Cocytus, sinners punish themselves. For example, two twins stand frozen in the ice near the front of this section,
109 butting their heads together. Those who committed Treachery are now punished by those whom they committed
110 Treachery against.
111      Finally, at the very center of Hell, is Lucifer himself. Satan has three constantly chewing mouths, in each of
112 which is a horrible sinner. In the left and right mouths are Brutus and Cassius, the two Roman Senators most
113 responsible for Julius Caesar's death. In the center mouth is Judas Iscariot, who betrayed Jesus of Nazareth. Brutus
114 and Cassius remain with their upper bodies exposed and their lower bodies in Satan's mouths. Judas's head,
115 however, is inside Satan's mouth, and thus he endures the place of worst torture in all of Hell. The journey through
116 Hell is complete.
117      Throughout every region of Hell mentioned in the *Inferno*, Dante carefully matches his punishments with
118 the types of sinners punished thereby. As Dr. David Noble stated in his lecture "Dante Alighieri—the *Divine*
119 *Comedy*," "Dante . . . for the first time sees God as a judge, not only as a miracle-worker and creator." When Dante
120 descended into Hell, he was a lost lonely traveler wandering through the valley of the shadow of death, but when he
121 rose again out of Hell, he was a firm believer in the absolute Justice of God. Thus, this absolute Justice is the theme
122 of the Inferno, and every sin is paid in full with its equal and just punishment. (John)

## Close Reading

1. What would be the best title for this essay?
   A. Biblical Truth
   B. Dante's Transformation in Hell
   C. Journey Proud
   D. Virgil the Traveler

2. What is the purpose of the beginning quote?
   A. The author wishes to increase readers' understanding of literature.
   B. The author believes novelists are very influential.
   C. The author draws readers into the world that Dante is experiencing.
   D. The author gives background on medieval Italy.

3. What organizational plan does the author employ?
   A. He offers a thesis at first and then argues the opposite.
   B. He defines the perimeters of his argument and then gives textual examples.
   C. He defines the perimeter of his argument and then offers personal examples.
   D. He asks a series of rhetorical questions.

4. How does the author "move" the reader through the essay?
   A. He gives a series of bullet points.
   B. He uses his own salvation experience as a rubric to power his essay.
   C. The readers moves, with Dante, through the layers of Hell.
   D. He moves readers into a deeper level of Hell and then offers a polemic.

5. The author finishes his essay with
   A. A summary statement.
   B. A new conclusion.
   C. A veiled warning.
   D. The way he began.

6. This essay can best be described as
   A. Analysis
   B. Synthesis
   C. Polemic
   D. Apology

7. The author
   A. Criticizes medieval Roman Catholicism as Dante journeys through Hell.
   B. Ties Dante's growth as a character to his journey into deeper levels of depravity.
   C. Argues for a religious experience.
   D. Concedes that Dante has an ecumenical view of Christianity.

8. The author is probably
   A. A homeschooler.
   B. A conservative Christian.
   C. A Hindu.
   D. An agnostic.

## Passage 2

1    John Knowles's psychological novel *A Separate Peace* is filled with many themes that pervade the work. One of
2    these themes is the common disdain for learning. Gene Forrester, Finny, Leper Lepellier, and practically every
3    young person in the book demonstrate a high level of distaste for study, a distaste that is clearly mirrored in
4    postmodern American culture. Yet, what a contrast this aversion is to the absolute emphasis put on learning during
5    the Renaissance. To provide irony in Knowles's book, everything takes place among Gothic- and Renaissance-style
6    architecture. Ever since it began, the Renaissance has been identified as a period in which the pursuit of learning was
7    the highest possible goal, and focus turned to the individual instead of to the community. Yet the Renaissance was
8    not born without forewarning. Progressive thinkers in the Middle Ages had been looking toward the rebirth of
9    classicism for years. One such thinker, Francis Bacon, is best known for his revolutionary essays, which shaped the
10   world of his descendants. As with many of his essays, Francis Bacon's essay "Of Studies" is ideological, but it
11   reinforces the high emphasis on learning seen in the Renaissance.
12          Bacon's views are summarized in a sentence that may accurately be titled the "thesis" for his essay "*Of
13   Studies*": "Studies serve for delight, for ornament, and for ability." Breaking this sentence into its constituent parts
14   reveals a more in-depth analysis of Bacon's opinions on the topic of studies and research. "Studies serve for
15   delight": Bacon believes that studies should be undertaken, in part, merely for the sake of studying. In other words,
16   research is intrinsically valuable as a means of entertainment. "For ornament": Bacon also believes that studies
17   should be undertaken so that the person studying may have the distinction of having studied. In an age before
18   official degrees were handed out by universities, this was a look toward academic decoration. "For ability": The
19   practical element of study is not entirely removed from Bacon's view, as evidenced by this final component of
20   Bacon's three-part statement. A person should study not only for fun and to distinguish oneself, but also because it
21   prepares the studier for other situations.
22          When looking at the wider Renaissance, one finds a view of learning remarkably similar to the opinion
23   espoused by Francis Bacon in his essay "Of Studies." "The Italian Renaissance had placed human beings once more
24   in the center of life's stage and infused thought and art with humanistic values." This focus on the individual also
25   applied to learning, which was viewed as particular to each person. Many began to focus on their specific passions
26   more than on a general education, which had been provided to the upper class since ancient times. "The Renaissance
27   is the period in European civilization immediately following the Middle Ages, conventionally held to have been
28   characterized by a surge of interest in classical learning and values." During this period, a man who was learned was
29   viewed as superior to one who was not. In some areas, learning began to achieve an almost equal status with wealth
30   as a social measure. "To the scholars and thinkers of the day, however, it was primarily a time of the revival of
31   classical learning and wisdom after a long period of cultural decline and stagnation." Learning was viewed as
32   important to the individual and to the society, but also to the interaction between the two. Learning was important so
33   that a person could impact the society, for if one did not understand history and literature, how could one make
34   intelligent moves in society? Study was entertaining, distinguishing, and practical.
35          As evidenced by the parallels between the ideas espoused in Bacon's essay "Of Studies" and those
36   expounded upon by Renaissance thinkers, it is evident that Francis Bacon was a progressive of his times who
37   encouraged the "rebirth" that was coming. As Bacon foresaw, study in the Renaissance was becoming a method of
38   entertainment, a system of social distinction, and a practically important value that was esteemed, sometimes, above
39   all else. "For expert men can execute, and perhaps judge of particulars, one by one; but the general counsels, and the
40   plots and marshalling of affairs, come best, from those that are learned." (John)

## Close Reading

1. What would be the best title for this essay?
   A. A Renaissance Theory of Education
   B. A Modern Education
   C. Francis Bacon
   D. John Knowles

2. How does the author begin the essay?
   A. Summary of argument
   B. Introduction to the argument
   C. Rhetorical questions
   D. A quote from a twentieth-century novel.

3. What is a possible criticism of such a beginning?
   A. American literature is the best resource to discover human nature.
   B. Never mention an author's name.
   C. Weak quote.
   D. Weak analogy.

4. What organizational plan does the author employ?
   A. Argument, Evidence, Counterargument
   B. Thesis, Supporting Textual Evidence, Conclusion
   C. Summary, Anecdotes
   D. Anecdotes, Commentary, Conclusion

5. Identify the evidentiary strength of this essay:
   A. Humor
   B. Hyperbole and allusion
   C. Extensive textual evidence
   D. Conflict and resolution

6. What is the author's primary strategy to create transitions?
   I. Using guide words like "As can be"
   II. Pausing for effect
   III. Double indent
   IV. Mentioning a word or thought from the preceding paragraph

   A. I and II
   B. III and IV
   C. II and III
   D. I and IV

7. The author is probably
   A. A homeschooler.
   B. A confessional Christian.
   C. A Hindu.
   D. An agnostic.

## Grammar and Usage

Choose the best grammar/usage form in bold sentence(s).

Passage 1, Line 107

   A. NONE
   B. The ninth and final circle of Hell contain those guilty of treachery.
   C. The ninth and final circle of Hell punish people guilty of treachery.
   D. The ninth and final circle of Hell entertain sinners guilty of treachery.

# Lesson 3
## SAT Essay

### Student Response 1

*Prompt:* Are advances in civilization tied to hard work or to intellect?

1  There comes a point in every civilization where the society needs to progress. The technology and knowledge need
2  to improve in order to continue to uphold and defend that society. Progress, however, does not improve simply
3  because of the inert desire of wanting it to improve, but rather because individuals that come once in a generation
4  have the ability to push progress forward. Intellects are the building blocks of progress and are the most important
5  quality of achievement.
6      Throughout history, numerous advancements have been made to progress society. The wheel, for instance,
7  was created to lessen the burden of workloads. An intellect with the ability to design the wheel is more important
8  than the determined worker who will do the same task as the intellect, but with an industrious disadvantage. In
9  corroboration with the famous adage "Brains over braun," the intellect uses one's ability to make a task easier
10 instead of mindlessly pining away at the same workload.
11     Great intellects, such as the creator of the wheel, rarely come more than once in a generation. Isaac
12 Newton, who developed the laws of gravity, quantified what no other person at the time period could have achieved.
13 Even the most determined mind could not have pioneered the laws of astrophysics by merely working hard. Albert
14 Einstein, who developed the theory of relativity, was not able to solve problems because he worked hard, but rather
15 because he had the inert ability to solve problems. Without Einstein's or Newton's intelligence, they would not have
16 been able to achieve their self-inspired revelations.
17     Societal progress is driven by innovation, and great innovation can only be made by great intellects. The
18 less intelligent but extremely determined can still forward industrial progress, but only the true intellects can alter
19 progress enough to change the lives of generations to come. (Willis)

### Student Response 2

*Prompt:* Is it necessary for us to fail in the little things to succeed in the big ones?

1      "You don't fail unless you give up, but you can't succeed unless you persevere through the desire to give
2  up," said daredevil Jeb Coreless. Failure brings success. My reasons for believing that failure brings success are the
3  following: We must fail to learn. We must overcome our challenge. When we see our success, we will not easily be
4  discouraged.
5      When I was younger, I challenged myself to learn how to dance; yet when I started taking lessons, I felt
6  incompetent to achieve my goal. **This feeling of incompetence came from my mistakes on the dance floor.** But
7  because I made mistakes, I persevered through the failures, and now I have succeeded in learning to dance. If I had
8  not met with failure by literally falling, I would not have had success.
9      After I learn how to do something by falling and learning the cause of my mistakes, I had to overcome the
10 conscious reminders of failure of which my fear reminds me. I must overcome my fear of failure to then master
11 basics and thereby gain success. (Luke)

### Close Reading

   1.  In Student Response 1
      A. Dissonance and warfare inevitably generate progress.
      B. Progress comes through luck.
      C. Intellect is the key ingredient in progress.
      D. Intellect is important, but hard work is more important.

   2.  In Response 2 the author organizes the essay
      A. By stating a rhetorical questions and then developing the thesis.
      B. By offering a series of anecdotes.
      C. By stating a thesis and offering several examples.
      D. By a series of bullet points.

3. Student Response Essay 1 can be improved by
   I. Giving more specific examples.
   II. Strengthening transitions.
   III. Removing personal examples.
   IV. Making the essay longer.
   V. Clearly stating the thesis and tying it to the topic.

   A. I, II, and V

   B. III and IV

   C. II and III

   D. V

4. Problems in Student Response Essay 2 include which of the following?
   I. Examples are not tied closely to the thesis.
   II. Transitions are weak.
   III. There are too many personal examples.
   IV. The essay is too short.
   V. The thesis is not clearly stated nor tied to the topic.

   A. I and II

   B. III and IV

   C. II and III

   D. I, II, IV, and V

   E. All

5. Where is the thesisof the Student Response 1?
   A. Lines 2–5     B. Lines 8–9     C. Line 18     D. Line 19

6. Where is the thesis of the Student Response 2?
   A. Lines 2–4     B. Lines 8–9     C. Line 10     D. Line 11

7. What is a significant stylistic problem in Student Essay 2?
   A. First person is used too much.

   B. Second-person pronouns are used.

   C. Transitions are weak.

   D. There are agreement problems.

8. Criticism of Student Response 2 should not include that
   I. The essay's position is unclear or limited; the critical thinking in the essay is weak and not supported by sufficient or relevant examples and details.
   II. The central idea is poorly defined.
   III. The essay is poorly organized, and in general the essay lacks coherence.
   IV. The language is ordinary and uninspiring.
   V. The sentence structure lacks variety and complexity.
   VI. There are serious grammar mistakes.

   A. I, II, & III

   B. I, II, III, IV, & V

   C. VI

   D. IV, V, & VI

   E. NONE

9. What score would the student responses receive?
   Student Response 1 receives ___. Student Response 2 receives ___.

## Grammar and Usage

Choose the best grammar/usage form in bold sentence(s).

Student Response 2, Lines 6–7
   A. NONE
   B. This feeling of incompetence came from my mistakes on the dance floor, but, because I made mistakes, I persevered the failures and now I have succeeded in learning to dance.
   C. Mistakes came from incompetence on the dance floor, but, persevering, I eventually learned to dance.
   D. This feeling of incompetence came from my mistakes on the dance floor; however, I made mistakes I persevered the failures and now I have succeeded in learning to dance.

# Lesson 4
## Reading: Document-Based Analysis

### Maryland Toleration Act (September 21, 1649)

1 Forasmuch as in a well governed and Christian Common Weath matters concerning Religion and the honor of God
2 ought in the first place to bee taken, into serious consideracion and endeavoured to bee settled, Be it therefore
3 ordered and enacted by the Right Honourable Cecilius Lord Baron of Baltemore absolute Lord and Proprietary of
4 this Province with the advise and consent of this Generall Assembly:
5     That whatsoever person or persons within this Province and the Islands thereunto belonging shall from
6 henceforth blaspheme God, that is Curse him, or deny our Saviour Jesus Christ to bee the sonne of God, or shall
7 deny the holy Trinity the father sonne and holy Ghost, or the Godhead of any of the said Three persons of the Trinity
8 or the Unity of the Godhead, or shall use or utter any reproachfull Speeches, words or language concerning the said
9 Holy Trinity, or any of the said three persons thereof, shalbe punished with death and confiscation or forfeiture of all
10 his or her lands and goods to the Lord Proprietary and his heires.
11     And bee it also Enacted by the Authority and with the advise and assent aforesaid, That whatsoever person
12 or persons shall from henceforth use or utter any reproachfull words or Speeches concerning the blessed Virgin
13 Mary the Mother of our Saviour or the holy Apostles or Evangelists or any of them shall in such case for the first
14 offence forfeit to the said Lord Proprietary and his heirs Lords and Proprietaries of this Province the summe of five
15 pound Sterling or the value thereof to be Levyed on the goods and chattells of every such person soe offending, but
16 in case such Offender or Offenders, shall not then have goods and chattells sufficient for the satisfyeing of such
17 forfeiture, or that the same bee not otherwise speedily satisfyed that then such Offender or Offenders shalbe
18 publiquely whipt and bee imprisoned during the pleasure of the Lord Proprietary or the Lieutenant or cheife
19 Governor of this Province for the time being. And that every such Offender or Offenders for every second offence
20 shall forfeit tenne pound sterling or the value thereof to bee levyed as aforesaid, or in case such offender or
21 Offenders shall not then have goods and chattells within this Province sufficient for that purpose then to bee
22 publiquely and severely whipt and imprisoned as before is expressed. And that every person or persons before
23 mentioned offending herein the third time, shall for such third Offence forfeit all his lands and Goods and bee for
24 ever banished and expelled out of this Province.
25     And be it also further Enacted by the same authority advise and assent that whatsoever person or persons
26 shall from henceforth uppon any occasion of Offence or otherwise in a reproachful manner or Way declare call or
27 denominate any person or persons whatsoever inhabiting, residing, traffiqueing, trading or comerceing within this
28 Province or within any the Ports, Harbors, Creeks or Havens to the same belonging an heritick, Scismatick, Idolator,
29 puritan, Independant, Prespiterian popish prest, Jesuite, Jesuited papist, Lutheran, Calvenist, Anabaptist, Brownist,
30 Antinomian, Barrowist, Roundhead, Separatist, or any other name or terme in a reproachfull manner relating to
31 matter of Religion shall for every such Offence forfeit and loose the somme of tenne shillings sterling or the value
32 thereof to bee levyed on the goods and chattells of every such Offender and Offenders, the one half thereof to be
33 forfeited and paid unto the person and persons of whom such reproachfull words are or shalbe spoken or uttered, and
34 the other half thereof to the Lord Proprietary and his heires Lords and Proprietaries of this Province. But if such
35 person or persons who shall at any time utter or speake any such reproachfull words or Language shall not have
36 Goods or Chattells sufficient and overt within this Province to bee taken to satisfie the penalty aforesaid or that the
37 same bee not otherwise speedily satisfyed, that then the person or persons soe offending shalbe publickly whipt, and
38 shall suffer imprisonment without baile or maineprise [bail] untill hee, shee or they respectively shall satisfy the
39 party soe offended or greived by such reproachfull Language by asking him or her respectively forgivenes
40 publiquely for such his Offence before the Magistrate of cheife Officer or Officers of the Towne or place where such
41 Offence shalbe given.
42     And be it further likewise Enacted by the Authority and consent aforesaid That every person and persons
43 within this Province that shall at any time hereafter prophane the Sabbath or Lords day called Sunday by frequent
44 swearing, drunkennes or by any uncivill or disorderly recreacion, or by working on that day when absolute necessity
45 doth not require it shall for every such first offence forfeit 2s 6d sterling or the value thereof, and for the second
46 offence 5s sterling or the value thereof, and for the third offence and soe for every time he shall offend in like
47 manner afterwards 10s sterling or the value thereof. And in case such offender and offenders shall not have
48 sufficient goods or chattells within this Province to satisfy any of the said Penalties respectively hereby imposed for

49 prophaning the Sabbath or Lords day called Sunday as aforesaid, That in Every such case the partie soe offending
50 shall for the first and second offence in that kinde be imprisoned till hee or shee shall publickly in open Court before
51 the cheife Commander Judge or Magistrate, of that County Towne or precinct where such offence shalbe committed
52 acknowledg the Scandall and offence he hath in that respect given against God and the good and civill Governement
53 of this Province, And for the third offence and for every time after shall also bee publickly whipt.
54     And whereas the inforceing of the conscience in matters of Religion hath frequently fallen out to be of
55 dangerous Consequence in those commonwealthes where it hath been practised, And for the more quiett and
56 peaceable governement of this Province, and the better to preserve mutuall Love and amity amongst the Inhabitants
57 thereof, Be it Therefore also by the Lord Proprietary with the advise and consent of this Assembly Ordeyned and
58 enacted (except as in this present Act is before Declared and sett forth) that noe person or persons whatsoever within
59 this Province, or the Islands, Ports, Harbors, Creekes, or havens thereunto belonging professing to beleive in Jesus
60 Christ, shall from henceforth bee any waies troubled, Molested or discountenanced for or in respect of his or her
61 religion nor in the free exercise thereof within this Province or the Islands thereunto belonging nor any way
62 compelled to the beleife or exercise of any other Religion against his or her consent, soe as they be not unfaithfull to
63 the Lord Proprietary, or molest or conspire against the civill Governement established or to bee established in this
64 Province under him or his heires. And that all and every person and persons that shall presume Contrary to this Act
65 and the true intent and meaning thereof directly or indirectly either in person or estate willfully to wrong disturbe
66 trouble or molest any person whatsoever within this Province professing to beleive in Jesus Christ for or in respect
67 of his or her religion or the free exercise thereof within this Province other than is provided for in this Act that such
68 person or persons soe offending, shalbe compelled to pay trebble damages to the party soe wronged or molested, and
69 for every such offence shall also forfeit 20s sterling in money or the value thereof, half thereof for the use of the
70 Lord Proprietary, and his heires Lords and Proprietaries of this Province, and the other half for the use of the party
71 soe wronged or molested as aforesaid, Or if the partie soe offending as aforesaid shall refuse or bee unable to
72 recompense the party soe wronged, or to satisfy such fyne or forfeiture, then such Offender shalbe severely punished
73 by publick whipping and imprisonment during the pleasure of the Lord Proprietary, or his Lieutenant or cheife
74 Governor of this Province for the tyme being without baile or maineprise.
75     And bee it further alsoe Enacted by the authority and consent aforesaid That the Sheriff or other Officer or
76 Officers from time to time to bee appointed and authorized for that purpose, of the County Towne or precinct where
77 every particular offence in this present Act conteyned shall happen at any time to bee committed and whereupon
78 there is hereby a forfeiture fyne or penalty imposed shall from time to time distraine and seise the goods and estate
79 of every such person soe offending as aforesaid against this present Act or any part thereof, and sell the same or any
80 part thereof for the full satisfaccion of such forfeiture, fine, or penalty as aforesaid, Restoring unto the partie soe
81 offending the Remainder or overplus of the said goods or estate after such satisfaccion soe made as aforesaid
82     The freemen have assented.

(http://avalon.law.yale.edu/18th_century/maryland_toleration.asp)

## Close Reading

1. What is the purpose of this message?
   A. To ensure religious liberty for all faiths.
   B. To require toleration for all Protestant faiths.
   C. To ensure religious liberty for all Trinitarian faiths, Roman Catholic and Protestant.
   D. To prosecute dissenting Christians.

2. Why would this act be necessary in 1649?
   I. Religion and the State were separated.
   II. Roman Catholicism was outlawed in England and in most colonies.
   III. French Canadians were threatening the English colonies.
   IV. Maryland was founded by and attracted Roman Catholics.

   A. I and II          C. I, II, and IV
   B. III and IV        D. I and IV

3. What is true about the Maryland Toleration Act?
   I. Today the Toleration Act seems restrictive, but in its day it offered more religious freedom for the citizens of Maryland than for those in England and in colonies like the Massachusetts Bay Colony.
   II. The Maryland Act of Toleration is an important stepping-stone to the religious freedom that became such an important characteristic of the United States.
   III. The Maryland Act opened the door for Quakers, Baptists, and other dissenting religious immigrants.

    A. I            C. III                       E. II and III
    B. II           D. I and II

4. Which group would benefit for this law?
   A. Jewish people                     C. Mormons
   B. Roman Catholics            D. Unitarians

## Words in Context

1. What is the meaning of *Proprietaries* in Line 70?
   A. Avocations                     C. Properties
   B. Penchants                    D. Demands

2. What is the meaning of *forfeiture* in Line 78?
   A. Rental                         C. Gain
   B. Damage                   D. Loss

# Lesson 5

## Math: Algebra, Arithmetic Problem Solving and Data Analysis, and Passport to Advanced Math

**Passport to Advanced Math**

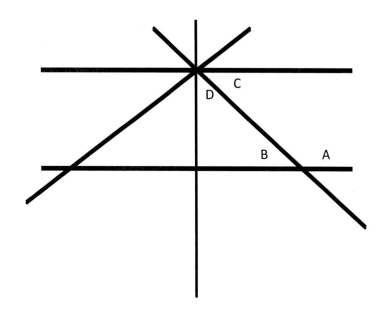

What is true about this diagram?
  I.   Angle C is equal to Angle B.
  II.  Angle A + Angle B = 360 degrees.
  III. Angle D is more than 90 degrees.

      A. I                           C. II and III
      B. I and II                    D. All

### Arithmetic Problem Solving

1.  Find two consecutive numbers such that a fifth of the larger shall equal the difference between a third and an eighth of the smaller.
    A.  25; 26                       C.  22; 23
    B.  23; 24                       D.  24; 25

2.  A is 24 years older than B, and A's age is as much above 50 as B's is below 40. What is the age of each?
    A.  A, 56 yrs.; B 32 yrs.        C.  A, 58 yrs.; B 34 yrs.
    B.  A, 57 yrs.; B 33 yrs.        D.  A, 59 yrs.; B 35 yrs.

3.  Find the number whose double added to 16 will be as much above 70 as the number itself is below 60.
    A.  38                           C.  42
    B.  40                           D.  36

4. A rabbit takes 5 leaps in the time it takes for a dog's 4 leaps, but 3 of the dog's leaps are equal to 4 of the rabbit's leaps. When the chase begins, the rabbit has a start of 20 of its leaps, so how many more leaps will the rabbit take before it is caught?
   A. 280 leaps
   B. 290 leaps
   C. 300 leaps
   D. 250 leaps

5. A greyhound takes 3 leaps in the time it takes for a rabbit's 5 leaps, but 2 of the greyhound's leaps are equal to 4 of the rabbit's. If the rabbit has a start of 48 of its leaps when the chase begins, how many leaps will the greyhound take to catch the rabbit?
   A. With 142 leaps
   B. With 144 leaps
   C. With 164 leaps
   D. With 146 leaps

6. A rabbit has a start of 40 of its leaps ahead of a dog when the chase begins. After how many more leaps will the rabbit be caught if 5 of its leaps equal 4 of the dog's, and if the rabbit takes 7 leaps while the dog takes 6?
   A. After 440 leaps
   B. After 500 leaps
   C. After 660 leaps
   D. After 560 leaps

# Chapter 24  Prospering in a Hostile Land Jeremiah 29:4–9

> *Memory Verse:* Seek the peace and prosperity of the city to which I have carried you into exile. Pray to the LORD for it, because if it prospers, you too will prosper. —Jeremiah 29:7

At the beginning of the twenty-first century, we Christians are called to be salt and light in a time and place that is woefully short of both. Without a doubt, we are called to be history makers in a world that wants none of it.

Above everything else, we must be hopeful. In the midst of chaos and despair, the early church was hopeful. People cannot live without hope. True history makers are not those whom you would expect—politicians, doctors, and lawyers. Real history makers are those who can invest in a dream. In spite of bleak conditions—ten thousand from Jeremiah's nation had been taken into Babylonian exile (597 BC), and ten years later Babylon would destroy Jerusalem and take all but the poorest into captivity (587/586)—Jeremiah was still able to have great hope. He had apocalyptic hope (based in history and revealed by God's promises). He understood who really had power: those who had hope in spite of the circumstances they faced. Jeremiah wrote a letter to the first exiles and told them to settle down in Babylon and seek peace there (Jeremiah 29:4–9).God told Jeremiah to buy a piece of land at Anathoth, three miles north of Jerusalem (Jeremiah 32). He did, thereby showing his confidence in the future of Judah. Even though Jeremiah would never get to enjoy that land (he was kidnapped to Egypt [Jer. 43]), he invested in it anyway. Apocalyptic hope causes us to invest in dreams we may never see consummated. People with apocalyptic hope are able to assert the sovereign and omnipotent will of God in all circumstances, no matter how bad things may be. They have an audacious belief about alternative possibilities that go under the name of hope. They see clearly that things are deeply wrong, but they still have hope. They do not have faith in mere humans, nor faith in human history, but a sure hope in God and in the history God is working out. Modern, existential hope of men like Viktor E. Frankl pales in the light of the hope of a committed Christian. "Was Du erlebst, kann keine Macht der Welt Dir rauben [What you have experienced, no power on earth can take from you]," Frankl writes (*Man's Search for Meaning* [New York: Pocket Books, 1963], 131). The truth is, young people, our hope is not based on human experiences; it is based on the promises of God.

But I ask you to invest in something you cannot see and might never see in your lifetime. A dream. A belief. That is the penultimate purpose of this book. That is ground zero for this course and for this world. The moment enough Christians understand and live this truth, that will be the moment the world will change.

## Journal Question

Describe yourself five years from now. Then, describe yourself twenty years from now. In your description, include your family, occupation, and spiritual life.

# Lesson 1
## Evidence-Based Reading and Writing

### Literary Choice

*Don Quixote*, with the full title *The Ingenious Gentleman Don Quixote of La Mancha*, is a Spanish novel by Miguel de Cervantes Saavedra. It follows the adventures of Don Quixote, a medieval Spanish aristocrat/knight. Quixote is accompanied by the unpretentious but acerbic Sancho Panza, his squire. Published in two volumes (1605–15), *Don Quixote* is the most important work of Spanish literature and has been translated into at least 48 languages. With his whimsical pretensions, Don Quixote is one of the major archetypical characters in Western literature.

### *Don Quixote*
### Miquel de Cervantes

### Chapter 3

1  Harassed by this reflection, he made haste with his scanty pothouse supper, and having finished it called the
2  landlord, and shutting himself into the stable with him, fell on his knees before him, saying, "From this spot I rise
3  not, valiant knight, until your courtesy grants me the boon I seek, one that will redound to your praise and the
4  benefit of the human race." The landlord, seeing his guest at his feet and hearing a speech of this kind, stood staring
5  at him in bewilderment, not knowing what to do or say, and entreating him to rise, but all to no purpose until he had
6  agreed to grant the boon demanded of him. "I looked for no less, my lord, from your High Magnificence," replied
7  Don Quixote, "and I have to tell you that the boon I have asked and your liberality has granted is that you shall dub
8  me knight to-morrow morning, and that to-night I shall watch my arms in the chapel of this your castle; thus
9  tomorrow, as I have said, will be accomplished what I so much desire, enabling me lawfully to roam through all the
10  four quarters of the world seeking adventures on behalf of those in distress, as is the duty of chivalry and of knights-
11  errant like myself, whose ambition is directed to such deeds."
12      The landlord, who, as has been mentioned, was something of a wag, and had already some suspicion of his
13  guest's want of wits, was quite convinced of it on hearing talk of this kind from him, and to make sport for the night
14  he determined to fall in with his humor. So he told him he was quite right in pursuing the object he had in view, and
15  that such a motive was natural and becoming in cavaliers as distinguished as he seemed and his gallant bearing
16  showed him to be; and that he himself in his younger days had followed the same honourable calling, roaming in
17  quest of adventures in various parts of the world, among others the Curing-grounds of Malaga, the Isles of Riaran,
18  the Precinct of Seville, the Little Market of Segovia, the Olivera of Valencia, the Rondilla of Granada, the Strand of
19  San Lucar, the Colt of Cordova, the Taverns of Toledo, and divers other quarters, where he had proved the
20  nimbleness of his feet and the lightness of his fingers, doing many wrongs, cheating many widows, ruining maids
21  and swindling minors, and, in short, bringing himself under the notice of almost every tribunal and court of justice in
22  Spain; until at last he had retired to this castle of his, where he was living upon his property and upon that of others;
23  and where he received all knights-errant of whatever rank or condition they might be, all for the great love he bore
24  them and that they might share their substance with him in return for his benevolence. He told him, moreover, that in
25  this castle of his there was no chapel in which he could watch his armour, as it had been pulled down in order to be
26  rebuilt, but that in a case of necessity it might, he knew, be watched anywhere, and he might watch it that night in a
27  courtyard of the castle, and in the morning, God willing, the requisite ceremonies might be performed so as to have
28  him dubbed a knight, and so thoroughly dubbed that nobody could be more so. He asked if he had any money with
29  him, to which Don Quixote replied that he had not a farthing, as in the histories of knights-errant he had never read
30  of any of them carrying any. On this point the landlord told him he was mistaken; for, though not recorded in the
31  histories, because in the author's opinion there was no need to mention anything so obvious and necessary as money
32  and clean shirts, it was not to be supposed therefore that they did not carry them, and he might regard it as certain
33  and established that all knights-errant (about whom there were so many full and unimpeachable books) carried well-
34  furnished purses in case of emergency, and likewise carried shirts and a little box of ointment to cure the wounds
35  they received. For in those plains and deserts where they engaged in combat and came out wounded, it was not
36  always that there was someone to cure them, unless indeed they had for a friend some sage magician to succour
37  them at once by fetching through the air upon a cloud some damsel or dwarf with a vial of water of such virtue that
38  by tasting one drop of it they were cured of their hurts and wounds in an instant and left as sound as if they had not
39  received any damage whatever. But in case this should not occur, the knights of old took care to see that their

40  squires were provided with money and other requisites, such as lint and ointments for healing purposes; and when it
41  happened that knights had no squires (which was rarely and seldom the case) they themselves carried everything in
42  cunning saddle-bags that were hardly seen on the horse's croup, as if it were something else of more importance,
43  because, unless for some such reason, carrying saddle-bags was not very favorably regarded among knights-errant.
44  He therefore advised him (and, as his godson so soon to be, he might even command him) never from that time forth
45  to travel without money and the usual requirements, and he would find the advantage of them when he least
46  expected it.

47  Don Quixote promised to follow his advice scrupulously, and it was arranged forthwith that he should
48  watch his armour in a large yard at one side of the inn; so, collecting it all together, Don Quixote placed it on a
49  trough that stood by the side of a well, and bracing his buckler on his arm he grasped his lance and began with a
50  stately air to march up and down in front of the trough, and as he began his march night began to fall.

51  The landlord told all the people who were in the inn about the craze of his guest, the watching of the armor,
52  and the dubbing ceremony he contemplated. Full of wonder at so strange a form of madness, they flocked to see it
53  from a distance, and observed with what composure he sometimes paced up and down, or sometimes, leaning on his
54  lance, gazed on his armour without taking his eyes off it for ever so long; and as the night closed in with a light from
55  the moon so brilliant that it might vie with his that lent it, everything the novice knight did was plainly seen by all.

56  Meanwhile one of the carriers who were in the inn thought fit to water his team, and it was necessary to
57  remove Don Quixote's armour as it lay on the trough; but he seeing the other approach hailed him in a loud voice,
58  "O thou, whoever thou art, rash knight that comest to lay hands on the armour of the most valorous errant that ever
59  girt on sword, have a care what thou dost; touch it not unless thou wouldst lay down thy life as the penalty of thy
60  rashness." The carrier gave no heed to these words (and he would have done better to heed them if he had been
61  heedful of his health), but seizing it by the straps flung the armour some distance from him. Seeing this, Don
62  Quixote raised his eyes to heaven, and fixing his thoughts, apparently, upon his lady Dulcinea, exclaimed, "Aid me,
63  lady mine, in this the first encounter that presents itself to this breast which thou holdest in subjection; let not thy
64  favour and protection fail me in this first jeopardy;" and, with these words and others to the same purpose, dropping
65  his buckler he lifted his lance with both hands and with it smote such a blow on the carrier's head that he stretched
66  him on the ground, so stunned that had he followed it up with a second there would have been no need of a surgeon
67  to cure him. This done, he picked up his armour and returned to his beat with the same serenity as before.

68  Shortly after this, another, not knowing what had happened (for the carrier still lay senseless), came with
69  the same object of giving water to his mules, and was proceeding to remove the armour in order to clear the trough,
70  when Don Quixote, without uttering a word or imploring aid from anyone, once more dropped his buckler and once
71  more lifted his lance, and without actually breaking the second carrier's head into pieces, made more than three of it,
72  for he laid it open in four. At the noise all the people of the inn ran to the spot, and among them the landlord. Seeing
73  this, Don Quixote braced his buckler on his arm, and with his hand on his sword exclaimed, "O Lady of Beauty,
74  strength and support of my faint heart, it is time for thee to turn the eyes of thy greatness on this thy captive knight
75  on the brink of so mighty an adventure." By this he felt himself so inspired that he would not have flinched if all the
76  carriers in the world had assailed him. The comrades of the wounded perceiving the plight they were in began from
77  a distance to shower stones on Don Quixote, who screened himself as best he could with his buckler, not daring to
78  quit the trough and leave his armour unprotected. The landlord shouted to them to leave him alone, for he had
79  already told them that he was mad, and as a madman he would not be accountable even if he killed them all. Still
80  louder shouted Don Quixote, calling them knaves and traitors, and the lord of the castle, who allowed knights-errant
81  to be treated in this fashion, a villain and a low-born knight whom, had he received the order of knighthood, he
82  would call to account for his treachery. "But of you," he cried, "base and vile rabble, I make no account; fling,
83  strike, come on, do all ye can against me, ye shall see what the reward of your folly and insolence will be." This he
84  uttered with so much spirit and boldness that he filled his assailants with a terrible fear, and as much for this reason
85  as at the persuasion of the landlord they left off stoning him, and he allowed them to carry off the wounded, and
86  with the same calmness and composure as before resumed the watch over his armour.

87  But these freaks of his guest were not much to the liking of the landlord, so he determined to cut matters
88  short and confer upon him at once the unlucky order of knighthood before any further misadventure could occur; so,
89  going up to him, he apologized for the rudeness which, without his knowledge, had been offered to him by these low
90  people, who, however, had been well punished for their audacity. As he had already told him, he said, there was no
91  chapel in the castle, nor was it needed for what remained to be done, for, as he understood the ceremonial of the
92  order, the whole point of being dubbed a knight lay in the accolade and in the slap on the shoulder, and that could be
93  administered in the middle of a field; and that he had now done all that was needful as to watching the armor, for all
94  requirements were satisfied by a watch of two hours only, while he had been more than four about it. Don Quixote
95  believed it all, and told him he stood there ready to obey him, and to make an end of it with as much despatch as

96 possible; for, if he were again attacked, and felt himself to be dubbed knight, he would not, he thought, leave a soul
97 alive in the castle, except such as out of respect he might spare at his bidding.
98        Thus warned and menaced, the castellan forthwith brought out a book in which he used to enter the straw
99 and barley he served out to the carriers, and, with a lad carrying a candle-end, and the two damsels already
100 mentioned, he returned to where Don Quixote stood, and bade him kneel down. Then, reading from his account-
101 book as if he were repeating some devout prayer, in the middle of his delivery he raised his hand and gave him a
102 sturdy blow on the neck, and then, with his own sword, a smart slap on the shoulder, all the while muttering between
103 his teeth as if he was saying his prayers. Having done this, he directed one of the ladies to gird on his sword, which
104 she did with great self-possession and gravity, and not a little was required to prevent a burst of laughter at each
105 stage of the ceremony; but what they had already seen of the novice knight's prowess kept their laughter within
106 bounds. On girding him with the sword the worthy lady said to him, "May God make your worship a very fortunate
107 knight, and grant you success in battle." Don Quixote asked her name in order that he might from that time forward
108 know to whom he was beholden for the favour he had received, as he meant to confer upon her some portion of the
109 honour he acquired by the might of his arm. She answered with great humility that she was called La Tolosa, and
110 that she was the daughter of a cobbler of Toledo who lived in the stalls of Sanchobienaya, and that wherever she
111 might be she would serve and esteem him as her lord. Don Quixote said in reply that she would do him a favour if
112 thenceforward she assumed the "Don" and called herself Dona Tolosa. She promised she would, and then the other
113 buckled on his spur, and with her followed almost the same conversation as with the lady of the sword. He asked her
114 name, and she said it was La Molinera, and that she was the daughter of a respectable miller of Antequera; and of
115 her likewise Don Quixote requested that she would adopt the "Don" and call herself Dona Molinera, making offers
116 to her further services and favours.
117        Having thus, with hot haste and speed, brought to a conclusion these never-till-now-seen ceremonies, Don
118 Quixote was on thorns until he saw himself on horseback sallying forth in quest of adventures; and saddling
119 Rocinante at once he mounted, and embracing his host, as he returned thanks for his kindness in knighting him, he
120 addressed him in language so extraordinary that it is impossible to convey an idea of it or report it. The landlord, to
121 get him out of the inn, replied with no less rhetoric though with shorter words, and without calling upon him to pay
122 the reckoning let him go with a Godspeed.

(http://www.spanisharts.com/books/quijote/chapter3.htm)

## Source Analysis

1. In this passage, which of the following statements best describes Don Quixote?
   - I.   Quixote is a bubbling idiot/fool.
   - II.  Quixote is a brave and earnest fool.
   - III. Quixote is a serious, self-important, sincere, self-effacing, slightly senile elderly knight on a mission.

       A.  I only                C.  III only
       B.  II only              D.  II and III

2. The narrative technique?
   A. Omniscient Narration          C. Third Person Objective
   B. Limited Omniscient            D. First Person

3. The landlord's reaction to Don Quixote may best described as
   A. Irritation                    C. Astonishment
   B. Fear                       D. Dread

4. What is the literary purpose of the landlord?
   A. Antagonist                  C. Protagonist
   B. Foil                       D. Extra

5. The book is an allegory or
   A. Polemic
   B. Tirade                    C. Poem
                              D. Parable

6. To be "quixotic" is to
   A. To be whimsical.
   B. To be sarcastic.
   C. To be daunting.
   D. To be creative.

## Words in Context

1. What is the meaning of *requisite* in Line 27?
   A. Obligatory
   B. Optional
   C. Ceremonial
   D. Redundant

2. What is the meaning of *errant* in Line 33?
   A. Pejorative
   B. Perfunctory
   C. Wayward
   D. Focused

3. What is the meaning of *succour/succor* in Line 36?
   A. Assistance
   B. Obstacle
   C. Remedial
   D. Rambunctious

# Lesson 2
## Critical Reading and Writing

### Passage 1

Read the following passage and answer accompanying questions:

1　But these freaks of his guest were not much to the liking of the landlord, so he determined to cut matters short and
2　confer upon him at once the unlucky order of knighthood before any further misadventure could occur; so, going up
3　to him, he apologized for the rudeness which, without his knowledge, had been offered to him by these low people,
4　who, however, had been well punished for their audacity. As he had already told him, he said, there was no chapel in
5　the castle, nor was it needed for what remained to be done, for, as he understood the ceremonial of the order, the
6　whole point of being dubbed a knight lay in the accolade and in the slap on the shoulder, and that could be
7　administered in the middle of a field; and that he had now done all that was needful as to watching the armor, for all
8　requirements were satisfied by a watch of two hours only, while he had been more than four about it. Don Quixote
9　believed it all, and told him he stood there ready to obey him, and to make an end of it with as much dispatch as
10　possible; for, if he were again attacked, and felt himself to be dubbed knight, he would not, he thought, leave a soul
11　alive in the castle, except such as out of respect he might spare at his bidding.
12　　　　Thus warned and menaced, the castellan forthwith brought out a book in which he used to enter the straw
13　and barley he served out to the carriers, and, with a lad carrying a candle-end, and the two damsels already
14　mentioned, he returned to where Don Quixote stood, and bade him kneel down. Then, reading from his account-
15　book as if he were repeating some devout prayer, in the middle of his delivery he raised his hand and gave him a
16　sturdy blow on the neck, and then, with his own sword, a smart slap on the shoulder, all the while muttering between
17　his teeth as if he was saying his prayers. Having done this, he directed one of the ladies to gird on his sword, which
18　she did with great self-possession and gravity, and not a little was required to prevent a burst of laughter at each
19　stage of the ceremony; but what they had already seen of the novice knight's prowess kept their laughter within
20　bounds. On girding him with the sword the worthy lady said to him, "May God make your worship a very fortunate
21　knight, and grant you success in battle." Don Quixote asked her name in order that he might from that time forward
22　know to whom he was beholden for the favour he had received, as he meant to confer upon her some portion of the
23　honour he acquired by the might of his arm. She answered with great humility that she was called La Tolosa, and
24　that she was the daughter of a cobbler of Toledo who lived in the stalls of Sanchobienaya, and that wherever she
25　might be she would serve and esteem him as her lord. Don Quixote said in reply that she would do him a favour if
26　thenceforward she assumed the "Don" and called herself Dona Tolosa. She promised she would, and then the other
27　buckled on his spur, and with her followed almost the same conversation as with the lady of the sword. He asked her
28　name, and she said it was La Molinera, and that she was the daughter of a respectable miller of Antequera; and of
29　her likewise Don Quixote requested that she would adopt the "Don" and call herself Dona Molinera, making offers
30　to her further services and favours. (from *Don Quixote*, chap. 3)

### Command of Evidence

1. Choose the best title for this passage:
   A. Don Quixote: The Hateful Knight　　　C. The Persistent Castellan
   B. The Reluctant Squire　　　D. The Beginning of all Things

2. Which of the following statements is true?
   A. Don Quixote approached the landlord with humility and circumspection.
   B. Don Quixote was full of perfidy.
   C. The landlord reluctantly granted Don Quixote knighthood.
   D. Don Quixote turned back to his home.

3. What is the tone of this passage?
   A. Serious
   B. Vituperative
   C. Humorous
   D. Sardonic

## Passage 2

### Sin in Christopher Marlowe's *Dr. Faustus*

1  "My God, my God, look not so fierce on me! Adders and serpents, let me breathe a while! Ugly hell, gape not!
2  Come not, Lucifer!" This desperate line is uttered by the title character of Christopher Marlowe's famous play,
3  *Doctor Faustus*, as he witnesses hell's gaping mouth ready to swallow him eternally. This speech reveals a man who
4  has fallen so far into the depths of despair that he can travel no further. Yet this descent is no instantaneous fall but
5  rather a long journey that continues slowly but surely downhill throughout the entire play. In *Doctor Faustus*,
6  Christopher Marlowe develops his plot in such a way so as to reflect the development of sin itself.
7      The exposition of the play mirrors the inception of sin. In the beginning of Marlowe's work, Faustus is
8  merely an ambitious scholar with an insatiable longing for knowledge. Although this at first glance seems harmless,
9  it leads to his desire to learn black magic. Similarly, sin is often born when a seemingly harmless enterprise becomes
10  tainted with a corrupt motive or desire. For example, the fall of man recounted in Genesis 3 of the Christian Bible
11  begins with Adam and Eve's longing for knowledge. This in and of itself is not sinful, until it extends into the
12  realms of forbidden knowledge. Through desiring forbidden knowledge, they, like Faustus, sin.
13      The rising action of the play also mirrors the development of sin. Faustus begins his twenty-four years of
14  unlimited power and "happiness" by amusing himself with rather simple questions and harmless entertainments. In
15  the end, however, he ends up indulging in absolute immorality, as exemplified in his desire to sleep with the
16  purportedly most beautiful woman who has ever lived on earth, Helen of Troy. Similarly, the development of sin
17  was a downward spiral that begins at mostly moral activities and ends at utter depravity. Support for this is seen in
18  Romans 1 of the Christian Bible, where Paul speaks of unbelief and its consequences. At first the sinful humans
19  described there try to be wise without God. In the same way, Faustus attempts to gain knowledge through
20  Mephistopheles's teachings, not through the Bible.
21      Finally, the climax of the play mirrors the culmination of sin. At the pinnacle of Marlowe's work, Faustus
22  is dragged off to hell by Mephistopheles, Lucifer, and other demons. Similarly, the culmination of sin is that a man
23  is doomed to hell. "For the wages of sin is death," as Paul writes in Romans 6 of the Christian Bible. The climax of
24  the tragedy and the culmination of sin are entirely the same: damnation to eternal torture in hell.
25      Through his careful maneuvering of the various twists and turns of plot development, Christopher Marlowe
26  patterns the story of Doctor Faustus after the development of sin itself. From the exposition through the rising action
27  to the climax of the play, Doctor Faustus matches the inception, development, and culmination of sin according to
28  Christian theology: "O, it strikes, it strikes! Now, body, turn to air, or Lucifer will bear thee quick to hell! O soul, be
29  changed into little water drops and fall into the ocean, ne'er be found!" (John)

## Command of Evidence

1. Choose the best thesis for this passage:
   A. Through his careful maneuvering of the various twists and turns of plot development, Christopher
      Marlowe patterns the story of Doctor Faustus after the development of sin itself.
   B. The rising action of the play also mirrors the development of sin.
   C. Finally, the climax of the play mirrors the culmination of sin
   D. In Doctor Faustus, Christopher Marlowe develops his plot in such a way so as to reflect the
      development of sin itself.

2. Which of the following statements is true about Passage 2?
   A. Faustus is a victim.
   B. Thes story of Faustus is the story of the destructiveness of sin.
   C. Marlowe's play is mostly autobiographical.
   D. The play is a parody of Elizabethan England.

## Words in Context

1. The word *inception* in Line 7 means
   A. Commencement
   B. Termination
   C. Cessation
   D. Moderation

2. The word *insatiable* in Lines 8 means
   A. Satisfied
   B. Fulfilled
   C. Inviolate
   D. Unquenchable

# Lesson 3
## SAT Essay

### Student Response 1

*Prompt:* Recount an incident or time when you experienced failure. How did it affect you, and what lessons did you learn?

1      I approach this lesson with extreme pain in the back of my legs. From the top of my thighs, down to the
2  back of my calf, I regret learning this lesson. It was nearly $90^0$ the day before the SAT's, so instead of studying
3  inside, I decided to study outside at the beach. It was perfect weather at the beach, and as I spread out my towel, I
4  knew this was the right decision. My siblings hurriedly passed around the sunscreen, and I waited for them to finish.
5  After five minutes, I finally received the sunscreen.
6      Let me explain something: I've a pattern for applying sunscreen. I sunscreen my arms, then my shoulders,
7  my neck, my face, and last, my legs. The problem with this, as I've now learned, is that by the time I get to the back
8  of my legs, what little sunscreen I have left for my face, is gone. (Actually, this is stretching the truth a little: enough
9  was left to leave a pristine sunscreen handprint which, much to my dismay, didn't burn, leaving a gleaming white
10 handprint among the backs of my glowing red legs.) Nonetheless, after finishing, I lay down on my towel and
11 cracked open my SAT study guide. Life was good.
12     Two hours of study (and a short nap) later, we were packing up to go home. As I stood up and prepared to
13 shake off my towel, I heard my mother sigh loudly.
14     "You did it again," she said.
15     (Unfortunately, this wasn't a first for me.) I wrinkled my nose and turned my head to inspect. Sure enough,
16 my legs were red. I puckered my face but didn't say anything. In such circumstances I'm not sure what to say.
17     The thing about sunburn is, it never hurts immediately. It's like a mosquito bite: it doesn't itch until you
18 realize it's there, and the more you think about it, the more it itches.
19     I thought about it a lot.
20     By the time I arrived home, it was unbearably itchy. I fled to the medicine closet, fished out some lotion,
21 and lathered it excessively on my burning legs. It didn't really help.
22     Now, my parents always recommend two things when I'm sunburned:
23         1.  Apply aloe vera.
24         2.  Drink lots of water.
25 So I did. After running to the store for the aloe, I generously applied it every two hours or so. It was magnificent!
26 However, I'm getting sidetracked; this lesson isn't about sunburn treatment.
27     The next morning was the SAT. Before leaving I rubbed on aloe and packed a generous amount of water
28 bottles (perhaps five). I was determined to rid myself of this malady as quickly as possible.
29     The problem began as I walked into the school. It was relatively humid inside, and as I sat down at my
30 designated seat, the aloe on the back of my legs began melting to form glue-like paste. This didn't bother me at first,
31 but then I tried adjusting my legs.
32     I couldn't.
33     The aloe vera was sticky like glue! My legs stuck, suctioned to the chair by this heaven-sent monstrosity! I
34 tried not to panic. I was fine sitting here for the first 20 minutes of the test, and there were only 2 hours and 40
35 minutes left. I'd be fine, . . . right?
36     Here's where the double hit kicks in: remember advice 2? Well, there aren't many breaks during the SAT's,
37 and by the time the first one arrived, I really needed to go. I sat there struggling silently for a moment before finally
38 jumping up. With a loud popping sound, my legs unsealed. Everyone stared. I skulked outside the classroom with a
39 red face. It was mortifying. Unfortunately, that's how the remainder of the SAT's went. I stuck to the seat during
40 test time, and I ran to the restroom during break time. By the time SAT's ended, I had decided that sunburn was
41 much worse than the SAT's. (Sydney)

## Student Response 2

*Prompt:* What is most necessary to succeed: intelligence or determination?

1     We are surrounded by stories of success through impossible odds throughout the whole of our lives.
2     Whether the stories are from history, literature, or family, the most popular question that arises after the telling of
3     such a story is "How did they succeed, what was it that pulled them through?"
4     In the gym where I run is a photograph with a quote. The picture is of a man running up a steep flight of
5     endless stairs, sweating and exhausted, but still going. The quote reads, "The difference between those who succeed
6     and those who don't, is not a lack of strength, of training, or of brainpower, but a lack of perseverance." I believe
7     that perseverance and determination gets you through a race, whether it is long or short, a literal race, or a race you
8     must run in your life.
9     **Many say that it is impossible to make wise and intelligent choices with just determination, that you**
10     **will just blunder into rocks and keep hitting against them, not getting anywhere.** But if we truly had the
11     knowledge of how hard a task would be, if we truly realized and calculated how great a challenge we were taking
12     on, wouldn't that cause us to falter and even turn from the hard work, feeling we cannot succeed, even when we
13     have not even tried yet?
14     Part of the beauty of J. R. R. Tolkien's *Lord of the Rings* trilogy is the innocence of small Frodo when he
15     declares at the council of Elrond, "I will go." He volunteers to go and do a task that the cleverest of them could not
16     have succeeded at. Though he "does not know the way" and doesn't have the "smarts," he is determined, and he
17     does succeed to fulfill his promise. Determination is what gets him up Mount Doom, whether it was his own
18     determination, or that of his friend, Samwise Gamgee. He does not calculate the cost as the other "smart people"
19     did; he just knew that he could succeed.
20     Many people feel cheated when they have a friend or relative who achieves more than they can because
21     they are just "so smart." The truth is, these "so smart" friends and relatives miss out on a lot of life's lessons by not
22     knowing how to work hard and keep up their endurance. Life's best lessons are learned through hard work and
23     determination. You become a better person when you have struggled and succeeded than if you have no obstacles.
24     Why is the saying "If at first you don't succeed, try, try again" so popular? Because sticking with things, seeing
25     them through even though it is strenuous, and not giving up—that is one of the most desirable character traits a
26     person can have.
27     We hear of athletes in sports making amazing comebacks and meeting extraordinary goals. In the movie
28     *Cinderella Man* starring Russell Crowe, a good boxer breaks his hand, is fired, is caught up in the Great Depression,
29     and then loses everything except his family. He can barely feed his family, much less himself. But when he gets one
30     more chance in the boxing ring, he takes it; despite his broken hand, he goes on to win back his name. He is broken,
31     beaten, and facing one of the most formidable boxers for his last fight. But he remembers that he is fighting for his
32     family, and he becomes determined.
33     How do they do it? Determination. Perseverance.
34     Sure, it is good to be smart. But in the end, when you have nothing left but determination, it will bring you
35     through. Determination gets us through the race, pushes us to win the battle, and teaches us valuable lessons along
36     the way. (Eva)

## Close Reading

1.  In Student Response 1
    A. The student dreaded the SAT and ate too much the day before.
    B. The student regrettably was sunburned the day before the SAT.
    C. The student missed her SAT exam.
    D. The student put the wrong medicine on her sunburn and missed the SAT.

2.  In Student Response 2
    A. The student argues that determination is more important than intelligence.
    B. The student argues that determination and intelligence are equally important.
    C. The student argues that intelligence is more important than determination.
    D. The student argues that neither determination nor intelligence is important.

3.  In Response 1 the author organizes her essay
    A. Chronologically.                   C. Stream of consciousness.
    B. Topically.                         D. Alphabetically.

4.  In Response 2 the author organizes her essay
    A. By stating a rhetorical questions and then offering a series of anecdotes from literature and real life.
    B. By offering a series of anecdotes from literature and real life.
    C. By stating a thesis and offering several examples.
    D. By a series of bullet points.

5.  Student Response Essay 1 can be improved by
    I.   Giving more specific examples.
    II.  Strengthening transitions.
    III. Removing personal examples.
    IV.  Making the essay longer.
    V.   Clearly stating the thesis and tying it to the topic.

        A. I, II, IV, and V        C. II and III
        B. III and IV              D. V

6.  Problems in Student Response Essay 2 include which of the following:
    I.   Examples are not tied closely to the thesis.
    II.  Transitions are weak.
    III. There are too many personal examples.
    IV.  The essay is too short.
    V.   The thesis is not clearly stated nor tied to the topic.

        A. I                 C. II and III
        B. II               D. I, II, IV, and V

7.  Where is the main point of the Student Response 1?
    A. Lines 3–5                          C. Lines 13–15
    B. Lines 8–9                          D. NONE

8.  Where is the main point of the Student Response 2?
    A. Lines 2–4                          C. Lines 18–20
    B. Lines 8–9                          D. Lines 32–34

9. What is a significant stylistic problem in Student Essay 2?
   A. First person and third person are used interchangeably.
   B. Second-person pronouns are used.
   C. Transitions are weak.
   D. There are agreement problems.

10. Criticism of Student Response 1 is that
    I. The essay's position is unclear or limited. The critical thinking in the essay is weak and not supported by sufficient or relevant examples and details.
    II. The central idea is poorly defined.
    III. The essay is poorly organized, and in general the essay lacks coherence.
    IV. The language is ordinary and uninspiring.
    V. The sentence structure lacks variety and complexity.
    VI. There are serious grammar mistakes.

    A. I, II, and III                  C. VI
    B. I, II, III, IV, and V           D. IV, V, and VI

11. Criticism of Student Response 2 is that
    I. The essay's position is unclear or limited. The critical thinking in the essay is weak and not supported by sufficient or relevant examples and details.
    II. The central idea is poorly defined.
    III. The essay is poorly organized, and in general the essay lacks coherence.
    IV. The language is ordinary and uninspiring,
    V. The sentence structure lacks variety and complexity,
    VI. There are serious grammar mistakes.

    A. I, II, and III                  D. IV, V, and VI
    B. I, II, III, IV, and V           E. NONE
    C. VI

12. What score would the student responses receive?
    Student Response 1 receives __. Student Response 2 receives __.

## Grammar and Usage

Choose the best grammar/usage form in bold sentence(s).

Student Response 2, Lines 9–10

A. NONE
B. Many say that it is impossible to make wise and intelligent choices with just determination, which you will just blunder into rocks and keep hitting against them, not getting anywhere.
C. Many say that it is impossible to make wise and intelligent choices with just determination that you will just blunder into rocks and keep hitting against them, not getting anywhere.
D. Many say that it is impossible to make wise and intelligent choices with just determination, that one will just blunder into rocks and keep hitting against them, not getting anywhere.

# Lesson 4
## Reading: Document-Based Analysis

### "What to the Slave Is the Fourth of July?"
### Frederick Douglass (July 5, 1852)

(Extract from a speech delivered by Frederick Douglass at Rochester, N.Y.)

1   *Fellow Citizens*:
2       Pardon me, allow me to ask, why am I called upon to speak here today? What have I or those I represent to
3   do with your national independence? Are the great principles of political freedom and of natural justice, embodied in
4   that Declaration of Independence, extended to us? And am I, therefore, called upon to bring our humble offering to
5   the national altar, and to confess the benefits, and express devout gratitude for the blessings resulting from your
6   independence to us?
7       Would to God, both for your sakes and ours, which an affirmative answer could be truthfully returned to
8   these questions. Then would my task be light, and my burden easy and delightful. For who is there so cold that a
9   nation's sympathy could not warm him? Who so obdurate and dead to the claims of gratitude, which would not
10   thankfully acknowledge such priceless benefits? Who so stolid and selfish that would not give his voice to swell the
11   hallelujahs of a nation's jubilee, when the chains of servitude had been torn from his limbs? I am not that man. In a
12   case like that, the dumb might eloquently speak, and the "lame man leap like a hart."
13       But such is not the state of the case. I say it with a sad sense of disparity between us. I am not included
14   within the pale of this glorious anniversary! Your high independence only reveals the immeasurable distance
15   between us. The blessings in which you this day rejoice are not enjoyed in common. The rich inheritance of justice,
16   liberty, prosperity, and independence bequeathed by your fathers is shared by you, not by me. The sunlight that
17   brought life and healing to you has brought stripes and death to me. This Fourth of July is yours, not mine. You may
18   rejoice, I must mourn. To drag a man in fetters into the grand illuminated temple of liberty, and call upon him to join
19   you in joyous anthems, were inhuman mockery and sacrilegious irony. Do you mean, citizens, to mock me, by
20   asking me to speak today? If so, there is a parallel to your conduct. And let me warn you, that it is dangerous to copy
21   the example of a nation whose crimes, towering up to heaven, were thrown down by the breath of the Almighty,
22   burying that nation in irrecoverable ruin. I can to-day take up the lament of a peeled and woe-smitten people.
        (http://teachingamericanhistory.org/library/document/what-to-the-slave-is-the-fourth-of-july/)

## Close Reading

1. What is the purpose of this speech?
   A. To ensure religious liberty for all faiths
   B. To require toleration for all Protestant faiths
   C. To show the hypocrisy of white Americans
   D. To encourage Americans to grant more rights to African Americans

2. Why would this speech be necessary in 1852?
   I. Douglass was a slave.
   II. Slavery importation was still legal.
   III. Slavery was legal in the United States.
   IV. Abraham Lincoln has just been elected.

   A. I and II                    C. II and III
   B. III                          D. I and IV

3. Which group would benefit from this speech?
   A. African Americans
   B. Southern planters
   C. Mormons
   D. Native Americans

4. The best interpretation of "Would to God, both for your sakes and ours, that an affirmative answer could be truthfully returned to these questions. Then would my task be light, and my burden easy and delightful" (Lines 6–7)?
   A. Douglass is a loyal American and is willing to overlook certain social injustices like slavery in order to honor a greater cause: American independence.
   B. Douglass abhors slavery and its effect on blacks, and is conflicted when he considers the freedoms granted other Americans, but he still would rather live in the United States than any other country.
   C. Douglass is grieved and angry that he, a member of an enslaved race, is asked to address a mostly free audience enjoying the benefits of the Declaration of Independence.
   D. Douglas is amused when he considers the irony of a freed slave speaking to an audience of free Americans.

5. Which lines provide the best evidence for the answer to the previous question?
   A. Lines 1–2
   B. Lines 2–5
   C. Lines 13–18
   D. Lines 19–21.

## Words in Context

1. What is the meaning of *devout* in Line 5?
   A. Insincere
   B. Earnest
   C. Hypocritical
   D. Redundant

2. What is the meaning of *bequeathed* in Line 16?
   A. Inherited
   B. Won
   C. Removed
   D. Bestowed

3. What is the meaning of *sacrilegious irony* in Line 19?
   A. Profound
   B. Obstinate
   C. Irreverent
   D. Obdurate

4. What is the meaning of *lament* in line 22?
   A. Dirge
   B. Song
   C. Essay
   D. Chant

# Lesson 5
## Math: Algebra, Arithmetic Problem Solving and Data Analysis, and Passport to Advanced Math

### Arithmetic Problem Solving

1. The fourth and eighth of a number are together equal to 36. What is the number?
   A. 96
   B. 95
   C. 106
   D. 28

2. A man left half his estate to his widow, and a fifth to his daughter. If they both together received $28,000, what was the value of his estate?
   A. $60,000
   B. $35,000
   C. $40,000
   D. $38,000

3. Henry gave a third of his marbles to one boy, and a fourth to another boy. He finds that he gave the boys a total of 14 marbles. How many did he have at first?
   A. 22
   B. 25
   C. 21
   D. 24

4. Two men own a third and two-fifths of a mill respectively. If their part of the property is worth $22,000, what is the value of the mill?
   A. $30,000
   B. $32,000
   C. $28,000
   D. $18,000

5. A fruit seller sold one-fourth of his oranges in the forenoon, and three-fifths of them in the afternoon. If he sold a total of 255 oranges, how many did he have at the start?
   A. 280
   B. 300
   C. 320
   D. 340

6. The half, third, and fifth of a number are together equal to 93. Find the number.
   A. 85
   B. 90
   C. 95
   D. 88

7. Mr. A bought one-fourth of an estate of land, Mr. B one-half, and Mr. C one-sixth. If they together bought 55,000 square feet, how large was the estate property?
   A. 40,000 sq. ft.
   B. 90,000 sq. ft.
   C. 50,000 sq. ft.
   D. 60,000 sq. ft

8. The wind broke off two-sevenths of a pine tree, and afterward two-fifths (of the original tree) more. If the parts broken off measured 48 feet, how high was the tree at first?
   A. 56 ft.
   B. 38 ft.
   C. 70 ft.
   D. 72 ft.

9. A man spaded up three-eighths of his garden, and his son spaded two-ninths of it. In all they spaded 43 square rods. How large was the garden?
   A. 68 sq. rods
   B. 70 sq. rods
   C. 72 sq. rods
   D. 74 sq. rods

10. A four-digit number has $W$ as the thousands digit, $X$ as the hundreds digit, $Y$ as the tens digit, and $Z$ as the ones digit. Which of the following is a picture of the number?
    A. $10^3W + 10^2X + 10Y + Z$
    B. $10^3W + 10^2X + 10^0Z + Y$
    C. $100W + 10X + Y + D$
    D. $1000W + 100X + 10Z + Y$

# Chapter 25   Song of the Redeemed
# Isaiah 35

> *Memory Verse:*
>
> The desert and the parched land will be glad;
>   the wilderness will rejoice and blossom.
> Like the crocus, it will burst into bloom;
>   it will rejoice greatly and shout for joy.
> The glory of Lebanon will be given to it,
>   the splendor of Carmel and Sharon;
> they will see the glory of the LORD,
>   the splendor of our God. —Isaiah 35:1–2

The prophet Isaiah wrote Isaiah 35 soon after the death of the mighty King Uzziah. Under the long reign of Uzziah (ca. 783–742 BC), in fame second only to Solomon's, Judah reached the summit of its power. Uzziah built up the economic resources of the country as well as its military strength. He conquered the Philistines and the Arabians, and he received tribute from the Ammonites; Uzziah fortified the country and reorganized and reequipped the army. "In Jerusalem he made devices invented for use on the towers and on the corner defenses so that soldiers could shoot arrows and hurl large stones from the walls" (2 Chronicles 26:15). His success as king, administrator, and commander in chief of the army made him ruler over the largest realm of Judah since the division of the kingdom into north and south.

But Uzziah's strength became his weakness. "He grew proud, to his destruction," and attempted to usurp the power of the priesthood, even entering the temple of the Lord to burn incense on the altar, a privilege reserved for the priest (26:16 NRSV). Azariah, the chief priest, followed by eighty priests, pleaded with Uzziah: "Leave the sanctuary!" (26:18–21). Uzziah refused, and God struck him with leprosy.

In these post-Christian times, let this be a warning. Presidents and kings go and come, but our Lord never changes and is always here. While God is merciful and loving, he does not tolerate violation of his Word. King Uzziah found a direct correlation between his acceptance of God's authority and word and Judah's prosperity. In other words, Judah prospered as its leaders obeyed God; likewise America will prosper if its leaders obey God.

It was into a world in transition that Isaiah brought his message. Isaiah was born and lived his whole life in Judah. He was married to a prophetess and had two children of promise (7:3; 8:3). Isaiah was a man who gave his prophetic warnings to a world that did not listen.

## Journal Question

Rewrite Isaiah 35 to reflect your own life. For instance, it might be something like this:

> The muddy soccer field and my math scores will be better;
>   my life so full of failure will yet be redeemed.
> Like the crocus, it will burst into bloom;
>   I will rejoice greatly and shout for joy.
> I shall yet make the soccer team;
>   I shall yet do better in math.

Continue by writing your own song of redemption!

# Lesson 1
## Evidence-Based Reading and Writing

### Literary Choice

#### *Silas Marner*

*Silas Marner*, by George Eliot (pen name for Mary Ann Evans), is one of the most successful novels of the nineteenth century. The main theme concerns redemption. Poor, old, odd Silas Marner is charged for perfidy that he did not commit. In personal disappointment and hurt, he withdraws from society and becomes a hermit. Only later in the novel, after he finds and cares for an orphan girl, is his life changed. Here is the first part of chapter 1.

1　　　In the days when the spinning-wheels hummed busily in the farmhouses—and even great ladies, clothed in
2　silk and thread-lace, had their toy spinning-wheels of polished oak—there might be seen in districts far away among
3　the lanes, or deep in the bosom of the hills, certain pallid undersized men, who, by the side of the brawny country-
4　folk, looked like the remnants of a disinherited race. The shepherd's dog barked fiercely when one of these alien-
5　looking men appeared on the upland, dark against the early winter sunset; for what dog likes a figure bent under a
6　heavy bag?—and these pale men rarely stirred abroad without that mysterious burden. The shepherd himself, though
7　he had good reason to believe that the bag held nothing but flaxen thread, or else the long rolls of strong linen spun
8　from that thread, was not quite sure that this trade of weaving, indispensable though it was, could be carried on
9　entirely without the help of the Evil One. In that far-off time superstition clung easily round every person or thing
10　that was at all unwonted, or even intermittent and occasional merely, like the visits of the peddler or the knife-
11　grinder. No one knew where wandering men had their homes or their origin; and how was a man to be explained
12　unless you at least knew somebody who knew his father and mother? To the peasants of old times, the world outside
13　their own direct experience was a region of vagueness and mystery: to their untraveled thought a state of wandering
14　was a conception as dim as the winter life of the swallows that came back with the spring; and even a settler, if he
15　came from distant parts, hardly ever ceased to be viewed with a remnant of distrust, which would have prevented
16　any surprise if a long course of inoffensive conduct on his part had ended in the commission of a crime; especially if
17　he had any reputation for knowledge, or showed any skill in handicraft. All cleverness, whether in the rapid use of
18　that difficult instrument the tongue, or in some other art unfamiliar to villagers, was in itself suspicious: honest folk,
19　born and bred in a visible manner, were mostly not overwise or clever—at least, not beyond such a matter as
20　knowing the signs of the weather; and the process by which rapidity and dexterity of any kind were acquired was so
21　wholly hidden, that they partook of the nature of conjuring. In this way it came to pass that those scattered linen-
22　weavers—emigrants from the town into the country—were to the last regarded as aliens by their rustic neighbors,
23　and usually contracted the eccentric habits which belong to a state of loneliness.
24　　　In the early years of this century, such a linen-weaver, named Silas Marner, worked at his vocation in a
25　stone cottage that stood among the nutty hedgerows near the village of Raveloe, and not far from the edge of a
26　deserted stone-pit. The questionable sound of Silas's loom, so unlike the natural cheerful trotting of the winnowing-
27　machine, or the simpler rhythm of the flail, had a half-fearful fascination for the Raveloe boys, who would often
28　leave off their nutting or birds'-nesting to peep in at the window of the stone cottage, counterbalancing a certain awe
29　at the mysterious action of the loom, by a pleasant sense of scornful superiority, drawn from the mockery of its
30　alternating noises, along with the bent, tread-mill attitude of the weaver. But sometimes it happened that Marner,
31　pausing to adjust an irregularity in his thread, became aware of the small scoundrels, and, though chary of his time,
32　he liked their intrusion so ill that he would descend from his loom, and, opening the door, would fix on them a gaze
33　that was always enough to make them take to their legs in terror. For how was it possible to believe that those large
34　brown protuberant eyes in Silas Marner's pale face really saw nothing very distinctly that was not close to them, and
35　not rather that their dreadful stare could dart cramp, or rickets, or a wry mouth at any boy who happened to be in the
36　rear? They had, perhaps, heard their fathers and mothers hint that Silas Marner could cure folks' rheumatism if he
37　had a mind, and add, still more darkly, that if you could only speak the devil fair enough, he might save you the cost
38　of the doctor. Such strange lingering echoes of the old demon-worship might perhaps even now be caught by the
39　diligent listener among the grey-haired peasantry; for the rude mind with difficulty associates the ideas of power and
40　benignity. A shadowy conception of power that by much persuasion can be induced to refrain from inflicting harm,
41　is the shape most easily taken by the sense of the Invisible in the minds of men who have always been pressed close
42　by primitive wants, and to whom a life of hard toil has never been illuminated by any enthusiastic religious faith. To

43  them pain and mishap present a far wider range of possibilities than gladness and enjoyment: their imagination is
44  almost barren of the images that feed desire and hope, but is all overgrown by recollections that are a perpetual
45  pasture to fear. "Is there anything you can fancy that you would like to eat?" I once said to an old laboring man, who
46  was in his last illness, and who had refused all the food his wife had offered him. "No," he answered, "I've never
47  been used to nothing but common victual, and I can't eat that." Experience had bred no fancies in him that could
48  raise the phantasm of appetite.

(http://etc.usf.edu/lit2go/196/silas-marner/4233/part-1-chapter-1/)

## Source Analysis

1.  The author describes the protagonist Silas Marner as
    A.  An ordinary man who deserves no special attention.
    B.  A recluse who has odd habits.
    C.  An immoral, wild man.
    D.  NONE

2.  What lines support this (above) characterization of the protagonist?
    A. Lines 6–9.                    C. Lines 26–30
    B. Lines 9–12                    D. Lines 40–42.

## Words in Context

1.  What is the meaning of *pallid* in Line 3?
    A.  Obscure                      C.  Shallow
    B.  Sallow                       D.  Innocent

2.  What is the meaning of *dexterity* in Line 20?
    A.  Clumsiness                   C.  Adroitness
    B.  Perspicuity                  D.  Sanguinity

3.  What is the meaning of *phantasm* Line 48?
    A.  Apparition                   C.  Idol
    B.  Icon                         D.  Goblin

# Lesson 2

## Critical Reading and Writing

### Command of Evidence

Read the following passage and answer accompanying questions:

1 In today's society, image is everything. We wake up, turn on the TV, and images immediately bombard us. Teens
2 post image-filled posters all over their rooms. **Billboards whizz by us on our way to work or school.**
3 Advertisements are posted at the work bulletin board, and telephone poles are dripping with image-filled ads. We
4 have clearly become an image-based culture, so it is no wonder that Allen Ginsberg claimed, "Whoever controls the
5 media—the images—controls the culture."
6     **Because our society is immersed in images, they greatly affect our culture today.** Last year I witnessed
7 what an amazing and far-reaching effect images can have on our culture. The big hit last year in women's fashion,
8 the "bump-it," was advertised in every other TV commercial across the country. The bump-it, a hairpiece that
9 supposedly gives hair volume and body, was all the rave. Every teenage girl dreamed of buying one and many did—
10 my sister included. She saw the pictures on the bump-it commercial of a gorgeous young lady with silky hair and a
11 strange, but considered by most, beautiful lump on her head. This lump, of course, was caused by the bump-it. The
12 commercial showed panoramic views of multiple young ladies with "voluminous" hair. The camera zoomed in and
13 out, the music sounded, and everyone looked happy and fashionable. The bump-it company, however, did not stop
14 at television commercials. The bump-it image was disseminated in all the popular magazines and ads. The women of
15 our culture were in awe. They saw the images. They wanted that hair. So, influenced by these images, my sister and
16 her friends along with almost every other teenage girl in the country went out and bought the $40 bump-it. My sister
17 was ecstatic. She was finally going to look like the images that had bombarded her for months. She took her bump-it
18 to her room. By the end of the day, however, she was close to tears. The bump-it was a disaster and, I must admit,
19 quite amusing. She emerged from the bedroom, and her head looked like a tumor was growing out of it. All of the
20 teenage girls agreed that they were duped by images once again, and quickly did away with their bump-its. Clearly,
21 whoever "controlled the images [of the bump-it company] controlled the [teenage girl] culture" (for a short time
22 anyway.)
23     **George Orwell's famous novel, *1984*, further illuminates the far-reaching effect of on a culture.** The
24 society in Orwell's *1984* is mercilessly controlled by a huge and inexorable government called "Big Brother." This
25 government has control of every aspect of its citizen's lives. Big Brother decides who marries whom, when sexual
26 intercourse is appropriate, who works for whom, and even where one lives. Big Brother is able to wield such
27 complete control over its citizens through images. The citizens of this society begin to rely and trust in their
28 government, Big Brother, because the government bombards them with the image of a benevolent and a strong-
29 faced man who is said to be the omniscient (though elusive) leader of the government. The citizens are also forced to
30 keep a giant telescreen in every room. These telescreens constantly bombard them with image-filled advertisements
31 and propaganda designed to make the Big-Brother government appear to be in charge, successful, and benevolent.
32 Sadly, because of these constant images, the young generation in the Big-Brother society has faith in their monstrous
33 government and relies on it to solve all of their problems.
34     Undoubtedly, culture is not only influenced, but is also manipulated, by images. The far-reaching effects
35 of culture can be seen in both my sister's bump-it experience and through the reliance of Orwell's citizens on their
36 big government. My sister and her friends relied on images to determine their actions, just as the citizens of the Big-
37 Brother society relied on the telescreen images to determine their actions. Images in today's society, and in Orwell's
38 Big-Brother society, determined the citizens' actions, which, in turn, determined the citizens' culture. (Sarah)

## Close Reading

1. The following statement is the thesis of this essay:
   A. Media images are powerful creators of culture but not as important as politics.
   B. Whoever controls the media images controls culture.
   C. *1984* is an important book for everyone to read.
   D. NONE

2. The author offers the anecdote in Lines 6–21 to
   A. Illustrate the impact of the media on everyday life.
   B. Show how shallow and irresponsible teenagers can be.
   C. Warn readers about "bump-its."
   D. Alert consumers to fraud.

3. The author mentions George Orwell's novel *1984* to
   A. Promote twentieth-century British literature.
   B. Warn readers about the evil of Nazism.
   C. Suggest one outcome of unshackled media control of culture.
   D. Warn readers about the dangers of "Big Brother."

## Grammar and Usage

Choose the best grammar/usage form in bold sentence(s).

1. Line 2
   A. NONE.
   B. Billboards whizz by us on our way to work or to school.
   C. Billboards whizz by us going to work or to school.
   D. Billboards whizz by us on our way to work and to school.

2. Line 6
   A. NONE
   B. Our society, immersed in images, greatly affects our culture.
   C. Our media-saturated society greatly affects our culture.
   D. Images in today's society greatly affect our culture.

3. Line 22
   A. NONE
   B. George Orwell's famous novel, *1984*, further illuminates the far-reaching effect images have on a culture.
   C. George Orwell's famous novel, *1984*, farther illuminates the far-reaching effect images has on a culture.
   D. George Orwell's famous novel, *1984*, further illuminates the far-reaching affect images has on a culture.

## Words in Context

What does *omniscient* mean in Line 29?
A. All-powerful
B. Innovative
C. Vituperative
D. Sagacious

The following are two analyses of John F. Kennedy's inaugural address at the Capitol Building on a snowy Friday, January 20, 1964 (http://www.bartleby.com/124/pres56.html).

## Passage 1

1  In order to fully comprehend a piece of writing, it is crucial to understand the purpose and intent of the writer.
2  Because of the vast amount of rhetorical devices used in John F. Kennedy's inaugural address, it is easy to become
3  bogged down in how he used rhetorical devices to support his purpose and consequently forget the purpose itself.
4  Because of this, one should not break down the speech into tiny incoherent bits of rhetorical devices, but should
5  rather examine the rhetorical devices while keeping the purpose of the speech as a whole in mind. Reading this
6  speech, it becomes apparent that the purpose of the speech is to further unity and idealistic change in a world of
7  turmoil and division. An underlying theme of reverence and formality is also apparent throughout. Therefore, in
8  analyzing the most prevalent rhetorical devices, one must consider how these devices fit and further these prevailing
9  purposes and themes.
10      The most prevalent rhetorical device that Kennedy incorporates into his inauguration address is parallelism.
11  The abundant use of parallelism gives the speech a sense of coherence, direction, and ultimately, unity. For example,
12  the sentence "born in this century, tempered by war, disciplined by a hard and bitter peace, proud of our ancient
13  heritage" is very direct and coherent. No words are wasted, and the statements all share the same structure, thus
14  helping to convey a feeling of unity and harmony. Not only short statements but also whole paragraphs are united by
15  parallel structure. All four of the paragraphs from the thirteenth to the seventeenth start with the words "Let both
16  sides." This conveys unification on an even larger scale. In these parallel paragraphs, Kennedy is urging "those
17  nations who would make themselves our adversary" to cooperate with our endeavors and share our dreams. This
18  urgency requires unity on a large scale and consequently parallelism on a large scale.
19      Another very prevalent rhetorical device in this speech is antithesis. The use of antithesis in this particular
20  speech helps to further the purpose of idealism and change. For example, the first sentence, "We observe today not a
21  victory of party but a celebration of freedom," tells the reader that previously a change in administration was thought
22  of as a victory and not a celebration, but that is not the case anymore. In the statements "Let both sides explore what
23  problems unite us instead of belaboring those problems which divide us" and "Let both sides seek to invoke the
24  wonders of science instead of it terrors" the phrase "instead of" not only creates antithesis, but also creates a feeling
25  of improvement and change. These hortative sentences are also effective in bringing the audience closer to the
26  speaker, enabling the audience to trust John F. Kennedy and his idealism.
27      Though unity and change are the main purpose of this speech, reverence and formality also underlie the entire
28  work. Kennedy's use of archaic language such as "foe, asunder, writ, and forbear" gives the writing a reverent,
29  formal characteristic. Also, the figures of speech and use of imagery make us deeply revere our country and our
30  freedom. For example, phrases such as "riding the tiger," "dark powers of destruction," "chains of poverty, "and
31  "torch of freedom" help us vividly see others' desperate state and our unwavering liberty. This pathos-filled
32  language and imagery make us not only respect our country but also our heritage and history.
33      Clearly, through the rhetorical devices of parallelism, antithesis, archaic language, and imagery, John F.
34  Kennedy was able to clearly and eloquently portray his purpose—the purpose of unity and idealism. Although the
35  text is replete with many additional rhetorical devices, analyzing the purpose and function of only the prevalent
36  devices and how they contributed to the entirety of the speech helped us to understand not only what Kennedy is
37  saying but also how and why he says what he does. (Sarah)

## Passage 2

1   After winning the presidential election of 1961 by a small margin, John F. Kennedy began his presidency with a
2   strong start. His inaugural address, concise and memorable, blended his great patriotism and passion for his position.
3   While the speech's respectful eloquence is appropriate for the occasion of an inauguration, its youthful energy and
4   look to the future make it distinctly John F. Kennedy's. Above all, Kennedy delivered potent words that not only
5   reminded Americans of their blessings and duty but joined together a nation not yet enthusiastic about their next
6   president. Although much skepticism confronted Kennedy around his election, age, and religion, he quickly proved
7   his nation wrong in exactly 1,343 words.
8       Regardless of the topic Kennedy addressed, he never failed to clarify his position. Initially, he makes his
9   case of clarification. "We observe today not a victory of party but a celebration of freedom—symbolizing an end as
10  well as a beginning—signifying renewal as well as change." Kennedy never lost sight of his audience and their
11  expectations of him. He made it clear that he stood before them for a greater purpose than politics. He was here to
12  remind Americans of their duty: "We dare not forget today that we are the heirs of that first revolution; . . . we dare
13  not meet a powerful challenge at odds and split asunder." He is here to join nations for a greater cause: "To those old
14  allies whose cultural and spiritual origins we share, we pledge the loyalty of faithful friends; . . . we offer a special
15  pledge to convert our good words into good deeds—in a new alliance . . . both sides begin anew the quest for
16  peace." He was here to make a difference. Kennedy made it clear that their compassion as a nation was "not because
17  the communists may be doing it, not because we seek their votes, but because it is right." Filled with both respect
18  and conviction, Kennedy used a combination of patriotic and declarative sentences to establish the driving force
19  behind his presidency.
20      Kennedy's use of repetitive words, including parallelism, emphasized the key points of his speech. For
21  example, he frequently began his sentences with "We dare not," "Let both sides," "To those," and "So let us." These
22  are sentences that imply conviction. Ultimately, if Kennedy could not win the hearts of Americans through his plans
23  toward the future, he sought to win their hearts through the common heritage they all possessed. At times Kennedy
24  appropriately used old-fashioned speech such as "For I have sworn before you and Almighty God the same solemn
25  oath our forebears prescribed nearly a century and three-quarters ago." This use of language may have seemed
26  outdated for such a young president, but maybe America needed a little old-fashioned talk to move them forward.
27      Kennedy's speech also had many uses of antithesis in parallel grammatical structures: "To those old allies,"
28  . . . "to those new states"; "Ask not what your country can do for you—ask what you can do for your country." The
29  prevalent use of opposite suggests that Kennedy aimed to join peoples together instead of isolate himself with the
30  American people.
31      In addition, Kennedy employed a variety of sentence structures. His sentences ranged from six words to
32  eighty words. A large proportion of the sentences are on the shorter side. This could have been in an effort to hold
33  his audience's attention. Long, complex sentences might have lost an already less-enthused crowd. On the other
34  hand, though, Kennedy makes use of quite a few complex sentences containing a subordinate clause. These
35  sentences, though lengthy, suggest a hidden and brewing energy that this youthful president promised to continue
36  throughout his administration.
37      At the end of an inspiring, convincing, and rallying address, Kennedy concluded by challenging his nation
38  to be the generation they were called to be. His call to action, known as an antithesis, is still well-remembered today:
39  "And so, my fellow Americans: ask not what your country can do for you—ask what you can do for your country.
40  My fellow citizens of the world: ask not what America will do for you but what together we can do for the freedom
41  of man." Throughout his short speech, Kennedy spoke of each topic in the highest regard and respect. More
42  importantly, he challenged himself and his nation in a youthful vigor that looked to the future. (Callie)

1. Both of the above passages argue that
   A. President Kennedy used rhetorical devices effectively to present a powerful speech.
   B. In spite of some major flaws, President Kennedy's inaugural speech was still effective.
   C. Rhetorical devices are incidentally important to this speech.
   D. President Kennedy's credibility was damaged by his controversial stand on the Vietnam War.

3. Kennedy uses the following rhetorical devices:
   A. Imagery
   B. Complex Sentences
   C. Antithesis
   D. All of the Above

4. Which is true? While both passages argue that Kennedy's speech is effective, they use two different organizational strategies to argue their points:
   A. Passage 2 use moves systematically through the speech, offering numerous examples of rhetorical devices. Passage 1 compares Kennedy's inaugural speech to Lincoln's first inaugural.
   B. Passage 1 uses different rhetorical devices to move the essay argument to a logical conclusion. Passage 2 followings a chronological analysis, describing the speech as it unfolds and offering several relevant rhetorical devices.
   C. Passage 1 moves systematically through the speech, highlighting rhetorical devices. Passage 2 does the same but highlights antithesis as a major rhetorical strategy.
   D. Passage 1 offers a few rhetorical devices but insists that the argument (logos) is the main strength of the speech. Passage 2 develops its argument by mentioning the most important element and moving to the least.

## Word in Context

In Line 38 of Passage 2, *antithesis* most likely means
   A. Converse.
   B. Similar.
   C. Intrepid.
   D. Inverted.

# Lesson 3
## SAT Essay

### Student Response 1

*Prompt:* Is bilingual education or class instruction and discussion in African American vernacular English (or Ebonics, as it is often called) a viable alternative to conducting classes in standard American English? Write an essay explaining your position.

1     What unites a group of people is communication. If there was no similar language, thoroughly
2 understanding each other's opinions and thoughts would be nearly impossible without a translator. In America, we
3 have a variety of different cultures, and understanding English for foreigners can be difficult. They may forever have
4 an accent when they speak, however, they must learn to be grammatically correct. It is possible to communicate in
5 what is described as broken English, but that is harder to understand and lacks the smooth and fluent sound of
6 American English. African American vernacular English, also known as Ebonics, is not suitable for class instruction
7 and discussion. Many other cultures are learning standard American English, as they should, and African Americans
8 are still part of our society just as much as other people. Also, standardized tests that have sections dedicated to
9 grammar, and writing would be difficult for African American students who learn Ebonics in the classroom. In
10 addition, it weakens the unity of the bonds of communication in the United States.
11     America is known for the opportunity to pursue the American Dream. Thus various cultures from Europe,
12 Africa, and Asia have immigrated in hopes of finding a better future. The United States is home to a various number
13 of cultures that should all be treasured and preserved. Preserving, however, does not involve allowing different
14 forms of English to be used and taught in classrooms. Just because many Asians learn British English doesn't mean
15 British English is what should be taught here. Similarly, African American vernacular English should be excluded
16 from class instruction. It is unfair and nonsensical to allow one culture to use its form of speech, while excluding
17 others. When immigrants come to America, they must be willing to adopt some of the American customs, language
18 being one of them. African Americans are no different from the other groups of immigrants because, truthfully, they
19 are all members of American society. Special treatment toward their language is not necessary to respect their
20 culture.
21     Standardized testing is a big part of the American school system to determine if a student meets the
22 learning standards and college entrance. If African American vernacular English is taught instead of standard
23 American English, how are those students to know and meet standards on grammar and writing? Ebonics should
24 almost be treated as just another foreign language. It should not be used as standard American English. Having
25 foreigners learn Ebonics does not make sense. In America, the standard language should be standard American
26 English. For this reason, standardized tests should remain the same and all be in standard American English. If
27 students were taught Ebonics, they would likely do poorly on the standardized tests, and creating a separate test
28 would take away from the fairness.
29     Third, because of the multitude of diverse cultures in America, it is necessary for us to find and protect all
30 forms of unity. Language is one form. Having foreigners as well as African Americans learn standard American
31 English allows us to find common ground for communication. Ebonics is a term commonly used by those who wish
32 to emphasize the fact that Ebonics takes root and has connections with African countries. It is not wrong for African
33 Americans to learn Ebonics since it is part of their culture, which is to be respected, but having it taught in schools
34 as the main language is a whole different matter. Allowing a culture to use a language that comes from external
35 countries is the same as allowing, for example, Chinese to be taught as the main language in school. There are
36 immersion schools where a language is taught all day, but those students are still expected to meet the standard
37 American English standards. School boards may allow Ebonics to be taught in schools, yet the students must still
38 meet the standards of American English.
39     Ebonics, or African American vernacular English, should not be the only language taught in schools. It is
40 possible to use for bilingual education, since it is a language of the African American culture. However, if students
41 are taught Ebonics, it is necessary to still meet the standard American English standards. Part of the African
42 American culture is their own language, which can be spoken in their own homes and among each other. The
43 students must still be able to communicate with people outside of their own culture, so a bilingual education is
44 necessary. Although it can be difficult to understand whether or not Ebonics should be taught, it is still a language

45  that belongs to a culture. Therefore, the people should be able to chose whether they want their children or want
46  themselves to learn Ebonics. It uses many slang terms and is difficult for a person who does not understand such
47  words, thus it is a language. If Ebonics is used for bilingual education, it is crucial to still be able to communicate in
48  standard American English with the rest of the public. (Abby)


## Student Response 2

*Prompt:* Choose a controversial community. Examine its structure and purpose, and argue for or against its value to its members and to the larger community.

1
2       Drugs, sex, rough language, and the like are some of the controversial topics used in rap and hip-hop
3   music. The music of hip-hop forms a community, but whether one agrees with the ideas promoted by such music is
4   a choice. However, this genre of music does satisfy the requirements of a community. The people are united for a
5   common purpose or goal, and they are involved in forming music with such themes and similar instruments. The
6   structure of the community involves the music producers as well as the listeners or supporters. Together they work
7   toward spreading their music. Although the themes may be controversial and can be considered morally incorrect,
8   the idea that this group of individuals is working for a common goal and share a common characteristic makes them
9   a community. However, the value is what can be debated. Personally, I see the hip-hop community as impacting
10  itself as well as the larger community negatively. It supports illegal behavior, spreads derogatory language, and
11  harms the moral code of society.
12      Many of the rap lyrics involve the discussion of substance abuse. For example, getting high while smoking
13  weed is considered cool. Snorting cocaine in the bathroom is considered fun. Binge drinking, prescription pills,
14  smoking, and such things all are mentioned as the common things to do. By allowing such music to be spread, it is
15  encouraging individuals to break the law or form unhealthy habits. Notice how the rap music focuses on the high
16  feeling of drugs, but never mentions the withdrawal symptoms or side effects one may develop. It is pure
17  propaganda to support illegal dealing of substances, which only causes people harm.
18      The language used in hip-hop lyrics is also not to be supported. Besides the cussing and mentioning of
19  drugs, racially offensive terms are used. The "n-word" used to describe African American people is still being used.
20  Many African Americans themselves are involved in producing rap music, yet they continue to use words that are
21  racially offensive to their own race. Swear words are treated as regular vocabulary, and people who listen to rap
22  music eventually become accustomed to such speech. The grammar is incorrect, and many slang terms are used. A
23  famous rapper credited for his influence in hip-hop music goes by the stage name of Fifty Cent. He doesn't add the *s*
24  at the end, although grammatically speaking it should be Fifty Cents. Grammar mistakes such as this become a part
25  of listeners' minds, and it becomes their normal to talk in such an improper way. The language itself is spreading a
26  bad influence on the listeners, which negatively impacts society.
27      With lyrics relating to substance abuse, sex, and incorrect language, the music created by the hip-hop
28  community is negatively affecting its listeners as well as the larger community. When listens become wrapped up in
29  such themes and informal way of speaking, it becomes their reality. They are motivated to try drugs or drinking for
30  the intent of getting drunk, which leads to danger and trouble with the law. Not only are they putting their own
31  health at risk; they are putting others around them at risk as well. They are liable to commit crimes or assault others
32  when the limbic system or animal instinct of the brain takes control. Spreading such ideas, this community harms its
33  members as well as others. The purpose, possibly, is to create music that people enjoy or will purchase. However,
34  there are many ways to do this. Rap music itself, as in the style of using the beats, can be enjoyable for many.
35  However, the problem begins with the lyrics. What is being promoted and placed in the minds of the youth is where
36  hip-hop and rap music goes wrong. It harms the moral code that society should have and encourages negative
37  behavior and dangerous decisions.
38      The value of the music to the hip-hop community itself I cannot assess. **I understand that is the way they**
39  **earn money, and maybe that's what they really believe to be correct.** To its own members, it hurts them as well.
40  The people who listen to such music and decide it will be fun or cool to try doing drugs, going to clubs, and so on,
41  only harm their health as well as their future. However, it is certain it negatively impacts the larger community.
42  Spreading promiscuous ideas to the future generations is wrong and negatively impacts society. Ultimately,
43  however, it is very unlikely such music will disappear. It has become such a large part of the music industry, and
44  some people truly believe it is correct and support spreading such ideas. The value to the larger community,
45  however, is little since it negatively impacts the future generations and its members. (Abby)

## Close Reading

1. In Student Response 1
   A. Ebonics must never be taught.
   B. Ebonics may be used, but standard English must be taught.
   C. African Americans should be allowed to speak and write anyway they wish.
   D. Spanish, not Ebonics, should be taught in school.

2. In Student Response 2
   A. Hip-hop music is better than rock and roll.
   B. Hip-hop is an indigenous African American music and therefore should be taught.
   C. Hip-hop is harmless.
   D. Hip-hop music is harmful to all who participate and does not sustain a separate culture.

3. In Student Response 1, the author organizes the essay
   A. By stating a rhetorical question and then developing the thesis.
   B. By offering a series of anecdotes.
   C. By moving from general to specific arguments.
   D. By a series of bullet points.

4. In Student Response 2 the author organizes her essay:
   A. By stating a rhetorical questions and then developing her thesis
   B. By offering a series of anecdotes
   C. By moving from general to specific arguments
   D. By a series of bullet points

5. What is a problem in Student Response 1?
   I. No specific examples are given.
   II. Transitions are weak.
   III. There are too many personal examples.
   IV. The essay is too short.
   V. The thesis is not clearly stated nor tied to the topic.

   A. I and II        C. II and III        E. All
   B. III and IV      D. V

6. What is a problem in Student Response Essay 2?
   I. Examples are not tied closely to the thesis.
   II. Transitions are weak.
   III. There are too many personal examples.
   IV. The essay is too long.
   V. The thesis is not clearly stated nor tied to the topic.

   A. I and II        C. IV and V          E. All
   B. III and IV      D. I, II, IV, and V

7. Where is the main point of the Student Response 1?
   A. Lines 3–4            C. Line 18
   B. Lines 8–9            D. Lines 44–46

8. Where is the main point of the Student Response 2?
   A. Line 3               C. Lines 12–13
   B. Lines 8–9            D. Lines 41–45

9. What is a significant stylistic problem in Student Response 1?
   I. First-person and third-person pronouns are both used.
   II. Second-person pronouns are used.
   III. Transitions are weak.
   IV. There are agreement problems.
   V. Present-tense and past-tense verbs are both used.

   A. I and II                          C. I and V
   B. III and IV                        D. I, II, III, and IV

10. What is a significant stylistic problem in Student Response 2?
    I. First-person and third-person pronouns are both used.
    II. Second-person pronouns are used.
    III. Transitions are weak.
    IV. There are agreement problems.
    V. Present and past tense verbs are both used.

    A. I and II                         C. I and V
    B. III and IV                       D. NONE

11. Where is evidence for this problem (question 9, above) in Student Response 1?
    A. Lines 1–4                        C. Lines 12–14
    B. Lines 8–9                        D. Lines 40–44

12. What is the problem with Student Response 1, Lines 21–28?
    A. The facts are wrong.
    B. The student is not credentialed to make such speculation.
    C. The paragraph is too long.
    D. Nobody believes the evidence.

13. What score would the student responses receive?
    Student Response 1 receives __. Student Response 2 receives __.

## Grammar and Usage

Choose the best grammar/usage form in bold sentence(s).

In Student Response 2, Lines 38–39:

A. NONE
B. I understand that is the way they earn money, and maybe that's what they really believe to be correct.
C. I understand that is the way they earn money, and thats what they really believe to be correct.
D. I understand that is the way they earn money, but maybe thats what they really believe to be correct.

# Lesson 4
## Reading: Document-Based Analysis

### Jefferson's Letter to Meriwether Lewis
### Thomas Jefferson (June 20, 1803)

1    To Meriwether Lewis, esquire, captain of the first regiment of infantry of the United States of America:

2

3        Your situation as secretary of the president of the United States, has made you acquainted with the objects
4    of my confidential message of January 18, 1803, to the legislature; you have seen the act they passed, which, though
5    expressed in general terms, was meant to sanction those objects, and you are appointed to carry them to execution.
6        Instruments for ascertaining, by celestial observations, the geography of the country through which you
7    will pass, have already been provided. Light articles for barter and presents among the Indians, arms for your
8    attendants, say from ten to twelve men, boats, tents, and other traveling apparatus, with ammunition, medicine,
9    surgical instruments and provisions, you will have prepared, with such aids as the secretary at war can yield in his
10    department; and from him also you will receive authority to engage among our troops, by voluntary agreement, the
11    attendants abovementioned; over whom you, as their commanding officer, are invested with all the powers the laws
12    give in such a case.
13        As your movements, while within the limits of the United States, will be better directed by occasional
14    communications, adapted to circumstances as they arise, they will not be noticed here. What follows will respect
15    your proceedings after your departure from the United States.
16        Your mission has been communicated to the ministers here from France, Spain, and great Briton, and
17    through them to their governments; and such assurances given them as to its objects, as we trust will satisfy them.
18    The country of Louisiana having ceded by Spain to France, the passport you have from the minister of France, the
19    representative of the present sovereign of the country, will be a protection with all its subjects; and that from the
20    Minister of England will entitle you to the friendly aid of any traders of that allegiance with whom you may happen
21    to meet.
22        The object of your mission is to explore the Missouri River, and such principal streams of it, as, by its
23    course and communication with the waters of the Pacific Ocean, whether the Columbia, Oregon, Colorado, or any
24    other river, may offer the most direct and practicable water-communication across the continent, for the purposes of
25    commerce.
26        Beginning at the mouth of the Missouri, you will take observations of latitude and longitude, at all
27    remarkable points on the river, and especially at the mouths of rivers, at rapids, at islands, and other places and
28    objects distinguished by such natural marks and characters, of a durable kind, as that they may with certainty be
29    recognized hereafter. The courses of the river between these points of observation may be supplied by the compass,
30    the log-line, and by time, corrected by the observations themselves. The variations of the needle, too, in different
31    places, should be noticed.
32        The interesting points of the portage between the heads of the Missouri, and of the water offering the best
33    communication with the Pacific ocean, should also be fixed by observation; and the course of that water to the
34    ocean, in the same manner as that of the Missouri.
35        Your observations are to be taken with great pains and accuracy; to be entered distinctly and intelligibly for
36    others as well as yourself; to comprehend all the elements necessary, with the aid of the usual tables, to fix the
37    latitude and longitude of the places at which they were taken; and are to be rendered to the war-office, for the
38    purpose of having the calculations made concurrently by proper persons within the United States. Several copies of
39    these, as well as of your other notes, should be made at leisure times, and put into the care of the most trustworthy of
40    your attendants to guard, by multiplying them against the accidental losses to which they will be exposed. A further
41    guard would be, that one of these copies be on the circular membranes of the paper of the birch, as less liable to
42    injury from damp than common paper.
43        The commerce which may be carried on with the people inhabiting the line you will pursue, renders a
44    knowledge of those people important. You will therefore endeavor to make yourself acquainted, as far as a diligent
45    pursuit of your journey shall admit, with the names of the nations and their numbers;
46        the extent and limits of their possessions;
47        their relations with other tribes or nations;

48    their language, traditions, monuments;

49    their ordinary occupations in agriculture, fishing, hunting, war, arts, and the implements for these;

50    their food, clothing, and domestic accommodations:

51    the diseases prevalent among them, and the remedies they use;

52    moral and physical circumstances which distinguish them from the tribes we know;

53    peculiarities in their laws, customs, and dispositions;

54    and articles of commerce they may need or furnish, and to what extent.

55    And, considering the interest which every nation has in extending and strengthening the authority of reason
56    and justice among the people around them, it will be useful to acquire what knowledge you can of the state of
57    morality, religion, and information among them; as it may better enable those who may endeavor to civilize and
58    instruct them, to adapt their measures to the existing notions and practices of those on whom they are to operate.

59    Other objects worthy of notice will be

60    the soil and face of the country, its growth and vegetable productions, especially those not of the United States;

61    the animals of the country generally, and especially those not known in the United States;

62    the remains and accounts of any which may be deemed rare or extinct;

63    the mineral productions of every kind, but more particularly metals, lime-stone, pit-coal and saltpetre; salines
64        and mineral waters, noting the temperature of the last, and such circumstances as may indicate their
65        character;

66    volcanic appearances;

67    climate, as characterized by the thermometer, by the proportion of rainy, cloudy, and clear days; by lightning,
68        hail, snow, ice; by the access and recess of frost; by the winds prevailing at different seasons; the dates at
69        which particular plants put forth, or lose their flower or leaf; times of appearance of particular birds,
70        reptiles or insects.

71    Although your route will be along the channel of the Missouri, yet you will endeavor to inform yourself, by
72    inquiry, of the character and extent of the country watered by its branches, and especially on its southern side. The
73    North river, or Rio Bravo, which runs into the gulf of Mexico, and the North river, or Rio Colorado, which runs into
74    the gulf of California, are understood to be the principal streams heading opposite to the waters of the Missouri, and
75    running southwardly. Whether the dividing grounds between the Missouri and them are mountains or flat lands,
76    what are their distance from the Missouri, the character of the intermediate country, and the people inhabiting it, are
77    worthy of particular inquiry. The northern waters of the Missouri are less to be inquired after, because they have
78    been ascertained to a considerable degree, and are still in a course of ascertainment by English traders and travelers;
79    but if you can learn any thing certain of the most northern source of the Mississippi, and of its position relatively to
80    the Lake of the Woods, it will be interesting to us. Some account too of the path of the Canadian traders from the
81    Mississippi, at the mouth of the Ouisconsin to where it strikes the Missouri, and of the soil and rivers in its course, is
82    desirable.

83    In all your intercourse with the natives, treat them in the most friendly and conciliatory manner which their
84    own conduct will admit; allay all jealousies as to the object of your journey; satisfy them of its innocence; make
85    them acquainted with the position, extent, character, peaceable and commercial dispositions of the United States, of
86    our wish to be neighborly, friendly, and useful to them, and of our dispositions to a commercial intercourse with
87    them; confer with them on the points most convenient as mutual emporiums, and the articles of most desirable
88    interchange for them and us. If a few of their influential chiefs, within practicable distance, wish to visit us, arrange
89    such a visit with them, and furnish them with authority to call on our officers on their entering the United States, to
90    have them conveyed to this place at the public expense. If any of them should wish to have some of their young
91    people brought up with us, and taught such arts as may be useful to them, we will receive, instruct, and take care of
92    them. Such a mission, whether of influential chiefs, or of young people, would give some security to your own
93    party. Carry with you some matter of the kine-pox, inform those of them with whom you may be of its efficacy as a
94    preservative from the small-pox, and instruct and encourage them in the use of it. This may be especially done
95    wherever you winter.

96    As it is impossible for us to foresee in what manner you will be received by those people, whether with
97    hospitality or hostility, so is it impossible to prescribe the exact degree of perseverance with which you are to pursue
98    your journey. We value too much the lives of citizens to offer them to probable destruction. Your numbers will be
99    sufficient to secure you against the unauthorized opposition of individuals, or of small parties; but if a superior
100   force, authorized, or not authorized, by a nation, should be arrayed against your further passage, and inflexibly
101   determined to arrest it, you must decline its further pursuit and return. In the loss of yourselves we should lose also
102   the information you will have acquired. By returning safely with that, you may enable us to renew the essay with
103   better calculated means. To your own discretion, therefore, must be left the degree of danger you may risk, and the

104 point at which you should decline, only saying, we wish you to err on the side of your safety, and to bring back your
105 party safe, even if it be with less information.

106       As far up the Missouri as the white settlements extend, an intercourse will probably be found to exist
107 between them and the Spanish post of St. Louis opposite Cahokia, or St. Genevieve opposite Kaskaskia. From still
108 further up the river the traders may furnish a conveyance for letters. Beyond that you may perhaps be able to engage
109 Indians to bring letters for the government to Cahokia, or Kaskaskia, on promising that they shall there receive such
110 special compensation as your shall have stipulated with them. Avail yourself of these means to communicate to us,
111 at seasonable intervals, a copy of your journal, notes and observations of every kind, putting into cypher whatever
112 might do injury if betrayed.

113       Should you reach the Pacific ocean, inform yourself of the circumstances which may decide whether the
114 furs of those parts may not be collected as advantageously at the head of the Missouri (convenient as is supposed to
115 the waters of the Colorado and Oregon or Columbia) as at Nootka Sound, or any other point of that coast; and that
116 trade be consequently conducted through the Missouri and United States more beneficially than by the
117 circumnavigation now practiced.

118       On your arrival on that coast, endeavor to learn if there be any port within your reach frequented by the sea
119 vessels of any nation, and to send two of your trusty people back by sea, in such way as shall appear practicable,
120 with a copy of your notes; and should you be of opinion that the return of your party by the way they went will be
121 imminently dangerous, then ship the whole, and return by sea, by the way either of Cape Horn, or the Cape of Good
122 Hope, as you shall be able. As you will be without money, clothes, or provisions, you must endeavor to use the
123 credit of the United States to obtain them; for which purpose open letters of credit shall be furnished you,
124 authorizing you to draw on the executive of the United States, or any of its officers, in any part of the world, on
125 which draughts can be disposed of, and to apply with our recommendations to the consuls, agents, merchants, or
126 citizens of any nation with which we have intercourse, assuring them, in our name, that any aids they may furnish
127 you shall be honorably repaid, and on demand. Our consuls, Thomas Hewes, at Batavia, in Java, William Buchanan,
128 in the Isles of France and Bourbon, and John Elmslie, at the Cape of Good Hope, will be able to supply your
129 necessities, by draughts on us.

130       Should you find it safe to return by the way you go, after sending two of our party round by sea, or with
131 your whole party, if no conveyance by sea can be found, do so; making such observations on your return as may
132 serve to supply, correct, or confirm those made on your outward journey.

133       On reentering the United States and reaching a place of safety, discharge any of your attendants who may
134 desire and deserve it, procuring for them immediate payment of all arrears of pay and clothing which may have
135 incurred since their departure, and assure them that they shall be recommended to the liberality of the legislature for
136 the grant of a soldier's portion of land each, as proposed in my message to congress, and repair yourself, with your
137 papers, to the seat of government.

138       To provide, on the accident of your death, against anarchy, dispersion, and the consequent danger to your
139 party, and total failure of the enterprise, you are hereby authorized, by any instrument signed and written in your
140 own hand, to name the person among them who shall succeed to the command on your decease, and by like
141 instruments to change the nomination, from time to time, as further experience of the characters accompanying you
142 shall point out superior fitness; and all the powers and authorities given to yourself are, in the event of your death,
143 transferred to, and vested in the successor so named, with further power to him and his successors, in like manner to
144 name each his successor, who, on the death of his predecessor, shall be invested with all the powers and authorities
145 given to yourself. Given under my hand at the city of Washington, this twentieth day of June, 1803.
146
147 Thomas Jefferson, President of the United States of America
                  (http://www.monticello.org/site/jefferson/jeffersons-instructions-to-meriwether-lewis)

1. What is the purpose of this message?
   I. To give instructions to the Lewis and Clark Expedition
   II. To raise money to buy the Louisiana Purchase
   III. To encourage Congress to support Jefferson's proposal

   A. I                        C. I and III
   B. I and II                 D. All

2. What genre form is this document?
   A. Essay                    C. Letter
   B. Speech                   D. Regulation

3. What are possible reasons why Jefferson wrote this document?
   I. Natural resources were in danger.
   II. To make sure the Lewis and Clark Expedition accomplished Jefferson's goals
   III. To protect the Native Americans in the area
   IV. To make sure America laid claim to Oregon

   A. I and II                 C. II
   B. III and IV               D. All

4. Why did President Jefferson show such concern about Native American relations?
   I. Native Americans were the majority in all the territory that Lewis and Clark would visit.
   II. Jefferson admired Native American culture and sought to know more about it.
   III. Jefferson wished to annihilate native people groups.

   A. I                        C. III
   B. I and II                 D. All

5. Passages that support the above statement include
   I. Lines 1–12               III. Lines 79-84
   II. Lines 41–52             IV. Lines 132–39

   A. I                        C. I and IV
   B. II                       D. II and III

## Words in Context

1. What is the meaning of *arrears* in Line 134?
   A. Liability                C. Debts
   B. Remorse                  D. Assets

2. What is the meaning of *anarchy* in Line 138?
   A. Mayhem                   C. Solitude
   B. Order                    D. Platitude

3. What is the meaning of *dispersion* in Line 138?
   A. Absorption               C. Dilution
   B. Diffusion                D. Dilation

# Lesson 5
## Math: Algebra, Arithmetic Problem Solving and Data Analysis, and Passport to Advanced Math

### Data Analysis

**Food Sales**

Values are in hundreds

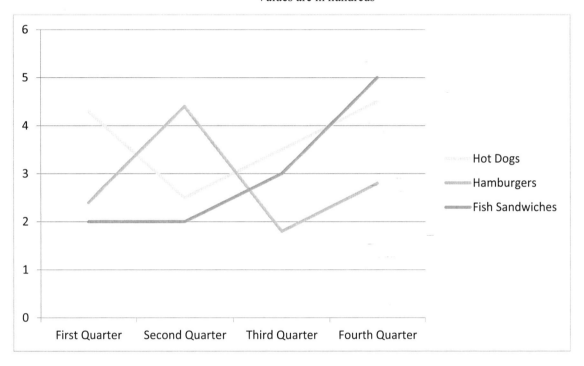

1. From the above chart, what conclusions are true?
   I. Hot dogs and hamburgers sold best in the second quarter.
   II. Fish sandwich sales steadily increased from the middle of the second quarter
   III. Hamburger and hot dog sales were the same in the early part of the third quarter.

   | A. I only | C. II and III |
   |-----------|---------------|
   | B. II only | D. All |

2. Which of the following scenarios *may* explain the data?
   I. Customers preferred hot dogs and hamburgers until the middle of the second quarter. Fish sandwich purchases increased in the middle of the second quarter because this business is in a predominately conservative Roman Catholic district, and Easter arrived late in April.
   II. On May 1 a major beef retailer reported that the majority of its beef products and bi-products were tainted with a toxic pesticide. Thousands of pounds of hamburger were recalled.
   III. All sales increased in the fourth quarter because baseball season began.

   | A. I only | C. III only |
   |-----------|-------------|
   | B. I and II only | D. All |

## Algebra

If $w$ and $x$ are positive integers such that $w = x^2$, which of the following could be the value of $w$?

A. 2
B. 4

C. 8
D. 10

## Arithmetic Problem Solving

1. Mr. A's investment in business is $15,000 more than Mr. B's. If Mr. A invests three times as much as Mr. B, how much is each man's investment?

   A. $22,500; $7,500
   B. $22,000; $7,000

   C. $28,000; $9,000
   D. $18,500; $7,500

2. A man drew out of the bank $27, in equal numbers of half-dollars, quarters, dimes, and nickels. What was the number?

   A. 30
   B. 28

   C. 32
   D. 34

# Answers

## Chapter 1

**Lesson 1**

Close Reading: 1C. 2A. 3A. 4B. 5B. 6D. 7A. 8C. 9A. 10D. 11A. 12A. 13C.

Command of Evidence, Student Response 1: 1B. 2B. 3B. Student Response 2: 1A. 2B. 3D.

Words in Context: 1B. 2D.

**Lesson 2**

Command of Evidence, Passage 1: 1D. 2B. 3C. 4D. 5A. 6B. 7B. Passage 2: 1C, 2D, 3A, 4D, 5C, 6B, 7D, 8B.

Grammar and Usage: 1B, 2D.

**Lesson 3**

Student Responses: 1D. 2C. 3A. 4E. 5A. 6C. 7A. 8D. 9, Response 1 score 2; Response 2 score 3.

Grammar and Usage: 1C. 2D.

**Lesson 4**

Reading: 1A. 2B. 3B. 4A. 5C. 6B. 7B.

**Lesson 5**

Math: Chart, D.

Algebra: 1B. 2D. 3A. 4A. 5C. 6D.

## Chapter 2

**Lesson 1**

Close Reading: 1B. 2A. 3C. 4A. 5B. 6B. 7A. 8D. 9B.

Command of Evidence, Student Response: 1B. 2A. 3D. 4A.

**Lesson 2**

Passage 1: 1C. 2C. 3B. 4D. 5B. 6B. Passage 2: 1D. 2C. 3B. 4C. 5B. 6D.

Grammar and Usage: 1C. 2B. –

**Lesson 3**

Student Responses: 1A. 2C. 3D. 4E. 5D. 6A. 7B. 8, Response 1 score 3; Response 2 score 3.

**Lesson 4**

Reading: 1A. 2D.

Words in Context: 1C. 2A. 3C. 4D. 5A. 6B. 7B.

**Lesson 5**

Math: 1B. 2B.

Arithmetic: 1C. 2B. 3A. 4C. 5B. 6D. 7A. 8C.

## Chapter 3

**Lesson 1**

Analysis: 1D. 2A. 3C. 4B.

Source Analysis: A.

**Lesson 2**

Command of Evidence: 1C. 2D. 3C.

Words in Context: C.

Analyzing a Source. A.

**Lesson 3**

Student Response score 4.

Grammar and Usage: 1B. 2D.

**Lesson 4**

Reading: 1C. 2A.

Words in Context: 1D. 2B.

**Lesson 5**

Arithmetic: A.

Algebra: C.

Data Analysis: 1A. 2B.

# Chapter 4

**Lesson 1**
>Close Reading: D
>Words in Context: 1C. 2A
>Source Analysis: D

**Lesson 2**
>Command of Evidence: 1B. 2C. 3A. 4C. 5E.
>Words in Context: 1C. 2A. 3B.

**Lesson 3**
>Essay: 1C. 2A. 3A. 4E. 5, score 4.
>Grammar and Usage: 1D. 2A.

**Lesson 4**
>Reading: 1C. 2A. 3D. 4A. 5C.
>Words in Context: 1D. 2B. 3A. 4B.

**Lesson 5**
>Math: 1E. 2E. 3C. 4A.

# Chapter 5

**Lesson 1**
>Close Reading: 1E. 2A. 3B.
>Words in Context: 1A. 2C.
>Source Analysis: D.

**Lesson 2**
>Command of Evidence: 1D. 2D. 3C. 4B. 5A. 6D. 7C. 8A.
>Words in Context: 1B. 2C. 3D. 4A.

**Lesson 3**
>SAT Essay: 1B. 2D. 3B.
>Student Essay: 1C. 2E. 3C. 4D. 5A. 6, score 3.
>Grammar and Usage: 1D. 2C.

**Lesson 4**
>Reading: 1D. 2B. 3D. 4E. 5D.

**Lesson 5**
>Arithmetic: 1D. 2B. 3C. 4A. 5E. 6A. 7C.
>Data Analysis: D

# Chapter 6

**Lesson 1**
>Close Reading: 1E. 2B. 3A. 4C.
>Words in Context: 1A. 2C. 3D. 4B. 5C.
>Source Analysis: D.

**Lesson 2**
>Command of Evidence: 1D. 2D. 3E.
>Data Analysis: 1A. 2D. 3C. 4D. 5E. 6D.

**Lesson 3**
>Student Response: 1A. 2F. 3E. 4C. 5B. 6A. 7A. 8D. 9B. 11B. 12, score 3 because it is somewhat off topic.

**Lesson 4**
>Reading: 1C. 2A. 3C. 4B. 5A. 6C.

**Lesson 5**
>Arithmetic: 1A. 2C. 3D. 4D. 5B. 6C.
>Chart: 1B. 2B.

# Chapter 7

**Lesson 1**
Close Reading: 1A. 2E. 3B. 4C. 5A. 6C. 7D. 8C.
Chart: 1A. 2C.
Source Analysis: D.

**Lesson 2**
Command of Evidence: 1A. 2A. 3B. 4B. 5A. 6B.
Words in Context: 1C. 2B. 3D. 4D. 5A. 6B. 7B.

**Lesson 3**
Essay: 1C. 2D. 3A. 4C. 5D. 6A. 7B. 8A. 9B. 10, score 3.

**Lesson 4**
Reading: 1D. 2C. 3B. 4D.
Words in Context: 1B. 2A.

**Lesson 5**
Algebra: 1B. 2A. 3D. 4C. 5B. 6D.
Data Analysis: A.

# Chapter 8

**Lesson 1**
Passage 1, Close Reading: 1D. 2C. 3B. 4A. 5C.
Passage 2, Close Reading: 1D. 2D.
Source Analysis: 1C. 2B.

**Lesson 2**
Close Reading: 1D. 2C. 3B. 4B. 5A. 6C.
Words in Context: 1C. 2A.

**Lesson 3**
Close Reading: 1E. 2A. 3D. 4A. 5A. 6A. 7C. 8D. 9D. 10C. 11C. 12B. 13A. 14, score 3, slightly off topic.

**Lesson 4**
Reading: 1C. 2A. 3C. 4B.
Words in Context: 1C. 2A. 3D.

**Lesson 5**
Data Analysis: 1D. 2C.
Algebra: 1C. 2A. 3B. 4D. 5A. 6C. 7C. 8D. 9A.

# Chapter 9

**Lesson 1**
Close Reading: 1C. 2A. 3A. 4C. 5D. 6B.
Source Analysis: 1C. 2C. 3E. 4C.

**Lesson 2**
Command of Evidence: 1A. 2C. 3B. 4D. 5C. 6D. 7A. 8C. 9B. 10E. 11A.

**Lesson 3**
Essay: 1D. 2C. 3B. 4D. 5C.
Grammar and Usage: 1B. 3D.

**Lesson 4**
Reading: 1B. 2B. 3B. 4C. 5A. 6C.
Data Analysis: 1C. 2B. 3B. 4A.
Words in Context: 1C. 2C. 3A. 4B. 5D. 6C.

**Lesson 5**
Math: 1B. 2A.
Algebra: 1B. 2A. 3C. 4D.

# Chapter 10

**Lesson 1**
Close Reading: 1A. 2B. 3C. 4A. 5C. 6A. 7D.
Command of Evidence: 1A. 2C. 3A. 4B. 5A.
Words in Context: 1B. 2A.
**Lesson 2**
Command of Evidence: 1D. 2A. 3C. 4C. 5A. 6C. 7C. 8C. 9C. 10A. 11B.
**Lesson 3**
Essay: 1B. 2C. 3C. 4A. 5B. 6D. 7C.
Grammar and Usage: 1D. 2B.
**Lesson 4**
Reading: 1C. 2A. 3C. 4C.
Data Analysis: 1C. 2A. 3B.
**Lesson 5**
Math: D.
Algebra: 1C. 2C. 3A. 4D. 5C. 6C.

# Chapter 11

**Lesson 1**
Close Reading: 1B. 2A. 3B. 4C. 5A. 6B.
Command of Evidence: 1C. 2D. 3C. 4A.
**Lesson 2**
Command of Evidence: 1B. 2C. 3C. 4A. 5B. 6D. 7B. 8E. 9B. 10D.
Words in Context: 1C. 2B. 3D. 4C.
**Lesson 3**
Essay: 1C. 2B. 3C. 4D. 5B. 6A. 7C. 8A. 9A. 10A. 11, score 3. 12, score 2.
**Lesson 4**
Reading: 1D. 2A. 3C. 4D. 5B.
**Lesson 5**
Arithmetic: 1D. 2B. 3A. 4D. 5B. 6C. 7C.
Data Analysis: 1B. 2A. 3D.

# Chapter 12

**Lesson 1**
Close Reading: 1B. 2A. 3C. 4B. 5D. 6C. 7B.
Source Analysis: 1C. 2C.
Words in Context: 1C. 2A. 3C.
**Lesson 2**
Close Reading: 1A. 2C. 3D. 4A.
Grammar and Usage: 1B. 2C.
Words in Context:     1C. 2A. 3B.
**Lesson 3**
Essay: 1C. 2B. 3A. 4B. 5E. 6D. 7D. 8D. 9A. 10, score 2.
Grammar and Usage: 1C. 2D.
**Lesson 4**
Reading: 1B. 2C. 3D. 4D. 5C. 6B. 7D.
Words in Context: 1C. 2A. 3D. 4C. 5A. 6C.
**Lesson 5**
Math: 1A. 2C.
Arithmetic: 1C. 2A. 3A. 4B.

# Chapter 13

**Lesson 1**

Close Reading: 1B. 2A. 3A. 4D. 5C. 6A.

**Lesson 2**

Close Reading: 1B. 2C. 3C. 4A.

**Lesson 3**

Essay: 1A. 2C. 3B. 4D. 5B. 6A. 7, score 3.

Grammar and Usage: 1C. 2D.

**Lesson 4**

Reading: 1A. 2A. 3C. 4D. 5B. 6A. 7C.

**Lesson 5**

Arithmetic: 1C. 2B. 3C. 4A. 5D. 6B. 7A.

Algebra: C.

# Chapter 14

**Lesson 1**

Close Reading: 1B. 2A. 3A. 4D. 5C. 6B. 7C.

Command of Evidence: 1B. 2D. 3A. 4D.

Words in Context: 1C. 2A. 3D. 4B.

**Lesson 2**

Command of Evidence, Passage 1: 1C. 2A. 3D. 4A. 5D.

Command of Evidence, Passage 2: 1B. 2C. 3A. 4B. 5A.

Grammar and Usage: 1C. 2D.

**Lesson 3**

Close Reading: 1A. 2B. 3C. 4B. 5D. 6D. 7B. 8B. 9B. 10C. 11, Response 1 score 3; Response 2 score 4.

Grammar and Usage: 1D. 2D.

**Lesson 4**

Reading: 1C. 2C. 3A. 4D. 5B.

Words in Context. 1B. 2A. 3D. 4B.

**Lesson 5**

Analyzing Data: 1B. 2C.

Arithmetic: 1A. 2C. 3A. 4B.

# Chapter 15

**Lesson 1**

Close Reading (Speech): 1D. 2C. 3A. 4A. 5D. 6C.

Command of Evidence (Student Response): 1A. 2C. 3A. 4A.

Words in Context: 1C. 2A. 3D. 4A. 5C. 6C. 7D. 8B.

Grammar and Usage: 1D. 2B.

**Lesson 2**

Close Reading, Passage 1: 1A. 2C. 3B. 4A. 5A. 6A.

Close Reading, Passage 2: 1C. 2A. 3B. 4D.

Grammar and Usage: 1B. 2C.

**Lesson 3**

Essay: 1A. 2C. 3D. 4A. 5A. 6B. 7C. 8C. 9D. 10D. 11A. 12A. 13, Response 1 score 2; Response 2 score 3.

**Lesson 4**

Reading: 1C. 2A. 3B. 4C. 5D.

Words in Context: 1C. 2C.

**Lesson 5**

Math: 1A. 2C.

Arithmetic: 1D. 2B. 3B. 4A. 5C.

# Chapter 16

**Lesson 1**

    Close Reading (Poem): 1C. 2A. 3D. 4C. 5A. 6C.

    Command of Evidence (Student Response): 1B. 2C. 3A. 4D. 5B. 6D. 7D.

    Words in Context: 1C. 2A.

**Lesson 2**

    Close Reading, Passage 1: 1C. 2A. 3C. 4A. 5A. 6B.

    Close Reading, Passage 2: 1C. 2B. 3A.

    Grammar and Usage: 1D. 2B.

**Lesson 3**

    Essay: 1B. 2D. 3A.

    Student Response: 1D. 2E. 3E. 4B. 5A. 6D. 7, score 4.

    Grammar and Usage: C.

**Lesson 4**

    Reading: 1A. 2B. 3C. 4A. 5D. 6C. 7C. 8D.

    Words in Context: 1C. 2C. 3A. 4D.

**Lesson 5**

    Math: 1C. 2A.

    Arithmetic: 1D. 2B. 3A. 4C.

    Algebra: 1A. 2C.

# Chapter 17

**Lesson 1**

    Close Reading (Poem): 1D. 2B. 3D. 4A. 5C. 6A. 7B.

    Command of Evidence (Student Response): 1D. 2C. 3A. 4D. 5A.

    Grammar and Usage: 1C. 2B.

**Lesson 2**

    Close Reading, Passage 1: 1D. 2A. 3C. 4B. 5A. 6D.

    Close Reading, Passage 2: 1C. 2C. 3C.

    Grammar and Usage: 1C. 2D.

**Lesson 3**

    Close Reading, Essay 1: 1B. 2D. 3A. 4C. 5D. 6, score 3.

    Close Reading, Essay 2: 1B. 2D. 3A. 4D. 5, score 3.

    Grammar and Usage: 1B. 2D.

**Lesson 4**

    Close Reading: 1B. 2D. 3A.

    Words in Context, Passage 1: 1C. 2A. 3C. 4D. 5B. 6A.

    Words in Context, Passage 2: 1C. 2C. 3D.

**Lesson 5**

    Math: C.

    Arithmetic: 1A. 2B. 3D. 4B.

# Chapter 18

**Lesson 1**

Close Reading (Poem): 1C. 2B. 3C. 4A. 5C. 6C. 7D.

Command of Evidence (Student Response): 1B. 2B. 3C. 4C. 5A. 6B. 7A. 8C. 9B. 10C. 11D. 12A.

Words in Context: 1C. 2D. 3A.

**Lesson 2**

Close Reading, Passage 1: 1C. 2A. 3D. 4B. 5C. 6A. 7C. 8B.

Close Reading, Passage 2: 1B. 2D. 3C. 4C.

**Lesson 3**

Close Reading, Essay 1: 1A. 2D. 3A. 4C. 5C. 6, score 2.

Close Reading, Essay 2: 1B. 2C. 3A. 4C. 5, score 4.

Grammar and Usage: C.

**Lesson 4**

Close Reading: 1D. 2A. 3C. 4B. 5A. 6D.

**Lesson 5**

Math: D.

Arithmetic: 1C. 2B. 3D.

Data Analysis: 1D. 2B. 3A.

Algebra: 1D. 2C.

# Chapter 19

**Lesson 1**

Close Reading (Mark Twain): 1B. 2C. 3D. 4A. 5D. 6B. 7A.

Command of Evidence (Student Response): 1C. 2A. 3B. 4D. 5B. 6C. 7C.

Grammar and Usage: 1B. 2D.

**Lesson 2**

Passage 1: 1C. 2D. 3B. 4C. 5A. 6A. 7A. 8C. 9D. 10C.

Passage 2: 1B. 2C. 3A.

**Lesson 3**

Close Reading: 1C. 2C. 3C. 4D. 5D. 6B. 7C. 8C. 9, Response 1 score 4; Response 2 score 3.

Grammar and Usage: C

**Lesson 4**

Close Reading: 1C. 2B. 3C. 4B. 5D. 6C. 7C. 8B.

Words in Context: 1C. 2D.

**Lesson 5**

Data Analysis: C.

Arithmetic: 1B. 2C.

Algebra: 1C. 2A. 3D. 4A.

# Chapter 20

**Lesson 1**
    Close Reading: 1D. 2C. 3D. 4A. 5B. 6A. 7D. 8B.
    Command of Evidence: 1B. 2D. 3D. 4A. 5B. 6B.
    Words in Context: 1B. 2B. 3D.
    Grammar and Usage: 1C. 2B.

**Lesson 2**
    Passage 1: 1D. 2C. 3D. 4C. 5A.
    Passage 2: 1B. 2A. 3B. 4C. 5C.
    Grammar and Usage: D.

**Lesson 3**
    Close Reading: 1A. 2A. 3D. 4D. 5A. 6C. 7, Response 1 score 3; Response 2 score 2.
    Grammar and Usage: 1C. 2B.

**Lesson 4**
    Close Reading: 1B. 2C. 3A. 4C.

**Lesson 5**
    Math: 1A. 2D.
    Arithmetic: 1A. 2B.
    Algebra: 1A. 2C. 3B. 4D.

# Chapter 21

**Lesson 1**
    Close Reading: 1B. 2A. 3A. 4C. 5B. 6C. 7A. 8C.
    Command of Evidence (Student Response): 1D. 2A.
    Words in Context: 1C. 2B.

**Lesson 2**
    Close Reading, Passage 1: 1C. 2B. 3C. 4D. 5B. 6D.
    Close Reading, Passage 2: 1D. 2A. 3B. 4D. 5B.

**Lesson 3**
    Close Reading: 1D. 2A. 3B. 4B. 5C. 6A. 7D. 8, Response 1 score 2; Response 2 score 3.
    Grammar and Usage: 1D. 2C.

**Lesson 4**
    Close Reading: 1C. 2B. 3B. 4B. 5C.
    Words in Context: 1A. 2C. 3B.

**Lesson 5**
    Math: 1C. 2A. 3D. 4A.
    Arithmetic: 1C. 2A. 3D.
    Algebra: 1B. 2A. 3C.

# Chapter 22

**Lesson 1**

Close Reading: 1B. 2D. 3A. 4C. 5B. 6B. 7A. 8B.

Command of Evidence: 1B. 2B. 3C. 4D. 5C. 6A.

**Lesson 2**

Close Reading, Passage 1: 1C. 2D. 3C. 4D. 5C. 6A. 7B.

Close Reading, Passage 2: 1B. 2B. 3B. 4C. 5C. 6C.

Grammar and Usage: B

**Lesson 3**

Close Reading: 1C. 2C. 3D. 4D. 5D. 6D. 7B. 8D. 9, Response 1 score 2; Response 2 score 2.

Grammar and Usage: B.

**Lesson 4**

Close Reading: 1C. 2A. 3C.

Words in Context: 1C. 2D.

**Lesson 5**

Math (chart): 1C. 2D.

Arithmetic: 1C. 2D. 3B. 4C. 5A. 6A. 7C. 8D. 9B.

# Chapter 23

**Lesson 1**

Close Reading: 1B. 2A. 3A. 4A. 5B. 6C. 7D. 8A. 9C. 10B. 11A.

Command of Evidence (Student Response): 1B. 2A. 3C. 4B. 5D. 6C.

Words in Context: 1C. 2A. 3D. 4C. 5A. 6C. 7A.

Grammar and usage: 1C. 2D.

**Lesson 2**

Close Reading, Passage 1: 1B. 2C. 3B. 4C. 3C. 6A. 7B. 8B.

Close Reading, Passage 2: 1A. 2D. 3D. 4B. 5C. 6D. 7B.

Grammar and Usage: A

**Lesson 3**

Close Reading: 1C. 2C. 3D. 4E. 5A. 6A. 7A. 8C. 9, Response 1 score 3; Response 2 score 2.

Grammar and Usage: C

**Lesson 4**

Close Reading: 1C. 2C. 3D. 4B.

Words in Context: 1C. 2D.

**Lesson 5**

Math: A.

Arithmetic: 1D. 2B. 3A. 4C. 5B. 6D.

# Chapter 24

**Lesson 1**

Source Analysis: 1C. 2A. 3C. 4B. 5D. 6A.
Words in Context: 1A. 2C. 3A.

**Lesson 2**

Command of Evidence, Passage 1: 1C. 2C. 3C.
Command of Evidence, Passage 2: 1D. 2B.
Words in Context: 1A. 2D.

**Lesson 3**

Close Reading: 1B. 2A. 3C. 4A. 5A. 6B. 7D. 8D. 9B. 10B. 11E. 12, Response 1 score 2; Response 2 score 4.
Grammar and Usage: D

**Lesson 4**

Close Reading: 1D. 2B. 3A. 4C. 5C.
Words in Context: 1B. 2D. 3C. 4A.

**Lesson 5**

Arithmetic: 1A. 2C. 3D. 4A. 5B. 6B. 7D. 8C. 9C. 10A.

# Chapter 25

**Lesson 1**

Source Analysis: 1B. 2C.
Words in Context: 1B. 2C. 3A.

**Lesson 2**

Close Reading: 1B. 2A. 3C.
Grammar and Usage: 1C. 2C. 3B.
Word in Context: D.
Passage 1 and Passage 2: 1A. 3D. 4B.
Word in Context: A.

**Lesson 3**

Close Reading: 1B. 2D. 3C. 4C. 5D. 6C. 7D. 8D. 9C. 10D. 11A. 12B.
   13, Response 1 score 4; Response 2 score 4.
Grammar and Usage: B.

**Lesson 4**

Jefferson to Lewis: 1A. 2C. 3C. 4B. 5D.
Words in Context: 1C. 2A. 3B.

**Lesson 5**

Data Analysis: 1C. 2B.
Algebra: B.
Arithmetic: 1A. 2A.

# Notes